Business Communication: In Person, In Print, Online, 8e

Current, fast-paced, & interesting—*Just like business itself*.

Take advantage of the following **free** resources! They'll help you succeed in this course and in your career by helping you better understand business communication topics and how they apply in the real-world.

www.bizcominthenews.com

BizCom in the News – Companion Blog

Visit the companion blog (www.bizcominthenews.com) to find relevant news stories related to each chapter topic. Updated at least three times a week, the blog describes current news stories, offers links for additional reading, and provides discussion questions to help you understand and apply topics in a real-world setting.

Like us **on Facebook and** *Follow us* **on Twitter!**

facebook **Facebook.com/BizComInTheNews**
twitter **@BizComInTheNews**

CourseMate Study Resources

CourseMate is a unique website, created to support this text, to make cours~~e~~ come alive with interactive learning, study, and exam preparation tools. Cou~~rse~~ delivers what you need, including an interactive eBook, an interactive gloss~~ary~~ videos, KnowNOW! and more!

Through CourseMate, you can access the following *free* **resources!**

- • **Flashcards**
- • **Key Terms**
- • **Learning Objectives**

Find even more when you log in through www.cengagebrain.com.

Business Communication: In Person, In Print, Online, 8e

Current, fast-paced, & interesting – *Just like business itself.*

The business world is evolving rapidly, and you deserve a textbook that keeps pace. **Business Communication: In Person, In Print, Online** presents innovative content that reflects the variety of communication technology used in today's workplace. The text moves beyond describing new media to helping you use social media and other emerging communication technologies. With engaging examples and an innovative, visual format, this edition grabs your attention and makes you want to read.

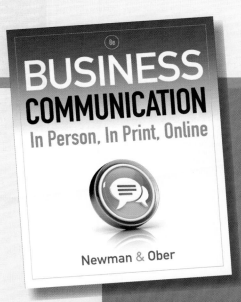

Business Communication: In Person, In Print, Online achieves the following:

- **Reflects how people communicate in business today.**

- **Illustrates principles with current, real-world examples.**

- **Engages readers with creative visuals and an accessible writing style.**

- **Reinforces learning and promotes skill-building with a variety of online resources.**

Reflects How People Communicate in Business Today

Business Communication: In Person, In Print, Online prepares you for challenging situations you will face in the digital workplace. Effective, accurate written and oral communication skills are still paramount. But in today's competitive business environment, you need to be more than a successful communicator; you need to use communication to differentiate yourself.

Prepares You for Today's Digital Workplace

Get more familiar with communicating through social media.

- Sending important information in a meeting
- Providing instant reminders[24]

Social Media

Perhaps the more interesting technologies for communication are **social media**. **Web 2.0**, which encourages online interaction, has opened the door for people to participate on the web. This is quite different from the one-way communication of the early Internet, when companies would post brochure-like websites for people to consume.

The real value of social media for companies is the opportunity to connect with people online. Social media is about the *conversation*. To promote interaction, companies use 2.0 technologies, for example, blogs, wikis, video, and social networking sites. These tools are used on the Internet (for the public), on a company's **intranet** (for employee access only), and on **extranets** (private networks for people outside the company, e.g., customers or franchisees). Examples of social media are shown in Figure 6.

For many companies, social media focuses on **user-generated content (UGC)**, also called **consumer-generated media (CGM)**. This content can be blog entries, product reviews, videos, or other messages posted about a company. As we discussed earlier in the Glassdoor example, this content isn't always positive. In Chapter 7, we'll explore how to respond to negative online comments.

The Fortune Global 100 companies are using social media actively. Seventy-nine percent are using at least one of four main social platforms—Twitter, videos, Facebook, and blogs—to communicate with customers.[25] Of these tools, Twitter is the most frequently used.[26] As a student, you may not be excited about Twitter (the average Twitter user is 39 years old),[27] but this has proved useful for companies,

After introducing a few examples here, we'll discuss social media—and other technologies—where relevant throughout the book. For example, we'll explore wikis for team communication; social networking for interpersonal communication; email, blogs, and instant messaging for written communication; user-generated content for customer communication; and video for oral presentations.

Companies use social media to have a conversation with internal and external audiences.

as we'll discuss later. The Fortune Global 100's frequency of social media activity is shown in Figure 7.[28]

Visit the author's blog at www.bizcominthenews.com for current communication examples.

Blogs Companies use blogs to connect with employees and customers. Successful blogs are updated regularly with news or commentary, and many encourage interactivity through comments, email subscriptions, and RSS (Really Simple Syndication) feeds to share news and other content.

Wegmans, a regional supermarket, has an active blog called "Fresh Stories" to educate and engage customers—and keep them coming back. The blog includes videos, photos, and posts by CEO Danny Wegman. In one recent post, the CEO wrote,

> With the spring season upon us (*we hope!* It's been a cold April in the Rochester area), I wanted to kick off the season with a fresh story from the farm. I'm hoping you'll start sharing your growing stories and questions as we experience this new season together![29]

With a blog, a CEO can build direct relationships with customers and personalize the company, particularly with a conversational style such as Danny W

The Wegmans blog also allows open comments, which are not alwa Following the earthquake and tsunami disasters in Japan, one custo

Learn how to listen to and engage online audiences.

new content

New Content Helps You:

- **Move from *diversity* to *inclusion*.**

- **Adapt communication to multicultural and international audiences.**

- **Participate in online (web) meetings and videoconferences.**

- **Create PowerPoint® "decks" and represent ideas using creative graphics.**

- **Manage your online reputation.**

Understand how to communicate ethically and avoid legal consequences of communication.

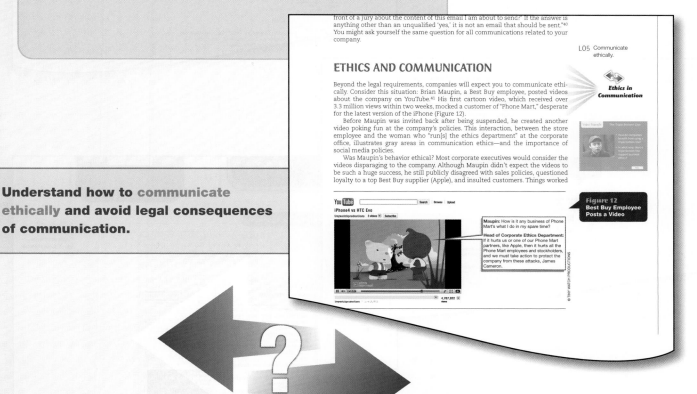

front of a jury about the content of this email I am about to send?' If the answer is anything other than an unqualified 'yes,' it is not an email that should be sent."⁴⁰ You might ask yourself the same question for all communications related to your company.

L05 Communicate ethically.

ETHICS AND COMMUNICATION

Beyond the legal requirements, companies will expect you to communicate ethically. Consider this situation: Brian Maupin, a Best Buy employee, posted videos about the company on YouTube.⁴¹ His first cartoon video, which received over 3.3 million views within two weeks, mocked a customer of "Phone Mart," desperate for the latest version of the iPhone (Figure 12).

Before Maupin was invited back after being suspended, he created another video poking fun at the company's policies. This interaction, between the store employee and the woman who "run[s] the ethics department" at the corporate office, illustrates gray areas in communication ethics—and the importance of social media policies.

Was Maupin's behavior ethical? Most corporate executives would consider the videos disparaging to the company. Although Maupin didn't expect the videos to be such a huge success, he still publicly disagreed with sales policies, questioned loyalty to a top Best Buy supplier (Apple), and insulted customers. Things worked

Figure 12
Best Buy Employee Posts a Video

Current, fast-paced, & interesting – Just like business itself.

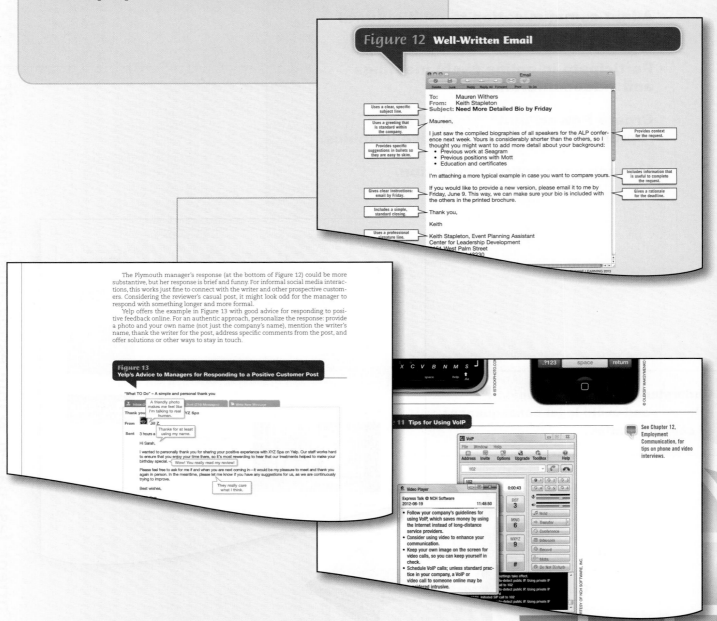

Figure 12 Well-Written Email

Uses a clear, specific subject line.

Uses a greeting that is standard within the company.

Provides specific suggestions in bullets so they are easy to skim.

Gives clear instructions: email by Friday.

Includes a simple, standard closing.

Uses a professional signature line.

Provides context for the request.

Includes information that is useful to complete the request.

Gives a rationale for the deadline.

To: Mauren Withers
From: Keith Stapleton
Subject: **Need More Detailed Bio by Friday**

Maureen,

I just saw the compiled biographies of all speakers for the ALP conference next week. Yours is considerably shorter than the others, so I thought you might want to add more detail about your background:
- Previous work at Seagram
- Previous positions with Mott
- Education and certificates

I'm attaching a more typical example in case you want to compare yours.

If you would like to provide a new version, please email it to me by Friday, June 9. This way, we can make sure your bio is included with the others in the printed brochure.

Thank you,

Keith

Keith Stapleton, Event Planning Assistant
Center for Leadership Development

The Plymouth manager's response (at the bottom of Figure 12) could be more substantive, but her response is brief and funny. For informal social media interactions, this works just fine to connect with the writer and other prospective customers. Considering the reviewer's casual post, it might look odd for the manager to respond with something longer and more formal.

Yelp offers the example in Figure 13 with good advice for responding to positive feedback online. For an authentic approach, personalize the response: provide a photo and your own name (not just the company's name), mention the writer's name, thank the writer for the post, address specific comments from the post, and offer solutions or other ways to stay in touch.

Figure 13
Yelp's Advice to Managers for Responding to a Positive Customer Post

"What TO Do" – A simple and personal thank you

A friendly photo makes me feel like I'm talking to real human.

Thanks for at least using my name.

Wow! You really read my review!

They really care what I think.

Thank you ... XYZ Spa

From Jill Z.

Sent 3 hours a...

Hi Sarah,

I wanted to personally thank you for sharing your positive experience with XYZ Spa on Yelp. Our staff works hard to ensure that you enjoy your time there, so it's most rewarding to hear that our treatments helped to make your birthday special.

Please feel free to ask for me if and when you are next coming in—it would be my pleasure to meet and thank you again in person. In the meantime, please let me know if you have any suggestions for us, as we are continuously trying to improve.

Best wishes,

11 Tips for Using VoIP

- Follow your company's guidelines for using VoIP, which saves money by using the Internet instead of long-distance service providers.
- Consider using video to enhance your communication.
- Keep your own image on the screen for video calls, so you can keep yourself in check.
- Schedule VoIP calls; unless standard practice in your company, a VoIP or video call to someone online may be considered intrusive.

See Chapter 12, Employment Communication, for tips on phone and video interviews.

Illustrates Principles with Current, Real-World Examples

Business Communication: In Person, In Print, Online is *interesting* to read. Principles and skills come alive with many examples of communication at work. You'll learn how companies use communication to their advantage—and how companies struggle with communication.

> **Sample annotated letters, emails, blog posts, and other messages illustrate what works well and what could be improved.**

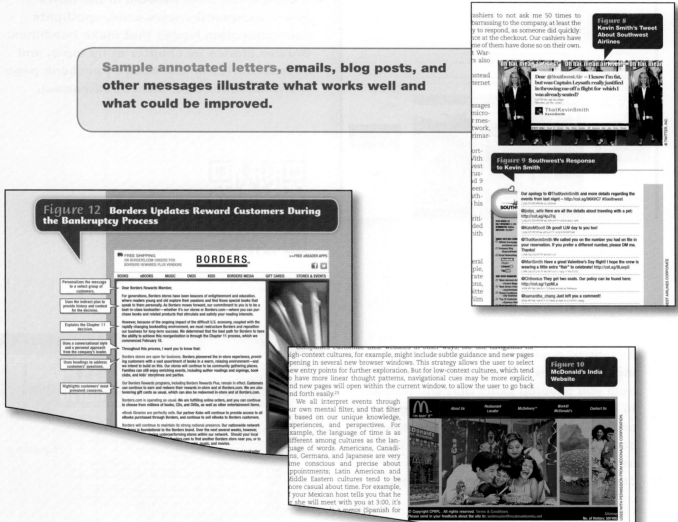

Figure 8 Kevin Smith's Tweet About Southwest Airlines

Figure 9 Southwest's Response to Kevin Smith

Figure 12 Borders Updates Reward Customers During the Bankruptcy Process

Figure 10 McDonald's India Website

• **Examples are integrated right into the paragraph text, such as Best Buy's suspension of an employee for a video posted on YouTube, Toyota's response to safety recalls, McDonald's adaptation to international markets, Google's strategy for hiring, and more.**

Illustrates Principles with Current, Real-World Examples

- A companion blog, **BizCom in the News** (www.bizcominthenews.com), spotlights communication issues that make headlines. Browse stories by chapter or by topic, and access stories on the book's Facebook page (www.facebook.com/bizcominthenews).

Scan This!

- **Expanded end-of-chapter exercises** include six new company scenarios that help you develop skills that will transfer to the workplace. For example, Aggresshop prepares you to respond to a customer complaint on the company's blog and select the appropriate channel to communicate organizational change.

Chapter 1 | Understanding Business Communication   33

Company Scenario

Aggresshop

Imagine you work for Aggresshop, an upscale women's clothing boutique with 16 stores throughout the United States. At www.cengagebrain.com, you'll find Aggresshop's company blog for customers and employees.

As you'll read in the scenario, Aggresshop is experiencing many customer complaints about its sales associates' overly aggressive techniques (two posts are shown below). The CEO decides to change the sales compensation structure to address this issue.

On the blog, you'll see examples of several communication concepts discussed in Chapter 1: directions of communication, communication media, barriers to communication, and ethics in communication. This scenario will also help you learn to do the following:

- respond to customer complaints on a company blog.
- ...ed communication channels.

Engages with Creative Visuals & an Accessible Writing Style

With strong visual appeal, this edition encourages you to read. Where appropriate, content is presented visually—in tables and graphics. Written in a professional, conversational style, **Business Communication: In Person, In Print, Online** aids comprehension and reflects business writing in companies today.

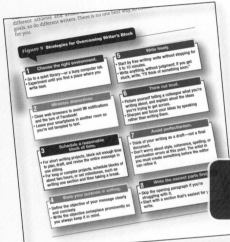

Creative visuals enhance your learning experience and aid in retention.

- **Engaging model documents** help you learn the many types of writing—both in print and online. Models provide marginal callouts with detailed writing instructions.

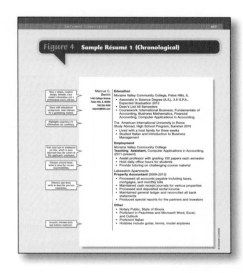

Current, fast-paced, & interesting – *Just like business itself.*

Reinforces Learning & Promotes Skill-Building with a Variety of Innovative Digital Resources

The eighth edition of Business Communication: In Person, In Print, Online integrates the most advanced new technology for efficient and effective study opportunities.

CengageNOW™ is an integrated, online learning system that gives you more control over your success. This innovative, intuitive tool combines the best of current technology to help you plan and study more effectively.

digital tools

CengageNOW:

- **A diagnostic Personalized Study Plan** helps you identify troublesome concepts and creates individualized study plans for better class preparation and grades.

- **With CengageNOW** you also get PowerPoint® slides, videos, digital flash cards, games, and an integrated ebook to make studying business communication more effective and convenient.

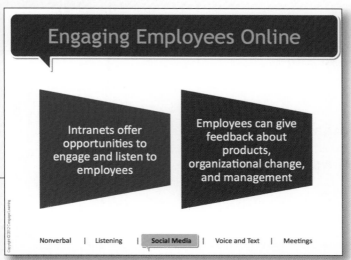

Innovative Digital Resources

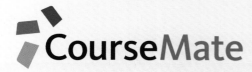 **Course**Mate

CourseMate is a unique website, created to support this text, to make course concepts come alive with interactive learning, study, and exam preparation tools. CourseMate delivers what you need, including an interactive eBook, quizzes, videos, KnowNOW!, Career Transitions interactive tool, and more!

Through CourseMate, you can access the following resources!

- **Pretests**
- **Posttests**
- **PowerPoint study slides**
- **Flash cards**
- **Multimedia company scenarios**
- **BizComInTheNews.com**

Log in through www.cengagebrain.com to see what is available.

digital tools

Helpful tools including flash cards, crossword puzzles, and videos are at your fingertips!

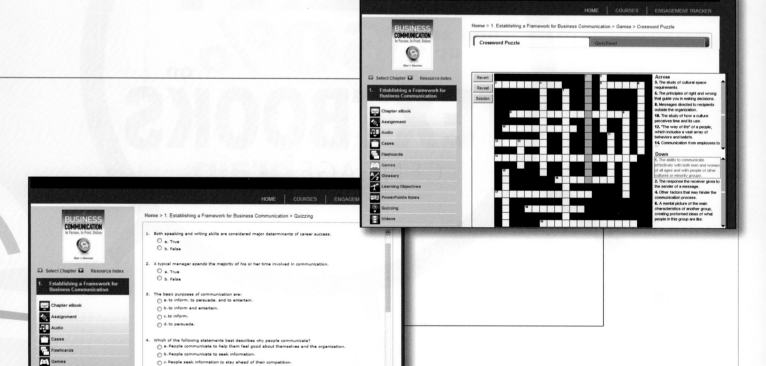

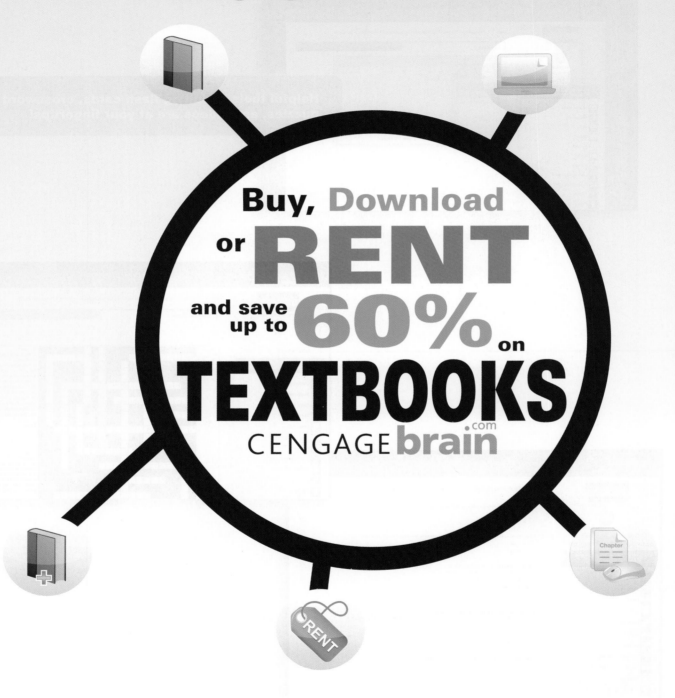

8e

Business Communication

In Person, In Print, Online

8e

Business Communication

In Person, In Print, Online

AMY NEWMAN

Cornell University

SCOT OBER

Ball State University

SOUTH-WESTERN
CENGAGE Learning®

Australia • Brazil • Japan • Korea • Mexico • Singapore • Spain • United Kingdom • United States

SOUTH-WESTERN
CENGAGE Learning

Business Communication:
In Person, In Print, Online 8e
Newman   Ober

Vice President of Editorial, Business: Jack W. Calhoun

Publisher: Erin Joyner

Acquisitions Editor: Jason Fremder

Senior Developmental Editor: Mary Emmons

Editorial Assistant: Megan Fischer

Marketing Manager: Michelle Lockard

Sr. Marketing Communications Manager: Sarah Greber

Sr. Content Project Manager: Cliff Kallemeyn

Media Editor: John Rich

Manufacturing Planner: Ron Montgomery

Production Service: MPS Limited, a Macmillan Company

Art Director: Stacy Shirley

Rights Acquisitions Specialist: Sam Marshall

Senior Rights Acquisitions Specialist: Deanna Ettinger

Photo Researcher: Terri Miller/E-Visual Communications, Inc.

For product information and technology assistance, contact us at
Cengage Learning Customer & Sales Support, 1-800-354-9706

For permission to use material from this text or product, submit all requests online at **www.cengage.com/permissions**
Further permissions questions can be emailed to
permissionrequest@cengage.com

Library of Congress Control Number: 2011941238

ISBN-13: 978-1-111-53316-8

ISBN-10: 1-111-53316-4

South-Western
5191 Natorp Boulevard
Mason, OH 45040
USA

Cengage Learning products are represented in Canada by Nelson Education, Ltd.

For your course and learning solutions, visit **www.cengage.com**
Purchase any of our products at your local college store or at our preferred online store **www.cengagebrain.com**

Back Cover Icons: © iStockphoto.com/Giorgio Magini

Printed in China
2 3 4 5 6 7   16 15 14 13

Brief Contents

Contents

Part 2   DEVELOPING YOUR BUSINESS WRITING SKILLS   105

5   Revising Your Writing   140

Part 3   WRITTEN MESSAGES   181

Part 4   REPORT WRITING   285

10 Writing the Report 324

Part 5   ORAL AND EMPLOYMENT COMMUNICATION   367

11 Oral Presentation 366

REFERENCE MANUAL 467

Introducing Amy Newman

Amy Newman specializes in business communication at the Cornell University School of Hotel Administration. As a senior lecturer, she teaches two required communication courses: a freshman business writing and oral communication class and an upper-level persuasive communication class. Amy also teaches an elective, Corporate Communication, which focuses on communication strategy, crisis communication, and social media.

Amy was an adjunct instructor at Ithaca College; Milano, The New School for Management and Urban Policy in New York City; and eCornell, where she taught classes online. She has won several awards for excellence in teaching and student advising and grants to develop technology-based learning solutions.

Amy's research focuses on social media and other communication technologies. She has published articles

and delivered presentations about instant messaging, email, and social media. Her current work examines hospitality managers' perspectives on social media and the ethical implications of social media participation.

Prior to joining Cornell, Amy spent 20 years working for large companies, such as Canon, Reuters, Scholastic, and MCI. Internally, she held senior-level management positions in human resources and leadership development. As an external consultant, Amy worked to improve communication and employee performance in hospitality, technology, education, publishing, financial services, and entertainment companies.

A graduate of Cornell University and Milano, Amy is co-author of *Business Communication: In Person, In Print, Online, 8e*. Amy has developed several multimedia company scenarios to accompany the book and maintains a blog, BizCom in the News.

Acknowledgments

Business Communication: In Person, In Print, Online was inspired by my teaching and learning from students at Cornell, and I am grateful for how they have shaped my thinking about business communication and who I am as an instructor. I thank my faculty colleagues for their extraordinary support and guidance in my teaching and professional development: Judi Brownell, Daphne Jameson, David Lennox, Craig Snow, and Maria Loukianenko Wolfe. I also extend my sincere thanks to Cornell Student Services staff Curtis Ferguson and Molly deRoos for their input on chapter content.

Throughout the revision process, I have consulted many colleagues, friends, and family for valuable feedback on book content and, when needed, a sympathetic ear: Joshua Bronstein, Daniel Meyerson, Laura Newman, Crystal Thomas, and my wonderful, encouraging husband, Ed Marion. I dedicate this book to my mother, who passed the year before publication and who taught me my first word: hot.

Several research assistants contributed to this edition and its supplements. Without their help, the book would not have the currency and life that I intended: Katie Satinsky, Grace Lee, Abigail Needles, and Zachary Ruben.

The following instructors participated in the editorial review board for the eighth edition. Throughout each stage of the revision process, they offered creative input that shaped the chapter content and dynamic design. I thank each of them for their valuable feedback and suggestions:

Kate Archard, *University of Massachusetts, Boston*
Fiona Barnes, *University of Florida*
Christina Bergenholtz, *Quinsigamond Community College*
David Bolton, *University of Maryland*
Dominic Bruni, *University of Wisconsin, Oshkosh*
Marilyn Chalupa, *Ball State University*
Cindi Costa, *Mohave Community College*
Melissa Diegnau, *Riverland Community College*
Peggy Fisher, *Ball State University*

Jorge Gaytan, *North Carolina, AT&T*
Bill Graham, *Seton Hall University*
Valerie Gray, *Harrisburg Area Community College*
Mary Groves, *University of Nevada, Reno*
Gloria Lessman, *Bellevue University*
Karen Messina, *SUNY Orange*
Bill McPherson, *Indiana University-Purdue*
Jean Anna Sellers, *Fort Hays State University*
Stacey Short, *Northern Illinois University*
Lynn Staley, *University of Missouri, St. Louis*
Sanci C. Teague, *Western Kentucky Community and Technical College*

I would also like to acknowledge the following reviewers for their thoughtful contributions on previous editions:

Lisa Barley, *Eastern Michigan University*
Lia Barone, *Norwalk Community College*
Carl Bridges, *Arthur Andersen Consulting*
Annette Briscoe, *Indiana University Southeast*
Mitchel T. Burchfield, *Southwest Texas Junior College*
Janice Burke, *South Suburban College*
Leila Chambers, *Cuesta College*
G. Jay Christensen, *California State University, Northridge*
Cheryl Christiansen, *California State University, Stanislaus*
Connie Clark, *Lane Community College*
Miriam Coleman, *Western Michigan University*

Anne Hutta Colvin, *Montgomery County Community College*
Doris L. Cost, *Metropolitan State College of Denver*
L. Ben Crane, *Temple University*
Ava Cross, *Ryerson Polytechnic University*
Nancy J. Daugherty, *Indiana University-Purdue University, Indianapolis*
Rosemarie Dittmer, *Northeastern University*
Gary Donnelly, *Casper College*
Graham N. Drake, *State University of New York, Geneseo*
Kay Durden, *The University of Tennessee at Martin*

Laura Eurich, *University of Colorado at Colorado Springs*
Mary Groves, *University of Nevada, Reno*
Phillip A. Holcomb, *Angelo State University*
Larry R. Honl, *University of Wisconsin, Eau Claire*
Kristi Kelly, *Florida Gulf Coast University*
Margaret Kilcoyne, *Northwestern State University*
Michelle Kirtley Johnston, *Loyola University*
Alice Kinder, *Virginia Polytechnic Institute and State University*
Emogene King, *Tyler Junior College*
Richard N. Kleeberg, *Solano Community College*
Patricia Laidler, *Massasoit Community College*
Lowell Lamberton, *Central Oregon Community College*
E. Jay Larson, *Lewis and Clark State College*
Kimberly Laux, *Saginaw Valley State University*
Michael Liberman, *East Stroudsburg University*
Julie MacDonald, *Northwestern State University*
Marsha C. Markman, *California Lutheran University*
Beryl McEwen, *North Carolina A&T State University*
Diana McKowen, *Indiana University, Bloomington*
Maureen McLaughlin, *Highline Community College*
Sylvia A. Miller, *Cameron University*
Billie Miller-Cooper, *Cosumnes River College*
Russell Moore, *Western Kentucky University*
Wayne Moore, *Indiana University of Pennsylvania*
Gerald W. Morton, *Auburn University of Montgomery*
Danell Moses, *Western Carolina University, Cullowhee, NC*

Jaunett Neighbors, *Central Virginia Community College*
Judy Nixon, *University of Tennessee at Chattanooga*
Rosemary Olds, *Des Moines Area Community College*
Richard O. Pompian, *Boise State University*
Rebecca Pope-Ruark, *Elon University*
Karen Sterkel Powell, *Colorado State University*
Seamus Reilly, *University of Illinois*
Carla Rineer, *Millersville University*
Jeanette Ritzenthaler, *New Hampshire College*
Betty Robbins, *University of Oklahoma*
Joan C. Roderick, *Southwest Texas State University*
Mary Jane Ryals, *Florida State University*
Lacye Prewitt Schmidt, *State Technical Institute of Memphis*
Jean Anna Sellers, *Fort Hays State University*
Sue Seymour, *Cameron University*
Sherry Sherrill, *Forsyth Technical Community College*
John R. Sinton, *Finger Lakes Community College*
Curtis J. Smith, *Finger Lakes Community College*
Craig E. Stanley, *California State University, Sacramento*
Ted O. Stoddard, *Brigham Young University*
Vincent C. Trofi, *Providence College*
Deborah A. Valentine, *Emory University*
Randall L. Waller, *Baylor University*
Maria W. Warren, *University of West Florida*
Michael R. Wunsch, *Northern Arizona University*
Annette Wyandotte, *Indiana University, Southeast*
Betty Rogers Youngkin, *University of Dayton*

Several business communication instructors devoted time and energy to making this edition a success. Because of their professionalism and creativity, the eighth edition will provide an enhanced teaching and learning experience for adopters. Maria Loukianenko Wolfe developed innovative activities to create valuable instructor's guides that enhance class interaction and learning. Elizabeth Christensen of Sinclair Community College and David Lennox of Cornell wrote a comprehensive test bank to reinforce students' learning. In addition, I value the excellent contributions of Karen Howie, Northwestern Michigan College, who developed digital content for the CourseMate website.

Finally, I am grateful to the inspiring team at Cengage Learning. It is a true pleasure to work with this team and their staff, who nurtured the book from a list of ideas to printed copy and every step along the way:

Erin Joyner, Publisher, Business and Computers
Jason Fremder, Acquisitions Editor
Michelle Lockard, Marketing Manager
Cliff Kallemeyn, Content Project Manager
Mary Emmons, Senior Developmental Editor
John Rich, Media Editor
Stacy Shirley, Senior Art Director

Amy Newman

8e

Business Communication

In Person, In Print, Online

Stimulus (1) Filter (1) Message (1) Medium (1) Destination (1) Directions of Communication (1) The Formal Communication Network (1) Downward Communication (1) **Understanding Business Communication** (1) Upward Communication (1) Lateral (or Horizontal) Communication (1) The Informal Communication Network (1) Communication Media Choices (1) Communication Barriers (1) Verbal Barriers (1) Nonverbal Barriers (1) Potential Legal Consequences of Communication (1) What Affects Ethical Behavior (1) Framework for Ethical Decision Making

LEARNING OBJECTIVES

After you have finished this chapter, you should be able to

LO1   Identify the components of communication.

LO2   Identify the major verbal and nonverbal barriers to communication.

LO3   Describe criteria for choosing communication media.

LO4   Avoid potential legal consequences of communication.

LO5   Communicate ethically.

The Learning Objectives (LOs) will help you learn the material. You'll see references to the LOs throughout the chapter.

"You can set up an iChat, but you don't know how people think."

— RYAN BINGHAM, GEORGE CLOONEY'S CHARACTER IN *UP IN THE AIR*

Chapter Introduction: Communication in the Movie *Up in the Air*

I n the movie *Up in the Air*, Anna Kendrick's character, Natalie, proposes videoconferencing as a way to reduce travel costs. It's an innovative suggestion, but not appropriate for her company's work—to communicate to employees that their job has been eliminated (a nice way of saying, "You're fired"). A more experienced employee at the company, played by George Clooney, thinks the idea is ridiculous.

Most reasonable people would agree. People prefer to receive bad news in person.[1,2] As technology is increasingly used for communication, choosing the right media is more important than ever.

Despite the research—and common sense—the persuasive Natalie gets a chance to prove herself and trains company employees to deliver the bad news by video. Spoiler alert: The system doesn't work out too well in the end. And poor Natalie gets a taste of her own medicine when her boyfriend breaks up with her via text message.

Communicating in Person in *Up in the Air*

© DALE ROBINETTE/© DREAMWORKS PICTURES/ COURTESY EVERETT COLLECTION

COMMUNICATING IN ORGANIZATIONS

Walk through the halls of any organization—a start-up company, a Fortune 500 giant, a state government office, or a not-for-profit organization—and what do you see? Managers and other employees drafting emails, attending meetings, reading articles online, writing reports, conducting interviews, talking on the phone, and making presentations. In short, you see people *communicating*.

> Communication is necessary for an organization to achieve its goals.

People in organizations work together to achieve a common goal that can only be reached through communication. Groups of people must interact in order to communicate their ideas, needs, expertise, and plans. Communication is how people share information, coordinate activities, and make better decisions. Understanding how communication works in companies and how to communicate competently will make you more effective in every aspect of business.

But many employees lack the communication skills required by their employers. Consider these recent research findings:

- Employees are "ill prepared" for the workforce, according to a recent study of employers, shown in Figure 1. More than 31% of respondents found a "high need" for written and oral communication skills (and other topics covered in this book, such as ethics, professionalism, diversity, and teamwork), but do not offer training.[3]

- In a 2010 study, communication was ranked as the top skill employers seek in job candidates. Employers also noted analytical skills, the ability to work in a team, technical skills, and a strong work ethic as important qualifications.[4]

- "People who cannot write and communicate clearly will not be hired and are unlikely to last long enough to be considered for promotion," reports The College Board, based on a survey of human resource directors.[5]

- The College Board also reports that one-third of employees in U.S. blue-chip companies write poorly, and companies spend as much as $3.1 billion each year on remedial writing training.[6]

- On a more positive note, companies that are considered highly effective communicators had 47% higher returns to shareholders than companies considered the least effective communicators. This study, by Towers Watson, a global professional services firm, calls communication "a leading indicator of financial performance and a driver of employee engagement."[7]

- Employees who are happy with how their company communicates difficult decisions are twice as likely to be motivated to work for the company and four times as likely to recommend their company.[8]

Figure 1
Employees "Ill Prepared" for Workforce

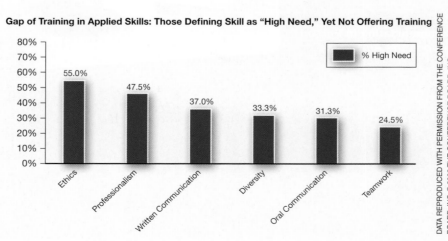

Gap of Training in Applied Skills: Those Defining Skill as "High Need," Yet Not Offering Training

■ % High Need

Ethics	55.0%
Professionalism	47.5%
Written Communication	37.0%
Diversity	33.3%
Oral Communication	31.3%
Teamwork	24.5%

Clearly, good communication skills are crucial to your success in an organization. Competence in writing and speaking will help you get hired, perform well, and earn promotions. If you decide to go into business for yourself, writing and speaking skills will help you find investors, promote your product, and manage your employees. These same skills will also help you achieve your personal and social goals.

It's no wonder that, according to Mark H. McCormack, chairman of International Management Group and best-selling author of *What They Don't Teach You at Harvard Business School*, "People's written communications are probably more revealing than any other single item in the workplace."[9]

Communication is the process of sending and receiving messages—sometimes through spoken or written words, and sometimes nonverbally through facial expressions, gestures, and voice qualities. If someone sends a message to you, and you receive it, communication will have taken place. However, in this example, only if you understand Chinese will the communication have been successful.[10]

Communication is sending and receiving verbal and nonverbal messages.

International Communication

Communication is successful only when you understand the message. These Chinese symbols mean *crisis*.

© CENGAGE LEARNING 2013

THE COMPONENTS OF COMMUNICATION

L01 Identify the components of communication.

How does communication happen among people and throughout an organization? In this section, we'll discuss the communication model (or process) and the directions of communication within a company.

The Communication Model

The communication model consists of five components: the stimulus, filter, message, medium, and destination. Ideally, the process ends with feedback to the sender, although feedback is not necessary for communication to have taken place. Consider the example of a company opening a new store in Los Angeles, California. Imagine that you are the VP, business development, and need to announce this decision to all employees. Other stakeholders—for example, customers, investors, and suppliers—will have to be informed too, but let's use the example of internal communication here. Figure 2 shows how communication might happen in this situation.

The Stimulus

For communication to take place, there first must be a **stimulus**, an event that creates within an individual the need to communicate. This stimulus can be internal or external. An internal stimulus is simply an idea that forms within your mind. External stimuli come to you through your sensory organs, for example, your eyes and ears. A stimulus for communicating in business might be an email message you just read, a bit of gossip you heard over lunch, or even the hot air generated by an overworked heating system (or colleague!).

Step 1: A stimulus creates a need to communicate.

The Filter

If everyone had the same perception of events, your job of communicating would be easier; you could assume that your perception of reality was accurate and that others would understand your motives and intent. But each of us has a unique perception of reality, based on our individual experiences, culture, emotions at the

Step 2: Our knowledge, experience, and viewpoints act as filters to help us interpret (decode) the stimulus.

Figure 2
Internal Communication Process: Opening a New Store

Feedback

Stimulus	Filter	Message	Medium	Destination
As the VP, business development, you and the rest of the management team decide at a monthly meeting to open a new store in Los Angeles. The company wants to expand into a new market and has research that indicates Los Angeles is a good choice.	You interpret this stimulus (the information about the new store) and decide whether and how to communicate it. Most likely, you perceive the store opening as good news—more revenue—and want employees to be excited about it.	Next, you create a message—the information to be communicated. Knowing your audience of employees, you tailor the message to what is important to them (for example, new job opportunities).	Because employees are dispersed around the country, you decide an email is the best way to communicate the news quickly and consistently. You also create a page on the company's intranet site for employees to get more information, find updates, and ask you questions.	Next, employees receive your messages (which creates a new stimulus for them). At this point, you hope for the best: that the messages achieved their objectives.

Feedback
Employees may respond to the news by asking questions through the intranet page. As the VP, business development, you'll want feedback to make sure your message was received as you intended and to see what follow-up communication you may need.

Noise Employees may be too busy to pay attention to the news, or they may delete the email without reading it. Noise is any distraction during the communication process. **Noise**

© CENGAGE LEARNING 2013

---

moment, personality, knowledge, socioeconomic status, and a host of other variables. Each variable acts as a **filter** in shaping a person's unique impressions of reality.

The brain attempts to make sense of the stimulus.

Once your brain receives a message, you interpret the message and decide how to respond. Our example of opening a new store would probably be received positively. But how do you think employees reacted to Starbucks' decision to close 900 underperforming stores in 2008 and 2009? If you worked at one of those stores, you would have been concerned about losing your job, but if you were an investor, you might have been happy about the news, believing that Starbucks was making a smart business decision.

Starbucks' investors and employees reacted differently to the news that 900 underperforming stores were closing.

© RICHARD LEVINE/ALAMY

Step 3: We formulate (encode) a verbal or nonverbal response to the stimulus.

The Message
Whether a communication achieves the sender's objectives depends on how well you construct the **message** (the information to be communicated). The purpose and content of your message may be clear, but communication success also

depends on how well you know your **audience** (who receives your communication) and how much you adapt your message to the audience.

The Medium

Once the sender has encoded a message, the next step in the process is to transmit that message to the receiver. At this point, the sender must choose the **medium**— how the message is transmitted. Oral messages might be transmitted through a staff meeting, individual meeting, telephone conversation, voice mail, podcast, conference call, videoconference, or even less formally, through the company grapevine. Written messages might be transmitted through an email, a report, a blog post, a web page, a brochure, a bulletin board notice, or a company newsletter. Nonverbal messages might be transmitted through facial expressions, gestures, or body movement. As we'll discuss later in this chapter, choosing the right medium for your audience, message, and objectives is critical to the success of your communication.

 Step 4: We select the form of the message (medium).

The Destination

The message is transmitted and then enters the sensory environment of the receiver (the **destination** or audience), at which point control passes from the sender to the receiver. Once the message reaches its destination, you have no guarantee that communication will actually occur. Your audience may misinterpret your message or miss it entirely. Assuming your message is transmitted, it then becomes the source, or stimulus, for the next communication episode, and the process begins again.

 Step 5: The message reaches its destination and, if successful, is perceived accurately by the receiver.

The Dynamic Nature of Communication

Although these components are presented in steps, you probably know from your own experience that communication is not a linear, static process. Rarely does communication flow neatly from one stage to the next with the senders and receivers easily identified at any given point.

 Communication is not a linear, static process.

   Two or more people often send and receive messages simultaneously. For example, the look on your face when you receive a message may send a new message to the sender that you understand, agree with, or are baffled by the message being sent. And your feedback may prompt the sender to modify his or her intended message. The model helps us understand each step of the process—but communication is far more complicated than presented here.

Directions of Communication

For an organization to be successful, communication must flow freely through formal and informal channels.

The Formal Communication Network

Three types of communication make up an organization's **formal communication network**: downward, upward, and lateral. Information may be transmitted in these directions, which we'll illustrate with Starbucks' organization chart, shown in Figure 3.[11]

Downward Communication **Downward communication** is the flow of information from managers to their employees (people who report to them). From the Starbucks organization chart, we could assume that Howard Schultz, as CEO and president, communicates downward to his direct reports. When Starbucks decided to close stores, for example, he would have communicated this message to Cliff

Figure 3
Starbucks' Organization Chart

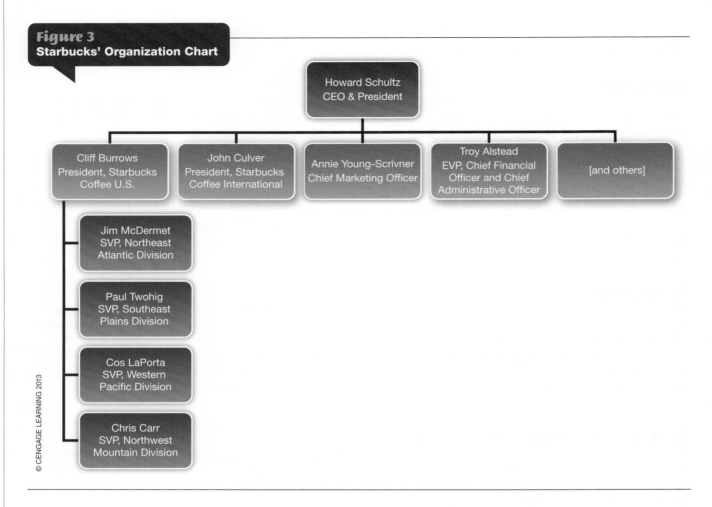

© CENGAGE LEARNING 2013

Burrows (president, Starbucks Coffee U.S.), who would then have communicated the bad news to his direct reports: Jim McDermet, Paul Twohig, and the others. This is called **cascading communication**, where information flows from one level in an organization down to another.

Employees have many justifiable complaints about their managers' communication. A Florida State University study proves the adage "Employees don't leave a company; they leave a manager."[12] Some of the disappointing results are shown in Figure 4.

Another issue with downward communication is that managers assume their employees receive and understand their messages. From our discussion on filters—and probably from your own experience—you know this isn't always the case. Employees pay attention to their manager's messages, but managers need

Figure 4
In FSU Study, Employees Rate Their Supervisors

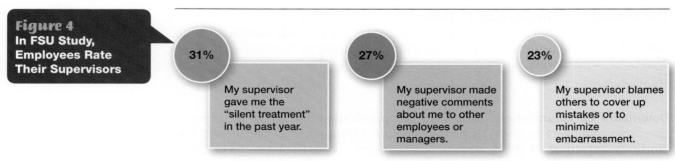

Source: Barry Ray, "Who's Afraid of the Big Bad Boss?" Florida State University News, December 4, 2006.

feedback from employees to determine whether their messages are received as intended.

Upward Communication **Upward communication** is the flow of information from lower-level employees to upper-level employees or managers. Upward communication provides upper management with feedback about their communication, suggestions for improving the business, and information needed for decision making. Encouraging employees to voice their opinions and concerns is one of the most important parts of a manager's job.

In the Starbucks example, Troy Alstead, as chief financial officer, probably gave oral and written financial reports to Howard Schultz to tell him which stores were underperforming. Lower-level employees may have expressed their frustration about the closings through formal upward communication channels, for example, during team meetings.

Lateral (or Horizontal) Communication **Lateral communication** (also called **horizontal communication**) is the flow of information among peers within an organization. Through lateral communication, employees create a more cohesive work unit by coordinating work, sharing plans and activities, negotiating differences, and developing interpersonal support. At Starbucks, managers responsible for closing a store probably communicated with each other to coordinate messages and timing—and perhaps to console each other during the process.

Lateral communication can be challenging in an organization because you're trying to influence people but have no management authority over them. This is particularly difficult when the lateral communication is **cross-functional**—across different departments, divisions, or branches. In these situations, you'll need to rely on your relationship-building and persuasive communication skills to rally support and accomplish your goals.

The Informal Communication Network

The **informal communication network** (or **grapevine**) transmits information through unofficial channels within the organization. Employees share what's happening in the company in person (while eating in the cafeteria or refilling their coffee cup) and online (on social networking sites and blogs). The informal communication network transmits information through unofficial channels within the organization.

Without good formal communication, the grapevine will take over. People need information, particularly when they fear change that may affect them: layoffs, benefit cuts, or organizational restructurings. Although the grapevine is surprisingly accurate (75% to 90% according to some studies),[13] managers who let the grapevine function as employees' main source of information miss out on the chance to convey their own messages.

Websites such as Glassdoor provide a public forum for current and former employees to voice their opinions about companies. As you can imagine, employees posted negative comments during the layoffs at Starbucks. This is potentially embarrassing for a company, but there's little management can do about the site—or any informal communication network.

Rather than trying to eliminate the grapevine (a futile effort), competent managers pay attention to it and act promptly to counteract false rumors. They use the formal communication network (meetings, email, the intranet, and newsletters) to ensure that all news—positive and negative—gets out to employees as quickly and as completely as possible. Savvy managers also identify key influencers in an organization to get accurate messages infused into the grapevine.

The free flow of information within the organization allows managers to stop rumors and communicate their own messages to employees. However, managers face additional challenges at work: verbal and nonverbal barriers to communication.

L02   Identify the
      major verbal and
      nonverbal barriers
      to communication.

COMMUNICATION BARRIERS

Considering the complexity of the communication process and the many communication channels, your messages may not always be received exactly as you intend. As we discussed in the section about communication filters, your messages may not be received at all, or they may be received incompletely or inaccurately. Some of the obstacles to effective and efficient communication are verbal; others are nonverbal.

Verbal Barriers

Verbal barriers are related to what you write or say. They include inadequate knowledge or vocabulary, differences in interpretation, language differences, inappropriate use of expressions, overabstraction and ambiguity, and polarization.

Inadequate Knowledge or Vocabulary

You must know enough about both your topic and your audience to express yourself precisely and appropriately.

Before you can communicate an idea, you must first *have* the idea and know enough about it. Assume, for example, that you're John Culver, president, Starbucks Coffee International. In your role, you'll need to inform international employees of the U.S. store closings. The decision may not affect international stores directly, but employees should be aware of the move and should hear the rationale from you—not public news organizations. You know all of the background information and are ready to announce the change to staff. Or are you?

Have you analyzed your audience? Do you know whether international employees already know about the closings, so you can decide how much background information to include? Do you know how much detail about the decision to provide? Employees should know why these 900 stores were selected, but do they need to see the financial performance of each? How personal should your communication be? Are international employees worried about their own jobs? Should you reassure them about the company's plans in other countries, or would that just worry them more? The answers to these questions will be important for you to achieve your communication objectives.

Differences in Interpretation

Sometimes senders and receivers attribute different meanings to the same word or attribute the same meaning to different words. When this happens, miscommunication can occur.

A word's denotation defines its meaning; its connotation indicates our associations with the word.

Every word has both a denotative and a connotative meaning. **Denotation** refers to the literal, dictionary meaning of a word. **Connotation** refers to the subjective, emotional meaning that you attach to a word. For example, the denotative meaning of the word *plastic* is "a synthetic material that can be easily molded into different forms." For some people, the word also has a negative connotative meaning—"cheap or artificial substitute"—or they associate the term with its environmental impact. For other people, the word means a credit card, as in "He used plastic to pay the bill."

Most interpretation problems occur because people ascribe different connotative meanings to a word. Do you have a positive, neutral, or negative reaction to the terms *broad, bad, aggressive, workaholic, corporate raider, head-hunter, golden parachute,* or *wasted?* Are your reactions likely to be the same as everyone else's? Some terms cause an emotional reaction that turns off the receiver and could harm your relationship.

International Communication

Language Differences

International businesspeople say that you can buy in your native language anywhere in the world, but you can sell only in the local language. Most communication between U.S. or Canadian firms and international firms is in English; in other cases, an interpreter (for oral communication) or translator (for written communication) may be used. But even with such services, problems can occur.

To ensure that the intended meaning is not lost in translation, important documents should first be translated into the second language and then retranslated into English. Of course, communication difficulties arise even among native English speakers. A British advertisement for Electrolux vacuum cleaners displayed the headline "Nothing Sucks like an Electrolux." Copywriters in the United States and Canada would never use this wording!

Poor translations can result in unintended meanings, as shown in this sign in China.

Inappropriate Use of Expressions

The intended meaning of an expression differs from its literal interpretation. Examples of expressions include slang, jargon, and euphemisms.

- **Slang** is an expression, often short-lived, identified with a specific group of people. Business has its own slang, such as *24/7, bandwidth, bottom line, strategic fit,* and *window of opportunity.* Using slang that your audience understands serves as a communication shortcut. But issues arise when the sender uses slang that receivers don't understand, either because they're excluded from a group or because of language differences.

 Use slang, jargon, and euphemisms cautiously.

- **Jargon** is the technical terminology used within specialized groups—sometimes called "the pros' prose." Technology, for example, has spawned a whole new vocabulary. Do you know the meaning of these common computer terms?

OS	FAQ	JPEG	retweet
POS	Trojan horse	VoIP	AI
SEO	hacker	followers	spam
thumbnail	HTML	patch	CAD

   As with slang, the problem is not in using jargon—jargon provides a very precise and efficient way of communicating with those familiar with it. The problem comes when we use jargon just to impress others, which can alienate people.

- **Euphemisms** are expressions used instead of words that may be offensive or inappropriate. Sensitive communicators use euphemisms when appropriate; for example, some consider "passed away" more pleasant than "died."

   Euphemisms, like slang and jargon, shouldn't be overused. Euphemisms for firing people have become a corporate joke; now companies downsize, right-size, smartsize, rationalize, amortize, reduce, redeploy, reorganize, restructure, offshore, outsource, and outplace. In the movie *Up in the Air*, George Clooney's character advises Natalie, the new hire, "Never say 'fired.'" Instead, she says,

Figure 5
Euphemisms Used to Fire Employees

"We're going to make a few changes around here, and one of them is you."

"I was fired from my second post-high-school job working for a dry cleaning establishment. My boss actually said, 'You're not dry cleaning material.'"

© CENGAGE LEARNING 2013

"You've been let go." On a website, employees posted memorable expressions that managers used to tell them they were fired (see Figure 5).[14]

Overabstraction and Ambiguity

An **abstract word** identifies an idea or a feeling instead of a concrete object. For example, *communication* is an abstract word, but *newspaper* is a **concrete word**, a word that identifies something that can be seen or touched. Abstract words are necessary to describe things you cannot see or touch, but we run into difficulty when we use too many abstract words or when we use too high a level of abstraction. The higher the level of abstraction, the more difficult it is for the receiver to visualize exactly what the sender has in mind. For example, which sentence communicates more information: "I acquired an asset at the store" or "I bought a printer at Fletcher Electronics"?

The word *transportation* is abstract; the word *car* is concrete.

Ambiguous terms such as *a few, some, several*, and *far away*, may be too broad for business communication. What does ASAP (as soon as possible) mean to you? Does it mean within the hour, by the end of the day, or something else? A more specific deadline, for example, January 20 at 3:00 P.M., will improve your chances of getting what you need when you need it.

Polarization

Thinking in terms of all or nothing limits our choices.

Not every situation has two opposite and distinct poles—usually we can see gray areas. Of course, there are some true dichotomies. You are either human or nonhuman, and your company either will or will not close an office. But most aspects of life involve more than two alternatives.

Is a speaker telling the truth or lying? What the speaker says may be true, but she may selectively omit information and give an inaccurate impression. Most likely, the answer lies somewhere in between. Likewise, you are not necessarily either tall or short, rich or poor, smart or dumb. Competent communicators avoid inappropriate either/or logic and instead make the effort to search for middle-ground words to best describe a situation.

What you do not say may also communicate a message.

When we talk about verbal barriers to communication, let's remember that what you do *not* say can also cause issues in communication. What if you congratulated only one of the three people after a company presentation? How would the other two presenters feel—even though you said nothing negative about their performance? Or suppose you tell one of them, "You really did an outstanding job this time." The presenter's reaction might be, "What was wrong with my performance last time?"

Nonverbal Barriers

Not all communication difficulties are related to what you write or say. Some are related to how you act. Nonverbal barriers to communication include inappropriate or conflicting signals, differences in perception, inappropriate emotions, and distractions.

Inappropriate or Conflicting Signals

People will usually believe what we do rather than what we say.

Suppose a well-qualified applicant for an auditing position submits a résumé with a typographical error or shows up to an interview in jeans. When verbal and nonverbal signals conflict, we tend to believe the nonverbal messages because they are more difficult to manipulate than verbal messages.

Many nonverbal signals vary from culture to culture—both within the United States and internationally. What is appropriate in one context might not be appropriate in another. We'll explore this further when we discuss intercultural communication in the next chapter.

Differences in Perception

Even when they hear the same presentation or read the same report, people of different ages, socioeconomic backgrounds, cultures, and so forth may form very different perceptions. How people perceive a message contributes to the mental filter we discussed earlier.

When employees receive an email from the company president, they'll probably react differently based on their experience, knowledge, and points of view. One employee may be so intimidated by the president that he accepts everything the president says, whereas another employee may have such negative feelings about the president that she believes nothing the president says.

Inappropriate Emotions

In most cases, a moderate level of emotional involvement intensifies the communication and makes it more personal. However, too much emotional involvement can be an obstacle to communication. For example, excessive anger can create an emotionally charged environment that makes reasonable discussion impossible. Likewise, prejudice (automatically rejecting certain people or ideas), stereotyping (placing individuals into categories), and boredom all hinder effective communication. These emotions tend to close your mind to new ideas and cause you to reject or ignore information that is contrary to your prevailing belief. Keeping an objective, open mind is important for effective communication—and for you to develop as a person.

 It's typically better to rely on logic instead of emotions when communicating.

 Information overload is an increasingly serious issue at work.

Distractions

Environmental or competing elements that hinder your ability to concentrate can affect communication. Such distractions are called **noise**, which you saw in the communication model (Figure 2). Examples of *environmental* noise are poor acoustics, extreme temperature, uncomfortable seating, or even your coworker's body odor. Examples of *competing* noise are too many projects, meetings, or emails.

Communication technologies themselves can cause distractions. Can you watch TV, text, and IM all at the same time? You may think you're good at multitasking, but a Stanford University study concludes the opposite: "Heavy multitaskers are lousy at multitasking."[15] Another study conducted at the University of London's Institute of Psychiatry found that "an average worker's functioning IQ falls 10 points when distracted by ringing telephones and incoming emails."[16]

Competent communicators try to avoid verbal and nonverbal barriers that might cause misunderstandings. They also choose the best communication media for their messages.

Multitasking may diminish your ability to communicate effectively.

© JGI/BLEND IMAGES/GETTY IMAGES

L03   Describe criteria for choosing communication media.

COMMUNICATION MEDIA CHOICES

As a business communicator, you have many options (channels or media) through which you can communicate a message. The real challenge is deciding which medium to use for your communication.

Traditional Communication Channels

Traditional forms of oral and written communication still exist in all organizations today.

Travel brochures, a traditional form of written communication, use photos of exotic destinations to lure customers.

© ART DIRECTORS & TRIP/ALAMY

Traditional Written Communication

Organizations still print slick, colorful brochures; internal newsletters for employees without computer access; financial statements for customers who don't choose the online option; solicitation letters; and periodicals such as magazines, journals, and newspapers. Complex reports also may be printed because they're difficult to read on a computer screen.

How much longer will some of these print communications exist? It's hard to say. In an office environment today, you'll likely receive few interoffice memos and postal letters. These communications are considered more official and formal, so you may receive important information about your pay or benefits, or you may send your cover letter and résumé through the mail, but not much else. Many companies no longer have printed letterhead with the company's name and logo; when you print a memo or letter, you'll insert the logo from a digital file. You may receive a report that you'll print, but it will probably come as an email attachment.

 Face-to-face is the best medium for building relationships.

Traditional Oral Communication

Fortunately, people do still meet in person. Face-to-face meetings are the most personal form of business communication and the best choice for building relationships. Traditional meetings include one-on-one (individual), small group (team), or large group gatherings.

At many organizations, flip charts and handouts are still used during meetings and training programs. Some companies don't have technology available in all meeting rooms, and some believe computers during meetings hinder communication. At times, low-tech options may be best to stay within organizational norms and to achieve your communication goals.

Communication Technologies

Technology-Based Communication Media

Technology has changed workplace communication, providing many options for sending a message. Depending on the type of message, you may choose from a variety of communication technologies.

Email, Phone, Voice Mail

 Email is often the default communication channel in organizations.

Although they are technology based, email, the phone, and voice mail are considered more conventional channels of communication. Email is so pervasive in organizations that it has become the default choice for communication.[17] And yet, one study showed a decline in numbers of email messages received, possibly because of increased use of instant messaging and social networking sites.[18] Landline office phones persist, but who knows for how long, considering cell phones—increasingly smartphones—have replaced so many home phones. People still call each other at work, but sending an email to someone in the next cubicle is common. It's no surprise that most people believe email is used too often instead of face-to-face communication.[19]

In Chapters 3 and 4, we'll discuss how to leave effective voice mails and write effective emails.

Instant and Text Messaging

Instant messaging (IM) and texting are becoming increasingly popular at work. For short messages and quick questions, these channels are ideal.[20] Of course, with smartphones, email may give you an instant response as well, but this varies by organization and people. As you probably know, the real value of IMing is "presence awareness"—you know when someone is available to respond immediately. Although some people consider IM an annoying interruption at work, people who use IM at the office report fewer disruptions[21] and believe that IM saves time and provides timely, relevant information.[22] One analyst predicts that by 2015, approximately 95% of employees will use IM as their primary communication tool for voice, video, and text chatting.[23]

Texting is still considered quite informal for communicating at work. And texting in front of other people—particularly during class!—may be considered rude. But it's useful for these business tasks:

- Confirming deliveries
- Sending product alerts
- Providing fast client contact
- Advertising your new product or service
- Sending important information in a meeting
- Providing instant reminders[24]

Social Media

Perhaps the more interesting technologies for communication are **social media. Web 2.0**, which encourages online interaction, has opened the door for people to participate on the web. This is quite different from the one-way communication of the early Internet, when companies would post brochure-like websites for people to consume.

The real value of social media for companies is the opportunity to connect with people online. Social media is about the *conversation*. To promote interaction, companies use 2.0 technologies, for example, blogs, wikis, video, and social networking sites. These tools are used on the Internet (for the public), on a company's **intranet** (for employee access only), and on **extranets** (private networks for people outside the company, e.g., customers or franchisees). Examples of social media are shown in Figure 6.

For many companies, social media focuses on **user-generated content (UGC)**, also called **consumer-generated media (CGM)**. This content can be blog entries, product reviews, videos, or other messages posted about a company. As we discussed earlier in the Glassdoor example, this content isn't always positive. In Chapter 7, we'll explore how to respond to negative online comments.

The Fortune Global 100 companies are using social media actively. Seventy-nine percent are using at least one of four main social platforms—Twitter, videos, Facebook, and blogs—to communicate with customers.[25] Of these tools, Twitter is the most frequently used.[26] As a student, you may not be excited about Twitter (the average Twitter user is 39 years old),[27] but this has proved useful for companies,

> After introducing a few examples here, we'll discuss social media—and other technologies—where relevant throughout the book. For example, we'll explore wikis for team communication; social networking for interpersonal communication; email, blogs, and instant messaging for written communication; user-generated content for customer communication; and video for oral presentations.

Companies use social media to have a conversation with internal and external audiences.

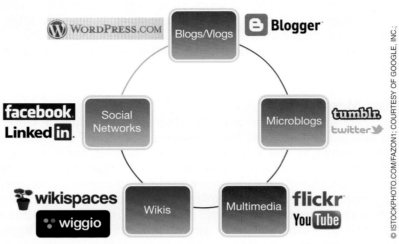

**Figure 6
Social Media
Examples**

as we'll discuss later. The Fortune Global 100's frequency of social media activity is shown in Figure 7.[28]

  Visit the author's blog at www.bizcominthenews.com for current communication examples.

Blogs Companies use blogs to connect with employees and customers. Successful blogs are updated regularly with news or commentary, and many encourage interactivity through comments, email subscriptions, and RSS (Really Simple Syndication) feeds to share news and other content.

Wegmans, a regional supermarket, has an active blog called "Fresh Stories" to educate and engage customers—and keep them coming back. The blog includes videos, photos, and posts by CEO Danny Wegman. In one recent post, the CEO wrote,

> With the spring season upon us (*we hope!* It's been a cold April in the Rochester area), I wanted to kick off the season with a fresh story from the farm. I'm hoping you'll start sharing your growing stories and questions as we experience this new season together![29]

With a blog, a CEO can build direct relationships with customers and personalize the company, particularly with a conversational style such as Danny Wegman's.

The Wegmans blog also allows open comments, which are not always positive. Following the earthquake and tsunami disasters in Japan, one customer wrote,

**Figure 7
How Fortune
Global 100 Use
Social Media**

FREQUENCY OF ACTIVITY

82% Percentage of Fortune 100 companies using their Twitter account per week
27 tweets on average per week

68% Percentage of Fortune 100 companies using their YouTube account per month
10 videos on average per month

59% Percentage of Fortune 100 companies using their Facebook page per week
3.6 posts on average per week

36% Percentage of Fortune 100 companies using their corporate blog per month
7 posts on average per month

"I would like to see Wegmans train their cashiers to not ask me 50 times to donate. . . . NO MEANS NO." Although this is embarrassing to the company, at least the open blog gives representatives the opportunity to respond, as someone did quickly: "We're sorry to hear about your recent experience at the checkout. Our cashiers have not been instructed to ask for donations, but some of them have done so on their own. We'll share your comments with our folks at Warrington."[30] Negative comments from customers also give companies the chance to improve service.

A **vlog** is simply a video form of a blog. Instead of primarily text, this type of blog is like Internet television.

Microblogs **Microblogs** are used for short messages with timely information. Twitter, a popular microblogging site, allows for only 140 characters per message. Although Twitter feels like a social network, relationships with "followers" are weak and primarily one-way (for updates only).[31,32]

As a business tool, Twitter is useful for reporting news and connecting with customers. With a well-established, online presence, Southwest Airlines, for example, can quickly respond to customers' concerns. The tweets in Figures 8 and 9 illustrate a partial Twitter exchange between Kevin Smith, popular movie director, and Southwest Airlines after Smith was asked to give up his seat for being "too fat to fly."

Although most companies avoid public criticism, Southwest's active online presence provided a forum for the company to apologize to Smith and present its perspective on the incident.

Multimedia **Multimedia** may incorporate several forms of media. Corporate videos, for example, can promote products and services, illustrate product functionality, address crisis situations, and excite prospective employees. Deloitte Consulting held a contest—the Deloitte Film Festival—for employees to create videos showing what it's like to work at the company. The videos were fun for employees to create and watch, and examples posted on YouTube became an effective recruiting tool.

Figure 8
Kevin Smith's Tweet About Southwest Airlines

© TWITTER, INC.

Figure 9 Southwest's Response to Kevin Smith

© SOUTHWEST AIRLINES CORPORATE

Flickr is an increasingly popular site for hosting videos and photos. Anyone can post photos on Flickr, and it can be useful for businesses. Just as companies have a "channel" on YouTube, they can create a "group" on Flickr to promote their products.

If you have used iTunes, you know what a **podcast** is. People download and listen to these audio and video files at their desktop computers or on the go. Companies use podcasts to provide portable audio or video content about their products and services.

Wikis **Wikis** are online spaces where people collaborate. Wikipedia, for example, allows people to edit a web page to co-create content. Within a company, wikis allow workgroups to share documents and track revisions, schedule team meetings, communicate online, and manage deadlines. In Chapter 2, we'll discuss how you can create and use a wiki for working in a small group.

Social networking is a subset of social media.

Social Networking If you're on Facebook, you're familiar with **social networking**. Under the social media umbrella, social networking sites are for communities of people who share common interests or activities. You may be surprised to learn that the average Facebook user is 38 years old.[33] Clearly, this site has evolved from its college roots. Some companies have a Facebook page to connect with customers, while others participate in other social networking sites such as MySpace. As a business student, you might be registered on LinkedIn, a professional networking site.

Social networking tools are sometimes integrated into other social media platforms. For example, companies install programs that mirror social networking sites on their intranets to connect employees within the organization. In Chapter 3, we'll look at social networking in more detail.

Choosing Communication Media

Given all of these media choices, which is best for your message? You should always consider your audience and communication objectives first. What do you want your audience to do, think, or feel differently as a result of your message, and what's the best medium to achieve this?

Although perceptions of communication media vary, we can think of our choices along the continuum shown in Figure 10.

Do you agree with this sequence? From your own experience and perspective, which would you move, and why? For example, is a text message more personal than an email because it's sent immediately to someone's phone?

Figure 10 **Continuum of Communication Media**

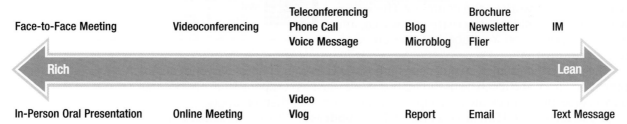

The richest medium is a face-to-face (in-person) conversation or meeting, where you are physically present and have the most communication cues, such as body language.

Rich media are more interactive than lean media. You have the opportunity for two-way communication: the receiver can ask questions and express opinions easily in person.

Rich media are best for difficult, complex, or emotional messages, such as decisions that people won't agree with, highly technical information, or changes that negatively affect people.

You might find media *roughly* in this order along the continuum.

Face-to-Face Meeting	Videoconferencing	Teleconferencing Phone Call Voice Message	Blog Microblog	Brochure Newsletter Flier	IM

Rich ←————————————————————————————→ **Lean**

In-Person Oral Presentation	Online Meeting	Video Vlog	Report	Email	Text Message

Lean media do not allow for many cues to complement and enrich your message. Written communication typically is leaner than oral communication.

With little opportunity for two-way communication, lean media are one-way and static.

Lean media are best for routine, neutral, simple messages, such as a regular meeting request, a weekly report, or a product update.

Relationship Considerations	Logistical Considerations
• What is your relationship with the audience? Do you have a strong, existing relationship, or are you building a new one? • Is the communication neutral, positive, or potentially bad news? How is the audience likely to react? • To what extent do you want immediate feedback? Will this communication be one-way or two-way? • What would your audience prefer? What are the organizational norms for this type of communication? If you're responding to a message, in what form did you receive it? • At what level of the organization is the receiver? Is this person senior, junior, or at your level? • Is this message confidential or private in some way? • Do you need the message or conversation documented?	• How long is the message? How complex is the information? • How many people will receive the message? • How urgent is the message? Do the receivers need it immediately? • Where are the receivers located? • What is most practical and efficient? • How easily will the receivers understand your message? What's their primary language and reading proficiency? • What access to technology does your audience have?

Figure 11
Considerations for Choosing Communication Media

© CENGAGE LEARNING 2013

As you plan your messages, you also might find the considerations in Figure 11 useful.

Companies often will use multiple communication channels as part of a large communication strategy. Sending multiple messages through a variety of communication media helps the company reach different audiences. To announce a company acquisition, for example, executives may hold a conference call with analysts, meet with the management team in person, send an email to all employees, and post a video on the company intranet. This coordination is part of a strategic communication plan, typically created at senior levels in an organization.

Convergence of Communication Media

Technology is blurring many forms of communication—oral and written, face-to-face and online. Imagine that you're meeting with a customer in person and send a text to someone back at the office to ask a quick product question. Or, you're on a phone call and respond to an IM. These examples could be considered **multicommunicating**, or **synchronous** (at the same time), overlapping conversations.[34]

Multicommunicating can be effective—up to a point. As you can imagine, with too many conversations going at the same time, it's easy to get confused. And you can be effective at multicommunicating only if people around you tolerate this. In some work situations, texting during a meeting may be acceptable, but not in others. Pay attention to what your respected peers do, and adjust your behavior to match theirs.

Communication technologies themselves are also connecting and converging. **Mashups**, for example, are web applications or pages that combine content from different sources. **Geolocation** services such as Foursquare and Gowalla display mashups based on where you are. Some programs allow you to open an email and listen to an attached voice message or open a text and watch a video. What will distinguish email, IM, and texting in the future if communication becomes more and more immediate? This remains to be seen.

LO4　Avoid potential legal consequences of communication.

POTENTIAL LEGAL CONSEQUENCES OF COMMUNICATION

In a business environment, we need to consider legal consequences—and other repercussions—of our communication. When you work for a company, anything you write and say may become public if your company is sued or is part of a government investigation. During legal discovery, the company must produce evidence related to an inquiry, including emails, IMs, recorded phone conversations, voice mail messages, and other communications the attorneys believe are relevant. According to an American Management Association (AMA) study, 24% of companies have had email subpoenaed in lawsuits.[35] This may include emails employees wrote using personal email addresses, such as Gmail, and believed were private.

In 2010, when the U.S. Securities and Exchange Commission sued Goldman Sachs for fraud related to the financial crisis, the company produced mounds of documentation. Within the 200 million pages Goldman submitted were email messages that investigators called into question. In some emails, Goldman executives seem to be boasting about profits in the midst of the U.S. housing market collapse.[36]

Goldman's emails also were embarrassing because of the profanity used. During congressional hearings, management was repeatedly questioned about obscene language used in their messages. Since then, the company has banned profanity in emails—and has implemented software to scan emails for obscene words and warn the writer before messages are sent.[37]

Employee emails may become public if your company is sued or is part of a government investigation, as these Goldman Sachs executives learned during congressional hearings.

© JIM WATSON/AFP/GETTY IMAGES

In the Goldman case, email messages became public as part of a broader investigation; however, messages themselves may be the impetus for a lawsuit. The AMA study also found that 15% of U.S. companies fought legal claims based on employees' email.[38]

When you join a company, you will probably sign several policies about communicating at work. These are designed to protect the company against lawsuits, public relations nightmares, and breaches of confidentiality, privacy, and security. Your company may provide guidelines, such as the following examples from Time Warner Cable's (TWC) social media policy:

• Follow copyright, fair use, and financial disclosure laws.

• Don't publish confidential or other proprietary information.

- Don't cite or reference clients, partners, or suppliers without their prior approval. When a reference is made, where possible, link back to the source.

- When communicating online, behave professionally and with the utmost respect for those individuals involved in the discussion. Ethnic slurs, personal insults, foul language, or conduct that would not be acceptable in TWC's workplace should not be used.

- On social networks where you identify yourself as an employee of TWC, be mindful that the content posted will be visible to coworkers, customers, and partners. Make sure the information posted is the most professional reflection of your opinions and beliefs.

- Do not insult or disparage TWC, its products and services, or any fellow employees, even if specific names are not mentioned.[39]

You can protect yourself and your company by paying careful attention to what you put in writing and what you say. A law firm suggests asking yourself, "'Would I be comfortable two years from now being cross-examined in federal court in front of a jury about the content of this email I am about to send?' If the answer is anything other than an unqualified 'yes,' it is not an email that should be sent."[40] You might ask yourself the same question for all communications related to your company.

LO5 Communicate ethically.

ETHICS AND COMMUNICATION

Beyond the legal requirements, companies will expect you to communicate ethically. Consider this situation: Brian Maupin, a Best Buy employee, posted videos about the company on YouTube.[41] His first cartoon video, which received over 3.3 million views within two weeks, mocked a customer of "Phone Mart," desperate for the latest version of the iPhone (Figure 12).

Ethics in Communication

Before Maupin was invited back after being suspended, he created another video poking fun at the company's policies. This interaction, between the store employee and the woman who "run[s] the ethics department" at the corporate office, illustrates gray areas in communication ethics—and the importance of social media policies.

Was Maupin's behavior ethical? Most corporate executives would consider the videos disparaging to the company. Although Maupin didn't expect the videos to be such a huge success, he still publicly disagreed with sales policies, questioned loyalty to a top Best Buy supplier (Apple), and insulted customers. Things worked

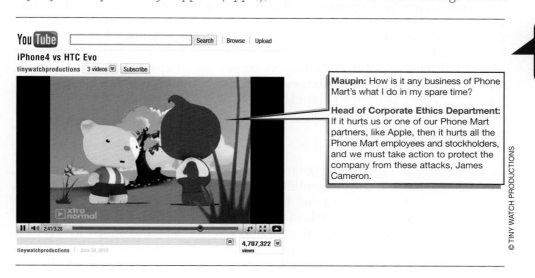

Figure 12
Best Buy Employee Posts a Video

© TINY WATCH PRODUCTIONS

out fine for Maupin, but negative comments about your company—or people—are best kept private.

Each of us has a personal code of **ethics**, or system of moral principles, that go beyond legal rules to tell us how to act. Our ethics represent our personal belief about whether something is right or wrong. As children, we begin forming our ethical standards based on how we perceive the behavior of our parents, other adults, and our peer group.

Let's consider three types of ethics:

Consider professional, social, and individual ethics.

- **Professional ethics** are defined by an organization (such as Best Buy or The Public Relations Society of America). Employees and members are expected to follow these guidelines, which define what is right or wrong in the workplace—often beyond established laws. For example, 95% of Fortune 500 companies protect their employees from discrimination in the workplace based on sexual orientation. This goes beyond the U.S. federal legal requirement.[42]

- **Social ethics** are defined by society. For example, although accepting gifts from suppliers is strictly frowned upon in North American societies, this practice may be commonplace and accepted in other societies.

- **Individual ethics** are defined by the person and are based on family values, heritage, personal experience, and other factors. For example, most universities have guidelines to deter plagiarism. In addition to the guidelines that represent professional ethics, you probably have your own beliefs about cheating.

What Affects Ethical Behavior

According to ethicists, when people make unethical decisions, they do so for one of three reasons:

1. We do what's most convenient—in other words, we take the easy route.
2. We do what we must to win. Some people think that embracing ethics would limit their ability to succeed. They believe that "good guys finish last."
3. We rationalize our choices. We decide that the decision we make depends upon the particular circumstances (this is called **situational ethics**).

Ethics are affected by the corporate culture.

The corporate culture affects ethics. If everyone spends time during the workday on Facebook, you are likely to also (the "everybody-does-it" defense). If managers are aware of unethical practices and don't stop them, they are condoning these actions.

How much freedom an organization gives an employee to behave unethically also affects behavior. At fast-food restaurants, for example, one employee takes your order and receives your payment, and another employee fills the order. This means that the person filling your order doesn't handle the money, and the person who handles the money doesn't fill your order. In this case, less opportunity for theft occurs.

When a strict code of ethics is in effect and enforced, employees have fewer opportunities to be unethical. Employees know what is expected of them and what happens if they fail to live up to these expectations, which is why a clearer policy at Best Buy may have helped Brian Maupin.

Ethics Pays

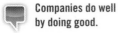
Companies do well by doing good.

Companies that are considered the most ethical outperform the S&P 500 and FTSE 100. The Ethisphere Institute identifies an annual list of ethical companies based on their corporate citizenship and responsibility, innovation that contributes to the public well-being, executive leadership and tone from the top, and other criteria. Gap Inc., for example, appears on the Ethisphere list—and on the list of "Best Corporate Citizens," published by *Corporate Responsibility Magazine*. On its website, shown in Figure 13, you can see how Gap promotes its social responsibility.[43]

Many companies are including **corporate social responsibility (CSR)** into their business model. CSR (or being socially responsible) means that companies consider the public's interest in their business practices. CSR extends beyond a solely numbers-driven measurement of success and instead encourages focus on a triple bottom line of people, planet, profit. Progressive companies consider CSR good for business—and the right thing to do.

Framework for Ethical Decision Making

When faced with an ethical decision, consider the factors shown in Figure 14.

In addition to ethical decisions, we face communications that challenge us to be responsible and appropriate. When a recent law school graduate, Dianna, sent emails to her prospective employer (a criminal defense attorney),[44] she didn't think about the consequences. In an email, she stated that she decided not to accept the firm's job offer. However, William, her hiring manager, had a different perspective: that she had already accepted the job. He said that he had finished preparing a computer and ordering office supplies for her. If William's version is true, most people would probably agree that Dianna's decision was unethical.

Figure 13 Gap Promotes Its Social Responsibility

© GAP INC.

Figure 14 Framework for Ethical Decision Making

1. Is the action legal? If the decision does not comply with workplace laws, such as workplace safety, equal opportunity, privacy, and sexual harassment, then don't do it.

2. Does the action comply with your company's policies and guidelines? This may be the time to re-read documentation or ask your manager or human resources representative.

3. Who will be affected by your decision and how? Determine who has an important stake in the outcome of your decision. Stakeholders might include employees, customers, suppliers, and the wider community. What is at stake for each?

4. Does the action comply with the company values? Even without a formal code of conduct policy, is the decision consistent with general business practices?

5. How will you feel after the decision is known? What if your actions were published on the company intranet or in the local paper? Could you face yourself in the mirror?

© CENGAGE LEARNING 2013

You'll find this entire email exchange on www .bizcominthenews.com, under Company Samples.

Beyond the ethics of the decision, were Dianna and William's communications responsible and appropriate? Dianna sent an email and left a voice mail message at 9:30 P.M., when William would not likely be in the office. She certainly could have chosen a more appropriate medium for her message, perhaps a phone call during business hours. William responded to Dianna's email with anger, writing that her email "smacks of immaturity." Dianna could have let it go, but she responded, questioning William's legal knowledge. Not to be outdone, William responded and warned her to avoid "pissing off more experienced lawyers." Did the exchange end there? Of course not. Dianna sent one final email with three words: "bla bla bla." William then forwarded the email chain, which was forwarded again and again, until it became viral and made ABC Nightly News. Both Dianna and William could have taken the high road and ended the exchange earlier. Their angry, belittling, back-and-forth dialog did not reflect professional business behavior.

Communicating Ethically

According to one communication professor,

> Much of what is controversial in the workplace today revolves around ethics and the way people express their views. . . . Ethics is inextricably tied to communication. The rhetorical acts of persuading or of simply passing on information are deeply influenced by individual ethical perspectives.[45]

When communicating, we constantly make decisions with ethical implications.

When communicating, we constantly make decisions regarding what information to include and what information to exclude from our messages. For the information that is included, we make conscious decisions about how to phrase the message, how much to emphasize each point, and how to organize the message. According to one business survey, 63% of the managers surveyed stated that misleading communications had undermined their trust in companies.[46]

Communication decisions have legal and ethical dimensions—both for you as the writer and for the organization. For example, BMW, the German automobile maker, was required to pay a $2 million judgment awarded to a U.S. car buyer because it had failed to inform him that paint had been damaged and then retouched.[47]

Competent communicators ensure that their oral and written messages are ethical, both in terms of what is communicated and in terms of what is left unsaid.

INTRODUCING THE 3PS (PURPOSE, PROCESS, PRODUCT) MODEL

Every chapter in this text concludes with a 3Ps model to illustrate important communication concepts covered in the chapter. These short case studies, which relate to each chapter introduction, include the *purpose,* the *process,* and the *product* (the 3Ps). The *purpose* defines the situation and discusses the need for a particular communication task. The *process* is a series of questions that provides step-by-step guidance for accomplishing the specific communication task. Finally, the *product* is the result—the final communication.

The 3Ps model guides you step-by-step through a typical communication by posing and answering relevant questions about each aspect of the message.

The 3Ps model demonstrates examples of communication so that you can see the *process* of communicating, not just the results. This approach helps you focus on one aspect of your communication at a time. Using the 3Ps in your own communication will help you produce messages more easily and deliver a better result. Pay particular attention to the questions in the *process* section, and ask yourself similar questions as you prepare your own messages.

An Ethical Decision from the Movie *Up in the Air*

The 3Ps In Action

Purpose

The movie *Up in the Air* profiles a consulting firm hired by other companies to communicate layoff decisions to employees. Of course, this isn't a real firm, and people might question the ethics of an outside company giving employees such bad news.

Imagine that you are a graduating senior and have received a job offer to work for this company as an entry-level auditor in the accounting office. You like the position, but you are disturbed by its ruthless reputation of firing the employees of other firms. You have to decide whether to accept the job, despite your concerns about the company.

Process

To help you decide whether to accept the job, you use the Framework for Ethical Decision Making. You choose the following questions because they are most relevant to the situation:

1. **Is the action legal?**
   Yes, both the company's work and my position at the company are legal. As long as companies don't discriminate against employees, they can legally downsize for business reasons.

2. **Who will be affected by my decision and how?**
   Employees will still be laid off whether I take the job or not. My decision, technically, won't directly affect people who lose their jobs.

3. **Is this job in line with my values?**
   I wish that companies could avoid downsizing staff (perhaps with more strategic planning and better management). But I realize that downsizing is a reality of working in business.

   On the other hand, employees should hear bad news from someone they know and trust—for example, their supervisor—not from someone outside the company. This just doesn't feel right to me.

4. **How will I feel after the decision is known?**
   If I take the job, I probably won't feel too good. I want to be proud of the company I work for instead of embarrassed about what they do. I'm concerned about explaining the company's business to my family. What would my parents say?

Product

Based on the answers to these questions, you decide not to accept the job. When you call the hiring manager to turn down the job, you don't mention your ethical dilemma; instead, you state your appreciation for the offer and focus on your decision.

The 3Ps In Practice

Media Choices in the Movie *Up in the Air*

Purpose

The company profiled in the movie *Up in the Air* is looking to save costs, and Natalie, a recent college graduate, has an idea to accomplish this goal: communicate layoff decisions through videoconferencing technology rather than flying consultants out to meet with people in person. You are Natalie's manager (but more reasonable than Natalie's manager in the movie), and you want to explain to Natalie why her idea is not an appropriate medium for telling people the bad news.

Process

1. What criteria will you use to determine the best communication medium for a message?
2. Why are face-to-face meetings (a rich medium) most commonly used for the layoff discussions?
3. What are the downsides of Natalie's suggestion to use videoconferencing?
4. How will you explain your rationale to Natalie?
5. What medium will you use for your message to Natalie? Consider an email, a memo, or a face-to-face meeting. Why did you choose this option?

Product

Using the medium you chose in response to the last question above (email, memo, or face-to-face meeting), prepare your communication to Natalie. Explain to her why videoconferencing is not a suitable medium for announcing a layoff decision.

Summary

L01   Identify the components of communication.

The components of communication explain how communication happens. The communication process begins with a stimulus, which is filtered by the receiver, who creates a message transmitted through a medium. If your message is successful, the receiver (destination) provides feedback to the sender. These components of communication are used in both formal and informal communication networks. The formal communication network consists of downward, upward, and lateral (horizontal) communication. The informal communication network (the grapevine) consists of information transmitted through unofficial channels.

L02   Identify the major verbal and nonverbal barriers to communication.

Barriers may interfere with effective communication. Examples of verbal barriers are inadequate knowledge or vocabulary, differences in interpretation, language differences, inappropriate use of expressions, overabstraction and ambiguity, and polarization. Examples of nonverbal barriers are inappropriate or conflicting signals, differences in perception, inappropriate emotions, and distractions.

L03   Describe criteria for choosing communication media.

Verbal communication includes oral and written communication. Traditional communication channels, such as face-to-face meetings and letters, still exist, but technology-based communication, such as social media, are increasingly popular for business communication. When deciding which channel (medium) to use for your message, first identify your audience and communication objectives. Consider lean channels for routine and neutral messages and rich channels for complex messages and bad news.

L04   Avoid potential legal consequences of communication.

Although communication is essential to all organizations, oral and written communication may have negative consequences as well. Email and other messages may be part of a legal discovery process, and inappropriate communication may be the impetus for litigation. To avoid these damaging situations, follow your company's guidelines and policies regarding email and other communication.

L05   Communicate ethically.

Beyond the legal requirements, we all have our own system of moral practices that guide our behavior. At the company level, corporate social responsibility (CSR) has become part of progressive organizations' communication strategy. At the personal level, you're responsible for behaving ethically, which includes how you communicate at work. The Framework for Ethical Decision Making will help guide your behavior and ensure that you communicate ethically.

Exercises

1. Identify communication components in a current news story.

Use a current news item to identify the five components of the communication process. You may use examples from the author's blog www.bizcominthenews.com. After reading background information about the story, choose one aspect of communication and identify the stimulus, filter, message, medium, feedback, and noise. You may add your own assumptions if you don't have enough details from the story.

L01 Identify the components of communication.

2. Examine your own communication filters.

Looking at the same news story you explored above, list at least ten ways you personally are filtering the information you receive. Consider such factors as your individual experiences, culture, emotions at the moment, personality, knowledge, socioeconomic status, and demographic variables.

3. Create an organization chart to identify a company's formal communication network.

Think of an organization where you've worked recently. Create an organization chart for two or three levels of employees. Then add arrows to identify the three directions of the formal communication network.

4. Describe a company's grapevine.

For the same organization you explored in the previous question, consider the informal communication network. With a partner, discuss how you heard about unofficial information about the company. How accurate do you think this information was? Was senior management plugged into the grapevine? Do you have examples of how management responded to information spread through the grapevine? If management ignored the grapevine, what do you think should have been done instead?

LO2 Identify the major verbal and nonverbal barriers to communication.

5. Identify communication barriers between a manager and an employee.

Watch Scene 13, "Flair," from the movie *Office Space*. This communication does not go very well. Identify the verbal and nonverbal barriers of communication in this scene.

Scene from the movie *Office Space*

6. Identify communication barriers between a retail sales representative and a customer.

Watch the video clip from the fictitious retail store, Aggresshop. Identify the verbal and nonverbal barriers of communication in this scene. Think about the interaction from both perspectives: the sales associate's and the shopper's.

7. Discuss communication barriers.

Which category of communication barriers—verbal or nonverbal—do you believe is easier to overcome? Why? Share your thoughts with the rest of the class.

Scene from the Aggresshop video

8. Adapt jargon for your audience.

Think of a topic you know well (e.g., a sport, a hobby, or an academic subject). Write an email to a colleague who is also an expert on the subject. Include at least six jargon terms that flow easily into the context of your email.

Now assume that you are sending the same email to someone who is not at all familiar with the topic. Revise your original message to make it appropriate for this reader. Which email is longer? Which is more effective? Why?

9. Analyze print communication.

Find an example of print communication, for example, a flyer on campus, a newsletter, or a magazine ad. With a partner, discuss why the creator of the message may have chosen a print medium. In your opinion, was this the best choice? What technology-based media may have worked instead or could supplement the printed message?

10. Explore how a company uses social media.

What's your favorite company? Spend some time exploring how the company uses social media. Does it have a customer blog, Facebook page, Twitter account, and other online places to connect with constituencies? Now compare this company's online presence to one of its close competitors' online presence. Which has more online activity, for example, more followers on Twitter, more people who "like" it on Facebook, or more blogs targeted to different audiences? In small groups, discuss findings about each of your favorite companies.

11. Choose communication media for different audiences.

Imagine that you're the CEO of a retail store such as Aggresshop (described at the end of this chapter and at www.cengagebrain.com). Let's say you're planning to redesign each of the 16 stores in the United States. As part of this effort, you'll need to close stores for two weeks at a time. Working in teams, identify in the communication plan template below which medium you would use to communicate with each audience. You may have multiple communications for some audiences. Include the rationale for your decisions.

Audience	Communication Medium (or Media)	Rationale for Choosing the Communication Medium
Store managers		
Store sales representatives		
Corporate office employees		
VIP customers		
Other customers		
Suppliers		

12. Choose how to a reject a job offer.

We'll discuss employment communication in Chapter 12; for now, consider a situation in which you're offered a summer internship but decide not to accept it. With a partner, discuss the most appropriate communication channel to use for your message. Would you use a different channel if you received the offer by email or by phone?

13. Give your manager advice about communication media.

For this exercise, you'll help your manager be a better communicator. Let's say you're lucky enough to have a good working relationship with your manager, and he or she tells you—before the rest of the team—that your department will be moving from

L03 Describe criteria for choosing communication media.

downtown Chicago to a suburb. This is a major change and will be bad news for most people.

In response to this email from your manager, write a reply to suggest that he also hold a face-to-face meeting for employees. Explain why you think this is important.

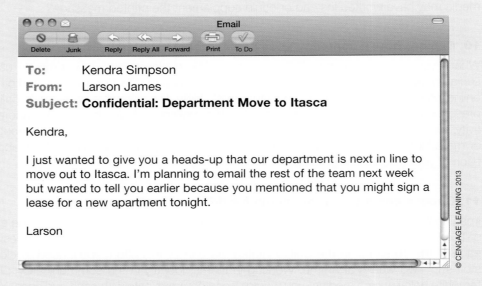

L04 Avoid potential legal consequences of communication.

14. Research a lawsuit about communication.

Find an example of a company that was sued because of its communication. Research the situation with a particular focus on the communication that was called into question (e.g., email messages, unclear reports, or discriminatory language).

Imagine that you're a consultant who was hired by one of the company's competitors. The competitor would like to avoid a similar situation and wants to hear what you learned about the case. Prepare and deliver a short presentation to class, summarizing the main points. Focus on how the company can avoid a similar lawsuit.

15. Write a policy about email use.

Draft a policy about employees' email use. Consider what would be important for a company to communicate to employees about their email communication. Next, search the Internet to find a sample policy about appropriate use of email. You may find one on your school's website (perhaps you had to read and sign a policy when you first enrolled). Compare your draft to the sample. Did you miss any important points? Revise your policy if necessary.

Then, in small groups, discuss your policy and be honest about how your use of email may violate the policy. Now that you know what is expected, would you handle email differently? Why or why not?

L05 Communicate ethically.

16. Respond to an email that suggests an unethical practice.

Imagine that you're an intern for the law firm Dewey, Wright, and Howe. As part of a team, you're developing an Orientation Plan for future interns. Your team receives the email on the next page from the HR recruiter at the firm.

In small groups, first discuss the situation and why this is an ethical dilemma. Then, on your own, write an email to respond to Mark's suggestion. You will want to balance ethics with tone to avoid accusing Mark of anything inappropriate and potentially making him feel defensive. When you're finished, share your draft with your group members and compare emails. Which works best and why?

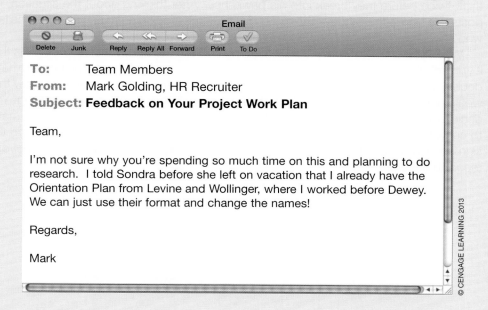

To: Team Members
From: Mark Golding, HR Recruiter
Subject: **Feedback on Your Project Work Plan**

Team,

I'm not sure why you're spending so much time on this and planning to do research. I told Sondra before she left on vacation that I already have the Orientation Plan from Levine and Wollinger, where I worked before Dewey. We can just use their format and change the names!

Regards,

Mark

© CENGAGE LEARNING 2013

17. Discuss ethical dilemmas.

Working in small groups and using the guidelines for ethical decision making discussed in this chapter, decide what you would do in each of the following situations:

1. *Confidentiality:* Your boss told you that one of your employees will have to be laid off because of budget cuts, but this information is confidential for the time being. You know that the employee just received a job offer from another company but is planning to reject the offer.

2. *Copyright Issues:* During peer reviews in a class, you read another student's paper and noticed two paragraphs of information that sounded familiar. The content appears to be quoted directly from a textbook used in your Introduction to Marketing class.

3. *Employment:* You accepted a job but received an offer for a much better job two days later.

4. *Hiring:* A Colombian candidate is the most qualified for a job, but the position requires quite a bit of face-to-face and telephone communication with customers, and you're concerned that customers won't understand his accent.

5. *Academic Integrity:* A friend asks you to proofread and correct his 12-page Financial Accounting report, which is due online in two hours. You notice lots of grammatical and typographical errors.

6. *Merit-Based Pay:* An employee has performed well all year and deserves a pay raise. However, she is at the top of her grade scale and can't be promoted.

18. Address a questionable business tactic.

You work part-time at a busy pawnshop in central San Antonio. A number of neighborhood stores have been burglarized in recent years, and the owner wants criminals to think twice before they break into his pawnshop. After thinking about the situation, he posts this sign in the window one night: "$10,000 reward offered to any officer of the law who shoots and kills someone attempting to rob this property."

When you come to work the next morning and see the sign, your first thought is that it will probably be an effective deterrent. As the day goes on, however, you begin to have doubts about the ethics of posting such a sign. Although you don't know of any law that would apply to this situation, you're not sure that your boss is doing the right thing. You decide to speak with him. To prepare for this discussion, list the points you might make to convince the boss to take the sign down. Next, list the points in favor of leaving the sign up. If you were in charge, what would you do? Explain your answer in a brief oral report to the class.

Each chapter ends with a company scenario available at www.cengagebrain.com. This first scenario, Aggresshop, is also used at the end of Chapter 8, Bad-News Messages.

Company Scenario

Aggresshop

Imagine you work for Aggresshop, an upscale women's clothing boutique with 16 stores throughout the United States. At www.cengagebrain.com, you'll find Aggresshop's company blog for customers and employees.

As you'll read in the scenario, Aggresshop is experiencing many customer complaints about its sales associates' overly aggressive techniques (two posts are shown below). The CEO decides to change the sales compensation structure to address this issue.

On the blog, you'll see examples of several communication concepts discussed in Chapter 1: directions of communication, communication media, barriers to communication, and ethics in communication. This scenario will also help you learn to do the following:

- Respond to customer complaints on a company blog.
- Communicate a change internally.
- Tailor message content and tone for different audiences and communication channels.

To help you practice your business communication, your instructor may assign the following activities now or later in the semester:

- Write customer service standards for Aggresshop sales associates.
- Respond to customer comments on the blog.
- Write an article for customers on the blog.

CATEGORIES
Complaints
Compliments

COMPANY INFORMATION
Welcome, Aggresshop Customers!
About Aggresshop
Employees' Entrance
Management's Entrance

No fighting in front of the customer, please!

I was at the register waiting to check out, and two of the sales associates had an argument in front of me about who gets the sale. I guess one of them suggested the dress, but the other one got me a different size. Whatever! Why don't they just split it?

Check out this video

My boyfriend filmed me in an Aggresshop in San Diego, and this is what happened! All of the customer complaints are true!

Aggresshop video on YouTube

Notes

1. Rana Tassabehji and Maria Vakola, "Business Email: The Killer Impact," *Communications of the ACM* 48 (2005): 64–70.

2. Harris International and Whitepages.com, "Survey Shows Most Adults Want Tough Talks Face to Face," February 27, 2007, www.whitepagesinc.com/press/article/000000073, accessed July 12, 2010.

3. Jill Casner-Lotto, Elyse Rosenblum, and Mary Wright, "The Ill-Prepared U.S. Workforce," Consortium: Corporate Voices for Working Families, The Conference Board, SHRM, and ASTD, 2009, www.shrm.org/Research/SurveyFindings/Articles/Documents/BED-09Workforce_RR.pdf, accessed July 6, 2010.

4. "Employers Rank Communication Skills First Among Job Candidate Skills and Qualities," National Association of Colleges and Employers, January 21, 2010, http://www.vscpa.com/Content/57969.aspx, accessed July 6, 2010.

5. "Writing: A Ticket to Work . . . Or a Ticket Out?" The College Board, The National Commission on Writing, September 2004, www.collegeboard.com/prod_downloads/writingcom/writing-ticket-to-work.pdf, accessed July 6, 2010.

6. Sam Dillon. "What Corporate America Can't Build: A Sentence," *The New York Times*, December 7, 2004, www.nytimes.com/2004/12/07/business/07write.html, accessed July 6, 2010.

7. "Capitalizing on Effective Communication. Communication ROI Study Report," Watson Wyatt, 2009/2010, www.towerswatson.com/assets/pdf/670/NA-2009-14890.pdf, accessed July 6, 2010.

8. "Writing: A Ticket to Work . . . Or a Ticket Out?"

9. Mark H. McCormack, "Words You Use Tell a Lot About You," *Arizona Republic*, April 13, 2000, p. D4.

10. Although many believe that the Chinese word for crisis is made up of elements that mean "danger" and "opportunity," linguists and sinologists have debunked this myth. See, for example, Victor H. Mair, "How a misunderstanding about Chinese characters has led many astray," September 2009, http://www.pinyin.info/chinese/crisis.html, accessed October 22, 2011.

11. Starbucks, www.starbucks.com, accessed July 8, 2010.

12. Barry Ray, "Who's Afraid of the Big Bad Boss? Plenty of Us, New FSU Study Shows." Florida State University News, December 4, 2006, www.fsu.edu/news/2006/12/04/bad.boss/, accessed July 7, 2010. Study by Wayne Hochwarter, an associate professor of management in FSU's College of Business.

13. Suzanne M. Crampton, John W. Hodge, and Jitendra M. Mishra, "The Informal Network: Factors Influencing Grapevine Activity," *Public Personnel Management* 27 (1998): 568–584.

14. Ragan Communications Forum, "Have you been fired?" www.myragan.com, accessed July 10, 2010.

15. Clare Baldwin, "Media Multitasking Doesn't Work Say Researchers," Reuters, August 24, 2009, http://uk.reuters.com/article/2009/08/24/tech-us-multitasking-stanford-idUKTRE57N55D20090824, accessed September 25, 2010.

16. Jack Trout, "Beware Of 'Infomania.'" Forbes.com. August 11, 2006. www.forbes.com/fdc/welcome_mjx.shtml, accessed July 8, 2010.

17. "'We Never Talk Anymore.' Survey Reveals Few Executives Use Telephone or Meet in Person at Work," OfficeTeam, January 18, 2006, www.honeycombconnect.com/Human_Resources/document_6389.ashx?page=page_74&datasource=68, accessed July 29, 2010.

18. Sara Radicati, "Business User Survey, 2009," The Radicati Group, Inc. www.radicati.com/wp/wp-content/uploads/2009/11/Business-User-Survey-2009-Executive-Summary1.pdf, accessed July 29, 2010.

19. Thomas W. Jackson, Anthony Burgess, and Janet Edwards, "A Simple Approach to Improving Email Communication," *Communications of the ACM* 49 (June 2006): 107–109.

20. Judi Brownell and Amy Newman, "Hospitality Managers and Communication Technologies: Challenges and Solutions." *Cornell Hospitality Research* 9 (December 2009).

21. R. Kelly Garrett and James N. Danziger, "IM = Interruption Management? Instant Messaging and Disruption in the Workplace," *Journal of Computer-Mediated Communication* 13 (2007): article 2.

22. Eulynn Shiu and Amanda Lenhart, "How Americans Use Instant Messaging," Pew Internet & American Life Project, September 2004, www.pewinternet.org/Reports/2004/How-Americans-Use-Instant-Messaging.aspx, accessed July 29, 2009.

23. Gartner, "Hype Cycle for Emerging Technologies, 2008 [ID Number: G00159496]," www.gartner.com/technology/research/methodologies/hypeCycles.jsp, accessed May 20, 2009.

24. "Ten Ways to Use Texting for Business," Inc.com, www.inc.com/ss/ten-ways-use-texting-business, accessed July 12, 2010.

25. "Social Media in Business: Fortune 100 Statistics," iStrategy 2010 with data from Burson-Marsteller, June 7, 2010, http://misterthibodeau.posterous.com/istrategy-2010-blog-archive-social-media-in-b, accessed July 14, 2010.

26. Ibid.

27. "Study: Ages of Social Network Users," Pingdom with data from Google Ad Planner, February 16, 2010, http://royal.pingdom.com/2010/02/16/study-ages-of-social-network-users/, accessed July 14, 2010.

28. iStrategy 2010.

29. Danny Wegman, "Down on the Farm: Watching Our Tomatoes Grow," Wegmans Blog, May 3, 2011, www.wegmans.com/blog/, accessed May 12, 2011.

30. Colleen Wegman, "Responding to the Crisis in Japan and How You Can Help," Wegmans Blog, March 17, 2011, www.wegmans.com/blog/, accessed May 12, 2011.

31. Dan Zarrella. "Is Twitter a Social Network?" HubSpot blog, June 22, 2009, http://blog.hubspot.com/blog/tabid/6307/Default.aspx?Author=Dan%20Zarrella&BBPage=7, accessed July 12, 2010.

32. Antone Gonsalves, "Twitter Is About News, Not Social Media," *Information Week*, May 5, 2010, www.informationweek.com/news/windows/microsoft_news/224700842, accessed July 17, 2010.

33. Pingdom.

34. N. Lamar Reinsch, Jr., et al., "Multi-communicating: A Practice Whose Time Has Come?" *Academy of Management Review* 33 (2008): 391–408.

35. American Management Association and the ePolicy Institute, 2006. "Workplace E-mail, Instant Messaging and Blog Survey," www.epolicyinstitute.com/survey2006Summary.pdf, accessed July 20, 2009.

36. "Goldman Disputes Assertions About E-mails," CBS News, April 24, 2010, www.cbsnews.com/stories/2010/04/24/business/main6428758.shtml, accessed September 18, 2010.

37. Cassell Bryan-Low and Aaron Lucchetti, "George Carlin Never Would've Cut It at the New Goldman Sachs," *The Wall Street Journal*, July 29, 2010, http://online.wsj.com/article/SB1000142405274870 489500457539555067240 6796.html, accessed July 29, 2010.

38. American Management Association.

39. Lydia Dishman, "Social Media Policies: The Good, The Mediocre, and the Ugly," Fast Company, June 9, 2010, www.fastcompany.com/1668368/social-media-policies-the-good-the-bad-and-the-ugly, accessed February 22, 2011.

40. Douglas C. Northup and Ronald J. Stolkin, "Legal Issues Affecting Business E-mails." Fennemore Craig, June 13, 2007, www.fclaw.com/newsletter/materials/BusinessEmailsUpdate6-13-07.pdf, accessed July 19, 2010.

41. MG Siegler, "Best Buy Trying to Fire Employee Over Those Hilarious EVO versus iPhone Videos," TechCrunch, July 1, 2010, http://techcrunch.com/2010/07/01/best-buy-iphone-4-evo-4g/, accessed September 11, 2010.

42. Equality Forum, "Fortune 500 Project," www.equalityforum.com/fortune500/, accessed July 19, 2010.

43. "2010 World's Most Ethical Companies," Ethisphere, http://ethisphere.com/wme2010/, accessed July 19, 2010.

44. Jack Tapper, "The 'Bla Bla Bla' Heard 'Round the World," ABC News/Nightline, February 18, 2006, http://abcnews.go.com/Nightline/story?id=1635472, accessed July 20, 2010.

45. Betsy Stevens, "Teaching Communication with Ethics-Based Cases," *Business Communication Quarterly* (September 1996): 6.

46. "What Has Undermined Your Trust in Companies?" *USA Today*, February 10, 2003, p. 1B.

47. "State Court Cuts Punitive Award in BMW Car Case," *Wall Street Journal*, May 12, 1997, p. B5.

Chapter 2

Work Team Communication (2) Conflict (2) Conformity (2) Consensus (2) Giving Constructive Feedback (2) Conflict Resolution (2) Collaboration on Team Writing Projects (2) Applying Strategies for Team Writing (2) Team and Intercultural Communication (2) Commenting on Peers' Writing (2) Using Technology for Work in Teams (2) Intercultural Communication (2) Cultural Differences (2) Group-Oriented Behavior (2) Strategies for Communicating Across Cultures (2) Diversity Within the United States (2) The Value of Diversity (2) Ethnicity Issues in Communication (2) Gender Issues in Communication (2) Communicating with People with Disabilities (2) Communicating Across Generations

LEARNING OBJECTIVES

After you have finished this chapter, you should be able to

LO1   Communicate effectively and ethically in small groups.

LO2   Collaborate to improve team writing.

LO3   Communicate with intercultural audiences.

LO4   Communicate with diverse populations.

"We embrace diversity . . . to better serve our consumers by better reflecting the communities we serve."

— THE WALT DISNEY COMPANY

Chapter Introduction: Diversity at Disney

Many companies say they "value diversity"—just as they say, "Employees are our greatest asset"—but Disney means it. With a U.S. employee population that is 40% Latino, Black, and Asian, Disney secured a spot on Diversity Inc's Top 50 Companies for Diversity.[1] Although this diversity may be most obvious at lower levels of the company, 21% of Disney management is minority.[2] The company also scored 100% on the Human Rights Campaign Foundation's Corporate Equality Index.[3]

Beyond the numbers, Disney's philosophy reflects its commitment:

Disney views the development of a diverse workforce as a business imperative and a catalyst to achieve better performance. . . . We believe that a diversity of opinions, ideas, and perspectives enhances our internal creativity and the company's vitality.[4]

Disney puts this philosophy into action with several programs to ensure an inclusive working environment for its Cast Members and Imagineers—what the company calls its employees.[5] A Diversity Leadership Advisory Board established at all Disney Resorts raises awareness and discusses issues of diversity. Diversity Resource Groups consist of employees who provide input into product and service development.[6] And Disney has a structured mentoring process, including training for mentors and metrics to assess performance.[7]

Its diverse employee population and these initiatives reflect Disney's strong focus on corporate responsibility. But this approach is also a smart marketing move to ensure that Disney reflects and reaches its diverse customer base around the world.

© UNIVERSITY OF CENTRAL FLORIDA/UCF CONSERVATORY THEATRE

University of Central Florida Recipients of the Disney Diversity Scholarship

L01   Communicate effectively and ethically in small groups.

WORK TEAM COMMUNICATION

By definition, people who work in organizations communicate with other people. Working in small groups and with diverse groups of people is one of most enriching—and sometimes one of the most challenging—aspects of a business environment. In this chapter, we'll explore ways to get the most out of your experience working with and learning from others.

A **team** is a group of individuals who depend on each other to accomplish a common objective. Teams are often more creative and accomplish more work than individuals working alone; a group's total output exceeds the sum of each individual's contribution. As a manager, if you work well as part of a team and can resolve conflicts, you will likely be seen as an effective leader with potential for promotion.[8]

On the other hand, teams can waste time, accomplish little work, and create a toxic environment. If you have worked as part of a team, you know all too well that people don't always contribute equally. Someone you might call a "slacker" is practicing **social loafing**, the psychological term for avoiding individual responsibility in a group setting.

Two to seven members—with five as an ideal—seems to work best for effective work teams.[9] Smaller teams often lack diversity of skills and interests to function well, and larger teams struggle with managing their interactions because two or three people may dominate discussions and make key decisions.

The Variables of Group Communication

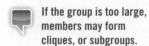
If the group is too large, members may form cliques, or subgroups.

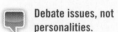
Debate issues, not personalities.

Three factors—conflict, conformity, and consensus—greatly affect a team's performance and how much team members enjoy working together. Let's consider a situation when these variables would come into play. Imagine that you worked for Disney when a young boy was killed by a bus at the Florida park.[10] To address this tragedy, you are working on a crisis management team with managers from several departments: transportation, public relations, human resources, and legal. To be successful, this crisis team needs to navigate the variables that shape group communication, explained in Figure 1.

Initial Group Goals

Teams work more effectively when the members know each other well—their strengths and weaknesses, work styles, experiences, attitudes, and so on. Starting off by getting to know each other improves the social dimension of your work and may not only make tasks go more smoothly but may help you enjoy the team experience more.

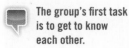
The group's first task is to get to know each other.

Small talk about friends, family, and social activities before and after meetings is natural and helps to establish a supportive and open environment. Even in online meeting environments, you can post a profile to introduce yourself or spend time IMing to learn about each other.

Too often, decisions just happen on a team; members may go along with what they think everyone else wants. Instead, teams should agree on how they'll operate and make decisions; for example, consider discussing the following early on with your team:

- What if someone misses a deliverable or team meeting? How should he or she notify the team? What will be the consequences?

- What if someone needs help completing a task? How should he or she handle this situation?

Figure 1 The Variables of Group Communication

Conflict: Should teams avoid conflict?

- Many group leaders work hard to avoid **conflict**, but conflict is what group meetings are all about. On the Disney crisis team, you would want people to voice different opinions. The head of transportation might be confident about bus safety, while the attorney is more cautious and suggests stopping all bus routes until the cause of the accident is properly understood. Without conflict, teams miss out on productive discussion and debate.
- However, healthy conflict is about *issues*, not about *personalities*. Interpersonal conflict, such as personal attacks, can doom a team. If the head of transportation took the attorney's advice personally ("You don't know anything about transportation, and I've been doing this for 15 years"), the situation could get ugly.

Conformity: Should team members try to conform?

- **Conformity** is agreement to ideas, rules, or principles. Crisis team members can disagree about whether the buses should be suspended, but certain fundamental issues, such as when the group meets, should be agreed to by everyone.
- However, too much conformity can result in **groupthink**, when people think similarly without independent thought. Groupthink stifles opposing ideas and the free flow of information.
- If the pressure to conform is too great, negative information and contrary opinions are never even brought out into the open and discussed. What if the attorney never raises the question of suspending buses? The team could make a bad decision, which might be apparent if another accident happened at the park.

Consensus: Should teams always strive for consensus?

- **Consensus** means reaching a decision that best reflects the thinking of all team members. Consensus is not necessarily a unanimous vote or even a majority vote. With a majority vote, only the members of the majority are happy with the end result; people in the minority may have to accept something they don't like at all. But with a consensus decision, people who have reservations can still support the idea. For example, the Disney team might agree to suspend the bus routes for only two days.
- Not every decision needs to have the support of every member. This would be too difficult and take too long. The team should decide which decisions are important enough to get everyone on board.

© CENGAGE LEARNING 2013

- What if two team members are having a conflict? How should it be resolved?
- Which decisions will be most important for our team? How should we make those decisions?

Giving Constructive Feedback

Giving and receiving constructive feedback is critical to work through team problems. These proven methods for giving and receiving criticism work equally well for giving and receiving praise.[11]

 Giving and receiving feedback should be a part of every team's culture.

Acknowledge the Need for Feedback

Imagine a work environment—or a class—where you never receive feedback on your performance. How would you know what you do well and what skills you need to develop? Feedback is the only way to find out what needs to be improved. Your team must agree that giving and receiving feedback is part of your team's culture—how you'll work together. This way, no one will be surprised when he or she receives feedback.

Give Both Positive and Negative Feedback

Many people take good work for granted and give feedback only when they notice problems. In one study, 67% of employees said they received too little positive

Figure 2
How to Give Positive and Negative Feedback

| Be descriptive. State objectively what you saw or heard. Give specific, recent examples from your own observations, if possible. | Avoid labels. Words like *unprofessional, irresponsible*, and *lazy* are labels that we attach to behaviors. Instead, describe the behaviors and drop the labels. | Don't exaggerate. Be exact. To say, "You never finish work on time" is probably untrue and unfair. | Speak for yourself. Don't refer to absent, anonymous people ("A lot of people here don't like it when you . . ."). | Use "I" statements. Instead of saying "You often submit work late," say, "I get annoyed when you submit work late because it holds up the rest of the team." "I" statements create an adult/peer relationship. |

© CENGAGE LEARNING 2013

feedback.[12] Hearing only complaints can be demoralizing and might discourage people from making any changes at all. Always try to balance positive and constructive feedback. Figure 2 suggests ways to give both positive and constructive feedback.

Use "I" statements to describe how someone's behavior affects you. This approach focuses on your reaction and helps avoid attacking or blaming the other person. Use the guidelines in Figure 3, but adapt the model to your own language, so you're authentic and sound natural.[13]

 "I" statements tell specifically how someone's behavior affects you.

Conflict Resolution

As discussed earlier, conflicts are a natural and effective part of the team process—until they become personal or disruptive. Most conflicts in groups can be prevented if a group spends time developing itself into a team, getting to know each other, establishing ground rules, and discussing norms for group behavior. However, no matter how much planning is done or how conscientiously team members work, conflicts occasionally show up.

 React to problems appropriately, consider them "group" problems, and have realistic expectations about the group process.

Problems rarely disappear on their own. However, you should neither overreact nor underreact to group problems. Some behaviors are only fleeting disruptions and can be ignored. Others are chronic and disruptive and must be resolved. If someone is late to a meeting once, you can probably let it go. If this continues, it should be addressed.

Think of each problem as a group problem. It's tempting to defuse conflicts by making a scapegoat of one member—for example, "We'd be finished with this report now if Sam had done his part; you never can depend on him." Rarely is one person solely responsible for the success or failure of a group effort. Were the expectations of Sam clear to him? Was he waiting for data from someone else? Did he need help but couldn't get it from the rest of the team? What is the team's role in encouraging or allowing behavior, and what can each of you do differently to encourage more constructive behavior?

At the same time, be realistic about team performance. Don't assume responsibility for others' happiness. You're responsible for being a fully contributing member of the team, behaving ethically, and treating others with respect. But the purpose of the group is not to develop lifelong friendships or to solve other people's

Sequence	Explanation
"When you . . ."	Start with a "When you . . ." statement that describes the behavior without judgment, exaggeration, labeling, attribution, or motives. Just state the facts as specifically as possible.
"I feel . . ."	Tell how the behavior affects you. If you need more than a word or two to describe the feeling, it's probably just some variation of joy, sorrow, anger, or fear.
"Because I . . ."	Now say why you are affected that way. Describe the connection between the facts you observed and the feelings they provoke in you.
(Pause for discussion.)	Let the other person respond.
"I would like . . ."	Describe the change you want the other person to consider . . .
"Because . . ."	. . . and why you think the change will help alleviate the problem.
"What do you think?"	Listen to the other person's response. Be prepared to discuss options and compromise on a solution.

Figure 3
Using "I" Statements When Giving Feedback

How the feedback will work: "When you [do this], I feel [this way], because [of such and such]." (Pause for discussion.) "What I would like you to consider is [doing X], because I think it will accomplish [Y]. What do you think?"

Example: "When you submit work late, I get angry because it delays the rest of the project. We needed your research today in order to start the report outline." (Pause for discussion.) "I'd like you to consider finding some way to finish work on time, so we can be more productive and meet our tight deadlines. What do you think?"

© CENGAGE LEARNING 2013

time-management or personal problems. If someone is sick, you may decide to extend a deadline, but you do not need to spend 20 minutes of a meeting talking about the illness.

Competent communicators welcome all contributions from group members, even if they disagree. This contributes to productive conflict where team members evaluate each contribution objectively against team goals and respond in a non-threatening, constructive way. If the atmosphere temporarily becomes tense, you can make a light comment, laugh, or offer a compliment to restore harmony and move the group forward.

However, if interpersonal conflict develops into a permanent part of the group interactions, it's best to address the conflict directly. Working through the conflict as a team may not be fun, but it will bring you to greater understanding and a higher level of productivity. It takes a brave manager to say, "I'd like to talk about how we interact with each other at these meetings. It seems like we often end up fighting—it's not productive, and someone usually gets hurt. Does anyone else feel that way? What can we do differently?"

The Ethical Dimension of Team Communication

Ethics in Communication

 Concentrate on group goals rather than individual goals.

When you agree to participate on a team, you accept certain standards of ethical behavior. One of these standards is to put the good of the team ahead of personal gain. Effective team performance requires members to set aside private agendas and avoid advocating positions that might benefit them personally but that would not be best for the team. In baseball, team ethics are clear. If a runner is on base, the batter may bunt the ball, knowing he'll probably be thrown out (i.e., the pitcher will get the ball to first base before he gets there). The batter makes the sacrifice for the good of the team, so that the teammate can advance a base.

Team members also have an ethical responsibility to respect each other's integrity and emotional needs. Everyone's ideas should be treated with respect, and no one should feel a loss of self-esteem. Team members should be encouraged to produce their best work, rather than feel criticized for not performing up to standard. When a baseball player hits a home run, the entire team celebrates. When a player strikes out, you'll never see team members criticizing him.

New York Yankee Alex Rodriguez affected the entire team when he admitted steroid use.

© AL MESSERSCHMIDT/GETTY IMAGES

Finally, each member has an ethical responsibility to promote the team's well-being—refraining from destructive gossip, dominating meetings, and sabotaging work. When New York Yankee Alex Rodriguez admitted using performance-enhancing steroids, for example, his behavior created controversy and bruised the reputation of the entire team. One team member's behavior can undermine the team's ability to reach its goals.

LO2 Collaborate to improve team writing.

💬 Writing as part of a team is a common task in organizations.

COLLABORATION ON TEAM WRITING PROJECTS

The increasing complexity of the workplace makes it difficult for any one person to have the time or expertise to write long or complex documents on his or her own. Team writing is common in organizations for sales proposals, recommendation reports, websites, financial analyses, and other projects that require input from people in different functions or departments.

Applying Strategies for Team Writing

Let's take an example of a start-up business. If you and two friends want to open an ice cream store and need funding—from either a bank or private investors—you would write a business plan. You would probably all do extensive research to make sure the business is feasible. Then, you might have one person write the financial projections, another write the marketing plan, and so on, until you complete the business plan. No one person will have expertise in all areas of planning your new business. When you present your idea to investors, each of you will create slides for your part of the presentation. And later, when you create a website, you may divide up the writing for that, too. Consider the steps in Figure 4 when writing as part of a team.

Figure 5 shows the start of a simple project plan. You can create something much more detailed, or keep it simple and build on these steps.

Figure 4 Steps for Team Writing

Identify Project Requirements
- Determine project goals: who is the audience, and what result do you want?
- Identify project components: what research do you need, what topics will you cover, and what deliverables will you produce?
- Decide how you'll share information: how will you collaborate online, and when will you meet in person?

Create a Project Plan
- Divide work fairly: which tasks suit each team member's strengths and interests?
- Create a project plan: who will complete which task by when? (See Figure 5 for a sample.)

Draft the Writing
- Begin with an outline: what major sections in what order will be included in the final product?
- Agree on a writing style: if different people write different sections, what style will you use (e.g., how formal, direct, or indirect)?
- Share information: if one person will create the entire first draft for consistency, how will each team member provide his or her expertise?

Revise the Writing
- Allow enough time for editing the draft: finishing a first draft the day before a project is due does not leave enough time.
- Provide feedback: see the tips for commenting on peers' writing (Figure 6).
- Make sure you have a single "voice" in the project: the final report should be coherent and cohesive.
- Have each team member review the entire draft: look for errors in content (gaps or repetition) and effective writing style.

Finalize the Project
- Have everyone proofread the final document: you are all responsible for the final version.
- Be clear about delivery: who will submit the final version, in what format, and by when?

Writing a Business Plan		
Who	**Task**	**By When**
Madeline	Create wiki.	April 20
Madeline	Draft an outline for the business plan.	April 22
Griffin	Draft company overview section (mission, vision, etc.).	April 24
Beata	Draft management profiles.	April 24
Madeline	Research local ice cream shops and other businesses for competitive analysis section.	April 30
[To be continued . . .]		

Figure 5
Example of a Simple Project Plan

Commenting on Peers' Writing

Commenting on your peers' writing is useful for both of you. Your peer receives feedback to improve his or her writing, and you practice techniques to objectively evaluate others'—and eventually your own—writing. When done effectively,

Figure 6
Tips for Commenting on Peer Writing

- Read first for meaning; comment on the large issues first—the information, organization, relevance for the audience, and overall clarity.
- Assume the role of reader—not instructor. Your job is to help the writer, not to grade the assignment.
- Point out sections that you liked, as well as those you disliked, explaining specifically why you thought they were effective or ineffective (not "I liked this part," but "You did a good job of explaining this difficult concept").
- Use "I" language (not "You need to make this clearer," but "I was confused here").
- Comment helpfully—but sparingly. You don't need to point out the same misspelling a dozen times.
- Emphasize the *writer* when giving positive feedback, and emphasize the *text* (rather than the writer) when giving negative feedback: "I'm glad *you* used the most current data from the annual report." "*This argument* would be more persuasive for me if it contained the most current data."
- Avoid taking over the text. Accept that you are reading someone else's writing—not your own. Make constructive suggestions, but avoid making decisions or demands.

Communication Technologies

providing each other feedback can build a sense of community within the team. Follow the tips in Figure 6 for commenting on peer writing.

Using Technology for Work in Teams

Although working in teams can be a challenge, technology such as wikis and Google Docs can help you manage documents and deadlines—and may improve your team communication. As introduced in Chapter 1, wikis are websites where groups of people collaborate on projects and edit each other's content. At Leap-Frog, the toy maker, a team of researchers, product designers, and engineers uses a wiki to "log new product ideas, track concepts over the course of their development, and spark better collaboration between team members."[14]

More businesses are adopting wikis to produce these useful results:[15,16]

- **Improved work processes.** Wikis make it easy to share information, monitor contributions, and track who makes revisions to which documents when.
- **Better collaboration.** Because wikis include interactive tools, such as chat and blogging, team members can communicate easily.
- **More contributions.** Wikis level the playing field, allowing users to contribute equally from anywhere in the world.
- **Better work outcomes.** With greater collaboration and contribution, users can expect better project results.
- **Improved knowledge management.** Because information is stored in one central place, knowledge is more easily retrieved and retained. Knowledge retention is particularly important for high-turnover organizations and as the workforce ages and more people retire.
- **Less email.** Case studies show that employees participating in a wiki receive less email and experience a more organized flow of communication.
- **Fewer meetings.** With better online communication and editing, wikis may reduce the number of in-person meetings.

The technology behind wikis is relatively simple. Designed as a website, wikis are fairly intuitive to use and can incorporate links, video, message boards, and other web features. With wikis, you can control who can access and edit which information, ensuring privacy and security. MediaWiki, Wiggio, Wikispaces—and even Google Sites—are all free and offer enough functionality for small

A happy customer with one of LeapFrog's interactive toys. Product teams at the toy maker use wikis to collaborate on new product designs.

Wikis are easy to use and can be created for no cost.

team projects, whereas enterprise wikis offer more functionality and control for large companies and major projects.

An example of a wiki created in Wiggio (www.wiggio.com) for a marketing project is shown in Figure 7. Although it looks like a typical website, the wiki has an important distinction: any member can post to the site and edit content. Wiggio offers additional functionality, such as polling and sending voice and text messages to your group members.

You can see how wikis might improve your team communication. In an online environment, according to the author of the book *Wikipatterns*, "Errors can be fixed immediately by anyone who notices them, and differing viewpoints can be worked out in a more natural manner. People can work together to reach a balance of viewpoints through a dialog that takes place as they edit, instead of putting forth versions that each feels is final."[17] You might find collaborating online an easier place to give feedback and address differences.

Google Docs is a good alternative to a wiki for smaller and shorter projects. You can use Google Docs to

Figure 7
Sample Wiki Homepage and Polling Feature

COURTESY OF WIGGIO

share documents and revise each other's work. However, with Google *Sites*, which is more like a wiki, you can use multiple Google applications and other functionality in one place.

If you're using Microsoft applications rather than Google Docs, you can still show revisions using the "Track Changes" feature. Although this type of sharing doesn't offer the functionality—or the benefits—of using a wiki, this solution may be just enough for simple projects. However, when a project is more complex and requires input from multiple people, a wiki has far more options for you to collaborate and build your team online.

INTERCULTURAL COMMUNICATION

International Communication

Working with others becomes even more complex—and interesting—when colleagues work in other countries. **Intercultural communication** (or **cross-cultural communication**) takes place between people from different cultures, when a message is created by someone from one culture to be understood by someone from another culture. More broadly, **multiculturalism** refers to appreciating diversity among people, typically beyond differences in countries of origin.

To be successful in today's global, multicultural business environment, managers need to appreciate differences among people. Although English may be the standard language for business, by no means do we have one standard for all business communication. If you want to do business abroad, you need to understand different cultures and adapt to the local language of business.

L03 Communicate with intercultural audiences.

 International business would not be possible without international communication.

According to an old joke, What do you call someone who speaks three languages? Trilingual. What do you call someone who speaks two languages? Bilingual. What do you call someone who speaks one language? American.

When we talk about **culture**, we mean the customary traits, attitudes, and behaviors of a group of people. **Ethnocentrism** is the belief that an individual's own cultural group is superior. This attitude hinders communication, understanding, and goodwill between business partners. Such arrogance is not only counterproductive but also unrealistic, considering that the U.S. population represents less than 5% of the world population.

Diversity has a profound effect on our lives and poses new opportunities and challenges for managers: opportunities to expand our own thinking and learn about other cultures—and challenges in communication. Although you'll learn in this chapter about communicating with people from different cultures, keep in mind that each member of a culture is an individual. We generalize here to teach broad principles for communication, but you should always adapt to individuals, who may think, feel, and act quite differently from the cultural norm or stereotype.

Cultures differ not only in their verbal languages but also in their nonverbal languages.

Cultural Differences

Cultures differ widely in the traits they value. For example, Figure 8 shows that international cultures vary in how much they emphasize individualism, time

**Figure 8
Cultural Values**

Value	High	Low
Individualism: Cultures in which people see themselves first as individuals and believe that their own interests take priority.	United States Canada Great Britain Australia Netherlands	Japan China Mexico Greece Hong Kong
Time Orientation: Cultures that perceive time as a scarce resource and that tend to be impatient.	United States Switzerland	Pacific Rim and Middle Eastern countries
Power Distance: Cultures in which management decisions are made by the boss simply because he or she is the boss.	France Spain Japan Mexico Brazil	United States Israel Germany Ireland Sweden
Uncertainty Avoidance: Cultures in which people want predictable and certain futures.	Israel Japan Italy Argentina	United States Canada Australia Singapore
Formality: Cultures that attach considerable importance to tradition, ceremony, social rules, and rank.	China India Latin American countries	United States Canada Scandinavian countries
Materialism: Cultures that emphasize assertiveness and the acquisition of money and material objects.	Japan Austria Italy	Scandinavian countries
Context Sensitivity: Cultures that emphasize the surrounding circumstances (or context), make extensive use of body language, and take the time to build relationships and establish trust.	Asian and African countries	Northern European countries

To learn more about cultural differences, read Geert Hofstede, *Culture's Consequences: Comparing Values, Behaviors, Institutions and Organizations Across Nations*, 2nd ed. (Thousand Oaks, CA: Sage Publications).

orientation, power distance, uncertainty avoidance, formality, materialism, and context sensitivity.[18]

You can use the Geert Hofstede model to compare your own culture with another.[19] Figure 9 compares the United States with South Korea, showing some of the cultural traits from Figure 8 and a new dimension: masculinity. You may find the Geert Hofstede model helpful to understand differences among you, your class-mates, and your coworkers.

We can look at communication differences even more deeply through a lens of "high-context" and "low-context" cultures, the last value listed in Figure 8. According to anthropologist Edward T. Hall, high-context cultures rely less on words used and more on subtle actions and reactions of communicators. Communication for these cultures is more implicit and emphasizes relationships among people. Silence is not unusual in these cultures, as it could have great meaning. Low-context cultures, on the other hand, rely on more explicit communication—the words people use. In low-con-text cultures, tasks are more important than relationships, so peo-ple use a direct style of communication, which we'll explore more when we discuss how to organize a message.[20]

Let's see how McDonald's adapts its website to cultures around the world. The company's Indian website, shown in Figure 10, shows groups of people interacting.[21] This might appeal to the In-dian people, who are part of a collectivist society. The emphasis here is on family and relationships.

Contrast the Indian website with two designed for individualist societies—the Germans and the Swiss (Figure 11). In both of these examples, products and promotions are emphasized rather than people. The German example focuses on McDonald's signature hamburger, while the Swiss example highlights a popular Monop-oly game.[22] McDonald's digital strategy is to have dynamic content on their websites, which each country updates frequently to best communicate messages for its own culture.

Companies customize their websites in other ways, too. Site navigation for high-context cultures, for example, might include subtle guidance and new pages opening in several new browser windows. This strategy allows the user to select new entry points for further exploration. But for low-context cultures, which tend to have more linear thought patterns, navigational cues may be more explicit, and new pages will open within the current window, to allow the user to go back and forth easily.[23]

We all interpret events through our own mental filter, and that filter is based on our unique knowledge, experiences, and perspectives. For example, the language of time is as different among cultures as the lan-guage of words. Americans, Canadi-ans, Germans, and Japanese are very time conscious and precise about appointments; Latin American and Middle Eastern cultures tend to be more casual about time. For example, if your Mexican host tells you that he or she will meet with you at 3:00, it's most likely *más o menos* (Spanish for "more or less") 3:00.

Figure 9
Comparing Cultural Dimensions

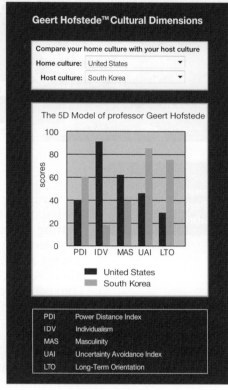

USED BY PERMISSION. GEERT HOFSTEDE, "CULTURE'S CONSEQUENCES: COMPARING VALUES, BEHAVIORS, INSTITUTIONS AND ORGANIZATIONS ACROSS NATIONS", SECOND EDITION. THOUSAND OAKS, CALIFORNIA: SAGE PUBLICATIONS, 2001, ISBN 0-8039-7323-3.

Figure 10
McDonald's India Website

USED WITH PERMISSION FROM MCDONALD'S CORPORATION.

Figure 11
McDonald's Germany and Switzerland Websites

Businesspeople in both Asian and Latin American countries tend to favor long negotiations and slow deliberations. They exchange pleasantries for a while before getting down to business. Similarly, many non-Western cultures use silence during meetings to contemplate a decision, whereas businesspeople from the United States and Canada tend to have little tolerance for silence in business negotiations. As a result, Americans and Canadians may rush in and offer compromises and counterproposals that would have been unnecessary if they were more comfortable with the silence—and more patient.

> Very few nonverbal messages have universal meanings.

Body language, especially gestures and eye contact, also varies among cultures. For example, our sign for "okay"—forming a circle with our forefinger and thumb—means "zero" in France, "money" in Japan, and a vulgarity in Brazil (Figure 12).[24] Americans and Canadians consider eye contact important. In Asian and many Latin American countries, however, looking a colleague full in the eye is considered an irritating sign of poor upbringing.

Figure 12
Same Sign, Different Meanings

OK sign
France: you're a zero;
Japan: please give me coins;
Brazil: an obscene gesture;
Mediterranean countries: an obscene gesture

Thumb and forefinger
Most countries: money;
France: something is perfect;
Mediterranean: a vulgar gesture

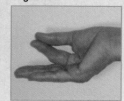

Thumbs-up
Australia: up yours;
Germany: the number one;
Japan: the number five;
Saudi Arabia: I'm winning;
Ghana: an insult;
Malaysia: the thumb is used to point rather than the finger

Thumbs-down
Most countries: something is wrong or bad

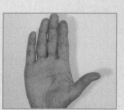

Open palm
Greece: an insult dating to ancient times;
West Africa: You have five fathers, an insult akin to calling someone a bastard

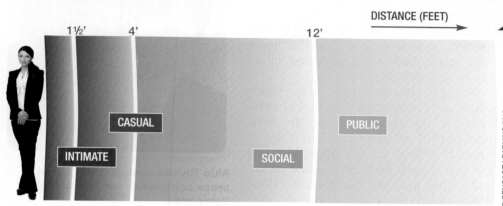

DISTANCE (FEET)

1½'   4'   12'

INTIMATE

CASUAL

SOCIAL

PUBLIC

© ISTOCKPHOTO.COM/JOSHUA HODGE PHOTOGRAPHY

© CENGAGE LEARNING 2013

Figure 13
Personal Spaces for Social Interaction

Touching behavior is very culture specific. Many Asians do not like to be touched except for a brief handshake in greeting. However, handshakes in much of Europe tend to last much longer than in the United States and Canada, and Europeans tend to shake hands every time they see each other, perhaps several times a day. In much of Europe, men often kiss each other upon greeting; if you don't know this custom, you might react inappropriately and embarrass yourself.

Our feelings about space are partly an outgrowth of our culture and partly a result of geography and economics. For example, Americans and Canadians are used to wide-open spaces and tend to move about expansively, using hand and arm motions for emphasis. But in Japan, which has much smaller living and working spaces, such abrupt and extensive body movements are not typical. Likewise, Americans and Canadians tend to sit face to face so that they can maintain eye contact, whereas the Chinese and Japanese (to whom eye contact is not so important) tend to sit side by side during negotiations.

Also, the sense of personal space differs among cultures. In the United States and Canada, most business exchanges occur at about five feet, within the "social zone," which is closer than the "public zone," but farther than the "intimate zone" (see Figure 13). However, both in Middle Eastern and Latin American countries, this distance is too far. Businesspeople there tend to stand close enough to feel your breath as you speak. Most Americans and Canadians will back away unconsciously from such close contact.

Finally, social behavior is very culture dependent. For example, in the Japanese culture, who bows first upon meeting, how deeply the person bows, and how long the bow is held depend on one's status.

Before you travel or interact with people from other countries, become familiar with these and other customs, for example, giving (and accepting) gifts, exchanging business cards, the degree of formality expected, and how people entertain.

 When in doubt about how to act, follow the lead of your host.

Group-Oriented Behavior

As shown earlier, the business environment in capitalistic societies, such as the United States and Canada, places great value on how individuals contribute to an organization. Individual effort is often stressed more than group effort, and a competitive atmosphere prevails. But in other cultures, originality and independence of judgment are not valued as highly as teamwork. The Japanese say, "A nail standing out will be hammered down." The Japanese go to great lengths to reach decisions through group consensus.

Closely related to the concept of group-oriented behavior is the notion of "saving face." People save face when they avoid embarrassment. When Akio Toyoda,

 Expect negotiations to take longer when unanimous agreement rather than majority rule is the norm.

The Toyoda family changed the company name to Toyota in 1937 for its clearer sound and more favorable number of strokes for writing the name.[25]

the Japanese president of Toyota Motor Corporation, apologized for many vehicle recalls starting in 2009, he demonstrated emotion and great humility—far more than might have been expected of an American business leader.

Human relationships are highly valued in Japanese cultures and are embodied in the concept of *wa*, the Japanese pursuit of harmony. This concept makes it difficult for the Japanese to say "no" to a request because it would be impolite. They are very reluctant to offend others—even if they unintentionally mislead them instead. A "yes" to a Japanese

Akio Toyoda apologizes at recall press conference for Toyota Motor Company.

might mean "Yes, I understand you" rather than "Yes, I agree." To an American, the Japanese style of communication may seem too indirect and verbose. At one point during Toyoda's testimony before Congress, the committee chair said, "What I'm trying to find out: is that a yes or a no?" To Japanese viewers, this sounded rude and disrespectful.[26]

Latin Americans also tend to avoid an outright "no" in their business dealings, preferring instead a milder, less explicit response. For successful intercultural communications, you have to read between the lines because what is left unsaid or unwritten may be just as important as what is said or written.

Strategies for Communicating Across Cultures

When communicating with people from different cultures, whether abroad or at home, use the following strategies.

Maintain Formality

Compared to U.S. and Canadian cultures, most other cultures value and respect a much more formal approach to business dealings. Call others by their titles and family names unless specifically asked to do otherwise. By both verbal and nonverbal clues, convey an attitude of propriety and decorum. Although you may think these strategies sound cold, most other cultures consider these appropriate.

Show Respect

Showing respect is probably the easiest strategy to exhibit—and one of the most important.

When interacting with people from other cultures, withhold judgment. Although different from your own, attitudes held by an entire culture are probably based on sound reasoning. Listen carefully to what is being communicated, trying to understand the other person's feelings. Learn about your host country—its geography, form of government, largest cities, culture, current events, and so on.

Expect to adapt to different cultures. For Japanese business practices, it is not uncommon for the evening's entertainment to extend beyond dinner. You can expect a second round of drinks or an invitation to a coffee shop. Refusing a drink during social business engagements may even be considered rude or impolite. If you're not a drinker, think about how you would handle the situation in advance.

Communicate Clearly

To make your oral and written messages understood, follow these guidelines:

- Avoid slang, jargon, and other figures of speech. Expressions such as "They'll eat that up" or "out in left field" can confuse even a fluent English speaker.
- Be specific and illustrate your points with concrete examples.

- Provide and solicit feedback, summarize frequently, write a summary of points covered in a meeting, ask your counterpart for his or her understanding, and encourage questions.

- Use a variety of media: handouts (distributed before the meeting to allow time for reading), visuals, models, and so on.

- Use humor sparingly; humor is risky—it may be lost on your counterpart, or worse, it may offend someone.

- Speak plainly and slowly (but not so slowly as to be condescending); choose your words carefully.

People who know more about, and are more comfortable with, different cultures are more effective managers because they reap the benefits of international business and avoid misunderstandings.

DIVERSITY WITHIN THE UNITED STATES

L04 Communicate with diverse populations.

 Cultural diversity provides a rich work environment.

Of course, we have much diversity within the United States. Each year, the United States becomes even more diverse, which creates tremendous opportunities for companies—and a few challenges for business communicators.

The Value of Diversity

Imagine a work environment where everyone is exactly the same. How would you allocate work when everyone has the same skills? How would you generate new ideas when everyone thinks similarly?

Diversity among employees provides richness and strength for an organization. People from varied backgrounds and perspectives help companies solve problems, make better decisions, and create a much more interesting work environment.

Companies recognize the need for diversity and actively seek employees from different backgrounds. Cox Communications, a broadband communications and entertainment company, advertises regularly to show that its diverse workforce is a competitive advantage (Figure 14).

Many companies today go beyond thinking about diversity— which tends to focus on numbers of people—and

Figure 14
Cox Communications Promotes Diversity Through Advertisements

Who makes our company tick? Perhaps the better question is who doesn't?

Cox Communications believes the strength of our company lies in the diversity of our people. It's a philosophy that translates into success. For ourselves, our customers and, more importantly, our society.

We're all connected.

COX   COX Business·   COX Media·

COURTESY OF COX COMMUNICATIONS

strive for **inclusion**. Do all employees feel included and welcomed in their work environment? Are they able to contribute fully to an organization, or do invisible barriers prevent people from participating in relevant meetings, making significant decisions, getting their ideas implemented—and, perhaps most important, getting promoted? Focusing on an inclusive work environment ensures that all employees can reach their full potential with a company.

As you look at companies' websites, you'll see that many of them refer to both diversity and inclusion. State Farm, the insurance company, is a good example of how companies describe these values (Figure 15). The company defines diversity and inclusion as follows:

> **Diversity** is the collective strength of experiences, skills, talents, perspectives, and cultures that each agent and employee brings to State Farm. It's how we create a dynamic business environment to serve our customers.

> **Inclusion** is about respecting and valuing the unique dimension each agent and employee adds to the organization. We recognize that agents and employees are at their creative and productive best when they work in an inclusive work environment.[27]

As you might expect, communication, particularly language, is an important part of an inclusive working environment. Unbiased or neutral language treats

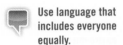

Use language that includes everyone equally.

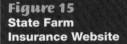

Figure 15
State Farm Insurance Website

everyone equally, making no unwarranted assumptions about any group of people. Consider the types of bias in this report:

> The distribution center was the scene of a confrontation today when two ladies from the morning shift accused a foreman of sexual harassment. Marta Maria Valdez, a Hispanic inspector, and Margaret Sawyer, an assembly-line worker, accused Mr. Engerrand of making suggestive comments. Mr. Engerrand, who is 62 years old and an epileptic, denied the charges and said he thought the girls were trying to cheat the company with their demand for a cash award.

Were you able to identify these instances of bias or discriminatory language?

- The women were referred to as *ladies* and *girls*, although the men in the company probably are not referred to as *gentlemen* and *boys*.
- The term *foreman* (and all other *-man* occupational titles) has a sexist connotation.
- The two women were identified by their first and last names, without a personal title, while the man was identified by a personal title and last name only.
- Valdez's ethnicity, Engerrand's age, and Engerrand's disability were identified, although they are irrelevant to the situation.

Respectful communicators make sure that their writing is free of unbiased language.

Refer to groups of people according to their preferences.

Ethnicity Issues in Communication

Whether you belong to the majority culture or to one of the minority cultures where you work, you will interact and socialize with people different from yourself. In fact, the term *minority* is becoming something of a misnomer. The non-Hispanic White population in the United States is expected to decline from 64.7% of the population in 2010 to less than the majority (46.3%) in 2050.[28] Also, most of us represent the minority of some group. If not race, we may be in the minority for our ethnicity, religion, age, sexual orientation, ability, geographic location, or other groups.

Terminology used to refer to groups is constantly evolving. The 2010 U.S. Census Form allowed people to select from several categories to identify their origin and race (Figures 16 and 17).[29] But even these categories may not apply to how each person prefers to be identified. Some White Americans prefer the term *European American* or *Caucasian*, and some Asian Americans prefer to be identified by their country of origin—for example, *Chinese American* or *Indonesian American*. Others prefer different designations.

Figure 16 Question 8 on the 2010 U.S. Census Form

8. Is Person 1 of Hispanic, Latino, or Spanish origin?

- [ ] No, not of Hispanic, Latino, or Spanish origin
- [ ] Yes, Mexican, Mexican Am., Chicano
- [ ] Yes, Puerto Rican
- [ ] Yes, Cuban
- [ ] Yes, another Hispanic, Latino, or Spanish origin — *Print origin, for example, Argentinean, Colombian, Dominican, Nicaraguan, Salvadoran, Spaniard, and so on.*

Source: United States Census 2010, "Explore the Form," http://2010.census.gov/2010census/about/interactive-form.php

Figure 17 Question 9 on the 2010 U.S. Census Form

9. What is Person 1's race? *Mark ⊠ one or more boxes.*

- [ ] White
- [ ] Black, African Am., or Negro
- [ ] American Indian or Alaska Native — *Print name of enrolled or principal tribe.*

- [ ] Asian Indian
- [ ] Chinese
- [ ] Filipino
- [ ] Other Asian — *Print race, for example, Hmong, Laotian, Thai, Pakistani, Cambodian, and so on.*
- [ ] Japanese
- [ ] Korean
- [ ] Vietnamese
- [ ] Native Hawaiian
- [ ] Guamanian or Chamorro
- [ ] Samoan
- [ ] Other Pacific Islander — *Print race, for example, Fijian, Tongan, and so on.*

- [ ] Some other race — *Print race.*

Source: United States Census 2010, "Explore the Form," http://2010.census.gov/2010census/about/interactive-form.php

When communicating about minorities—or "people of color"—in the United States, we should realize that what we call ourselves is not a trivial matter. The terms used to refer to other groups are not ours to establish. And it's easy enough to use terms that others prefer.

We should also realize that ethnicity is not a characteristic limited to people of color; White Americans are ethnic, too. Every ethnic and racial group in the world—which includes 7 billion of us—has its own physical and cultural characteristics. Of course, every person within an ethnic group has his or her own individual characteristics as well.

No wonder communicating about ethnic and racial topics can be emotionally charged. Yet we must learn to communicate comfortably and honestly with one another. If we use the wrong terminology, make an unfair assumption, or present only one side of the story, our readers or listeners will let us know soon enough.

Gender Issues in Communication

 Men and women often communicate differently based on learned behavior.

Of course, more differences exist within each gender group than between groups. We should be careful not to stereotype and wrongly assume that *all* women or *all* men communicate or behave in one way. And yet, recognizing that common differences do exist may help us understand each other better and improve communication overall (see Figure 18).[30]

Figure 18
Differences in Male and Female Communication Patterns

- Women communicate largely to build rapport; men communicate primarily to preserve independence and status by displaying knowledge and skill.
- Men prefer to work out their problems by themselves, whereas women prefer to talk out solutions with another person.
- Women are more likely to compliment the work of a coworker; men are more likely to be critical.
- Men tend to interrupt to dominate a conversation or to change the subject; women tend to interrupt to agree with or to support what another person is saying.
- Men tend to be more directive in their conversation, whereas women emphasize politeness.
- Men are more interested than women in calling attention to their own accomplishments.
- Men tend to dominate discussions during meetings.
- Men tend to internalize successes and to externalize failures: "That's one of my strengths." "We should have been given more time."
- Women tend to externalize successes and to internalize failures: "I was lucky." "I'm just not good at that."
- In the workplace, men speak differently to other men than they do to women, and women speak differently to other women than they do to men.

© CENGAGE LEARNING 2013

Recognize that these differences often (but not always) exist. Thus, a woman should not take it personally if a male coworker fails to praise her work; he may simply be engaging in gender-typical behavior. If a male manager feels that a female colleague is more interested in relating to others in the group and seeking consensus than in solving the problem, she may simply be engaging in gender-typical behavior. Again, these patterns may be typical, but they certainly don't apply to everyone.

In addition to accepting potential differences between the sexes, we can improve working relationships by avoiding sexist language. Follow these strategies for using inclusive, gender-neutral language.

1. Use neutral job titles to avoid implying that a job is held by only men or only women.

Instead of	Use
chairman	chair, chairperson
salesman	sales representative, sales associate
male nurse	nurse
waitress	server
stewardess	flight attendant
businessmen	employees, managers

2. Avoid words and phrases that unnecessarily imply gender.

Instead of	Use
best man for the job	best person for the job
executives and their wives	executives and their partners
you guys	everyone
housewife	homemaker
manmade	artificial, manufactured
mankind	people, human beings
manpower	human resources, employees

3. Use appropriate personal titles and salutations.
   - If a woman has a professional title, use it (Dr. Martha Ralston, the Rev. Deborah Connell).
   - Follow a woman's preference in being addressed as *Miss, Mrs.,* or *Ms.*
   - If a woman's marital status or her preference is unknown, use *Ms.*
   - If you do not know the reader's gender, use a gender-neutral salutation (Dear Investor, Dear Neighbor, Dear Customer, Dear Policyholder). Or, you may use the full name in the salutation (Dear Chris Andrews, Dear Terry Brooks).

4. Avoid *he* or *his* as generic pronouns (e.g., "Each manager must evaluate *his* employees annually"). This is debatable, but is easy enough to work around with these alternatives:
   - Use plural nouns and pronouns. "All managers must evaluate their employees annually." (But not: "Each manager must evaluate *their* employees annually," which uses a plural pronoun to refer to a singular noun.)
   - Use second-person pronouns *(you, your)*. "You must evaluate your employees annually."
   - Omit the pronoun. "Each manager must evaluate employees annually."
   - Use *his or her* (sparingly). "Each manager must evaluate his or her employees annually."

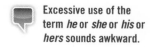
Excessive use of the term *he* or *she* or *his* or *hers* sounds awkward.

With all of these alternatives, avoid using "one" as a singular pronoun (e.g., "One must evaluate one's employees annually"). This is considered too formal for business communication in the United States.

Communicating with People with Disabilities

Since the Americans with Disabilities Act (ADA) of 1990 was passed, more people who have disabilities have entered the workplace and contributed to organizations.

 Notice the unnecessary hyphen in "differently-abled" on the Toys "R" Us website.

Effective managers go beyond the legal requirements of hiring and accommodating people with disabilities. One way to think about people is that we're all "differently abled"—each with strengths as well as areas that need development. You may have a great eye for design but need help with construction. Toys "R" Us recognizes this with a marketing campaign for "differently-abled kids." As you can see on the website (Figure 19), the company promotes toys to improve auditory, social, language, and other skills that need improvement. The perspective that no one is perfect may help you communicate with people at work.

Reasonable changes in how you communicate with people are typically expected and appreciated. For example, when being introduced to someone who uses a wheelchair, bend over slightly to be closer to eye level. If the person is able to extend his or her hand for a handshake, offer your hand. For lengthy conversations, sit down so that you are both eye to eye. People who use wheelchairs may see their wheelchairs as extensions of their personal space, so avoid touching or leaning on their wheelchairs.

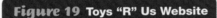

Figure 19 Toys "R" Us Website

Most hearing-impaired people use a combination of hearing and lip reading. Face the person to whom you're speaking, and speak a bit slower (but not louder) than usual. When talking with a person who is blind, communicate in words rather than in gestures or glances. As you approach him or her, make your presence known; in a group, address the person by name to start the conversation. Identify yourself and use your normal voice and speed.

Everyone needs help at one time or another. If someone with a disability seems to need assistance, ask whether help is wanted, and follow the person's wishes. But resist the temptation to take too much care of an individual with a disability. Don't be annoying or patronizing.

Always, everywhere, avoid using language like "Are you deaf?" "He's a little slow," or "What are you, blind?" Jokes about people with disabilities don't go over too well. President Obama—on a late-night TV show—compared his poor bowling skills to the Special Olympics. Even before the show aired, the President called the chair of the board of Special Olympics to apologize for the comment (Figure 20).[31]

Instead of using potentially disparaging language, use "people-first language," which respects people's dignity and avoids labels.[32] With people-first language, you identify the person before his or her disability; for example, say, "Alejandro is a sophomore who has epilepsy" rather than referring to "the epileptic"—there's much more to Alejandro than his disability. Also avoid referring to someone as "handicapped." We still have "handicapped" parking spaces—an outdated term—but, when referring to people, a handicap may imply a limitation and a disadvantage.

When making presentations, consider the needs of those with disabilities—in terms of seating, visual support, and other factors. As always when communicating, the best advice is to know your audience. Also, see the "unseen." Recognize that some disabilities are invisible. Be alert and sensitive to colleagues who may have allergies, addictions, or other life-threatening (or even fatal) conditions.

Accept accommodations as a normal part of the workplace. We all need accommodations of some sort, not necessarily a wheelchair but perhaps an ergonomic office chair or a special keyboard. Accommodations are worth the little trouble it takes to include everyone as fully contributing members of the organization.

 Making reasonable accommodations for workers who have disabilities is part of today's workplace.

**Figure 20
President Obama's Gaffe**

© AP IMAGES/GERALD HERBERT

President Obama: I bowled a 129.
Jay Leno (laughing): Oh . . . that's very good, Mr. President.
President Obama: It was like Special Olympics or something.

Communicating Across Generations

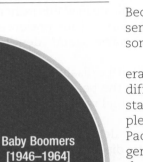

"HOUSEHOLD DATA, ANNUAL AVERAGES," BUREAU OF LABOR STATISTICS, U.S. DEPARTMENT OF LABOR.

Because people are living longer, more generations are represented in the workforce. You may find yourself working with someone from one of four generations (Figure 21).[33]

Much has been written about differences among the generations, but according to recent research, some of these differences—particularly the negative effects—may be overstated. According to one study of approximately 100,000 people in 34 countries within North America, Europe, and Asia Pacific, 42% of employees say they have experienced intergenerational conflict at work, but the same percentage say that generational differences *improve* productivity. These numbers are very consistent by generation and geographic region. Between 68% and 75% of employees do adapt their communication style for colleagues from different generations (Figure 22); however, the method people prefer for communicating (e.g., face-to-face or email) is similar across generations and countries.[34]

It's best to be aware of potential differences but—as discussed throughout this section—not to judge people based only on their age. Assuming that an older worker doesn't understand technology or that a younger worker doesn't understand the business is unfair to individuals and may lead to bad business decisions. Also, avoid age-biased language, such as referring to people as "old," "senior citizens," or worse.

We are all members of different groups with different customs, values, and attitudes. If you think of your audience as individuals, rather than as stereotypical members of some particular group, you will avoid bias and instead will contribute to an inclusive work environment. The value of diversity in business far outweighs the few challenges of communication.

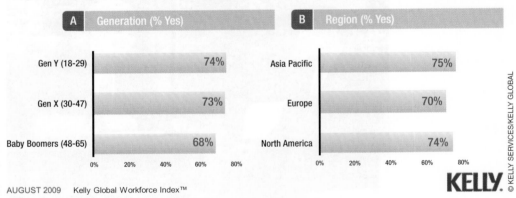

Do you adapt your communication style to colleagues from different generations?

AUGUST 2009   Kelly Global Workforce Index™

KELLY.

© KELLY SERVICES/KELLY GLOBAL WORKFORCE INDEX™

Addressing Disrespectful Comments

Purpose

Imagine that you work for an amusement park and overhear three employees who report to you talking in the employee cafeteria. You hear one say, "This morning, I think I got every old guy wanting to relive his childhood." Another employee says, "Yeah, well, I had to help two Wheelies get up the handicapped ramp. But at least I made a few kids applaud."

   You decide to address these comments.

Process

1. Why are the employees' comments inappropriate?

These comments do not reflect the company's values or the expectations of employees.

2. What is the best way to address the situation?

Although a few other people are in the cafeteria, I'd like to address the situation immediately. I'll be careful about embarrassing anyone, but I need to be clear that these comments are unacceptable.

3. What will you do and say?

Using "I" messages, I'll sit down with the employees, reflect what I heard, and explain how it affected me. I want employees to understand that I take this situation very seriously.

Product

I'll begin by saying something like this: "I just overheard your conversation, and I have to say that I'm surprised to hear you talking this way."

   Next, I'll wait for a response to see whether the employees immediately understand what I'm referring to—they might.

   I'll ask questions to encourage employees to think about the impact of their language, for example, "How do you think a guest would react if he or she overheard you talking? How would a new employee react?" and "What do you see as the company's values in terms of how we treat guests?"

   Finally, I'll ask employees to use more respectful language when on company time and when representing the organization.

   After my discussion with the employees, I may follow up by holding individual meetings, placing a note in each employee's file, or possibly taking corrective or disciplinary action.

Tailoring a Message to Different Audiences

Purpose

Imagine that you work for an amusement park in the U.S. corporate office. You just read an article on the company blog about "Waterway Cleanup," employees' volunteer work to remove debris from the U.S. coastline. This paragraph from the article gives you an idea:

> Employees did a great job on Sunday—and had a lot of fun—cleaning up trash on Long Beach Island. Most of the litter collected was plastic, disposable items. If you can't participate in one of our Waterway Cleanups, you can contribute to cleaner oceans by using reusable instead of disposable products, such as coffee cups, shopping bags, and water bottles.

You decide to create a poster to encourage amusement park guests to choose reusable coffee cups, shopping bags, and water bottles. Because you work for both U.S. and Brazilian parks, you create two posters to reflect cultural differences.

Process

1. From studying Geert Hofstede's cultural dimensions, what differences exist between the United States and Brazil that may be relevant to your communication?
2. How can you use words to relate to each audience?
3. What images will you use for each audience?

Product

Sketch two versions of the poster: one for parks in the United States and one for parks in Brazil.

Summary

L01   Communicate effectively and ethically in small groups.

Teams can accomplish more and better quality work in less time than individuals can *if* the teams function properly. Otherwise, teams can waste time and cause interpersonal conflicts. Conflict about ideas is a helpful part of the group process, but interpersonal conflicts are detrimental. Consensus and conformity can lead to productivity, but too much focus on either can lead to groupthink.

   When a team first forms, group members should get to know each other and decide how they'll operate. They should acknowledge the need for positive and negative feedback and know how to give productive feedback, particularly on team writing. When problems arise, group members should react to them appropriately, consider them as group problems, and be realistic about what to expect from the group.

L02   Collaborate to improve team writing.

For group writing projects, team members should identify project requirements, create a project plan, draft the writing, revise the writing, and finalize the project.

   Teams may find it useful to create a wiki for team writing projects. Wikis can lead to improved work processes, more contributions, better work outcomes, and fewer meetings.

L03   Communicate with intercultural audiences.

Understanding cultural differences is essential to success in a global business environment. Although individuals often defy stereotypes, consider differences in context sensitivity, feelings about space, group-oriented behavior, and other factors. When communicating with people from other cultures, maintain formality, show respect, and write and speak clearly.

L04   Communicate with diverse populations.

In the United States, the population is becoming increasingly diverse. This diversity brings great value to companies and encourages us to appreciate differences and create an inclusive workplace. You can demonstrate respect through your language choices about ethnicity, gender, ability, age, and other variables among employees.

Exercises

1. Analyze a team's communication.

Think about a recent situation when you worked as part of a team. In retrospect, what worked well about the communication, and what could have been improved? Call or meet with one of your former team members to talk through your assessment and find out how he or she viewed the experience. What can you learn from this experience that may help you work with teams in the future?

L01 Communicate effectively and ethically in small groups.

2. Explain a team's communication.

After analyzing a team's communication, briefly describe for the class (in two or three minutes) the purpose of the team and how well you functioned. Describe how the variables of group communication—conflict, conformity, and consensus—were or were not incorporated. Was groupthink an issue? How did the other team member view the experience? In what ways was this similar or different from your own, and why do you think this might be?

3. Provide feedback.

Imagine that you're working as part of a team to create a five-year marketing plan. Everyone had agreed to have his or her part drafted by the time your team met today. What would be an appropriate response to each of the following situations at today's meeting? Discuss your responses in small groups.

a. Fred did not have his part ready (although this is the first time he has been late).

b. Thales did not have his part ready (the third time this year he has missed a deadline).

c. Anita not only had her part completed but also had drafted an attractive design for the final document.

d. Sunggong was 45 minutes late for the meeting because his car had skidded into a ditch as a result of last night's snowstorm.

e. Elvira left a message that she would have to miss the meeting because she was working on another report, which is due tomorrow.

Jim wraps Dwight's desk in Christmas paper in an episode of _The Office_.

© CHRIS HASTON/© NBC/COURTESY EVERETT COLLECTION

4. Identify poor team behavior.

Watch an episode of _The Office_ on NBC. This crew lacks many skills for effective teamwork! See how many flaws in their interactions you can identify. For example, what incidents of disruptive, interpersonal conflict do you observe? How do individuals demonstrate a lack of respect for each other? How do they provide feedback to each other?

5. Comment on a peer's writing.

Use the "Tips for Commenting on Peer Writing" to provide feedback on another student's writing. Exchange draft documents with another student and use "Track Changes" in Microsoft Word to make comments. After

LO2   Collaborate to improve team writing.

you have commented on each other's work, review each other's suggestions. Then, discuss your reactions to the other's feedback. To what extent do you feel that your partner followed the tips presented in this chapter? How could your partner have given you better feedback?

6. Create a project plan.

Working in groups of four or five, imagine that you are creating a new website for a local business. First, choose a business that all of you know well. Next, complete the first two steps for team writing: identify project requirements and create a project plan.

Identify Project Requirements

- Determine project goals: who is the audience, and what result do you want?
- Identify project components: what research do you need, what topics will you cover, and what deliverables will you produce?
- Decide how you'll share information: how will you collaborate online, and when will you meet in person?

Create a Project Plan

- Divide work fairly: which tasks suit each team member's strengths and interests?
- Create a project plan: who will complete which task by when?

© CENGAGE LEARNING 2013

7. Contribute to Wikipedia.

To experience a wiki, contribute to an article on Wikipedia. Find a topic that you consider yourself an expert on, for example, your college, your neighborhood, a sport, or a game. Make one or two changes to a relevant article on Wikipedia. In one week, track your contribution: did it hold, or was it changed by someone else?

8. Set up a wiki.

Set up a wiki for a class project or campus organization. Take the lead to structure the site, post initial content, and encourage everyone to participate. If you have already used wikis with teams, try a different site (e.g., Wiggio, Google Sites, or Wikispaces) to experience a new approach and to see whether you prefer one to another.

9. Improve how you use a wiki.

Review a wiki you or another team used recently for a project. In retrospect, how could you have organized the files differently to improve the work process? What tools could you have used but didn't (e.g., the chat feature or the calendar)? To prepare for a possible future team project, send an email to your former team members with your ideas for how you could use a wiki next time. If you have time, meet with your team to discuss your ideas for your next wiki experience.

10. Interpret two messages from international offices.

Imagine that you work for the law firm Dewey, Wright, and Howe as an intern. With a team of employees, you are working on an orientation program for new interns. Part of your plan is to have interns do research online about the firm before their date of hire. You believe this research, which will take about two hours, will give new interns a jump start before they start working.

In response to your draft Orientation Plan, you receive two emails from partners in the firm—the first from the German office and the second from Japan. From these messages, you realize that Mr. Yamashita misunderstood your intent: he thought your plan

L03 Communicate with intercultural audiences.

 These email messages are part of the company scenario Dewey, Wright, and Howe, available at www.cengagebrain.com.

was for interns to come to the office before their start date, whereas you meant only for them to do research online.

Working in small groups, discuss how you interpret these messages. What feedback are the partners giving you? Consider cultural differences discussed in this chapter.

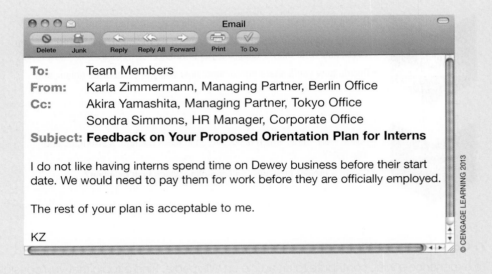

To: Team Members
From: Karla Zimmermann, Managing Partner, Berlin Office
Cc: Akira Yamashita, Managing Partner, Tokyo Office
         Sondra Simmons, HR Manager, Corporate Office
Subject: **Feedback on Your Proposed Orientation Plan for Interns**

I do not like having interns spend time on Dewey business before their start date. We would need to pay them for work before they are officially employed.

The rest of your plan is acceptable to me.

KZ

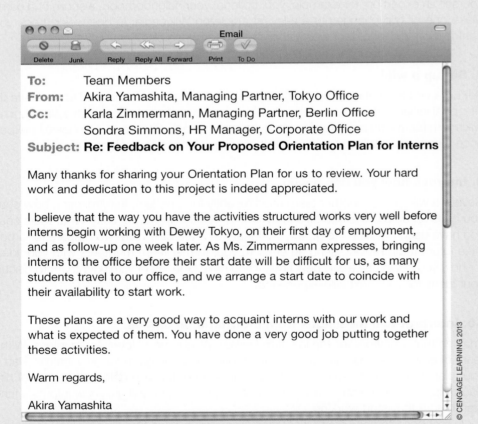

To: Team Members
From: Akira Yamashita, Managing Partner, Tokyo Office
Cc: Karla Zimmermann, Managing Partner, Berlin Office
         Sondra Simmons, HR Manager, Corporate Office
Subject: **Re: Feedback on Your Proposed Orientation Plan for Interns**

Many thanks for sharing your Orientation Plan for us to review. Your hard work and dedication to this project is indeed appreciated.

I believe that the way you have the activities structured works very well before interns begin working with Dewey Tokyo, on their first day of employment, and as follow-up one week later. As Ms. Zimmermann expresses, bringing interns to the office before their start date will be difficult for us, as many students travel to our office, and we arrange a start date to coincide with their availability to start work.

These plans are a very good way to acquaint interns with our work and what is expected of them. You have done a very good job putting together these activities.

Warm regards,

Akira Yamashita

11. Adapt to cultural differences in email responses.

After you discuss your interpretation of the emails in the previous exercise, individually write separate email responses to Ms. Zimmermann and Mr. Yamashita. How can you address their concerns about the Orientation Plan, while adapting your communication style for cultural differences?

12. Research international communication and write an advice memo.

Working with a teammate, select a country for your research. Using three or more Internet sites, outline cultural differences of the country that might impact international business dealings. Look for differences regarding customs, use of space, hand gestures, time orientation, social behavior, how business is conducted, and other business-related issues. Write a memo with your advice to someone planning to travel to this country for business.

13. Present cultural differences to the class.

Choose one or two students from your class to discuss their experience traveling internationally. The students may use the following questions to guide their ten-minute presentation:

- What country did you visit, and what was the reason for your trip?
- What surprised you most about the people? What were the most obvious differences you noticed from your own culture?
- How do you interpret the cultural values of the region? Review the following dimensions discussed in this chapter: individualism, time orientation, power distance, uncertainty avoidance, formality, materialism, and context sensitivity.
- What observations did you make about the people's feelings about space and group-oriented behavior?
- What advice would you give to someone planning to do business in the region?

14. Analyze an intercultural situation.

Joe arrived 15 minutes late for his appointment with Itaru Nakamura, sales manager for a small manufacturer to which Joe's firm hoped to sell parts. "Sorry to be late," he apologized, "but you know how the local drivers are. At any rate, since I'm late, let's get right down to brass tacks." Joe began to pace back and forth in the small office. "The way I see it, if you and I can come to some agreement this afternoon, we'll be able to get the rest to agree. After all, who knows more about this than you and I do?" Joe sat down opposite his colleague and looked him straight in the eye. "So what do you say? Can we agree on the basics and let our assistants hammer out the details?" His colleague was silent for a few moments, then said, "Yes."

Discuss Joe's intercultural skills. Specifically, what mistakes did he make? What did Nakamura's response probably mean?

15. Analyze how well a company adapts to international audiences.

Choose a large, global company and explore their website. Do you find multiple versions of the company's site for different countries? In what ways does the company adapt its writing style, use of graphics, and other features to adapt to different cultures? Write a brief report on your findings, and include screenshots of the company's website(s) to illustrate your points.

L04 Communicate with
     diverse populations.

16. Learn about someone's cultural background.

Interview a partner about one aspect of his or her cultural background. First, ask your partner which aspect of his or her cultural identity (e.g., race, ethnicity, sex, religion, socioeconomic background, age) he or she feels comfortable discussing.

You might ask questions such as the following:

- In what ways do you identify with this characteristic?
- How, if at all, do you think this characteristic distinguishes you from other people?
- How do you feel similar to others who share this characteristic? Within your group, what differences do you observe?
- In what ways does your background influence how you communicate with others?
- In a work environment, in what ways have you seen this characteristic contribute to your performance and business relationships?

Next, switch roles, so you can share information about one aspect of your own background.

17. Respond to domestic intercultural issues.

As a manager, how would you respond to each of the following situations? What kind of helpful advice can you give to each party?

a. Alton gets angry when several of the people he works with talk among themselves in their native language. He suspects they are talking and laughing about him. As a result, he tends to avoid them and to complain about them to others.

b. Jason, a slightly built office worker, feels intimidated when talking to his supervisor, a much larger man who is of a different racial background. As a result, he often is unable to negotiate effectively.

c. Raisa is embarrassed when she must talk to Roger, a subordinate who has a major facial disfigurement. She doesn't know how to look at him. As a result, she tends to avoid meeting with him face to face.

d. Sheila, the only female manager on staff, gets incensed whenever her colleague Alex apologizes to her after using profanity during a meeting.

e. When Jim arrived as the only male real estate agent in a small office, it was made clear to him that he would have to get his own coffee and clean up after himself— just like everyone else. Yet whenever the FedEx truck delivers a heavy carton, the women always ask him to lift the package.

18. Use inclusive language.

Revise the following sentences to eliminate biased language.

a. The mayor opened contract talks with the union representing local policemen.

b. While the salesmen are at the convention, their wives will be treated to a tour of the city's landmarks.

c. Our company gives each foreman the day off on his birthday.

d. Our public relations director, Heather Marshall, will ask her young secretary, Bonita Carwell, to take notes during the president's speech.

e. Neither Mr. Batista nor his secretary, Doris Hawkins, had met the new family.

19. Discuss your views of using inclusive language.

In small groups, discuss your views about the previous sentences. If you worked for a company and read or overheard each of these statements, would you be offended? Do you believe others might be offended? Discuss the value—and potential downsides—of using inclusive language.

20. Use gender-neutral language.

Identify at least one gender-neutral word for each of the following words:

a. Policeman

b. Clergyman

c. Fireman

d. Salesman

e. Mailman

f. Bellman

g. Handyman

h. Repairman

i. Manhole cover

j. Waiter

Company Scenario

Dewey, Wright, and Howe LLP

Dewey, Wright, and Howe

Dewey, Wright, and Howe is an international law firm that hires college interns. This company scenario, described at www.cengagebrain.com, challenges you to face many of the issues discussed in Chapter 2. Working through the activities for Dewey, Wright, and Howe, you'll have the opportunity to do the following:

• Collaborate in a wiki to produce team results.
• Practice participating in meetings and giving and receiving feedback.
• Manage conflict in a multicultural environment.

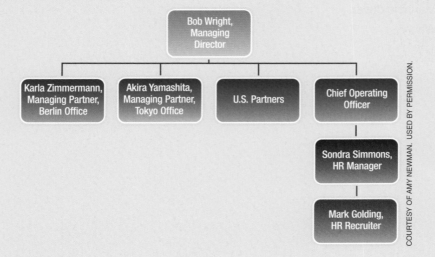

Your team of interns at Dewey is asked to create an Orientation Plan for new hires— and you'll run into a few obstacles along the way: conflicting messages, different communication styles, and a questionable ethical situation. But don't worry—you'll have plenty of direction with a detailed work plan, and you'll rely on your team members for good, sound advice throughout the process.

Notes

1. DiversityInc., "Top 50 Companies for Diversity," www.diversityinc.com/article/5464/No-29-The-Walt-Disney-Co/, accessed June 26, 2010.

2. DiversityInc.

3. Human Rights Campaign, "Corporate Equality Index 2010," www.hrc.org/issues/cei.htm, accessed June 26, 2010.

4. The Walt Disney Corporation, "Corporate Responsibility Report," http://disney.go.com/crreport/workplaces/disneyoperations/diversity.html, accessed June 26, 2010.

5. The Walt Disney Corporation, "Corporate Responsibility Fiscal Year 2009 Interim Update," http://corporate.disney.go.com/media/responsibility/FY09_CR_Update_Final.pdf, accessed June 26, 2010.

6. The Walt Disney Corporation, "Corporate Responsibility Report."

7. DiversityInc.

8. "Conflict Resolution: Don't Get Mad, Get Promoted," *Training* (June 2002): 20.

9. John R. Pierce, "Communication," *Scientific American* 227 (September 1972): 36.

10. Michael Schneider, "Boy Killed by Bus on Disney Property Identified," Associated Press, April 2, 2010, www.msnbc.msn.com/id/36137020/ns/travel-news/t/boy-killed-bus-disney-property-identified/, accessed December 11, 2010.

11. Peter R. Scholtes, *The Team Handbook: How to Use Teams to Improve* (Madison, WI: Joiner Associates, 1988), pp. 6.23–6.28.

12. "Managers Are Ignoring Their Employees," Leadership IQ, December 2, 2009, www.leadershipiq.com, accessed July 15, 2010.

13. Adapted from Peter R. Scholtes, *The Team Handbook, Second Edition* (Madison, WI: Joiner Associates, 1996), pp. 6.27. Reprinted with permission.

14. Stewart Mader, *Wikipatterns* (Indianapolis, Ind.: Wiley, 2008).

15. A. Majchrzak, C. Wagner, and D. Yates, "Corporate Wiki Users: Results of a Survey." *Proceedings of the 2006 International Symposium on Wikis,* Odense, Denmark, 2006.

16. Collaborative Writing, http://en.wikipedia.org/wiki/Collaborative_writing, accessed on July 14, 2010.

17. Stewart Mader.

18. A. J. DuBrin. *Human Relations* (Upper Saddle River, NJ: Prentice-Hall, 1997). Adapted with permission.

19. Geert Hofstede, *Culture's Consequences: Comparing Values, Behaviors, Institutions and Organizations Across Nations*, Second Edition (Thousand Oaks, California: SAGE Publications, 2001).

20. Elizabeth A. Tuleja. *Intercultural Communication for Business*, Managerial Communication Series, James S. O'Rourke IV, editor (South-Western, Canada, 2005).

21. McDonald's India Home Page, www.mcdonaldsindia.net, accessed July 19, 2010.

22. McDonald's Germany Home Page, www.mcdonalds.de and Switzerland Home Page, www.mcdonalds.ch/, accessed March 2011.

23. Elizabeth Würtz. "A Cross-Cultural Analysis of Websites from High-Context Cultures and Low-Context Cultures," *Journal of Computer-Mediated Communication*, 11(1), 2005.

24. Atlanta Committee for Olympic Games, by Sam Ward, *USA Today.* Taken from Ben Brown, "Atlanta Out to Mind Its Manners," *USA Today*, March 14, 1996, p. 7c.

25. "Toyota Motor Company," The Yamasa Institute, www.yamasa.org.acjs/network/english/newsletter/issue30.html, accessed December 27, 2010.

26. Roland Kelts, "Toyota and Trust: Was the Akio Toyoda Apology Lost in Translation?," CS Monitor, February 25, 2011, www.csmonitor.com/Commentary/Opinion/2010/0225/Toyota-and-trust-Was-the-Akio-Toyoda-apology-lost-in-translation, accessed March 11, 2011.

27. State Farm Insurance Website, "Diversity and Inclusion," www.statefarm.com/aboutus/diversity/diversity.asp, accessed April 2, 2011.

28. Jennifer M. Ortman and Christine E. Guarneri, "United States Population Projections: 2000 to 2050," U.S. Census Bureau, www.census.gov/population/www/projections/2009projections.html, accessed March 11, 2011.

29. United States Census 2010, "Explore the Form," http://2010.census.gov/2010census/about/interactive-form.php/, accessed December 13, 2010.

30. Jennifer Coates, *Women, Men, and Language,* (New York: Longman, 1986); Deborah Tannen, *You Just Don't Understand,* (New York: Ballantine, 1990); John Gray, *Men Are from Mars, Women Are from Venus* (New York: HarperCollins, 1992); Patti Hathaway, *Giving and Receiving Feedback,* rev. ed. (Menlo Park, CA: Crisp Publications, 1998); and Deborah Tannen, *Talking from 9 to 5* (New York: William Morrow, 1994).

31. Jake Tapper and Huma Khan, "Obama Apologizes for Calling His Bad Bowling 'Like the Special Olympics,'" ABC News, March 20, 2009, http://abcnews.go.com/Politics/story?id=7129997&page=1, accessed on July 15, 2010.

32. Washington State Developmental Disabilities Council, "The Missing Page in Your Stylebook," www.ddc.wa.gov/Publications/090720_RespectfulLanguage.pdf, accessed July 15, 2010.

33. "Household Data, Annual Averages," Bureau of Labor Statistics, U.S. Department of Labor, www.bls.gov/cps/cpsaat5.pdf, accessed February 15, 2011.

34. Kelly Services. "Kelly Global Workforce Index," http://www.kellyservices.com/web/training/refresh_training_site/en/pages/zmag_kgwi_testpage.html, accessed July 19, 2010.

Chapter 3

Nonverbal Communication (3) Body Movement (3) Physical Appearance (3) Voice Qualities (3) Listening (3) The Value of Listening (3) The Problem of Poor Listening (3) Interpersonal Communication Skills (3) Keys to Better Listening (3) Using Social Media to Build Business Relationships (3) Engaging Customers Online (3) Engaging Employees Online (3) Communicating by Voice and Text Messaging (3) Business Meetings (3) The Case for Face-to-Face (3) Planning the Meeting (3) Prepare an Agenda (3) Encourage Participation and Facilitate Discussion (3) Participating in the Meeting (3) Following Up the Meeting

LEARNING OBJECTIVES

After you have finished this chapter, you should be able to

LO1   Explain the meaning and importance of nonverbal messages.

LO2   Listen effectively in business situations.

LO3   Use social media to build business relationships.

LO4   Use voice technologies and texting effectively in business situations.

LO5   Plan, facilitate, and participate in a business meeting.

"It's more about interaction and conversation rather than Management communicating TO employees. This is not a top-down communication channel."

— TOBIAS HUEBSCHER, INTERNAL COMMUNICATIONS, eBAY, EUROPE

Chapter Introduction: Meetings at eBay

How can a company connect employees to each other—and to the business? Internal communication experts at eBay Europe have found a way.

Each week, more than 400 employees meet face-to-face within locations and virtually (via videoconference) with colleagues in other European offices. Employees hear business updates, ask questions—and argue over rival football teams.

Getting employees to participate in optional meetings can be tough, but Tobias Huebscher, Internal Communications at eBay Europe, found an approach that works. First, to pique employees' interest, he led a competition to decorate the meeting rooms:

> It was a competition we ran among staff to come up with their favourite comic book characters. The most popular were awarded cash to decorate the rooms with memorabilia—bought on eBay of course.

Huebscher also attributes the success of the team meetings to scheduling a set time each week, covering important content during the meetings, having well-structured presentations with humor, allowing lots of time for discussion, and not recording the presentations so people are encouraged to participate.

These meetings foster interaction among employees at different locations and different levels within the company. Building these relationships goes a long way in helping employees understand the business and navigate organizational change.[1]

Virtual Meetings at eBay

© LIEW CHEON FONG – HTTP://LIEWCF.COM; © eBAY GMBH

LO1   Explain the meaning
and importance of
nonverbal messages.

Nonverbal messages are
unwritten and unspoken.

Cultures differ in the
importance they attach
to eye contact.

*International
Communication*

NONVERBAL COMMUNICATION

Not all communication at work is spoken, heard, written, or read—in other words, verbal. According to management expert Peter Drucker, "The most important thing in communication is to hear what isn't being said."[2] A nonverbal message is any message that is not written or spoken. You may use a nonverbal message with a verbal message (smiling as you greet a colleague), or alone (sitting in the back of the classroom). Nonverbal messages are typically more spontaneous than verbal messages, but they're not necessarily less important. The six most common types of nonverbal communication in business are discussed in the following sections.

Body Movement

By far, the most expressive part of your body is your face—particularly your eyes. Research shows that receivers read facial expressions quite consistently. In fact, many of these expressions have the same meaning across different cultures.[3] Eye contact and eye movements tell you a lot about a person, although—as we discussed earlier—maintaining eye contact is not perceived as important (or even polite) in some cultures. Facial expressions tell us much about a person. Paul Ekman, known as the lie detector, claims that facial expressions are universal—not cultural. He has isolated 43 facial muscles that, among other variables, tell us whether a smile is genuine.[4]

In Figure 1, can you tell which smile is real? If you guessed the one on the left, you are correct. One clue is how the woman contracts the many muscles in the corners of her eyes, which is hard to fake unless the smile is genuine.[5]

Gestures are hand and upper-body movements that—in addition to or instead of words—add important information to face-to-face interactions. As the game of charades proves, you can communicate quite a bit without using oral or written signals. More typically, gestures are used to help illustrate and reinforce your verbal message. A Chicago psychiatrist studied former President Bill Clinton's grand jury testimony about his relationship with Monica Lewinsky. Dr. Alan Hirsch found that the president touched his nose once every four minutes when he gave answers that later were shown to be false. By contrast, he did not touch his nose at all when he gave truthful answers.[6]

**Figure 1
Which Smile Is
Genuine?**

AMY SNYDER, © EXPLORATORIUM, WWW.EXPLROATORIUM.EDU

Body stance (e.g., your posture, where you place your arms and legs, and how you distribute your weight) is another form of nonverbal communication. For example, leaning slightly toward someone would probably convey interest and involvement in the interaction. On the other hand, leaning back with arms folded across the chest might be taken (and intended) as a sign of boredom or defiance. In Figure 2, a scene from the TV show, *The Office*, Oscar and Angela don't look too impressed with Kevin.

Figure 2
Sending Negative Messages in *The Office*

© PAUL DRINKWATER/© NBC/COURTESY: EVERETT COLLECTION

Physical Appearance

Our culture places great value on physical appearance. TV, magazines, and the Internet are filled with advertisements for personal-care products, and the ads typically feature attractive users of these products. Attractive people tend to be seen as more intelligent, more likable, and more persuasive than unattractive people.[7] In addition, people believed to be attractive earn more money.[8]

With its "Campaign for Real Beauty," Dove created a highly successful, viral advertising campaign. In one video, Dove Evolution, with over 12 million views, the company shows how a plain-looking woman is transformed with makeup and Photoshop. Dove also struck a chord with people by featuring curvy women in its advertisements, perhaps—in a small way—challenging our American perceptions of beauty.

Your appearance is particularly important for making a good first impression. Although you can't change all of your physical features, make choices that enhance your professional image in the business environment, such as using clothing, jewelry, and hairstyle to emphasize your strong points.

In its Dove Evolution viral video, Dove reveals how physical appearance is enhanced with makeup and Photoshop.

REPRODUCED WITH KIND PERMISSION OF UNILEVER PLC AND GROUP COMPANIES.

Voice Qualities

Your tone of voice can emphasize, subordinate, or even contradict your verbal messages.

No one speaks in a monotone. To illustrate, read the following sentence aloud, each time emphasizing the italicized word. Note how the meaning changes with each reading.

- *Allison* missed the donor meeting. (Answers the question "Who missed the meeting?")
- Allison *missed* the donor meeting. (Emphasizes that Allison wasn't at the meeting.)
- Allison missed the *donor* meeting. (Clarifies which meeting Allison missed.)

Voice qualities such as volume, speed, pitch, tone, and accent carry both intentional and unintentional messages. For example, when you are nervous, you tend to speak faster and at a higher pitch. People who speak too softly risk being interrupted or ignored, whereas people who speak too loudly are often seen as being pushy or insecure.

International Communication

A significant number of voice qualities are universal across all human cultures. One study showed that "vocalizations communicating the so-called 'basic emotions' (anger, disgust, fear, joy, sadness, and surprise)" were recognized across two very different cultures.[9] Around the world, adults use higher-pitched voices when speaking to children, when greeting others, and during courtship.[10]

Time

International Communication

The meaning we attach to time depends on our culture, our status, and the specific situation.

How do you feel when you're late for an appointment? When others are late? The meaning given to time varies greatly by culture, with Americans and Canadians being much more time-conscious than members of South American or Middle Eastern cultures.

Time is related not only to culture but also to status within the organization. You would be much less likely to keep your manager waiting for an appointment than you would someone who reports to you.

Time is also situation-specific. Although you normally might not worry about being five minutes late for a staff meeting, you would probably arrive early if you were the first presenter or meeting with a prospective client for the first time. Are you more likely to be late if you can text message your lunch date? Some people feel justified in being five minutes late so long as they send a text—but not everyone will be forgiving.

Touch

Touch is the first sense we develop, acquired even before birth. Some touches, such as those made by a physician during an examination, are purely physical; others, such as a handshake, are a friendly sign of willingness to communicate; and still others indicate intimacy.

International Communication

The importance of touching behavior varies widely by culture. One international study found that in typical social exchanges, people from San Juan, Puerto Rico, touched an average of 180 times an hour; those in Paris touched 110 times per hour; those in Gainesville, Florida, touched 2 times per hour; and those in London touched not at all.[11]

Because of litigation in the United States, touching in the office has become an issue for many companies. Although handshakes are certainly appropriate, in most companies—depending on the organizational culture—any other touching is frowned upon.

Space and Territory

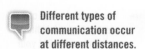
Different types of communication occur at different distances.

When you are on a crowded elevator, you probably look down, up, or straight ahead—anything to avoid looking at the other people. Most people in the U.S. culture are uncomfortable in such close proximity to strangers. In Chapter 2, we discussed cultural differences regarding space; now, let's look more closely at how Americans use space to interact with others (Figure 3).

Competent communicators recognize their own personal space needs and the needs of others. Look for cues from others, such as people backing away or moving their chairs, to determine whether they prefer more or less space. Try to accommodate differences to make people feel comfortable.

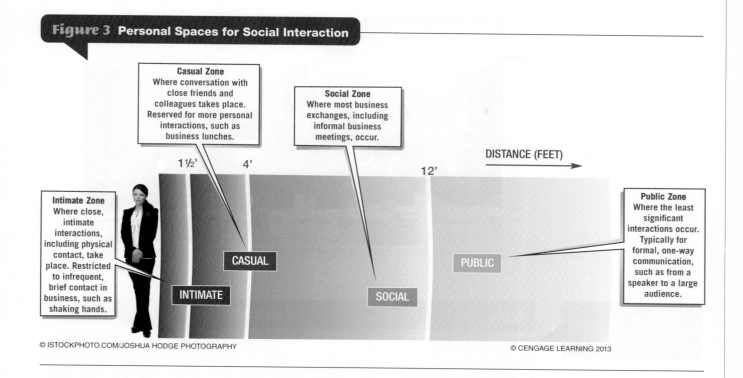

Figure 3 Personal Spaces for Social Interaction

Casual Zone
Where conversation with close friends and colleagues takes place. Reserved for more personal interactions, such as business lunches.

Social Zone
Where most business exchanges, including informal business meetings, occur.

DISTANCE (FEET)

1½'   4'   12'

Intimate Zone
Where close, intimate interactions, including physical contact, take place. Restricted to infrequent, brief contact in business, such as shaking hands.

CASUAL

INTIMATE

PUBLIC

SOCIAL

Public Zone
Where the least significant interactions occur. Typically for formal, one-way communication, such as from a speaker to a large audience.

© ISTOCKPHOTO.COM/JOSHUA HODGE PHOTOGRAPHY

© CENGAGE LEARNING 2013

LISTENING

L02   Listen effectively in business situations.

Across continents or across a conference table, effective communication requires both sending and receiving messages. Whether you are making a formal presentation to 500 people or speaking with one person over lunch, listening is essential to understanding.

Listening involves much more than just hearing. You can hear and not listen (just as you can listen and not understand). Hearing is a passive process, whereas listening is an active process. When you *perceive* a sound, you're merely aware of it; you don't necessarily comprehend it. When you *listen,* you interpret and assign meaning to the sound.

 There is a difference between hearing and listening.

When your car is operating normally, even though you *hear* the sound of the engine as you're driving, you're barely aware of it; you tune it out. But the minute the engine begins to make a strange sound—not necessarily louder or harsher, but just *different*—you tune back in, listening intently to determine the problem. You *heard* the normal hum of the engine but *listened* to the strange noise.

The Value of Listening

Listening is essential to business. Imagine trying to tell your manager about a potential new client, an idea to save money, or a product safety issue—and being ignored.

Good listening in business improves tasks and relationships.

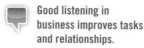

Ethics in Communication

Toyota was criticized for ignoring potential safety issues that led to millions of car recalls beginning in 2009. In Chapter 2, we discussed president Akio Toyoda's response to these recalls. Investigators believed some issues may have been avoided if Toyota had listened and responded properly to customer complaints.

Effective managers know that good listening improves tasks and relationships (Figure 4).[12]

Toyota executives testify before the U.S. Congress after failing to listen and respond to customer complaints about safety issues.

© MARK WILSON/GETTY IMAGES

Figure 4
How Listening Improves Business

Tasks	Relationships
Improves problem solving	Increases interpersonal trust
Improves product and service design	Improves customer service and loyalty
Improves accuracy of communication	Increases employee commitment and morale
Reduces misunderstandings about new tasks	Encourages timely feedback
Increases frequency of sharing information	Increases perceptions of integrity

© CENGAGE LEARNING 2013

The Problem of Poor Listening Skills

 Although listening is the communication skill we use most frequently, most people have not been taught how to listen effectively.

Listening is the communication skill we use the most. White-collar workers typically devote at least 40 percent of their workdays to listening. Yet immediately after hearing a ten-minute oral presentation, the average person retains only 50 percent of the information. Forty-eight hours later, only 25 percent of what was heard can be recalled.[13] Listening is probably the least developed of the four verbal communication skills (writing, reading, speaking, and listening).

Why are we such poor listeners? First, most people have simply not been taught how to listen well. Think back to your early years in school. Chances are that reading, writing, and perhaps speaking were heavily stressed in your education. But how much formal training have you had in listening? If you're typical, the answer is "Not much."

Another factor that contributes to poor listening skills is the disparity between how quickly we speak and how quickly our brains process data. We can think about four times faster than we can speak. When listening to others, our minds begin to wander, and we lose our ability to concentrate on what is being said.

Ineffective listening can result in lost sales and productivity, hurt feelings, low morale, and in the Toyota example, safety issues and a damaged corporate image.

 Poor listeners may not be aware of their weakness.

Still, poor listening skills are not as readily apparent as poor speaking or writing skills. It's easy to spot a poor speaker or writer but much more difficult to spot a poor listener because a poor listener can fake attention—and may not even know this is a weakness.

Keys to Better Listening

The good news is that you can improve your listening skills. To listen more effectively, give the speaker your undivided attention, stay open-minded, avoid interrupting, and involve yourself in the communication.

Give the Speaker Your Undivided Attention

It's easy to get distracted. During a business presentation, the audience may tune the speaker out and let their minds wander. During a job interview, the recruiter may take phone calls. Or, during class, you may doodle or think about an upcoming exam.

In a working environment, some distractions are easier than others to eliminate. A messy office, with lots of toys to play with, can diffuse your focus when you're listening on the phone. This is within your control. But in a cubicle or open environment, you can't control all of the noise and diversions around you. Your coworker may be typing loudly, talking on the phone, or clipping his toenails (true story!). Your best bet is to use your proficient communication skills to explain how the behavior is affecting your work and politely request a change.

This office worker may have trouble listening because of all of the distractions in her work space.

Mental distractions are even more difficult to eliminate. But with practice and effort, you can discipline yourself to postpone thinking about how tired you are or how much you're looking forward to a social event. Temporarily banishing competing thoughts will allow you to give the speaker your undivided attention.

Try to focus on the content of the message. Although a speaker's nonverbal communication, such as dress and body language, can be distracting, don't let unimportant factors prevent you from listening openly. Delivery skills can steal our attention—sometimes more than they should. If someone is nervous or speaks too softly, challenge yourself to listen beyond these surface issues. Almost always, *what* is said is more important than *how* it is said.

 Pay more attention to what the speaker says than to how he or she says it.

Also, avoid dismissing a topic simply because it's uninteresting or not presented in an exciting way. "Boring" does not mean unimportant. Information that's boring or difficult to follow may prove to be useful and well worth your effort to give it your full attention.

Stay Open-Minded

Regardless of whom you're listening to or what the topic is, keep your emotions in check. Listen objectively and empathetically. Be willing to accept new information and new points of view, regardless of whether they mesh with your existing beliefs. Concentrate on the content of the message rather than on its source.

Don't look at the situation as a win–lose proposition; that is, don't consider that the speaker wins and you lose if you concede the merits of his or her position. Instead, think of it as a win–win situation: the speaker wins by convincing you of the merits of his or her position, and you win by gaining new information and insights that will help you perform your job more effectively.

 Keeping an open mind results in a win–win situation.

We tend to jump to conclusions too quickly. Instead, try to understand *why* the speaker is arguing a particular point of view and what facts or experience convinced the speaker to adopt this position. When you assume this empathetic frame of reference, you will likely realize that the speaker is not entirely wrong. Evaluating a message objectively will help you learn the most when you disagree with someone.

Don't Interrupt

Perhaps because of time pressures, we sometimes get impatient. As soon as we've figured out what a person is going to say, we tend to interrupt to finish the speaker's

 Interrupting a speaker creates a barrier to effective communication.

sentence, particularly when he or she speaks slowly. Or, as soon as we can think of a counterargument, we tend to rush right in—regardless of whether the speaker has finished or even paused for a breath.

Interruptions have many negative consequences. First, they are rude. Second, instead of speeding up the exchange, interruptions may drag it out because they interfere with the speaker's train of thought, causing backtracking. But the most serious negative consequence is the message an interruption sends: "I have the right to interrupt you because what I have to say is more important than what you have to say." Of course, this hinders effective communication.

There is a difference between listening and simply waiting to speak. Even if you're too polite to interrupt, don't simply wait for the first opportunity to barge in with your version of the truth. If you're constantly planning what you'll say next, you can hardly listen attentively to what the other person is saying.

Americans tend to have low tolerance for silence. But waiting a moment or two after someone has finished before you respond has several positive effects—especially in an emotional exchange. It gives the person speaking a chance to elaborate, which could draw out further insights. It also helps create a quieter, calmer, more respectful atmosphere, one that is more conducive to solving the problem.

Involve Yourself

As we have said, hearing is passive, whereas listening is active. You should be *doing* something while the other person is speaking (and we don't mean doodling, texting, or staring out the window).

 Involve yourself mentally in what the speaker is saying.

The best listeners are active listeners. They focus on the content of what's said as well as the underlying emotions. When they respond, they convey their understanding of both without judgment.

Much of what you should be doing when someone is speaking is mental. Summarize to yourself what the speaker is saying; create what experts call an **internal paraphrase** of the speaker's comments. We process information much faster than the speaker can present it, so use that extra time for more active listening.

Some listeners find it helpful to jot down points, translating their mental notes into written notes. If you do, keep your notes brief; don't become so busy writing down the facts that you miss the message. Concentrate on the main ideas; if you get them, you'll be more likely to remember the supporting details later. Recognize also that even if a detail or two of the speaker's message might be inaccurate or irrelevant, the major points may still be valid. Evaluate the validity of the overall argument; don't get bogged down in trivia.

Listen for what you need. Constantly ask yourself, How does this point affect *me*? How can I use this information to further my goals or to help me perform my job more effectively? Personalizing the information will help you concentrate more easily and weigh the evidence more objectively—even if the topic is difficult to follow or uninteresting and even if the speaker has some annoying mannerisms or an unpleasant personality.

Encourage the speaker by letting him or her know that you're actively involved in the interaction. Maintain eye contact, nod in agreement, lean forward, and use encouraging phrases such as "Uh huh" or "I see." In a conversation, ensure that your mental paraphrases are on target by summarizing aloud for the speaker what you think you're hearing. Consider three levels of responding, each with increasing involvement (Figure 5).

How you respond depends on the speaker and your listening skills. To repeat what someone says feels like parroting; it demonstrates that you are hearing but not necessarily listening. Paraphrasing is better: this approach shows that you are interpreting the message and restating it in your own words. Sometimes reflecting is best: you are telling the person that you hear, understand, and care about the underlying message. This is particularly appropriate if you see someone visibly upset (and may be inappropriate for other interactions). Reflecting may open up

```
Sender          Receiver
                ┌──────────────────┐  ┌────────┐
                │ "You're not going │  │ Repeat │
                │ to finish the     │  └────────┘
                │ research by       │
                │ Friday."          │
                └──────────────────┘
┌────────────┐  ┌──────────────────┐  ┌───────────┐
│ "I'm not   │  │ "You won't be    │  │ Paraphrase│
│ going to   │──│ done with your   │  └───────────┘
│ finish the │  │ section on time."│
│ research   │  └──────────────────┘
│ by Friday."│  ┌──────────────────┐  ┌────────┐
└────────────┘  │ "You seem worried│  │ Reflect│
                │ about missing the│  └────────┘
                │ deadline."       │
                └──────────────────┘
```

© CENGAGE LEARNING 2013

Figure 5
Three Levels of Responding

the discussion and encourage the person to talk more about what's happening and how you can help solve the issue.

Even in formal presentation settings, you can demonstrate your attention to the speaker with nonverbal communication such as maintaining eye contact, nodding, and smiling when appropriate. This sends the message that you are interested in what the speaker has to say and want to hear more.

Of course, we lose body language in online communication, but many of these principles for effective listening apply to online interactions, which we'll discuss next.

USING SOCIAL MEDIA TO BUILD BUSINESS RELATIONSHIPS

Ask anyone responsible for social media for a company, and he or she will likely say the same thing: it's all about the "conversation." Building meaningful relationships with customers and employees online requires good interpersonal communication, particularly listening.

Engaging Customers Online

Listening is the first objective described in *Groundswell*, a book about capitalizing on social technologies. According to Forrester Research, which provided the groundwork for the book, listening is "learning from what your customers are saying. It's tapping into that conversation. They're talking about your company. If you can listen, the information flows back in the other direction."[14,15]

JetBlue Airways sees the value of connecting with customers through social media:

> Our Twitter desk is a much more economical way to communicate with customers than handling emails or phone calls; you can handle . . . our five Twitter streams at a time vs. taking one phone call at a time.

> We built a database of most common questions and answers, and it's not often that people have to make a phone call to someone else within the company and say "Hey, we got this tweet; what do we do with it?" People call it social media, but we actually see it as the opposite of media; it's direct communication with the brand on a one-to-one level.[16]

For JetBlue, social media creates a collaborative, cost-effective way to interact with customers. As you can see from JetBlue's Twitter page, the company frequently listens and responds, as in the examples in Figure 6.[17]

Communication Technologies

L03 Use social media to build business relationships.

Smart companies listen to customers by engaging them online.

Figure 6
JetBlue Listens and
Responds Through
Twitter

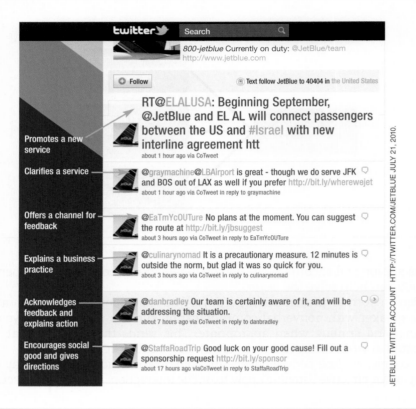

Promotes a new service
Clarifies a service
Offers a channel for feedback
Explains a business practice
Acknowledges feedback and explains action
Encourages social good and gives directions

JETBLUE TWITTER ACCOUNT HTTP://TWITTER.COM/JETBLUE JULY 21, 2010.

Listening online isn't just about having a presence—it's about engaging customers. A recent study looked at large brands and analyzed how they are using social technologies, such as Facebook, wikis, and Flickr; and content distribution sites, such as Facebook Connect and ShareThis (Figure 7). The "Wallflower" brands,

Figure 7
Customer Engage-
ment Online

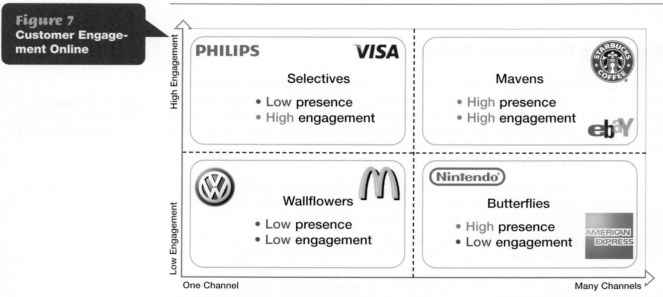

such as McDonald's, use one social tool but do little to connect with customers. The "Mavens," such as Starbucks, are active on many sites and heavily engage customers.[18]

When customers are listened to online, they are more likely to contribute to social media sites, providing valuable feedback to companies. TripAdvisor, the travel review site, sends email to people who post a review. By telling customers how many people read their review, TripAdvisor acknowledges online feedback, increasing the likelihood that customers will continue to participate in online conversations. Similar to listening in person, engaging customers online encourages people to give more frequent and better feedback.

Just as for in-person communication, if you provide an avenue for people to provide feedback online, you must respond. Many companies now offer online chat, a nice service for customers browsing a website. But consider the following entertaining exchange with a telephone system company:

> **Customer:** All I want to be able to do is call in and out of the building.
> **Customer:** Hello?
> **Customer:** Is anybody there?
> **Nicole:** *You're local provider will be able to assist you.*
> **Customer:** So you can't answer my question?
> **Customer:** (You spelled "you're" incorrectly, by the way. It's "your." Just so you know, for the future.)

If companies don't handle online chat well, they may be better off sticking with a toll-free number.

Engaging Employees Online

Smart companies find ways to engage employees online as well as in face-to-face communication. Considered "internal customers," employees also have valuable feedback that companies should hear.

An intranet site is a good way to encourage employees to participate in the conversation about the company—and to keep their comments internal. Rather than posting embarrassing information about a company on public websites, employees can give feedback about products, organizational changes, management, and more on an employee-only intranet site.

 Intranets offer opportunities to engage and listen to employees.

As we saw in Chapter 1, Best Buy hasn't been 100% successful (Brian Maupin posted several public videos), but the company has made strides in opening the door to employees. Best Buy implemented a "listening chair" with online employee surveys. Employees participate in decisions by responding to questions such as "Do you think the Geek Squad uniform needs updating?"

Later in the book, we'll discuss more about engaging audiences online.

Online employee surveys encourage Best Buy employees to share feedback about their work environment.

© JODI HILTON

Communication Technologies

LO4 Use voice technologies and texting effectively in business situations.

COMMUNICATING BY VOICE AND TEXT MESSAGING

Voice technologies and text messaging are good choices for interpersonal communication at work. A richer medium than email, the telephone allows you to convey and hear tone of voice, one of the cues for interpreting messages. But the telephone—and certainly text messaging—is not nearly as rich as face-to-face communication, which includes nonverbal cues such as gestures and body language. Without these cues, your voice and etiquette are more important when you use an office phone, smartphone, text messaging, and **VoIP** (Voice over Internet Protocol, such as Skype or Google Voice) for business communication. Figures 8 through 11 provide tips for using these technologies.

Figure 8
Tips for Using an Office Telephone

Office Telephone

1) **Receiving and Ending Calls**
   - Answer within two or three rings.
   - Use your company's standard greeting, or use a greeting similar to your manager's.
   - Take notes to remember important information.
   - Follow your company's norm when ending the call; not everyone says a formal "Goodbye" in business.

2) **Setting up a Greeting for Voice Mail**
   - Use your company's standard greeting (less than 15 seconds).
   - Consider separate greetings for internal and external callers if your system allows it.
   - Change your greeting when you're out of the office.

3) **Making Outgoing Calls**
   - Be respectful of timing; don't call at 4:55 P.M. when the office closes at 5 P.M., and don't call late at night if you may reach someone's smartphone at home.
   - Prepare to speak with the person directly and to leave a voice mail message—you never know which.
   - Plan what you will say for important calls; prepare your first couple of sentences.
   - Leave a complete but brief voice mail message: your name, the reason you're calling, and your phone number.

4) **Convey a Positive, Professional Image**
   - Use your natural voice, but make sure you don't sound bored; try smiling when you answer the phone.
   - Give the caller your full attention; people can hear if you're typing or moving papers.
   - Avoid eating or chewing gum while on the phone.
   - Avoid using office phones for personal calls.
   - Avoid saying anything that you might regret; conversations could be recorded.

"Good morning, this is Tre Thompson in Xerox Accounting. How may I help you?"

"Hello, you've reached Tre Thompson at Xerox. I'm traveling this week, but I will check my messages and get back to you as soon as I can. Thank you."

© HEMERA TECHNOLOGIES/JUPITERIMAGES

Figure 9 Tips for Using a Smartphone

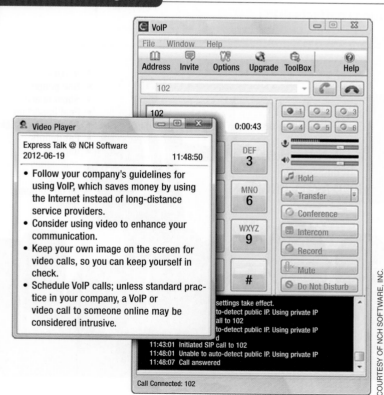

Smartphone

- Use the office phone principles that apply to work-related calls on your smartphone.
- Avoid talking in public for important work-related calls.
- Schedule time for important calls, so you can arrange for a private, quiet place to talk.
- Avoid taking calls during meetings; unless this is the norm in your company, it's likely considered rude.
- Avoid using your company-paid smartphone for personal calls unless this is allowed.
- Be mindful of people around you; don't block traffic—or get hit by it!
- Avoid talking on the phone while driving.

© ISTOCKPHOTO.COM/DSGPRO

Figure 10 Tips for Text Messaging

Text Messaging

- Send texts to people at or below your level in the organization—or to your manager if you know this is acceptable to him or her.
- Reserve texts for quick messages that require an immediate response, usually for logistical information; don't send texts for heavy content or important business decisions.
- Avoid texting during meetings unless this is acceptable at your company.
- Use informal language, but know that anything you write may become public.
- Never text while driving; this is dangerous and not worth the risk.

"Board mtg. starts in 2 hrs. Can you pls. send John the PPT?"

© OLEKSIY MAKSYMENKO PHOTOGRAPHY/ALAMY

Figure 11 Tips for Using VoIP

Express Talk @ NCH Software
2012-06-19   11:48:50

- Follow your company's guidelines for using VoIP, which saves money by using the Internet instead of long-distance service providers.
- Consider using video to enhance your communication.
- Keep your own image on the screen for video calls, so you can keep yourself in check.
- Schedule VoIP calls; unless standard practice in your company, a VoIP or video call to someone online may be considered intrusive.

COURTESY OF NCH SOFTWARE, INC.

See Chapter 12, Employment Communication, for tips on phone and video interviews.

LO5 Plan, facilitate, and
participate in a
business meeting.

Effective managers
know how to run and
participate in business
meetings.

Use face-to-face
meetings for the most
important business
interactions.

BUSINESS MEETINGS

Meetings in organizations take many forms and serve many purposes. Whether in person or through technology, people meet to share information about the business, provide team progress updates, solicit and provide input, solve problems, make decisions—and start, maintain, and sometimes end relationships.

Unfortunately, many meetings are unnecessary and poorly run. Seventy-five percent of employees who attend meetings say they could be more effective.[19] The cartoon in Figure 12 shows what a joke meetings have become in many organizations.

Meetings can work well. After choosing an appropriate meeting format, an effective communicator plans, facilitates and participates in, and follows up a meeting.

Determining the Meeting Format

Choosing an appropriate format for your meeting is an important part of good meeting planning. In some cases, logistics, such as people working in different locations and time zones, will drive how you meet. In other cases, your meeting purpose, for example, trying to close a deal, will determine how you meet. Your company also will have standard practices, and people within the company will have personal preferences. All of these factors—and research about effective meetings—will help you decide on a structure for your meeting.

The Case for Face-to-Face

With all of the technology available, most people prefer face-to-face meetings. A global Kelly Services study found that between 74% and 82% of employees prefer face-to-face communication with their colleagues and coworkers.[20] A Harvard Business Review group study of 2,300 managers from North America, Asia, and Europe found that more than 50% of managers preferred face-to-face communication—even if it means traveling—for the following purposes:[21]

- Meeting new (94%) or existing clients (69%) to sell business
- Negotiating contracts (82%)

**Figure 12
Meeting Humor**

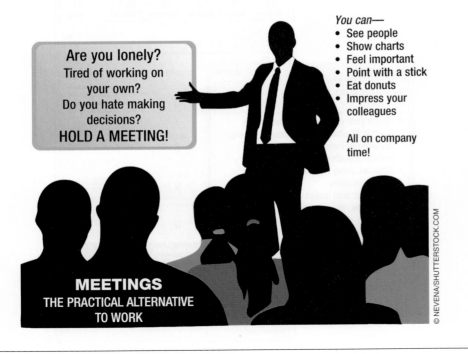

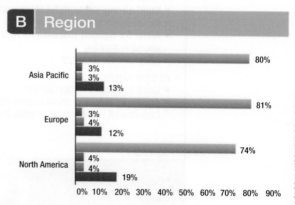
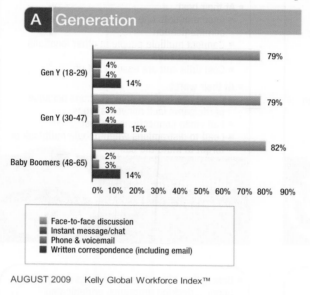

Figure 13 **Preferences for Communicating with Colleagues**

In communicating with your colleagues and coworkers, which method do you prefer?

A Generation

Gen Y (18-29): 4%, 4%, 14%, 79%

Gen Y (30-47): 3%, 4%, 15%, 79%

Baby Boomers (48-65): 2%, 3%, 14%, 82%

0% 10% 20% 30% 40% 50% 60% 70% 80% 90%

- Face-to-face discussion
- Instant message/chat
- Phone & voicemail
- Written correspondence (including email)

B Region

Asia Pacific: 3%, 3%, 13%, 80%

Europe: 3%, 4%, 12%, 81%

North America: 4%, 4%, 19%, 74%

0% 10% 20% 30% 40% 50% 60% 70% 80% 90%

AUGUST 2009   Kelly Global Workforce Index™

KELLY.

© KELLY SERVICES/KELLY GLOBAL WORKFORCE INDEX™

- Interviewing senior staff for key appointments (81%)
- Understanding and listening to important customers (69%)
- Identifying growth opportunities (55%)
- Building relationships/managing geographically dispersed teams (55%)
- Initiating discussions with merger and acquisition targets (52%)

Only 20% of managers in this study agreed with the statement "You can achieve the same results with virtual meetings as you can with in-person meetings."[22]

Clearly, some of the most important business dealings are handled in person. This makes sense, considering what we discussed in Chapter 1: face-to-face is the richest medium and the best choice for interpersonal communication. Plus, face-to-face communication is strongly preferred over other forms of communication by three generations of workers and employees in Asia, Europe, and North America (Figure 13).

And yet, managers are using new technologies for meetings and expect to do so more in the future. The Harvard Business Review group study also found that most managers anticipate participating in more or the same number of teleconferences or audio conferences and videoconferences, but in-person meetings that require travel will decrease or stay the same.[23] Budget restrictions on travel are expected to push meeting technologies as a more popular choice in the future.[24]

Considering Alternatives

Although the best choice for many situations, face-to-face meetings are not always practical or ideal for all business purposes. Figure 14 compares the best and worst of face-to-face and virtual meetings (**conference calls**, **online meetings**, and **videoconferences**).

Communication Technologies

Figure 14 Comparison of Four Meeting Formats

- **Description:** In-person meetings for any number of people
- **At their best:**
  - Build strong, meaningful relationships
  - Increase social interaction
  - Allow for difficult discussions and complex decision making
  - Keep people focused
- **At their worst:**
  - Lead to excessive socializing
  - Are expensive and show unproven return on investment (when large groups travel)

Face-to-Face Meetings

- **Description:** Audio conference calls for people in two or more locations (often through speakerphone)
- **At their best:**
  - Accommodate one-way and two-way communication
  - Connect multiple people in other locations on one medium
  - Cost little and are easy to set up
- **At their worst:**
  - Cause overlapping conversations because participants lack nonverbal cues
  - Fail when connections are lost
  - Lead to distractions when people multitask or forget to mute the call

Conference Calls

- **Description:** Web-based meetings using a service such as WebEx or GoToMeeting
- **At their best:**
  - Allow teams to work on documents together (with screen-sharing capabilities)
  - Provide an inexpensive alternative to a face-to-face presentation (with PowerPoint driven by one or more people)
  - Are free for small groups and limited use
- **At their worst:**
  - Fail because of the technology, which sometimes requires a separate telephone connection
  - Lead to distractions (as with conference calls)

Online Meetings

- **Description:** Video-based meetings using smartphones, desktop programs, or dedicated services such as telepresence suites
- **At their best:**
  - Provide the best alternative to face-to-face meetings
  - Feel like a face-to-face meeting (telepresence)
  - Cost little (smartphones and desktop systems)
- **At their worst:**
  - Fail because of technology problems (or people using the technology!)
  - Require equipment that's too expensive for most businesses (telepresence)

Videoconferences

 Consider alternatives when face-to-face meetings aren't practical.

Some companies use virtual, three-dimensional environments, such as Second Life, for meetings (Figure 15). Although broad adoption has been slow, Second Life is far less expensive than in-person meetings and provides a simulated environment for companies to test new ideas. IBM, for example, held one conference that saved the company $320,000 in travel expenses and lost productivity. Other companies, such as CIGNA and Children's Memorial Hospital in Chicago, have used Second Life for training and disaster planning.[25] The technology isn't for everyone, but with proper planning and for the right purpose, Second Life presents a viable alternative to the traditional meeting.

Planning the Meeting

Even ignoring technology and travel expenses, when you add up the hourly salaries of people planning and attending a meeting, the cost can be considerable. Managers must make sure they are getting their money's worth from a meeting, and that requires careful planning: identifying the purpose and determining whether a meeting is necessary, deciding who should attend, preparing an agenda, and planning the logistics.

Figure 15 Virtual Meeting in Second Life

COURTESY OF INTERNATIONAL BUSINESS MACHINES CORPORATION, © INTERNATIONAL BUSINESS MACHINES CORPORATION.

Identify Your Purpose

The first step is always to determine your purpose. The more specific you can be, the better results you will get. A purpose such as "to discuss how to make our marketing staff more effective" is vague and doesn't identify a clear outcome. These purpose statements are clearer and more specific:

- To decide whether to implement a new rewards program for the marketing staff
- To finalize the work schedule for July
- To prioritize candidates for the IT analyst position

Determine Whether a Meeting Is Necessary

Sometimes meetings are not the most efficient means of communication. For one-way communication that doesn't require input or feedback, such as a monthly status update, perhaps sending an email or posting a podcast on the intranet is best. Similarly, it doesn't make sense to use the weekly staff meeting of ten people to hold a long discussion involving only one or two of the members. A phone call or smaller meeting would accomplish that task more quickly and at less cost.

 Determine whether a meeting is the best way to accomplish your goal.

Decide Who Should Attend

Everyone you invite to your meeting should have a specific reason for attending. Ideally, you will include only those people who can contribute to the meeting. Who will make the decision? Who will implement the decision? Who will contribute ideas? Who can provide background information? On the one hand, you want to include all who can contribute to solving the problem; on the other hand, you want to keep the meeting to a manageable number of people. For videoconferences, who is invited is even more important: each connection to a location costs money.

Everyone at the meeting should have a specific reason for being there.

Meeting invitations—like wedding invitations—can cause friction. You may want to keep your meeting small but feel obligated to include someone. Of course, you want to avoid hurt feelings, but you should balance this with your goal: to run an efficient, productive meeting. Speaking with someone ahead of time about whether he or she needs to attend or involving your manager in the decision may be useful.

Although getting everyone to agree on the same goal can be challenging, avoid excluding people just to prevent conflict. Instead, speak separately with decision makers and cynics ahead of time to help rally their support during the meeting.

Prepare an Agenda

With your purpose and participants set, you need to decide what topics the meeting will cover and in what order. This list of topics, or **agenda**, will accomplish two

 An agenda helps focus the attention of both the facilitator and the participants.

things: it will help you prepare for the meeting, and it will help you run the meeting by keeping everyone focused on the schedule.

Knowing what topics will be discussed will also help participants plan for the meeting by reviewing background information, bringing documentation, and preparing questions. You also may assign topics for participants to lead (with their permission, of course). By doing this, you'll engage more people in the meeting and share some of the responsibility.

Send the agenda before the meeting is scheduled, so people know what to expect and have enough time to prepare. Ideally, you would send the agenda with a calendar invitation that automatically schedules a time when everyone is available. If you schedule the meeting far in advance, you may want to send a reminder a day or two before the date. The sample email in Figure 16, to the team who will select a new IT analyst, encourages people to come to the meeting ready to contribute.

Figure 16
Sample Email to Prepare for a Meeting

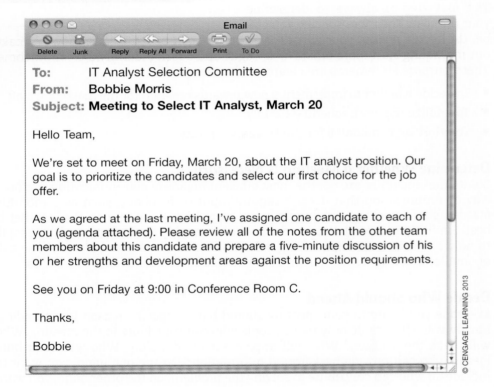

To: IT Analyst Selection Committee
From: Bobbie Morris
Subject: **Meeting to Select IT Analyst, March 20**

Hello Team,

We're set to meet on Friday, March 20, about the IT analyst position. Our goal is to prioritize the candidates and select our first choice for the job offer.

As we agreed at the last meeting, I've assigned one candidate to each of you (agenda attached). Please review all of the notes from the other team members about this candidate and prepare a five-minute discussion of his or her strengths and development areas against the position requirements.

See you on Friday at 9:00 in Conference Room C.

Thanks,

Bobbie

© CENGAGE LEARNING 2013

The more specific the agenda you can provide, the better. Figure 17 is an example of a detailed agenda.

Notice that this agenda isn't set for one hour. Although one hour is often the default time, some meetings need more or less time and should be scheduled accordingly. People may be more likely to stick with the agenda if the times are not typical. Also, most of the work will be done outside the meeting. The short time frames keep people focused on why they are meeting: to make a decision.

Arrange Logistics

Coordinating a meeting—whether face-to-face or virtual—requires thoughtful preparation. Figure 18 offers suggestions to get your meeting off to a good start.

IT Analyst Selection Team Meeting
Purpose: To prioritize the candidates and select our first choice for the job offer
March 20
Conference Room C
9:00 – 9:45 A.M.

Topic	Who	Timing
Review requirements of the IT analyst position	Yuri	9:00 – 9:05
Candidate 1		
• Review feedback gathered	Kelly	9:05 – 9:10
• Discuss qualifications	Everyone	9:10 – 9:15
Candidate 2		
• Review feedback gathered	David	9:15 – 9:20
• Discuss qualifications	Everyone	9:20 – 9:25
Candidate 3		
• Review feedback gathered	Eun	9:25 – 9:30
• Discuss qualifications	Everyone	9:30 – 9:35
Agree on the top candidate (and possibly a backup)	Everyone	9:35 – 9:40
Recap and agree on next steps	Yuri	9:40 – 9:45

© CENGAGE LEARNING 2013

Face-to-Face Meetings	Virtual Meetings
• **Schedule a room.** Choose a room large enough for people to feel comfortable, and include the location in your meeting invitation.	• **Prepare the main meeting room.** If you have several people in one location, use the face-to-face meeting guidelines.
• **Send an online meeting invitation.** Use your company's calendar system or a program such as Doodle (www.doodle.com) to schedule meetings easily.	• **Send instructions with your meeting invitation.** Include detailed instructions for using the technology, and encourage people to log on early.
• **Check the seating arrangement.** Make sure you have enough chairs, and place them to facilitate interaction (facing each other as much as possible).	• **Practice using the technology.** Call a colleague in another room to adjust sound, lighting, and camera positioning. Practice navigating the system seamlessly.
• **Check the technology.** Practice using whatever technology you'll need during the meeting. Make sure everything works properly.	• **Bring all contact numbers.** Have technical support and all participants' emails and phone numbers with you just in case.
• **Send materials in advance.** Help people prepare for the meeting by sending your agenda and perhaps handouts or slides ahead of time.	• **Log on five to ten minutes early.** Greet people as they enter, and make sure they can see and hear.
• **Welcome people.** Greet people as they join the meeting, and introduce people who do not know each other.	• **Have a backup plan.** For a videoconference, bring a speakerphone in case the system fails. For an online meeting, prepare to email materials in case participants can't see them.

© CENGAGE LEARNING 2013

Facilitating the Meeting

After all of the planning, a manager's job is to facilitate the meeting, making sure that goals are met through strong organization and active participation.

Follow the Agenda

An efficient leader begins and ends meetings on time.

Within the first few minutes, you'll set the stage for the meeting. Starting on time tells people you're serious about the topic, value their time, and expect them to be prompt for future meetings. Depending on the organizational culture and people, you may spend a few minutes socializing, but don't let this go on too long. The most efficient meetings get down to business on time and save socialization for just before and a few minutes after the meeting.

Use the agenda as your guide throughout the meeting. Keep track of time and refer to the schedule throughout the meeting. Bring copies or display the agenda so that everyone can see the progress you're making. Be respectful of people's time and end when you plan to. People often have back-to-back meetings and need to get somewhere else quickly.

Encourage Participation and Facilitate Discussion

Good facilitation is key to keeping a meeting on track and achieving its objective.

Several strategies will help you keep the meeting focused and productive:

- State the purpose of the meeting and review the agenda upfront.

  Example: "Thank you, everyone, for coming on time. I'm looking forward to hearing your feedback on the three candidates for the IT analyst position. By the end of the meeting, we'll know which candidate will receive an offer—and we may identify a backup candidate. Here are copies of the agenda. I'd like to start by reviewing the job qualifications, and then we'll review each candidate before we agree on our top choice."

- Manage time efficiently but tactfully.

  Example: "Kelly, I'm getting concerned about time. Maybe we should move on to Candidate 2 at this point."

  Example: "It sounds like we're not 100% clear where this position will be located. Why don't I check with HR and follow up with you separately, so we can continue discussing Candidate 3's qualifications?"

- Be flexible to avoid cutting off valuable discussion.

  Example: "We're running a little behind schedule, but I think this discussion is important. Do you want to schedule time for tomorrow, so we can talk more about this?"

- Encourage participation from everyone.

  Example (before the meeting): "David, I'm really looking forward to hearing whether you think these candidates have the technical skills for the job."

  Example (during the meeting): "Eun, what did you think about Candidate 2's interpersonal skills?"

  Example (during the meeting): "Kelly, we haven't heard much from you about Candidate 3. What do you think?"

- Summarize the meeting and next steps.

  Example: "So, it sounds like we all agree to extend an offer to Candidate 2. If she doesn't accept, then we'll start a new search. I'll call her today and will let you know by email what she says. Thanks for a productive meeting, everyone."

Participating in the Meeting

Communication Technologies

Meetings rely on good facilitation and participation. As a meeting participant, follow the guidelines in Figure 19 to be perceived as a professional who is engaged in the conversation—for both face-to-face and virtual meetings.

All Meetings	Virtual Meetings
• Arrive on time and prepared. • Don't bring food. • Turn off your smartphone. • Introduce yourself to new people. • Avoid side conversations. • Participate fully. • Don't interrupt others. • Stick to relevant topics. • Stay focused and engaged. • Support others' comments. • Disagree respectfully.	• Practice with the technology ahead of time to make sure the system works on your computer. • Avoid loud plaid or striped clothing, which can look distorted on video. • Log on a minute or two before the meeting start time. • Minimize background noises such as shuffling papers or tapping on the desk. • Mute your phone when you're not speaking. • Avoid multitasking—you may miss an important point or a question directed to you! • Allow a little extra time before you speak, so you don't overlap others' comments. • State your name when you speak (for teleconference calls without video). • Speak and act naturally—no need to talk loudly or exaggerate your gestures.

Figure 19
Guidelines for Meeting Participants

© CENGAGE LEARNING 2013

During some meeting situations, you may use your smartphone. You may find a text or IM useful to get a quick answer during a meeting—multicommunicating, as we discussed earlier. But you should do this only if your organizational culture allows it. If you are unsure, you might consider asking permission first.

Mute and hold buttons are important for conference calls. Mute buttons prevent embarrassing situations such as 15 people hearing you flush the toilet (another true story!). Hold buttons should not be used because music playing in the background may interrupt the call for everyone.

Following Up the Meeting

Regular or informal meetings may require only a short email as a follow-up to what was decided. Formal meetings or meetings where controversial ideas were discussed may require a more formal summary.

Minutes are an official record of the meeting; they summarize what was discussed, what decisions were made, and what actions participants will take. Generally, they should emphasize what was *decided* at the meeting, not what was *said* by the members.

 Formal meetings require formal minutes of what took place.

Figure 20 is an example of meeting minutes—sent by email—for a development committee at a not-for-profit organization. To keep this simple, the writer added minutes in blue type to the agenda. From reading these, you can tell that the meeting was fairly informal for a group of people who meet regularly.[26]

Sending minutes within 24 hours shows meeting participants that their contributions are valued. Minutes may be sent by email or posted to an intranet or wiki.

 The minutes should be accurate, objective, and complete.

With good planning, strong facilitation, and timely follow-up, you might hold meetings that people *want* to attend.

Figure 20   Sample Meeting Minutes

Identifies the meeting title and date.

Identifies who attended the meeting.

Uses the original agenda, with clear main topics, as the starting point.

Adds notes in blue type.

Identifies clear responsibilities for action items.

Could be clearer here. What was the outcome of these suggestions? Who will follow up on these ideas?

Documents a clear decision here.

Shows flexibility for discussion by moving a topic to a future meeting.

Confirms upcoming meeting dates.

DEVELOPMENT COMMITTEE: FEBRUARY 2, 5:00 TO 6:30 P.M.
MEETING MINUTES

Attended: Rose, Jean, Larry, Laura, Arlene

1. Donor Appreciation Event (March 16)
   - Guest speaker will be Melanie DiPaolo.
   - Invitations will be sent out February 5.
   - Rose and Jean visited and approved the venue.
   - Arlene suggested Party Plus on Turrey Avenue for paper goods.

2. Spring Gala (June 3)
   a. Auctioneer and children's pre-event show
      - Calvin Chatsworth agreed to be auctioneer at no charge.
      - Sesame Workshop contacted for pre-event puppet show; waiting for a reply.

   b. Live and silent auction
      - Auction forms and letters now available for solicitation.
      - Arlene will donate Yankee tickets.
      - Larry will work on getting restaurant gift certificates.

   c. Pro-bono printer/graphic designer
      - Arlene suggested talking with board and committee members.
        - Members may have connections to major corporations, which likely have business relationships with outside printing companies.
        - Printing companies may give us free or discounted invitation printing/mailing.
      - Rose suggested contacting Fred; he created a lovely flyer for the Latino event.

   d. Other decisions to be made
      - Dress code: "Business casual: leave your heels at home" on invitation.
      - Ticket price: $175pp down from $200pp; lower cost may attract more guests.
      - Invitation wording/theme for the event: Several options—need feedback from entire committee.

3. Tennis Event?
   - Topic will be discussed at future development meeting.

4. Next meeting dates
   - Meetings will be on Tuesdays at 5:00–6:30 p.m.
   - Schedule set for February 2, March 9, April 13, May 18, and June 15.

The
3Ps
In Action

Listening to Customers

Purpose

Imagine that you're working as a customer service intern at an online auction company. Part of your job is to take phone calls from unhappy customers. One customer is particularly upset and tells you about his experience:

> I was the winning bid for a pair of Ugg boots, but it's been two weeks, and I still haven't received them. My daughter's birthday is in two days, and if I don't get them tomorrow, I won't have the present I promised for her!

Process

1. **What is your objective in handling this phone call?**
   I need to understand the situation and try to neutralize the customer's emotion. If he followed the correct procedure but still didn't receive the boots, I will help resolve the situation.

2. **What limitations do you have in listening to or helping the customer?**
   I won't recite our policy—which is likely to make the customer angrier—but I do need to understand whether he has contacted the seller. Usually, these disputes are best resolved by the buyer communicating directly with the seller.

3. **What listening skills will be most useful during the conversation?**
   I will avoid simply repeating what he says; rather, I'll paraphrase some information and reflect emotion to ensure that I understand what happened and acknowledge how upset he is. I'll stay calm and focused on the situation to avoid fueling his anger, which would make the situation worse.

4. **How will you end the conversation?**
   I will end by making sure the plan to resolve the issue is clear—and I'll try to end on a positive note.

Product

Here's how the conversation goes:

Caller: I was the winning bid for a pair of Ugg boots, but it's been two weeks, and I still haven't received them. My daughter's birthday is in two days, and if I don't get them tomorrow, I won't have the present I promised for her!

Me: I'm sorry you haven't received the boots yet. Will you please tell me the item number, so I can look this up and see what's happening?

Caller: What kind of a company are you running that you take people's money but don't deliver the item?!

Me: I understand that you're upset with your daughter's birthday coming up so soon. I'd like to be able to help you.

Caller: What can you possibly do at this point to help me?? Just send me the boots.

Me: I wish I could send you the boots. We'll have to see what's happening with the seller. Let's look at the information and see what the hold-up is. Will you give me the item number?

Caller: [Sigh] Okay, it's 330506558696.

Me: Thank you. I'll be with you in just a minute.
[pause]

Me: Okay, is this Mr. Espinosa?

Caller: Yes.

Me: Mr. Espinosa, I see that your payment went through PayPal just yesterday. [pause]

Caller: Well, I was out of town for a while, but I still need them by tomorrow!

Me: I understand that you're on a tight deadline now. Have you contacted the seller to see whether she can send the boots by express mail? That might be your best bet at this point.

Caller: But I paid only for regular shipping!

Me: I've seen this situation before, where a customer needs an item more quickly than originally planned. You could contact the seller immediately and see whether the boots can be sent out today.

Caller: Well, okay, I guess I'll try that. There's nothing at all you can do??

Me: I wish I could. The seller has the item and will know whether it can be shipped to you today. I hope she can!

Caller: Okay, I'll contact her now.

Me: Good. I hope this works out for you and that your daughter gets the boots in time for her birthday.

Caller: Thank you for your help.

Me: Thank you for calling us. Goodbye.

Planning a Meeting

Purpose

Imagine that you manage the customer service division at an online auction company. As part of your job, you're evaluating the current frequently asked questions on the Customer Support page of the website. You continually update these questions to give customers quick answers and to prevent unnecessary contact with the customer service associates.

You're planning a meeting with five customer service associates at the company headquarters to decide what, if any, changes to make to the current questions. You have some data about which current questions are accessed most frequently on the website, and you would like to hear from the associates what additional questions they typically receive by email and by chat. To plan the meeting, you prepare an email to the associates.

Process

1. What is the purpose of this meeting, and why is a meeting necessary?
2. What is the best format for the meeting (in person, teleconference, online, or video-conference)? Why is this format the best choice?
3. What will you include in the meeting agenda? How can you make sure the agenda is detailed enough?
4. How can you inspire associates to come to the meeting prepared?
5. What else will you include in your email?

Product

Write an email to the customer service associates.

Summary

L01   Explain the meaning and importance of nonverbal messages.

Nonverbal communication includes body movement, physical appearance, voice qualities, time, touch, and space and territory. Cultures differ greatly in terms of how they interpret nonverbal behavior.

L02   Listen effectively in business situations.

Listening has many positive benefits for business but is the least developed verbal communication skill. Whether listening to a formal presentation or conversing with one or two people, you can learn to listen more effectively by giving the speaker your undivided attention, staying open-minded about the speaker and the topic, avoiding interrupting the speaker, and involving yourself actively in the communication.

L03   Use social media to build business relationships.

Like listening in person, listening online is important to build business relationships. Companies that truly engage customers and employees through social media develop stronger connections with these audiences and receive more valuable feedback. When companies offer online channels for customers, they must respond—or prepare to lose credibility.

L04   Use voice technologies and texting effectively in business situations.

The office phone, smartphone, texting, and VoIP all have a place in business communication. Use the telephone for richer communication that requires more cues for understanding; text messaging for short messages, typically around logistics; and VoIP to reduce call expenses; for example, to international offices. Follow the norms of your company for each medium.

L05   Plan, facilitate, and participate in a business meeting.

Planning a business meeting requires determining your purpose, deciding whether a meeting is necessary, and identifying what format is most appropriate. You must then decide who should attend, prepare your agenda, and arrange logistics. When facilitating and participating in a meeting, follow the agenda and encourage and contribute to discussion. Follow up the meeting with detailed minutes that summarize discussion, decisions, and actions.

Exercises

L01   Explain the meaning and importance of nonverbal messages.

1. Identify facial expressions.

Find a partner and take turns telling each other a three-minute story. When each of you tells your story, try to exaggerate, as if you were on stage and telling the story to a live audience. As you watch your partner, take notes on facial expressions you see, and identify what emotion each expression conveys (e.g., anger, excitement, disgust). Pay particular attention to your partner's nose, mouth (lips and tongue), eyes (eyebrows and eyelids), and forehead.

As an alternative to this exercise, watch a few minutes of your favorite stand-up comedian online. What facial expressions do you see, and which emotions does he or she convey?

2. Communicate without talking.

This is your big chance to be a star! In front of the class, use only nonverbal communication to convey the following emotions.

a. Surprise
b. Anger
c. Sorrow
d. Puzzlement
e. Boredom

   See whether the class can guess your emotion. This will give you practice in matching your nonverbal language to your message.

3. Use your voice tone to convey emotions.

With a partner, repeat the following groups of sentences, conveying a different emotion each time. Change the order, and see if your partner can guess which emotion you're expressing.

Today is my birthday. (excited)	I didn't get the Bank of America job. (disappointed)
Today is my birthday. (sad)	I didn't get the Bank of America job. (angry)
Today is my birthday. (anxious)	I didn't get the Bank of America job. (indifferent)
Today is my birthday. (surprised)	I didn't get the Bank of America job. (surprised)

4. Analyze time norms.

Think back to a meeting you attended recently—either at school or at a workplace. Did everyone arrive at the same time? How do you interpret the behavior of those who arrived first and last? Would you draw any conclusions about their status in the group or their culture, which may have influenced their perception of time? How does your own perspective on time factor into your analysis?

5. Listen to key ideas and compare notes.

Watch a few minutes of a news report with the class. As you're listening, take notes about the most important points. In small groups, compare a few examples. In what ways are your notes different or similar? Did you miss important points that your classmates wrote down? If so, why do you think this is the case?

LO2   Listen effectively in business situations.

6. See how nonverbal communication affects a speaker.

Working in groups of three or four, have one person tell a three-minute story to the rest of the group. As he or she tells the story, demonstrate negative nonverbal communication: roll your eyes, cross your arms, frown, turn away, and lean back in your chair. Ask the storyteller what effect this had on him or her. Was he or she able to continue the story? It probably didn't feel very good!

   Now give the storyteller a fair chance. This time, when he or she tells a story (the same or a different one), practice good nonverbal listening skills by nodding your head, smiling, and expressing other emotions that track with the story. What effect does your nonverbal communication have on the speaker? (It should encourage him or her to continue talking and want to say more.)

7. Observe someone listening.

Working in groups of three, have one person talk about a difficult decision he or she needs to make. As he or she describes the situation, have a second person listen, using skills discussed in this chapter. The listener does not need to give advice or help the speaker solve the problem; he or she merely needs to listen. The third person in your group should take notes on how the listener uses the skills in Figure 21.

After about five minutes of conversation, have both the speaker and observer give feedback to the listener. Which skills were used most effectively, and which skills could the listener improve?

If you have time, switch roles so everyone has a chance to practice listening skills.

Figure 21
Checklist for Listening Skills Feedback

Skills	Rating
• Gives the speaker his or her undivided attention	1 2 3 4 5
• Stays open-minded	1 2 3 4 5
• Doesn't interrupt	1 2 3 4 5
• Involves himself or herself by doing the following:	
– Maintains eye contact	1 2 3 4 5
– Nods in agreement	1 2 3 4 5
– Leans forward	1 2 3 4 5
– Uses encouraging phrases ("Uh huh," "I see")	1 2 3 4 5
– Responds (paraphrases and reflects)	1 2 3 4 5

© CENGAGE LEARNING 2013

L03 Use social media to build business relationships.

8. Practice an active listening response.

For each of the following statements, write down three responses: one that repeats the content, one that paraphrases the content, and one that reflects both the content and the possible underlying emotion.

- I can't believe I wasn't chosen for the hockey team.
- I didn't think I'd get a call back for a second interview, but I did!
- My family is visiting this weekend, and I have two exams on Monday.
- I didn't get the promotion to senior financial assistant.

Figure 22
Sony Tweets to Engage Customers

SONY make.believe
Sony Sony
Enjoy, have a blast! RT @LevenRambin: Just got a @sony NEX-3 Camera with lenses. Watch out, I'm the new paparazzi on the block.
6 hours ago

SONY make.believe
Sony Sony
Cool! Are you into 3D gaming or movies? RT @chadstray: Just purchased a 46" 3-D @Sony Bravia! So pumped for it to arrive. #awesome
7 hours ago

SONY make.believe
Sony Sony
@CadeRageous Have fun! If you're a @foursquare user, don't forget to check in to the @PlayStation lounge: http://ow.ly/4rSqo
7 hours ago

CadeRageous Cade ↻ by Sony
@Sony heading to Sony Style and the PlayStation lounge today in nyc! Have to show friends what heaven is like.
11 hours ago

© TWITTER, INC.

9. Analyze how Sony uses Twitter to engage customers.

As a company interested in engaging customers online, Sony is active on Twitter. Review the tweets in Figure 22, and in small groups, discuss how effectively Sony is listening and responding to consumers. Do you find the tweets engaging? Why or why not?

Now imagine that you are responsible for Sony's Twitter account. Write two tweets (up to 140 characters) to engage customers: one to promote a new product (your choice) and one to respond to a tweet by Brinda Durii (Figure 23).

Figure 23
Tweet About Sony

BrindaDurii2827 Brinda Duril
@Ethan_Anderton **sony makes the best laptops out there**
http://bit.ly/gH7WnJ?=mtq0
1 minute ago

© TWITTER, INC.

10. Help a company improve how it listens to customers online.

Think about one of your favorite companies—or a company where you might like to work—and analyze their social media presence and engagement. Does it have a Facebook page, Twitter account, blog, or other ways to connect with customers online? If it does have a presence, what do you think of the way the company interacts with customers? Does their approach encourage you to contribute? Do you believe that customers feel *listened to* online?

Write a one- or two-page memo to the company's vice president of social media with your recommendations. Submit this to your instructor.

11. Propose a way to include employees' input.

Imagine that you are the vice president of employee communication at a large financial services company. Management is considering redesigning the office space for customer service associates to reduce noise but keep an open environment. As part of the process, you propose an online survey to hear employees' opinions. Write a one- or two-page proposal to the rest of the management team (your peers) to implement a survey on the company's intranet. Convince the rest of the team that this is a good idea by explaining your rationale and providing enough detail so that they understand how the survey would work. Be honest about the downsides of your idea; after all, asking employees for their opinions can be risky.

12. Leave a voice mail message.

Imagine that you applied for a job and received this voice mail message from the company's HR manager:

> Hello. This is Marley Catona from Bank on Me. We received your cover letter and résumé, and I'd like to schedule a phone interview with you. Will you please tell me what times you're available this Friday for a half-hour call? You can reach me at 555-1212. Thank you.

Leave a response on another student's phone. Plan your message in advance, but try to sound natural. You'll want to express your enthusiasm for the interview and give specific times when you're available.

Use the checklist in Figure 24 to give each other feedback.

LO4   Use voice technologies and texting effectively in business situations.

 This voice mail relates to the Bank on Me company scenario available at www.cengagebrain.com.

© CENGAGE LEARNING 2013

Figure 24
Checklist for Voice Mail Message Feedback

❑ Thanks Ms. Catona for the call

❑ Includes all relevant information:
  ○ First and last name
  ○ Reason for calling (responding to Ms. Catona's message)
  ○ Times available on Friday

❑ Avoids extraneous information and fillers (e.g., overuse of "uh," "um")

❑ Uses an appropriate tone:
  ○ Professional
  ○ Enthusiastic
  ○ Natural
  ○ Confident, but not overly confident

❑ Ends the call clearly and professionally

❑ Other: _____

13. Evaluate a telephone greeting.

Working in teams of three, exchange cell phone numbers, call each other, and listen to the voice mail greetings. Give the other students feedback about their greetings. Do they sound professional? Is the message clear? How can it be improved? After you receive feedback, re-record your greeting and have your classmates call you again to check the revised version.

14. Practice using VoIP.

If you don't have much experience using VoIP, such as Skype or Google Voice, try calling another student or a coworker. Both services are free, have simple sign-up procedures, and include optional video.

Talk for a few minutes online. What differences do you notice between VoIP and talking on a cell phone? Discuss what you learned with the rest of the class, and then, as a group, generate a list of tips for people using VoIP.

L05   Plan, facilitate, and participate in a business meeting.

15. Determine the best meeting format.

For each of the following scenarios, identify which format—face-to-face, conference call, online meeting, or videoconference—would work best.

- You want to close a sale with a new client.
- You have a weekly meeting with housekeeping staff at the Arlington, Virginia, hotel.
- You call a meeting to discuss cost-cutting ideas with your counterparts in three different states.

- You need to teach the new IT analyst, who works in a different office, how to operate a proprietary system.
- You need to tell employees who report to you but work in different locations that the company is planning to downsize.

16. Evaluate a business meeting.

Attend a business meeting at work, a city council meeting in your community, a student organization meeting at school, or some other meeting. Observe the meeting and evaluate how well the facilitator plans and runs the meeting. Write an email to the facilitator to recommend improvements, according to what you learned in this chapter.

17. Plan a business meeting.

Working in groups of five, choose one of these scenarios for the next three exercises. For the scenario you and your team members choose, prepare an email and detailed agenda to send to the other meeting participants.

Scenario 1

Imagine that you are a dean at your college, which does not celebrate Martin Luther King, Jr.'s birthday with a paid holiday. You want the support of the college's four other deans to make the third Monday in January a holiday for all college employees and students. Invite your four colleagues to a meeting.

Scenario 2

Imagine that you work as a sales associate for your local Gap store. The work schedule is always set a month in advance, but you want more flexibility. You ask the four other sales associates in the store to meet with you, so you can convince them to plan the schedule only one week in advance. You would need the store manager's approval to do this, but you decide to get your coworkers on board first.

18. Facilitate a face-to-face meeting.

Use one of the scenarios in the previous exercise to practice facilitating and participating in a meeting.

Have each person assume the role of another participant. Determine who will lead the meeting (the dean or the sales associate calling the meeting). Conduct a 10- to 15-minute meeting. Following the meeting, evaluate its effectiveness. Did you achieve your objective? Explain your answer.

19. Write meeting minutes.

To summarize the meeting for your colleagues in the previous scenario, write up the meeting minutes. Each of you in the group should prepare minutes separately. Then, as a group, compare your minutes. Which are best and why?

20. Participate in an online meeting.

Sign up for free versions of WebEx, GoToMeeting, or another service to practice participating in an online meeting. In groups of four or five, have one person take the role of facilitator to schedule a time and send an invitation to the rest of the team.

During the meeting, discuss the benefits and obstacles of using the tool for an organization where you worked recently. In what ways could the service be useful for the organization? In what ways is the service not appropriate for this particular organization?

Company Scenario

In The Loop
Soup Kitchen

In the Loop Soup Kitchen

In the Loop is a not-for-profit community kitchen that provides a safe, warm place for locals to get a healthy meal. This scenario presents a crisis situation—someone enters the facility with a gun—and challenges you to:

- Analyze Twitter use in a crisis situation.
- Practice leaving a voice mail message during a crisis.
- Write internal and external messages to address a sensitive situation.
- Take a proactive, strategic approach to crisis communication.

At www.cengagebrain.com, you'll find:

- Information about the situation:
  - The Scoop (overview of the scenario)
  - Organization background (vision, mission, organizational structure)

- Communications during the situation:
  - Voice mail message (from the executive director)
  - Twitter page (tweets written by an intern, shown here)

If you were the assistant director of In the Loop and had to handle this situation in the executive director's absence, what would you do? Your instructor may assign you to do the following to practice your interpersonal communication skills:

- Analyze the intern's use of Twitter in this situation and meet with Chris, the intern, to understand his perspective and to present your own ideas.
- Write a few tweets that would communicate that all is well at In the Loop and to continue building relationships with your key audiences.
- Leave a voice mail message for Emilio, the executive director (in response to his message, which you can listen to online).

These communications—and others for this scenario—will test your ability to build relationships in a difficult situation.

Notes

1. Marc Wright, "Ebay reinvents team briefings," www.simply-communicate.com, accessed July 25, 2010.

2. Peter F. Drucker, quoted by Bill Moyers in *A World of Ideas* (Garden City: Doubleday, 1990).

3. Judee K. Burgoon and Thomas Saine, *The Unspoken Dialogue: An Introduction to Nonverbal Communication* (Boston: Houghton Mifflin, 1978).

4. Judy Foreman, "A Conversation with Paul Ekman; the 43 Facial Muscles That Reveal Even the Most Fleeting Emotions," New York Times Online, August 5, 2003, http://nytimes.com/2003/08/05/health/conversation-with-paul-ekman-43-facial-muscles-that-reveal-even-most-fleeting.html, accessed April 21, 2011.

5. Robin Marks, "The Eyes Have It," QUEST Community Science Blog, January 24, 2008, www.kqed.org/quest/blog/2008/01/24/the-eyes-have-it/, accessed July 20, 2010.

6. Buck Wolf, "The Pinocchio Effect," ABCNews.com Home Page, December 17, 2000, http://abcnews.go.com/sections/us/WolfFiles/wolffiles68.html, accessed September 11, 2003.

7. Timothy A. Judge, Charlice Hurst, and Lauren S. Simon, "Does It Pay to Be Smart, Attractive, or Confident (or All Three)?" *Journal of Applied Psychology* 94 (2009): 742–755.

8. Timothy A. Judge, Charlice Hurst, and Lauren S. Simon, "Does It Pay to Be Smart."

9. Disa A. Sauter et al., "Cross-Cultural Recognition of Basic Emotions through Nonverbal Emotional Vocalizations," *Proceedings of the National Academy of Sciences of the United States of America*, November 4, 2009, www.pnas.org/content/107/6/2408.full, accessed July 22, 2010.

10. David B. Givens, "Tones of Voice," *The Nonverbal Dictionary of Gestures, Signs, and Body Language Cues*, 2002, http://sirpabs.ilahas.com/ebooks/Body%20Language.pdf, accessed July 21, 2010.

11. Curt Suplee, "Get Outta My Face," *Washington Post*, June 9, 1999, p. H-1.

12. Judi Brownell, "Fostering Service Excellence through Listening: What Hospitality Managers Need to Know," The Center for Hospitality Research, *Cornell Hospitality Report* 9 (April 2009).

13. Ralph G. Nichols, "Listening Is a Ten-Part Skill," *Nation's Business*, September 1987, p. 40; and "Listen Up!" *American Salesman*, July 1987, p. 29.

14. Josh Bernoff, "Five Objectives in the Groundswell (Listening)," Forrester's Consumer Forum 2007, April 7, 2008, www.youtube.com/watch?v=xC8JU_aEvgg, accessed July 21, 2010.

15. Charlene Li, Josh Bernoff, *Groundswell: Winning in a World Transformed by Social Technologies* (Harvard Business Press, 2011).

16. Marty St. George, vice president of marketing and commercial at JetBlue, quoted in "How JetBlue Became One of the Hottest Brands in America," by Rupal Parekh, http://adage.com/article/cmo-strategy/jetblue-hottest-brands-america/144799/, accessed July 21, 2010.

17. JetBlue Twitter Page, http://twitter.com/JETBLUE, July 21, 2010, accessed July 21, 2010.

18. Erick Schonfeld, "The Most Engaged Brands on the Web," (study by Charlene Li and WetPaint), *TechCrunch*, July 20, 2009, http://techcrunch.com/2009/07/20/the-most-engaged-brands-on-the-web/, accessed on July 21, 2010.

19. Hubert B. Herring, "Endless Meetings: The Black Holes of the Workday," *New York Times*, June 18, 2006, p. E7.

20. Kelly Services, "Kelly Global Workforce Index," www.smartmanager.us, accessed July 19, 2010.

21. Harvard Business Review Analytic Services, "Managing Across Distance in Today's Economic Climate: The Value of Face-to-Face Communication," June 2009 survey.

22. Harvard Business Review Analytic Services.

23. Harvard Business Review Analytic Services.

24. Tracy Paurowski, "American Express Business Travel Launches Online Travel Management Scorecard," March 23, 2010, http://home3.americanexpress.com/corp/pc/2010/mtnm.asp, accessed July 24, 2010.

25. "Second Life Work/Success Stories," http://wiki.secondlife.com, accessed December 17, 2010.

26. Published with permission from the author.

Chapter 4

Audience Analysis (4) Who Is the Primary Audience? (4) What Is Your Relationship with the Audience? (4) How Will the Audience Likely React? (4) What Does the Audience Already Know? (4) What Is Unique About the Audience? (4) **The Writing Process** (4) **Planning** (4) Purpose (4) Content (4) Organization (4) **Drafting** (4) Letting Go (4) **Overcoming Writer's Block** (4) **Writing for Different Media** (4) **Revising** (4) Revising for Content (4) **Revising for Style** (4) Revising for Correctness (4) **Proofreading**

LEARNING OBJECTIVES

After you have finished this chapter, you should be able to

L01 Analyze the audience for your communication.

L02 Plan the purpose, content, and organization of your message.

L03 Compose the first draft of your message.

L04 Revise for content, style, and correctness.

L05 Proofread your message.

"This [company] sign is both disappointing and anti-social."

— CAREY ALEXANDER,
THE CONSUMERIST, ABOUT POORLY
WRITTEN RESTAURANT SIGN

Part 2

Chapter Introduction: Bad Writing Is Bad Business

Bad writing is bad business. Here are just a few examples of how poor writing affects the bottom line:

- An attorney and her law firm were hit with a $6.6 million suit because a lease agreement was "inartfully written and done so in a confusing fashion, which lends itself to ambiguities and disagreements."[1]

- A computer company lost $35 million partly because of poorly written instructions. The company admitted that customers were dissatisfied because of "manuals which did not offer the first-time user adequate assistance."[2]

- U.S. states spend $221 million annually—paid by taxpayers—on remedial writing instruction for state employees. "It's impossible to calculate the ultimate cost of lost productivity because people have to read things two and three times," said former Arkansas governor Mike Huckabee.[3]

- A confusing comma almost cost a cable TV company $1 million Canadian. The company won the case on appeal, but not before an unnecessary lawsuit about just one comma in a 14-page contract.[4]

Other errors are hard to quantify. Consider the sign pictured here—adapted from a real sign posted in a national fast-food restaurant window. This one is so funny, it's sad.

A sign riddled with errors caused embarrassment to a fast-food restaurant chain.

AN OVERVIEW OF THE WRITING PROCESS

When faced with a writing task, some people just start writing. They try to do everything at once: choose the best words, organize into paragraphs, format, proofread—all at the same time. This may seem like the most efficient writing process, but it's not. In fact, you might be bogged down with details that will prevent you from moving forward and producing the best product. Instead, writing in steps is the better strategy and will save you time in the long run. For example, spending planning time up front gives you a sense of where you want to go. With clear goals, it's more likely your writing will accomplish those goals. And if you save a separate step for proofreading, you'll catch more errors.

Although you may vary this process for different writing projects, business writers typically perform the following five steps (see Figure 1).

The amount of time you devote to each step depends on the complexity, length, and importance of the writing project. You may go through all the steps when writing a business plan, but not when answering an email inviting you to a meeting.

 The writing process consists of analyzing the audience, planning, drafting, revising, and proofreading.

Figure 1 The Writing Process

Audience Analysis: Studying the needs, experiences, background, personality, and other aspects of the receiver.

Planning: Determining the purpose of the message, what information you need to give the reader, and in what order to present it.

SEPS Email to All Employees

• Announce the system.

• Describe the purpose.

• List goals achieved.

• Close on a positive note.

Drafting: Composing a first draft of a message.

On behalf of senior managers at Sony, I am pleased to introduce our new performance management process, **SEPS** (Sony Employee Performance System). We are continuing to focus on employee performance and development by giving you new tools and resources to use for the performance management process.

SEPS will provide a unified, consistent, organizational platform for managing and developing employee performance. This process is consistent with, and reinforces, our existing performance systems; **SEPS** builds upon the performance management needs and philosophies of each of the divisions, while improving consi... divisions. Rather than an off-the...

Revising: Editing for content, style, and correctness.

On behalf of senior managers at Sony, I am pleased to introduce our new performance management process, **SEPS** (Sony Employee Performance System). We are continuing to focus on employee performance and develop-ment by giving you new tools and resources ~~to use~~ for the performance management process.

SEPS will provide a unified, consistent, ~~organizational~~ platform for managing and developing employee performance. The process ~~is consistent with, and~~ reinforces, ~~our~~ our existing performance systems; **SEPS** builds ~~upon~~-on the performance management needs and philosophies of ~~each of the~~ ~~divisions~~-division, while improvi... across ~~divisions~~-all groups. Rat...

Proofreading: Checking for content, typographical, and format errors.

Email

To: All Sony Employees
From: Warren Saliano
Subject: SEPS: New Performance Management System

On behalf of senior managers at Sony, I pleased to introduce our new performance management Process SEPS (Sony Employee Performance System). We are continuing to focus on employee performance and development by giving you new tools for the performance management process.

SEPS will provide a unified, consistent plat-form for managing and developing employee performance. This process reinforces our existing performance systems; **SEPS** builds on the performance management needs and philosophies of each division, while improving consistency across all groups. Rather than an

AUDIENCE ANALYSIS

L01 Analyze the audience for your communication.

Your first step is to consider your audience for the message—the reader or readers of your writing. Your audience may be just one person or a group of diverse people all over the world. We can't always understand our audience perfectly, but we do our best to anticipate what they need and how they might react to our message. For a strategic-level communication—for example, announcing a big change in a company, such as a merger or acquisition—multiple messages would be sent to different audiences. Here, we'll consider just one message at a time.

An audience analysis will help you understand your message from the reader's perspective. This process gives you a sense of the audience's potential mental filters and how to adjust your message accordingly.

Let's take an example of moving an office from downtown Chicago to a suburb. In Figure 2, you can see how analyzing an audience helps the writer tailor a message.

Figure 2 Audience Analysis Example (Moving the Office to the Suburbs)

Who is the audience?	What is your relationship with the audience?	How will the audience likely react?	What does the audience already know?	What is unique about the audience?
• Primary audience: employees in the Chicago office, who will be moving • Secondary audience: employees in the Boston office, who may be concerned that they will move next	• As the Chicago office manager, I know these employees well and have credibility with them. • My tone will be respectful and conversational.	• Employees who live near the new location will be happy, but most will not. This is a big change for everyone. • I will get to the main point quickly and will explain the rationale for the move and include lots of evidence to support the decision.	• Employees know this was a possibility because we have been looking to reduce costs. • I will refer to previous discussions about ways to reduce costs. • I will be honest and say that the Boston location may move as well.	• Many employees don't have cars, so I'll emphasize the public transportation options. • Many employees are paid minimum wage, so I'll emphasize less expensive housing options in the area.

© CENGAGE LEARNING 2013

Who Is the Primary Audience?

When you have more than one audience, you need to identify your **primary audience** (e.g., the decision maker) and your **secondary audience** (others who will also read and be affected by your message). Focus on the primary audience, but try to satisfy the needs of the secondary audience as well. If this is too much to accomplish with one message, write separate messages to different audiences. For example, a sales letter to a major client should be tailored to that client's needs.

What Is Your Relationship with the Audience?

Does your audience know you? If your audience doesn't know you, establish your credibility by assuming a professional tone, and give enough evidence to support your claims. Are you writing to someone inside or outside the organization? If outside, your message may be more formal and contain more background information and less jargon than if you are writing to someone inside the organization.

 Your relationship with the reader determines the tone and content of your message.

What is your status in relation to your audience? Communications to your manager obviously are vital to your success in the organization. Typically, these messages are a little more formal, less authoritarian in tone, and filled with more information than communications to peers or people who report to you. Also, these messages are typically "front-loaded"—that is, they use a direct organizational style and present the major idea in the first paragraph. Study your manager's own messages to understand his or her preferred style, and adapt your own message accordingly.

When you communicate with people who report to you, be respectful rather than patronizing. Try to instill a sense of collaboration, and include employees in your message rather than talk down to them. For example, use "we" when you refer to the company or department, but avoid platitudes such as "Employees are our greatest assets." Be sincere and think about how your employees might react to your message. When praising or criticizing, focus on specific behaviors, not the person. As always, praise in public, but criticize in private.

How Will the Audience Likely React?

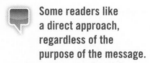

Some readers like a direct approach, regardless of the purpose of the message.

If the reader's initial reaction to both you and your topic is likely to be *positive,* your job is relatively easy. You can use a direct approach—beginning with the most important information (e.g., your conclusions or recommendations)—and then provide details. If the reader's initial reaction is likely to be *neutral,* you may want to use the first few lines of the message to get the reader's attention and convince him or her that what you have to say is important and that your reasoning is sound. Make sure your message is short and easy to read and that any requested action is easy to take.

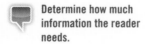

If you expect readers to react negatively, present extensive evidence and expert testimony.

Suppose, however, that you expect your reader's reaction—either to your topic or to you personally—to be *negative.* Now you have a real sales job. Your best strategy is to call on external evidence and expert opinion to bolster your position. Use polite, conservative language, and suggest ways the readers can cooperate without appearing to "give in."

If you anticipate that your reader will oppose your proposal, consider providing more evidence. Instead of one example, give two or three. Instead of quoting one external source, quote several. Begin with the areas of agreement, stress how the audience will benefit, and try to anticipate and answer any objections the reader might have. Through logic, evidence, and tone, build a case for your position.

What Does the Audience Already Know?

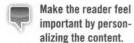

Determine how much information the reader needs.

Understanding what the audience already knows helps you decide how much content to include and what writing style is most appropriate. When writing to multiple audiences, adapt to the key decision maker (the primary audience). In general, it is better to provide too much rather than too little information.

What Is Unique About the Audience?

Make the reader feel important by personalizing the content.

The success or failure of a message often depends on little things—the extra touches that say to the reader, "You're important, and I've taken the time to learn some things about you."

What can you learn about the interests or demographics of your audience that you can build into your message? What questions and concerns can you anticipate and address in your message?

Example of Audience Analysis

To illustrate the crucial role that audience analysis plays in communication, assume that you are a marketing manager at Seaside Resorts, a chain of small hotels along the California, Oregon, and Washington coasts. You know that many of the larger hotel chains have instituted frequent-stay (or loyalty) programs, which reward repeat customers with free stays or other perks.

You want to write a message recommending a similar plan for your hotel. Assume that Cynthia Haney, your immediate manager and the vice president of marketing, will be the only reader of your email and has the authority to approve or reject your proposal. Let's look at three versions of Haney and how you could adjust your message to each (Figure 3).

Figure 3
Audience Analysis: Adjusting a Written Message for Seaside Resorts

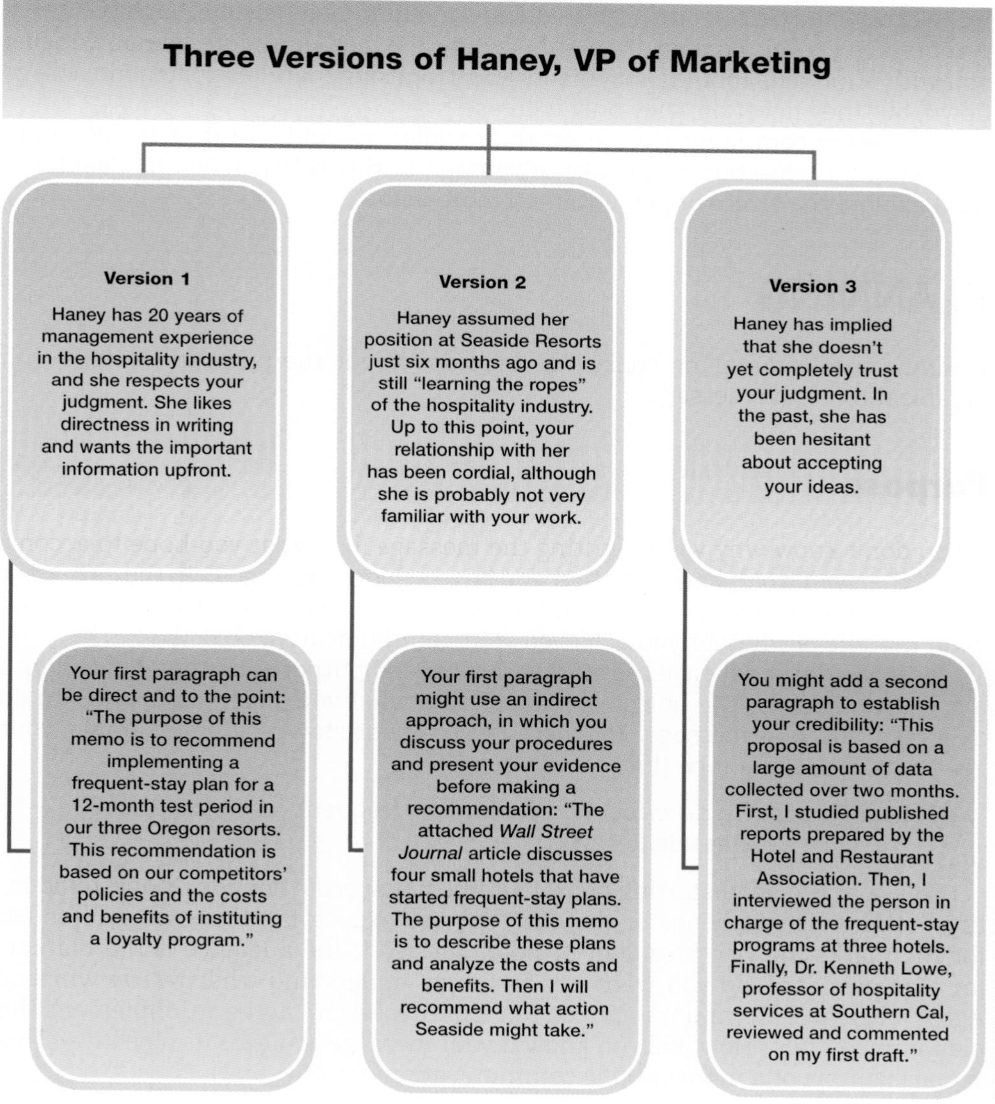

Three Versions of Haney, VP of Marketing

Version 1

Haney has 20 years of management experience in the hospitality industry, and she respects your judgment. She likes directness in writing and wants the important information upfront.

Version 2

Haney assumed her position at Seaside Resorts just six months ago and is still "learning the ropes" of the hospitality industry. Up to this point, your relationship with her has been cordial, although she is probably not very familiar with your work.

Version 3

Haney has implied that she doesn't yet completely trust your judgment. In the past, she has been hesitant about accepting your ideas.

Your first paragraph can be direct and to the point: "The purpose of this memo is to recommend implementing a frequent-stay plan for a 12-month test period in our three Oregon resorts. This recommendation is based on our competitors' policies and the costs and benefits of instituting a loyalty program."

Your first paragraph might use an indirect approach, in which you discuss your procedures and present your evidence before making a recommendation: "The attached *Wall Street Journal* article discusses four small hotels that have started frequent-stay plans. The purpose of this memo is to describe these plans and analyze the costs and benefits. Then I will recommend what action Seaside might take."

You might add a second paragraph to establish your credibility: "This proposal is based on a large amount of data collected over two months. First, I studied published reports prepared by the Hotel and Restaurant Association. Then, I interviewed the person in charge of the frequent-stay programs at three hotels. Finally, Dr. Kenneth Lowe, professor of hospitality services at Southern Cal, reviewed and commented on my first draft."

© CENGAGE LEARNING 2013

As you can see in Figure 3, the type, amount, and organization of information you include in your message reflect what you know (or can learn) about your audience.

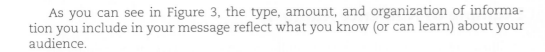

Ethical Persuasion

Ethics in Communication

Every message you write seeks to persuade—and should be handled ethically.

Any business communication—no matter how routine—involves more than just dumping information on your audience. Persuasion is a major purpose of any communication. Whether your goal is to sell, motivate, or convey bad news, you'll want the same outcome: to influence others' behaviors, thoughts, or feelings.

Persuasion, of course, is not **coercion**—far from it. In some cases, people may be forced to do something, but they can't be forced to believe something. They must be persuaded in ways that are agreeable to them. The word **persuade** stems from a Latin root that means *agreeable*.

As business communicators, we have a responsibility to act ethically in building relationships with our audience. For example, during the subprime mortgage crisis, mortgage lenders' behavior was called into question. Imagine wanting to buy a house and being convinced that you can afford one—even though you can't. A mortgage broker gains your trust by acting the part of a professional, enticing you with affordable monthly payments and promising that these payments will go down, but they never do; they only increase.[5]

Competent communicators know their audience—and ensure that their audience knows them—but never take advantage of this relationship. In Chapter 7, we'll explore the ethics of persuasion in more detail.

L02 Plan the purpose, content, and organization of your message.

PLANNING

Planning involves making conscious decisions about the purpose, content, and organization of the message.

Purpose

The purpose should be specific enough to serve as a yardstick for judging the success of the message.

If you don't know why you're writing the message (i.e., what you hope to accomplish), then you won't know whether you have achieved your goal. In the end, what matters is not how well crafted your message was or how well it was formatted; what matters is whether you achieved your communication objective.

Most writers find it easier to start with a general purpose and then refine it into a specific objective. The objective should state what you expect the reader to do as a result of your message. For the hotel frequent-stay program example, your general purpose might be this:

General Purpose: To describe the benefits of a frequent-stay program at Seaside Resorts.

This goal is a good starting point, but it is not specific enough. It doesn't identify the intended audience or the outcome you expect. Is the message intended for the marketing vice president or hotel guests? If the audience is the marketing vice president, do you want her to simply understand what you've written? Agree with you? Commit resources for more research? Agree to implement the plan immediately? How will you know if your message achieves its objective? This is one example of a more specific communication objective:

Specific Purpose: To persuade Cynthia to approve developing and implementing a frequent-stay plan for a 12-month test period in Seaside's three Oregon resorts.

This purpose is now specific enough to guide you in writing the message and evaluating its success.

Figure 4 shows additional examples of general-purpose statements converted to more useful objectives.

General-Purpose Statement	Specific Communication Objective
To communicate the office move.	To explain the rationale and process for the move to employees, while maintaining morale and minimizing employee turnover.
To apply for the sales associate position.	To convince the HR manager to call me for an interview based on my qualifications for the job.
To deny a customer's request for a replacement iPod.	To maintain the customer's goodwill by helping her understand the rationale for the decision and convincing her that the denial is reasonable.

Figure 4
Identifying a Communication Objective

These communication objectives state what you expect the audience to do and how you hope people will feel after reading your message. A clear-cut objective lets you focus on the content and organization.

A clearly stated objective helps you avoid including irrelevant and distracting information.

Content

After you analyze your audience and identify the objective of your message, the next step is to decide what information to include. For simple messages, such as a quick text or routine email, this step is easy. However, many communication projects require many decisions about what to include. How much background information is needed? What statistical data best supports the conclusions? Is expert opinion needed? Would examples, anecdotes, or graphics help comprehension? Will research be necessary, or do you have what you need?

The trick is to include enough information so that you don't lose or confuse the reader, yet avoid including irrelevant material that wastes the reader's time and obscures important data. Different writers use different methods for identifying what information is needed. Some simply jot down notes on the points they plan to cover.

For all but the simplest communications, the one thing you should *not* do is to start drafting immediately, deciding as you write what information to include. Instead, start with at least a preliminary outline of your message—whether it's in your head, in a typed outline, or as notes on a piece of paper.

Do not start writing until you have planned what you want to say.

One useful strategy is **brainstorming**—jotting down ideas, facts, possible leads, and anything else you think might be helpful in constructing your message. Aim for quantity, not quality. Don't evaluate your output until you run out of ideas. Then begin to refine, delete, combine, and revise your ideas to form your message.

Another approach is **mind mapping** (also called *clustering*), a process that avoids the step-by-step limitations of lists. Instead, you write the purpose of your message in the middle of a page and circle it. Then, as you think of possible points to add, write them down and link them with a line either to the main purpose or to another point. As you think of other details, add them where you think they might fit. This

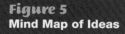

Figure 5
Mind Map of Ideas

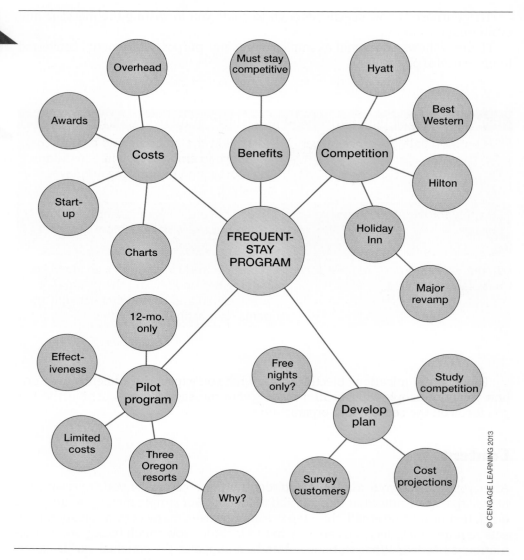

© CENGAGE LEARNING 2013

visual outline offers flexibility and encourages free thinking. Figure 5 shows an example of mind mapping for the frequent-stay idea.

You may use computer graphics for this process, but many people find writing by hand more freeing. Either way, by putting your ideas down and showing how they relate, you're beginning to organize your message, which is the next step in the planning process.

Organization

After you have brainstormed around a main idea, you need to organize your points into an outline. The **organization** of a message indicates the order in which you'll discuss each topic.

First, classify or group related ideas. Next, differentiate between the major and minor points so that you can line up minor ideas and evidence to support the

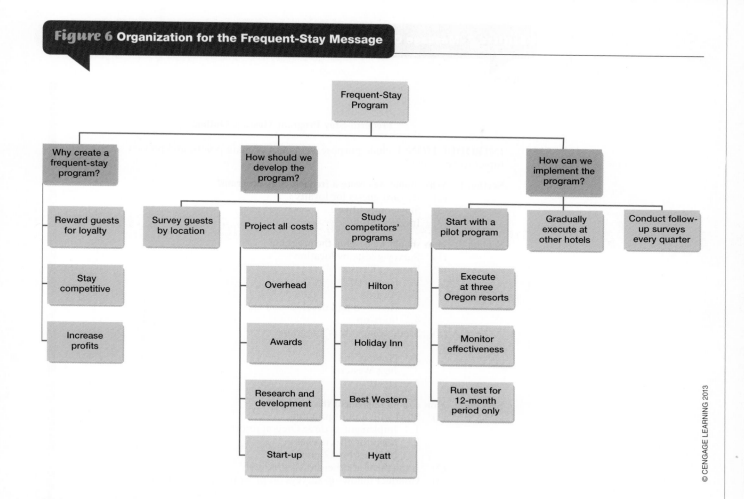

Figure 6 Organization for the Frequent-Stay Message

© CENGAGE LEARNING 2013

major ideas. The diagram in Figure 6 shows the frequent-stay idea shaping up into a well-organized message.

Rather than create a hierarchical diagram, you may present your ideas in outline format, shown in Figure 7. Of course, you may skip some of these steps for shorter and less important business writing.

As mentioned earlier, the most effective sequence for the major ideas depends partly on the reaction you expect from your audience. For most business communication, audiences expect to see the main point up front (the direct approach): your conclusion or recommendation first, with explanations following. However, if you expect a negative response, you may decide to use an indirect approach, with the reasons presented first and the conclusion after.

For longer written communications (e.g., long memos, articles, or reports), consider writing your introductory paragraph first. For the direct approach, the introduction explains why you're writing (the **purpose**), what your conclusions are (your **main points**), and what topics the reader can expect (the **preview**). For the indirect approach, you also will cover these points, but you would provide more background information—and discuss your purpose and main points later in the introduction. Compare two approaches for an introductory paragraph for the frequent-stay

 Organize according to how you expect the reader to react.

Figure 7 Message Organization in Outline Format

Frequent-Stay Program Message Outline

INTRODUCTION: Include purpose, summary of main points, and preview of topics to be covered.

Section 1:   Why should we create a frequent-stay program?
- (1)   Reward guests for loyalty
- (2)   Stay competitive
- (3)   Increase profits

Section 2:   How should we develop the program?
- (1)   Survey guests by location
- (2)   Project all costs
  1.   Overhead
  2.   Awards
  3.   Research and development
  4.   Start-up
- (3)   Study competitors' programs
  1.   Hilton
  2.   Holiday Inn
  3.   Best Western
  4.   Hyatt

Section 3:   How can we implement the program?
- (1)   Start with a pilot program
  1.   Implement at three Oregon resorts
  2.   Monitor effectiveness
  3.   Run test for 12 months
- (2)   Implement at other hotels gradually
- (3)   Conduct follow-up surveys on programs every quarter

Conclusion: Summarize points, request action, and provide contact information.

© CENGAGE LEARNING 2013

proposal (Figure 8). These build on our earlier examples of analyzing the audience (Figure 3).

In the indirect introduction example, notice how much softer the tone is for the reader. The main point is more of an invitation than a recommendation.

In Chapter 5, we'll discuss more about paragraph unity, coherence, and length—also important elements of organization.

L03 Compose the first draft of your message.

DRAFTING

After planning your message, you're finally ready to begin **drafting**—composing a preliminary version of a message. The more work you did to plan and organize your message, the easier this step will be. Again, don't begin writing too soon. People who believe they have weak writing skills tend to jump in and get it over with as quickly as possible. Instead, follow each of the five steps of the writing process to ease the journey and improve your final product.

Figure 8   Direct and Indirect Introductory Paragraphs

Direct Approach

Background: The VP is experienced and respects you.

Purpose statement

The purpose of this memo is to recommend implementing a frequent-stay plan for a 12-month test period in our three Oregon resorts. This recommendation is based on our competitors' policies and the costs and benefits of instituting a loyalty program.

Main points

Implementing a similar program will keep us competitive in the Oregon market and may significantly increase guest loyalty and profits.

Preview of topics to be covered

In this memo, I'll discuss why we should establish a frequent-stay program, how we should develop the program, and how we can implement the program for our guests.

Indirect Approach

Background: The VP is new and doesn't know you well.

A recent *Wall Street Journal* article discusses four small hotels that have started frequent-stay plans. I became interested in this idea for Seaside and would like to share with you my research about these programs. My research shows that 77% of our competitors have a frequent-stay program, and a recent survey shows that nearly half of the 5,000 respondents choose specific hotels (even if they are more expensive) in order to accrue hotel loyalty points. In this memo, I'll describe frequent-stay plans and then analyze the costs and benefits for Seaside. After reviewing this information, I hope that you will consider piloting a frequent-stay program at our three Oregon resorts.

Purpose statement

Preview of topics to be covered

Main point

© CENGAGE LEARNING 2013

Letting Go

Probably the most important thing to remember about drafting is to just let go—let your ideas flow as quickly as possible, without worrying about style, correctness, or format. Separate the drafting stage from the revising stage. Although some people revise as they create, most find it easier to first get their ideas down in rough-draft form, and then revise. It's much easier to polish a page full of writing than a page full of *nothing*. As one writing authority has noted,

> Writing is art. Rewriting is craft. Mix the two at your peril. If you let your inner editor . . . into the process too early, it's liable to overpower your artist, blocking your creative flow.[6]

So avoid moving from author to editor too quickly. Your first draft is just that— a *draft*. Don't expect perfection, and don't strive for it. Instead, write in narrative form all the points you identified in the planning stage.

 Do not combine drafting and revising. They involve two separate skills and two separate mindsets.

 Employ the power of positive thinking: you can write well!

Overcoming Writer's Block

If a report is due in five weeks, some managers (and students) spend four weeks worrying about the task and one week (or less!) actually writing the report. Similarly, when given 45 minutes to write an email, some people spend 35 minutes anxiously staring at a blank screen and 10 minutes actually writing. These people are experiencing **writer's block**—the inability to focus on the writing process and to draft a message. Typical causes of writer's block follow:

- *Procrastination:* Putting off what we dislike doing.
- *Impatience:* Getting bored with the naturally slow pace of the writing process.
- *Perfectionism:* Believing that our draft must be perfect the first time.

Once these factors interfere with creativity, writers may start to question their ability, which makes it even harder to tackle writing.

Try the strategies in Figure 9 for avoiding writer's block at least once; then build into your writing routine those strategies that work best for you. Just as different athletes and artists use different strategies for accomplishing their goals, so do different writers. There is no one best way, so choose what works best for you.

 Business writers usually have a built-in purpose for writing something, so the writing process may come more easily.

Figure 9 Strategies for Overcoming Writer's Block

1 Choose the right environment.
- Go to a quiet library—or a busy computer lab.
- Experiment until you find a place where you write best.

2 Minimize distractions.
- Close web browsers to avoid IM notifications and the lure of Facebook!
- Leave your smartphone in another room so you're not tempted to text.

3 Schedule a reasonable block of time.
- For short writing projects, block out enough time to plan, draft, and revise the entire message in one sitting.
- For long or complex projects, schedule blocks of about two hours, or set milestones, such as writing one section and then taking a break.

4 State your purpose in writing.
- Define the objective of your message clearly and concisely.
- Write the objective someplace prominently so you always keep it in mind.

5 Write freely.
- Start by free writing: write without stopping for 5 to 10 minutes.
- Write anything, without judgment; if you get stuck, write, "I'll think of something soon."

6 Think out loud.
- Picture yourself telling a colleague what you're writing about, and explain aloud the ideas you're trying to get across.
- Sharpen and focus your ideas by speaking rather than writing them.

7 Avoid perfectionism.
- Think of your writing as a draft—not a final document.
- Don't worry about style, coherence, spelling, or punctuation errors at this point. The artist in you must create something before the editor can refine it.

8 Write the easiest parts first.
- Skip the opening paragraph if you're struggling with it.
- Start with a section that's easiest for you to write.

Writing for Different Media

In Chapter 1, we discussed several options for conveying your message. How you draft your message depends on which medium you choose. In this chapter, we'll look at writing guidelines for four typical media choices for business communication: email, memos, letters, and the Internet.

Writing Email Messages

Email is so pervasive in organizations that many people don't consider it writing—but of course it is. In business, emails can be one-word confirmations or longer messages with attachments. Email is the default communication choice in many organizations, with middle managers receiving about 100 messages a day.[7,8] With people receiving so many messages, how you write emails will determine whether yours are read and understood.

Emails tend to be more concise and—even if sent outside the organization—are often less formal than letters. Here are a few guidelines for drafting email messages:

Communication Technologies

Follow your organization's conventions for email.

- Follow your company's standards for salutations. Use "Dear," "Hi," "Hello," or "Good morning" as salutations, depending on what people in your organization typically use. If you're writing an email to a prospective employer, err on the side of formality with "Dear Ms. Unger," followed by a comma. Although a comma after "Hi" as in, "Hi, Jasmine," is technically correct, you may find that few people in your company use this as a convention. Also, most people will skip the salutation (and signature) after one round of emails. It's silly to continue using someone's name for quick response emails.

- Use a descriptive, attention-grabbing subject line, such as those in Figure 10. Research tells us people often delete or read email based on the subject line alone.[9]

- Don't copy the world. People already receive too many emails, so be respectful and copy only those people who need to know about your message. Consider the people who are copied as your secondary audience, and adjust your message accordingly.

- Use "BCC" (blind computer copy) sparingly. In some organizations, using BCC to send people a copy of your email without others knowing about it is considered sneaky. This can become an ethical issue—and can come back to bite you if the person on BCC replies to all. A better alternative is to be open about who else is seeing the message or, if you must, forward an email after it has been sent.

Ethics in Communication

- Keep emails short. Some managers believe emails should be no longer than what fits on a desktop computer screen; others think anything more than a paragraph is too much, particularly for emails received on smartphones. For messages longer than about 300 words, use attachments instead.

- Keep paragraphs short. You may lose your audience with dense paragraphs in email. Keep them shorter—even single-sentence paragraphs are acceptable in email—to improve readability.

"EOM" in the subject line indicates "end of message," so the reader doesn't have to open the message.[10]

Uncommon Goods, the gifts cataloger, uses catchy subject lines to distinguish their emails from the rest. "Don't lick this email" encouraged readers to open the message and find delicious-looking parfaits.[11]

Here are more examples of clear, specific subject lines:

- Today's meeting changed from 3:00 to 3:30 p.m. (EOM)
- Need your input on the proposal revisions by 7/14
- Do you want to include Marjorie in the meeting?
- Customer has a question about shipping fees
- Revised performance objectives for your approval

**Figure 10
Descriptive Email Subject Lines**

- Make emails skimmable. Particularly for email, which people read quickly, make sure your main points are clear and up front. Bulleted lists are common in email.
- Use an appropriate tone. Emails can be formal or informal. Typically, more formal emails are sent to people you don't know well or those far more senior to you in an organization.
- Provide context. Initiating an email and responding to one require different approaches. When you initiate an email, provide enough context for the reader, just as you would in a memo or letter. Although email is fast, we still need to consider—and clearly communicate—our purpose for writing. When responding, consider including parts of the original email so that the receiver understands your reply.
- Follow conventions for closings and signatures. Similar to salutations, use standard phrases that reflect your organization's culture. See what other people use, for example, "I hope all is well," or "Please let me know if you have any questions." Before you type your name at the end of the email, include a brief closing. For more formal emails, end with "Best regards," "Regards," "All the best," or simply "Best." For less formal emails, you may simply write, "Thanks" or nothing before your name. In some organizations or departments, people may omit their name entirely—it just depends on the culture.
- Use a signature line. You may set up a personalized signature line for emails that you send. Typically, this includes your name, title, company, and possibly your phone number. If your company has guidelines, follow what's required. If not, keep your signature line simple and professional: avoid fancy fonts, colors, and backgrounds for business email.

Compare the emails in Figures 11 and 12 to see how these criteria are met.

Figure 11 Poorly Written Email

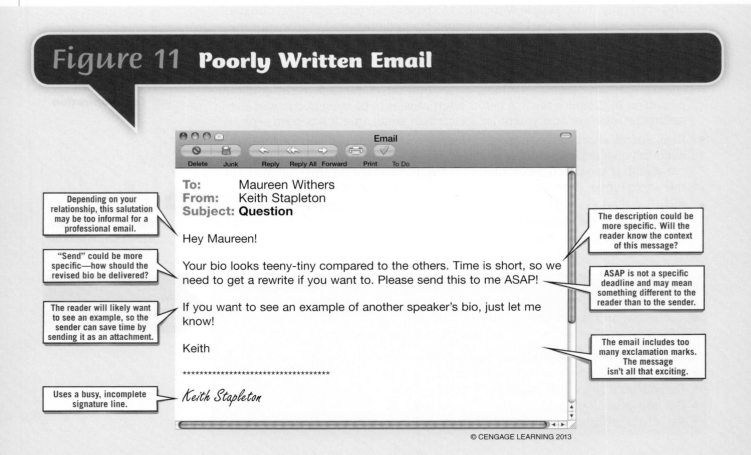

In addition to conforming to organizational norms for email, you should pay attention to variations by country and region. Cultural differences discussed in Chapter 2 are as apparent in email messages as in any business communication. For example, in cultures that emphasize relationships rather than tasks, you may see longer emails with more personal information. Although an email from a U.S. manager may jump right into the main point, an email from a Latin American manager may start with a longer introduction about the weather or an update about the family.

Email presents many challenges for communication—and cultural differences add even more possibilities for misunderstandings.

Writing Memos

Email has replaced almost all **memos**—written messages to people within an organization. Today, memos are reserved for more formal messages that are longer than one page (and are attached to short emails) or for short messages that serve as cover notes (and are attached to printed material), as in the example in

International Communication

Figure 12 Well-Written Email

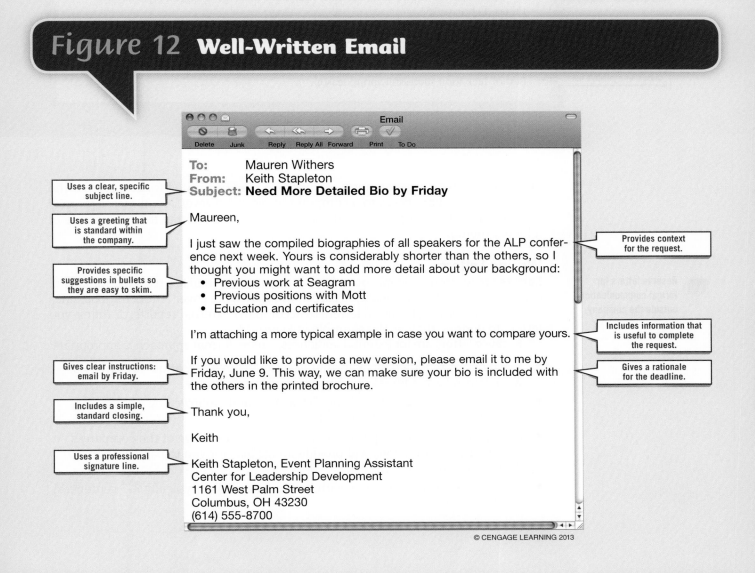

Uses a clear, specific subject line.

Uses a greeting that is standard within the company.

Provides specific suggestions in bullets so they are easy to skim.

Gives clear instructions: email by Friday.

Includes a simple, standard closing.

Uses a professional signature line.

Provides context for the request.

Includes information that is useful to complete the request.

Gives a rationale for the deadline.

To: Mauren Withers
From: Keith Stapleton
Subject: **Need More Detailed Bio by Friday**

Maureen,

I just saw the compiled biographies of all speakers for the ALP conference next week. Yours is considerably shorter than the others, so I thought you might want to add more detail about your background:
• Previous work at Seagram
• Previous positions with Mott
• Education and certificates

I'm attaching a more typical example in case you want to compare yours.

If you would like to provide a new version, please email it to me by Friday, June 9. This way, we can make sure your bio is included with the others in the printed brochure.

Thank you,

Keith

Keith Stapleton, Event Planning Assistant
Center for Leadership Development
1161 West Palm Street
Columbus, OH 43230
(614) 555-8700

Figure 13   Sample Short Cover Memo

Is printed on paper with a company logo.

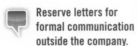

Includes standard memo heading with the writer's initials.

To: Store Managers
From: Andrea Jewel, CEO A.J.
Subject: Spring Catalog
Date: February 8, 2013

Refers to attached printed materials (a good reason to send a printed memo).

Attached is a preview copy of our spring catalog. I'm very proud of our Design Team, who created a beautiful representation of Aggresshop's most unique clothing and accessories.

Asks for feedback by email, which is the more typical communication medium for the company.

You will receive 100 copies of the catalog in your store by February 20. If you would like more than 100 copies, please contact Maryanne (msunger@aggresshop.com) by Friday, February 15.

Includes information related to the printed catalogs; this also may be sent by email.

Catalogs will be shipped to customers on February 22—one week earlier this year in response to your requests.

Closes on a positive note.

Best of luck for a successful spring season.

COURTESY OF AMY NEWMAN

Figure 13. In some organizations, memos also may be printed for employees who do not have regular access to a computer at work; however, email messages may be printed for this purpose as well. See the Reference Manual for an example of a longer memo.

Writing Letters

Reserve letters for formal communication outside the company.

Letters are written to people outside your organization and are reserved for formal communication. In your business career, you may write cover letters for jobs, sales letters to customers, proposal letters to accompany external reports, or thank-you letters to donors, such as the example in Figure 14.

Because letters are for external audiences, a more formal approach is appropriate:

- Use block or modified block format (see the Reference Manual for samples) with your return address and the date.
- Use a formal salutation, typically, "Dear Mr. Patel," followed by a colon (although commas are often used).
- Print your letter on company stationery or with an image of the company's logo. Many organizations will provide image files for you to paste into a document online.
- Use a more formal approach, with longer paragraphs (typically 3–7 sentences) and few bulleted lists.

Figure 14 Sample Letter

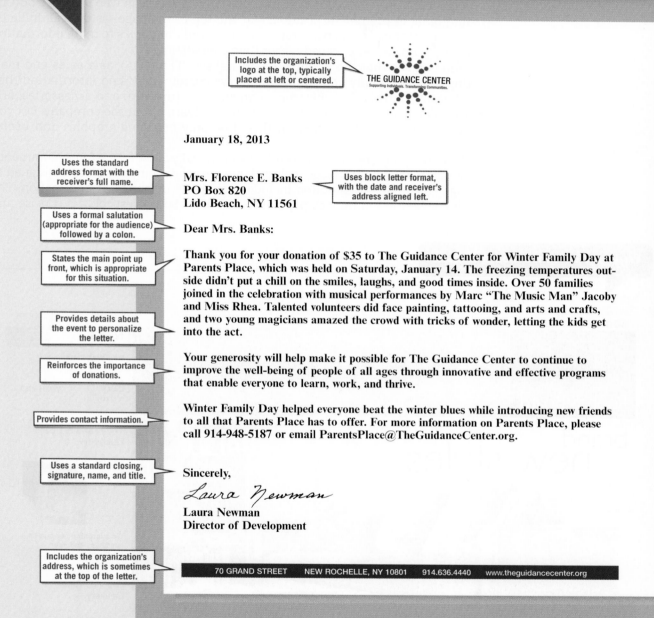

Includes the organization's logo at the top, typically placed at left or centered.

THE GUIDANCE CENTER
Supporting Individuals. Transforming Communities.

January 18, 2013

Uses the standard address format with the receiver's full name.

Mrs. Florence E. Banks
PO Box 820
Lido Beach, NY 11561

Uses block letter format, with the date and receiver's address aligned left.

Uses a formal salutation (appropriate for the audience) followed by a colon.

Dear Mrs. Banks:

States the main point up front, which is appropriate for this situation.

Thank you for your donation of $35 to The Guidance Center for Winter Family Day at Parents Place, which was held on Saturday, January 14. The freezing temperatures outside didn't put a chill on the smiles, laughs, and good times inside. Over 50 families joined in the celebration with musical performances by Marc "The Music Man" Jacoby and Miss Rhea. Talented volunteers did face painting, tattooing, and arts and crafts, and two young magicians amazed the crowd with tricks of wonder, letting the kids get into the act.

Provides details about the event to personalize the letter.

Reinforces the importance of donations.

Your generosity will help make it possible for The Guidance Center to continue to improve the well-being of people of all ages through innovative and effective programs that enable everyone to learn, work, and thrive.

Provides contact information.

Winter Family Day helped everyone beat the winter blues while introducing new friends to all that Parents Place has to offer. For more information on Parents Place, please call 914-948-5187 or email ParentsPlace@TheGuidanceCenter.org.

Uses a standard closing, signature, name, and title.

Sincerely,

Laura Newman

Laura Newman
Director of Development

Includes the organization's address, which is sometimes at the top of the letter.

70 GRAND STREET   NEW ROCHELLE, NY 10801   914.636.4440   www.theguidancecenter.org

- Use a professional closing, such as "Sincerely" or "Regards," and then leave a few lines to sign your name above your full typed name. Your title and division may follow your name.

Writing for the Web
Web writing takes many forms for business communication: websites, blogs, tweets, Facebook pages, and more. Here, we'll focus on writing for company websites and blogs.

Communication Technologies

Static websites, intended only for people to retrieve information, can be useful but are least ideal for business communication. Effective online communication from companies today has less writing and includes more interactivity—if not social media functionality, then other ways to connect with customers.

Less text is preferable for websites. Typically, people scan web pages, so putting main points in prominent positions—at the top of the page—is critical. Bulleted text, short sentences and paragraphs, simple words, and links to more information will keep your reader engaged rather than overwhelmed.

You can see that the Room & Board website (Figure 15), as a sales and marketing tool, is visually appealing and allows customers to find information they need easily. On this site, customers can shop for furniture and accessories, find a store, get customer service information, and learn about the company. But you won't find long blocks of text on this site—only engaging graphics and useful content.

Blogs use far more text than websites and typically allow for customer comments. Although many opinion blogs include longer articles, company blogs—designed to engage customers—more often include short posts or blurbs of information. The writing style for Southwest's popular "Nuts About Southwest" blog is concise and

Figure 15 Room & Board Website

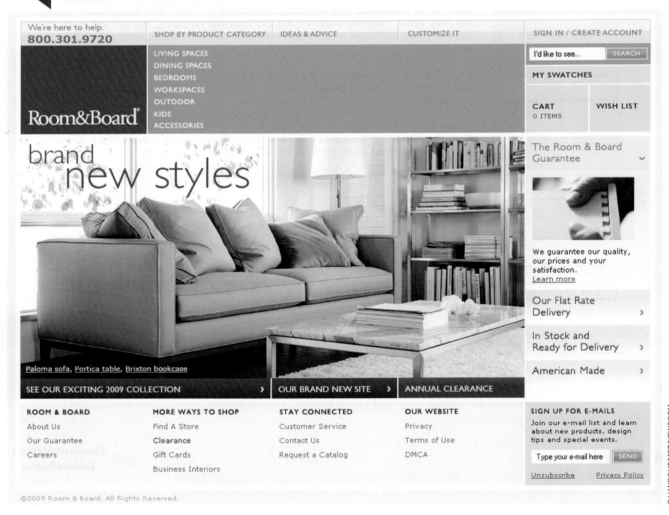

Figure 16 Nuts About Southwest Blog

Engages the viewer with bold graphics and a theme.

Integrates Twitter stream for a more seamless presence on the web.

Personalizes the entries from real people who work at Southwest.

Uses a conversational style, which is appropriate for the company's culture—and for web writing.

Makes it easy to share the post.

© SOUTHWEST AIRLINES CORPORATE

quite personal (Figure 16). This approach is most likely to encourage interactivity with customers, which we discussed in Chapter 3.

Concise writing, short paragraphs, and a conversational style are hallmarks of writing for the web. Well-written web pages are highly skimmable, with graphics, headings, bullets, and links to encourage people to read more or visit other parts of the company's website.

REVISING

Revising refers to modifying a message to make improvements. Having the raw material—your first draft—in front of you, you can now refine it into the most effective message possible, considering its importance and your time constraints.

If possible, put your draft away for some time—the longer the better. This break helps you distance yourself from your writing. If you revise immediately, you'll remember what you meant to say rather than what you actually wrote, which may prevent you from spotting errors.

For important writing projects, solicit comments about your draft from colleagues as part of the revision process. This step may prevent embarrassment for you and your company.

Although we have discussed revising as the fourth step of the writing process, it involves several substeps. Revise first for content, then for style, and finally for correctness.

Revising for Content

After an appropriate time interval, first reread your purpose statement and then the entire draft to get an overview of your message. Ask yourself such questions as these:

- Is the content appropriate for the purpose I've identified?
- Will the purpose of the message be clear to the reader?

LO4 Revise for content, style, and correctness.

 Ensure that all needed information——and only needed information——is included.

- Have I been sensitive to how the reader might react?
- Is all the information necessary?
- Is important information missing?
- Is the order of my main points logical?

Although you may be proud of your first draft, don't be afraid of making changes to improve your writing—even if it means striking out whole sections and starting again from scratch. The goal is to produce the best possible message.

Revising for Style

Next, read each paragraph again (aloud, if possible). Reading aloud gives you a feel for the rhythm and flow of your writing. Long sentences that made sense as you wrote them may leave you out of breath when you read them aloud.

Revising for Correctness

See the Language Arts Basics section of the Reference Manual for guidelines.

The final phase of revising is **editing**, ensuring that the writing conforms to standard English. Editing involves checking for correctness—identifying problems with grammar, spelling, punctuation, and word usage. Unfortunately, you can't rely solely on your computer's grammar and spell checker. These tools aren't 100% accurate, and they miss the context of your writing. Take responsibility to catch your own errors that may reflect negatively on your credibility or cause misunderstandings, as we saw in the introduction to this chapter.

L05   Proofread your message.

Typographical errors may reflect negatively on your credibility.

PROOFREADING

Proofreading is the final quality-control check for your message. A reader may not know whether an incorrect word resulted from a simple typo or from the writer's ignorance of correct usage. And even one such error can have adverse effects. In the *Boston Herald*, Continental Airlines advertised one-way fares from Boston to Los Angeles for $48, although the actual one-way fare was $148. That typographical error cost Continental $4 million: it sold 20,000 round-trip tickets at a loss of $200 each.[12]

Make sure your final product is the best possible reflection of you. Proofread for content, typographical, and formatting errors.

- **Content Errors:** First, read through your message quickly, checking for content errors. Was any material omitted unintentionally? As you revise, you may move, delete, or duplicate text. Check to be sure that your message *makes sense*.
- **Typographical Errors:** Next, read through your message slowly, checking for typographical errors. Look carefully for these hard-to-spot errors:

Look for Hard-to-Spot Errors

- Misused words that spellcheckers won't flag—for example, "I took the data *form* last month's report."
- Repeated or omitted words, such as articles (*the, a, an*).
- Proper names and numbers.
- Titles and headings, particularly if you use "all caps," which some spellcheckers skip (although you can change this option).

- **Formatting Errors:** Visually inspect the message for appropriate format. Are all the parts included and in the correct position? Does the message look attractive on the page or online?

Use these tips to catch more errors in your writing:

> **Catch More Errors**
>
> - Proofread in print—never on the computer screen.
> - Print on yellow or pink paper to see your work differently.
> - Wait a few hours or overnight after your last revision before you start proofreading.
> - Use a ruler to guide and slow down your eyes as you proofread.
> - Read backwards, one sentence at a time.

After you make changes, be sure to proofread again. By correcting one mistake, you might inadvertently introduce another. You're finished proofreading only when you read through the entire message without making any changes.

The Checklist for the Writing Process summarizes the five steps discussed in this chapter.

Checklist for the Writing Process   GO

1. Audience Analysis
- ☑ Who is the primary audience?
- ☑ What is your relationship with the audience?
- ☑ How will the audience likely react?
- ☑ What does the audience already know?
- ☑ What is unique about the audience?

2. Planning
- ☑ Determine the specific purpose of the message. What response do you want from the reader?
- ☑ Determine what information to include in the message, given its purpose and your analysis of the audience.
- ☑ Organize the information according to the reader's expected reaction:
  - ☑ Direct approach (expected positive or neutral reaction): present the major idea first, followed by supporting details.
  - ☑ Indirect approach (expected negative reaction): present the reasons first, followed by the major idea.

3. Drafting
- ☑ Choose a productive work environment, and schedule a reasonable block of time to devote to the drafting phase.
- ☑ Let your ideas flow as quickly as possible, without worrying about style, correctness, or format. If helpful, write the easiest parts first.
- ☑ Do not expect a perfect first draft; avoid the urge to revise at this stage.
- ☑ If possible, leave a time gap between writing and revising the draft.

4. Revising
- ☑ Revise for content: check for unnecessary information, omitted information, and organization.
- ☑ Revise for style: try reading your message aloud.
- ☑ Revise for correctness: use correct grammar, mechanics, punctuation, and word choice (see the Reference Manual).

5. Proofreading
- ☑ Proofread for content, typographical, and formatting errors.

The 3Ps In Action

Responding to the Embarrassing Sign at a National Fast-Food Restaurant

Purpose

Imagine that you own the restaurant where the embarrassing sign appeared in the window (described in the chapter introduction). The sign was posted at about noon, but you didn't see it until 2:00 p.m. because you were visiting one of your other locations. As soon as you see the sign, you remove it, but the damage has been done: when you check your email, you see this message from a local reporter.

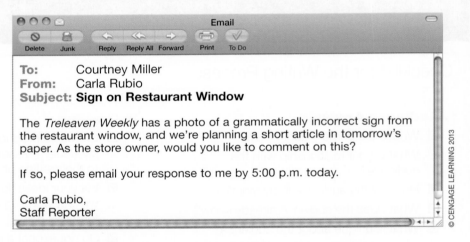

To: Courtney Miller
From: Carla Rubio
Subject: **Sign on Restaurant Window**

The *Treleaven Weekly* has a photo of a grammatically incorrect sign from the restaurant window, and we're planning a short article in tomorrow's paper. As the store owner, would you like to comment on this?

If so, please email your response to me by 5:00 p.m. today.

Carla Rubio,
Staff Reporter

© CENGAGE LEARNING 2013

You decide to respond so that the article will include your perspective.

Process

1. **What is the purpose of your message?**
   To restore the restaurant's credibility.

2. **Describe your primary audience.**
   Carla Rubio, the reporter. She is on a deadline and wants my perspective for a well-balanced story.

3. **Do you have a secondary audience for your email? If so, describe this group.**
   Yes, current and potential customers are my secondary audience. Customers may or may not have seen the sign, but those who did may have found it appalling or funny. The public is another audience—people who may never eat at the restaurant but may form a negative impression about the company because of this incident.

4. Considering your purpose, what are your main points for the response to the reporter?

- Thank her for the opportunity to respond.
- Express my concern about the situation, but encourage readers (customers and the public) to keep the sign in perspective—try not to make this a bigger deal than it is already.
- Assure readers that the company takes literacy seriously.
- Explain a plan for improving employees' writing skills.
- Assure readers that the restaurant is open, and the meat supply is restocked.

5. What medium will you use for your message?

I'll reply to the reporter's email, as she requested. If I don't get a confirmation by 4:30 p.m., I will call her to make sure she received it in time.

Product

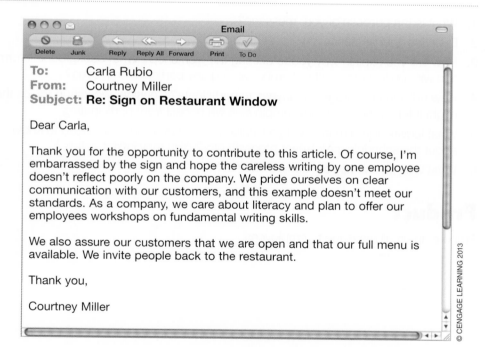

To: Carla Rubio
From: Courtney Miller
Subject: Re: Sign on Restaurant Window

Dear Carla,

Thank you for the opportunity to contribute to this article. Of course, I'm embarrassed by the sign and hope the careless writing by one employee doesn't reflect poorly on the company. We pride ourselves on clear communication with our customers, and this example doesn't meet our standards. As a company, we care about literacy and plan to offer our employees workshops on fundamental writing skills.

We also assure our customers that we are open and that our full menu is available. We invite people back to the restaurant.

Thank you,

Courtney Miller

Announcing Writing Skills Workshops

Purpose

After the embarrassing sign incident at the restaurant you own, you decide to offer employees a six-week fundamental writing skills workshop. A local business communication instructor, who has experience teaching writing skills at Treleaven Community College, will facilitate the sessions. To encourage employees to attend these optional sessions, write an email that explains why you're offering the workshop and why employees should participate.

Process

1. What is the purpose of your message?
2. Describe your audience.
3. How will you explain why you're offering the workshop? What background information will you include—without embarrassing any particular employee?
4. How will you encourage employees to participate? Consider workshop topics that might interest them and how employees will benefit from participating.
5. What logistical information will you include? What do employees need to know about the schedule, enrollment process, etc.? (You may invent details.)
6. What will you use as your subject line?

Product

Prepare an email message to employees.

Summary

L01   Analyze the audience for your communication.

Before writing, carefully analyze your audience. Identify who the audience is (both primary and secondary), determine what the audience already knows, consider your relationship with the audience, anticipate the audience's likely reaction, and identify any unique characteristics of the audience.

L02   Plan the purpose, content, and organization of your message.

Identify the general purpose and then the specific purpose of your message. Based on your audience analysis, determine what information to include and in what order. Determine whether a direct or indirect organizational plan is more likely to achieve your goals.

L03   Compose the first draft of your message.

Select an appropriate environment for drafting, and schedule enough time. Concentrate on getting the information down without worrying about style, correctness, or format. Leave a time gap between writing and revising the draft. Adjust your writing for different media. Follow organizational conventions for email, write memos for longer messages and when email is not practical, use a more formal style for letters, and work toward interactivity for the Internet.

L04   Revise for content, style, and correctness.

Revise first for content to determine whether the right amount of information is included in a logical order. Then revise for style to ensure that your message reads well for your audience. Finally, revise for correctness, being sure to avoid any errors in grammar, mechanics, punctuation, and word choice.

L05   Proofread your message.

Read through your message carefully to catch content, typographical, and formatting errors.

Exercises

1. Complete an audience analysis of housekeeping staff.

Imagine that you work for a small, independent hotel. Management has decided to change housekeepers' hours from 8:00 a.m.–4:00 p.m. to 8:30 a.m.–4:30 p.m. Using the five audience analysis questions in Figure 2, analyze the housekeeping staff. How does your analysis affect your approach for communicating the message?

L01 Analyze the audience for your communication.

2. Analyze an instructor as the audience.

If you were a business communication instructor and received this email from a student, how would you react? Analyze your instructor as an audience for this student's message, and consider changes the student might make to achieve his or her purpose.

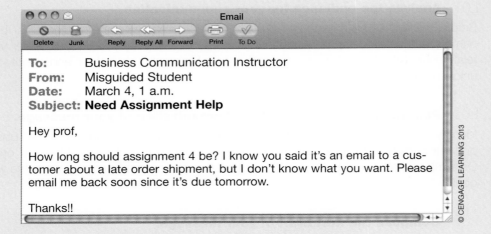

To: Business Communication Instructor
From: Misguided Student
Date: March 4, 1 a.m.
Subject: **Need Assignment Help**

Hey prof,

How long should assignment 4 be? I know you said it's an email to a customer about a late order shipment, but I don't know what you want. Please email me back soon since it's due tomorrow.

Thanks!!

© CENGAGE LEARNING 2013

3. Discuss a company's public statement.

When Bank of America was criticized for using "robo-signers" (employees who signed hundreds of foreclosure documents a day without reading them), the company issued this statement:

> Bank of America has extended our review of foreclosure documents to all fifty states. We will stop foreclosure sales until our assessment has been satisfactorily completed. Our ongoing assessment shows the basis for our past foreclosure decisions is accurate. We continue to serve the interests of our customers, investors and communities. Providing solutions for distressed homeowners remains our primary focus.[13]

Critics said that robo-signers—without properly reviewing documents—determined whether people would lose their homes. Critics also said this was unfair and may have forced some people to leave their homes unnecessarily. In small groups, identify and analyze the audience for the company's statement, which was published on the Bank of America website. Who are the company's primary and secondary audiences for the statement? How appropriate is the wording, considering the situation?

4. Evaluate audience focus in a company message.

After the oil spill in the Gulf of Mexico, Bob Dudley was appointed as British Petroleum's first American CEO. In a speech to business leaders in London, Dudley said the following in his closing comments:

Conclusion

> I will conclude with one related observation about this last aspect of the crisis, the political and media attention it generated.

> Over 87 days as the oil kept flowing into the ocean, it frequently felt as if we were the only story on the news, 24/7. I have seen figures that in some months fully 30% of the 24-hour news coverage was devoted to the incident.[14]

He went on to say the following:

> As I said at the outset, this was a human tragedy and a terrible event with major environmental and economic impacts. It was an accident from which we must and will learn.

We were certainly not perfect in our response. But we have tried to do the right thing, and we are making significant changes to our organisation as a result of the accident.[15]

Notice the British spelling of "organisation."

Some people criticized the conclusion of Dudley's speech, believing Dudley attacked the media rather than taking full responsibility for the oil spill.[16] What do you think, based on this excerpt? Complete an analysis of Dudley's primary and secondary audiences for the speech—business leaders and the public—and then discuss your assessment in small groups.

5. Identify general-purpose statements and communication objectives for several situations.

L02 Plan the purpose, content, and organization of your message.

Read the following situations and write a general-purpose statement and a specific communication objective—the results you want—for each.

- As the manager of a small retail clothing store, you write an email to let employees know they're getting a $1 per hour wage increase.
- As the assistant manager of a movie theater, you write an email to tell a customer you found the earring she lost the night before.
- As a newly hired advertising director, you write an email to the president of the company requesting a 10% increase in your advertising budget.
- As a CEO, you write a blog post on your investor website about your company's falling stock price.
- As a marketing manager, you write a letter to customers announcing a new product that will be available in your store starting next month.
- As a student, you write a letter to your college newspaper editor about the increase in tuition costs.
- As a warehouse manager, you write an email to an employee about the facility being left unlocked last night.

6. Plan the organization of messages.

For the situations in Exercise 5, imagine what the audience reaction might be and whether a direct or an indirect organizational plan would be better. Explain your answers.

7. Brainstorm new ice cream flavors.

Working in groups of three or four—without censoring your ideas—come up with as many new ice cream flavors as you can. Make a list of all the suggestions, and then share your list with the other groups in the class. How does your list compare to the other groups' lists? How big is the combined list? Which group generated the most ideas? What do they believe contributed to their success?

8. Organize a restaurant review.

Prepare to write a review of a restaurant or a dining facility on campus. Use the process outlined in this chapter:

- Brainstorm ideas. What do you think is important to include in your review? Draw a mind map.
- Create a hierarchy of ideas. How will you organize your main and supporting points?
- Develop an outline. Write a more detailed, sequential plan for your restaurant review.

LO3 Compose the
     first draft of your
     message.

9. Write a draft restaurant review.

Now that you have your outline for Exercise 8, draft your restaurant review. Practice free writing for this activity to avoid moving to the revision stage too quickly. Don't worry about formatting for this exercise; just practice moving from an outline to a written document.

10. Write a draft email to the sales team at Herman Miller.

Using the principles discussed for effective email communication, write a draft email to a team of sales associates. Imagine that you work for Herman Miller, a company that sells high-end office furniture. Today, the associates typically make phone calls and send online brochures to prospective clients. You believe that you can increase sales if the associates make personal visits instead. In your email, encourage associates to visit at least three businesses each week.

Use a respectful, encouraging tone, and provide enough reasons to convince the sales associates that personal visits will increase business. Invent whatever details you need to make your email realistic.

11. Write a company memo to announce a new organizational structure.

Imagine that you have just purchased a company and have brought in an entirely new management team—five of your classmates. In a separate message to employees, you have communicated the rationale for the changes. Now, you would like to introduce your new team to the rest of the organization.

Write a two-page memo. After a brief introduction, in which you refer to previous communications about the change, include a short paragraph (about 50 words) for the five new executive team members. In each paragraph, include the following information: executive's name, new title, and previous experience. You may invent whatever details you would like.

12. Format a letter.

You have just finished collecting donations for the American Cancer Society. To thank people for donating, you will send individual letters. Using guidelines in the Reference Manual, format your letter. You do not need to write the letter; just create the template with the date, addresses, salutation, and closing. You may create your own letterhead or use a standard return address.

13. Write blog posts.

Imagine that you work for Southwest Airlines and have been asked to write a few entries on their Nuts About Southwest blog. Write three short posts (about 50 words each). Write one post about a recent national holiday, one post to encourage viewers to visit your website, and one post to link to a recent news story about the company.

LO4 Revise for
     content, style,
     and correctness.

14. Revise your email to sales associates at Herman Miller.

Revise your draft email to Herman Miller sales associates (from Exercise 10). What changes will you make to improve the message? Follow these steps for the revision process:

a. Read the email once, revising for content. Make sure that all needed information is included, no unneeded information is included, and the information is presented in a logical sequence.

b. Read the email a second time, revising for style. Make sure that the words, sentences, paragraphs, and overall tone are appropriate.

c. Read the email a third time, revising for correctness. Make sure that grammar, mechanics, punctuation, and word choice are error free.

15. Revise another student's Herman Miller email.

Exchange draft Herman Miller emails with other students in class (so that you're not revising the paper of the person who is revising yours). Using the process described in Exercise 14, revise the other student's message, and then return the paper to the writer with your changes.

16. Revise a previous message.

Bring in a one-page message (email, memo, or letter) you have written in the past. Exchange papers with other students (so that you're not revising the paper of the person who is revising yours). Spend a few minutes asking the writer to give you background information about the message: purpose, audience, and so on. Then, follow the three-step revision process described in Exercise 14.

Return the paper to the writer. Then, using the revisions of your paper as a guide only (after all, *you* are the author), prepare a final version of the message. Submit both the marked-up version and the final version of your paper to your instructor.

17. Revise an email gone wrong.

When you read this email, you'll know that it was sent in anger. (This is adapted from a real email for a similar situation.)

First, discuss the issues in class. What went wrong? How would the audience (university employees) likely have reacted to this message? What was the intended communication objective? Did it likely achieve that objective?

Next, revise the message. The request is legitimate, but the approach and tone are not. Also consider the timing. How much time will people need to file or delete messages from their inboxes (probably more than one day)?

Finally, compare your version with two others in class. How do they differ? What are the best parts of each version?

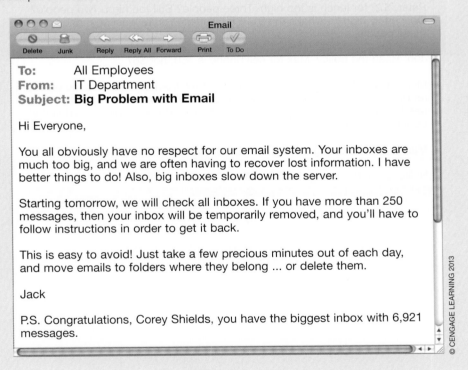

To: All Employees
From: IT Department
Subject: **Big Problem with Email**

Hi Everyone,

You all obviously have no respect for our email system. Your inboxes are much too big, and we are often having to recover lost information. I have better things to do! Also, big inboxes slow down the server.

Starting tomorrow, we will check all inboxes. If you have more than 250 messages, then your inbox will be temporarily removed, and you'll have to follow instructions in order to get it back.

This is easy to avoid! Just take a few precious minutes out of each day, and move emails to folders where they belong ... or delete them.

Jack

P.S. Congratulations, Corey Shields, you have the biggest inbox with 6,921 messages.

© CENGAGE LEARNING 2013

18. Revise another email gone wrong.

Another angry writer sent the email below to employees of a news agency. (This is adapted from a real message—and the original was much longer.) Use the same process as above to revise this email.

First, discuss the issues in class. What went wrong? How would the audience likely have reacted to this message? What was the intended communication objective? Did it likely achieve that objective?

Next, revise the message. The purpose is legitimate: to improve how people file expense reports. But the approach and tone could be much improved.

Finally, compare your version with two others in class. How do they differ? What are the best parts of each version?

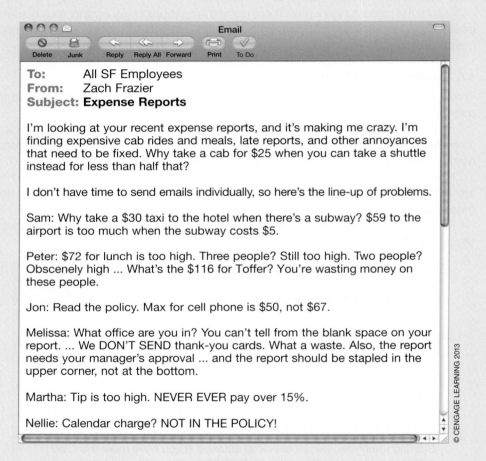

To: All SF Employees
From: Zach Frazier
Subject: **Expense Reports**

I'm looking at your recent expense reports, and it's making me crazy. I'm finding expensive cab rides and meals, late reports, and other annoyances that need to be fixed. Why take a cab for $25 when you can take a shuttle instead for less than half that?

I don't have time to send emails individually, so here's the line-up of problems.

Sam: Why take a $30 taxi to the hotel when there's a subway? $59 to the airport is too much when the subway costs $5.

Peter: $72 for lunch is too high. Three people? Still too high. Two people? Obscenely high ... What's the $116 for Toffer? You're wasting money on these people.

Jon: Read the policy. Max for cell phone is $50, not $67.

Melissa: What office are you in? You can't tell from the blank space on your report. ... We DON'T SEND thank-you cards. What a waste. Also, the report needs your manager's approval ... and the report should be stapled in the upper corner, not at the bottom.

Martha: Tip is too high. NEVER EVER pay over 15%.

Nellie: Calendar charge? NOT IN THE POLICY!

© CENGAGE LEARNING 2013

19. Proofread a letter.

Assume that you are Michael Land, and you wrote and typed the following letter. Proofread the letter, using the line numbers to indicate the position of each error. Proofread for content, typographical errors, and format. For each error, indicate by a "yes" or "no" whether the error would have been identified by a computer's spelling checker. How many errors can you find?

1. April 31 2011
2. Mr. Thomas Johnson, Manger
3. JoAnn @ Friends, Inc.
4. 1323 Charleston Avenue
5. Minneapolis, MI 55402

6. Dear Mr. Thomas:

7. As a writing consultant, I have often aksed aud-
8. iences to locate all teh errors in this letter.
9. I am allways surprized if the find all the errors.
10. The result being that we all need more practical
11. advise in how to proof read.

12. To aviod these types of error, you must ensure that
13. that you review your documents carefully. I have
14. preparred the enclosed exercises for each of you
15. to in your efforts at JoAnne & Freinds, Inc.

16. Would you be willing to try this out on you own
17. workers and let me know the results.

18. Sincerly Yours

19. Mr. Michael Land,
20. Writing Consultant

L05 Proofread your
message.

20. Proofread a job posting.

Review this passage, and see how many errors you can find. Look for spelling, formatting, and punctuation errors.

Finance Management Trainee

Program Overview

Bank on Me; a financial services company based in NYC; is now recruit a select number of candidates for its finance management training program. This is a comprehensive two year financial training program to provyde you with experience in the magor financial areas of the bank.

In addition to ongoing classroom training, the trainees complete projects in one or more of the following area:
- Analyzing and reporting on internal operations
- Forecasting financial trends
- Developing models and performing financial analyze of investments
- Supporting the corporations internal planning and management accounting functions
- Prepare external reports for shareholders and regulatory authorities
- Providing guidance on acounting policy issues and/or taxation issues

Position Qualification
- Associates or bachelors degre
- Financial course work
- At least on summer of finance related experience
- Minimum 3.5 GPA
- Demonstrated leadership experience
- Spanish language, a plus
- Microsoft Excel proficiency
- Strong comumnication skills
- Excellent attention detail

About Bank on Me

Founded in 1964, Bank on Me offer consumer and commercial banking services in 630 branches throughout the North east U.S. We offer personal and busines checking accounts, loans, credet cards, and other financial products. We also provide home lons and assistance to commercial property owners and investors. At Bank on Me we prid ourselves on superior customer service and have won several service awards to demonstrates this commitment.

Contact Information

Please send your cover letter and resume to the following:
Marley Catona
Recruting Officer
Bank on Me
555 New York Ave.
New York, NY 10022

Company Scenario

Writeaway Hotels

Imagine that you work for Writeaway Hotels as a catering director. If you had just 30 minutes between meetings to respond to an inbox full of email, how would you start? The Writeaway Hotels email and IM simulation allows you to practice the following skills:

- Reading and prioritizing email
- Making decisions about whether and how to respond to email
- Writing messages under pressure
- Evaluating the effectiveness of email you receive

Your instructor may assign a role for you to play from the Writeaway Hotels group.

Who's Who

To practice drafting email messages, you can start by responding to these. If you were Pat Gibson and received these messages, how would you respond? The first is from an upset client; the second is from your general manager.

Missed Conference Call   Inbox | X

☆ Diana **to** me   show details 8:51 AM (0 minutes ago)   ↩ Reply ▼

Pat,

Why weren't you on the conference call this morning with Bill? We just talked about this yesterday, so I'm sure you knew about it. I was embarrassed that you weren't on.

This brings up a bigger issue. I'm glad business is going so well for you and that you have a lot of new clients. But I'm starting to feel like I'm getting less attention now, and I want to make sure that we can maintain the good working relationship we've had in the past.

Diana

Checking In   Inbox | X

☆ Janet **to** me   show details 8:58 AM (0 minutes ago)   ↩ Reply ▼

Hello Pat,

I'm just checking in because I noticed that today is your one-year anniversary with us! How's it going??

Janet

Notes

1. Shannon P. Duffy, "Attorney Hit With $6.6 Million Malpractice Verdict," Law.com, April 23, 2007, www.law.com/jsp/article.jsp?id= 900005479433&slreturn=1&hbxlog, accessed July 29, 2010.

2. Dorothy Ferenbaugh, John Greenwald, Carol Fletcher, "How Does This #%*@! Thing Work? Instruction Manuals," *Time Magazine*, June 18, 1984, www.time .com/time/magazine/article/ 0,9171,951198,00.html, accessed July 29, 2010.

3. "Report: States pay $221 million for bad writing," Associated Press, July 4, 2005, www.msnbc.msn.com/ id/8459345/ns/us_news/t/report- states-pay-million-bad-writing/, accessed July 29, 2010.

4. "The, case, of, the, million, dollar, comma," *The Register*, October 26, 2006, www.theregister .co.uk/2006/10/26/the_case_of_the_ million_dollar_comma/, accessed July 29, 2010.

5. Ryan Barnes, "The Fuel that Fed the Subprime Meltdown," Investo- pedia, www.investopedia.com/ articles/07/subprime-overview .asp#axzz1PyMT3pZe, accessed November 27, 2010.

6. Marshall Cook, "Seven Steps to Better Manuscripts," *Writer's Digest*, September 1987, p. 30.

7. OfficeTeam, "'We Never Talk Any- more.' Survey Reveals Few Ex- ecutives Use Telephone or Meet in Person at Work," January 18, 2006, www.officeteam.com, accessed July 29, 2009.

8. Sara Radicati, "Business User Sur- vey, 2009," The Radicati Group, Inc., http://www.radicati.com, accessed July 29, 2010.

9. EmailStatCenter, http://www .emailstatcenter.com/SubjectLines .html, accessed July 29, 2009.

10. David Shipley and Will Schwalbe, *SEND: Why People Email So Badly and How to Do It Better*, (New York: Knopf, 2008).

11. Sherry Chiger, "Emails We Love: The Subject Was Subject Lines," The Big Fat Marketing Blog, July 23, 2010, http://bigfatmarketingblog. com/2010/07/23/emails-we-love- the-subject-was-subject-lines/, accessed July 28, 2010.

12. Julie Schmit, "Continental's $4 Mil- lion Typo," *USA Today*, May 25, 1993, p. B1.

13. Statement from Bank of America Home Loans, http://mediaroom .bankofamerica.com, accessed November 6, 2010.

14. Bob Dudley, Speech to CBI Annual Conference, British Petroleum, October 25, 2010, www.bp.com/ genericarticle.do?categoryId= 98&contentId=7065742, accessed November 3, 2010.

15. Bob Dudley, Speech to CBI Annual Conference, British Petroleum.

16. "Countdown with Keith Olber- mann," MSNBC, "Worst Person In The World: Bob Dudley," October 25, 2010.

Chapter 5

Choosing the Right Words (5) Write Clearly (5) Write Concisely (5) Writing Effective Sentences (5) Use a Variety of Sentence Types (5) **Revising Your Writing** (5) Use Active and Passive Voice Appropriately (5) Use Parallel Structure (5) Developing Logical Paragraphs (5) Keep Paragraphs Unified and Coherent (5) Creating an Appropriate Tone (5) Write Confidently (5) Use a Courteous and Sincere Tone (5) Use Appropriate Emphasis and Subordination (5) Use Positive Language

LEARNING OBJECTIVES

After you have finished this chapter, you should be able to

L01 Choose the right words for your message.

L02 Write effective sentences.

L03 Develop logical paragraphs.

L04 Convey an appropriate tone.

"From a business communication standpoint, less is more."

— GARY DAVIS,
VICE PRESIDENT OF
CORPORATE COMMUNICATIONS,
WORLD WRESTLING ENTERTAINMENT
(STAMFORD, CONNECTICUT)

Chapter Introduction: Business Communication at World Wrestling Entertainment

No matter who manages to stay in the ring—or who lands outside—Gary Davis uses positive language to describe the situation. He is vice president of corporate communications for World Wrestling Entertainment (WWE), which arranges more than 300 professional wrestling events every year worldwide.

Whether drafting a routine announcement or explaining the company's response to an unexpected problem, the WWE executive emphasizes that "the key is to write as if the glass is half full. If you do that, your message will come out positive." Another way Davis helps audiences grasp his meaning is by writing simply and concisely. "Although it is very easy to overwrite, to say too much, to be too flowery, this obscures what you're trying to say," he notes. "From a business communication standpoint, less is more."

Demonstrating the power of concrete, positive language, Davis wrote a letter showcasing the Smackdown Your Vote! initiative. The letter quoted WWE stars talking about registering young voters. The result: Hundreds of thousands of young voters are becoming involved in the election process—and the WWE is enhancing its credibility with key audiences.

At World Wrestling Entertainment, they know that the key to writing is using simple, concise language.

WHAT DO WE MEAN BY STYLE?

If you study the six Language Arts Basics modules in the Reference Manual at the end of this book, you will know how to express yourself *correctly* in most business writing situations; that is, you will know how to avoid major errors in grammar, spelling, punctuation, and word usage. But a technically correct message may still not achieve its objective, because it may lack style.

By **style**, we mean how an idea is expressed (not its *substance*). Style consists of words the writer uses and how those words are combined into sentences, paragraphs, and complete messages.

While writing the first draft of a message, you should be more concerned with content than with style. Your major objective should be to get your ideas down in some form, without worrying about style and mechanics. (**Mechanics** are elements in communication that show up only in writing, for example, spelling, punctuation, abbreviations, capitalization, number expression, and word division.) Apply the principles of style shown in Figure 1 as you write messages that are assigned in later chapters and on the job.

 See the Reference Manual for a review of Language Arts Basics (LAB) modules.

 Your writing can be error free and still lack style, but it cannot have style unless it is error free.

Figure 1 Principles of Style

Words	Sentences	Paragraphs	Tone
• Write clearly. • Write concisely.	• Use a variety of sentence types. • Use active and passive voice appropriately. • Use parallel structure.	• Keep paragraphs unified and coherent. • Control paragraph length.	• Write confidently. • Use a courteous and sincere tone. • Use appropriate emphasis and subordination. • Use positive language. • Stress the "you" attitude.

© CENGAGE LEARNING 2013

L01   Choose the right words for your message.

CHOOSING THE RIGHT WORDS

As the building blocks for writing, words can make or break your message. Clear, concise writing is essential for business communication.

Write Clearly

The most basic guideline for writing is to write clearly—to write messages the reader can understand and act on. You can achieve clarity by following these guidelines:

- Be accurate and complete.
- Use familiar words.
- Use specific, concrete language.
- Avoid dangling expressions.
- Avoid clichés, slang, and unnecessary jargon.

Be Accurate and Complete

Your credibility as a writer depends on the accuracy of your message. If a writer is careless, doesn't prepare, or intentionally misleads the reader, the damage is immediate and long lasting.

These headlines use correct grammar, but are they accurate?[1]

Headlines Gone Wrong
Iraqi Head Seeks Arms
Police Begin Campaign to Run Down Jaywalkers
Red Tape Holds Up New Bridges
Farmer Bill Dies in House
Teacher Strikes Idle Kids
New Study of Obesity Looks for Larger Test Group
Kids Make Nutritious Snacks
Typhoon Rips Through Cemetery; Hundreds Dead

Accuracy is critical in business writing. It involves more than freedom from errors.

Accuracy means presenting information truthfully—and much more. For example, consider the following sentence from a memo to a firm's investors:

> The executive committee of Mitchell Financial Services met on Thursday, May 28, to determine how to resolve the distribution fiasco.

What if the reader knows that May 28 fell on a Wednesday this year—not on a Thursday? Immediately, the reader may suspect everything else in the message and think, "If the writer made this error that I *did* catch, how many errors that I *didn't* catch are lurking there?"

Now consider more subtle shades of truth. The sentence implies that the committee met, perhaps in an emergency session, for the *sole* purpose of resolving the distribution fiasco. But suppose this was only one of five agenda items being discussed at a regularly scheduled meeting. Is the statement still accurate? Suppose the actual agenda listed the topic as "Discussion of Recent Distribution Problems." Is *fiasco* the same as *problems*?

The accuracy of a message depends on what is said, how it is said, and what is left unsaid. Competent writers assess the ethical dimensions of their writing and use integrity, fairness, and good judgment to make sure their communication is ethical.

When the oil spill disaster in the Gulf of Mexico became public in 2010, Tony Hayward, former CEO of British Petroleum, said, "The Gulf of Mexico is a very big ocean. The amount of volume of oil and dispersant we are putting into it is tiny in relation to the total water volume."[2] Hayward was highly criticized for this comment. Can you understand why?

Closely related to accuracy is completeness. A message that lacks important information may create inaccurate impressions. A message is complete when it contains all the information the reader needs—no more and no less—to react appropriately.

Ethical communicators make sure the overall tone of their message is accurate.

Ethics in Communication

Write to express, not to impress.

Use Familiar Words

To make your message easy to understand, use words familiar to you and your readers. The expression "Write to express, not to impress" is a good guide for business communication.

A Princeton University study, "Consequences of Erudite Vernacular Utilized Irrespective of Necessity: Problems with Using Long Words Needlessly," found that undergraduates use more complex words in papers to sound more intelligent. However, according to the researcher, this strategy achieves the opposite effect:

> It turns out that somewhere between two-thirds and three-quarters of people (depending on how you ask) admit to deliberately replacing short words with longer words in their writing in an attempt to sound smarter. . . . The problem is that this strategy backfires—such writing is reliably judged to come from less intelligent authors.[3]

Of course, long words are sometimes useful in business communication and should be used when appropriate. The larger your vocabulary and the more you know about your reader, the better equipped you will be to choose and use correctly those words that are familiar to your reader.

Short and simple words are more likely to be understood, less likely to be misused, and less likely to distract the reader. Literary authors often write to *impress*; they select words to amuse, excite, or anger. Business writers, on the other hand, write to *express*; they want to achieve *comprehension*. They want their readers to focus on their information, not on how they convey their information. Using short, simple words helps achieve this goal.

 Use language that you and your reader understand.

NOT Our utilization of adulterated water precipitated the interminable delays.

BUT Our use of impure water caused the long delays.

Our guideline is not to use *only* short and simple words but to *prefer* short and simple words. (As Mark Twain, who was paid by the word for his writing, noted, "I never write *metropolis* for seven cents because I can get the same price for *city*.")

Here are some examples of needlessly long words, gleaned from various business documents, with their preferred shorter substitutes:

Long	Short
ascertain	learn
modification	change
endeavor	try
substantial	large
enumerate	list
termination	end
initiate	start
utilization	use

 More than 70% of the words in Lincoln's Gettysburg Address (190 out of 267) are only one syllable long.

You may still use long words, but use them in moderation. And when a shorter alternative works just as well, choose that one for business writing.

Use Specific, Concrete Language

In Chapter 1, we discussed the communication barriers caused by overabstraction and ambiguity. When possible, choose *specific* words (words that have a definite, unambiguous meaning) and *concrete* words (words that bring a definite picture to your reader's mind).

NOT The vehicle broke down several times recently.

BUT The delivery van broke down three times last week.

In the first version, what does the reader imagine when he or she reads the word *vehicle*—a golf cart? Automobile? Boat? Space shuttle? And how many times is *several*—two? Three? Fifteen? What is *recently*? The revision tells precisely what happened.

Sometimes we do not need such specific information. For example, in "The president answered *several* questions from the audience," the specific number of questions is probably not important. But in most business situations, you should watch out for words like *several, recently, a number of, substantial, a few,* and *a lot of.* You may need to be more exact.

Concrete words give the reader a specific mental picture of what you mean. Compare these descriptions—and how persuasive each is.

 Concrete words present a vivid picture.

Which is more specific and concrete?	
"Friendly's Mac & Cheese Quesadilla meal for kids has a lot of calories."	"Friendly's Mac & Cheese Quesadilla meal for kids has 2,270 calories—the equivalent of 45.5 Glazed Munchkins from Dunkin' Donuts."[4]

Of course, the version on the right is more specific and concrete, telling us the number of calories and comparing the meal to donuts. This description gives parents more information about a meal they may order for their child.

NOT The vice president was bored by the presentation.

BUT The vice president kept yawning and looking at her watch.

Bored is an abstract concept. "Yawning and looking at her watch" paints a more vivid picture.

Specific terms tell readers how to react. Watch out for terms like *emotional meeting* (anger or gratitude?), *bright color* (red or yellow?), *new equipment* (projector or computer?), and *change in price* (increase or decrease?).

Avoid Dangling Expressions

A **dangling expression** is any part of a sentence that doesn't logically fit in with the rest of the sentence. Its relationship with the other parts of the sentence is unclear; it *dangles.* The two most common types of dangling expressions are misplaced modifiers and unclear antecedents. To correct dangling expressions, use one or more of these techniques:

- Make the subject of the sentence the doer of the action expressed in the introductory clause.
- Move the expression closer to the word that it modifies.
- Make sure that the specific word to which a pronoun refers *(its antecedent)* is clear.
- Otherwise revise the sentence for coherence.

NOT After reading the proposal, a few problems occurred to me. *(As written, the sentence implies that "a few problems" read the proposal.)*

BUT After reading the proposal, I noted a few problems.

NOT Dr. López gave a presentation on the use of drugs in our auditorium. *(Are drugs being used in the auditorium?)*

BUT Dr. López gave a presentation in our auditorium on the use of drugs.

NOT Ming explained the proposal to Joy, but she was not happy with it. *(Who was not happy—Ming or Joy?)*

BUT Ming explained the proposal to Joy, but Joy was not happy with it.

Avoid Clichés, Slang, and Unnecessary Jargon

A **cliché** is an expression that has become monotonous through overuse. Because audiences have heard a cliché many times, using clichés may send the message that the writer is uncreative, unoriginal—and couldn't be bothered to tailor the message to the audience.

NOT ▶ Enclosed please find an application form that you should return at your earliest convenience.

BUT ▶ Please return the enclosed application form before May 15.

Avoid these trite expressions in your writing:

Picture a person seeing "thank you for your recent letter" in all 15 letters he or she reads that day. How sincere and original does it sound?

According to our records	If you have any other questions
Company policy requires	Thank you for your attention to this matter
Do not hesitate to	Our records indicate that
For your information	Please be advised that

As noted earlier, slang is an informal expression, often short-lived, that is identified with a specific group of people. If you understand each word in an expression but still don't understand what it means in context, chances are you're having trouble with a slang expression. For example, read the following sentence:

International Communication

It turns my stomach the way you can break your neck and beat your brains out around here, and they still stab you in the back.

To anyone unfamiliar with American slang (a nonnative speaker, perhaps), this sentence might seem to be about the body because it refers to the stomach, neck, brains, and back. The real meaning, of course, is something like this:

I am really upset that this company ignores hard work and loyalty when making promotion decisions.

Avoid terms like these in most business writing:

Clichés and buzzwords go in and out of style too quickly to serve as effective components of written business communication.

can of worms	gut feeling	play up to
chew out	keep your cool	security blanket
go for broke	pay through the nose	wiped out

As a joke, one manager created an IM away message filled with business slang (Figure 2).[5]

Figure 2
Business Slang in an Away Message

I am away tending to a fire drill at the moment. If you would like, we can table this discussion by taking this correspondence offline at a later date. That way, we can both be in the loop, have our ducks in a row, and be on the same page moving forward, ensuring that we're comparing apples to apples, which, hopefully, will represent the lowest hanging fruit. This will also guarantee that it's kept from the back burner, yielding timely, actionable deliverables, which will encompass fresh, out-of-the-box thinking, synergistically moving the needle for whatever comes down the pike. Net-net, our success will manifest itself on the bottom line, I assure you. Although nothing will be etched in stone, let's regroup to run the numbers ASAP, say COB or EOD, whichever comes first. Until then we can remain in a holding pattern.

© OCULO/SHUTTERSTOCK.COM

As discussed in Chapter 1, jargon is technical vocabulary used within a special group. Every field has its own specialized words, and jargon offers a precise and efficient way of communicating with people in the same field. But problems arise when jargon is used to communicate with someone who doesn't understand it. Does the NRA refer to the National Rifle Association or the National Restaurant Association?

Closely related to jargon are *buzzwords*, which are important-sounding expressions used mainly to impress other people. Because buzzwords are so often used by government officials and high-ranking businesspeople—people whose comments are "newsworthy"—these expressions get much media attention. They become instant clichés and then go out of fashion just as quickly.

Be especially careful of turning nouns and other types of words into verbs by adding *-ize*. Such words as *operationalize, prioritize, commoditize,* and *maximize* quickly become tiresome.

Write Concisely

As part of its "Plain Language" initiative, the U.S. government has been working on clearer, more concise writing to the public. Compare the before-and-after examples in Figure 3.[6]

In this revision, the most important parts of the message are preserved. Is anything lost in translation? Not much. When you revise, avoid redundancy, wordy expressions, hidden verbs and nouns, and other "space eaters."

Avoid Redundancy and Wordy Expressions

A **redundancy** is the unnecessary repetition of an idea that has already been expressed or intimated.

NOT Signing both copies of the lease is a necessary requirement.

BUT Signing both copies of the lease is necessary.

Figure 3 **Revision for Plain Language**

The Department of Health and Human Services has taken a six-page article and replaced it with a single, foldout brochure, conveying the same information. Here is an excerpt.

Losing Weight Safely

Before
The Dietary Guidelines for Americans recommends a half-hour or more of moderate physical activity on most days, preferably every day. The activity can include brisk walking, calisthenics, home care, gardening, moderate sports exercise, and dancing.

After
Do at least 30 minutes of exercise, like brisk walking, most days of the week.

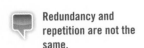

Redundancy and repetition are not the same.

Make every word count.

> **NOT** Combine the ingredients together.

> **BUT** Combine the ingredients.

A *requirement* is by definition *necessary*, so only one of the words is needed. And to *combine* means to bring *together*, so using both words is redundant. Don't confuse redundancy and repetition. Repetition—using the same word more than once—is occasionally effective for emphasis (as we will discuss later in this chapter). Redundancies, however, serve no purpose and should always be avoided.

Also avoid these common redundancies:

Instead of ...	Use ...
new innovation	innovation
combine together	combine
divide up	divide
plan ahead	plan
any and all	any *or* all
11:00 A.M. in the morning	11:00 A.M.
different types	types
basic fundamentals	basic *or* fundamentals
each and every day	each *or* every
repeat again	repeat
free gift	gift

© CENGAGE LEARNING 2013

Also avoid adding a noun when an abbreviation already stands for that noun, for example, *ATM* machine (ATM stands for "automated teller machine"), *PIN num-ber*, and *HIV virus*.

Use the fewest words that will achieve your objective.

Although wordy expressions are not necessarily writing errors (as redundancies are), they do slow the pace of the communication and should be avoided. Substitute one word for a phrase whenever possible.

> **NOT** In view of the fact that the model failed twice during the time that we tested it, we are at this point in time searching for other options.

> **BUT** Because the model failed twice when tested, we are searching for other options.

The original sentence contains 28 words; the revised sentence, 13. You've "saved" 15 words. In his book, *Revising Business Prose*, Richard Lanham speaks of the "lard factor": the percentage of words saved by "getting rid of the lard" in a sentence. In this case, 54% of the original sentence was "lard":

$$28 - 13 = 15$$

$$15 / 28 = 54\%$$

Lard fattens a sentence without providing any "nutrition." Lanham suggests, "Think of a lard factor (LF) of 1/3 to 1/2 as normal, and don't stop revising until you've removed it."[7]

Here are examples of other wordy phrases and their preferred one-word substitutes:

Instead of ...	Use ...
are of the opinion that	believe
in the event of	if
due to the fact that	because
pertaining to	about
for the purpose of	for *or* to
with regard to	about
in order to	to

© CENGAGE LEARNING 2013

Overusing prepositions also can cause wordiness (excessive word use). Consider these examples and their shorter equivalents:

Wordy	Better
The cover of the book	The book cover
Department of Human Resources	Human Resources Department
The tiles on the floor	The floor tiles
Our benefits for employees	Employee benefits
The battery in my smartphone	My smartphone battery

Avoid Hidden Verbs and Hidden Subjects

A hidden verb is a verb that has been changed into a noun form, thereby weakening the action. Verbs are *action* words and should convey the main action in the sentence. They provide interest and forward movement. Consider this example:

 Changing verbs to nouns produces weak, uninteresting sentences.

NOT Carl made an announcement that he will give consideration to our request.

BUT Carl announced that he will consider our request.

What is the real action? It is not that Carl *made* something or that he will *give* something. The real action is hiding in the nouns: Carl *announced* and will *consider*. These two verb forms, then, should be the main verbs in the sentence. Notice that the revised sentence is much more direct—and four words shorter (LF = 33%). Here are some other actions that should be conveyed by verbs instead of being hidden in nouns:

arrived at the conclusion (concluded)	has a requirement for (requires)
came to an agreement (agreed)	held a meeting (met)
gave a demonstration of (demonstrated)	made a payment (paid)

A pronoun in an expletive does not stand for any noun.

Like verbs, subjects play a prominent role in a sentence and should stand out, rather than being obscured by an expletive at the beginning. An **expletive** is an expression, such as *there is* or *it is*, that begins a clause or sentence and for which the pronoun has no antecedent. Because the topic of a sentence beginning with an expletive is not immediately clear, you should use such sentences sparingly in business writing. Avoiding expletives also contributes to conciseness.

NOT There was no indication that it is necessary to include John in the meeting.

BUT No one indicated that John should be included in the meeting.

Business writers sometimes use expletives to avoid a clear subject. Consider these variations, with particular attention to the changes in subjects and verbs:

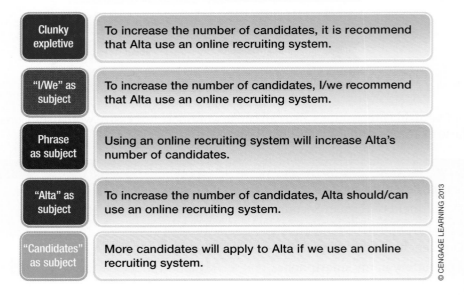

Clunky expletive	To increase the number of candidates, it is recommend that Alta use an online recruiting system.
"I/We" as subject	To increase the number of candidates, I/we recommend that Alta use an online recruiting system.
Phrase as subject	Using an online recruiting system will increase Alta's number of candidates.
"Alta" as subject	To increase the number of candidates, Alta should/can use an online recruiting system.
"Candidates" as subject	More candidates will apply to Alta if we use an online recruiting system.

© CENGAGE LEARNING 2013

All of these variations are grammatically correct—but they emphasize different subjects. For example, the first variation, with no clear subject, might be used to distance the source from the advice, which may be appropriate in some situations. In the second variation, the source takes ownership for the advice. The third, fourth, and fifth variations all clarify the subject and avoid the expletive in the first sentence. Notice how each of these three variations emphasizes different subjects: using the online recruiting system, Alta, and candidates, respectively. A writer would choose the variation that suits his or her purpose.

Imply or Condense

Sometimes you do not need to explicitly state certain information; you can imply it instead. In other situations, you can use adjectives and adverbs instead of clauses to convey the needed information in a more concise format.

NOT We have received your recent email and are happy to provide the data you requested.

BUT We are happy to provide the data you recently requested.

NOT This brochure, which is available free of charge, will answer your questions.

BUT This free brochure will answer your questions.

WRITING EFFECTIVE SENTENCES

L02 Write effective sentences.

A sentence has a subject and predicate and expresses at least one complete thought. Beyond these attributes, however, sentences vary widely in style, length, and effect.

Sentences are also very flexible; you can move sentence parts around, add and delete information, and substitute words to express different ideas and emphasize different points. To build effective sentences, use a variety of sentence types, use active and passive voice appropriately, and use parallel structure.

Use a Variety of Sentence Types

The three sentence types—simple, compound, and complex—are all appropriate for business writing.

Simple Sentence

A **simple sentence** contains one independent clause (i.e., a clause that can stand alone as a complete thought). Because it presents a single idea and is usually short, a simple sentence is often used for emphasis. Although a simple sentence contains only one independent clause, it may have a compound subject or compound verb (or both). All of the following sentences are simple:

 Use a simple sentence for emphasis.

- I quit.
- Employees can enroll in the company's 401(k) plan.
- Both part- and full-time employees can enroll in the company's 401(k) plan and in an Individual Retirement Account.

Compound Sentence

A **compound sentence** contains two or more independent clauses. Because each clause presents a complete idea, each idea receives *equal* emphasis. (If the two ideas are not closely related, they should be presented in two separate sentences.) Here are three compound sentences:

 Use a compound sentence to show coordinate (equal) relationships.

- Stacey listened, and I nodded.
- Morris Technologies made a major acquisition last year, but it turned out to be a mistake.
- Westmoreland Mines moved its headquarters to Prescott in 1984; however, it stayed there only five years and then moved back to Globe.

Complex Sentence

A **complex sentence** contains one independent clause and at least one dependent clause. For example, in the first sentence below, "the scanner will save valuable input time" is an independent clause because it makes sense by itself. "Although it cost $235" is a dependent clause because it does not make sense by itself.

 Use a complex sentence to express subordinate relationships.

- Although it cost $235, the scanner will save valuable input time.
- George Bosley, who is the new CEO at Hubbell, made the decision.
- I will move to Austin when I start my new job.

The dependent clause provides additional, but *subordinate*, information related to the independent clause.

Use a variety of sentence patterns and lengths.

Sentence Variety

Using a variety of sentence patterns and sentence lengths keeps your writing interesting. Note how simplistic and choppy too many short sentences can be and how boring and difficult too many long sentences can be.

Too Choppy:

Golden Nugget will not purchase the Claridge Hotel. The hotel is 60 years old. The asking price was $110 million. It was not considered too high. Golden Nugget had wanted some commitments from New Jersey regulators. The regulators were unwilling to provide such commitments. Some observers believe the refusal was not the real reason for the decision. They blame the weak Atlantic City economy for the cancellation. Golden Nugget purchased the Stake House in Las Vegas in 2000. It lost money on that purchase. It does not want to repeat its mistake in Atlantic City.

(Average sentence length = 8 words)

Too Difficult:

Golden Nugget will not purchase the Claridge Hotel, which is 60 years old, for an asking price of $110 million, which was not considered too high, because the company had wanted some commitments from New Jersey regulators, and the regulators were unwilling to provide such commitments. Some observers believe the refusal was not the real reason for the decision but rather that the weak Atlantic City economy was responsible for the cancellation; and since Golden Nugget purchased the Stake House in Las Vegas in 2000 and lost money on that purchase, it does not want to repeat its mistake in Atlantic City.

(Average sentence length = 50 words)

The sentences in these paragraphs should be revised to show relationships between ideas more clearly, to keep readers interested, and to improve readability. Use simple sentences for emphasis and variety, compound sentences for coordinate (equal) relationships, and complex sentences for subordinate relationships.

More Variety:

Golden Nugget will not purchase the 60-year-old Claridge Hotel, even though the $110 million asking price was not considered too high. The company had wanted some commitments from New Jersey regulators, which the regulators were unwilling to provide. However, some observers blame the cancellation on the weak Atlantic City economy. Golden Nugget lost money on its 2000 purchase of the Stake House in Las Vegas, and it does not want to repeat its mistake in Atlantic City.

(Average sentence length = 20 words)

The first two sentences in the revision are complex, the third is simple, and the last sentence is compound. The lengths of the four sentences range from 12 to 27 words. To write effective sentences, use different sentence patterns and lengths. Most sentences in good business writing range from 16 to 22 words.

© CENGAGE LEARNING 2013

Use Active and Passive Voice Appropriately

 In active sentences, the subject performs the action; in passive sentences, the subject receives the action.

Voice is the aspect of a verb that shows whether the subject of the sentence acts or is acted on. In the **active voice**, the subject *performs* the action expressed by the verb. In the **passive voice**, the subject *receives* the action expressed by the verb.

ACTIVE Old Navy offers a full refund on all orders.

PASSIVE A full refund on all orders is offered by Old Navy.

ACTIVE Shoemacher & Doerr audited the books last quarter.

PASSIVE The books were audited last quarter by Shoemacher & Doerr.

Passive sentences add some form of the verb *to be* to the main verb, so passive sentences are always somewhat longer than active sentences. In the first set of sentences, for example, compare *offers* in the active sentence with *is offered by* in the passive sentence.

In active sentences, the subject is the doer of the action; in passive sentences, the subject is the receiver of the action. Because the subject gets more emphasis than other nouns in a sentence, active sentences emphasize the doer, while passive sentences emphasize the receiver. In the second set of sentences, both versions are correct, depending on whether the writer wanted to emphasize *Shoemacher & Doerr* or *the books*.

Use active sentences most of the time in business writing, just as you naturally use active sentences in most of your conversations. Note that verb *voice* (active or passive) has nothing to do with verb *tense*, which shows the time of the action. As the following sentences show, the action in both active and passive sentences can occur in the past, present, or future.

NOT A very logical argument was presented by Hal. *(Passive voice, past tense)*

BUT Hal presented a very logical argument. *(Active voice, past tense)*

NOT An 18% increase will be reported by the eastern region. *(Passive voice, future tense)*

BUT The eastern region will report an 18% increase. *(Active voice, future tense)*

Passive sentences are most appropriate when you want to emphasize the *receiver* of the action, when the person doing the action is either unknown or unimportant, or when you want to be tactful in conveying negative information. All the following sentences are appropriately stated in the passive voice:

Passive sentences are generally more effective than active sentences for conveying negative information.

- Protective legislation was blamed for the drop in imports. *(Emphasizes the receiver of the action)*
- Transportation to the construction site will be provided. *(Downplays the unimportant doer of the action)*
- Several complaints have been received regarding the new policy. *(Conveys negative news tactfully)*

Use Parallel Structure

The term **parallelism** means using similar grammatical structure for similar ideas—that is, matching adjectives with adjectives, nouns with nouns, infinitives with infinitives, and so on. Much widely quoted writing uses parallelism—for example, Julius Caesar's "I came, I saw, I conquered" and Abraham Lincoln's "government of the people, by the people, and for the people."

Parallelism refers to consistency.

Parallel structure links ideas and adds a pleasing rhythm to sentences and paragraphs, which enhances coherence.

NOT The new dispatcher is competent and a fast worker.

BUT The new dispatcher is competent and fast.

NOT The new grade of paper is lightweight, nonporous, and it is inexpensive.

BUT The new grade of paper is lightweight, nonporous, and inexpensive.

NOT The training program will cover vacation and sick leaves, how to resolve grievances, and managing your workstation.

BUT The training program will cover vacation and sick leaves, grievance resolution, and workstation management.

NOT One management consultant recommended either selling the children's furniture division or its conversion into a children's toy division.

BUT One management consultant recommended either selling the children's furniture division or converting it into a children's toy division.

NOT Gwen is not only proficient in Microsoft Word but also in Excel.

BUT Gwen is proficient not only in Microsoft Word but also in Excel.

In the last two sets of sentences above, note that correlative conjunctions (such as *both/and, either/or,* and *not only/but also*) must be followed by words in parallel form.

Be especially careful to use parallel structure in report headings and presentation slide titles that have equal weight and in numbered and bulleted lists. Two examples of revisions for parallel phrasing in bulleted lists are shown in Figure 4.

Figure 4   Revising for Parallel Phrasing

Before	After
Agenda: Planning for Independent Research • What is independent research? • Reasons we should use independent research for this project • Starting the process	**Agenda: Planning for Independent Research** • What is independent research? • Why is independent research appropriate for this project? • How should we begin the research process?
What is the process for conducting independent research? • Pick a topic • Faculty sponsor • Setting up a timeline • Resources • Figure out a method • Data study • You should deliver results	**What is the process for conducting independent research?** **D.I.S.C.U.S.S.** • Discover topic • Identify faculty sponsor • Set up timeline • Consult resources • Use methods • Study data • Shape deliverables

© CENGAGE LEARNING 2013

L03 Develop logical paragraphs.

DEVELOPING LOGICAL PARAGRAPHS

A paragraph is a group of related sentences that focus on one main idea. The main idea is often identified in the first sentence of the paragraph—the **topic sentence**. The body of the paragraph supports this main idea by giving more information, analysis, or examples. A paragraph is typically part of a longer message, although one paragraph may be an entire email.

Paragraphs organize a topic into manageable units of information for the reader. Readers need a cue to tell them when they have finished a topic so they can pause and refocus their attention on the next topic. Effective paragraphs are unified, coherent, and an appropriate length.

 **Use a new paragraph to signal a change in direction.**

Keep Paragraphs Unified and Coherent

Although closely related, unity and coherence are not the same. A paragraph has **unity** when all its parts work together to develop a single idea consistently and logically. A paragraph has **coherence** when each sentence links smoothly to the sentences before and after it.

Unity

A unified paragraph gives information that is directly related to the topic, presents this information in a logical order, and omits irrelevant details. The following excerpt is a middle paragraph in a memo arguing against the proposal that Collins, a baby-food manufacturer, should expand into producing food for adults:

> **NOT** ▶ [1] We cannot focus our attention on both ends of the age spectrum. [2] In a recent survey, two-thirds of the under-35 age group named Collins as the first company that came to mind for the category "baby-food products." [3] For more than 50 years, we have spent millions of dollars annually to identify our company as the baby-food company, and market research shows that we have been successful. [4] Last year, we introduced Peas 'n' Pears, our most successful baby-food introduction ever. [5] To now seek to position ourselves as a producer of food for adults would simply be incongruous. [6] Our well-defined image in the marketplace would make producing food for adults risky.

Before reading further, rearrange these sentences to make the sequence of ideas more logical. As written, the paragraph lacks unity. You may decide that the overall topic of the paragraph is Collins' well-defined image as a baby-food producer. So Sentence 6 would be the best topic sentence. You might also decide that Sentence 4 brings in extra information that weakens paragraph unity and should be left out. The most unified paragraph, then, would be Sentences 6, 3, 2, 5, and 1, as shown here:

> **BUT** ▶ Our well-defined image in the marketplace would make producing food for adults risky. For more than 50 years, we have spent millions of dollars annually to identify our company as the baby-food company, and market research shows that we have been successful. In a recent survey, two-thirds of the under-35 age group named Collins as the first company that came to mind for the category "baby-food products." To now seek to position ourselves as a producer of food for adults would simply be incongruous. We cannot focus our attention on both ends of the age spectrum.

A topic sentence is especially helpful in a long paragraph, for the reader as well as the writer. Placed at the beginning of the paragraph, the topic sentence tells the reader the main point of the paragraph and encourages the writer to keep focused on one topic to ensure paragraph unity.

 The topic sentence usually goes at the beginning of the paragraph.

Coherence

A coherent paragraph weaves sentences together so that the discussion is integrated. The reader never needs to pause to puzzle out the relationships or reread to get the intended meaning. To achieve coherence, use transitional words, use pronouns, and repeat key words and ideas.

 Coherence is achieved by using transitional words, pronouns, repetition, and parallelism.

Transitional words help the reader see relationships between sentences. Such words may be as simple as *first* and other indicators of sequence.

Ten years ago, Collins tried to overcome market resistance to its new line of baby clothes. *First*, it mounted a multimillion-dollar ad campaign featuring the Mason quintuplets. *Next*, it sponsored a Collins Baby look-alike contest. *Then* it sponsored two network specials featuring Dr. Benjamin Spock. *Finally*, it brought in the Madison Avenue firm of Morgan & Modine to broaden its image.

The words *first, next, then,* and *finally* clearly signal step-by-step movement. Now note the use of transitional words in the following paragraph:

I recognize, *however*, that Collins cannot thrive on baby food alone. *To begin with*, since we already control 73% of the market, further gains will be difficult. *Also*, the current baby boom is slowing. *Therefore*, we must expand our product line.

These transitional words act as road signs, indicating where the message is headed and letting the reader know what to expect. Here are some commonly used transitional expressions grouped by the relationships they express:

Relationship	Transitional Expressions
addition	also, besides, furthermore, in addition, too
cause and effect	as a result, because, consequently, therefore
comparison	in the same way, likewise, similarly
contrast	although, but, however, nevertheless, on the other hand, still
illustration	for example, for instance, in other words, to illustrate
sequence	first, second, third, then, next, finally
summary/conclusion	at last, finally, in conclusion, therefore, to summarize
time	meanwhile, next, since, soon, then

A second way to achieve coherence is to use pronouns. Because pronouns stand for words already named, using pronouns binds sentences and ideas together. The pronouns are italicized here:

If Collins branches out with additional food products, one possibility would be a fruit snack for youngsters. Funny Fruits were tested in Columbus last summer, and *they* were a big hit. Roger Johnson, national marketing manager, says *he* hopes to build new food categories into a $200 million business. *He* is also exploring the possibility of acquiring other established name brands. *These* acquired brands would let Collins expand faster than if *it* had to develop a new product of *its* own.

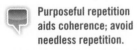
Purposeful repetition aids coherence; avoid needless repetition.

A third way to achieve coherence is to repeat key words. In a misguided attempt to appear interesting, writers sometimes use different terms for the same idea. For example, in discussing a proposed merger, a writer may at different points use *merger, combination, union, association,* and *acquisition.* Or a writer may use the words *administrator, manager, supervisor,* and *executive* all to refer to the same person. Such "elegant variation" only confuses the reader, who has no way of knowing whether the writer is referring to the same concept or to slightly different variations of that concept.

Avoid needless repetition, but use purposeful repetition to link ideas and thus promote paragraph coherence. Here is a good example:

Collins has taken several *steps* recently to enhance profits and project a stronger leadership position. One of these *steps* is streamlining operations. Collins' line of children's clothes was *unprofitable*, so it discontinued the line. Its four produce farms were also *unprofitable*, so it hired an outside professional *team* to manage them. This *team* eventually recommended selling the farms.

Ensure paragraph unity by developing only one topic per paragraph and by presenting the information in logical order. Ensure paragraph coherence by using transitional words and pronouns and by repeating key words.

Control Paragraph Length

How long should a paragraph of business writing be? As with other considerations, the needs of the reader, rather than the convenience of the writer, should determine the answer. Paragraphs should help the reader by signaling a new idea, as well as by providing a physical break.

 Excessively long paragraphs look boring and difficult.

Long blocks of unbroken text look boring and may unintentionally obscure an important idea buried in the middle. On the other hand, a series of extremely short paragraphs can weaken coherence by obscuring underlying relationships. Compare the messages in Figure 5. Which is more inviting to read? Information is easier to digest when broken into small chunks with paragraph breaks, headings, bullets, and in this example, sub-bullets.

 See the Reference Manual for a full version of the memo in Figure 5.

Figure 5
Comparing Paragraph Length: Which Is More Inviting to Read?

Our goal is to transition the organization as smoothly as possible. Over the next 90 days, we will implement the transition plan. By October 15, we will transfer sales representatives to new divisions. Each sales representative will be moved from our current regional teams to a new team: consumer, small business, or corporate. Managers will work closely with representatives to determine strengths, experience, and preferences. By October 31, we will identify account type. All sales representatives will categorize current accounts for the new divisions: consumer, small business, and corporate. By November 30, we will transition accounts to new teams. Where accounts are changing sales representatives, we will follow this process. For small business accounts, the former and new sales representative will send an email to the account contact, followed by a phone call and visit (if possible) by the new sales representative. For corporate accounts, the former sales representative will send an email and schedule a conference call or visit by the account contact and new sales representative.

Our goal is to transition the organization as smoothly as possible. Over the next 90 days, we will implement the transition plan:

- **Transfer sales representatives to new divisions (by October 15)**

  Each sales representative will be moved from our current regional teams to a new team: consumer, small business, or corporate. Managers will work closely with representatives to determine strengths, experience, and preferences.

- **Identify account type (by October 31)**

  All sales representatives will categorize current accounts for the new divisions: consumer, small business, and corporate.

- **Transition accounts to new teams (by November 30)**

  Where accounts are changing sales representatives, we will follow this process:

  - For small business accounts, the former and new sales representative will send an email to the account contact, followed by a phone call and visit (if possible) by the new sales representative.
  - For corporate accounts, the former sales representative will send an email and schedule a conference call or visit by the account contact and new sales representative.

There are no fixed rules for paragraph length, and occasionally one- or ten-sentence paragraphs might be effective. However, most paragraphs of good business writers fall into the 60- to 80-word range—long enough for a topic sentence and three or four supporting sentences.

A paragraph is both a logical unit and a visual unit. It is logical in that it discusses only one topic. It is visual in that the end of the paragraph signals readers to pause and digest the information (or, perhaps, just to rest). Although a single paragraph should never discuss more than one major topic, complex topics may need to be divided into several paragraphs. Your purpose and the needs of your reader should ultimately determine paragraph length.

L04 Convey an appropriate tone.

CREATING AN APPROPRIATE TONE

After choosing the right words to create effective sentences and then combining these sentences into logical paragraphs, we can now examine the tone of the complete message—the complete email, memo, letter, report, blog post, and so on.

Tone in writing refers to the writer's attitude toward both the reader and the subject of the message. The overall tone of your written message affects your reader, just as your tone of voice affects your listener during a conversation. Follow these guidelines to achieve an appropriate tone in business writing:

- Write confidently.
- Use a courteous and sincere tone.
- Use appropriate emphasis and subordination.
- Use positive language.
- Stress the "you" attitude.

Write Confidently

To achieve your communication objective, your message should convey a professional, confident attitude. The more confident you are about your writing, the more likely your audience will understand your explanation, accept your decision, or complete your request.

Avoid using language that makes you sound unsure of yourself. Be especially wary of beginning sentences with "I hope," "If you agree," "I think," and other self-conscious terms.

NOT If you'd like to take advantage of this offer, call our toll-free number.

BUT To take advantage of this offer, call our toll-free number.

NOT I hope that you will agree that my qualifications match your job needs.

BUT My qualifications match your job needs in the following respects.

In some situations, the best strategy is simply to omit information. Why focus on your lack of work experience in a cover letter or imply that your product may need to be returned?

NOT Let us know if you experience any other problems.

BUT Your Skullcandy headphones should now provide you with several years of clear audio enjoyment.

Figure 6 Inappropriate Tone in an Email

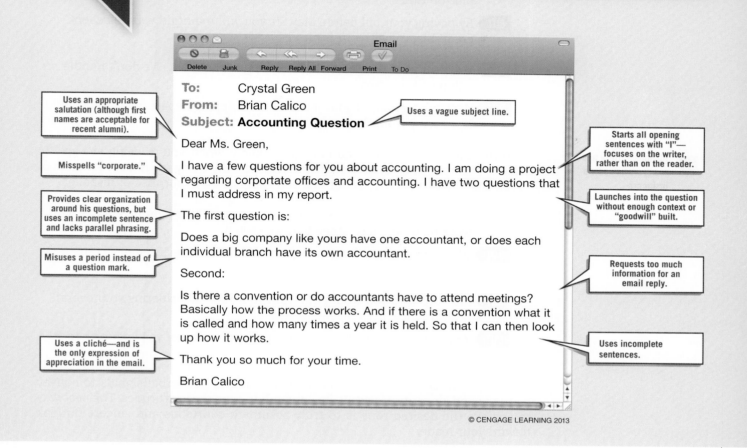

To: Crystal Green
From: Brian Calico
Subject: Accounting Question

Dear Ms. Green,

I have a few questions for you about accounting. I am doing a project regarding corpratate offices and accounting. I have two questions that I must address in my report.

The first question is:

Does a big company like yours have one accountant, or does each individual branch have its own accountant.

Second:

Is there a convention or do accountants have to attend meetings? Basically how the process works. And if there is a convention what it is called and how many times a year it is held. So that I can then look up how it works.

Thank you so much for your time.

Brian Calico

Callouts:
- Uses an appropriate salutation (although first names are acceptable for recent alumni).
- Misspells "corporate."
- Provides clear organization around his questions, but uses an incomplete sentence and lacks parallel phrasing.
- Misuses a period instead of a question mark.
- Uses a cliché—and is the only expression of appreciation in the email.
- Uses a vague subject line.
- Starts all opening sentences with "I"—focuses on the writer, rather than on the reader.
- Launches into the question without enough context or "goodwill" built.
- Requests too much information for an email reply.
- Uses incomplete sentences.

© CENGAGE LEARNING 2013

A word of caution: Do not appear *overconfident*; avoid sounding presumptuous or arrogant. Be especially wary of using such strong phrases as "I know that" and "I am sure you will agree that."

NOT I'm sure that you'll agree our offer is reasonable.

BUT This solution should give you the data you need while still protecting the privacy of our clients.

Consider the email in Figure 6, sent from a student to a recent alumnus.[8] The receiver found the email to be presumptuous and inappropriate.

Competent communicators are *confident* communicators. They write with conviction, yet avoid appearing pushy or presumptuous.

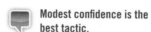 Modest confidence is the best tactic.

Use a Courteous and Sincere Tone

A tone of courtesy and sincerity builds goodwill for you and your organization and increases the likelihood that your message will achieve its objective. For example, lecturing the reader or filling a letter with **platitudes** (trite, obvious statements) implies a condescending attitude. Also, readers are likely to find offensive such

 A platitude is a statement so obvious that including it in a message would insult the reader.

expressions as "you failed to," "we find it difficult to believe that," "you surely don't expect," or "your complaint."

> **NOT** ▶ Companies like ours cannot survive unless our customers pay their bills on time.

> **BUT** ▶ By paying your bill before May 30, you will maintain your excellent credit history with our firm.

> **NOT** ▶ You sent your complaint to the wrong department. We don't handle shipping problems.

> **BUT** ▶ We have forwarded your letter to the shipping department. You should be hearing from them within the week.

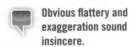
Obvious flattery and exaggeration sound insincere.

Your reader is sophisticated enough to know when you're being sincere. To achieve a sincere tone, avoid exaggeration (especially using too many modifiers or too strong modifiers), obvious flattery, and expressions of surprise or disbelief.

> **NOT** ▶ Your satisfaction means more to us than making a profit, and we will work night and day to see that we earn it.

> **BUT** ▶ We value your goodwill and have taken these specific steps to ensure your satisfaction.

> **NOT** ▶ I'm surprised you would question your raise, considering your overall performance last year.

> **BUT** ▶ Your raise was based on an objective evaluation of your performance last year.

Competent communicators use both verbal and nonverbal signals to convey courtesy and sincerity. However, it is difficult to fake these attitudes. The best way to achieve the desired tone is to truly assume a courteous and sincere outlook toward your reader.

Use Appropriate Emphasis and Subordination

Not all ideas are equal. Some are more important and more persuasive than others. Assume, for example, that you have been asked to evaluate and compare the Copy Cat and the Repro 100 photocopier and then to write a memo recommending one for purchase. Assume that the two brands are alike in all important respects except these:

Feature	Copy Cat	Repro 100
Speed (copies per minute)	15	10
Cost	$2,750	$2,100
Enlargement/Reduction?	Yes	No

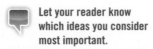
Let your reader know which ideas you consider most important.

As you can see, the Copy Cat has greater speed and more features. A casual observer might think you should recommend the Copy Cat on the basis of its additional advantages. Suppose, however, that most of your photocopying involves fewer than five copies of each original, all of them full-sized. Under these conditions, you might conclude that the Repro 100's lower cost outweighs the Copy Cat's higher speed and additional features; you therefore decide to recommend purchasing the Repro 100.

If you want your recommendation to be credible, you must make sure your reader views the relative importance of each feature the same way you do. To do so, use appropriate emphasis and subordination techniques.

Techniques of Emphasis

To emphasize an idea, use any of the following strategies (to subordinate an idea, simply use the opposite strategy):

- Put the idea in a short, simple sentence. However, if you need a complex sentence to convey the needed information, put the more important idea in the independent clause. (The ideas communicated in each independent clause of a *compound* sentence receive *equal* emphasis.)

 To subordinate an idea, put it in the dependent clause.

> **SIMPLE** ▶ The Repro 100 is the better photocopier for our purposes.

> **COMPLEX** ▶ Although the Copy Cat is faster, 98% of our copying requires fewer than five copies per original. *(The independent clause emphasizes that speed is not a crucial consideration for us.)*

- Place the major idea first or last. The first paragraph of a message receives the most emphasis, the last paragraph receives less emphasis, and the middle paragraphs receive the least emphasis. Similarly, the middle sentences within a paragraph receive less emphasis than the first sentence in a paragraph.

> The first criterion examined was cost. The Copy Cat sells for $2,750, and the Repro 100 sells for $2,100, or 24% less than the cost of the Copy Cat.

- Make the noun you want to emphasize the subject of the sentence. In other words, use active voice to emphasize the doer of the action and passive voice to emphasize the receiver.

> **ACTIVE** ▶ The Repro 100 costs 24% less than the Copy Cat.
> *(Emphasizes the Repro 100 rather than the Copy Cat)*

> **PASSIVE** ▶ The relative costs of the two models were compared first.
> *(Emphasizes the relative costs rather than the two models)*

- Devote more space to the idea.

> The two models were judged according to three criteria: cost, speed, and enlargement/reduction capabilities. Total cost is an important consideration for our firm because of the large number of copiers we use and our large volume of copying. Last year, our firm used 358 photocopiers and duplicated more than 6.5 million pages. Thus, regardless of the speed or features of a particular model, if it is too expensive to operate, it will not serve our purposes.

- Use language that directly implies importance, such as *most important, major,* or *primary*. Use terms such as *least important* or *a minor point* to subordinate an idea.

> The most important factor for us is cost. The service contract is a minor concern.

- Use repetition (within reason).

> However, the Copy Cat is expensive—expensive to purchase and expensive to operate.

- Use mechanical means (within reason)—enumeration, italics, second color, indenting from left and right margins, or other elements of design—to emphasize key ideas.

> But the most important criterion is cost, and the Repro 100 costs *24% less than* the Copy Cat.

The Ethical Dimension

Use emphasis and subordination to show your reader how important you consider each idea. Your goal is *not* to mislead the reader. If you believe that the Repro 100 is the *slightly* better choice, avoid intentionally misleading your reader into concluding that it is *clearly* the better choice. Achieve your communication objectives using fair tactics and sound business judgment.

Use Positive Language

By using positive instead of negative words, you are more likely to achieve your objectives. Positive language also helps to build goodwill and usually provides more information to your reader. Note the differences in tone and detail in the following sentences:

NOT The briefcase is not made of cheap imitation leather.

BUT The briefcase is made of 100% belt leather for years of durable service.

NOT We cannot ship your merchandise until we receive your check.

BUT As soon as we receive your check, we will ship your merchandise.

NOT I do not yet have any work experience.

BUT My two terms as secretary of the Management Club taught me the importance of accurate recordkeeping and gave me experience in working as part of a team.

Avoid negative-sounding words.

Expressions like *cannot* and *will not* are not the only ones that convey negative messages. Other words, like *mistake, damage, failure, refuse,* and *deny,* also carry negative connotations and should be avoided when possible.

Negative language also often has the opposite effect of what is intended. "Do not think of elephants." What are you thinking of now?

NOT Failure to follow the directions may cause the blender to malfunction.

BUT Following the directions will ensure many years of carefree service from your blender.

NOT We apologize for this error.

BUT We appreciate your telling us about this issue.

NOT We close at 7:00 P.M. on Fridays.

BUT We're open until 7:00 P.M. on Fridays to give you time to shop after work.

You'll find the entire email exchange on the author's blog, www .bizcominthenews.com, under Samples for Chapter 5.

Stress what is true and what *can* be done rather than what is not true and cannot be done. Of course, negative language is strong and has a place in business writing, but unless the situation clearly calls for negative language, you are more likely to achieve your objective by stressing the positive.

A journalism student learned the hard way that negative language often produces negative results. Steve Jobs, former CEO of Apple, was notorious for responding to emails personally—sometimes with curt replies. When the journalism student sent Jobs an email, an unkind exchange began.[9]

Although the student began with a positive introductory paragraph complimenting Apple's products, she used a critical subject line and strong language throughout. Apparently, she had contacted Apple's Media Relations Department for help with a class project but didn't get a response. She wrote that her questions were "vital to my academic grade as a student journalist" and used negative language that could, understandably, turn off the CEO of the company: "I have called countless times," "the Media Relations Department fails," "I have repeatedly told them," "ignored my needs," and "hypocrisy." Perhaps the worst offense was the student's email tagline: "Sent via BlackBerry from T-Mobile" (Apple's competition).

Steve Jobs responded with characteristic brevity—and the exchange continued. He first denied responsibility for the student's academic success, to which the student responded, among other missives, "I am on deadline." After more back-and-forth emails, Jobs, of course, had the last word: "Please leave us alone."

You have to admire the student's determination. She was persistent—although she may have found better success by focusing on more positive language and, as we'll discuss next, stressing the "you" attitude, rather than her own goals.

Stress the "You" Attitude

Are you more interested in how well *you* perform in this course or in how well your classmates perform? When you hear a television commercial, are you more interested in how the product will benefit *you* or in how your purchase of the product will benefit the sponsor? If you're like most people reading or hearing a message, your conscious or unconscious reaction is likely to be "What's in it for *me*?"

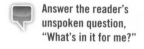
Answer the reader's unspoken question, "What's in it for me?"

Knowing that this is true provides you with a powerful strategy for structuring your messages to increase their impact: stress the "you" attitude, not the "me" attitude.

The **"you" attitude** emphasizes what the *receiver* (the listener or the reader) wants to know and how he or she will be affected by the message. It requires developing **empathy**—the ability to project yourself into another person's position and to understand that person's situation and feelings. To avoid sounding selfish and uninterested, focus on the reader—adopt the "you" attitude.

> **NOT** ▶ I am shipping your order this afternoon.
>
> **BUT** ▶ You should receive your order by Friday.

> **NOT** ▶ We will be open on Sundays from 1:00 to 5:00 P.M., beginning May 15.
>
> **BUT** ▶ You will be able to shop on Sundays from 1:00 to 5:00 P.M., beginning May 15.

Receiver Benefits

An important component of the "you" attitude is the concept of **receiver benefits**—emphasizing how the *receiver* (the reader or the listener) will benefit from doing as you ask. Sometimes, especially when asking a favor or refusing a request, the best we can do is to show how *someone* (not necessarily the reader) will benefit. But whenever possible, we should show how someone *other than ourselves* benefits from our request or from our decision.

> **NOT** ▶ We cannot afford to purchase an ad in your organization's directory.
>
> **BUT** ▶ Advertising exclusively on television allows us to offer consumers like you the lowest prices on their cosmetics.

NOT Our decorative fireplace has an oak mantel and is portable.

BUT Whether entertaining in your living room or den, you can still enjoy the ambience of a blazing fire because our decorative fireplace is portable. Simply take it with you from room to room.

Note that the revised sentences, which stress reader benefits, are longer than the original sentences—because they contain *more information*. But they do not contain unnecessary words. You can add information and still write concisely.

Exceptions

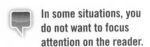

In some situations, you do not want to focus attention on the reader.

Stressing the "you" attitude focuses the attention on the reader, which is right where the attention should be—most of the time. However, when you refuse someone's request, disagree with someone, or talk about someone's mistakes or shortcomings, avoid connecting the reader too closely with the negative information. In these situations, avoid second-person pronouns (*you* and *your*), and use passive sentences or other subordinating techniques to stress the receiver of the action rather than the doer.

NOT You should have included more supporting evidence in your presentation.

BUT Including more supporting evidence would have made the presentation more convincing.

NOT You failed to return the merchandise within the 10-day period.

BUT We are happy to give a full refund on all merchandise that is returned within 10 days.

Note that neither of the revised sentences contains the word *you*. Instead, the revisions separate the reader from the negative information, making the message more tactful and palatable.

The Checklist for Revising Your Writing summarizes principles of style, which goes beyond *correctness*. Style involves choosing the right words, writing effective sentences, developing logical paragraphs, and setting an appropriate tone.

At first, you may find it difficult and time-consuming to revise your writing using these criteria. But your time spent will pay off: soon, you'll apply these principles unconsciously and will see a big improvement in your writing.

Checklist for Revising Your Writing   GO

Words

☑ **Write clearly.** Be accurate and complete; use familiar words; use specific, concrete language; avoid dangling expressions; and avoid clichés, slang, and unnecessary jargon.

☑ **Write concisely.** Avoid redundancy and wordy expressions, avoid hidden subjects and hidden verbs, and imply or condense when appropriate.

Sentences

☑ **Use a variety of sentence types.** Use simple sentences for emphasis, compound sentences for coordinate relationships, and complex sentences for subordinate relationships.

☑ **Use active and passive voice appropriately.** Use active voice in general and to emphasize the doer of the action; use passive voice to emphasize the receiver.

☑ **Use parallel structure.** Match adjectives with adjectives, nouns with nouns, infinitives with infinitives, and so on.

Paragraphs

☑ **Keep paragraphs unified and coherent.** Develop a single idea consistently and logically; use transitional words, pronouns, and repetition when appropriate.

☑ **Control paragraph length.** Use a variety of paragraph lengths.

Overall Tone

☑ **Write confidently.** Avoid sounding self-conscious, but also avoid sounding arrogant or presumptuous.

☑ **Use a courteous and sincere tone.** Avoid platitudes, exaggeration, obvious flattery, and expressions of surprise or disbelief.

☑ **Use appropriate emphasis and subordination.** Emphasize and subordinate through the use of sentence structure, position, verb voice, amount of space, language, repetition, and mechanical means.

☑ **Use positive language.** Stress what you *can* do or what *is* true rather than what you cannot do or what is not true.

☑ **Stress the "you" attitude.** Emphasize what the receiver wants to know and how the receiver will be affected by the message; stress receiver benefits.

Revising Content for an Entertainment Company Website

Purpose

Imagine that you work for an entertainment company as a web writer. You're responsible for all content on the website, but you don't write everything yourself. For example, for the "Company Information" page, you received the following blurb from the Television division.

> **TELEVISED ENTERTAINMENT**
>
> Each and every week there are over 11 million viewers who tune in to watch over fifteen hours of programming in the US and there is even more programming around the world. Join the millions watching today!

The blurb explains the large scope of the business but needs editing to be ready for the company website.

Process

You ask yourself the following questions as you start this editing job.

1. **What do you want to accomplish with the Company Information section of the website?**
   Encourage financial investment and advertising sponsorship.

2. **Who are your primary and secondary audiences?**
   External audiences—investors and the media. Television viewers may find this page, but they are not the primary audience for the Company Information section of the website.

3. **What tone is appropriate for this section of the website?**
   A professional, conversational tone—not too "salesy," but not too formal either. The draft isn't too formal, but the end of the first paragraph ("Join the millions watching today!") is a bit too much with the exclamation mark. The purpose of this part of the website is to provide information—not present a marketing pitch.

4. **How else can you improve the blurb?**
   I can remove wordiness and improve the sentence structure. I also can provide data about our growth, which may be important to potential investors and advertisers.

5. **What other changes are needed for accuracy?**
   Punctuation and number expressions need to be corrected.

Product

> **TELEVISED ENTERTAINMENT**
>
> Each week in the United States, more than 11 million viewers tune in to watch over 15 hours of programming. In Canada and Europe, an additional 4 million viewers watch our shows. Our viewership has more than doubled since January 2010, and we expect this trend to continue.

Revising an Email to Employees

Purpose

Imagine that you work for an entertainment company and have asked an intern to draft an email to employees about a summer dress code. The email will be distributed to 300 employees in the corporate office. You will allow employees to dress more casually during the warm weather, but you also want to give them clear guidelines on what is and is not acceptable to wear in the office. You receive the draft from the intern, but it needs work.

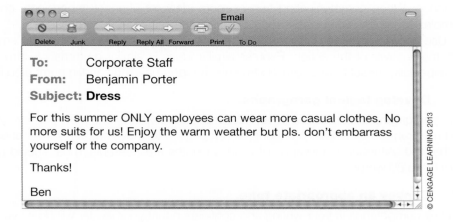

To: Corporate Staff
From: Benjamin Porter
Subject: Dress

For this summer ONLY employees can wear more casual clothes. No more suits for us! Enjoy the warm weather but pls. don't embarrass yourself or the company.

Thanks!

Ben

© CENGAGE LEARNING 2013

Process

1. What do you want to accomplish with this email?
2. What, specifically, do employees need to know?
3. What works well in this email draft?
4. What could be improved in this message?

Product

Rewrite the draft email for employees.

Summary

LO1   Choose the right words for your message.

Achieve clarity by making your message accurate, by using familiar words, and by avoiding dangling expressions and unnecessary jargon. Write to express—not to impress. Use longer words only if they express your idea more clearly. Use specific, concrete language and avoid clichés, slang, and buzzwords.

To achieve conciseness, make every word count. Avoid redundancy, wordy expressions, and hidden verbs and subjects. Sometimes you may imply rather than explicitly state certain information. In other situations, use adjectives or adverbs instead of clauses to convey information more concisely.

LO2   Write effective sentences.

Because they present a single idea and are usually short, prefer simple sentences for emphasis. Use compound sentences to communicate two or more ideas of equal importance. When communicating two or more ideas of unequal importance, choose complex sentences and place the subordinate idea in the dependent clause.

Use active voice to emphasize the doer of the action and passive voice to emphasize the receiver of the action. Express similar ideas in similar grammatical structure. Be especially careful to use parallel structure in report headings and in numbered lists.

LO3   Develop logical paragraphs.

Your paragraphs should be unified and coherent. Develop only one topic per paragraph, and use transitional words, pronouns, and repetition to move smoothly from one idea to the next. Although paragraphs of various lengths are desirable, most should range from 60 to 80 words.

LO4   Convey an appropriate tone.

Convey competence in your writing and confidence that your reader will do as you ask or will accept your decision. Avoid, however, sounding presumptuous or arrogant. Use a tone of courtesy and sincerity to build goodwill and to help you achieve your objectives.

Use emphasis and subordination to develop a common frame of reference between you and the reader. Positive rather than negative words are more likely to help you achieve your communication objective. Keep the emphasis on the reader—stressing what the reader needs to know and how the reader will be affected by the message.

Exercises

LO1   Choose the right words for your message.

1. Announce a new initiative using clear, simple language.

As the CEO of a growing business, you want to help employees save for retirement. Many of your employees receive minimum wage and have little experience with investing money. Write a simple, clear email to employees explaining what a 401(k) plan is, why employees should participate, and how it will work at your company. You may need to research 401(k) plans first; you will find information at sites such as www.irs.gov and Wikipedia.

For this new initiative, you will probably have in-person meetings, too, to explain the new plan. Imagine that this email is a starting point.

2. Write clearly and avoid slang.

These two sentences are filled with business slang and clichés. Revise them using simple, clear language.

> Using the synergies amongst our competitors, we can formulate a program that not only capitalizes on the strengths of each of our respective constituencies but that raises the bar to a new level for each and every one of us.
>
> At the end of the day, we need to think outside the box to look for low-hanging fruit, or we'll never reach our end goal.

3. Revise to eliminate dangling expressions.

Revise these sentences to eliminate dangling expressions.

a. Driving through Chicago in the fog, the street signs were hard to read.

b. The Federal Reserve banks maintain excellent relations with the major financial institutions, but they are still not doing as much as they had expected.

c. To become law, the governor must sign the bill by the end of the session.

d. While drilling a hole to bring in the wiring, a crack was created in the wall.

e. After attending the meeting, the minutes were prepared by the administrative assistant.

f. After resting in bed for several weeks, the doctor told the actor the plastic surgery was successful.

g. Although the owners have changed, they continue to expand.

h. Sitting in a diner on Main Street, hamburgers were enjoyed by the soccer team.

i. Purchased in Italy, I brought home several bottles of fantastic red wine.

j. To try out for *American Idol*, an entry form must be completed while you wait in line.

4. Choose concrete language.

When the U.S. government spent $700 billion in stimulus funding in 2008, the public had difficulty grasping this amount of money. Zephyr Teachout, an associate professor of law, tried to make this amount more tangible.[10] Which of the following concrete descriptions helps you grasp the magnitude of $700 billion? Under what circumstances might you use one description over another? Discuss your ideas in small groups.

a. It could pay for 2,000 McDonald's apple pies for every single American.

b. It is nine times the amount spent on education in 2007.

c. It is one-third of the total amount of money received by the federal government in 2007, including Social Security, income tax, corporate tax, and all other receipts.

d. It is $120 billion more than that spent on Social Security benefits.

e. It is almost 3 billion nonrefundable bus fares from Durham to San Francisco.

f. It is 35 times the amount spent on all foreign aid in most years.

g. It is more zeros than the calculator that comes with my computer allows.

h. It is 7,000 times bigger than the Sierra Club's yearly budget.

i. According to some estimates, it is three times what it would cost, over 10 years, to reduce oil dependency by 20%.

j. It is over twice the amount of all money given to all charitable organizations in the United States in any given year.

k. It is more than $100 for every person in the world.

5. Analyze a simple explanation of a complex topic.

Watch one or two videos by the company Common Craft, which creates short videos to make complex topics easy to understand.[11] Go to www.commoncraft.com or search YouTube for "Common Craft," and choose a topic that interests you. What about the video helps you understand the topic? Consider the use of words and graphics to explain abstract topics. Giving specific examples from the video, write a one-page analysis and submit it to your instructor.

6. Use simple language.

Revise this paragraph to make it more understandable.

> The privileged juvenile was filled with abundant glee when her fashion mogul employer designated her as the contemporary representative of an ostentatious couture line. Although she was temporarily employed for the summer for an internship in the design department, her adolescent ambition was to enrich her life as a model. Subsequent to altering her hair, administering makeup, and adorning herself with the fashion designer's creations, she advanced in front of the photographer's lenses, beginning the succession of fulfilling her dreams.

7. Use specific and concrete words.

Revise this paragraph to use more specific, concrete language. You may make up information.

> To stimulate sales, Apple is lowering prices substantially on its line of electronic items. Sometime soon, it will ship out to most of its stores various electronic accessories to hand out to select lucky customers as a promotion for the sale. Markdowns will range from very little on its MacBook line to a great deal on certain iPod devices. Apple plans to rely on Internet marketing to let people know of these price reductions. In particular, it is considering using a popular celebrity to publicize the new pricing strategy.

8. Eliminate wordy expressions.

Revise the following sentences to eliminate wordy phrases by substituting a single word wherever possible. You may find other opportunities to tighten for conciseness.

a. Push the red button in the event that you see smoke rising from the cooking surface.

b. More than 40% of the people polled are of the opinion that government spending should be reduced.

c. Please send me more information pertaining to your new line of pesticides.

d. Due to the fact that two of the three highway lanes were closed for repairs, I was nearly 20 minutes late for my appointment.

e. Chef Ramsay, who was formerly my instructor at culinary school, is in today's society the owner of several restaurants, which are all over the world.

f. The newest sports automobile trend is to install seats made out of leather.

g. Google is now taking applications for job positions at this point in time, in spite of the fact that they just laid off employees.

h. We have the ability to vote for the best performer on TV by text messaging the on-screen telephone number.

9. Eliminate hidden verbs and hidden subjects.

Revise the following sentences to eliminate hidden verbs and hidden subjects.

a. The jury needs to carry out a review of the case to make a decision about whether the actress has a violation of her alcohol probation.

b. For our road trip during spring break, we must undertake the calculations of our driving travel time from California to New York.

c. If you cannot make the payment for the $135 tickets, you will not be able to make backstage visitations for the Lollapalooza concerts.

d. After much deliberation, the group came to a decision about how to make a response to the lawsuit.

e. Although Hugh wanted to offer an explanation of his actions, his boss refused to listen.

f. If confused about the assignment, there are some diagrams that you should review.

g. It is our intent to complete the project by Friday at 3:00 P.M.

h. There are four principles of marketing that we need to consider.

10. Identify types of sentences.

What type of sentence—simple, compound, or complex—is each of the following? Internal punctuation has been omitted to avoid giving hints. Compare your answers to others' in the class.

a. Now that she has found her true love "The Bachelorette" wants women everywhere to know that it is worth it to wait for the right guy.

b. Hillary went to see the new branch manager but the manager had gone to lunch.

c. The new single from the band's album is out on Tuesday while the demo version which you can download on iTunes will be available on Monday.

d. You will have 12 hours to complete the job.

e. I will try to get the project finished and shipped to you by tomorrow.

LO2 Write effective sentences.

f.   Everyone seems to be feeding off the intensity at the physically challenging football camp particularly the defensive tackles who often sport aggressive expressions.

g.   The milestone homer provided an encouraging lift during a trying stretch for the baseball team.

h.   Walking down the street with my sister I saw two men dressed in dark suits running out of the bank.

i.   See the coach and turn in your gear.

j.   Please clean your room when you have finished your homework.

k.   The fifth order arrives today it should be the last one.

11. Practice writing different types of sentences.

Write a simple, a compound, and a complex sentence that incorporates both items of information in each bullet. For the complex sentences, emphasize the first idea in each item.

a.   The new smartphone will be available on Wednesday / The smartphone will have more features than the older model.

b.   The captain got promoted to a major today / He will lead the army into battle.

c.   Tim was promoted / Tim was assigned additional responsibilities.

d.   Eileen is our corporate counsel / Eileen will draft the letter for us.

12. Practice sentence variety.

Rewrite the following paragraph by varying sentence types and sentence lengths to keep the writing interesting.

> Smartfood was founded by Ann Withey, Andrew Martin, and Ken Meyers in 1984. The product was the first snack food to combine white cheddar cheese and popcorn. Ann Withey perfected the Smartfood recipe in her home kitchen after much trial and error. Smartfood sales were reportedly only $35,000 in 1985. During that time, the product was available only in New England. By 1988, sales had soared to $10 million. This attracted the attention of Frito-Lay. The snack-food giant bought Smartfood in 1989 for $15 million. Since the purchase, Frito-Lay has not tampered with the popular Smartfood formula. It has used its marketing expertise to keep sales growing, despite the growing number of challengers crowding the cheesy popcorn market.

13. Vary sentence length.

Write a long sentence (40 to 50 words) about a company or person you admire. Then revise the sentence so that it contains 10 or fewer words. Finally, rewrite the sentence so that it contains 16 to 22 words. Which sentence is the most effective? Why?

14. Use active and passive voice.

Working in groups of three, identify whether each of the following sentences is active or passive. Then, discuss whether the sentence uses active or passive voice appropriately and why. Next, change the sentences that use an inappropriate voice.

Sentence Example	Active or Passive Voice?	Appropriate Use? (If not, then rewrite the sentence.)
a. A very effective sales letter was written by Paul Mendelson.		
b. Our old office will be sold to a real estate developer.		
c. You failed to verify the figures on the quarterly report.		
d. The website designed by Catalina Graphics did not reflect our company's image.		

15. Check and revise sentences for parallel structure.

Determine whether the following sentences use parallel structure. Revise sentences as needed to make the structure parallel.

a. The executive at Ernst & Young writes reports quickly, accurately, and in detail.

b. The bride hates wearing heels, and on her wedding day, she just wanted to wear flats, be able to dance around, and be comfortable.

c. The store is planning to install a new point-of-sale system that is easier to operate, easier to repair, and cheaper to maintain than the current system.

d. Angelina's children like to go swimming, biking, and play tennis.

e. According to the survey, most employees prefer either holding the employee cafeteria open later or its hours to be kept the same.

f. The quarterback is expert not only in calling plays but also in throwing passes.

g. Our career guide will cover writing résumés, cover letters, and techniques for interviewing.

16. Guess the sentence order in this paragraph.

Can you identify the order of these sentences within one paragraph? *Hint:* The broadest statement will be the first sentence. Place a number (from 1 to 6) next to each sentence to represent its position within the paragraph.

L03 Develop logical paragraphs.

Both Kelvin Electronics and PC Richards pay a higher starting salary than we offer, and neither has the commission cap that we have in place.	
In addition to the turnover issue, our compensation is not competitive.	
We have had the same plan in place for over five years, and it's time to consider an update.	
In the past year, we have had a 40% turnover in sales staff.	
We need to reevaluate the sales compensation plan.	
During exit interviews, all of these staff identified compensation as the main reason they resigned.	

17. Order sentences into a logical paragraph.

From the following sentences, select the best topic sentence; then list the other sentences in an appropriate order.

a. The Accord has 17-inch alloy wheels.

b. The car's wide-opening doors provide easy access to the interior.

c. With an automatic reverse feature, the moonroof is safe.

d. The Accord is a good choice for today's active driver.

e. The Honda Accord is a well-designed, functional car that will attract attention.

f. In a variety of colors, the Accord will stand out in the crowd.

g. The one-touch power moonroof with tilt is easy to operate.

18. Use transitions for paragraph coherence.

Revisit the Honda Accord paragraph in the previous exercise. Now that you have sentences in a logical order, add transitions to improve coherence.

19. Insert transitions for paragraph coherence.

Insert logical transitions in the blanks to give the following paragraph coherence.

Bits 'n' Bytes is widening its lead over Desktop Computing in the computer-magazine war. _____ its revenues increased 27% last year, whereas Desktop Computing's increased only 16%. _____ its audited paid circulation increased to 600,000, compared to 450,000 for Desktop Computing. _____ Desktop Computing was able to increase both the ad rate and the number of ad pages last year. One note of worry _____ is Desktop Computing's decision to shut down its independent testing laboratory. Some industry leaders believe much of Desktop Computing's success has been due to its reliable product reviews. _____ Bits 'n' Bytes has just announced an agreement whereby Stanford University's world-famous engineering school will perform product testing for Bits 'n' Bytes.

20. Adjust paragraph length.

Read the following paragraph and determine how it might be divided into two or more shorter paragraphs to help the reader follow the complex topic being discussed.

Transforming a manuscript into a published book requires several steps. After the author submits the manuscript, the copy editor makes any needed grammatical or spelling changes. The author reviews these changes to be sure that they haven't altered the meaning of any sentences or sections. Next, the publisher begins the design process. At this point, designers select photographs and other artwork and create page layouts, which show how the pages will look when printed. The author and publisher review these page proofs for any errors. Only after all corrections have been made does the book get published. From start to finish, this process can take as long as a year.

L04 Convey an appropriate tone.

21. Revise to convey an appropriate tone.

Revise the paragraph to create a more confident, less presumptuous tone.

If you believe my proposal has merit, I hope that you will allocate $50,000 for a pilot study. It's possible that this pilot study will achieve my profit estimates so that we can implement the idea in other locations. Even though you have several other worthwhile projects to consider for funding, I know you will agree the proposal should be funded prior to January 1. Please call me before the end of the week to tell me that you've accepted my proposal.

22. Revise to convey a confident tone.

Revise the following sentences to convey an appropriately confident attitude.

a. Can you think of any reason not to buy a wristwatch for dressy occasions?

b. I hope you agree that my offer provides good value for the money.

c. Of course, I am confident that my offer provides good value for the money.

d. You might try to find a few minutes to visit our gallery on your next visit to galleries in this area.

23. Revise this passage to avoid platitudes, obvious flattery, and exaggeration.

You, our loyal and dedicated employees, have always been the most qualified and the hardest working in the industry. Because of your faithful and dependable service, I was quite surprised to learn yesterday that an organizational meeting for union representation was recently held here. You must realize that a company like ours cannot survive unless we hold labor costs down. I cannot believe that you don't appreciate the many benefits of working at Allied. We will immediately have to declare bankruptcy if a union is voted in. Please don't be fooled by empty rhetoric.

24. Vary emphasis in a memo.

Assume that you have evaluated two candidates for the position of sales assistant. This is what you have learned:

- Carl Barteolli has more sales experience.
- Elizabeth Larson has more appropriate formal training (earned a college degree in marketing and attended several three-week sales seminars).
- Elizabeth Larson's personality is a better fit for the corporate culture.

You must write a memo to Robert Underwood, the vice president, recommending one of these candidates. First, assume that personality is the most important criterion, and write a memo recommending Elizabeth Larson. Second, assume that experience is the most important criterion, and write a memo recommending Carl Barteolli. Use appropriate emphasis and subordination in each message. You may make up any reasonable information needed to complete the assignment.

25. Use positive language.

Revise the following paragraph to eliminate negative language.

We cannot issue a full refund at this time because you did not enclose a receipt or an authorized estimate. I'm sorry that we will have to delay your reimbursement. We are not like those insurance companies that promise you anything but then disappear when you have a claim. When we receive your receipt or estimate, we will not hold up your check. Our refusal to issue reimbursement without proper supporting evidence means that we do not have to charge you outlandish premiums for your automobile insurance.

26. Make a positive impression.

Revise the following signs often seen in stores:

a. "No shirt, no shoes, no service."

b. "American Express cards not accepted."

c. "No returns without receipts."

d. "No smoking."

e. "No dogs allowed."

27. Stress the "you" attitude in sentences.

Revise the following sentences to make the reader the center of attention.

a. I need the scholarship so I can go to a four-year college.

b. We have been providing affordable cleaning services to houses in the college town area for over a decade.

c. Our stores will be closed to all customers for the weekend to stock the shelves with discounted items in preparation for the holiday sales.

28. Stress the "you" attitude in a paragraph.

Revise the following paragraph to make the reader the center of attention.

> We are happy to announce that we are offering for sale an empty parcel of land at the corner of Mission and High Streets. We will be selling this parcel for $89,500, with a minimum down payment of $22,500. We have had the lot rezoned M-2 for student housing. We originally purchased this lot because of its proximity to the university and had planned to erect student housing, but our investment plans have changed. We still believe that our lot would make a profitable site for up to three 12-unit buildings.

29. Use a "you" attitude and positive language.

Rewrite this email from a facilities manager to country club members. How can you stress the "you" attitude and focus on good news without misleading members?

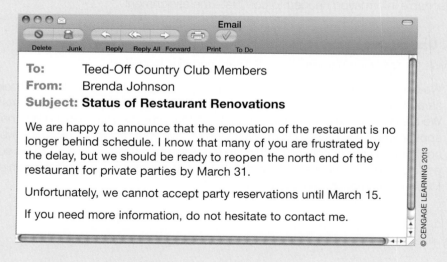

To:	Teed-Off Country Club Members
From:	Brenda Johnson
Subject:	**Status of Restaurant Renovations**

We are happy to announce that the renovation of the restaurant is no longer behind schedule. I know that many of you are frustrated by the delay, but we should be ready to reopen the north end of the restaurant for private parties by March 31.

Unfortunately, we cannot accept party reservations until March 15.

If you need more information, do not hesitate to contact me.

© CENGAGE LEARNING 2013

30. Emphasize receiver benefits.

Revise the following sentences to emphasize receiver benefits.

a. We have been in the business of repairing sewing machines for more than 40 years.

b. We need donations so that we can expand the free-food program in this community.

c. Company policy requires us to impose a 2% late charge when customers don't pay their bills on time.

d. Although the refund department is open from 9:00 A.M. to 5:00 P.M., it is closed from 1:00 P.M. to 2:00 P.M. so that our employees can take their lunch breaks.

Company Scenario

© ISTOCKPHOTO.COM/SIRIMO

Writeaway Hotels

COURTESY OF ED MARION, EDMARION.COM

Writeaway Hotels

Even in a fast-paced company like Writeaway Hotels, your writing reflects on your credibility as a business professional. Take this opportunity to revise some of the emails you created for this simulation in Chapter 4.

To do this, you might look over your sent messages and choose a few to edit. Or, you might sign into another student's email—for the character he or she played—and choose a few messages to edit. How can you improve your writing now that you have more time?

Another option is to practice by revising the following emails—sent by students who participated in this simulation in the past. For their future writing, what advice would you give these students? In the first email exchange, Pat responds to Diana, the upset client; in the second email, Pat responds to Ron, the HR manager. For the response to Ron, you might consider lessons learned about potential legal consequences of communication, discussed in Chapter 1.

Missed Conference Call   Inbox | X

☆ ● Diana1 Chavez to me   show details 9:45 AM (0 minutes ago)   ↩ Reply ▼

Pat,

Why weren't you on the conference call this morning with Bill? We just talked about this yesterday, so I'm sure you knew about it. I was embarrassed that you weren't on.

This brings up a bigger issue: I'm glad business is going so well for you and that you have a lot of new clients. But I'm starting to feel like I'm getting less attention now, and I want to make sure that we can maintain the good working relationship we've had in the past.

Diana

↩ Reply   → Forward   ● Diana1 is not available to chat

☆ ● Pat2 Gibson to Diana1   show details 9:46 AM (0 minutes ago)   ↩ Reply ▼

Diana Banana,

You know I love ya, babe! I had family issue that required my immediate attention. It won't happen again.

Pat

↩ Reply   → Forward   ● Diana1 is not available to chat

Confidential   Inbox | X

☆ ● Ron1 Harrison to me   show details 9:32 AM (15 minutes ago)   ↩ Reply ▼

Dear Pat,

We need to talk. Someone in your department filed a sexual harassment complaint, and I'd like to discuss it with you. Are you available tomorrow at 10:00? That time would work best for me. Please let me know asap.

Regards,
Ron

↩ Reply   → Forward   ● Ron1 is not available to chat

☆ ● Pat11 Gibson to Ron1   show details 9:33 AM (14 minutes ago)   ↩ Reply ▼

Hello Mr. Harrison,

Yes, that incident did occur in my department. I will definitely discuss the matter with you tomorrow morning at 10:00.

↩ Reply   → Forward   ● Ron1 is not available to chat

© CENGAGE LEARNING 2013

Notes

1. "Funny Headlines," www .plainlanguage.gov/examples/ humor/headlines.cfm, accessed July 30, 2010.
2. Tim Webb, "BP Boss Admits Job on the Line over Gulf Oil Spill," *The Guardian*, May 14, 2010, www .guardian.co.uk, accessed July 30, 2010.
3. Daniel M. Oppenheimer, "Consequences of Erudite Vernacular Utilized Irrespective of Necessity: Problems with Using Long Words Needlessly," *Applied Cognitive Psychology*, vol. 20, pp. 139–156 (2006). Quoted in Richard Morin, "Nerds Gone Wild," The 2006 Ig Nobel Awards, Pew Center Research Publications, October 6, 2006, http://pewresearch .org/pubs/72/nerds-gone-wild, accessed October 23, 2010.
4. Dave Zinczenko and Matt Goulding, "The 5 Worst Kids' Meals in America," July 23, 2010, http://today .msnbc.msn.com/id/38367754/ns/ today-today_health/t/worst-kids-meals-america/, accessed July 30, 2010.
5. "What Silly Sounding Business Jargon Do You Have to Hear al [sic] the Time? Discuss!" Mark Hanes, Response to LinkedIn Questions, August 18, 2008, www.linkedin.com, accessed August 2, 2010.
6. "Improving Communication from the Federal Government to the Public," Plain Language Action and Information Network (PLAIN), www.diversityrx.org/resources/ plain-language-improving-communication-federal-government-public, accessed August 1, 2010.
7. Richard A. Lanham, *Revising Business Prose* (New York: Scribner's, 1981), p. 2.
8. This example has been modified to protect the writer.
9. Adrian Chen, "Steve Jobs in Email Pissing Match with College Journalism Student," Gawker, September 17, 2010, www.gawker .com/5641211/steve-jobs-in-email-pissing-match-with-college-journalism-student, accessed October 19, 2010.
10. Zephyr Teachout, Selected from "How Much Is 700 Billion?" September 21, 2008, www .techpresident.com/node/6362, accessed August 2, 2010.
11. Common Craft Home Page, www.commoncraft.com, accessed August 2, 2010.

Chapter 6

Neutral and Positive Messages

LEARNING OBJECTIVES

After you have finished this chapter, you should be able to

L01 Compose a neutral message.

L02 Respond to a neutral message.

L03 Compose a goodwill message.

L04 Address customer comments online.

"Nordstrom has a reputation for personal service, but this is the first time I received a written thank-you note from any salesperson there—or from any store.[1]"

— NORDSTROM CUSTOMER

Chapter Introduction: Personal Communication at Nordstrom

Nordstrom, the luxury retailer, knows how to communicate with customers. With stiff competition in the luxury market, Nordstrom differentiates itself through exceptional service. The company's service reputation is so well known that businesses in other industries are sometimes called the "Nordstrom of...[the industry]." For example, Apple has been referred to as the "Nordstrom of Technology" for its attention to customers.[2]

Nordstrom's approach is low tech and personal. *The Nordstrom Way*, a book about Nordstrom's service culture, describes sales associates' relationships with customers. In one example, a customer at the Michigan Avenue store in Chicago told a salesperson, "I love the coat, but it's way too expensive. But if it ever goes on sale, will you please let me know." The salesperson made a note, called the customer when the price dropped, and shipped the coat to her. This was a routine request, but it received an extraordinary response.[3]

At Nordstrom, sales associates sometimes send handwritten notes to reflect their special relationships with customers. This is just one of the many ways Nordstrom has developed a legendary service reputation.

Nordstrom makes personalized customer communication a hallmark of its service.

© AP IMAGES/ELAINE THOMPSON

TYPES OF NEUTRAL AND POSITIVE MESSAGES

Business communication is often about routine topics. A small business owner asks for information from a supplier, a manager at a large corporation sends an email about a minor policy change, a customer calls a store for product information, a manager compliments an employee, or a customer writes positive comments about a company online. Although routine, these messages are important to run a business.

To distinguish these examples from more difficult communication—persuasive and bad-news messages covered in the next chapters—we'll refer to these as *neutral* or *positive* messages. These communications can be internal or external and may be presented in any communication medium.

PLANNING A NEUTRAL OR POSITIVE MESSAGE

 The direct style presents the major idea first, followed by explanations and details.

When a message conveys neutral or positive information to an audience who will likely be interested in what we have to say, we use a **direct organizational plan**. The main idea is stated first, followed by explanations and details, and then a friendly closing. Most neutral and positive messages follow the direct plan. In the example in Figure 1, Build-A-Bear Workshop announces a new store opening.[4]

Using a direct organizational plan for neutral and positive messages puts the major news first—where it stands out and gets the most attention. For busy media representatives, who receive many news releases each day, having the main points up front saves time and allows them to skim the message. The **indirect organizational plan**, in which the reasons are presented before the major idea, is sometimes used for bad-news and persuasive messages.

First determine whether a written message is needed.

A written message is not always the best medium for achieving your objective. As we discussed earlier, email is often overused in organizations; calling someone or walking down the hall to a colleague's office may work better in some cases. For quick interactions, an instant message or a text message may be enough.

However, for many situations, a written message will be the best choice. When you need to reach many employees, or you don't have a customer's phone number, or you need a record of your conversation, follow these guidelines for organizing your written message.

LO1 Compose a neutral message.

ORGANIZING A NEUTRAL MESSAGE

A message is neutral if you anticipate that the reader will do as you ask without having to be persuaded. For example, a request for specific information about an organization's product is neutral because all organizations appreciate the opportunity to promote their products. However, a request for free product samples might require a *persuasive* message to convince the company to do something that will cost money.

Figure 1   Build-A-Bear Press Release

Uses standard formatting and information for a company press release.

ORLANDO INTERNATIONAL AIRPORT

Contact
Shannon Lammert
314-423-8000 ext. 5379
314-556-8841 (cell)
Shannon@buildabear.com

Jill Saunders
314-423-8000 ext. 5293
314-422-4523 (cell)
JillS@buildabear.com

Includes a clear, specific title and subtitle to describe the positive news.

FOR IMMEDIATE RELEASE
Build-A-Bear Workshop to Open First Store at Airport
Build-A-Bear Workshop announces new store in Orlando International Airport

Summarizes main points in the first paragraph for the direct organizational plan.

ST. LOUIS (April 27, 2011) - Build-A-Bear Workshop®, the interactive entertainment retailer of customized stuffed animals, is teaming up with Orlando International Airport to open a new store in mid-May. Of the more than 400 operating locations around the world, this will be the first Build-A-Bear Workshop store located inside an airport.

Expresses enthusiasm with a quotation.

"We are very excited about our relationship with Orlando International Airport and to bring Build-A-Bear Workshop to this location," said Maxine Clark, founder and chief executive bear of Build-A-Bear Workshop. "Making a furry friend is a great way to celebrate a memorable vacation. We think this store is going to be a hit for traveling families."

Adds details and examples.

The Build-A-Bear Workshop store at Orlando International Airport will provide the same experience and interaction as mall-based Build-A-Bear Workshop retail locations. When Guests visit, they will choose from a variety of animals to make, including limited edition furry friends. They stuff their new friend, give it a heart filled with wishes, and make a personalized birth certificate. Guests can further personalize their new friend and choose from a wide selection of unique fashions and accessories.

Grab and go and new Build-A-Bear Workshop Craftshop™ items will also be offered at this store location to provide young Guests with fun activities to keep them occupied in the airport and during their flights. This assortment includes:

Uses bullet points for short, parallel points.

- Stickers
- Activity Books
- Coloring Books
- Make-Your-Own Card Kit

"Creating fun, long lasting memories is just part of the 'Orlando Experience' at Orlando International Airport (MCO), and it's also part of what Build-A-Bear Workshop brings to our airport. The addition allows passengers of all ages to take this one-of-a-kind experience in an airport with them on their travels," said Manager of Concessions for the Greater Orlando Aviation Authority, Linda Baratta.

Includes related information about the company.

The majority of Build-A-Bear Workshop stores are located within shopping malls. Build-A-Bear Workshop also has non-traditional store locations within three Major League Baseball ballparks, a store in the Saint Louis Zoo, a store in the Saint Louis Science Center, and stores located within select Rain Forest Café® and T-Rex Café locations. The first Build-A-Bear Workshop store in a hospital opened in March 2011 at Cook Children's Medical Center in Fort Worth, TX.

Major Idea First

When making a routine request, present the major idea—your request—clearly and directly in the first sentence or two. You may use a direct question, a statement, or a polite request to present the main idea. A polite request can take a period instead of a question mark, such as "May I please have your answer by March 3." Use a polite request when you expect the reader to respond by *acting* rather than by actually giving a yes-or-no answer.

 Use a direct question, polite request, or statement to present your request.

Always pose your request clearly and politely, and give any background information needed to set the stage. Following are examples of effective routine requests:

Direct Question

Does Black & Decker offer educational discounts? Blair Junior High School will soon replace approximately 50 portable electric drills used by our industrial technology students.

Statement

Please let me know how I might invest in your deferred money-market fund. As an American currently working in Bangkok, Thailand, I cannot easily take advantage of your automatic monthly deposit plan.

Polite Request

Would you please answer several questions about the work performance of Janice Henry. She has applied for the position of financial analyst at Citibank and gave your name as a reference.

© CENGAGE LEARNING 2013

Decide in advance how much detail you need. If you need only a one-sentence reply, phrase your request to elicit that response.

NOT ▶ Please explain the features of your Google Docs program.

BUT ▶ Does your Google Docs program automatically number lines and paragraphs?

 Do not ask more questions than are necessary. Make the questions easy to answer.

Remember that you are imposing on the goodwill of the reader. Ask as few questions as possible—and never ask for information that you can easily get on your own. If many questions *are* necessary, number them; most readers will answer questions in order and will be less likely to skip one unintentionally. Yes-or-no questions or short-answer questions are easy for the reader to answer, but when you need more information, use open-ended questions.

Arrange your questions in logical order (for example, order of importance, chronological order, or simple-to-complex order), word each question clearly and objectively (to avoid bias), and limit the content to one topic per question. If appropriate, assure the reader that the information provided will be treated confidentially.

Explanation and Details

 Explain why you're making the request.

Most of the time, you'll need to explain your initial request. Include background information (the reason for asking) either immediately before or after making the request.

For example, suppose you received the polite request asking about Janice Henry's job performance. Unless you were also told that the request came from a potential employer and that Janice Henry had given your name as a reference, you might be reluctant to provide such confidential information.

Or assume that you're writing to a former employer or professor asking for a letter of recommendation. You might need to give some background about yourself to jog the reader's memory. Put yourself in the reader's position. What information would you need to answer the request accurately and completely?

 If possible, show how others benefit from your receiving the requested information.

A reader is more likely to cooperate if you can show how responding to the request will benefit him or her.

Will you please complete our five-minute survey about your online banking needs. We're revamping our website to make it easier for you to navigate.

You can skip the benefits when they're obvious. An email asking employees to recycle their paper would probably not need to discuss the value of recycling, which most people already know.

Friendly Closing

Use a friendly, positive tone in your last paragraph. In your closing, express appreciation for the assistance, state and justify any deadlines, or offer to reciprocate. Make your closing specific to the purpose and original.

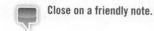 Close on a friendly note.

> **NOT** I need the information by October 1.

> **BUT** May I please have the product information by October 1, so I can include Kodak products in the next catalog.

> **NOT** Thank you in advance for your assistance in this matter.

> **BUT** Thank you for providing this information, which will help us make a fairer evaluation of Janice Henry's qualifications for this position.

> **NOT** Let me know how I can help you in the future.

> **BUT** Please let me know if I can return the favor by attending the meeting with Gupta Associates next week.

Figure 2 illustrates how *not* to write an effective routine request. This email has been modified but is very close to the original message. For an improved version, see Figure 3.

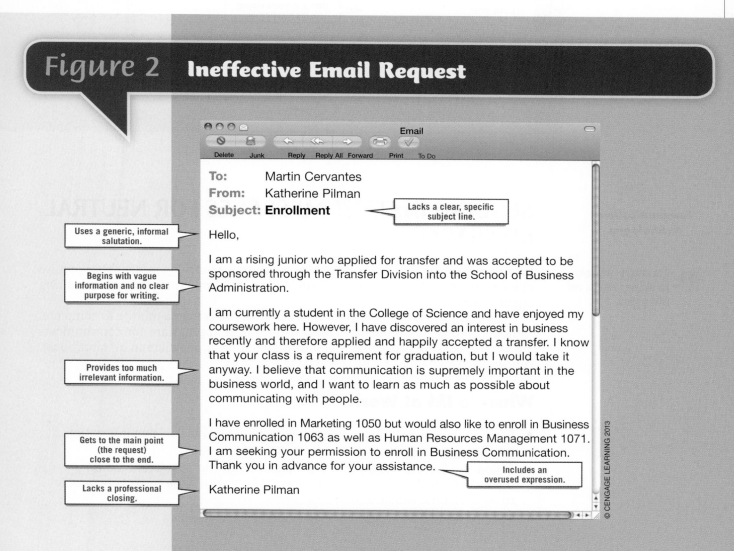

Figure 2   Ineffective Email Request

Figure 3   Revised Email Request

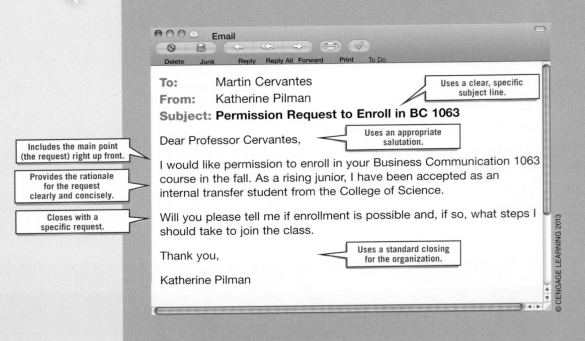

To: Martin Cervantes
From: Katherine Pilman
Subject: **Permission Request to Enroll in BC 1063**

Uses a clear, specific subject line.

Dear Professor Cervantes,

Uses an appropriate salutation.

Includes the main point (the request) right up front.

I would like permission to enroll in your Business Communication 1063 course in the fall. As a rising junior, I have been accepted as an internal transfer student from the College of Science.

Provides the rationale for the request clearly and concisely.

Closes with a specific request.

Will you please tell me if enrollment is possible and, if so, what steps I should take to join the class.

Thank you,

Uses a standard closing for the organization.

Katherine Pilman

© CENGAGE LEARNING 2013

Communication Technologies

Use instant messages for simple requests and information.

SENDING INSTANT MESSAGES FOR NEUTRAL MESSAGES

Instant messaging (IM) is a good choice for simple, neutral messages that require quick responses. The example in Figure 4 is an IM from a major global consulting organization.

This example, like most instant messages, took less than a minute to complete. Although proper grammar isn't used here, this is appropriate for communicating with coworkers you know well (but may not be appropriate in all situations). Follow these guidelines for effective IM use at work:

When to IM at Work

- Send an IM when you have a simple question, need to convey information quickly, or need a fast response from someone.
- Follow the culture within your organization. How do your peers use IM instead of email? For example, do they IM only with close coworkers or only to address time-sensitive issues?
- Keep IMs short. For longer messages, use email instead.

> Employee 1: do you know how to undo split screens?
> Employee 1: on excel?
> Employee 2: yup
> Employee 1: how?
> Employee 2: go into ... one sec
> Employee 2: ok highlight the column or row where the split is
> Employee 2: go into Window
> Employee 2: click freeze panes
> Employee 2: that should do it
> Employee 1: thanks!
> Employee 2: no prob

Figure 4
Sample IM for a Neutral Message

© CENGAGE LEARNING 2013

- Avoid using instant messaging for personal or confidential business information. Instant messages, like email, can be automatically saved on a computer or server.

- Avoid excessive personal messaging at work. This overuse is similar to making too many personal calls and may affect your productivity and damage your credibility.

How to IM at Work

- Create a professional screen name. The name you have from middle school is probably not acceptable in the business world. Make your screen name similar to your name, so people can recognize it easily. If you use a company-wide (enterprise) system to IM, you will be assigned a screen name.

- Follow the communication custom within your organization when initiating an IM. You may start by asking, "Is this a good time?" or "Got a sec?"

- Keep instant messages short and focused. You can say, "How's it going?" or "How are you?" but get to the point quickly. When you finish asking your question or making your point, say goodbye so that the recipient can get back to other work.

- Follow grammar, punctuation, and capitalization standards within the organization. If your manager follows good writing principles, you should follow suit. Even though IM is fast, your messages should still be reasonably error free.

- Avoid using abbreviations, such as "u" and "r," unless the recipient has used them first. Also, use emoticons such as smiley faces sparingly, and avoid elaborate fonts and colors.

- Follow your company's IM policy, and be aware of viruses and security risks. Avoid accepting IMs from people you don't know, and—as with email—don't open attachments unless you trust the source.

LO2   Respond to a neutral message.

RESPONDING TO A NEUTRAL MESSAGE

In this section, we'll look at responses to requests for information and neutral customer feedback. In the next chapter, we'll discuss how to respond to negative feedback from customers.

Follow these guidelines when responding to requests and other neutral messages:

- Respond promptly. You'll want prospective customers to receive your information before they make a purchase decision—and possibly go to a competitor. Research shows that customers expect a response within 24 hours, and satisfaction levels drop sharply if responses take longer.[5] However, quicker

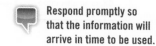
Respond promptly so that the information will arrive in time to be used.

responses are best. For requests posted online, for example, on Twitter, customers may expect a response within just an hour or two.

- Respond courteously. Your response represents the organization. A reply that sounds terse or burdened misses an opportunity to build goodwill.

  NOT Although we do not generally provide the type of information you requested, we have decided to do so in this case.

  BUT We are happy to provide the information you requested.

- Use a direct organizational plan. Make it easy for the reader to understand your response by putting the "good news"—the fact that you're responding favorably—up front. This pattern is the same as a neutral request.

  NOT I have received your request of June 26 asking me to speak at the meeting.

  BUT I would be pleased to speak at your Engineering Society meeting on August 8. Thank you for thinking of me.

- Answer all the questions asked or implied, using objective and clearly understood language.
- Personalize your response. Even if you start with a form letter, include your reader's name and tailor the message to specific requests.
- Promote your company, products, or services—within reason. You may choose a subtle sales approach when responding to simple requests.
- Close your response on a positive, friendly note. Avoid such clichés as "If you have additional questions, please don't hesitate to let me know." Use original wording, personalized especially for the reader.

In the example in Figure 5, the Garmin representative answers a quick question within the same day. The writer gives clear, concise information.

In the next example, Southside Brewery responds to a customer inquiry with personalized, thorough information (Figure 6).

Figure 5　Neutral Customer Question and Response

Judy's question is simple, and the urgency is clear.

This is Judy's main concern, which could be presented first.

Gives the most important part—the positive answer—up front.

Links to more detailed information.

Offers an alternative, depending on Judy's situation.

Ask Garmin: Will the Garminfone sync with Outlook?
June 18, 2010 – posted in Ask Garmin, On the Go.

Today's Ask Garmin question comes from Judy. "I cannot find the answer to my question anywhere. Maybe you can help. I want to pick up a Garminfone, but I cannot find out if it will sync with Outlook. This is a deal breaker for me."

Introduction can be omitted for an even more direct style.

Thanks for the great question, Judy. The really short answer to your question is yes. The Garminfone has on-device sync with Microsoft Exchange for Outlook email. If you're using a personal, non-enterprise version of Outlook, you can sync your email by first downloading the free sync software from the GarminAsus.com website. If you're on your company's enterprise server, you will need to contact your network administrator to obtain the necessary information about your network prior to being able to sync your Outlook email, contacts, and calendar.

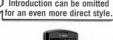

Figure 6

Personalized Response to a Customer's Inquiry

September 5, 2013

Mr. Derek Morris
13 Barnes Street
Dallas, TX 75202

> Uses the standard block-letter format on company stationery.

> Includes the standard letter salutation.

Dear Mr. Morris:

> Immediately addresses the customer's inquiry about a function on a specific date.

Southside Brewery would be delighted to host Moniker's office party. Thank you for thinking of us for your event. Yes, we have a private room that will accommodate up to 25 people, and we do have availability on December 9.

> Explains two options to meet the customer's needs.

> Attaches relevant information.

We offer two options for private parties: a full menu or a fixed-price limited menu. For the full menu, your guests would simply order from our regular lunch menu, and we would charge you accordingly. I have enclosed a menu for your reference. If you prefer a limited menu, we could offer a fixed price depending on the items you choose. For example, for $15 per person (not including beverages and dessert), your guests could choose from these items:

> Offers sample menu items in easy-to-read bullets.

- Southwest Chicken Salad
- Salmon Teriyaki
- Ground Beef Burger

> Encourages more customization.

If you prefer different menu items, we can work up pricing based on your preferences.

> Addresses another specific request.

You also asked about a special occasion cake, and we certainly can arrange this for you. We work closely with a bakery that would create something according to your specifications.

I would be happy to meet with you to talk about your requirements and to finalize arrangements.

> Closes on a positive note after an offer to meet in person.

Thanks again for your inquiry, and I hope to speak with you soon. You can call me at (215) 555-6760 or email me at ron@southsidebrewery.com.

Sincerely,

> Includes the standard letter closing with signature.

Ron Ramone

Enclosure

L03 Compose a goodwill
      message.

**Ethics in
Communication**

**International
Communication**

Follow guidelines for
goodwill messages: be
prompt, direct, sincere,
specific, and brief.

COMPOSING GOODWILL MESSAGES

People send **goodwill messages** out of a sense of kindness and to maintain or build relationships. With no true business objective, these messages convey congratulations, appreciation, or sympathy. Goodwill messages achieve their objective precisely because they have no ulterior motive. Even subtle sales promotion would make receivers suspect the sincerity of your message.

Of course, you may reap business advantages from goodwill messages. People naturally like to deal with businesses and with people who are friendly and who take the time to comment on noteworthy occasions. But this is not the goal of a sincere goodwill message.

Goodwill messages vary by culture. What may be appropriate, even expected, in one country may be improper in another. Also, what is emphasized in a goodwill message may differ by culture. In a study comparing Chinese and American graduation cards, Chinese messages reflected far more "process-focused themes" of hard work and continuous self-improvement, whereas American cards emphasized "person-focused themes," such as individual traits.[6] Ask your international host or a local colleague before writing goodwill messages to people from cultures you don't know well.

You may send a goodwill message by calling instead of writing—especially for minor occasions. But a written message, including a handwritten note, is more thoughtful, more appreciated, and more permanent. And because they require extra effort, and people receive fewer of them, written goodwill messages may be more meaningful than a phone call.

To write effective goodwill messages, follow the guidelines in Figure 7.

Figure 7 Guidelines for Goodwill Messages

Be prompt.

Send a goodwill message while the reason is still fresh in the reader's mind. A welcome note to a new employee, for example, should be sent within his or her first few days on the job.

Be direct.

State the major idea in the first sentence or two, even for sympathy notes; because the reader already knows the bad news, you don't need to shelter him or her from it.

Be specific.

If you're thanking or complimenting someone, mention a specific incident or anecdote. Personalize your message to avoid having it sound like a form letter.

Be sincere.

Avoid language that is too flowery or too strong (for example, "awesome" or "the best I've ever seen"). Use a conversational tone, as if you were speaking to the person directly, and focus on the reader—not on yourself. Take special care to spell names correctly and to make sure your facts are accurate. You may use exclamation marks, but don't overdo it.

Be brief.

You may not need an entire page to get your point across. A personal note card or a one-paragraph email may be plenty.

© CENGAGE LEARNING 2013

Recognition Notes

As discussed earlier, most employees believe they don't receive enough positive feedback at work. Messages should be sent to recognize when someone does a particularly good job. An email to specify what the person did and how it benefited the organization will go a long way in making people feel valued and improving employee morale. When appropriate, you might copy an employee's immediate supervisor.

Dear Javier,

You did a terrific job on the feasibility study for Barker Associates. Ron called me this morning to tell me it was the most thorough, detailed analysis he had received in years. He also complimented the easy-to-read report format.

I really appreciate your work on this project. You put in a lot of long hours in the past three months, and your dedication has certainly paid off. When Ron has another project in the pipeline, he'll definitely call us for the job!

Keep up the good work,

Maurice

Congratulatory Notes

Congratulatory notes should be sent for major business achievements—receiving a promotion, winning new business, announcing a retirement, receiving an award, opening a new branch, or celebrating an anniversary with the company. These notes are also appropriate for personal milestones—engagements, weddings, births, graduations, and other occasions. Congratulatory notes should be written both to employees within the company and to customers, suppliers, and others outside your company.

Congratulations, Tom, on being elected president of the United Way of Alberta County. I was happy to see the announcement in this morning's newspaper and to learn of your plans for the upcoming campaign.

Best wishes for a successful fund drive. This important community effort surely deserves everyone's full support.

Daniel

Dear Melody,

Congratulations on your new house. I saw the photos on Facebook, and it looks like a great spot—move-in ready!

I hope that you and Thad enjoy many happy years there.

Best,

Sam

Thank-You Notes

A note of thanks or appreciation may be valued more than a monetary reward. As Nordstrom sales associates know, a sincere, handwritten thank-you note is especially appreciated today, when people receive so many "personalized" computer-generated messages.

Thank-you notes (either typed or handwritten) should be sent whenever someone does you a favor—sends you a gift, writes a recommendation letter for you, gives you a scholarship, or interviews you for a job. Like the letter example in Chapter 4, the example in Figure 8 is from a not-for-profit organization.

Figure 8
Thank-You Note from a Not-for-Profit Organization

food bank
of the Southern Tier

May 18, 2011

Ms. Amy Newman
Cornell University
331 Statler Hall
Ithaca, NY 14853

Uses standard letter formatting and the organization's logo.

Dear Ms. Newman:

Begins with the main point, expressing appreciation.

Please accept my deepest gratitude for your generous in-kind gift of food. Your gift will help feed our Southern Tier neighbors in need. The Food Bank's network of hunger-relief agencies is currently serving more households than in previous years. Within the last year, existing clients needed assistance more frequently than before, and our network experienced an increase in first-time users, many of them employed but unable to make ends meet, as well as seniors who struggle to live on fixed incomes.

Shows the importance of the donation.

Personalizes the message to stress the "you" attitude.

Without people like you, we would not be able to keep up with the increasing demand for emergency food assistance. I am very thankful that we have such wonderful, caring donors who want to alleviate the stress that some families face.

Restates the appreciation.

Thank you for your generosity and support for the Food Bank's hunger-relief efforts.

Sincerely,

Uses a standard closing.

Natasha R. Thompson
President & CEO

Includes the initials of the person who typed the letter.

NRT/lce

Source: Food Bank of the Southern Tier. Reprinted by Permission.

Sympathy Notes

Expressions of sympathy or condolence to a person who is having a difficult time personally are especially tough to write but are also especially appreciated. People who have experienced serious health problems, a severe business setback, or the death of a loved one need to know that others are thinking of them and that they are not alone.

Some of the most difficult messages to write are those expressing sympathy over someone's death. These notes should be handwritten, whenever possible. They should not avoid mentioning the death, but they need not dwell on it. Most sympathy notes are short. Begin with an expression of sympathy, mention some specific quality or personal reminiscence about the deceased, and then close with an expression of comfort and affection. An offer to help, if genuine, is appropriate. Figure 9 expresses sympathy to the wife of a coworker who died.

 Begin by expressing sympathy, offer some personal memory of the deceased, and close by offering comfort.

Figure 9 Sympathy Note to an Employee's Spouse

Uses company letterhead. (Personal stationery or a store-bought card are also appropriate.)

November 14, 2012

Dear Katrina,

> Begins with an expression of sympathy and expresses the impact of the death.

I was so sorry to hear about Alan's death. This came as a terrible shock to his Southside friends and co-workers, many of whom knew Alan since our opening in 2001.

> Mentions specific qualities and a personal remembrance.

Alan will always be remembered for his diligence, his willingness to help others, and his sharp sense of humor. Alan's co-workers have been talking about his memorable speech at Southside's 10th Anniversary Dinner — what a great time that was for everyone, and Alan was a big part of it.

> Closes with a genuine, specific offer of help.

I wish you well during this difficult time and would like to help in any way I can. I know that you have been in touch with our HR department; if I can smooth the process, please call me directly at 555-7037.

Sincerely,
Victor

114 W. 115th Street
Chicago, IL 60628

**Communication
Technologies**

LO4 Address customer
comments online.

ADDRESSING CUSTOMER COMMENTS ONLINE

So far, we have discussed one-to-one requests and responses. But communication is often far more complex. For online customer communication—public comments on review sites, blogs, and social networks—the opportunities are greater and the stakes higher. Companies can win customers and build a positive reputation online, but slow and poorly written responses can lose customers and damage a company's image—with potentially millions of people watching.

Deciding Whether to Respond

Not all online comments require a company response.

Smart companies monitor the constant stream of social media posts and decide whether and how to respond to each. For large companies that can afford them, **aggregators** scan the web for comments about the company. These programs automatically collect and analyze the online messages. Smaller companies have staff members who use tools such as **Google Alerts** to search the web for conversations about their company.

The flowchart shown in Figure 10, typical for organizations that pay attention to online customer feedback, helps guide a company's response.[7] As you can see from the flowchart, companies won't necessarily respond to every online post. For "Happy" customers whose posts are positive and truthful, you may or may not

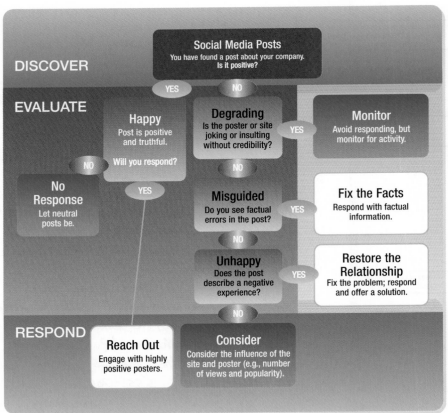

**Figure 10
Social Media
Response
Guidelines**

Figure 11 Neutral Customer Online Post

Tiffany P.
Stockton, CA

★★★★☆

We tend to forget this place exists, but then a special occasion comes up, and we are reminded again. We've attended a wedding rehearsal dinner here, had an anniversary dinner here, and even had our engagement dinner here. It's a cozy little place with exceptionally good service. The food is delicious although sometimes lacks in quantity. But they offer a full bar and a great variety of food as well as lovely desserts. This is a great place all around.

Source: Yelp.com. Reprinted by permission.

respond. However, if a post is *highly* positive, you may want to reply to engage the sender and highlight the good feedback.

For comments such as those in Figure 11, posted on the review site Yelp, management *could* respond but does not. This post can stand alone without negative repercussions for the company—or a missed opportunity to build on positive feedback.

Negative posts require more attention. We'll discuss these in Chapter 7.

Responding to Positive Reviews

The online comment shown in Figure 12 is highly positive and does warrant a management response to acknowledge the feedback.

Respond to highly positive online comments.

Figure 12
Highly Positive Online Post and Management's Response

Erik H.
Plymouth, MI

★★★★★

My favorite hangout in Plymouth. It's got a great European warm modern feel, and the staff is very friendly and professional. The food is very tasty and interesting.
A great place to meet with friends who are wine drinkers! Another hidden gem that is uniquely a part of Plymouth!

Was this review ...?   Useful ● (1)   Funny ●   Cool ● (1)

🔖 Bookmark   ✉ Send to a Friend   🔗 Link to This Review

Comment from Lisa O. of Grape Expectations
Wine Bar & Merchant   « Hide

 Thanks, Erik. Uh, we may need to check id next time you're in.... you look a little young in your photo!!

Source: Yelp.com. Reprinted by permission.

The Plymouth manager's response (at the bottom of Figure 12) could be more substantive, but her response is brief and funny. For informal social media interactions, this works just fine to connect with the writer and other prospective customers. Considering the reviewer's casual post, it might look odd for the manager to respond with something longer and more formal.

Yelp offers the example in Figure 13 with good advice for responding to positive feedback online. For an authentic approach, personalize the response: provide a photo and your own name (not just the company's name), mention the writer's name, thank the writer for the post, address specific comments from the post, and offer solutions or other ways to stay in touch.

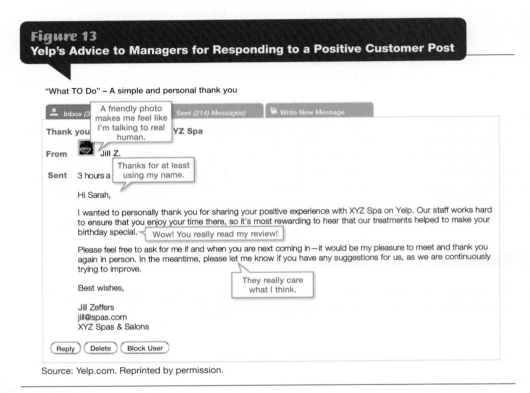

Figure 13
Yelp's Advice to Managers for Responding to a Positive Customer Post

Source: Yelp.com. Reprinted by permission.

Anticipating Customer Needs Online

 Anticipate customer needs on sites such as Twitter.

Sometimes simply responding to customers isn't enough. Companies can *anticipate* requests and offer suggestions on sites such as Twitter. Figure 14 shows an example of Wynn Encore in Las Vegas proactively interacting with a customer.

Figure 14 Anticipating Customer Needs on Twitter

- Shean702 tweets this message about his weekend plans in Las Vegas:[8]

  This weekend = room @venetianvegas dinner & drinks
  @LavoLasVegas on Friday. Saturday is dinner @EncoreLasVegas
  drinks @SurrenderVegas #Vegas
  about 22 hours ago via twidroid

- With the tag "@EncoreLasVegas," the Wynn Encore Tweeter finds the tweet and asks a follow-up question:[9]

  @shean702 where are you dining at Encore on Saturday? ^JB
  about 14 hours ago via CoTweet in reply to shean702

  Following

- Shean responds with the name of the restaurant, Switch Steak:

  @WynnLasVegas switch steak! I have heard great things but
  never been! #staycation
  about 13 hours ago via twidroid in reply to WynnLasVegas

- The Wynn Tweeter then makes an unsolicited recommendation:

  EXPLORE
  DISCOVE

  Wynn Las Vegas
  designed to be e
  discovered, to ex
  of each and ever

  @shean702 try the Kobe-style beef
  carpaccio, grilled baby octopus, dry-
  aged NY strip w/bacon-mushroom
  crust, or Montana bison rib-eye. ^JB
  about 12 hours ago via UberTweet in reply to shean702

  award-winning rooms &
  suites, signature restaurants,
  exciting leisure activities &
  nightly entertainment.

  800   346,037   1,744
  following   followers listed

  Tweets   3,852

- Shean responds with his gratitude:

  @WynnLasVegas wow! That all sounds incredible!!! I will check it
  out and let you know how it goes!!!
  about 11 hours ago via twidroid in reply to WynnLasVegas

© TWITTER.COM

Speed is critical in online communication. This Wynn interaction takes place within 11 hours—slower than a phone conversation but probably faster than an email exchange for several messages. Responses are even faster with location-based apps such as Foursquare, which tell companies when potential customers are near their store. Companies have to decide how "proactive" to be without being intrusive. These decisions will only get more complex as new apps are developed and privacy is increasingly challenged.

Responding to a Request for Information

Purpose

Imagine that you are the director of customer service for a department store. You receive the following email from a customer:

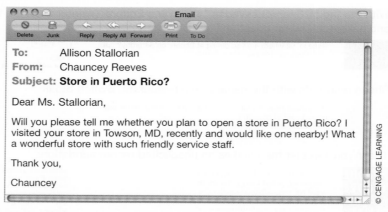

To: Allison Stallorian
From: Chauncey Reeves
Subject: **Store in Puerto Rico?**

Dear Ms. Stallorian,

Will you please tell me whether you plan to open a store in Puerto Rico? I visited your store in Towson, MD, recently and would like one nearby! What a wonderful store with such friendly service staff.

Thank you,

Chauncey

Reply to this email with the requested information.

Process

1. What is the purpose of your email?
To respond to the question about the company's plans to open a store in Puerto Rico and to thank him for visiting the store.

2. Describe your audience.
A satisfied customer who may become a loyal customer.

3. What information will you provide in your email?
- Yes, we will open a store in Puerto Rico.
- We don't have an opening date yet, but the information will be on the company website.

Product

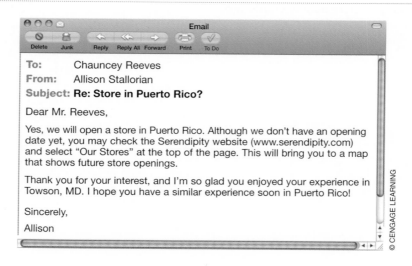

To: Chauncey Reeves
From: Allison Stallorian
Subject: **Re: Store in Puerto Rico?**

Dear Mr. Reeves,

Yes, we will open a store in Puerto Rico. Although we don't have an opening date yet, you may check the Serendipity website (www.serendipity.com) and select "Our Stores" at the top of the page. This will bring you to a map that shows future store openings.

Thank you for your interest, and I'm so glad you enjoyed your experience in Towson, MD. I hope you have a similar experience soon in Puerto Rico!

Sincerely,

Allison

Responding to Online Feedback

The 3Ps In Practice

Purpose

Imagine that you are the director of customer service for a department store. While monitoring the web for comments about your store, you see this post on an online review site. Decide whether and how to respond to this comment.

> Just got back from Serendipity Rack in Vegas. What a great store! I spent over $350, but I got such bargains. I bought designer shoes and a terrific winter coat that would have cost $350 alone full price. Tell all of your friends!

Process

1. Would you respond to this comment? Why or why not?
2. Assume that you will respond. What is the purpose of your response?
3. Describe your audience.
4. Write your opening line for the response.

Product

Write your full response and compare yours to responses written by other students. What differences do you see?

Summary

L01   Compose a neutral message.

When writing a neutral message, such as to request action or ask a question, present the major request early, along with reasons for making the request. Word your questions so that they are clear and easy to answer. Finally, close on a friendly note.

L02   Respond to a neutral message.

Answer neutral messages promptly and graciously. Grant the request early and answer all questions asked. Close on a positive and friendly note, and use original language.

L03   Compose a goodwill message.

Write goodwill messages to express congratulations, appreciation, or sympathy. Write promptly, using a direct pattern, and be sincere, specific, and brief.

L04   Address customer comments online.

Follow a strategy for responding to online comments. Highly positive comments may deserve a response, while neutral comments can be left alone.

Exercises

L01 Compose a neutral message.

1. Request alumni organization membership information.

Whether you're graduating this year or a few years from now, you may want to join a local alumni organization. Write an email to the head of the alumni association in the area you might live. Include specific questions about membership fees, club activities, benefits of joining, and the process for enrollment.

Compare the email you receive from the association with emails your classmates receive. Is the alumni association communicating consistently across regions (if there are multiple locations), and are representatives of the organization customizing emails to each of you?

2. Request health club membership information.

Research a local health club online. Look at all of the information on the club's website, and find one question that isn't answered online. For example, you might ask a question about cancelling membership, suspending membership temporarily, getting discounts for bringing in new members, or parking facilities. Write an email—or complete the club's online form—to submit your question. Before you send the question, print a copy for your instructor.

3. Request a recommendation letter.

As part of your application for a one-semester internship at American Express, you are asked to include a letter of recommendation from one of your business professors. You earned a good grade in MGT 382: Wage and Salary Administration, which you took three semesters ago from Dr. Dennis Thavinet in the management department at your school. Although you were not one of the most vocal students in class, Dr. Thavinet did commend you for your group project. American Express (at 1850 East Camelback Road, Phoenix, AZ 85017) wants to know especially about your ability to work well with others.

Compose (but do not send) an email message to Dr. Thavinet (djthavinet@marsu .edu), asking for a letter of recommendation. You would like him to respond within two weeks.

4. Write an email to a major supplier about an office move.

Imagine that you work for a T-shirt manufacturer. On March 11, your facility will move to a new location. You want to send a personalized email to your biggest supplier, Cotton Ware, to ensure a smooth transition. You are particularly concerned about this company because Harris Vinton, your main contact, is not the most responsive person.

Write an email to Harris explaining your move and asking him to hold shipments between March 5 and 12 to ensure that nothing is lost in the interim. You may invent the new address, phone number, and other details.

To make sure that Harris gets the message and complies with your request, find a way to politely ask for a response. How can you make sure that nothing gets shipped to the old address after March 4?

5. Write an email to employees about new security procedures.

Imagine that you work for a news organization. Because of recent bomb threats to your building, facility management will implement new security procedures. In the past, employees would walk to the elevators freely, but starting two weeks from today, employees will have to swipe ID cards to get access to the elevators.

Write an email to employees explaining the rationale for the new procedure, where to get an ID card, and how the process will work. Invent whatever details you believe employees will need in order to understand the change.

6. Respond to a request for information about school.

Imagine that you receive an email from a student at your former high school, asking you about life at your college. Read the message below, and then write a response.

LO2 Respond to a neutral message.

Email

Delete   Junk   Reply   Reply All   Forward   Print   To Do

To: _____
From: Penny Garzon
Subject: **Questions About College Life**

Hello _____,

I'm a sophomore at _____ high school, and I'd like to know more about _____ [college or university]. You might remember my sister, Marguerite Garzon, who graduated with you. She went to Ohio State University, but I'm looking at other options.

Will you please tell me how you like school and answer a few questions for me:
- How difficult is the work? Is the workload much more than what we have in high school? Is it manageable if I also have a part-time job during school?
- How accessible are the instructors at your school? Do they have time for you one-on-one?
- What's the social life like at your school? Are fraternities and sororities popular? What do people do for fun?
- Does your school have a debate club? I'm on the debate team in high school, and I'd like to join a club in college. What are my options?

Thanks for giving me your perspective. This will help me make a decision about whether to apply to your school.

Penny Garzon

© CENGAGE LEARNING

7. Evaluate responses to the request for information about school.

Compare responses to the previous exercise. When you look at two other students' responses to the same request for information, you'll likely see differences. Some differences may reflect high school experiences; you'll provide different information when using your high school as a common point of reference. Other differences may be because of your perceptions about college life.

Still other differences may reflect your writing style and the level of detail you provided. What differences do you see in your responses, and which versions work best and why?

8. Respond to a speaking request.

Imagine that your former employer invites you to come back and speak to their human resources department. They want to know your perspective as a former employee or intern. Read the following email, and write a response accepting the invitation.

```
 ● ● ● ✉                           Email                                 ⊖
  ⊘        🖨         ←    ≪     →      🖨      ✓
 Delete   Junk      Reply Reply All Forward  Print   To Do

 To:         _____
 From:       _____
 Subject: Request to Speak to Our HR Department

 Dear _____,

 We would like to invite you to speak to our human resources department
 about your work experience at _____. Your perspective will help us
 plan the intern program for next summer.

 If you accept, you'll speak as part of a panel discussion on Friday,
 October 14, 1:00-2:00 p.m., in the Statler Conference Room.

 Please let me know by September 9 whether you are available and willing
 to participate. I look forward to your response and will send more details
 if you accept.

 Thank you,

 _____
```

© CENGAGE LEARNING

9. Write a team response to a request.

You are a member of the Presidents' Council, which consists of the presidents of all on-campus student organizations. You just received a memo from Dr. Robin H. Hill, dean of students, wanting to know what types of social projects the student organizations on campus have been engaged in during the past year. The dean must report to the board of trustees on the important role played by student organizations—both in the life of the university and community and in the development of student leadership and social skills. She wants to include such information as student-run programs on drug and alcohol abuse, community service, and fundraising.

Working in groups of four, identify and summarize the types of social projects that student organizations at your institution have completed this year. Then organize your findings into a one-page memo to Dr. Hill. After writing your first draft, have each team member review and comment on the draft. Then revise as needed and submit. Use only factual data for this assignment.

10. Write a congratulations note.

Imagine that your former boss just won a "Manager of the Year" award. Handwrite a note congratulating the manager, and make it meaningful by referring to your own experience as his or her employee. Include whatever details and examples you believe are relevant when congratulating your boss for the award.

LO3   Compose a goodwill message.

11. Write a recognition email.

Imagine that you're a store manager for a local Costco. Brian, one of the sales associates who reports to you, has a reputation of going above and beyond to help customers. You just received a copy of this note, which a customer sent to Brian:

> Dear Brian,
>
> Thank you so much for your help with the Panda curtains. Thanks to your diligent follow-up, I found the size and color I wanted at the Birmingham store.
>
> I appreciate that you remembered to call me with the information, and even more, I appreciate your cheerful personality. In other stores, I sometimes feel like a burden to the sales staff, but you treated me like a real customer—someone who is important to Costco. I'll remember this next time I redecorate my house!
>
> Best wishes,
>
> Annan Pongsudhirak

As a good manager who takes the time to recognize employees' work, you write your own email to Brian. In addition to acknowledging this customer's feedback, include other examples of Brian's performance (which you can invent).

12. Write a thank-you note.

Imagine that you work for In the Loop Soup Kitchen, a local community kitchen. Earlier this week, a man came into the facility with a gun. Fortunately, no one was hurt, but people were frightened. Write a note to your local police department thanking them for their quick response and adept handling of the situation.

 You'll find more information about the company scenario, In the Loop, on www .cengagebrain.com

13. Decide whether to respond to online reviews.

Read three online reviews of a stereo system (Figure 15). If you were in charge of customer service, to which, if any, of these reviews would you respond? Why or why not? In small groups, discuss your rationale for whether to respond to each review. If you do choose to respond, what would you hope to accomplish with each reply?

LO4   Address customer comments online.

Figure 15 To Which Review(s) Would You Respond?

★★★★★ **Incredible sound!**
February 23, 2012 See all my reviews

Excellent sound with woofer -- feels like I'm in the stadium. I love Sony products. Wouldn't buy anything else. Easy to use and install.

★★☆☆☆ **Good for little over a year**
February 23, 2012 See all my reviews

The system worked great for the first year. Good sound quality. But it stopped working last week, of course right after the warranty expired. What a waste of money.

★★★☆☆ **Nice stereo.**
February 23, 2012 See all my reviews

Good sound, easy to listen to. I would recommend this for an amateur who likes listening to the radio.

© CENGAGE LEARNING 2013

14. Respond to a positive customer online post.

Refer to the five-star stereo review ("Incredible sound!") in Exercise 13. If you were a representative of the stereo company and read this response, how would you respond in a way that reinforces a positive customer opinion in your reply? Write your response using the Yelp guidelines in Figure 13.

15. Send an email response to a highly positive customer comment.

Imagine that you just found this comment about your new dog-training company online. Using the Yelp guidelines in Figure 13, write a response that shows appreciation for the comment.

★★★★★ **The Best $ You Could Spend**
February 21, 2012 See all my reviews

Doggie Do is the best! My Doberman, Oscar, wasn't house trained and took frequent nips at my 11-year-old son, but now he's a new dog. Amelia at Doggie Do immediately took control, and now Oscar is a well-behaved little pooch—and the rest of the family is much happier. I'd recommend Amelia to anyone having trouble breaking in a new pet.

© CENGAGE LEARNING 2013

16. Evaluate a company response to comments online.

Imagine that you are a manager at the department store JCPenney. A new employee, Marni, is responding to customer comments online and wants your advice on her draft. She says that she wants to keep responses short and doesn't see the point of adding anything. In an email to Marni, provide your feedback on her draft—and rewrite the response. Consider how you can personalize the response and perhaps engage the customer to tell you more about his or her experience.

Original post: "Ordering online with JCPenney is a breeze! What a great website—easy to find anything and easy to navigate. I love JCPenney!"

Draft company response: "Thank you. This is nice to read."

17. Anticipate a customer's needs.

Imagine that you manage the Twitter account for Nike. At least twice a day, you search for mentions of the company and questions about products and services. Today, you found this tweet.

chrisbushkin Chris Bush
does anyone know where i can get Nike Total 90 Supremacy's from .. Size 11 FB ..
18 seconds ago

© TWITTER.COM

This is a great opportunity to reach out to a potential customer proactively. You may invent information to include about the product. Just be sure to stay within Twitter's 140-character limit. If you want to refer to a web address, you may include a shortened link (using the web address "bit.ly").

Company Scenario

In The Loop Soup Kitchen

In the Loop

Let's revisit In the Loop, the soup kitchen in the midst of a crisis. You may recall that a gunman entered the facility, and fortunately, no one was hurt. Now it's your job, as the assistant director, to get the agency back to normal so that you can continue to serve the community. Encouraging people to return to In the Loop is crucial for the organization to fulfill its mission (shown below from the website):

In The Loop
Soup Kitchen

» About *In the Loop* Soup Kitchen
Mission
Our mission is to serve people in the Olpine community who need food and warmth. Through direct service and education, we strive to help people meet basic needs for survival.

Your instructor may assign the following for you to practice communicating neutral/positive messages:

- Write a news release to be posted on the In the Loop website and sent to news agencies. Your instructor may provide a sample template for you to use.

- Write an internal email to explain the situation to volunteers and encourage them to return to In the Loop.

- Create a crisis communication plan for handling potential situations in the future. You may use the template, below.

Communication Plan Template

Audience	Communication Objectives	Audience Background	Communication Medium	Message Timing

Notes

1. Beth Galleto, "Your Mother, the Marketing Expert," Words at Work, September 23, 2009, http://galletomedia.com/wordpress/?p=23, accessed December 17, 2010.
2. Michael Gartenberg, "Apple Is No Longer the Nordstrom of Tech, They're the 'New Nordstrom,'" Slash Gear, www.slashgear.com/apple-is-no-longer-the-nordstrom-of-tech-theyre-the-new-nordstrom-1963901/, accessed August 4, 2010.
3. Robert Spector and Patrick McCarthy, *The Nordstrom Way: The Inside Story of America's #1 Customer Service Company* (Hoboken: Wiley, 2005).
4. "Build-A-Bear Workshop to Open First Store at Airport," Build-A-Bear Press Release, April 27, 2011, www.reuters.com/article/2011/04/27/idUS205435+27-Apr-2011+BW20110427, accessed May 31, 2011.
5. Yoram M. Kalman and Sheizaf Rafaeli, "Email Chronemics: Unobtrusive Profiling of Response Times," *Proceedings of the 38th Hawaii International Conference on System Sciences,* 2005.
6. Karen Choi and Michael Ross, "Cultural Differences in Process and Person Focus: Congratulations on your Hard Work Versus Celebrating Your Exceptional Brain," *Journal of Experimental Social Psychology,* 2010, www.sciencedirect.com/science/article/pii/S0022103110002581, accessed January 11, 2011.
7. Adapted from Laura Bergells, Maniactive, "Social Media Mentions," www.slideshare.net/maniactive/social-media-response-flow-chart, accessed August 5, 2010, and from the U.S. Air Force Blog Assessment Flow Chart, www.af.mil/shared/media/document/AFD-091210-037.pdf, accessed May 20, 2011.
8. Shean702, Twitter, August 4, 2010, http://twitter.com/shean702, accessed August 5, 2010.
9. WynnLasVegas, Twitter, August 4, 2010, http://twitter.com/wynnlasvegas, accessed August 5, 2010.

LEARNING OBJECTIVES

After you have finished this chapter, you should be able to

LO1 Plan a persuasive message for your audience.

LO2 Write a short persuasive message.

LO3 Write a sales letter.

LO4 Write and respond to negative customer feedback.

"Toyota has always prided itself on building high-quality, durable cars that customers can depend on. And I know that we've let you down.[1]"

— TOYOTA MOTOR SALES PRESIDENT & COO JIM LENTZ

Chapter Introduction: Reactions to Toyota and Mattel Apologies

MediaCurves, a public perception research company, has business persuasion down to a science. On the company's website, participants evaluate commercials, news reports, and corporate messages.

The website includes several examples of company executives and celebrities, such as Tiger Woods, apologizing for wrongdoings and other missteps. As viewers watch these videos, they rate levels of likability, believability, and sincerity—all important aspects of persuasion.

Recent videos include Toyota Motor Corporation's executives apologizing after several automobile model recalls. One video shows Jim Lentz, U.S. division president and COO. Overall, both Toyota and non-Toyota owners reacted favorably to his apology, more favorably than to the message of Akio Toyoda, the company's president of Toyota worldwide. Viewers rated Lentz as more likable, believable, and sincere than Toyoda. While watching Toyoda's message, 54% of viewers identified their prevailing emotion as "skepticism"—not the best reaction for a company trying to repair its image.

In a crisis situation, making the perfect apology to a broad audience is nearly impossible. Particularly when a company has responsibility for wrongdoing, executives have to overcome justifiable criticism from the public. One possible explanation for viewers' lower ratings for Toyoda is the setting for Toyoda's apology: during the U.S. congressional hearings. You might imagine how this scene would influence public perceptions. Also, if MediaCurves' viewers are mostly American, certainly this could affect how they filter Toyoda's message.

Although Jim Lentz's apology was well received, viewers rated a message by Mattel CEO Bob Eckert as even more sincere. Like Lentz and Toyoda, Eckert was in a tough spot: millions of toys were recalled because of lead in the surface paint and magnets that could be swallowed. But, according to MediaCurves, Eckert did well. Viewers found him highly believable, which was critical to his ability to persuade the public that Mattel's toys are safe.

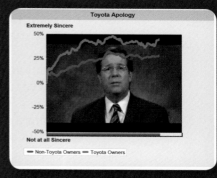

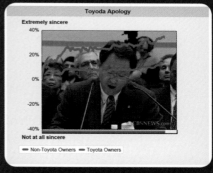

Viewers react to executives' apologies.

PLANNING PERSUASIVE MESSAGES

L01   Plan a persuasive
      message for your
      audience.

We use persuasion to motivate someone to do something or believe something that he or she would not otherwise have done. Every day people try to persuade you: companies advertise their products, friends convince you to go to the movies, and instructors encourage you to learn new concepts.

In a sense, all business communication involves persuasion. Even if your primary purpose is to inform, you still want your reader to accept your perspective and to believe the information you present.

As a manager, you need to persuade others to do what you want. To be successful, you must overcome resistance. People may resist your ideas for many reasons. Following are a few examples of persuasive messages and the resistance you may encounter.

Use persuasion when
the other person initially
resists your efforts.

Persuasive Message	Possible Resistance
You want your manager to give you a promotion.	Your manager may have budget restrictions or may believe your performance doesn't warrant a promotion.
You want to sell a new product to an existing customer.	The customer may be happy with the current product or may not want to spend more money.
You want an employee to work overtime.	The employee may have other plans or may believe your request is unfair or unnecessary.
You want a supplier to give you a discount on products.	The supplier may have sales targets he or she needs to reach, may not have authority to grant your request, or may be concerned about fairness to other customers.
You want a business to provide better service.	The business may not believe your negative feedback or may have national standards that can't be changed (for example, how many people work in local stores).

In each of these situations, you must find ways to overcome the resistance. This process begins with analyzing your audience.

ANALYZING YOUR AUDIENCE

You'll have the best chance of persuading your audience if you know your audience and adapt your message to them.

The better you know your
audience, the more likely
you will persuade them.

Knowing Your Audience

One distinction between advertising and persuasion is that persuasion is more personalized. Although advertisers can target a consumer based on, for example, other online purchases and websites visited, managers who know their audience personally can tailor a persuasive message to their specific needs.

In Chapter 4, you learned an approach for analyzing your audience. These five questions, shown again in Figure 1, are particularly useful for persuasive messages.

Figure 1 Audience Analysis

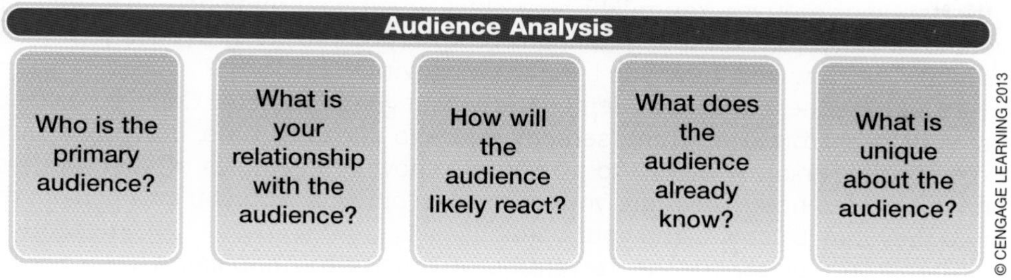

Audience Analysis				
Who is the primary audience?	What is your relationship with the audience?	How will the audience likely react?	What does the audience already know?	What is unique about the audience?

© CENGAGE LEARNING 2013

Let's say you manage a team of eight employees and—because of cutbacks—need to persuade each of them to take on additional responsibilities.

Example of Tailoring a Persuasive Message to Different Employees	
For an employee who . . .	*You might focus on how taking on additional responsibilities will . . .*
Is ambitious and wants to be promoted.	Make him or her eligible for higher-level positions in the future.
Is social and cares about the team.	Help the overall team performance.
Has a strong work ethic.	Increase his or her contribution to the organization.
Is an underperformer.	Maintain his or her status in the organization (by understanding that the new responsibilities are essential to the job).

Stress the "you" attitude to achieve the results you want. Audiences need to know "What's in it for me?" and you can address this if you know your audience well. Your job is to let the reader know the benefits of doing as you ask. Emphasize the reader, not your request or product.

NOT ▶ Our firm would like to do an energy audit of your business.

BUT ▶ An energy audit will tell you which investments will save the most money over time.

Applying Persuasion Principles

In his work *Rhetoric*, Aristotle identified three methods by which people can be persuaded:

- **Ethos**, an appeal based on credibility
- **Pathos**, an appeal based on emotion
- **Logos**, an appeal based on logic

These methods remain as relevant today as they were when Aristotle wrote about them more than two thousand years ago. As part of your process of analyzing your audience, you might consider which of these methods—or what combination—will work best to persuade each person or group.

Adapt your use of ethos, pathos, and logos to your audience and message.

Ethos: Appeal Based on Credibility

To persuade an audience who is skeptical about your character or ethics, focus on your credibility. In these situations, your audience may not know you well or may question your motives. You might hear clues about your audience's resistance to your credibility; for example, you might get questions such as, "What's your background?" or "How long have you been working with Wells Fargo?"

To address these concerns, demonstrate your good character. Consider discussing your background up front, sending your bio ahead of time, bringing a more experienced person with you to a meeting, showing examples of your work, or providing references. The more your audience connects with you as a person, the more they may trust you and your opinions.

The SPCA (Society for the Prevention of Cruelty to Animals), whose mission is "the advancement of safety and well-being of animals," uses credibility in this example by identifying the organization with famous celebrities, a common approach in advertising.

Mary Tyler Moore and Bernadette Peters Honor SPCA International

On Saturday, July 11, actresses Mary Tyler Moore and Bernadette Peters honored SPCA International at the annual "Broadway Barks" – a star-studded dog and cat adopt-a-thon in New York City hosted by Broadway Cares.

© SPCA INTERNATIONAL — WWW.SPCAI.ORG

Pathos: Appeal Based on Emotion

Some audiences are more persuaded by emotional appeals—and some topics lend themselves to more emotional appeals. As you might imagine, the SPCA often uses this approach to get people to adopt pets and donate money. Adorable—and tragic—stories and images of animals appeal to the SPCA's audience on an emotional level. Notice how pets' names are used in this story to personalize the animals. You also can connect with people emotionally through vivid language and, for an oral presentation, dynamic delivery.

Another Mission Complete!

After a long summer of sweltering heat that forces airlines to impose restrictions on animal travel in the Middle East, SPCA International's rescue experts were able to go back to Baghdad last week and save 18 U.S. soldiers' companions. Dusty, Zada, Demon, Stryker, Dude, Maggie, Stinky, and DH, along with twelve others, landed safely at Dulles International Airport in Virginia. Stryker (pictured here) has an especially sweet story of rescue and survival.

© SPCA INTERNATIONAL WWW.SPCAI.ORG

Logos: Appeal Based on Logic

To persuade some audiences, logical appeals—solid evidence and reasoning—work best. When an audience challenges your argument ("How can you be sure we'll get the results you promise?") or asks for data ("What's the return on investment for your proposal?"), focus on logical appeals. In this example, the SPCA uses evidence and reasoning to show—in concrete terms—the consequence of one unspayed animal and what your donation will achieve.

For many business communication situations, logic is the most effective form of persuasion. Aristotle defined the three aspects of logic this way:

- **Fact:** indisputably true
- **Inference:** probably true
- **Opinion:** possibly true

Factual data is most persuasive; however, inferences drawn on available data and expert opinion also may convince your audience.

Ethical Persuasion

Let's look at an example of questionable ethics in persuasive communication. You probably heard of scam emails that con people into sending money, either to help someone in trouble or in exchange for a large inheritance. Notice how the writer uses ethos, pathos, and logos to persuade the audience in the email example in Figure 2.

Ethics in Communication

Be wary of misuses of persuasion tactics.

Figure 2 Scam Email Uses Principles of Persuasion

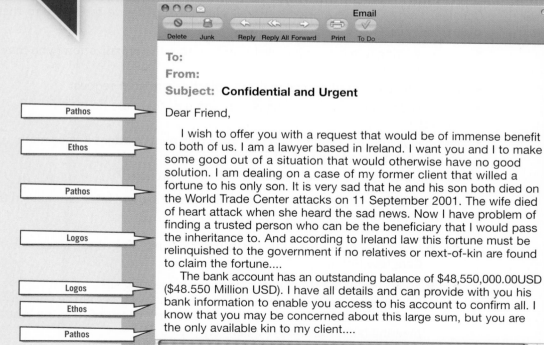

The many grammatical errors and awkward sentences should cause the receiver to question the writer's credibility.

This email goes on to promise a 40% share of the $48 million, but of course, there's a catch. When readers get in touch with the sender, they are asked for a "transaction fee" before they can receive the money. This could be a few thousand dollars—not much if you're expecting millions in return. In a similar scam, a 76-year-old Floridian sent $30,000 to someone in New York and $12,000 to what she believed to be the Central Bank of Nigeria.[2]

You might find it unbelievable that so many people fall for this blatant fraud. But this is persuasion at its worst. With an adept use of ethos, pathos, and logos, thousands of similar schemes swindle people out of millions of dollars. One scam-fighting organization estimates that people lose $200 million each year because of such emails.[3]

LO2 Write a short persuasive message.

WRITING A SHORT PERSUASIVE MESSAGE

In business, you'll write many types of persuasive messages. In this section, we'll discuss how to write a short message, for example, to present an idea or to request action. In later sections, we'll explore approaches to sales letters and negative online customer feedback—also challenging situations for persuasive writing.

To help you write messages to persuade an audience to accept your idea or fulfill your request, we'll discuss how to start the message, justify your idea or request, deal with obstacles, and motivate action.

Determining How to Start the Message

International Communication

In the past, it was common practice to organize all persuasive messages by using an indirect organizational plan—presenting the rationale first, followed by the major idea or request. Today, most persuasive messages in the United States have the main point up front with the direct organizational plan. However, messages in high-context countries, described in Chapter 2, tend to follow the indirect style. Determine which is best to achieve your objective.

Direct Plan—Present the Major Idea First

 Choose the direct plan for most persuasive messages to U.S. audiences.

Consider using the direct organizational plan for persuasive messages in these situations:

- You're writing to more senior-level people within the organization (who may not read your entire message).
- Your audience is predisposed to listen objectively to your request.
- The idea does not require strong persuasion (i.e., there are no major obstacles).
- The idea is long or complex (a reader may become impatient if your main point is buried in a long report).
- You know that your reader prefers the direct approach.

To use the direct style, present your recommendation and brief rationale in the first paragraph, followed by supporting evidence.

NOT I recommend we hold our Pittsburgh sales meeting at the Mark-Congress Hotel.

BUT I have evaluated three hotels as possible meeting sites for our Pittsburgh sales conference and recommend we meet at the Mark-Congress Hotel. The Mark-Congress is centrally located, has the best meeting facilities, and is moderately priced.

Figure 3   Direct Plan to Present an Idea

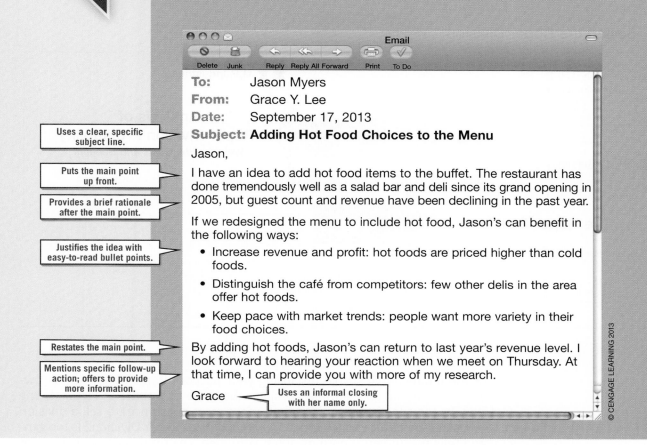

Uses a clear, specific subject line.

Puts the main point up front.

Provides a brief rationale after the main point.

Justifies the idea with easy-to-read bullet points.

Restates the main point.

Mentions specific follow-up action; offers to provide more information.

To: Jason Myers
From: Grace Y. Lee
Date: September 17, 2013
Subject: **Adding Hot Food Choices to the Menu**

Jason,

I have an idea to add hot food items to the buffet. The restaurant has done tremendously well as a salad bar and deli since its grand opening in 2005, but guest count and revenue have been declining in the past year.

If we redesigned the menu to include hot food, Jason's can benefit in the following ways:

- Increase revenue and profit: hot foods are priced higher than cold foods.
- Distinguish the café from competitors: few other delis in the area offer hot foods.
- Keep pace with market trends: people want more variety in their food choices.

By adding hot foods, Jason's can return to last year's revenue level. I look forward to hearing your reaction when we meet on Thursday. At that time, I can provide you with more of my research.

Grace

Uses an informal closing with her name only.

© CENGAGE LEARNING 2013

In the example in Figure 3, a restaurant employee presents an idea to improve the owner's business. After mentioning the problem (declining sales), she states her recommendation up front and then provides evidence to support her idea.

In Chapter 10, about writing reports, we'll see the Jason's Deli example as a longer, more formal proposal. In this example, Grace provides just enough information to get the owner interested in her idea.

Indirect Plan—Gain the Reader's Attention First

Unfortunately, your readers may initially resist your suggestions. Your job then is to explain the merits of your idea and how the reader will benefit. Because a reluctant reader is more likely to agree to an idea *after* he or she understands its merits, the indirect style will convince the reader before asking for action.

Consider using the indirect organizational plan in these situations:

- You're writing to colleagues or employees who report to you and may resist your message (but are likely to read your entire message).
- You're writing to someone outside the organization who may resist your message.
- You know that your reader prefers the indirect plan (e.g., someone from a high-context culture).

 Use the indirect plan when your audience may resist your message but will likely read it anyway and when you know that your audience prefers an indirect style.

Figure 4 Direct and Indirect Title Slides

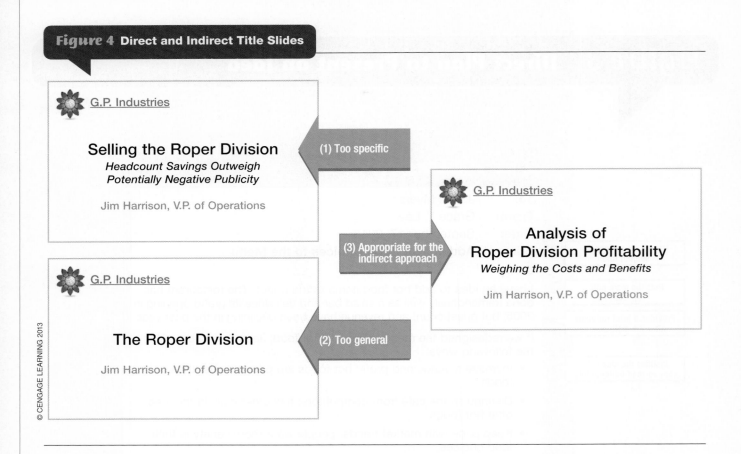

For the indirect style, avoid disclosing your purpose immediately. For a Pow-erPoint presentation, for example, compare the three title slides in Figure 4. The first may be too specific for an idea that might meet resistance (to sell a division of the business to reduce headcount). The second title, "Roper Division," is too general and tells the audience nothing about your idea. The third is probably best for the topic: the title provides context for the presentation but does not reveal the conclusion up front.

An opening that is interesting, relevant, and short will entice your audience to continue reading:

The opening statement must be interesting, relevant, and short.

- **Interesting:** A good opening sentence in a persuasive message grabs and keeps the reader's attention. A **rhetorical question** gets the reader thinking about the topic of your message but doesn't elicit a literal answer. Of course, yes-or-no questions or questions with obvious answers won't motivate someone to read on and may insult the reader's intelligence. An effective rhetorical question is "How much weight does the average Cedar Fitness Center member lose within a month of joining?" An unusual fact or unexpected statement also may draw the reader into the message. Or, you might want to write something that immediately establishes common ground between you and the reader.

- **Relevant:** Your opening statement must also be relevant to the purpose of your message. If it is too far off the topic or misleads the reader, you risk losing goodwill, and the reader may simply stop reading. At the very least, the reader will feel confused or deceived, making persuasion more difficult.

- **Short:** Often an opening paragraph of just one sentence will make the message inviting to read. Few readers have the patience to wade through a long introduction to figure out the purpose of the message.

Figure 5 Rhetorical Question Captures Attention

In Orissa death is spreading faster than relief. Those who have nothing to eat are dying of starvation. Those who can find something to eat are dying of diarrhoea and contamination. There's not enough dry land left to bury the rotting corpses leave alone sleep on. If we continue to ignore the problem hundreds will continue to die. ActionAid India is rushing plastic sheets, food, clothing and medicine to Orissa. If you'd like to help send us your contributions in cash or kind. Please draw your cheques in favour of ActionAid India Society and mail to 3, Rest House Road, P.B. 5406. Bangalore 560001. Alternatively, call 2990420 or 5586682. All contributions are exempt under Section 80G of the Income Tax Act.

ℤACTIONAID

A 200 km/hr. wind can blow away a whole State. What's it going to take to move a nation?

COURTESY OF ACTIONAID (HTTP://WWW.ACTIONAID.ORG/)

This catchy ad (Figure 5) highlighted the devastating cyclone in Orissa, India. Two simple sentences in bold type draw you in and keep you reading. The second sentence is a rhetorical question that doesn't expect an answer. The ad is relevant—focused on the message—and short. Smaller type at the top of the ad explains the request in more detail.

Whether you use a direct or an indirect style in the opening, you next have to convince the reader to accept your idea or fulfill your request.

Justifying Your Idea or Request

How you support your idea depends on what would persuade your audience, what is relevant to the situation, and what information you have available. Generally, the more evidence you can include, the better. However, for simple ideas presented in short messages, focus on your strongest supporting points and use a variety of evidence. A mix of facts and statistics, expert opinion, and examples (Figure 6) will prove that your idea is valid and that you know the subject well.

 Provide a variety of convincing evidence.

Figure 6 Types of Evidence

Facts and Statistics: Use objective statements and statistics that can be verified. Choose a few relevant data points to avoid overwhelming the reader.

Example: The Roper Division represents 34% of our overhead expenses.

Expert Opinion: Include experts to support your points, particularly if your credibility is in question.

Example: According to a recent study by Accenture's Supply Chain Management group...

Examples: Use relevant, representative cases or incidents to illustrate your points.

Example: When Maximus outsourced its logistics last year, the company saved...

© CENGAGE LEARNING 2013

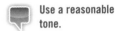

Use a reasonable tone.

Also, to convince your readers to accept your idea, you must be objective, specific, logical, and reasonable. Avoid emotionalism, obvious flattery, insincerity, and exaggeration. Let your evidence carry the weight of your argument.

NOT Moving our plant to Norfolk would result in considerable savings.

BUT Moving our plant to Norfolk would save nearly $175,000 annually.

NOT Why should it take a thousand phone calls to convince your computer to credit my account for $37.50?

BUT Even after five phone calls over the past three weeks, $37.50 has still not been credited to my account.

Favors require persuasion because the reader gets nothing tangible in return.

In some ways, justifying a persuasive request is more challenging because reader benefits are not always obvious. The email in Figure 7 illustrates a poorly written message from a student to her instructor requesting help revising her résumé.

If you're curious about whether "Jamie" (not her real name) received a response, she did. Within a few hours, she received comments about her résumé, which were probably helpful to her. However, she did not respond to her instructor to thank her for the assistance. Jamie's communication is unlikely to produce the same results in the future.

For your own requests, demonstrate professionalism by sending a carefully edited message and expressing enough gratitude to convince the reader to do what you ask—now and possibly in the future.

Figure 7 Poorly Written Persuasive Request

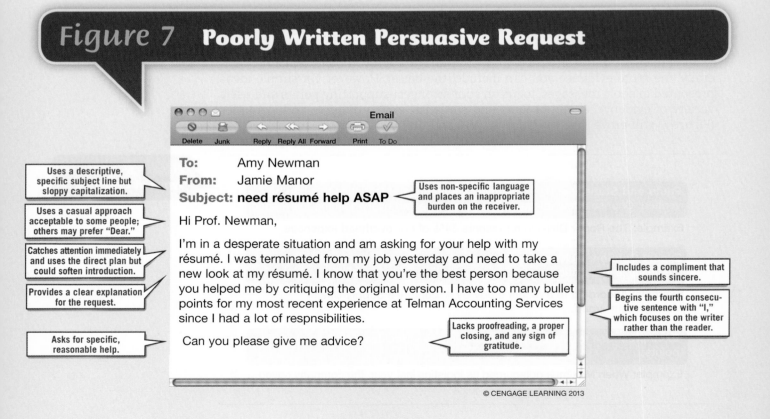

Dealing with Obstacles

Most business audiences are smart enough to know potential downsides of your idea. If you ignore obvious obstacles, you miss an opportunity to address them—and could insult your audience. Instead, identify potential audience objections ahead of time and prepare a counterargument to show that your request is reasonable despite these concerns.

In most cases, you can devote relatively little space to obstacles. Include these points in the same sentence as benefits to the reader, or in mid-paragraph.

However, if the obstacles are pressing—or you have a good response to them—you might address them up front. For example, Taylor Advisors, a consulting firm to financial companies, addresses potential objections prominently on their website.

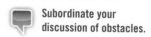

Subordinate your discussion of obstacles.

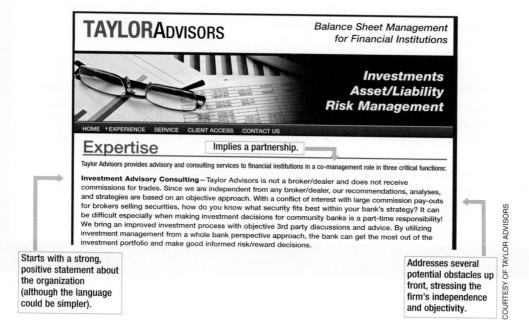

Starts with a strong, positive statement about the organization (although the language could be simpler).

Addresses several potential obstacles up front, stressing the firm's independence and objectivity.

COURTESY OF TAYLOR ADVISORS

Taylor Advisors shows readers that the company is aware of the obvious obstacles and can overcome them with a different investment strategy.

Motivating Action

Although your idea or request has been stated (direct organizational plan) or implied (indirect organizational plan) earlier, give a direct statement to motivate action late in the message—after most of the background information and reader benefits have been thoroughly covered. Make the specific action clear and easy to fulfill. Provide specific instructions on how and when the reader can complete the task; for example, ask for a meeting to discuss an idea in more detail, or state the time by when a request is needed.

You may use compliments, but only when they're sincere. Readers are rightfully suspicious when they receive a form letter saying they have been "selected" (along with thousands of others). Instead, a personalized request may be more persuasive: "We have selected only five advertising firms to participate on our panel. We included Madison Clark because of your 24 years of experience and your strong service reputation in the industry."

For a sincere tone, make any complimentary comments unique to the reader.

Use a confident, polite tone to ask for the desired action. You might acknowledge, "I know this is a busy time for you," but avoid weak statements, such as "If you don't want to do this, I understand." Don't let the reader off the hook too easily.

Checklist for Short Persuasive Messages   GO

Determine How to Start the Message

☑ **Direct Plan.** Use a direct organizational plan when writing to your manager and for most situations. Present the recommendation, along with the criteria or brief rationale, in the first paragraph.

☑ **Indirect Plan.** Use an indirect organizational plan when you expect a lot of resistance and when writing to people who prefer the indirect style. With an interesting, relevant, short statement, capture interest and motivate the reader to continue reading.

Justify Your Idea or Request

☑ Devote the major part of your message to justifying your message. Give enough background and evidence to enable the reader to make an informed decision.

☑ Use facts and statistics, expert opinion, and examples to support your points.

☑ Use an objective, logical, reasonable, and sincere tone.

☑ Present the evidence in terms of either direct or indirect reader benefits.

Deal with Obstacles

☑ Do not ignore obstacles or any negative aspects of your message. Instead, address them directly.

☑ In most cases, subordinate the discussion of obstacles by position and amount of space devoted to the topic.

Ask Confidently for Action

☑ State (or restate) the specific idea or request late in the message—after most of the benefits have been discussed.

☑ Make the desired action clear and easy for the reader to take, use a confident tone, do not apologize, and do not provide excuses.

☑ End on a forward-looking note, continuing to stress reader benefits.

Possibly most important, keep your request reasonable. Don't ask someone else to do something that you can or should do yourself.

The Checklist for Short Persuasive Messages summarizes these guidelines. Although you will not be able to use all these suggestions in each persuasive request, you should use them as an overall framework for structuring your persuasive message.

LO3 Write a sales letter.

WRITING A SALES LETTER

The heart of most business is sales—selling a product or service. Individual letters and form letters are common to reach prospective customers. In your career, you may write letters as a sales manager for a large company, as a development officer for a not-for-profit organization, or as the owner of your own start-up company. All of these situations require a special approach to persuasion—and involve ethical challenges.

Typically, the indirect organizational plan is used for sales letters. It is sometimes called the *AIDA* plan, because you first gain the reader's *attention*, then create *interest* in and *desire* for the benefits of your product, and finally motivate *action*.

Selecting a Central Selling Theme

Your first step is to become thoroughly familiar with your product, its competition, and your audience. Then, you must select a **central selling theme** for your letter. Rather than focus on all of your product's features, find one major reader benefit that you introduce early and emphasize throughout the letter. A basic law of direct-mail advertising could be labeled $E^2 = 0$, meaning that when you try to emphasize *everything,* you end up emphasizing *nothing.*[4]

With a sales letter, you have only a short time to make a lasting impression on your reader. Introduce your central selling theme early (in the opening sentence, if possible), and keep referring to it throughout the letter. In a classic American Express sales letter (Figure 8), we see a strong selling theme: exclusive benefits.[5]

Figure 8 American Express Sales Letter

AMERICAN EXPRESS TRAVEL RELATED SERVICES COMPANY, INC.
AMERICAN EXPRESS PLAZA, NEW YORK, NY 10004

Diane Shaib
Vice President
Marketing

Dear Mr. Masterson:

Quite frankly, the American Express® Card is not for everyone. And not everyone who applies for Cardmembership is approved.

However, because we believe you will benefit from Cardmembership, I've enclosed a special invitation for you to apply for the most honored and prestigious financial instrument available to people who travel, vacation, and entertain.

The American Express Card is the perfect example of the old adage, "You get what you pay for."

For example, you get a truly impressive array of extra privileges, all designed for your convenience and security:

- <u>A Worldwide Network of Travel Service Offices* is at Your Service</u>.
  Enjoy personal attention at any of the nearly 1,000 American
  Express Offices -- your "homes away from home" -- around the globe.

- <u>Cash Your Personal Check at Thousands of Locations.</u>
  Cash up to $250 at participating hotels and motels, and up to $1,000
  at most American Express Travel Service Offices all over the world.
  (Subject to cash availability and local regulations.)

- <u>Card Lost or Stolen? You'll Get a Quick Replacement</u>.
  If the Card is lost or stolen, an emergency replacement will be
  provided at any Travel Service Office in the world, usually by the end
  of the next business day.

- <u>Obtain Emergency Funds Instantly</u>. Once you've enrolled in this
  convenient service, our network of automated Travelers Cheque
  Dispensers lets you obtain up to $500 . . . in 60 seconds or less!

- <u>Carry $100,000 of Travel Accident Insurance</u>. Just charge your tickets
  to the Card, and you, your spouse, or dependent children under the
  age of 21 are automatically covered when traveling by common
  carrier on land, sea, or in the air. It's underwritten by Fireman's

(over, please)

*Of American Express Travel Related Services Company, Inc., its affiliates and Representatives.

Gaining the Reader's Attention

Review the earlier section on gaining the reader's attention when writing persuasive messages.

A reply to a request for product information from a potential customer is called a **solicited sales letter**. An **unsolicited sales letter**, on the other hand, promotes a company's products and is mailed to potential customers who have not expressed any interest. (Unsolicited sales letters are also called *prospecting letters*. Some recipients, of course, call them *spam* or *junk mail*.)

As we discussed earlier, you have only a line or two to grab the reader's attention. Then, you're lucky if the reader skims the rest of your message—either out of curiosity or because the opening sentence was especially intriguing.

The American Express letter immediately catches attention: "Quite frankly, the American Express Card is not for everyone. And not everyone who applies for

---

Fund Insurance Companies, San Rafael, California, for approximately 35¢ of the annual Cardmembership fee.

- Your Hotel Reservations Are Assured. As an American Express Cardmember, if you request, your hotel room will be held for you until check-out the following day, at nearly 8,000 participating hotels.

- Enjoy Special Express Hotel Service. Speedy check-in and check-out is available to Cardmembers at more than 1,000 hotels, including Hilton, Hyatt, Marriott, Sheraton, and more.

Extras like these only begin to tell the story of American Express Card security, emergency protection, and convenience. You'll also enjoy:

- Unequalled Hospitality. The Card is welcomed by the world's major airlines, car rental agencies, railroads, and cruise lines. Plus it pays for auto parts and servicing at thousands of locations nationwide.

- A Worldwide Welcome. Fine restaurants, hotels, resorts, and a host of other establishments around the world, and right in your hometown, recognize the Card and welcome your patronage.

- Purchasing Power. No need to carry large amounts of cash. The Card takes care of shopping needs, whether you're choosing a wardrobe, buying theater tickets, sending flowers, or hosting a dinner (even if you can't be there!)

- Financial Freedom. Unlike bank cards, the American Express Card imposes no preset spending limit. Purchases are approved based on your ability to pay as demonstrated by your past spending, payment patterns, and personal resources. So you are free to make your own decisions about when and where to use the Card.

In a few words, American Express Cardmembership is the most effective letter of introduction to the world of travel, entertainment, and the good life yet devised. Yet surprisingly, these benefits are all yours to enjoy for the modest fee of just $35 a year.

Why not apply for the membership today? All you have to do is fill out and mail the enclosed application. As soon as it is approved, we'll send along the Card, without delay.

Sincerely,

Diane Shaib

Diane Shaib
Vice President

P.S. Apply today and enjoy all the benefits of Cardmembership. Those listed here are just a handful of what's available. A full listing is included in the Guide to Cardmember Services you'll receive along with the Card.

Cardmembership is approved." The reader is drawn in: this is an exclusive sought-after offer! Notice how the company refers to "Cardmembership," which is an invented word, capitalized as if it's something unique and, again, reinforces the selling theme, exclusivity.

These opening sentences have proven effective, particularly for sales letters.

Technique	Item Promoted	Example
Rhetorical question	A high-priced car	*What is the difference between extravagance and luxury?*
Thought-provoking	An early-morning television news program	*Most of what we had to say about business this morning was unprintable.*
Unusual fact	A laundry detergent	*If your family is typical, you will wash one ton of laundry this year.*
Current event	A real estate company	*The new Arrow assembly plant will bring 1,700 new families to White Rock within three years.*
Anecdote	A weekly business magazine	*During six years of college, the one experience that helped me the most did not occur in the classroom.*
Direct challenge	A no-blot ballpoint pen	*Drop the enclosed Pointer pen on the floor, writing tip first, and then sign your name with it.*

As in persuasive requests, the opening of a sales letter should be interesting, short, and original. When possible, incorporate the central selling theme into your opening; and avoid irrelevant, obvious, or overused statements.

Sales letters, unlike other persuasive messages, may stretch sincerity—within reason. In the American Express letter, readers may or may not believe this is a "special invitation." This is probably acceptable for the purpose and audience.

But be careful about crossing an ethical line to draw people in. Phishing scams, which lure people into giving personal information, such as bank account numbers, computer passwords, or social security numbers, warn people of expired accounts or, ironically, security failures. Today, because people are more attuned to this type of fraud, they may react negatively to a sales letter with a questionable introduction, even if the business is legitimate.

For solicited sales letters, which respond to a customer inquiry, an attention-getting opening is not as crucial. Instead, you might begin by expressing appreciation for the customer's inquiry and then introduce the central selling theme.

 Many attention-getting openings consist of a one-sentence paragraph.

 **Ethics in Communication**

Creating Interest and Building Desire

If your opening sentence is directly related to your product, transitioning to features and reader benefits will be smooth and logical.

Interpreting Features

Most of your letter (typically, several paragraphs) will probably be devoted to creating interest and building desire for your product. The American Express letter does this well, with easy-to-skim bullets. The writer *interprets* services by showing how each aspect of the program benefits members. By focusing on **benefits** rather than **features** (how the card works), American Express makes the reader—not the product—the subject of the letter.

 Devote several paragraphs to interpreting the product's features.

Marketers refer to the benefit a user receives from a product or service as the **derived benefit**. American Express doesn't sell cards; it sells exclusivity.

Although emphasizing the derived benefit rather than product features is generally the preferred strategy, two situations call for emphasizing product features instead: when promoting a product to experts and when promoting expensive equipment. For example, if the car you're promoting to sports car enthusiasts achieves a maximum torque of 138 ft-lb at 3,000 rpm or produces 145 hp at 5,500 rpm, tell the reader that. You would sound condescending if you explained to such experts what this means.

Using Vivid Language and Graphics

Because people are so bombarded with advertising today, novel approaches are essential to differentiate your product or service from the pack. The website shown in Figure 9, with its bold language and eye-catching colors and graphics, invites readers to pay attention. "Boringissexy.com" is not a typical domain name for a bank.

Figure 9 Catchy Name and Bold Graphics Create Interest

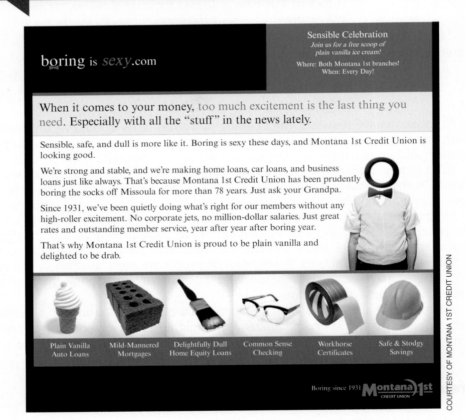

Use action verbs when talking about the product's features and benefits. Within reason, use colorful adjectives and adverbs and positive language, stressing what your product is, rather than what it is *not*.

> **NOT** The ski lodge isn't in one of those crowded resort areas.

> **BUT** The private ski lodge sits on the snow-capped peaks of the Canadian Rocky Mountains.

NOT ▶ A serving of our baked potato chips doesn't have high calories like the original chips.

BUT ▶ Our baked potato chips have 140 calories per serving—40% less than the original chips.

Using Objective, Ethical Language

To be convincing, you must present specific, objective evidence. For sales letters, even more than other persuasive messages, simply saying that a product is great is not enough. You must provide evidence to show *why* or *how* the product is great. Here is where you'll use all the data you gathered before you started to write. Avoid generalities, unsupported superlatives and claims, and too many or too strong adjectives and adverbs. Avoid stating or implying something your product is not, so your letter doesn't cross an ethical line.

Maintain credibility by providing specific facts and figures.

Ethics in Communication

NOT ▶ At $795, the Sherwood moped is the best buy on the market.

BUT ▶ The May issue of *Independent Consumer* rated the $795 Sherwood moped the year's best buy.

NOT ▶ Everyone enjoys the convenience of our Bread Baker.

BUT ▶ Our Bread Baker comes with one feature we don't think you'll ever use: a 30-day, no-questions-asked return policy.

Similar to a message proposing an idea, a sales letter should include a variety of evidence. If you were selling a Kindle, for example, you might include the evidence shown in Figure 10.[6,7]

Figure 10 Examples of Evidence

Facts and Statistics

Weighing only 8.7 ounces, the Amazon Kindle stores up to 3,500 books.

Expert Opinion

According to David Pogue, technology writer and commentator, "The Kindle is, of course, the world's most popular electronic book reader.... What makes the Kindle successful is the effortlessness of it.... The convenience is amazing."

Examples

As one customer says, "For years, I was unable to read regular books because of problems with my hands and failing eyesight, so the Kindle has been a great investment for me. Plus, the cost of books I currently own on my Kindle, had I bought them in the store, would have been $527.98; however, the cost of those books in electronic format was approximately $140—almost $390 in savings in less than a year!"

Subordinate price in your message.

Mentioning Price

If price is your central selling theme, introduce it early and emphasize it often. In most cases, however, price is not the central selling theme and should therefore be subordinated. Introduce the price late in the message, after most of the advantages of owning the product have been discussed. State it in a long complex or compound sentence, perhaps in a sentence that also mentions a reader benefit. In the American Express letter, the price is presented at the end of the second-to-last paragraph: "Yet surprisingly, these benefits are all yours to enjoy for the modest fee of just $35 a year."

Presenting the price in small units and comparing it to a familiar object may soften the expense. You can see this technique used at the website shown in Figure 11, which seeks donations for a children's residential treatment center. By using phrases such as "less than $1 per day" and by comparing this amount to a cup of coffee or a value burger, the organization makes a convincing argument for donating to its cause.

Figure 11 Comparing Donations to Small, Everyday Purchases

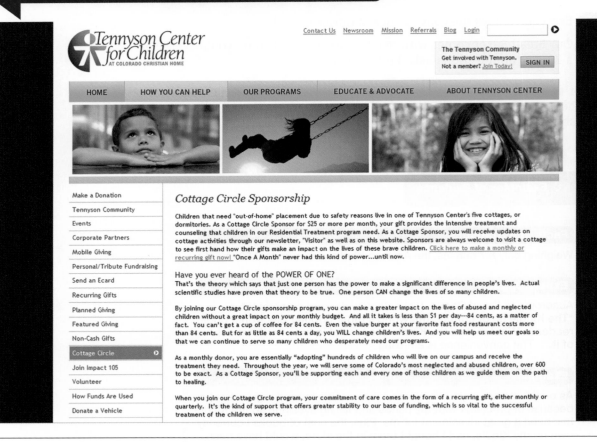

© TENNYSON CENTER FOR CHILDREN AT COLORADO CHRISTIAN HOME

Referring to Enclosures

Sometimes, an enclosure explains your product or service or inspires action. If you include an enclosure, subordinate your reference to it, and refer to some specific item in the enclosure to increase the likelihood of its being read.

NOT ▸ I have enclosed a sales brochure on this product.

BUT ▸ Take a look at our clearance items on page 7 of the enclosed brochure.

> **NOT** I have enclosed an order blank for your convenience.

> **BUT** Use the enclosed order blank to send us your order today. Within a week, you'll be wearing your new waterproof boots!

Motivating Action

Although the purpose of your letter should be apparent right from the start, delay making your specific request until late in the letter—after you have created interest and built desire for the product. Then state the specific action you want. In the American Express letter, the requested action is clear in the last paragraph: "Why not apply for Cardmembership today? All you have to do is fill out and mail the enclosed application."

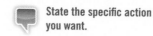
State the specific action you want.

If the desired action is an actual sale, make the action easy by including a toll-free number, a website link, or an order form. For high-priced items, it would be unreasonable to expect to make an actual sale by mail. It's unlikely that someone would phone in an order for a new car after reading a sales letter.

For high-end items, your goal is to get the reader to take just a small step toward purchasing—visiting a dealership for a test drive, calling for more information, or asking a sales representative to follow up. These steps are easy for the reader to take.

You might also provide an incentive for prompt action by, for example, offering a gift to the first 100 people who respond or by stressing the need to buy early while there is still a good selection, before the holiday rush, or during the three-day sale. Make your push for action *gently,* however. Any tactic that smacks of high-pressure selling is likely to increase reader resistance and, again, may lead the reader to question your ethics.

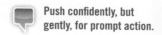
Push confidently, but gently, for prompt action.

Use confident language when asking for action, avoiding such hesitant phrases as, "If you want to save money" or "I hope you agree that this product will save you time." When asking the reader to part with money, mention a reader benefit in the same sentence.

> **NOT** Hurry! Hurry! Hurry! These sale prices won't be in effect long.

> **BUT** Call before September 30 to take advantage of our lowest prices of the year.

> **NOT** If you agree that this ice cream maker will make your summers more enjoyable, you can place your order by telephone.

> **BUT** To use your Jiffy Ice Cream Maker during the upcoming July 4 weekend, simply call our toll-free number today.

Consider putting an important marketing point in a postscript (P.S.). The American Express letter uses a P.S. to encourage a response ("Apply today . . .") and reinforce the selling theme (". . . enjoy all the benefits of Cardmembership"). Some studies have shown that people first read their name, then who signed the letter, and then the postscript—all before reading the introductory paragraph on the first page.[8] Because of this reading pattern, the P.S. should contain new and interesting information, as the American Express letter does.

Use the Checklist for Sales Letters to make your letters as persuasive as possible. With a well-written letter, you'll have a better chance of achieving your goals.

Checklist for Sales Letters

GO

Select a central selling theme—your product's most distinguishing feature—and refer to this throughout the letter.

Gain the Reader's Attention

☑ Make your opening brief, interesting, and original. Avoid obvious, misleading, and irrelevant statements.

☑ Use any of these openings: rhetorical question, thought-provoking statement, unusual fact, current event, anecdote, direct challenge, or some similar attention-getting device.

☑ Introduce (or at least lead up to) the central selling theme in the opening.

☑ If the letter is in response to a customer inquiry, begin by expressing appreciation for the inquiry and then introduce the central selling theme.

Create Interest and Build Desire

☑ Make the introduction of the product follow naturally from the attention-getter.

☑ *Interpret* the features of the product; instead of just describing the features, show how the reader will benefit from each feature. Let the reader picture owning, using, and enjoying the product.

☑ Use action-packed, positive language and engaging graphics. Provide objective, convincing evidence to support your claims—specific facts and figures, independent product reviews, endorsements, and so on.

☑ Continue to stress the central selling theme throughout.

☑ Subordinate price (unless price is the central selling theme). State price in small terms, in a long sentence, or in a sentence that also talks about benefits.

Motivate Action

☑ Make the desired action clear and easy to take.

☑ Ask confidently, avoiding the hesitant "If you'd like to . . ." or "I hope you agree that. . ."

☑ Encourage prompt action (but avoid a hard-sell approach).

☑ End your letter with a reminder of a reader benefit.

Communication Technologies

WRITING AND RESPONDING TO NEGATIVE CUSTOMER FEEDBACK

L04 Write and respond to negative customer feedback.

How you communicate your response is critical to service recovery.

Wouldn't it be great if all customers were happy all the time? Of course, this isn't the case. Throughout your career—both as a customer and as a provider of a product or service—you will have to address situations when expectations are not met. To convince a business that its product is faulty or to convince a customer that your product is *not* faulty requires another type of persuasion.

Sometimes, negative feedback is best handled in person or with a phone call. If you work for McKinsey Consulting and have a two-year relationship with a client for potentially millions of dollars in consulting fees, you would hope that the client would call with a complaint rather than post a rant on YouTube. Also, if you receive a complaint from a customer, you might call her rather than respond by letter to explain how you'll fix the problem. How you communicate your response is critical to **service recovery**—ideally, turning an upset customer into a loyal one. In situations such as these, you might improve your chances of rebuilding a relationship with personal communication.

However, for more transactional, high-volume businesses, where you don't necessarily know your customer, you may be more likely to see comments posted on social media sites. As we discussed in Chapter 6, responding to positive comments online is important, but the stakes are even higher with negative online feedback.

How well you handle negative customer feedback affects your company's image. When a customer has a negative service experience, the situation may be exacerbated in two ways: the customer writes about the experience on a public website, and the company mishandles the online comment. Increasingly, managers are concerned about their company's online reputation—how the company is perceived by the public on the Internet.

When the activist organization Greenpeace criticized Nestlé's use of palm oil, the company didn't handle it well. Environmentalists wanted Nestlé to drop its palm oil producer, which they claimed destroyed rain forests, a critical habitat for orangutans.[9]

The Facebook examples in Figure 12 show the company representative's failure to respond to public concerns.[10] Clearly, Nestlé isn't "engaging" customers, as we discussed in Chapter 3, but this situation is more critical: the company misses an opportunity to respond to negative feedback, and as a result, makes the situation far worse.

Figure 12
Nestlé's Poor Response—and Apology—to Public Criticism

 Kay Wilkinson Aaron Ludwig, how transparent are you! – You're just trying to cover your back. I've tweeted about this link because I was so shocked at your attitude to your 'fans'. This is in no way a positive thing and has reinforced what I always thought about Nestle. You have a negative reputation with many and with good reason. I suspect many others will have had the same reaction as me.
March 19, 2010 at 2:48pm

 Jennifer Krase nestle, you have much to learn about the internet. and about common human decency.
March 19, 2010 at 1:34pm

 Nestle @Paul Griffin – that's a new understanding of intellectual property rights. We'll muse on that. You can have what you like as your profile picture. But if it's an altered version of any of our logos, we'll remove it form this page.
March 19, 2010 at 2:53am

 Nestle Thanks for the lesson in manners. Consider yourself embraced. But it's our page, we set the rules, it was ever thus.
March 19, 2010 at 2:53am

Errors in Nestlé's posts (e.g., "form" rather than "from") are not excusable; however, because Nestlé is a Swiss company, the spelling of "apologise" is understandable.

 Nestle This (deleting logos) was one in a series of mistakes for which I would like to apologise. And for being rude. We've stopped deleting posts, and I have stopped being rude.
March 19, 2010 at 1:29pm

FACEBOOK.COM, MARCH 19, 2010.

These are real posts on Nestlé's Facebook page, so the grammar and punctuation do not represent professional business communication, but the point is clear: people are unhappy with Nestlé's response to the criticism. As you can see in the last post, the Nestlé representative has come around to apologize. The apology is a stark difference from the previous post, which is rude and sarcastic. Can you guess what happened to the Nestlé representative on the morning of March 19? Perhaps he was spoken to about proper communication via social media.

In a marketing campaign to protest Nestlé, "Kit Kat" is changed to "Killer."

In this section of the chapter, we'll look at principles for writing customer complaints (in letters and online) and responding to negative feedback.

Writing Customer Complaint Letters and Online Reviews

To present yourself as a credible customer with a complaint worth the company's attention, follow these principles for writing a complaint letter or negative online review:

- Consider an indirect style. Although you'll want to get to the issue quickly, asking for compensation in your first paragraph may turn off the reader. Instead, build your case gradually to convince the reader to fulfill your request.

  NOT Recently, I planned to take the bus to Houston, but it left early, and I'd like my $55 refunded.

  BUT Recently, I planned to take the bus to Houston, but I missed it because it left early.

 Provide specific evidence and use an objective tone.

- Give specific evidence about what went wrong. For the bus example, giving the specific location, date, and time—and witnesses—makes your argument more credible and persuasive. Avoid generalizations and vague descriptions.

  NOT The bus always leaves early.

  BUT On Thursday, September 14, I was scheduled to take the bus at 3:15 from Minor Hall. When I arrived at 3:05 with my luggage, two people told me they saw the bus leave at 3:00.

- Maintain a calm, objective tone. Your anger may be understandable, but it could hinder your ability to get a positive response from the company. Consider asking a friend for feedback or waiting a day before you mail or post angry feedback online.

NOT ▸ What's the deal with this?? Even Amanda, at your central office, said the bus left early, and she was upset about it too!

BUT ▸ I called the central office and spoke with Amanda, who called the driver on the other line and confirmed that the bus had left at 3:00. She said she was surprised the bus left before 3:15, which was its scheduled departure.

- Close with a confident, respectful tone. After you provide details, ask for reasonable compensation and a response.

NOT ▸ I hope you'll send me the $55 I paid for the ticket and $200 for my waiting time until I could catch a ride with a friend.

BUT ▸ I enclose the ticket and respectfully request $55 as reimbursement. Please send the check to my home address: 525 Simpson Hall, Dallas, TX, 74205.

With such clear explanations and an appropriate tone, this is a persuasive message to which any reasonable company would respond.

If you weren't requesting compensation for a dissatisfying bus experience, you could have instead posted a review online. Whether you post on the company's Facebook page or a public review site, such as Yelp, the audience is slightly different: a company representative may read your post, but your primary audience is the public—other customers considering taking the bus.

The same principles of organization, evidence, and tone apply for online reviews, but respect may be even more important for public comments. If your post is unreasonable or angry, you may embarrass yourself and regret it later. Also, you might want to give the company the opportunity to address major concerns more privately through a phone call, email, letter, direct message on Twitter, or feedback form on the company's website.

The review about a television, shown in Figure 13, is honest, measured, and reasonable. The customer isn't happy, but the feedback is clear and useful for other consumers—and the manufacturer.

Figure 13   Negative Online Review for a TV

(One star) **Good Color, but Terrible Visibility** ◂ Includes a specific title for the post.

February 4, 2013

> Uses the direct plan with the main point up front. This is appropriate for the public audience.

> Includes relevant positive information. Provides specific measurements to justify the point.

> Offers a comparison to explain the results.

The color is nice on this 40-inch TV, but it's difficult to see. The colors are accurate, but I can't see the picture from all angles. I see fine if I move from left and right of the set (at up to a 75-degree angle), but I can't watch TV in bed (at more than 20 degrees below eye level). I see only dark, muted colors, almost like a negative of a photo. I wouldn't buy this brand again, and I don't recommend this TV at all. ◂ Ends with a clear recommendation.

Responding to Negative Feedback

Respond to online feedback promptly to preserve the company's reputation.

Hearing negative feedback can be difficult but is a good opportunity to improve the business and rebuild a customer relationship. Ignoring the feedback or responding rudely will surely lose one already angry customer and, if it is posted online, may lose even more. Consider the negative review in Figure 14 and the owner's response in Figure 15, originally published on Yelp.

Clearly, this owner could have written a better response. She insults the guest personally, questions his credibility, and is terribly defensive. Her abundant use of exclamation points and capital letters and her lack of attention to detail and proper grammar only exacerbate her negative image as a small business owner. When this exchange was published on a Phoenix blog, it generated 600 comments within 10 days. Of course, everyone has an opinion online! Many comments are about the restaurant ("Not only will I never eat there, but if I hear anyone else planning on going there, I will steer them away as well") and about the owner's response ("Poor Amy just made a bad situation even worse. Swallow your pride, apologize, admit that the pizza you served Joel L. was a bad one, and invite him and a guest back for a complimentary meal").[11]

Figure 14 Negative Review of Amy's Baking Company

Elite '10
210
187
Joel L.
Phoenix, AZ
★☆☆☆☆

Reviews

In retrospect, I should have known better than to step foot into Amy's Baking Company (a.k.a. ABC Bistro).
-8 pm on a Saturday night, three tables are occupied
-a sign on the door indicates they're looking for an experienced line cook, a dishwasher, waitresses, you name it
-Pita Jungle, just a stone's throw away, is packed to the gills

These are all bad signs. They go ignored, however, because I'd eaten one thing all day, and I had drove here to try their pizza. Never, ever again.

…

I took a bite, and was immediately underwhelmed. The crust had very little character, was slightly sweet but had that store-bought quality to it. The pesto tasted okay, but the tomatoes were completely tasteless and overall, it just fell flat. It's margherita – the ingredients need to shine to make such a simple pizza. These ingredients were sub-par. After two small pieces, I decided I was wasting my calories and just gave up on it.

So I sat outside, not eating, and sat. And sat. Where the hell was the waitress? I glanced inside a few times, hoping to catch her eye, but she must have been occupied elsewhere.

The owner comes out. "How'd you like your pizza?" Instead of immediately responding, I asked how it had come out so quickly. In short, he told me another table had ordered it, decided they didn't want it, and it sat in the kitchen for two minutes, who in turn decided to send it out to me since I didn't order anything else.

Me: "Well, it didn't really taste fresh."

Him: "No, no, our pizzas are the best. Ask our customers. You're the first person since we've opened to ever not like our pizzas."

He got very defensive about the pizza, but I hadn't really launched a harsh criticism on the pizza, just said I didn't really enjoy it. So I sat some more, with an empty drink, and realized they wanted me gone. The owner wouldn't make eye contact with me. The server never came back out asking if I wanted something else. And they didn't refill my drink.

…

This is arrogance in its worst form. I can forgive bad food, but I cannot forgive misplaced arrogance and the blatant dismissal of a customer, whether you agree with them or not.

Perhaps the sign on the door should also say, "Wanted: New owner".

I cannot, for the life of me, recommend this restaurant to anyone.

Figure 15 Amy's Negative Response

---

amy b's Review

amy b
Scottsdale, AZ
⭐⭐⭐⭐⭐

All

Dear Joel,L. It is blatantly obvious to me why you were ALONE on a Saturday night!

Read any of the reviews that have been written about us and you will see that EVERYONE loves us!! The only people that don't is our "Competition". We knew you had been sent by another restaurant before you even ordered your $14.00 Pizza.

The Pizza was fresh and amazing. The reason the tomatoes had different texture was because I use three different heirloom tomatoes and some of them are sundried. So of course they are going to have different texture from the fresh ones!!! But perhaps you are only accustomed to tasting the ones that come "fresh from the can!"

Moving on to the "Store bought Dough"Comment. PLEASE!! My dough is made fresh every day from 100% organic ingredients. Perhaps your palate is not sophisticated enough to tell the difference.

As for you having the Patio all to yourself unless you have been living on another PLANET it is summertime in ARIZONA MORON!!! Only TRAMPS and LOSERS want to sit outside in 110 temperatures!!!!

We are hiring because we are so busy that we need to hire more people. You just so happened to come right after a huge rush. And the people did not change their mind for the Margarita Pizza they ordered. They were still enjoying their amazing Caesar salad and I thought perhaps you would appreciate not having to wait so long for your pizza. Which was just coming out of the OVEN.

I am the CHEF and the owner, and I am the one that made your PIZZA.

…

I would LOVE for anyone who reads this review to come to ABC and try our Pizza. If you don't like it then I guarantee you don't have to pay for it.

Now let's look at a better example of responding to negative reviews. If you owned the Lakes Inn and saw the online travel review in Figure 16, how would you respond?

Overall the review is positive, but the guest makes one negative comment that should be addressed. According to the Social Media Response Guidelines presented in Chapter 6, this guest could be considered "Unhappy." Also, it's smart to respond because a negative review may influence the decisions of millions of travelers.

Follow these guidelines when responding to negative online reviews:

- Show appreciation for the feedback. Thank the writer for the review—even negative comments give you the opportunity to respond and restore your company's reputation.

"Beautiful location but smells"

Figure 16
Lakes Inn Review

Courtney

March 11

This inn is at the top of Twin Lake, the perfect spot for boating and a terrific view of the lake and surrounding areas. But I noticed a musty smell throughout the inn. This wasn't as noticeable in our room, but it was very prevalent in the lobby and the restaurant. It was a real turn-off.

- Reinforce positive aspects of the review. Many reviews will include some positive points; highlight those for other readers.
- Address negative aspects directly. Explain the situation and what you will do to correct the situation. Then, follow through to use negative feedback to improve operations or service.
- Invite the customer to experience your product or service again. If you can contact the writer directly, you might offer a special discount to entice him or her to try your company again—and to have a better experience.

The manager of the Lakes Inn uses these principles to respond to the guest's review in Figure 17. Notice how the manager responds promptly (the same day), thanks the guest and acknowledges the feedback, apologizes where appropriate, explains how the problem will be fixed, and invites the guest to return.

Responding to customers' negative feedback is a make-or-break situation for business professionals. If handled well, you can win over a customer for life. If handled poorly, you risk losing much more than one dissatisfied customer.

Figure 17 Management Response to a Negative Review

March 11 — Responds within a day (critical for social media responses).

Addresses the guest by her username.

Dear Courtney,

Thanks the guest for the review and reinforces positive aspects up front.

Thank you for writing the review of Lakes Inn. I am glad that you enjoyed our beautiful location on Twin Lake.

Repeats and apologizes for the issue; provides a reason for the musty odor; provides an update (important for future potential guests).

I am sorry about the musty odor in the common areas. We had just finished cleaning the carpets, and the smell had lingered longer than we expected. Fortunately, the odor has dissipated today.

Describes specific actions the inn is taking to correct the issue.

I have circulated your comments to our facilities manager, who will work to improve this situation in the future.

Encourages the guest to return and will make a personal connection if she does.

Please let me know if you stay with us again. I would very much like to welcome you back to the inn.

© CENGAGE LEARNING 2013

A Sales Letter to Automobile Customers

The 3Ps In Action

Purpose

Imagine that you own a car dealership in Mesa, Arizona. After the recent car recalls, you have seen a significant decline in business and want to do everything possible to boost sales. Particularly, you focus on generating interest in the Billa model, which you want to sell before more inventory is delivered. You decide to write a letter to customers who have previously bought vehicles at your location.

Process

To plan the sales letter, you first answer the following questions.

1. **Who is my audience?**

   My audience is previous owners, who may be skeptical about buying another car because of the recall news.

2. **What will be my main selling theme?**

   I want to focus on why this is the best time to buy a Billa.

3. **How will I capture the reader's attention with something brief and original?**

   I will use the car slogan: "You are versatile. So is the Billa." Then, I will open the letter to emphasize my main selling theme: "Have you driven the Billa? Now is the time!"

4. **What features will I emphasize, and how will I describe them as benefits to customers?**

   Exterior: "With streamlined aerodynamics, the Billa's sleek exterior looks beautiful and provides maximum fuel efficiency."
   Safety: "Active headrests, patented safety system, and illuminating high beams protect your safety and put you at ease while you enjoy the drive."

5. **What action do I want customers to take, and how can I encourage them to act quickly?**

   I want customers to buy the Billa before the end of the month. "Purchase a Billa before June 30 to take advantage of our special offer: no money down and 0% APR financing for up to 60 months."

Product

BILLA

You are versatile. So is the Billa.

October 14, 2013

Mr. Jon Perez
11 Madison Way
Lincoln, NE 68504

Dear Mr. Perez:

Have you driven the Billa? Now is the time!

Purchase a Billa **before June 30** to take advantage of our special offer: no money down and 0% APR financing for up to 60 months. Choose from many options to build your own car.

Come experience the Billa firsthand to fully appreciate its unique features. With streamlined aerodynamics, the Billa's sleek exterior looks beautiful and provides maximum fuel efficiency. Active headrests, patented safety system, and illuminating high beams protect your safety and put you at ease while you enjoy the drive.

The Billa is like no other car you've driven. Just like you, the Billa is versatile—and it can be yours now. Come in for a ride.

Sincerely,

Marni Mendelson

Marni Mendelson
VP, U.S. Marketing

P.S. Visit your local dealer to take the Billa for a spin. Purchase a Billa before June 30 for no money down and 0% APR financing for up to 60 months. Take advantage of this great deal and drive away in a great car!

Requesting a Visit to Another Dealership

The **3Ps**

In Practice

Purpose

Imagine that you recently purchased a car dealership in Columbus, Ohio. After three months of working at the facility, you realize that you have much to learn. You would like to visit the dealership in Dayton, Ohio—one of the highest-producing operations in the company. You'll need approval from the regional director, Jalisa Jones, who manages several dealerships in the Midwest. Most of your communication with Jalisa has been by email, so you decide to send an email to her with this request.

Process

To plan your email, you first answer the following questions.

1. What is your main point? How will you clearly and concisely describe your request? Be as specific as possible.

2. What are your communication objectives? What, specifically, do you want Jalisa to do after she reads your email?

3. What are the key benefits of your idea—to you and to the company? How can you focus your email around these points?

4. How will you create interest? What would inspire Jalisa to accept your idea?

5. How can you justify your request? What evidence will you present to support your points? How can you quantify the costs? (Here's where you'll need some research—and some imagination.)

6. What obstacles should you address in your email? Realistically, what objections might the regional director have (e.g., travel expenses)? How will you address these in the email?

7. Will you use the direct or indirect plan to organize the email?

8. Write your opening paragraph. How will you describe your purpose and main points up front?

9. How will you summarize your main points and inspire action in your closing?

Product

Draft, revise, format, and proofread your email. Then submit your email and your responses to the process questions to your instructor.

Summary

LO1   Plan a persuasive message for your audience.

The more you know your audience, the more likely you can persuade them. Consider possible resistance and adapt your message accordingly. Use a mix of credibility, emotional appeal, and logical arguments, depending on your audience and the situation. However, be mindful about ethical lines. Never misuse someone's trust to persuade someone to do something that is ultimately not in his or her best interest.

LO2   Write a short persuasive message.

Use a direct writing style when writing to your manager and for most other persuasive messages. Present the idea or request, along with the criteria or a brief rationale, in the first paragraph. Use the indirect style when you expect considerable resistance and for people who prefer this style. First gain the reader's attention by using an opening paragraph that is relevant, interesting, and short. Then provide a variety of evidence—facts, expert opinion, and examples—to support your points. Discuss and minimize any obstacles to your idea, and finally, motivate action.

LO3   Write a sales letter.

For sales letters, introduce a central selling theme early and build on it throughout the message. Devote most of the message to showing how the reader will specifically benefit from owning the product or using the service. Subordinate the price, unless price is the central selling theme.

LO4   Write and respond to negative customer feedback.

Negative customer feedback presents an opportunity for businesses to improve but can be difficult to address online. To write a complaint letter or negative online review as a customer, use an appropriate tone and provide enough evidence to support your points. When responding to negative feedback, consider a personal approach if you know the customer; otherwise, respond online promptly, thank the customer and acknowledge the feedback, apologize where appropriate, explain how the problem will be fixed, and ask for repeat business.

Exercises

LO1 Plan a persuasive message for your audience.

1. Assess what is important to team members.

Think about a team you know well. It could be a volunteer organization, a small group at work, or a sports team. If you were introducing a new idea—one that team members might resist—what would be important to know about each team member that might influence how you tailor your message? You might consider questions such as the following:

- How long has this person been a part of the team?
- How important is the team to the person?
- What level of commitment to the team—rather than to the team member him- or herself—do you see?
- How might the person react to your idea?
- How will this person, specifically, be affected by the change?
- What questions or objections would this person have?

2. Analyze use of ethos, pathos, and logos in a sales call.

In the movie *Boiler Room,* Giovanni Ribisi's character (Seth) is a trainee working at a "chop shop"—a shady brokerage firm that sells stock in fake companies. The movie is based on a real company, previously on Long Island. During a sales call to a prospective customer (Harry), Seth uses credibility (ethos), emotional appeals (pathos), and logical arguments (logos)—but not in a professional, ethical way.

On the DVD, the sales call is at 1:04:28–1:07:56 (in scene 18). You will also find the clip under "Videos" on the author's blog (www.bizcominthenews.com).

As you watch the scene, how do you see Seth using credibility, emotional appeals, and logic to convince Harry to buy stock? Write down specific text that represents each strategy for persuasion. You may use this form for your notes.

Ethos	Pathos	Logos

3. Discuss the ethics of an advertisement.

On its website (Figure 18), a company promises to deposit cash into a customer's bank account within 24 hours. In small groups, discuss tactics this company uses to persuade its audience. How do you see credibility (ethos), emotional appeals (pathos), and logical arguments (logos) used? What is *not* being said that may ultimately turn out badly for a customer?

Figure 18
Website Using Questionable Ethics

PROMISE/CASHCENTER.COM
* No Credit Checks
* Hassle Free
* Cash in Minutes

Receive up to
$2500
deposited into your account!

Apply Today!

First Name   Last Name

Address

Email Address

Phone Number

- GET CASH NOW -

Apply Today!

© YURI ARCURS/SHUTTERSTOCK.COM; © TATIANA POPOVA/SHUTTERSTOCK.COM ; TERRI MILLER/E-VISUAL COMMUNICATIONS, INC.

4. Analyze a scripted video message on MediaCurves.com.

On MediaCurves.com, you'll find several examples of persuasive messages and will see viewers' reactions. Choose one message and analyze how people rate likability, believability, and sincerity.

Pay particular attention to the points at which viewers' ratings increase or dip. What do you believe accounts for these sometimes subtle changes? Discuss your analysis with a partner.

L02 Write a short persuasive message.

5. Write an article on a blog to warn people about quick cash businesses.

To discourage people from signing up at the "Promise Cash Center" site discussed in Exercise 3, write an online article. Imagine that you'll post your article on a site that warns consumers about questionable business practices. Your objective is to convince people that—even though fast cash sounds good—it's not in their best interest in the long term.

Consider these questions as you draft your article:

1. What evidence will you use? Research outside sources to support your view. Include data, expert opinion, and examples where relevant.
2. How will you organize your article—directly or indirectly?
3. What will you write up front to capture and keep the reader's attention?
4. How will you address potential obstacles or objections from readers?
5. What is a catchy title for your article?

6. Identify the organization of a persuasive letter.

When you graduate, you may receive communications from your school's alumni office. For example, the "Open Letter" from Georgia Tech's School of Electrical and Computer Engineering is posted on the school's website (Figure 19).[12]

How is the letter organized—using the direct or indirect approach? What specific examples in the text tell you it's organized in this way? Do you believe this is the best approach for this letter? Why or why not? Write a one-page summary of your analysis.

7. Rewrite an email requesting a favor.

Rewrite Jamie Manor's email in Figure 7. Write a persuasive request using the guidelines you studied in this chapter. See whether you could do a better job to encourage your instructor to review your résumé.

8. Write an email requesting a recommendation.

Imagine that you're interviewing for your ideal job. You're doing well in the process, and the HR manager has asked you for a letter of recommendation from one of your instructors. Write an email to the instructor who knows you best. You may invent details about the job for which you're interviewing.

9. Write an email to suggest an idea.

Similar to Grace Lee's suggestion in Figure 3, write an email to a current or previous employer. Think of an idea that would improve the business: a new procedure, an upgraded system, an innovative product, or some other way to increase sales, improve service, or increase operational efficiencies. Choose something simple enough to convey in a short message. Using the direct plan, put your main point up front, and be sure to use a clear, specific subject line to capture attention.

Figure 19 Georgia Tech Alumni Letter

Search | Contact Us | BuzzPort

GT Home > COE Home > ECE Home > Alumni and External Relations > An Open Letter to Alumni

COLLEGE OF ENGINEERING

School of Electrical and Computer Engineering

Great Minds Think Differently

alumni & external relations

Expand All | Collapse All

+ About ECE

+ Academics

+ Academic Enrichment

+ Research

+ Faculty & Staff

+ Alumni & External Relations

Open Letter from the Chair

Update Your Information With Us

GT Alumni Association

Professional Education

Advisory Board

Corporate Affairs Partnerships (CAP)

Gift Opportunities

Direct Involvement

+ Campuses

+ Media & Calendar

ECE Home

An Open Letter to Alumni of the School of Electrical and Computer Engineering (ECE)

Dear Fellow Alumnus/Alumna,

Thank you for visiting ECE's web site. Like me, you are a member of a rarified group of people who received a degree from our School. This community of people, now numbering over 15,500, continues to make significant and distinctive contributions to our profession and to many related fields.

What you have collectively accomplished is in large measure responsible for the ever-growing tradition and reputation of Georgia Tech and our School as one of the best engineering education and research institutions in the world. In like measure, that reputation enhances the value of all our degrees.

ECE has been working to strengthen its connection with our alumni over the past years. As the School Chair, I am committed to continuing this work, with the goal of making your connection with ECE a lifelong one that will be mutually beneficial.

You can remain involved with the School in many ways. First and foremost, please keep us posted on where you are and what you are doing through our Contact Alumni Affairs at ECE page. Also, keep abreast of what is going on at ECE through our bi annual alumni newsletter, *ECE Connection*, and our on-line newsletter *ECE Highlights*. Visit the institute's Alumni Affairs web site to find out about institute-wide events, continuing education opportunities, and local alumni clubs and activities.

Of course, financial support is always welcome. In fact, the financial contributions of ECE alumni represent a vital resource for the School's programs and services. If you would like to make a contribution, or have an idea for an innovative gift, please contact Martina Emmerson at 404.894.0274 or at martina.emmerson@ece.gatech.edu.

I appreciate your support and honor your continued involvement with the ECE family of faculty, students, staff, and alumni.

Best regards,

Gary S. May,
Professor and Steve W. Chaddick School Chair

Last revised on April 23, 2010

Van Leer Electrical Engineering Building • 777 Atlantic Drive NW • Atlanta, GA 30332-0250 • 404.894.2901 • Fax 404.894.4641
©1994-2010, School of Electrical and Computer Engineering at the Georgia Institute of Technology
GT Legal & Privacy Information

Internet | Protected

L03 Write a sales letter.

10. Write a magazine subscription letter.

Imagine that you work for your favorite magazine. Write a sales letter to encourage new subscriptions. As you're planning your letter, think carefully about your audience:

- Why would they want to subscribe to the magazine? What benefits would they gain?
- What can you offer to make a subscription attractive?
- What are the potential obstacles to your sale? How can you overcome them?
- How can you personalize the letter to your audience?

You'll want to use an indirect style for this letter, so think of a creative, catchy opening that would make your audience read on.

11. Write a fundraising letter to recent alumni.

Imagine that you're working for your college's alumni office. You're asked to write a letter to recent graduates (within the past three years) to inspire them to donate to your school. You may use the Georgia Tech example in Figure 19, but tailor the letter to your school—and to recent graduates. You also may consider that your letter will be sent directly to graduates; this is different from the Georgia Tech example, which is posted on the school website. Consider how this difference might affect the order, content, and tone of your letter.

12. Write a fundraising letter to older alumni.

Now rewrite the letter you wrote for Exercise 11. Adapt it for a new audience: people who graduated between 30 and 40 years ago. What will you change to persuade this cohort to donate to your school?

13. Analyze a sales letter or email you receive.

Be on the lookout for sales letters you receive at home or through email. Bring one to class so you can discuss the example with other students.

In small groups, discuss how the letter or email uses persuasion tactics discussed in this chapter. What works best about the example, and what could be improved? Will you—or did you—purchase the product or service being promoted? Why or why not?

Agree on the best letter or email within your group, and share it with the rest of the class.

14. Write text for a small business website.

If you were starting your own business, how would you represent your product or services on your website? You can use whatever business you'd like: home decorating, house painting, car repair, food delivery, home organizing, résumé editing, personal shopping, photography, or anything else that interests you.

You might start by exploring other small business websites. How do they present their business to the public? How do they organize their message? How do they use vivid language to draw people in?

Write one or two paragraphs about your product or service.

L04 Write and respond to negative customer feedback.

15. Write a complaint letter to a business owner.

Think about a negative customer service experience you had recently. Write a letter to the business owner or the company's customer service department explaining what happened. Be sure to use a credible tone and specific examples to persuade the owner that your experience is valid.

Also find a way to encourage a response from the company. You may ask for reasonable compensation, if appropriate.

16. Give feedback on someone else's letter.

After you complete Exercise 15, switch letters with a partner. Imagine that you're the business owner receiving this complaint. Use the following form to give feedback to your partner. Circle a rating for each question.

Feedback on a Customer Service Letter				
	Not at All	Somewhat	Yes	Definitely
1. The organization works well for the purpose. COMMENTS:	1	2	3	4
2. The tone is appropriate for the audience. COMMENTS:	1	2	3	4
3. Enough details and examples explain the situation. COMMENTS:	1	2	3	4
4. Requests for compensation are reasonable. COMMENTS:	1	2	3	4
5. Correct grammar and punctuation make the letter credible. COMMENTS:	1	2	3	4

17. Respond to a complaint letter.

Imagine that you own the business that is the subject of your peer's complaint in Exercise 15. Respond to the letter using principles discussed in this chapter. You may invent whatever details are necessary to win over the customer.

18. Evaluate negative online reviews.

Find online reviews for a product you would like to buy. Which of the reviews influences you most? What about these reviews do you find persuasive? Discuss your analysis with a partner in class.

19. Write a negative review online.

Now rewrite your customer complaint letter from Exercise 15 for an online review. For your post to an online review site, you have a different audience: the public. Consider making changes for a broader audience, who, like the business owner, cares about your credibility, tone, and details. But, unlike the business owner, this audience may make a buying decision based on your review.

20. Respond to another student's review.

Give the review you completed in the previous exercise to a partner in class. Imagine that you're the proprietor of the business—the owner or a manager who would be responsible for responding to online reviews. First, decide how you would respond to this post. Would you ignore it, write an online response, or try to call or email the customer directly? Then, talk with your partner about your decision. Is this what he or she would prefer? Why or why not?

Next, assume that you'll write a response online. Draft your response, and again ask your partner for feedback. Would he or she be satisfied with the response?

Finally, rewrite the response to perfect it with feedback from your partner.

> **Figure 20**
> **Dissatisfied Customers at the Hotel**

COURTESY OF AMY NEWMAN

21. Write an email to a customer who posted negative feedback.

Imagine that you work for the Colonnade Hotel and Resort, and a customer posted a video of his negative experience checking into the hotel (Figure 20).

The customer also posted a negative review of the hotel on a travel website (Figure 21).

Prepare an email to the customer, addressing his concerns. How can you win over this very angry customer?

22. Rewrite a management response.

In this chapter, we saw that Amy, of Amy's Baking Company, didn't do such a good job responding to a customer's review (Figures 14 and 15). Rewrite Amy's response to get a better reaction.

> **Figure 21**
> **Negative Review of the Colonnade**

Colonnade Hotel and Resort

"No available room for our parents' 50th anniversary!"

kward55

What a scam! My whole family (15 of us) made plans 8 months ago to celebrate my parents' anniversary together. We heard great things about the CHR (and it was beautiful), but when my wife, son, and I arrived at 10 p.m., we were told the hotel was overbooked, and we had to stay at another hotel 15 miles away. The front desk agent was nice enough (although she didn't look too happy about the situation), and CHR paid for our first night, but what a hassle! And my poor parents—this was their dream . . . to celebrate their 50th with their 3 children and 7 grandchildren from all over the country. My brother came in later than we did, and he and his wife were sent to yet another hotel in another direction. What's the point of making reservations far in advance and reserving with a credit card?? Every day, we were on the phone trying to make plans and taking taxis to and from the hotel to see each other. It was crazy. Check out our video on YouTube: http://www.youtube.com/watch?v=0qPeva-fiNA

© ISTOCKPHOTO.COM/SIRIMO

PersuadeCafé

PersuadeCaf

PersuadeCafé, a 220-store coffee and pastry company, is facing several challenges. The company is asking you—one of their smart, new employees—for ideas to improve the business. This scenario encourages you to do the following:

- Analyze company information to determine business priorities.
- Apply persuasive communication strategies to oral and written messages.
- Evaluate messages based on given criteria.
- Adjust communications based on feedback provided.
- Create visuals and a written proposal, including quantitative data, to support an argument.

On www.cengagebrain.com, you'll see PersuadeCafé's employee intranet site, shown below.

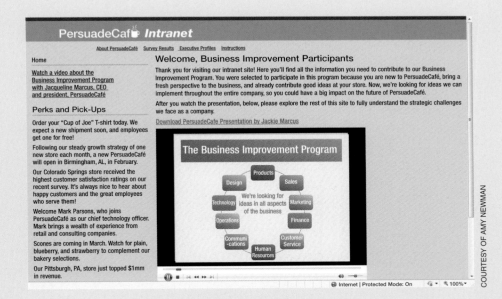

COURTESY OF AMY NEWMAN

The intranet includes information to help you propose a new business idea:

- Presentation by the company CEO and president, Jacqueline Marcus (PowerPoint and audio)
- Company background and menu
- Customer and employee survey results
- Executive profiles
- Assignment instructions

You can start by thinking of an idea you might propose to management and by analyzing the executive who will be most interested in your proposal. Your instructor may assign you to write a pitch memo and provide feedback to another student.

Notes

1. Jim Lentz, ToyotaUSA, "Toyota Talks to Customers About the Sticking Pedal Issue," February 1, 2010, YouTube, www.youtube.com/watch?v=ZCb2dEFBq7I, accessed on October 9, 2010.

2. Cassie Carothers, "Victims Still Falling Prey to Nigerian EMail Scam," Fox News, November 29, 2006, www.foxnews.com/story/0,2933,232500,00.html, accessed August 8, 2010.

3. Cassie Carothers.

4. Herschell Gordon Lewis, *Direct Mail Copy That Sells!* (Englewood Cliffs, NJ: Prentice-Hall, 1984), p. iii.

5. Used with permission from American Express. This letter is from a 1980s marketing campaign.

6. Amazon.com, Kindle Store, www.amazon.com, accessed August 11, 2010.

7. David Pogue, Pogue's Posts, Kindle Tag, New York Times blog, March 5 and July 2, 2009, http://pogue.blogs.nytimes.com/tag/kindle/, accessed August 11, 2010.

8. "Understanding How People Read Your Direct Mail Results in Higher Response Rates," The Lead Tree, May 6, 2010, www.theleadtree.com, accessed August 16, 2010. Original study in German: Professor Siegfried Vögele, "Eye Tracking," Institute for Direct Marketing in Munich, Germany, March 2005, www.braatz-text.de/INSIGHT_10_Augenkamera.pdf, accessed August 16, 2010.

9. "Orangutan Plight Protest at Nestle in York and Croydon," BBC News, March 17 2010, www.bbc.co.uk//2/hi/uk_news/england/8572062.stm, accessed May 27, 2011.

10. Matt Ridings, "Nestle/Facebook/Greenpeace Timeline," techguerilla talk, www.techguerilla.com/nestle-facebook-greenpeace-timeline-in-proces, accessed August 14, 2010.

11. Michele Laudig, "Ouch! Today's Hard Lesson on Yelp," Phoenix NewTimes Blog, August 2, 2010, http://blogs.phoenixnewtimes.com/bella/2010/08/ouch_todays_hard_lesson_on_yel.php, accessed August 11, 2010.

12. Gary S. May, "An Open Letter to Alumni of the School of Electrical and Computer Engineering (ECE)," Georgia Tech, www.ece.gatech.edu/alumni-exrel/letter.html, accessed October 9, 2010.

Chapter 8

Planning the Bad-News Message (8) Organizing to Suit Your Audience (8) Justifying Your Decision (8) Giving the Bad News (8) Closing on a Pleasant Note (8) **Bad-News Messages** (8) Composing Bad-News Replies (8) Rejecting an Idea (8) Refusing a Favor (8) Refusing a Customer Request (8) **Announcing Bad News** (8) Bad News About Normal Operations (8) Bad News About the Organization (8) Bad News About Jobs

LEARNING OBJECTIVES

After you have finished this chapter, you should be able to

LO1 Plan a bad-news message.

LO2 Write a message that rejects an idea.

LO3 Write a message that refuses a favor.

LO4 Write a message that refuses a customer request.

LO5 Write a bad-news announcement.

"Wow, what a way to destroy morale (if there was any of it left)."

— "JON," YAHOO! EMPLOYEE[1]

Chapter Introduction: Communicating Layoffs at Yahoo!

When Yahoo! laid off about 3,200 employees, the company's internal communications—and employees' criticism of them—were posted on several social media sites. Yahoo!'s process for layoffs included at least two steps: the CEO sent an email to all employees, and then managers met individually with affected employees. These steps are typical but didn't escape public scrutiny.

Jerry Yang, Yahoo!'s CEO at the time, communicated the decision in a series of emails to explain the rationale for the layoffs, acknowledge the difficulty of the decision, and thank employees. Although Yang probably had good intentions when writing these messages, employees took particular issue with his use of all lowercase letters, as in this excerpt:

> saying goodbye to colleagues and friends is never easy. they all are dedicated members of our yahoo! family, who worked beside us and shared our passion.

One study identified three main reasons employees found the use of lowercase inappropriate:

- Demonstrated a poor choice for Yang's position as CEO and for the negative message
- Indicated a lack of respect for employees
- Left a negative impression of Yang personally[2]

Employees' comments, as in the following example, reflected hurt and anger: "[S]eriously, is a shift key too much to ask when thousands are losing their jobs?"[3]

To prepare managers for individual meetings with employees, Yahoo! sent a PowerPoint presentation with guidelines. The advice to managers was appropriate, but unfortunately, these slides also became public and were criticized by one website as "Yahoo's secret layoff doublespeak."[4]

This situation is a hard lesson for business communicators: company executives should expect their negative messages to become public. No one likes bad news, and the Internet presents a forum for messages received by a few to be dissected by many.

L01   Plan a bad-news
       message.

PLANNING THE BAD-NEWS MESSAGE

At some point, we'll all be senders and receivers of bad news. Closing an office, discontinuing a product, denying credit, rejecting an offer—bad news is part of running a business.

Just as people don't like hearing bad news, few enjoying giving it—and most people don't do it well. Like persuasive messages, bad-news messages require careful planning. According to Andrew Grove, a founder of Intel Corporation, "The worse the news, the more effort should go into communicating it."[5] Grove should know: Intel, like most companies, has communicated its share of bad news, including thousands of layoffs.

How you write your messages won't change the news, but it may determine how your reader responds. Ideally, when you communicate bad news, your reader will agree with the message, but this won't always happen. Sometimes, the best you can do is to help the reader understand and accept the decision.

Every communication in business can be considered persuasive, and communicating bad news is no exception. However, when communicating bad news, the potential negative consequences are greatest: people who don't like the news or the way you present it are more likely to tell others—and post your written message—on social media sites, as in Yahoo!'s situation.

You have several goals in communicating bad news:

Your objectives are to convey the bad news and retain the reader's goodwill.

- Make your decision clear.
- Help your audience accept the message.
- Maintain a goodwill relationship.
- Prevent further unnecessary discussion.
- Preserve the company's image.
- Protect the company against lawsuits.

Communication Technologies

As we discussed in Chapter 1, the medium you choose for your message is critical. Most people prefer to give and receive bad news in person.[6,7] But this doesn't always happen. A restaurant server in England received this text message: "I think it is best you don't come back to work. I did not like the way you conducted the situation. It left a bad feeling, and it won't be long before you do it again." Apparently, this was a follow-up to her filing a sexual harassment complaint with the owner. An independent dispute-resolution group awarded the employee $120,000 paid by the company.[8]

When communicating bad news, you may achieve your purpose better with a personal visit or phone call than with a written message. Particularly if the news has serious consequences—for example, an employee's promotion wasn't approved, or his or her job has been relocated to another state—then a face-to-face meeting is most appropriate.

However, in-person meetings are not always practical. When meeting in person is too expensive because of travel, or when the news needs to be delivered quickly to many people, we have to choose another medium. For these and other situations, email may be the best choice.

Email is so pervasive in business that it is often used for communicating bad news. Compared to face-to-face meetings, email does have the following advantages for delivering bad news:

- Allows the sender to determine precise wording.
- Gives the reader time to absorb and understand the message before reacting.
- Ensures a consistent message when sent to many people.
- Controls the message time when sent to many people.
- Provides a permanent record of what was communicated.
- Ensures a more accurate and complete message.

This last point is a particularly interesting one, based on a study about delivering bad news by email rather than in person or by phone. The authors hypothesize that because communicating bad news is difficult, the sender often delays, distorts, or incompletely communicates the message. Email may provide just enough distance to help senders communicate more clearly.[9]

When deciding which medium to use for your message, you might consider how the original message was sent. For example, if you received a request over the phone, it's probably best to respond with a phone call rather than an email; otherwise, the receiver may think you're avoiding a more genuine response. But a quick IM request ("Can you please join the meeting at 2?") needs only a quick IM reply ("Sorry, I'm meeting with Ted at 2 and don't want to change it").

Organizing to Suit Your Audience

How you organize your bad-news message depends on the content of the message, your relationship with the reader, and the reader's expectations. An email telling employees that the company cafeteria will be closed on Thursday for cleaning can be written directly. If the company cafeteria will be closed permanently, however, your message would require more explanation and should probably be written using the indirect plan. Analyzing your audience, as you did in previous chapters, will help you decide on a direct or indirect plan.

Direct Plan—Present the Bad News Immediately

As discussed in Chapter 6, many requests are neutral; the writer simply wants a yes-or-no decision and wants to hear it directly. Use the direct plan in these situations:

- The bad news is about a small, insignificant issue that will unlikely elicit an emotional reaction from the reader. When the Internet browser Firefox fails, users get an amusing, direct message with clear solutions (Figure 1).

Figure 1 Firefox Error Message

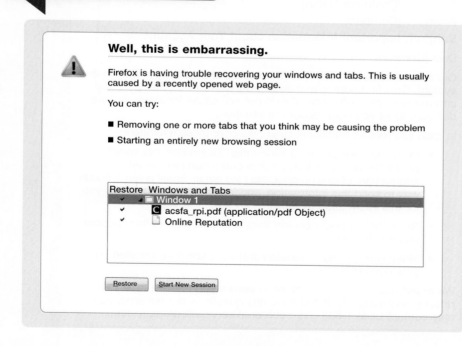

COURTESY OF FIREFOX BROWSER/ FIREFOX® IS A REGISTERED TRADEMARK OF THE MOZILLA FOUNDATION.

Choose the direct organizational plan for communicating bad news to your manager.

- The reader prefers directness. Managers typically prefer that *all* messages from employees be written using the direct plan.
- The reader expects a "no" response. Applicants for a popular reality TV show know that a letter (instead of a phone call) means bad news. An indirect plan in these cases only delays the inevitable rejection and may anger the receiver.
- The writer wants to emphasize the negative news. A forceful "no" may be in order if you're rejecting a proposal a second time or responding to an unreasonable request ("Although Mr. Jackson [the CEO] admires your ambition, it isn't appropriate for you, as an intern, to join his dinner with the Board of Directors on Wednesday"). Sometimes the news is too important for the reader to miss.

When a marketing company's list of email addresses was stolen, several of its clients sent email to their customers. Chase, Kroger, Brookstone, TiVo, and many others sent a message similar to that in Figure 2. The email uses the direct plan because it is a simple, important message.

The direct plan for bad-news messages is the same used for neutral and positive messages discussed in Chapter 6: present the major idea (the bad news) up front.

Figure 2   Email About a Security Breach

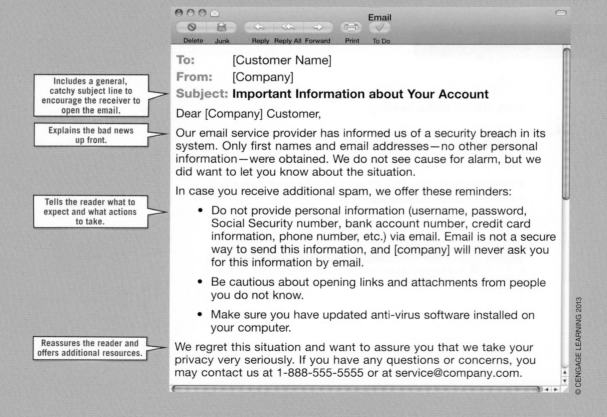

Includes a general, catchy subject line to encourage the receiver to open the email.

Explains the bad news up front.

Tells the reader what to expect and what actions to take.

Reassures the reader and offers additional resources.

To: [Customer Name]
From: [Company]
Subject: Important Information about Your Account

Dear [Company] Customer,

Our email service provider has informed us of a security breach in its system. Only first names and email addresses—no other personal information—were obtained. We do not see cause for alarm, but we did want to let you know about the situation.

In case you receive additional spam, we offer these reminders:

- Do not provide personal information (username, password, Social Security number, bank account number, credit card information, phone number, etc.) via email. Email is not a secure way to send this information, and [company] will never ask you for this information by email.
- Be cautious about opening links and attachments from people you do not know.
- Make sure you have updated anti-virus software installed on your computer.

We regret this situation and want to assure you that we take your privacy very seriously. If you have any questions or concerns, you may contact us at 1-888-555-5555 or at service@company.com.

To help readers accept your decision when using the direct plan, present a brief rationale along with the bad news in the first paragraph.

NOT The annual company picnic originally scheduled for August 3 at Riverside Park has been canceled.

BUT Because ongoing construction at Riverside Park might present safety hazards to our employees and their families, the annual company picnic originally scheduled for August 3 has been canceled.

State the message in language as positive as possible, while still maintaining honesty.

NOT Our compliance report will be late next month. (*too blunt*)
I am pleased to announce that our compliance report will be submitted on March 15. (*too positive*)

BUT Because we needed more time to resolve the Baton Rouge refinery problem, our compliance report will be submitted on March 15 rather than on March 1.

Then follow with an explanation and a friendly closing.

A message organized directly is not necessarily any shorter than one organized indirectly. Both messages may contain the same information in a different order. Compare these two examples (Figure 3).

 Direct messages are not necessarily shorter than indirect messages.

Figure 3
Comparing Direct and Indirect Organizational Plans

Situation: The program chair of the Downtown Marketing Club has written to ask you to be the luncheon speaker at its March 8 meeting, but because of a prior commitment, you must decline.

Scenario 1: You have a close relationship with the program chair. (103 words)	Scenario 2: You have never met the program chair. (101 words)
If I didn't have plans to be in Mexico on March 8, I would have enjoyed speaking to the Downtown Marketing Club. As you know, Hansdorf is opening an outlet in Nogales, and I'll be there March 7–14 interviewing marketing representatives and setting up sales territories.	As a long-time member of the Downtown Marketing Club, I've enjoyed the luncheon speakers the club sponsors each month. Monica Foote's December talk on trends in international marketing was especially interesting and helpful.
If you need a speaker during the summer, please keep me in mind. So far, my travel schedule is quite light during June, July, and August.	As you may know, Hansdorf is opening an outlet in Nogales, Mexico, and I'll be there March 7–14 interviewing marketing representatives and setting up sales territories. So, I unfortunately must decline your thoughtful invitation for March 8.
As a long-time member of the Downtown Marketing Club, I've enjoyed these luncheon speakers, and I hope you find someone else.	If you need a speaker during the summer, please keep me in mind. My travel schedule will be much lighter, and I would be happy to present during that time.
Best wishes for a successful year as program chair.	

© CENGAGE LEARNING 2013

On average, direct messages are shorter than indirect messages, but only because the direct plan is often used for simpler situations, which require little explanation and background information.

Indirect Plan—Buffer the Bad News

Although most business situations in the United States require the direct plan, you will find times when using the indirect plan is best. When presenting negative news using the indirect plan, you present the reasons first, then the negative news. You may want to use an indirect plan to communicate bad news to these audiences:

International Communication

A buffer lessens the impact of bad news.

- Employees who report to you, particularly when an employee is expecting a "yes" answer
- Customers, particularly when delivering news that may be disappointing, such as denying a request to return a high-priced item
- Readers who prefer the indirect plan, such as people in high-context cultures
- People you don't know, who may be turned off without some attempt at relationship building first

In these situations, putting the negative news in the first sentence might be too harsh, and your decision might sound unreasonable until the reader has heard the rationale. Instead, begin with a neutral and relevant statement—one that establishes or strengthens the reader–writer relationship. This statement serves as a **buffer** between the reader and the bad news that will follow (Figure 4).

Complex situations typically call for an indirect organizational plan and require more explanation than simpler situations.

Figure 4 Characteristics of Effective Opening Buffers

Situation: A manufacturer of home theater systems denies a request from a store owner (Parker Electronics) to provide a demonstration model for the store.

Neutral
- Does not convey the news immediately.
- Resists implying positive news, which is misleading.
- **Not neutral:** "Stores like Parker benefit from our policy of not providing demos of our home theater systems."
- **Misleading:** "Your store would be a great venue for a demo product."

Interesting
- Motivates the receiver to continue reading.
- Avoids obvious information.
- **Obvious:** "We have received your request for an in-store demo model."

Relevant
- Provides a smooth transition to the reasons that follow.
- Refers to the original request.
- **Irrelevant:** "Our new V12 system has received rave reviews from the December issue of *Consumer Reports*."

Supportive
- Establishes compatibility between the reader and writer.
- Avoids controversy and condescension.
- **Not supportive:** "You must realize how expensive it would be to supply a demo for every store that sells our products."

Short
- Gets to the main point quickly.
- **Too Long:** "As you may remember, for many years we provided in-store demos of our audio systems. We were happy to do this because we felt that customers needed to hear the surround effects and superior quality compared to competitors' systems. We discontinued this practice last year because ..."

Buffer Type	Example
Agreement	We both recognize the promotional possibilities of having in-store demos.
Appreciation	Thanks for letting us know of your success in selling our V12 Home Theater System. (*Avoid, however, thanking the reader for asking you to do something that you're going to refuse to do, which would sound insincere.*)
Compliment	Congratulations on having served the community of Greenville for ten years.
Facts	Three-fourths of our distributors sold at least 50% more V12 systems than the older A19 model.
General principle	We believe in giving our distributors a wide range of support in promoting our products.
Good news	Our upcoming 20% off sale will be heavily advertised and will likely increase traffic for the holiday season.
Understanding	We want to help you boost sales of the V12.

Figure 5
Types of Buffers

Buffers provide a smooth transition to the discussion of reasons.

Ethics in Communication

Let's look at better options for buffers in this situation (Figure 5).

We use a buffer in a sincere effort to help the reader accept the disappointing news, not to manipulate or confuse the reader. Imagine a situation where an employee is called into a manager's office and doesn't know what to expect. In the exchange in Figure 6, does the manager use buffers well, or is the employee simply rebuffed? A long, false buffer is not ethical communication.

Justifying Your Decision

Presumably, you reached your negative decision by analyzing all the relevant information. Whether you began with a direct or an indirect plan, now explain your

Focus on the reasons for the refusal rather than on the refusal itself.

Figure 6
Buffered or Rebuffed?

1 Manager: "Hi, Melissa, how are you doing today?"

2 Employee: "Great. I finished the Gap proposal yesterday, and I'm waiting for their response."

3 Manager: "How do you think the proposal turned out? You're so good at pricing and figuring out exactly what the client needs."

4 Employee: "Thank you. I enjoy writing proposals, and I'm confident about Gap."

5 Manager: "That's great. I'm glad to hear it. But ..."

6 Employee: "Yes? Is something wrong?"

7 Manager: "Well, no, nothing is wrong, but Paul called, and we didn't get the Gap project."

8 Employee: "We didn't? Why didn't you just say so?"

© CENGAGE LEARNING 2013

analysis to help convince the reader that your decision is reasonable. Most of your message should focus on the reasons rather than on the bad news itself.

For bad-news messages communicated using the direct plan, the reasons can be stated concisely and matter-of-factly. Indirectly written messages, however, require more careful planning—because the stakes are typically greater.

Provide a smooth transition from the opening buffer, and present the reasons honestly and convincingly. If possible, explain how the reasons benefit the reader or, at least, benefit someone other than your organization, as illustrated in these examples:

- You don't provide copies of company documents in order to protect the confidentiality of customer transactions.
- You raised prices of a product in order to use a greener manufacturing process.
- You don't exchange worn garments in order to offer better quality merchandise to your customers.

In a letter from 1956 (Figure 7), the New York Museum of Modern Art rejects an offer from Andy Warhol, one of the most popular and successful artists of our

**Figure 7
Andy Warhol
Rejection Letter**

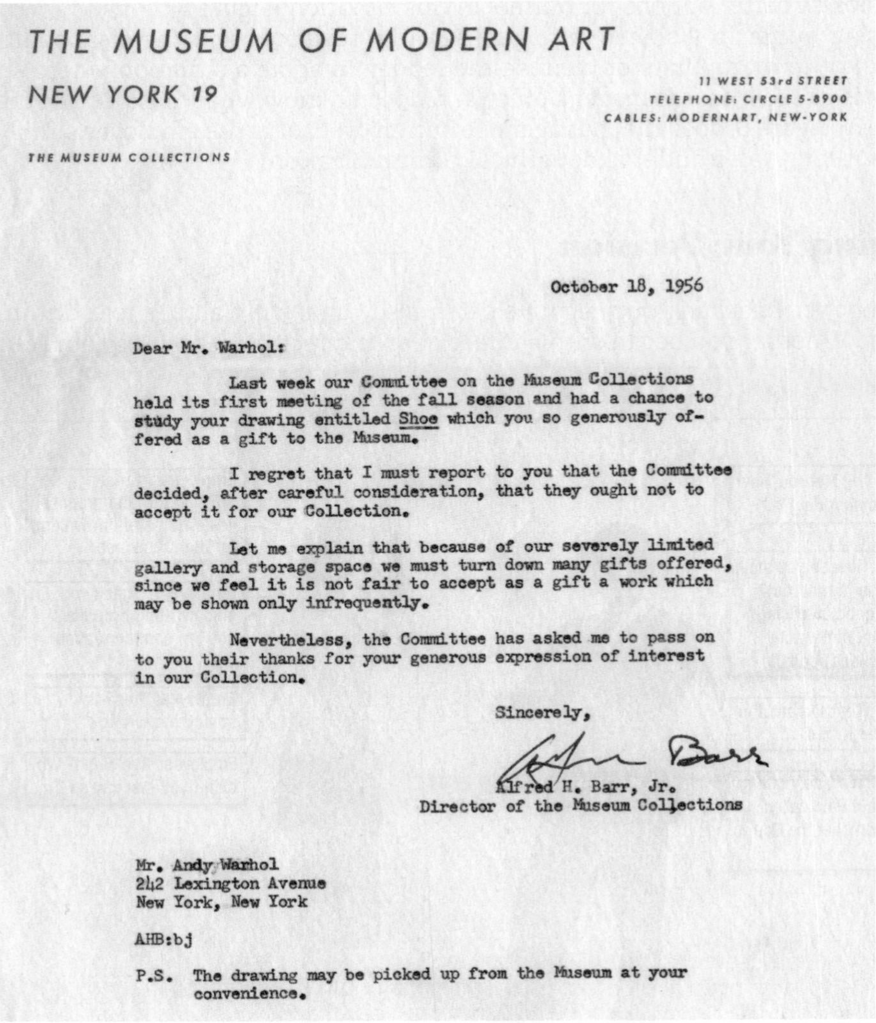

THE MUSEUM OF MODERN ART
NEW YORK 19

11 WEST 53rd STREET
TELEPHONE: CIRCLE 5-8900
CABLES: MODERNART, NEW-YORK

THE MUSEUM COLLECTIONS

October 18, 1956

Dear Mr. Warhol:

Last week our Committee on the Museum Collections held its first meeting of the fall season and had a chance to study your drawing entitled Shoe which you so generously offered as a gift to the Museum.

I regret that I must report to you that the Committee decided, after careful consideration, that they ought not to accept it for our Collection.

Let me explain that because of our severely limited gallery and storage space we must turn down many gifts offered, since we feel it is not fair to accept as a gift a work which may be shown only infrequently.

Nevertheless, the Committee has asked me to pass on to you their thanks for your generous expression of interest in our Collection.

Sincerely,

Alfred H. Barr, Jr.
Director of the Museum Collections

Mr. Andy Warhol
242 Lexington Avenue
New York, New York

AHB:bj

P.S. The drawing may be picked up from the Museum at your convenience.

time. According to the letter, the Museum's decision is based on their "severely limited gallery and storage space." This is a convincing argument—and much kinder than giving personal negative opinions about the drawing. Of course, the rejected drawing would be worth quite a bit of money today.

Presenting reader benefits keeps your decision from sounding selfish. Sometimes, however, granting the request is simply not in the company's best interests. In such situations, don't invent false reader benefits; instead, just provide whatever short explanation you can and let it go at that.

> Because this data would be of strategic importance to our competitors, we treat the information as confidential. Similar information about our entire industry (SIC Code 1473), however, is collected in the annual U.S. Census of Manufacturing. These census reports are available online for public access.

Show the reader that your decision was a *business* decision, not a personal one. Also show that the request was taken seriously, and don't hide behind company policy. People are turned off by hearing "That's just our policy" if it doesn't make sense to them. If the policy is a sound one, it was established for good reasons; therefore, explain the rationale for the policy.

NOT ▶ Company policy prohibits our providing an in-store demonstration product.

BUT ▶ We surveyed our dealers three years ago and found that the space taken up by in-store demos and the resulting traffic problems were not worth the effort. Dealers also had trouble selling demo products, even with large discounts.

The reasons justifying your decision should take up the major part of the message, but be concise, or your readers may become impatient. Do not belabor a point, and do not provide more background than is necessary. If you have several reasons for refusing a request, present the strongest ones first—where they will receive the most emphasis—and omit weak reasons. Why invite a rebuttal? Stick with your most convincing arguments.

Giving the Bad News

The bad news is communicated up front in directly written messages. But even in an indirectly written message, if you explained the reasons well, the bad news itself will come as no surprise; the decision will appear logical and reasonable—the *only* logical and reasonable decision that could have been made under the circumstances.

To retain the reader's goodwill, state the bad news in positive or neutral language, stressing what you *can* do rather than what you *cannot* do. Avoid writing *cannot, are not able to, impossible, unfortunately, sorry,* and *must refuse.* To subordinate the bad news, put it in the middle of a paragraph, and include in the same sentence (or immediately afterward) more reasons.

> In response to these dealer concerns, we eliminated in-store demonstrations and have instead increased our advertising efforts in the print media. We feature a two-page spread in each major Sunday newspaper, including your local paper, the *Greenville Courier.*

When using the indirect plan, phrase the bad news in impersonal language. Avoid *you* and *your* to distance the reader from the bad news; otherwise, the news may feel like a personal rejection. Also avoid *but* and *however* to introduce the bad news; most readers won't remember what was written before the *but*—only what was written after it.

 The reader should be able to infer the bad news before it is presented.

You do not need to apologize for making a rational business decision.

Resist the temptation to apologize for your decision. A reader faced with the same options and information would probably act similarly. Apologizing may unnecessarily weaken your position and make the reader question the decision.

In some situations, the refusal can be implied, making a direct statement of refusal unnecessary. But don't be evasive. If you think a positive, subordinated refusal might be misunderstood, go ahead and state it directly. However, even under these circumstances, you should use impersonal language and include reader benefits.

Closing on a Pleasant Note

Do not refer to the bad news in the closing; end on a positive, friendly, helpful note.

Any refusal, even when handled skillfully, has negative overtones. Therefore, you need to end your message on a more pleasant note. Figure 8 provides approaches to avoid and techniques to use when closing a bad-news message.

To sound sincere and helpful, make your ending original and positive. If you provide a counterproposal or offer other sources of help, provide all information the reader needs to follow through. If you include a sales promotion, make it subtle and reader oriented.

The Checklist for Bad-News Messages summarizes guidelines for writing these difficult messages. The rest of this chapter discusses strategies for writing bad-news replies and bad-news announcements.

**Figure 8
Closing a Bad-News Message**

Approaches to Avoid

Apologizing
Again, I am sorry that we were unable to grant this request.

Anticipating Problems
If you run into other problems, please write to me directly.

Inviting Needless Communication
If you have any further questions, please let me know.

Repeating the Bad News
Although we are unable to supply an in-store demo model, we do wish you much success during your holiday season.

Using a Cliché
If we can be of any further help, please don't hesitate to call us.

Revealing a Doubt
I trust that you now understand why we made this decision.

Sounding Selfish
Don't forget to feature the V12 prominently in your holiday display.

Techniques to Use

Offering Best Wishes
Best wishes for success during the holiday season. We have certainly enjoyed our ten-year relationship with Parker and look forward to continuing to serve your needs in the future.

Suggesting a Counterproposal
To provide increased publicity during the holidays, we would be happy to include a special 2-by-6-inch boxed notice of your sale in the *Greenville Courier* edition of our ad on Sunday, February 8. Just send us your copy by January 26.

Directing to Other Sources
To provide increased publicity for the holiday season, we would be happy to provide a demo of the A19 model.

Referring to Sales Promotions
You can be sure that the V12 we're introducing this month will draw many customers to your store during the holidays.

Checklist for Bad-News Messages

GO

Determine How to Start the Message

Direct Plan. Use a direct organizational plan when the bad news is insignificant, the reader prefers directness (such as your manager) or expects a "no" response, or you want to emphasize the bad news. Present the bad news, along with a brief rationale, in the first paragraph.

Indirect Plan. Use an indirect organizational plan when writing to people who report to you, customers, readers who prefer the indirect plan, or readers you don't know. Start by buffering the bad news, following these guidelines:

- ☑ Remember the purpose: to establish a common ground with the reader.
- ☑ Select an opening statement that is neutral, relevant, supportive, interesting, and short.
- ☑ Consider establishing a point of agreement, expressing appreciation, giving a sincere compliment, presenting a fact or general principle, giving good news, or showing understanding.
- ☑ Provide a smooth transition from the buffer to the reasons that follow.

Justify Your Decision

- ☑ If possible, stress reasons that benefit someone other than yourself.
- ☑ State reasons in positive language.
- ☑ Avoid relying on "company policy"; instead, explain the reason behind the policy.

- ☑ State reasons concisely to avoid reader impatience. Do not over explain.
- ☑ Present the strongest reasons first; avoid discussing weak reasons.

Give the Bad News

- ☑ If using the indirect plan, subordinate the bad news by putting it in the middle of a paragraph and discussing additional reasons.
- ☑ Present the bad news as a logical outcome of the reasons given.
- ☑ State the bad news in positive and impersonal language. Avoid terms such as *cannot* and *your*.
- ☑ Do not apologize.
- ☑ Make the refusal definite—by implication if appropriate; otherwise, by stating it directly.

Close on a Positive Note

- ☑ Make your closing original, friendly, off the topic of the bad news, and positive.
- ☑ Consider expressing best wishes, offering a counterproposal, suggesting other sources of help, or building in subtle sales promotion.
- ☑ Avoid anticipating problems, apologizing, inviting needless communication, referring to the bad news, repeating a cliché, revealing doubt, or sounding selfish.

COMPOSING BAD-NEWS REPLIES

Even the best written bad-news message can test a reader's goodwill. In this section, you'll learn principles for writing three types of negative replies while maintaining a positive relationship:

- Rejecting an idea
- Refusing a favor
- Refusing a customer request

LO2 Write a message that rejects an idea.

Rejecting an Idea

One of the more challenging bad-news messages to write is one that rejects someone's idea or proposal. Put yourself in the role of the person making the suggestion, for example, Grace Lee, who recommended that Jason's Deli and Restaurant add hot food items (presented in Chapter 7, Figure 3). Grace was excited about her idea and wants her suggestion to be accepted.

If Jason decides to reject Grace's idea, he'll be in a tough spot. He needs to explain his decision without discouraging Grace from submitting ideas in the future. If his communication is successful, Jason will achieve the following:

- Recognize Grace's hard work.
- Educate Grace by explaining business realities she may not know.
- Focus on business—not personal—reasons for the decision.
- Use the indirect plan to gradually persuade Grace that her idea isn't in the best interests of the company.

Let's see how Jason's message turned out (Figure 9). His email communicates bad news, but it's also a *persuasive* message. Like all bad-news messages, the email persuades the reader that the writer's position is reasonable.

Figure 9   Rejecting an Idea

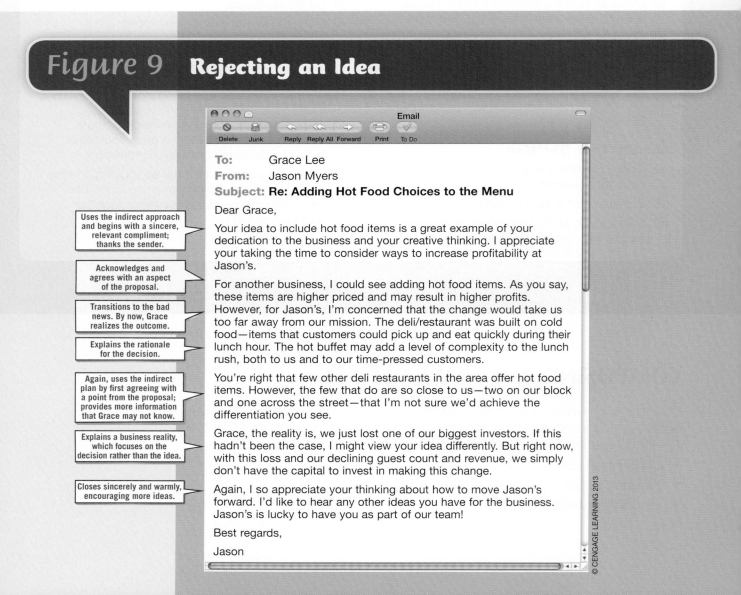

To: Grace Lee
From: Jason Myers
Subject: Re: Adding Hot Food Choices to the Menu

Dear Grace,

Uses the indirect approach and begins with a sincere, relevant compliment; thanks the sender.

Your idea to include hot food items is a great example of your dedication to the business and your creative thinking. I appreciate your taking the time to consider ways to increase profitability at Jason's.

Acknowledges and agrees with an aspect of the proposal.

Transitions to the bad news. By now, Grace realizes the outcome.

Explains the rationale for the decision.

For another business, I could see adding hot food items. As you say, these items are higher priced and may result in higher profits. However, for Jason's, I'm concerned that the change would take us too far away from our mission. The deli/restaurant was built on cold food—items that customers could pick up and eat quickly during their lunch hour. The hot buffet may add a level of complexity to the lunch rush, both to us and to our time-pressed customers.

Again, uses the indirect plan by first agreeing with a point from the proposal; provides more information that Grace may not know.

You're right that few other deli restaurants in the area offer hot food items. However, the few that do are so close to us—two on our block and one across the street—that I'm not sure we'd achieve the differentiation you see.

Explains a business reality, which focuses on the decision rather than the idea.

Grace, the reality is, we just lost one of our biggest investors. If this hadn't been the case, I might view your idea differently. But right now, with this loss and our declining guest count and revenue, we simply don't have the capital to invest in making this change.

Closes sincerely and warmly, encouraging more ideas.

Again, I so appreciate your thinking about how to move Jason's forward. I'd like to hear any other ideas you have for the business. Jason's is lucky to have you as part of our team!

Best regards,

Jason

© CENGAGE LEARNING 2013

Refusing a Favor

People rely on friends and coworkers in companies for favors. We do favors for each other out of service and because we may need a favor in return some day. But, for business or personal reasons, we cannot always accommodate requests.

How you write your message refusing a favor depends on the circumstances. If someone asks for a favor that requires a large time commitment, he or she probably wrote a thoughtful message trying to persuade you. In this case, an indirect plan for your response is most appropriate.

Most requests for favors, however, are routine, and you may write your response using the direct organizational plan. A colleague asking you to attend a meeting in her place, an employee asking for a deadline extension, or a business associate inviting you to lunch will not be deeply disappointed if you decline. The writer probably has not spent a great deal of energy composing the request; he or she simply wants a "yes" or "no" response.

Imagine a situation where an employee requests free conference admission for a planning committee. In Figure 10, Swati Mellone uses the direct plan to give her refusal in the first paragraph. After denying the request, she gives clear reasons for the decision and offers a possible alternative without making promises.

L03   Write a message that refuses a favor.

 When refusing routine requests, give the refusal in the first paragraph.

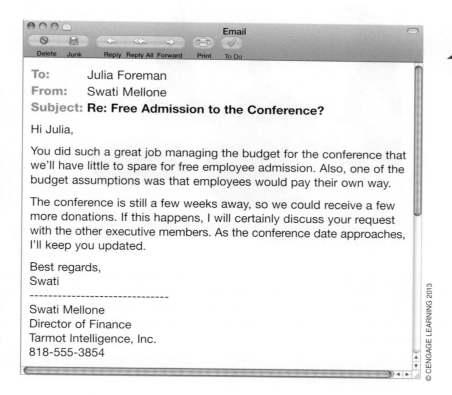

**Figure 10
Refusing a Favor
(Direct Plan)**

To: Julia Foreman
From: Swati Mellone
Subject: **Re: Free Admission to the Conference?**

Hi Julia,

You did such a great job managing the budget for the conference that we'll have little to spare for free employee admission. Also, one of the budget assumptions was that employees would pay their own way.

The conference is still a few weeks away, so we could receive a few more donations. If this happens, I will certainly discuss your request with the other executive members. As the conference date approaches, I'll keep you updated.

Best regards,
Swati

Swati Mellone
Director of Finance
Tarmot Intelligence, Inc.
818-555-3854

© CENGAGE LEARNING 2013

Refusing a Customer Request

The indirect plan is almost always used when refusing a customer's request because the reader (a dissatisfied customer) is emotionally involved in the situation. The customer is already upset by the failure of the product or service to live up to

L04   Write a message that refuses a customer request.

expectations. If you refuse the claim immediately, you risk losing the customer's goodwill—and, as discussed earlier, having the situation go viral through social media sites.

United Airlines made a big mistake when it mishandled a passenger's request to reimburse him for a broken guitar. Dave Carroll, a talented musician, wrote a catchy song with the verse, "United, you broke my Taylor guitar." The song, "United Breaks Guitars," became a YouTube sensation, with over 10 million views.[10]

The situation was exacerbated by United's poor customer service. On his blog, Carroll explains his frustration: "This stopped being about compensation when the airline flatly refused to consider the matter and . . . I committed to telling the rest of the story."[11] Carroll created two more videos and released a new album. This story was quite embarrassing for United Airlines and cost the company much more than the $3,500 price tag of a new Taylor guitar. By some estimates, the damage was $180 million, representing a 10% drop in share price because of bad press about the incident.[12]

Dave Carroll set his complaint about United Airlines to music—a viral video.

> **Use impersonal, neutral language to explain the basis for the refusal.**

Companies don't have to grant all requests, but they do have to handle the communication well. Always use a respectful tone with customers—even when the customer is at fault. To separate the reader from the refusal, begin with a buffer, using one of the techniques presented earlier (e.g., showing understanding).

Marathon runners like you depend on a resilient shoe that will hold up for many months under normal use.

When explaining the reasons for denying the request, do not accuse or lecture the reader. At the same time, however, don't appear to accept responsibility for the problem if the customer is at fault. Use impersonal, neutral language to explain why the request is being denied.

NOT ▶ The reason the handles ripped off your Samsonite luggage is that you overloaded it. The tag on the luggage clearly states that you should use the luggage only for clothing, with a maximum of 40 pounds. However, our engineers concluded that you had put at least 65 pounds of items in the luggage.

BUT On receiving your piece of Samsonite luggage, we sent it to our testing department. The engineers there found stretch marks on the leather and a frayed nylon stitching cord. They concluded that such wear could have been caused only by contents weighing substantially more than the 40-pound maximum weight that is stated on the luggage tag. Such use is beyond the "normal wear and tear" covered in our warranty.

Note that in the second example, the pronoun *you* is not used at all when discussing the bad news. By using third-person pronouns and the passive voice, the example avoids directly accusing the reader of misusing the product. The actual refusal, given in the last sentence, is conveyed in neutral language.

As with other bad-news messages, close on a friendly, forward-looking note. If you can offer a compromise, it will take the sting out of the rejection and show the customer that you are reasonable. Compromises also help the customer save face. Be careful, however, not to take responsibility.

 An offer of a compromise, however small, helps retain the reader's goodwill.

Although we replace luggage only when it is damaged in normal use, our repair shop tells me the damaged handle can easily be replaced. We would be happy to do so for $38.50, including return shipping. If you would like us to do this, please respond to this email, and we will return your repaired luggage within two weeks.

Somewhere in your letter you might include a subtle pitch for resale. Although the customer has had a negative experience with your product, you might remind him or her why he or she bought the product in the first place. But use this technique carefully; a strong pitch may simply annoy an already-unhappy customer.

ANNOUNCING BAD NEWS

L05   Write a bad-news announcement.

We just discussed strategies for writing negative replies. Often, however, we're presenting bad news about a new situation. Quite often, these messages go to a large internal or external audience. These are just some of the many examples of bad news that companies need to communicate:

 Bad-news announcements are not in response to any request.

- The company suffered a bad fiscal quarter.
- An executive is leaving.
- Employees will be laid off.
- A product is being discontinued.
- Prices are increasing.
- Stores will be closed or departments consolidated.
- The company has been acquired.
- The company is accused of wrongdoing.
- The company lost a big lawsuit.
- A product is being recalled.
- Service cannot be fulfilled.
- A fire caused damage.

Not every organizational change is negative for all audiences—for example, a company acquisition may be good news to shareholders and executives who will be retained, but bad news for employees who will be made redundant (a euphemism for fired). For this reason, messages about corporate change must be tailored to each audience affected, with particular attention paid to those affected negatively.

As with other bad-news messages, you must decide whether to use the direct or the indirect plan of organization. Consider how the bad news will affect your audience and your relationship with them.

Bad News About Normal Operations

Let's look at how a cabin tent manufacturer might communicate a price increase to different audiences (Figure 11). The increase is a routine message for the order department but requires more explanation for wholesalers and end users. Of course, a smart company would provide its order department with all communications so that customer service representatives can answer questions about the change properly.

Figure 11
Communicating a Price Increase to Different Audiences

Situation: Management has decided to increase by 10% the price of the Danforth cabin tent you manufacture. You have to notify your order department, your wholesalers, and a special retail customer. How would you adapt your message to these different audiences?

Order Department

To this group, the price change is routine. What matters most is how the procedures need to change, so you can probably send an email using the direct plan.

Effective March 1, the regular price of our Danforth cabin tent (Item R-885) changes from $148.99 to $164.99, an increase of 10%. Any order postmarked before March 1 should be billed at the lower price, regardless of when the order is actually shipped.

The new price will be shown in our spring catalog, and a notice is being sent immediately to all wholesalers. If you receive orders postmarked on or after March 1 but showing the old price, please notify the wholesaler before filling the order.

Wholesalers

Wholesalers probably won't be personally disappointed, so you may use the direct approach, but you do need to justify the price increase. The bad news is cushioned by presenting the reason (which is beyond your control) and including resale in the closing paragraph.

Because of the prolonged strike in South African mines, we now must purchase the chrome used in our Danforth cabin tent elsewhere at a higher cost. Thus, effective March 1, the regular price of the Danforth tent (Item R-885) will change from $148.99 to $164.99.

As a courtesy to our wholesalers, however, we are billing any orders postmarked prior to March 1 at the old price of $148.99. Please use the online form or call us at 800-555-9843 to place your order for what American Camper calls the "sock-it-to-me" tent.

Association for Backpackers and Campers

You have an exclusive marketing agreement with this organization. It promotes the Danforth cabin tent in each issue of *Field News*, its quarterly magazine, at no cost to you in exchange for your offering ABC members the wholesale price of $148.99 (a 26% savings).

This is a critical audience who may respond particularly negatively to the news. Use the indirect plan to communicate the price increase.

The popularity of the Danforth cabin tent that you feature in each issue of *Field News* is based partly on our exclusive use of a chrome frame. Chrome is twice as strong as aluminum, yet it weighs about the same.

Because of the prolonged strike in South African mines, we were faced with the choice of either switching to aluminum or securing the needed chrome elsewhere at a higher cost. We elected to continue using chrome in our tent. This decision to maintain quality has resulted in a change in the wholesale price of the Danforth cabin tent (Item R-885) from $148.99 to $164.99.

The Danforth tent promotion in the spring issue of *Field News* should be changed to reflect this new price. Because the spring issue usually arrives the last week of February, we will bill any orders postmarked before March 1 at the lower price of $148.99.

We have enjoyed serving ABC members, and we extend best wishes to your organization for another successful year of providing such valuable service to American backpackers and campers.

© CENGAGE LEARNING 2013

During difficult times, companies still can communicate effectively with customers. Borders, the second-largest bookstore operator in the United States, sent email to its reward customers when the company filed for Chapter 11 bankruptcy protection. Understandably, customers would have questions about how they would be affected during the company's restructuring. As you can see in Figure 12, the company did an excellent job of reassuring its most valuable customers—without glossing over the current situation.

Figure 12 Borders Updates Reward Customers During the Bankruptcy Process

FREE SHIPPING
ON BORDERS.COM ORDERS FOR
BORDERS REWARDS PLUS VENDORS

BORDERS™

>>FREE eREADER APPS

BOOKS   eBOOKS   MUSIC   DVDS   KIDS   BORDERS MEDIA   GIFT CARDS   STORES & EVENTS

Personalizes the message to a select group of customers.

Dear Borders Rewards Member,

Uses the indirect plan to provide history and context for the decision.

For generations, Borders stores have been beacons of enlightenment and education, where readers young and old explore their passions and find those special books that speak to them personally. As Borders moves forward, our commitment to you is to be a best-in-class bookseller—whether it's our stores or Borders.com—where you can purchase books and related products that stimulate and satisfy your reading interests.

Explains the Chapter 11 decision.

However, because of the ongoing impact of the difficult U.S. economy, coupled with the rapidly changing bookselling environment, we must restructure Borders and reposition our business for long-term success. We determined that the best path for Borders to have the ability to achieve this reorganization is through the Chapter 11 process, which we commenced February 16.

Uses a conversational style and a personal approach from the company's leader.

Throughout this process, I want you to know that:

Uses headings to address customers' questions.

Borders stores are open for business. Borders pioneered the in-store experience, providing customers with a vast assortment of books in a warm, relaxing environment—and we intend to build on this. Our stores will continue to be community gathering places. Families can still enjoy enriching events, including author readings and signings, book clubs, and kids' storytime and parties.

Highlights customers' most prevalent concerns.

Our Borders Rewards programs, including Borders Rewards Plus, remain in effect. Customers can continue to earn and redeem their rewards in-store and at Borders.com. We are also honoring gift cards as usual, which can also be redeemed in-store and at Borders.com.

Borders.com is operating as usual. We are fulfilling online orders, and you can continue to choose from millions of books, CDs, and DVDs, as well as other entertainment items.

eBook libraries are perfectly safe. Our partner Kobo will continue to provide access to all eBooks purchased through Borders, and continue to sell eBooks to Borders customers.

Borders will continue to maintain its strong national presence. Our nationwide network of stores is foundational to the Borders brand. Over the next several weeks, however, Borders will be closing underperforming stores within our network. Should your local store be affected, please visit Borders.com to find another Borders store near you, or to purchase from our incredible selection of books, music, and movies.

Reassures customers with a positive, forward-looking tone.

Over the next several months, we will build on our core strengths as a great bookseller with the goal of emerging as the destination of choice for the millions of customers who shop our stores each year.

Provides additional resources for customers.

For more information, please visit www.bordersreorganization.com. You may also call our Customer Care Center at (800) 770-7811, or contact them at ccare@borders.com.

Sincerely,

Is written by the president and CEO, demonstrating his personal commitment to customers and to the future of the company.

Mike Edwards
President and CEO, Borders, Inc.

Bad News About the Organization

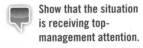

Show that the situation is receiving top-management attention.

If your organization is experiencing serious problems, your employees, customers, and investors should hear the news from you—not from a newspaper, a blog, or the grapevine. For serious problems that receive widespread attention, the company's public relations department will issue a news release.

In these cases, the company will communicate with several internal and external audiences. In a crisis situation, the management team needs a crisis communication plan to ensure clear, consistent messages to all internal and external constituencies.

Anything you write may be made public and could be taken out of context. When writing bad news about the company, choose your words carefully, but also recognize that you can't always control how your message is interpreted, as in the example in Figure 13.

Figure 13
Misinterpreting a President's Message

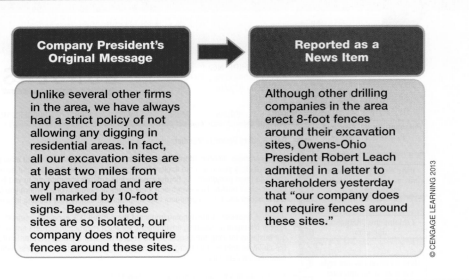

Company President's Original Message

Unlike several other firms in the area, we have always had a strict policy of not allowing any digging in residential areas. In fact, all our excavation sites are at least two miles from any paved road and are well marked by 10-foot signs. Because these sites are so isolated, our company does not require fences around these sites.

Reported as a News Item

Although other drilling companies in the area erect 8-foot fences around their excavation sites, Owens-Ohio President Robert Leach admitted in a letter to shareholders yesterday that "our company does not require fences around these sites."

© CENGAGE LEARNING 2013

The last sentence of the president's statement would have been more effective had it been worded in positive, impersonal language.

Fences are unnecessary in such isolated sites and, in fact, can cause safety hazards of their own. For example . . .

If the reader has already learned about the situation from other sources, your best strategy is to use a direct organizational plan. Confirm the bad news quickly and immediately provide information to help the reader understand the situation.

When you entered the building this morning, you probably saw the broken window in the lobby. The purpose of this memo is to let you know exactly what happened and to outline steps we are taking to ensure the continued safety of our employees who work during evening hours.

If the reader is hearing the news for the first time, your best strategy is to use the indirect plan, using a buffer opening and stressing the most positive aspects of the situation (in this case, the steps you're taking to prevent a recurrence of the problem).

As an employee working the night shift, your safety and well-being are of prime concern to us. In that spirit, I would like to discuss with you several steps we are taking as a result of . . .

Bad News About Jobs

One of the toughest parts of a manager's job is communicating bad news about employees' jobs. When decisions affect people personally—particularly their livelihood and their self-esteem—no one wants to be the messenger.

Companies regularly make decisions that have negative results for employees: they reduce benefits, relocate, change policies, and, possibly most dramatically, lay off employees. Maintaining employees' goodwill in these situations is just as important as maintaining customers' goodwill. Employees have the same ability to use traditional news channels and social media to gossip about the company, and with or without cause, they can sue you. In addition, of course, treating employees with respect is the right thing to do. At some point, your company hired these employees, hoping for a promising future with them.

 Pay as much attention to communicating bad news to employees as you would for customers.

When Yahoo! downsized, as you read in the chapter introduction, the CEO's email was criticized, particularly because of the lowercase lettering. But Yang's message followed many principles for effectively communicating negative information about jobs. The message in Figure 14 was posted on the Yahoo! website.[13]

You may wonder why this memo uses the direct organizational plan, and why this works well. Although employees likely reacted emotionally (one reason to use the indirect plan), they had expected the news. Starting with a buffer and placing the news at the end would feel manipulative to employees who know what's coming. When Intel laid off employees, CEO and President Paul Otellini also began his email to employees with the bad news up front:[14]

> This week we're taking an important and difficult step in our efficiency project: reducing the number of Intel managers by about 1,000 people worldwide. Only managers, ranging from senior to first-line, are affected. This step is important because it addresses a key problem we've found in our efficiency analysis—slow and ineffective decision making, resulting, in part, from too many management layers.

However, Starbucks' founder and CEO Howard Schultz used the indirect plan in his bad-news email to employees:[15]

> As you well know, these are very challenging times for everyone at Starbucks. We are working hard to navigate both a deteriorating global economy and the restructuring of our business. And we do so with the ever-present priority to preserve the culture and guiding principles of our company

 The direct and indirect plan can work equally well for bad news about jobs, depending on the company culture and whether employees are expecting the news.

Schultz's email to employees then discusses the decline in revenue and the need to "re-architect" the company's cost structure. The email then describes Starbucks' investment in health care benefits and stock options for employees. Finally, the email explains that 700 non-store employees will be laid off, and 6,000 store positions will be lost. Schultz builds his case for the bad news rather than presenting the layoff decisions up front. His email works equally well as the direct-plan messages and may be more appropriate to the situation, organizational culture, and management style.

All of these messages effectively follow principles for communicating bad news that affects employees' jobs. No manager wants to tell employees they're fired, but all managers likely will have to deliver this news at some point during their career.

Figure 14   Yahoo! Layoff Email

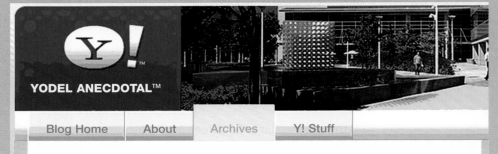

YODEL ANECDOTAL™

| Blog Home | About | Archives | Y! Stuff |

Tough times

Posted December 10th, 2008 at 11:06 am by Jerry Yang, CEO & Chief Yahoo

56 Comments / Filed in: General

As we announced in October, we've been aggressively managing our costs to bring them in line with the challenging economic conditions. Unfortunately, that means laying off employees — by far the toughest part of being a manager. Here's the email I sent to Yahoos today:

> **Refers to "yahoos," the term for employees at the company.**

yahoos,

today, most of our layoffs in the US are happening, and they've been underway in other regions around the world.

> **Uses the direct organizational plan, which is appropriate because employees know the bad news is coming.**

this is a tough time for all of us and i wanted to take a moment to reach out to you.

> **Acknowledges the difficulty of the decision.**

saying goodbye to colleagues and friends is never easy. they all are dedicated members of our yahoo! family, who worked beside us and shared our passion.

> **Sounds sincere and authentic.**

> **Clearly and simply explains the rationale for the decision.**

but as you all know, we must take actions to better perform in today's turbulent global economy. while we've found efficiencies in many parts of our business, laying off employees is unfortunately unavoidable. our difficult decision to let colleagues go reflects the changes we're having to make to better align costs with revenues — something businesses in virtually every sector are also having to do.

> **Again acknowledges the impact, thanks employees, and describes compensation to be provided.**

for those who are affected by these layoffs, i am extremely grateful for your contributions to yahoo!. we realize the impact this will have on you. that's why, consistent with our past practices, we're making every effort to support you with severance packages and other services.

> **Closes with a forward-looking approach (but isn't dismissive). Restates gratitude.**

the reductions we're making are very hard, but they are also very necessary — as we focus on the long-term health of our business. to those who are leaving us, i extend my heartfelt thanks on behalf of yahoos everywhere — you will be missed.

thanks,
jerry

> **Closes informally.**

Rejecting an Idea to Spin Off a Company Division

The
3Ps
In Action

Purpose

Imagine that you are division head of Photog, a website for sharing and storing photos and videos. Your company (Yippee) bought the website from Allupe in 2007 and has since integrated Photog into the business.

Imagine that a small team of people who worked for Allupe remains with the division today, and some believe Photog would be better off as an independent unit. This group wants to see Photog spun off from Yippee, with the possibility of being sold to a company such as Google or Microsoft.

Over the past four years, you have repeatedly heard arguments for this strategy, and you have tried to be clear that selling off Photog is not part of Yippee's plan. At this point, you decide to write an email to employees to put an end to the discussion and to reassure employees who worry what a sale might mean for them personally.

Process

1. **Describe your primary audience and the idea.**

   Employees who would like to see Photog spun off from Yippee. This group is highly vocal and loyal to the division and the company's founders. Seeing the final decision in writing may frustrate this group.

   These employees believe that Photog deserves more attention than Yippee provides. Additional funding and a clearer strategy, according to this group, would enable Photog to compete more successfully with growing sites such as Facebook, which dwarfs Photog's number of photos by about 40 billion.

   Some analysts value Photog between $2.2 and $4 billion, which the employees say would be a welcome contribution to Yippee's bottom line.

2. **Describe your secondary audience.**

   Employees who work within the Photog division but do not favor the idea of a spin-off. This group will be glad to see the final decision in writing.

3. **Brainstorm reasons why you might reject the idea. Then, after you've come up with several, order them with your most convincing argument first.**

   a. Photog is a profitable part of Yippee and an important part of Yippee's social media mission.

   b. Yippee needs Photog to compete with sites such as Google's Picasa and YouTube.

   c. Yippee will not relinquish the level of traffic the site brings to Yippee's suite of products.

   d. When Yippee bought Photog, it closed Yippee Photos, which will not likely be reinstated.

4. **Write your buffer opening—neutral, relevant, supportive, interesting, and short.**

   Over the past few years, we have had many discussions about whether Yippee should sell Photog. Photog is an important part of Yippee's suite of products and brings substantial revenue to the company.

5. **Write the closing for your letter—original, off the topic of the refusal, and positive.**

   I appreciate your commitment to Photog, and I know that the recommendation to spin off comes from a good place. We all want to succeed and grow as much as possible. Let's focus on what's ahead of us and stick to the plan.

Product

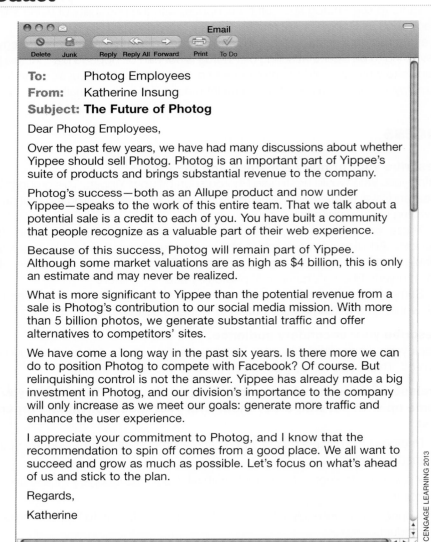

Email

Delete   Junk   Reply Reply All Forward   Print   To Do

To: Photog Employees
From: Katherine Insung
Subject: **The Future of Photog**

Dear Photog Employees,

Over the past few years, we have had many discussions about whether Yippee should sell Photog. Photog is an important part of Yippee's suite of products and brings substantial revenue to the company.

Photog's success—both as an Allupe product and now under Yippee—speaks to the work of this entire team. That we talk about a potential sale is a credit to each of you. You have built a community that people recognize as a valuable part of their web experience.

Because of this success, Photog will remain part of Yippee. Although some market valuations are as high as $4 billion, this is only an estimate and may never be realized.

What is more significant to Yippee than the potential revenue from a sale is Photog's contribution to our social media mission. With more than 5 billion photos, we generate substantial traffic and offer alternatives to competitors' sites.

We have come a long way in the past six years. Is there more we can do to position Photog to compete with Facebook? Of course. But relinquishing control is not the answer. Yippee has already made a big investment in Photog, and our division's importance to the company will only increase as we meet our goals: generate more traffic and enhance the user experience.

I appreciate your commitment to Photog, and I know that the recommendation to spin off comes from a good place. We all want to succeed and grow as much as possible. Let's focus on what's ahead of us and stick to the plan.

Regards,

Katherine

Announcing the Close of a Division

The
3Ps
In Practice

Purpose

Imagine that you are the head of Yippee's video division and have the unfortunate task of communicating to employees—by email—that the service will be discontinued. The company's plan is to archive current videos but no longer host new videos. With competing sites such as YouTube, Hulu, and Vimeo, Yippee does not see a competitive advantage and wants to invest in other services, such as email and photo sharing.

Process

1. What is the purpose of your message?
2. Describe your audience.
3. Should you use a direct or an indirect organizational plan? Why?
4. Write the first sentence of your email. Be professional, yet sensitive to employees' concerns.
5. How much space should you devote to discussing the reasons for the decision? Why?
6. Write the last sentence of your email. Strive for a forward-looking approach, but be careful not to minimize employees' feelings.

Product

Draft, revise, format, and proofread your email. Then submit both your answers to the process questions and your revised email to your instructor.

Summary

L01 Plan a bad-news message.

When writing a bad-news message, your goal is to convey the bad news and, at the same time, keep the reader's goodwill. A direct organizational plan is recommended when you are writing to your manager, the bad news is relatively insignificant, or you want to emphasize the bad news. When using the direct plan, state the bad news in positive language in the first paragraph, with a short buffer or a reason for the decision. Then present the explanation or reasons, and close on a friendly and positive note.

When writing to people who report to you, customers, people who prefer a less direct style, and people you don't know, consider using an indirect plan. This approach begins with a buffer—a neutral and relevant statement that helps establish or strengthen the reader–writer relationship. Next, explain the bad news and provide reasons. The reasons should be logical and, when possible, should identify a reader benefit. The bad news should be subordinated, using positive and impersonal language; apologies are not necessary. The closing should be friendly, positive, and off the topic.

L02 Write a message that rejects an idea.

When rejecting someone's idea, tact is especially important. Because the person presenting the idea believes it has merit, devote most of your message to presenting reasons for the rejection. Show that the proposal was carefully considered and that the rejection is based on business, not personal, beliefs.

L03 Write a message that refuses a favor.

Most requests for favors are routine and should receive a routine response written in the direct organizational plan. Give your refusal in the first paragraph, but be sensitive to the reader's feelings. Provide a quick, reasonable rationale for declining.

L04 Write a message that refuses a customer request.

Use the indirect plan when refusing a customer's request. The tone of your refusal must convey respect and consideration for the customer, even when the customer is at fault. When explaining the reasons for denying the request, do not accuse or lecture the reader. Close on a friendly, forward-looking note.

L05 Write a bad-news announcement.

Announcements of bad news may be either internal (addressed to employees) or external (addressed to those outside the organization). If the bad news will have little effect on the reader, use a direct organizational plan. If the reader will be personally affected by the announcement, consider an indirect plan (unless the reader is well aware of the bad news). Stress any positive aspects, such as steps you're taking to resolve the situation.

Exercises

L01 Plan a bad-news message.

1. Organize a bad-news message.

For the following situations, would you use the direct or indirect organizational plan for a written message? When you choose an organizational plan, you're making assumptions about your readers and how they might react. Discuss your ideas in small groups.

- After three on-site job interviews, you decline an offer for a summer internship with an alumnus of your college.

- After meeting a CEO at an on-campus job fair, you decline an interview with the company because it is not in your hometown.
- You decline a lunch invitation from a college friend who works for a competitor.
- You decline an employee's vacation request because he wants to be away during your busy season.
- You inform a supplier that you do not plan to renew your contract.
- You inform customers that a product has been discontinued.

2. Practice writing buffers.

For the situations in Exercise 1 for which you chose the indirect plan, write a buffer statement. Then compare your buffers with those of two other students. Which work best and why?

3. Discuss a situation when you received bad news.

In groups of three or four, discuss a situation when you received bad news. This could be anything work related or personal that is appropriate for you to discuss in class. Did the sender use the direct or indirect organizational plan to communicate the news to you? Did you find this approach effective? Why or why not? If not, what would have been a better approach?

4. Send an email rejecting an idea for online ordering.

Imagine that you run a local used bookstore, where you receive this email from a new employee:

L02 Write a message that rejects an idea.

> **Email**
>
> Delete   Junk   Reply Reply All Forward   Print   To Do
>
> **To:**   Ben Marcus
> **From:**   Amanda Choi
> **Subject: Expanding through online ordering**
> Hi Ben,
>
> I thought it would be a good idea to expand the website and offer online ordering. This could increase sales!
>
> Amanda

© CENGAGE LEARNING 2013

Write an email response to this employee rejecting the suggestion. You can invent whatever rationale you'd like, and keep in mind that this employee did not put a lot of thought into the suggestion.

5. Write a memo rejecting an idea to shorten wait lines.

You're new to the management staff of Cedar Point, a large amusement park in Sandusky, Ohio. Cedar Point is renowned for its 14 roller coasters and dozens of other exciting rides. Each ride can accommodate many people at once, so the lines don't stand still for very long.

Even so, on summer holidays and weekends, the wait for Cedar Point's most popular rides, such as the Millennium Force roller coaster, can be lengthy. In fact, when *Wall Street Journal* reporters sampled the midday waiting time at parks around the United States, they waited one hour for the two-minute Millennium Force ride. At the other end of the spectrum, the reporters waited only 11 minutes or less to jump on rides at

Coney Island in Brooklyn, New York, an old-fashioned park where the lines lengthen after dark.

Your boss, Cedar Point's top operational officer, has asked all employees to submit ideas for a system that would make the wait less onerous for customers. One employee suggests that parents with strollers be allowed to go to the front of the line, on the theory that this policy reduces the likelihood of noisy scenes with fussy kids.

You believe that other customers would resent this system; you also don't believe that it would dramatically affect either the wait or customers' perceptions of it. You decide to reject this idea. Write this memo, using your knowledge of bad-news replies (making up any details you need).

6. Write a blog post to reject an idea on behalf of Starbucks.

Imagine that you work for Starbucks. The company has a well-developed website, My Starbucks Idea, which gathers suggestions from customers and employees (www.mystarbucksidea.com). Review a few suggestions, and choose one for your negative response.

As you prepare your reply, you may need to do some research about the issue and about Starbucks' current practices. Then, write your response as a blog entry, which might be posted on the site (although Starbucks does not respond to all ideas posted).

7. Write an email refusing an employee's request.[16]

You manage the conventions department for a hotel, where you supervise an employee named Robert. Robert is responsible for meeting with companies that hold events at the hotel. This morning, you received the following email from Robert:

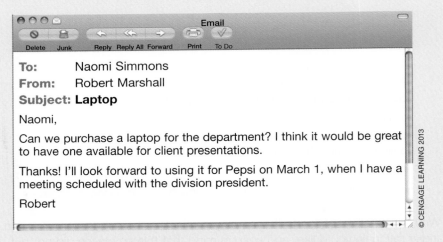

To: Naomi Simmons
From: Robert Marshall
Subject: Laptop

Naomi,

Can we purchase a laptop for the department? I think it would be great to have one available for client presentations.

Thanks! I'll look forward to using it for Pepsi on March 1, when I have a meeting scheduled with the division president.

Robert

You won't be able to approve this request for the following reasons:

- You have no budget for this capital expense. It's possible to budget for this next year, but you're not sure a laptop just for client presentations would be worth the expense. You really don't see the point because you recently spent a lot on printing beautiful materials, which Robert takes to clients with him.

- Robert started work at your company only one month ago. Although you encourage ideas, you do not like Robert's presumptuous tone.

- Also, you'd like to encourage Robert to put more time and thought into his ideas. Although not a huge expense, a laptop for your department would need to be justified—and Robert would benefit from supporting his suggestions more convincingly.

- His preliminary marketing plan was due on Wednesday, but he hasn't submitted it yet. You'd like him to focus on his current responsibilities as a priority.

- On the other hand, you hired Robert because of his strong work background and excellent skills, and you *hope* he will have a long career with your company. Also, the hiring process was lengthy and expensive, and you have no desire to go through it again. You don't want to discourage him.

Write an email to Robert that rejects his request.

Next, exchange emails with another student. At this point, your instructor may give you more information about Robert's perspective. If you were Robert, how would you react to the email? Provide feedback to the original writer.

8. Write a letter to refuse a favor for a colleague's son.

Assume the role of vice president of operations for Kolor Kosmetics, a small manufacturer in Biloxi, Mississippi. One of your colleagues from the local chamber of commerce, Dr. Andrea T. Mazzi, has written asking whether your firm can provide a summer internship in your department for her son Peter, a college sophomore who is interested in a manufacturing career. Kolor Kosmetics has no provisions for temporary summer employees and does not currently operate an internship program. Also, the factory shuts down for a two-week vacation every July.

Write a letter to Dr. Mazzi explaining why you are unable to provide a summer internship to her son Peter.

LO3 Write a message that refuses a favor.

9. Write an email denying a request for a salary advance.

Imagine that you own a website design firm, and an employee asks you for a favor: a one-month salary advance. This is one of your best employees, someone who has worked with you for over five years, and you know she's buying a house. But you cannot advance her the money for these reasons:

- It's against your company policy (according to your employee handbook).
- You want to be fair to everyone and cannot accommodate others' requests.
- You don't want this to set a precedent for this employee.
- You don't believe it's your responsibility.

Decide how you'll organize the email and which of these reasons you will present to the employee. You don't need to include everything unless you believe it will explain your rationale and maintain the employee's goodwill.

10. Write an email rejecting an exception.

Imagine that you work for a Fortune 500 investment bank. It's two weeks before the annual Take Our Sons and Daughters to Work Day, and one of your employees asks you for a favor. Although it's clearly stated on the company intranet and in the email reminder that employees may bring only two children to work, this employee wants to bring a third child.

The employee explains that his youngest child, Emanuel, has a strong interest in finance and would get a lot out of the experience of visiting you at work. He also wants to bring his two older children, who have participated for the past three years.

Acting as the HR Director for the investment bank, write an email denying the employee's request.

11. Write an email to turn down an invitation.

You are the purchasing manager at your firm and have received an email from Barbara Sorrels, one of your firm's major suppliers. She will be in town on October 13 and would like to take you out to dinner that evening. However, you have an early morning flight on October 14 to Kansas City and will need to pack and make last-minute preparations on the evening of the 13th. Write an email to Barbara declining her invitation.

L04 Write a message that refuses a customer request.

12. Write a letter refusing a customer's request for reimbursement.

As the president's assistant at the Ford Motor Company, you received a customer letter. The customer complains that her Ford Escort is a "lemon" and has cost her over $3,000 in repairs over a two-year period after the warranty expired. She wants to be reimbursed $3,000. You cannot grant her request; however, you can offer her a credit for $1,000 toward the purchase of a new Ford car.

Write a letter explaining the decision. Present your rationale in a way that acknowledges the customer's concerns yet avoids paying for past repairs.

13. Write an email refusing a customer's request for a refund.

On Twitter, a Whole Foods customer posted this tweet:

bbkendel Barb Kendel
Whole Foods' salad bar made me sick! Was ill all afternoon at work. Want $9.59 back.
5 Jun

© CENGAGE LEARNING 2013

As a representative for Whole Foods, you find this tweet and send the customer a direct message (DM) to obtain his email address. In your email to the customer, reject his request for a refund. You may invent your own rationale for the decision. Also try including a subtle sales promotion in your closing paragraph.

Exchange drafts with a partner in class and give each other feedback on the approach.

14. Write an email refusing a customer's request to waive a fee.

Imagine that you work for Bank of America's credit card division, and you're trying to resolve a complaint from a customer. Through an online form on the website, you receive a customer's message, requesting that the bank waive $75 of overdraft fees accrued over the past three months.

Your policy doesn't require you to waive these fees, although you have for some customers. However, you deny this customer's request for two primary reasons:

- The customer had similar overdraft fees in the previous quarter, so the customer is aware of these fees.
- The customer's account is overdue; a bill has not been paid in two months.

Write an email to communicate your decision to the customer.

15. Write an email about a pending lawsuit against the company.

L05 Write a bad-news announcement.

Imagine that you're the CEO of a chain of retail stores. Last week, you received notification of a lawsuit against your company. An employee who was terminated for poor performance last month is suing for wrongful discharge, claiming sex discrimination. You had hoped to keep this quiet, but you saw a report on the local news this morning about the suit. Embarrassed by the report and concerned about the company's image, you decide to do some damage control internally. You need employees to hear from you directly—to reassure them and to explain your side of the story.

Working in small groups, write a memo to store employees. When in your groups, first discuss your goals for this message, and then plan what you will include and how you will organize the message.

Assign one role to each student in your group: legal counsel, human resources representative, public relations manager, and the former employee's direct supervisor. As you play these roles, think about the concerns or questions a person in that position would have. How will you contribute to the development of this communication?

Here are a few facts of the case:

- Employee's Background Information: Amelie Cardon, sales associate, 28 years old, 2 years with the company, female.

- Performance Record: Received a poor performance review last year because of many customer complaints and a poor attendance record.

- Supervisor: Marilyn Simone, sales manager.

- News report: The reports on TV and in the local newspaper discuss details of Cardon's lawsuit, which includes accusations of being called names and receiving unfair treatment. Cardon claims she had no knowledge of customer complaints and had a perfect attendance record.

One of the biggest decisions you have as a team is to decide how many of these details to include in your memo to employees. How much do people need to know? You may invent more information to give employees a full sense of what is happening.

16. Write a memo announcing employee layoffs.

You are the SVP of human resources for a financial software company that has 7,500 employees. The company has decided to sell AccountSoft, one of its major products. The software has suffered declining sales for the past two years, and it no longer fits with the new mission of the company, which is to sell to small businesses and individuals, rather than larger accounting firms (currently 95% of AccountSoft's buyers).

You will have individual conversations with employees who are affected by the layoffs, but first you advise the CEO to send an email to all employees to announce the decision to sell AccountSoft and to prepare employees for the downsizing and what will happen next.

As you write this memo for the CEO to send under his name, consider that not all employees from the AccountSoft division will be laid off. The software developers will go to the acquiring firm, Accounting Support Services, Inc., but the sales and marketing staff (about 150 people) will be leaving the firm. This was your agreement with Accounting Support Services, as part of the acquisition deal.

Write the memo to communicate the decision clearly and help employees understand and accept the message.

17. Write an email to tell employees about a product recall.

As the vice president of public relations at GM, you just wrote the following news release about vehicle recalls.[17] Next, you will work with the vice president of human resources to communicate this news to employees. Rewrite this external message so that it is appropriate for your internal audience. Address your email to all GM employees.

 **News**

For Immediate Release

GM Recalls Crossovers for Safety Belt Inspection
Potential Second-Row Buckle Damage Leads to Voluntary Action

DETROIT - General Motors is voluntarily conducting a safety recall for 2009-2010 models of the Chevrolet Traverse, Buick Enclave, GMC Acadia and Saturn Outlook to inspect second-row safety belts for damage that in rare cases could make an occupant think the belt is properly latched when it isn't.

There are 243,403 vehicles involved in the recall, the majority in the United States with several thousand exported vehicles in Canada, Mexico, China and Saudi Arabia and small populations in other countries.

GM discovered damaged second-row safety belt buckles among warranty returns. There are no known cases where second-row safety belts have failed to perform properly in a crash.

Some vehicles may have a condition where the second-row seat side trim shield restricts the upward rotation of the seat belt buckle when the seat back is returned to a seating position after being folded flat. If the buckle makes contact with the seat frame, the buckle may receive cosmetic damage as the seat back is being returned to its upright position. When this occurs, the customer may notice that additional effort is required to return the seat to a seating position.

But if sufficient force is applied, the buckle cover could be pushed down the strap, exposing and partially depressing the red release button. The seat belt release button may not travel as much as designed when depressed. The buckle may not latch or unlatch and may appear to be jammed. In rare instances, the buckle may appear to latch when the latch mechanism is not fully engaged.

"Because of the potential for a false-latch condition, we want customers to return their vehicles to have the recall repair performed as soon as possible," said Jeff Boyer, GM executive director of safety.

Owners will begin receiving letters this month to schedule appointments with dealership service departments for a no-charge inspection and repair of the second-row belts. Dealer service personnel will reshape the side trim to allow easier belt clearance and inspect the second-row belt buckles for damage. Damaged buckles will be replaced free of charge.

18. Write a memo announcing no bonus.

You are the manager of a fitness equipment manufacturing plant called Muscles Galore located in Gary, Indiana. The plant has been in operation for seven years. Over the years your employees have been very productive, and sales have been high. Therefore, Muscles Galore has been able to give generous holiday bonuses (usually more than $1,000) to all of its employees for the last five years.

This year, however, because of a slow economy, you will not be able to offer the holiday bonus. Although the workers have been very productive, fitness equipment sales are down about 15% from last year. Your projections indicate that the economy is recovering, and sales should be up about 20% next year. If the projections are accurate, you should be able to offer the bonus again next year—but you won't make any promises.

Write a memo to your employees letting them know the bad news. Add details to make your message complete.

19. Write a letter announcing a decision not to renew a lease.

Assume the role of Gene Harley, the leasing manager of Northern Shopping Plaza. You have decided not to renew the lease of T-shirts Plus, which operates a tiny T-shirt decorating outlet in the mall. Three times in the past 13 months, the store's employees have left their heat-transfer machinery switched on after closing. Each time, the smoke activated the mall's smoke alarms and brought the fire department to the mall during the late-night hours. Although no damage has occurred, your insurance agent warns that the mall's rates will rise if this situation continues.

The lease that T-shirts Plus signed five years ago specifies that either party can decide not to renew. All that is required is written notification to the other party at least 90 days in advance of the yearly anniversary of the contract date. By writing this week, you will be providing adequate notice. Convey this information to the store's manager, Henry D. Curtis.

20. Write a letter about no longer volunteering.

You own Kitco Inc., a small financial consulting firm in Baton Rouge, Louisiana. For the last 12 years, some of your employees have voluntarily prepared and served a Thanksgiving meal at St. Benedict's homeless shelter in Baton Rouge. You paid for the turkeys, hams, and other trimmings to feed the 100–150 people; your employees cooked the food at their homes and served the meal at a local church. This meal has been greatly appreciated by the St. Benedict staff and anticipated by the poor and homeless people in the area. However, you are closing your office in Baton Rouge and moving to Dallas in early October; therefore, no one from your company will be available in Baton Rouge to prepare and serve the meal. You have enjoyed your partnership with the homeless shelter, and you plan to continue the tradition in Dallas. Although you cannot prepare and serve the meal, you will donate $250 to the shelter to cover the cost of buying the food. Write a letter to Pastor Sullivan DeMarco, giving him the bad news.

21. Write an email about a party cancellation.

Nobody likes a party more than Edgar Dunkirk, the president of Rockabilly Enterprises, a record label. In the early days, the company's holiday parties were legendary for their splendid food arrangements and outstanding entertainment (featuring the label's popular singing stars). Employees performed elaborate skits and competed for valuable prizes. These days, however, sales of the company's country and rockabilly recordings are down. In fact, Dunkirk recently had to lay off 150 of the company's 350 employees, the most severe austerity measure in the company's history.

Because so many employees had to be let go, including some who had helped Dunkirk found the company a decade ago, the president has decided that a lavish party would be inappropriate. He has therefore canceled the traditional holiday party. As Dunkirk's vice president of human resources, write an email communicating the news to Rockabilly's employees.

22. Write a product recall letter.

You have received two reports that users of your ten-stitch portable sewing machine, Sew-Now, have been injured when the needle broke off while sewing. One person was sewing lined denim, and the other was sewing drapery fabric—neither of which should have been used on this small machine. Fortunately, neither injury was serious. Although your firm accepts no responsibility for these injuries, you decide to recall all Sew-Now machines to have a stronger needle installed.

Owners should take their machines to the store where they purchased them. These stores have been notified and already have a supply of the replacement needles. The needle can be replaced while the customer waits. Alternatively, users can ship their machines to you prepaid. Other than shipping, there is no cost to the user.

Prepare a letter that will go out to the 1,750 Sew-Now purchasers. Customers can call your toll-free number if they have questions.

Company Scenario

Aggresshop

Let's revisit Aggresshop, the company struggling to improve customer service in its retail stores. As you read at the end of Chapter 1 and online, Aggresshop has received several customer complaints, and the CEO, Andrea Jewel, is taking action.

Imagine that you are part of the company management team and receive this email from Andrea about a change in compensation structure:

To: Aggresshop Managers
From: Andrea Jewel
Subject: New Commission Structure and Service Standards for Sales Associates

Aggresshop Managers,

As you know, Rob Cuervo, our HR director, has been working diligently to redesign the compensation structure for our sales associates. We appreciate all of your help during the past three months, particularly the store managers and associates we have consulted during this process.

At this point, we are ready to communicate the new guidelines. I realize that most of our sales associates will be unhappy about these changes. But we must stay true to our mission and customer commitment and, of course, be financially responsible. This email answers the following questions you may have:

- Why are we making this change?
- What is the new compensation structure?
- What are the new customer service standards?
- How will we communicate these changes?

Why are we making this change?

Most of you understand the impetus of this change, but I'd like to review this so we're giving consistent messages to sales associates in all 16 stores. Primarily, this change was inspired by two discoveries: negative feedback on the Aggresshop customer blog and large compensation payouts.

As we have all read on the customer blog, comments are overwhelmingly negative and surprisingly consistent about our associates' behavior in the stores. The YouTube video, in particular, has been an embarrassment to us. To make short-term sales transactions, our associates are being overly aggressive with customers and fighting with each other. We must fix this and the negative perception of our service.

The compensation structure for sales associates is likely contributing to the problem. When we designed the commission and bonus plans five years ago, we had all good intentions. We wanted to reward our associates generously, with a clear focus on selling more expensive items. The strategy worked: we have grown tremendously and now sell only high-end, luxury items. But now that we have such highly priced items, this structure is overly generous and pays far more than we intended. The bonus plan only exacerbates the problem.

What is the new compensation structure?

We have created a new commission plan more in line with industry standards and have eliminated the bonus plan entirely. Unlike other luxury boutique shops, we have decided to keep some commission-based compensation because we still want our sales associates engaged with our customers, and we see value in encouraging sales. The new commission structure for employees who work at least 35 hours per week is below.

New Commission Structure
(based on the dollar amount sold per store, per month)

$100,000 – $150,000	$150,001 – 200,000	$200,001 – $250,000	Over $250,000
.5%	1%	1.5%	2%

| ● ● ● ✉ | | | | Email | | | | ⬯ |

| ⊘ Delete | 🗃 Junk | | ↩ Reply | ↩↩ Reply All | → Forward | 🖨 Print | ✓ To Do | |

This new commission structure accomplishes a few objectives for us:
- Ensures more reasonable payouts for associates, with lower rates overall.
- Rewards store, rather than individual, performance to encourage more collaboration among sales associates.
- Recognizes only full-time associates' contribution to the store.
- Focuses on longer-term goals because commissions are based on monthly, rather than daily, performance.

I realize this system is imperfect, too. Not every store has the same opportunity to bring in sales, not all sales associates work equally hard to encourage sales, etc. But this structure will work better than our previous one, and we can make adjustments over time.

What are the new customer service standards?

In addition to the new commission plan, several of you thought it was important for us to be more specific about how we expect our sales associates to interact with customers. I thought this was a great idea, and Rob has worked with many of you and associates throughout the country to create our customer service standards. We will communicate these to sales associates as well.

How will we communicate these changes?

I understand these are difficult messages to communicate to our sales associates, and we may lose some of our top performers. But we cannot maintain a compensation structure that hurts our image and conflicts with our mission and customer commitment. Let's do our best to communicate these changes in a way that's transparent, yet firm. We'll implement a two-step process to announce the changes:
1. Our corporate communications director will send a memo to all sales associates.
2. Store managers will hold meetings with sales associates at each store.

Thank you again for your support with this change. Please let me know if there's anything I can do to help you communicate these messages to our associates, and I look forward to hearing your feedback.

Best regards,

Andrea

Andrea Jewel, Chief Executive Officer

Aggresshop Inc. | 555 Bonaventura Blvd. | San Diego, CA 92101 | Phone: (619) 555-1124 | Email: ajewel@aggresshop.com

Your role is to communicate the bad news, as we discussed in this chapter. Your instructor may ask you to complete two assignments, acting as two different roles within the organization:

- Write an internal memo to all sales associates (from the corporate communication director).
- Hold a face-to-face meeting with sales associates at one store (led by a store manager).

These assignments will challenge you to adjust your content for each message, taking into consideration how your audience—unhappy sales associates—is likely to react.

Notes

1. "jon," cited by Cynthia L. King, "Email Capitalization and CEO Ethos: Examining Online Responses to Yahoo's Layoff Email," *Proceedings of 74th Annual Convention of the Association for Business Communication*, Portsmouth, VA, November 4–7, 2009.

2. Cynthia L. King.

3. "Nancy L.," cited by Cynthia L. King.

4. "Yahoo's Secret Layoff Doublespeak Revealed!" Valleywag, http://gawker.com/5106184/yahoos-secret-layoff-doublespeak-revealed?tag=valleywag, accessed June 17, 2010.

5. Dianna Booher, *Communicate with Confidence: How to Say It Right the First Time and Every Time* (New York: McGraw-Hill, 1994).

6. Harris International and Whitepages.com, "Survey Shows Most Adults Want Tough Talks Face to Face," February 27, 2007, www.whitepagesinc.com/press/article/000000073, accessed July 12, 2010.

7. Rana Tassabehji and Maria Vakola, "Business Email: The Killer Impact," *Communications of the ACM* 48, no. 11 (November 2005): 64–70.

8. Sam Narisi, "Woman Fired via Text Message Wins 120k," *HR Tech News*, July 22, 2008, www.hrtechnews.com/woman-fired-over-text-message-wins-120k/, accessed August 14, 2010.

9. Stephanie Watts Sussman and Lee Sproull, "Straight Talk: Delivering Bad News through Electronic Communication," *Information Systems Research* 10, no. 2 (June 1999): 150–166.

10. David Carroll Music, "United Breaks Guitars Trilogy Story," www.davecarrollmusic.com/ubg/story/, accessed August 17, 2010.

11. Dave Carroll, "United Breaks Guitars Three: The Finale," www.davecarrollmusic.com/2010/03/united-breaks-guitars-song-3/, accessed April 19, 2011.

12. Ravi Sawhney, "Broken Guitar Has United Playing the Blues to the Tune of $180 Million," *Fast Company*, July 28, 2009, www.fastcompany.com/blog/ravi-sawhney/design-reach/youtube-serves-180-million-heartbreak, accessed April 19, 2011.

13. Jerry Yang, "Tough Times," Yodel Anecdotal, December 10, 2008, http://ycorpblog.com/2008/12/10/tough-times/, accessed January 15, 2011.

14. Paul Otellini, "Making Intel More Efficient," *eWEEK*, posted July 14, 2006, www.eweek.com/c/a/Desktops-and-Notebooks/Otellini-Memo-Making-Intel-More-Efficient/, accessed August 18, 2010.

15. Howard M. Schultz, Memo to Employees, from Meg Marco, "300 Starbucks Will Close, Brand New Fancy Jet Will Be Sold," February 2, 2009, http://consumerist.com/2009/02/300-starbucks-will-close-brand-new-fancy-jet-will-be-sold.html, accessed December 19, 2010.

16. Adapted and used with permission from David Lennox, Cornell University, School of Hotel Administration, August 17, 2010.

17. "GM Recalls Crossovers for Safety Belt Inspection," General Motors News, August 17, 2010, http://media.gm.com/content/media/us/en/news/news_detail.brand_gm.html/content/Pages/news/us/en/2010/Aug/0817_gm_safety, accessed August 19, 2010.

Chapter 9

LEARNING OBJECTIVES

After you have finished this chapter, you should be able to

L01 Find relevant sources for a report.

L02 Evaluate the quality of data.

L03 Develop a questionnaire and cover letter.

L04 Construct tables and charts.

L05 Interpret data for the report reader.

"The more McDonald's knows about the people it is serving, the more it is able to communicate messages which appeal to them."

— McDONALD'S, THE MARKETING PROCESS[1]

Chapter Introduction: International Market Research at McDonald's

In the Philippines, instead of "Would you like fries with that?" you might hear, "Would you like McSpaghetti with that?" (in Filipino, of course). Or maybe you'd prefer a Bacon Roll (bacon on a hard roll with ketchup) in England or—for you fish lovers—a McLobster Sandwich in Canada.[2] Just as McDonald's adapts its website to different cultures, the company offers different products in different countries.

McDonald's relies on market research data to determine which products will be successful with which consumers. What attracts an American parent with two children to McDonald's is quite different from what appeals to a South Korean teenager. The company's extensive research indicates the "key audiences" within a region and the best product mix for each group. Detailed market data answers important questions for the company:

- What products are well received?
- What prices are consumers willing to pay?
- What advertising do consumers currently read or watch?
- What restaurants do consumers visit?[3]

Meeting market demands is a moving target. Product mix is continuously adjusted to respond to changes in technology, legal requirements, the economy, and social preferences.[4] Companies that want to stay ahead of the competition use data to monitor their key audiences and make smart business decisions.

The Nürnburger, three bratwurst with mustard and grilled onions, is available in Germany.

© FLORIAN SEEFRIED/GETTY IMAGES

WHO READS AND WRITES REPORTS

Managers need information to make good business decisions, such as the following:

- A sales manager at General Motors headquarters uses information provided by field representatives to make sales projections. If hybrid car sales are up, manufacturing will ramp up to produce more.
- A vice president of information technology at CVS asks store managers to track wait times to determine how many cash registers are needed in each store.
- A human resources manager at The Home Depot surveys staff to pinpoint causes of low morale. If employees are unhappy with their opportunities for advancement, HR may implement a career development program.
- A product manager for Ben & Jerry's Ice Cream conducts market research to test a new flavor.
- A business development manager at Kroger reviews usage of their pilot gas station. If usage is high enough, the manager will recommend implementing stations at all stores.

 A wide variety of reports helps managers solve problems.

 For guidelines on preparing other types of business reports, see Common Types of Business Reports, in the Reference Manual at the end of this book.

These situations show why a wide variety of reports is essential to today's organization. Because managers don't always have the time, resources, or expertise, they often rely on others for information, analysis, and recommendations to help make decisions and solve problems. Reports travel upward, downward, and laterally within the organization, so reading and writing reports is a typical part of nearly every manager's responsibilities.

In any organization, unique problems and opportunities require **situational reports**, which are produced only once. These reports are often more challenging than ongoing reports, such as a weekly time log or monthly sales analysis, because they require the writer to start from scratch. For each report, writers need to determine what and how much information to include, and how best to organize and present the findings. These one-of-a-kind projects will be the focus of this chapter (see Figure 1 for an example).[5]

For our purposes, we define a **business report** as an organized presentation of information used to make decisions and solve problems (Figure 2). At work, you're likely to see many reports for a variety of audiences.

L01   Find relevant sources for a report.

FINDING SOURCES FOR YOUR REPORT

Before you collect any data, plan your approach:

1. Define the report purpose.
2. Analyze the intended audience.
3. Determine what data is needed to solve the problem or make a decision.

Your data will come from several sources. You may include data that you already have (either in your mind or from previous work), you may need to find data from other sources, or you may have to generate your own data.

Start the data-collection phase by **factoring** your problem—breaking it down to determine what data you need to collect. Let's say you own a small chain of restaurants and are considering offering healthier menu choices for children. What information would you need to make a decision? You might want answers to the following questions:

- What is the nutritional content of our current menu options for kids?
- What are the industry trends? How prevalent is the move toward healthier menus for kids?

Although the word *data* is technically the plural form of *datum*, in most cases in this text the term is used as a collective noun and takes a singular verb. The Usage Panel for the *American Heritage Dictionary* endorses this position.

Figure 1   Sample Situational Report

Includes a specific subject line about the situation.

Provides brief context and the report purpose up front.

Identifies criteria for comparing the information.

Uses a table to compare information easily.

States the recommendation and time frame clearly.

Uses an internal memo format.

To: Golden Lakes Condominium Association

From: Robert Fields, Grounds Committee Chair

Date: September 19, 2013

Subject: Comparing Bids to Resod the Recreation Building Grounds

The remodeling of the Golden Lakes Condominium recreation building has resulted in grass damage to the surrounding common areas. In response, I have investigated options for resodding these areas. The criteria for the project include the following:

1. Adequate sod for a 200-square-foot area

2. A price within the $4,500 budget

3. A guarantee

Four landscape companies have estimated the project. The following table shows the company, price, project length, and guarantee offered by each.

Company	Price ($)	Number of Days	Guarantee
Green Company	3,707	3	None
Landscape Professionals	3,984	2	6 inspections in 6 months Replacements at no cost
K-Mart Professional	4,000	3	6 inspections in 12 months Replacements at no cost
Luxury Landscape	4,439	3	6 inspections in 4 months Replacements at no cost

Although all four prices are within our budget, the K-Mart Professional Crew offers the best guarantee at a price comfortably below our budget for the resodding.

I recommend that we contract the K-Mart Professional Crew because the guarantee offers six inspections over a full year with sod replacement as necessary within that period at no extra cost. I also suggest that we have the work completed by November 20, when the condominium owners leave town and return to their winter homes.

© CENGAGE LEARNING 2013

**Figure 2
Criteria for a
Business Report**

Organized	The reader can locate information quickly. Content is presented in a logical order.
Well Supported	The reader can trust the information (facts and data). Where subjective judgments are made, as in drawing conclusions and making recommendations, they must be presented ethically and be based on information presented in the report.
Useful	The reader uses the report to make decisions and solve problems that affect the organization's success. Unlike some scientific and academic reports, business reports provide practical information that readers use to take action.

- How might customers respond to the change? Will they choose healthier meals? If so, what kinds of meals would they prefer?
- How much would healthier food cost?

In addition to guiding your research, your questions may ultimately serve as the major divisions of your report.

Research and report writing are a cost, just like other corporate expenses. How much information do you need to make a good decision? You do not want to provide a $100 answer to a $5 question, but neither do you want to provide a $5 answer to a $100 question. A sensible approach to research will keep you focused on your goal: providing enough information to feel confident in your decision.

Identifying Types of Data

The two major types of data you will use are secondary and primary data. **Secondary data** is data collected by someone else for some other purpose; it may be published or unpublished (Figure 3).

**Figure 3
Examples of
Secondary Data**

Published (widely disseminated)	Unpublished (not widely disseminated)
- Internet resources - Journal, magazine, and newspaper articles[6] - Books - Brochures and pamphlets - Technical reports	- Company records (reports and communications) - Legal documents (e.g., court records) - Personal files (e.g., expense records) - Medical records

Primary data is collected by the researcher to solve a specific problem. Because you are collecting the data yourself, you have more control over its accuracy, completeness, objectivity, and relevance. The three main methods of primary data collection are surveys, observation, and experimentation.

Although secondary and primary data are both important sources for business reports, we usually start our data collection by reviewing data that is already available—it costs less and saves time. Not all report situations require collecting new (primary) data, but it would be unusual to write a report that did not require some type of secondary data.

Let's refer back to our example of a restaurant offering healthier menu items for children. As the owner, you would certainly rely on secondary sources to learn about industry trends. There's no need for you to commission your own research when the National Restaurant Association and industry publications probably have published studies and articles about the topic. Also, studying secondary data can provide sources for additional published information and provide guidance for possible primary research.

For these reasons, our discussion of data collection first focuses on secondary sources. Secondary data is neither better than nor worse than primary data; it is simply *different*. One of the challenges is finding secondary data that is appropriate for your purpose.

Nearly all reporting tasks use secondary data.

Searching for Relevant Sources

You may be tempted to start all searches by Googling keywords, but you have better options available to you. Particularly as a student, you can access subscription-based information through your school's library. Databases such as Business Source Premier, ProQuest, and LexisNexis are good choices for business-related newspapers, magazines, and journals for your research. Figure 4 compares search results for Google, Google Scholar, and ProQuest.

Getting into Google may be easier than a library database, but you never know what you'll get. Library databases include information already evaluated by scholars and publishers. In the long run, a database will save you time and give you the best results for your report.

Evaluating Sources of Information

Once you find information that seems relevant to your research questions, you'll need to evaluate the quality of the sources. With higher quality sources, you'll write more credible reports and make better business decisions. Whether you're reading a research study or an article on a blog, you should look at the source critically.

L02 Evaluate the quality of data.

Communication Technologies

Evaluating Internet Resources
We know that anyone can post anything on the Internet. But even news agencies can be sloppy in checking their sources. As a fact-checking test, Mike Wise, a sports

Figure 4   Comparing Search Results

Situation: As a restaurant owner who is considering healthy menu choices, you could search for terms such as *healthy*, *food*, *trend*, and *children*.

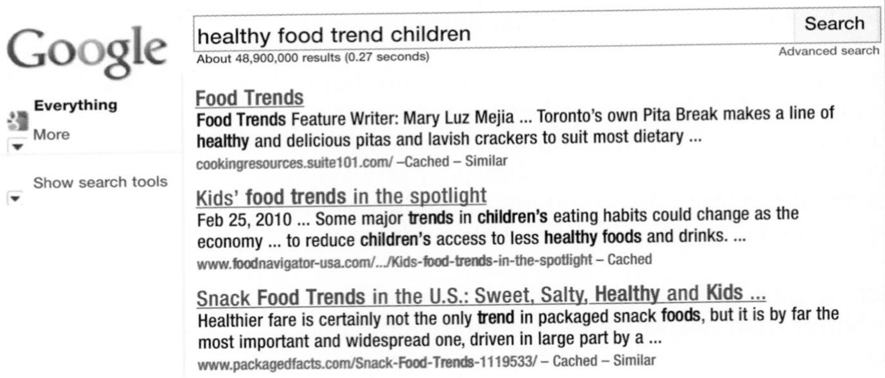

Google

healthy food trend children   [Search]
About 48,900,000 results (0.27 seconds)   Advanced search

Everything
More
Show search tools

Food Trends
Food Trends Feature Writer: Mary Luz Mejia ... Toronto's own Pita Break makes a line of **healthy** and delicious pitas and lavish crackers to suit most dietary ...
cookingresources.suite101.com/ –Cached – Similar

Kids' food trends in the spotlight
Feb 25, 2010 ... Some major **trends** in **children's** eating habits could change as the economy ... to reduce **children's** access to less **healthy foods** and drinks. ...
www.foodnavigator-usa.com/.../Kids-food-trends-in-the-spotlight – Cached

Snack Food Trends in the U.S.: Sweet, Salty, Healthy and Kids ...
Healthier fare is certainly not the only **trend** in packaged snack **foods**, but it is by far the most important and widespread one, driven in large part by a ...
www.packagedfacts.com/Snack-Food-Trends-1119533/ – Cached – Similar

Worst: This Google search yields an overwhelming 48.9 million results from companies, consumer organizations, and government agencies—too many and too varied to reasonably sort through. Advertisements on Google probably will not provide useful information for your search. You could limit your results by using Advanced Search or by changing your search terms, but using Google is still an unrefined approach, which may cause you to spend more time than you'd like finding reliable data.

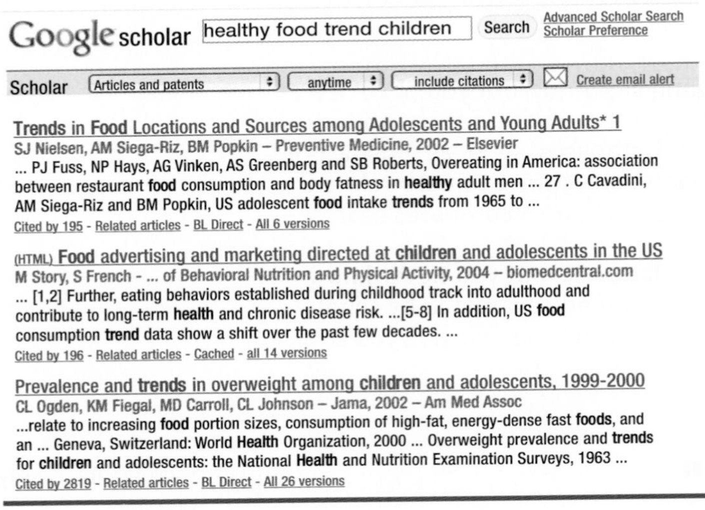

Google scholar

healthy food trend children   [Search]   Advanced Scholar Search   Scholar Preference

Scholar   [Articles and patents]   [anytime]   [include citations]   ☒ Create email alert

Trends in Food Locations and Sources among Adolescents and Young Adults* 1
SJ Nielsen, AM Siega-Riz, BM Popkin – Preventive Medicine, 2002 – Elsevier
... PJ Fuss, NP Hays, AG Vinken, AS Greenberg and SB Roberts, Overeating in America: association between restaurant **food** consumption and body fatness in **healthy** adult men ... 27 . C Cavadini, AM Siega-Riz and BM Popkin, US adolescent **food** intake **trends** from 1965 to ...
Cited by 195 - Related articles - BL Direct - All 6 versions

(HTML) **Food advertising and marketing directed at children and adolescents in the US**
M Story, S French - ... of Behavioral Nutrition and Physical Activity, 2004 – biomedcentral.com
... [1,2] Further, eating behaviors established during childhood track into adulthood and contribute to long-term **health** and chronic disease risk. ...[5-8] In addition, US **food** consumption **trend** data show a shift over the past few decades. ...
Cited by 196 - Related articles - Cached - all 14 versions

Prevalence and trends in overweight among children and adolescents, 1999-2000
CL Ogden, KM Fiegal, MD Carroll, CL Johnson – Jama, 2002 – Am Med Assoc
...relate to increasing **food** portion sizes, consumption of high-fat, energy-dense fast **foods**, and an ... Geneva, Switzerland: World **Health** Organization, 2000 ... Overweight prevalence and **trends** for **children** and adolescents: the National **Health** and Nutrition Examination Surveys, 1963 ...
Cited by 2819 - Related articles - BL Direct - All 26 versions

Better: Entering the same search terms in Google Scholar yields 361,000 results, which is still too many to read, but this list is prescreened for you with only academic articles. You also can more easily narrow your search by selecting dates and subject area (e.g., business).

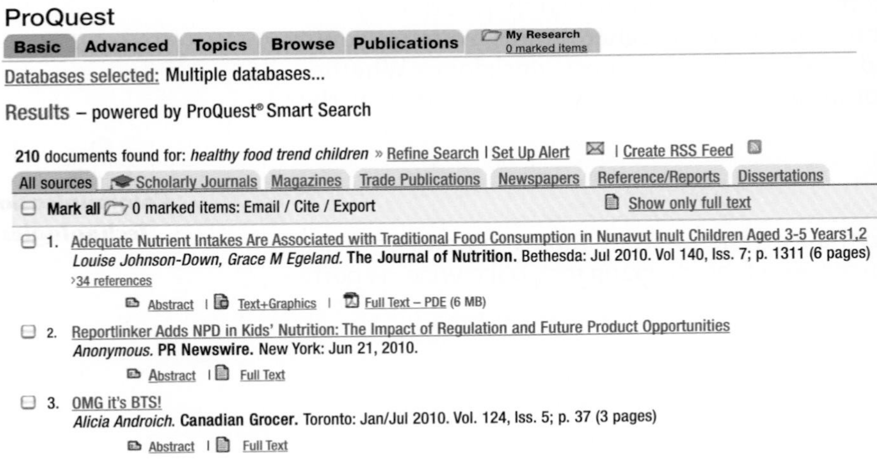

ProQuest

[Basic] [Advanced] [Topics] [Browse] [Publications]   My Research   0 marked items

Databases selected: Multiple databases...

Results – powered by ProQuest® Smart Search

210 documents found for: *healthy food trend children* » Refine Search | Set Up Alert ☒ | Create RSS Feed

All sources   Scholarly Journals   Magazines   Trade Publications   Newspapers   Reference/Reports   Dissertations

☐ Mark all ☐ 0 marked items: Email / Cite / Export   ☐ Show only full text

☐ 1.   Adequate Nutrient Intakes Are Associated with Traditional Food Consumption in Nunavut Inuit Children Aged 3-5 Years1,2
Louise Johnson-Down, Grace M Egeland. **The Journal of Nutrition.** Bethesda: Jul 2010. Vol 140, Iss. 7; p. 1311 (6 pages)
›34 references
☐ Abstract | ☐ Text+Graphics | ☐ Full Text – PDE (6 MB)

☐ 2.   Reportlinker Adds NPD in Kids' Nutrition: The Impact of Regulation and Future Product Opportunities
Anonymous. **PR Newswire.** New York: Jun 21, 2010.
☐ Abstract | ☐ Full Text

☐ 3.   OMG it's BTS!
Alicia Androich. **Canadian Grocer.** Toronto: Jan/Jul 2010. Vol. 124, Iss. 5; p. 37 (3 pages)
☐ Abstract | ☐ Full Text

Best: A library database, such as ProQuest, yields a manageable 210 articles, which can be sorted by date and type of publication. Like Google Scholar, these articles are prescreened and more likely to be reliable sources.

Clearly, this is your best bet for finding relevant, reliable sources.

columnist for *The Washington Post* sent a false tweet (Figure 5). The tweet refers to Pittsburgh Steelers quarterback Ben Roethlisberger, who was suspended for six games, not five.

Figure 5 False Tweet

The Washington Post didn't appreciate Wise's joke and suspended him for one month. However, the fake tweet was picked up by several media outlets, including *The Miami Herald* and *The Baltimore Sun*.[7,8] Wise posted another tweet (Figure 6), which sums up the incident fairly well.

Figure 6 Reflections on the False Tweet

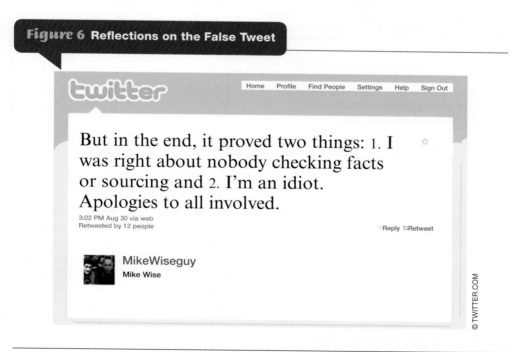

People have difficulty distinguishing the quality of sources. According to one study, 40% of Internet users don't know the difference between company-paid Internet sites and independent Internet sites. Another study concluded that people tend to evaluate the quality of Internet data according to the appearance and professionalism of the website itself,[9] but this is not a sufficient method.

**Figure 7
Evaluating Web
Sources**

Authority

- Is the author or organization identifiable? Look for links that say "Who We Are," "About This Site," or something similar.
- How credible are the site owners (e.g., experience, credentials, publications, press)?
- What other sites are linking to this site (search for "link: [site name]")?
- Do links on this site lead to other reputable sites?
- Is the domain extension (e.g., .edu, .gov, .org) appropriate for the content?

Accuracy and Reliability

- Have research sources been properly documented and cited?
- Do you find spelling errors or incorrect uses of grammar?
- Can background information be verified for accuracy?
- How long has the site been in existence (use the Internet Archive to check: www.archive.org)?

Purpose/Objectivity

- What is the purpose or motive for the site (e.g., educational, commercial, entertainment)? Is the site trying to sell you something?
- Do you see a clear distinction between opinion and fact?
- Who is the intended audience, and how is this reflected in the organization and presentation of the site?

Coverage

- Does the site cover a specific time period?
- Does the site cover one aspect of the topic, or does it cover the topic in depth?
- What information is included? What is omitted?
- Is the page completed or "under construction"?

Currency

- When was the site last updated or revised?
- How often is the site updated?
- Do you notice any dead links?

When you find content on the Internet, ask the questions in Figure 7 to evaluate the resource.[10]

You also may be tempted to use Wikipedia as an information source. Although librarians may advise against using Wikipedia, several studies demonstrate its reliability.[11] However, relying only on Wikipedia is sloppy for two reasons. First, anyone can post to this free, collaborative encyclopedia, so it may be a good starting point for research, but you should check all sources in the footnotes yourself. Second, you'll want a variety of sources; citing Wikipedia directly for anything other than definitions may tell your reader you didn't do your homework.

Evaluating Research Studies

Research studies may be a better source than web sources for a report, but they may not be appropriate for your purpose. Ask yourself the questions in Figure 8 about research you consider incorporating into your report.

Data that fails even one of these five tests should probably not be used in your report. At the very least, such data requires extra scrutiny and perhaps extra explanation in the report itself if you do choose to use it.

© CENGAGE LEARNING 2013

Figure 8
Evaluating Research Studies

What was the purpose of the study?

People who have a vested interest in the outcome of a study may take shortcuts to get the answer they want. But people who approach research with a genuine interest in answering a question are more likely to select their samples carefully, ask clear and unbiased questions, and analyze data objectively.

Example: Which study about children's food preferences is more trustworthy—one conducted by the U.S. National Institute of Health or one conducted by Sabrett Hot Dogs?

How was the data collected?

Were appropriate procedures used? Even if you're not an experienced researcher, you can make sure data was collected properly and from a large enough, representative sample.

Example: If you want to learn your customers' reactions to healthier menu items, you wouldn't ask only two guests who visited the restaurant on Saturday. You would ask a large percentage of your customers and include individuals and families, early and late diners, and so on.

How was the data analyzed?

As we'll see later in this chapter, how we analyze data depends on the type of data we collect. In some situations, even though the analysis is appropriate for the original study, it may not be appropriate for your particular purposes.

Example: Let's say you find a study about eating preferences by age. If the researchers used the broad category "younger than 21," the study won't help you understand how your target group (children 6–9 years old) responded.

How consistent is the data with that from other studies?

When you find the same general conclusions in several independent sources, you can have greater confidence in the data.

Example: If four studies conclude that children don't like fish unless it is fried, and a fifth study reached an opposite conclusion, you might be skeptical of the fifth study.

How old is the data?

Data that was true at the time it was collected may not be true today.

Example: A 1980 study of children's food preferences may not be relevant to your decision today, when more food choices are available, people are dining out more frequently, and people are more health conscious.

COLLECTING DATA THROUGH QUESTIONNAIRES

L03 Develop a questionnaire and cover letter.

If your research fails to find enough high-quality secondary data to help you make a decision, you will probably need to collect primary data.

A **survey** is a data-collection method that gathers information through questionnaires, telephone or email inquiries, or interviews. The **questionnaire** (a written instrument with questions to obtain information from recipients) is the most frequently used method in business research. For relatively little expense, the researcher can get a representative sampling over a large geographical area. It costs no more to send a questionnaire through the postal service or by email across the country than across the street.

 Don't confuse the terms *survey* and *questionnaire*: you conduct a survey by administering a questionnaire.

Also, the anonymity of a questionnaire increases the validity of some responses. When respondents aren't identified, they may give more complete and honest personal and financial information. In addition, no interviewer is present to possibly bias the results. Finally, respondents can answer at a time convenient for them, which is not always the case with telephone or interview studies.

The big disadvantage of questionnaires is the low response rate, and those who do respond may not be representative (typical) of the population. Extensive research has shown that respondents tend to be better educated, more intelligent, and more sociable, and have higher social status and a higher need for social approval than those who choose not to respond.[12] Thus, questionnaires should be used only under certain conditions (Figure 9).

The main disadvantage of surveys is a low response rate.

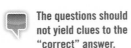
Figure 9
When to Mail Questionnaires

When the information can be provided easily and quickly

Questionnaires should contain mostly yes-or-no questions, check-off alternatives, or one- to two-word fill-in responses. People tend not to complete questionnaires that call for lengthy or complex responses.

When the target audience is homogeneous

To ensure a high response rate, your study must interest the respondents, and you must use language they understand. It is difficult to construct a questionnaire that would be clearly and uniformly understood by people with widely differing interests, education, and socioeconomic backgrounds.

When sufficient time is available

Three to four weeks is generally required from questionnaire mailing to final returns—including follow-ups of the nonrespondents. (Emailing questionnaires, of course, requires less total time.) A telephone survey, on the other hand, can often be completed in one day.

© CENGAGE LEARNING 2013

Constructing the Questionnaire

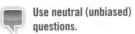
The questions should not yield clues to the "correct" answer.

Because the target audience has limited time, make sure that every question you ask is necessary. Each question should be essential to your research and yield information that you can't get from other sources (such as through library or online research). Follow the guidelines in Figure 10 for constructing a questionnaire. A well-designed questionnaire about guests' restaurant experience is shown in Figure 11.[13]

Use neutral (unbiased) questions.

To get valid and reliable data from your target audience, your language must be clear, precise, and understandable. Imagine spending time and money on a questionnaire and then making a decision based on invalid data. At best, you would have to disregard the data; at worst, you might decide, for example, to offer a product that few people buy. You are responsible for the quality of the information you include in your reports and presentations—and the collection process starts with neutral (unbiased) questions.

NOT Do you think our company should open an on-site child care center as a means of ensuring the welfare of our employees' small children?

_____yes

_____no

Figure 10
Constructing a
Questionnaire

Content

- Ask only for information that is not easily available elsewhere.

- Have a purpose for each question. Make sure that all questions directly help you solve a problem or make a decision. Avoid asking for unimportant or merely "interesting" information.

- Use precise wording so that no question can possibly be misunderstood. Use clear, simple language, and define unfamiliar or confusing terms.

- Use neutrally worded questions and deal with only one topic per question. Avoid loaded, leading, or multifaceted questions.

- Ensure that the response choices are both **exhaustive** (one appropriate response for each question) and **mutually exclusive** (no overlapping categories).

- Be careful about asking sensitive questions, such as information about age, salary, or morals. Consider using broad categories for such questions (instead of narrow, more specific categories).

- Pilot-test your questionnaire on a few people to check that all questions function as intended. Revise as needed.

Organization

- Arrange the questions in some logical order. Group questions that deal with a particular topic. If your questionnaire is long, divide it into sections.

- Arrange the alternatives for each question in some logical order—such as numerical, chronological, or alphabetical.

- Give the questionnaire a descriptive title, provide whatever directions are necessary, and include instructions for returning the questionnaire.

Format

- Use an easy-to-answer format. Check-off questions draw the most responses and are easiest to answer and tabulate. Use free-response items only when necessary.

- To increase the likelihood that your target audience will cooperate and take your study seriously, ensure that your questionnaire has a professional appearance: use a simple and attractive format and proofread carefully.

This wording of the question favors the "pro" side, which biases the responses. A more neutral question will result in more valid responses.

BUT ▸ Which one of the following possible additional benefits would you most prefer?

_____a dental insurance plan

_____an on-site child care center

_____three personal-leave days annually

_____other (please specify:_____)

Also be certain that each question contains a single idea.

NOT ▸ Our company should spend less money on advertising and more money on research and development.

_____agree

_____disagree

Figure 11
Questionnaire about Guests' Restaurant Experience

Personal space questionnaire

This restaurant and Cornell University are working together to study how to create better dining experiences. You can help by taking a moment to complete the following short survey. Please leave your completed survey in the check folder, or you may give it to the host as you depart. Thank you for your feedback!

> **Includes clear statements and defined choices.**

1. Please indicate your agreement with each of the following questions about your dining experience today.

   (1 — Strongly Disagree, 7 — Strongly Agree)

   I was pleased with my dining experience.
   1   2   3   4   5   6   7

   I had enough room at my table.
   1   2   3   4   5   6   7

   I was happy with my food.
   1   2   3   4   5   6   7

   This restaurant was a wise choice.
   1   2   3   4   5   6   7

   I felt rushed during my dining experience.
   1   2   3   4   5   6   7

   The servers did a good job for me.
   1   2   3   4   5   6   7

   I was uncomfortable in my seat.
   1   2   3   4   5   6   7

   The staff was friendly and hospitable.
   1   2   3   4   5   6   7

   My table was too close to other tables.
   1   2   3   4   5   6   7

   I was very dissatisfied by my experience.
   1   2   3   4   5   6   7

2. Is this your first visit to this restaurant?
   Yes   No
   If yes, how did you find out about this restaurant?

   _____

3. How likely are you to return to this restaurant?

   (1 — Very Unlikely, 7 — Very Likely)
   1   2   3   4   5   6   7

4. How likely are you to recommend this restaurant to others?

   (1 — Very Unlikely, 7 — Very Likely)
   1   2   3   4   5   6   7

> **Uses check-off items for sensitive information.**

5. Please tell us a little about yourself (to be completed by only one member of your party).
   You are: Male _____ Female _____
   Your age is: Under 25 _____   26-49 _____   50+ _____

6. How often do you eat out at a restaurant for dinner? (please choose one)
   More than twice a week   _____
   1–2 times a week   _____
   2–3 times a month   _____
   Once a month   _____
   Less than once a month _____

> **Uses a free-response question for more in-depth information.**

7. If you were the manager of this restaurant, what would you change about the experience?

   _____

> **Expresses appreciation.**

THANK YOU FOR PARTICIPATING AND FOR DINING WITH US TODAY.

Suppose the respondent believes that the company should spend more (or less) money on advertising *and* on research and development? How would he or she answer? The solution is to put each of the two ideas in a separate question.

Finally, ensure that your categories are mutually exclusive, with no overlap.

NOT In your opinion, what is the major cause of high employee turnover?

_____lack of air conditioning

_____noncompetitive financial package

_____poor health benefits

_____poor working conditions

_____weak management

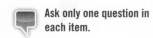

Ask only one question in each item.

The problem with this item is that the "lack of air conditioning" category overlaps with the "poor working conditions" category, and "noncompetitive financial package" overlaps with "poor health benefits." Also, all four of these probably overlap with "weak management." Intermingling categories will confuse the respondent and yield unreliable survey results.

Respondents may be hesitant to answer sensitive questions, for example, about their age or salary. Even worse, they may deliberately provide *inaccurate* responses. To improve your chances of getting sensitive information, try the following:

- Assure the respondent (in your cover letter or email) that the questionnaire is anonymous.
- Use broad categories (accurate estimates are better than incorrect data).
- Include a list of options rather than a fill-in response.

NOT What is your annual gross salary?

$_____

BUT Please check the category that best describes your annual salary:

_____Less than $25,000

_____$25,000–$40,000

_____$40,001–$70,000

_____More than $70,000

In the third category, "$40,001" is necessary to avoid overlap with the figure "$40,000" in the second category. Without this distinction, the categories would not be mutually exclusive.

Even experienced researchers find it difficult to spot ambiguities or other problems in their own questionnaires. Before sending the questionnaire to a large population, run a pilot test with a small sample of respondents, or, at a minimum, ask a colleague to edit your instrument with a critical eye. Then, you can make revisions before distributing the final version.

Writing the Cover Letter or Email

Unless you will distribute the questionnaires personally (in which case, you could explain the purpose and procedures in person), include a cover letter or email,

Figure 12   Email to Announce a Questionnaire

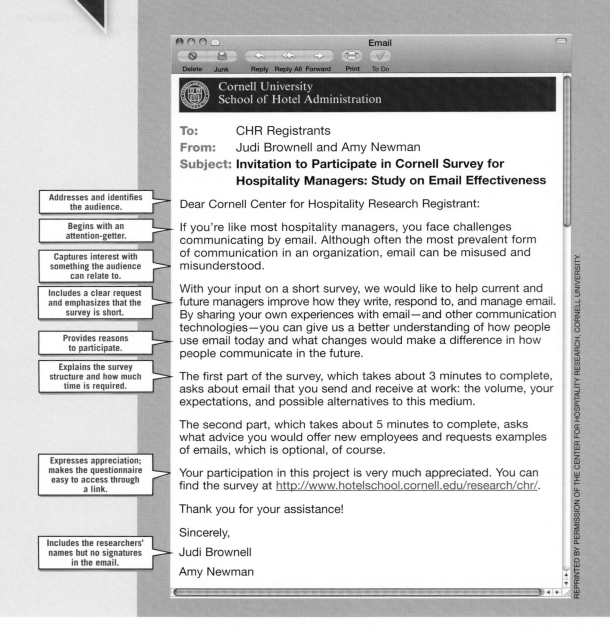

Cornell University
School of Hotel Administration

To: CHR Registrants
From: Judi Brownell and Amy Newman
Subject: Invitation to Participate in Cornell Survey for Hospitality Managers: Study on Email Effectiveness

Dear Cornell Center for Hospitality Research Registrant:

If you're like most hospitality managers, you face challenges communicating by email. Although often the most prevalent form of communication in an organization, email can be misused and misunderstood.

With your input on a short survey, we would like to help current and future managers improve how they write, respond to, and manage email. By sharing your own experiences with email—and other communication technologies—you can give us a better understanding of how people use email today and what changes would make a difference in how people communicate in the future.

The first part of the survey, which takes about 3 minutes to complete, asks about email that you send and receive at work: the volume, your expectations, and possible alternatives to this medium.

The second part, which takes about 5 minutes to complete, asks what advice you would offer new employees and requests examples of emails, which is optional, of course.

Your participation in this project is very much appreciated. You can find the survey at http://www.hotelschool.cornell.edu/research/chr/.

Thank you for your assistance!

Sincerely,

Judi Brownell

Amy Newman

Annotations:
- Addresses and identifies the audience.
- Begins with an attention-getter.
- Captures interest with something the audience can relate to.
- Includes a clear request and emphasizes that the survey is short.
- Provides reasons to participate.
- Explains the survey structure and how much time is required.
- Expresses appreciation; makes the questionnaire easy to access through a link.
- Includes the researchers' names but no signatures in the email.

L04 Construct tables and charts.

such as the one shown in Figure 12, with your questionnaire. The cover letter or email should be written as a persuasive message (see Chapter 7). Your job is to convince the reader that it's worth taking the time to complete the questionnaire.[14]

DISPLAYING QUANTITATIVE INFORMATION

At some point in the reporting process, you'll have enough data from your secondary and primary sources to help you make a decision. (Of course, during data analysis and report writing, you may realize that you need to collect more information.)

Next, your job is to convert your raw data (from your notes, copies of journal articles, completed questionnaires, recordings of interviews, and web links) into **information**—meaningful facts, statistics, and conclusions—that will help the reader of your report make a decision. In addition to interpreting your findings in narrative form, you will likely prepare **visual aids**—tables, charts, photographs, or other graphic materials—to improve comprehension and add interest. Some of these visuals may be used in presentation software, such as PowerPoint, to support an oral presentation.

Data analysis cannot be accomplished in one sitting. The more familiar you become with the data and the more you pore over it, the more different things you'll see. Data analysis is usually the part of the report process that requires the most time as well as the most skill. The more insight you can provide the reader about the *meaning* of the data you've collected and presented, the more helpful your report will be.

 Analysis and interpretation turn data into information.

Constructing Tables

 Tables are often the most economical way of presenting numerical data.

A **table** is an orderly arrangement of data into columns and rows. It represents the most basic form of statistical analysis and is useful for showing a large amount of numerical data in a small space. With a table, you can show numerical data in a more efficient and interesting way than with narrative text. A table also provides more information than a chart does, although with less visual impact. Because information is presented in vertical columns and horizontal rows, a table allows easy comparison of figures. However, trends are more obvious when presented in graphs.

Figure 13 shows a printout of an attitude-scale item (Question 9) on a questionnaire and the corresponding table constructed from this printout. Apex Company,

Computer Printout

**Figure 13
From Printout to Report Table**

Q.9 "APEX COMPANY IS AN ASSET TO OUR COMMUNITY"

VALUE LABEL	VALUE	FREQ	PCT	VALID PCT	CUM PCT
Strongly agree	1	41	15.0	15.1	15.1
Agree	2	175	63.8	64.6	79.7
No opinion	3	34	12.4	12.6	92.3
Disagree	4	15	5.5	5.5	97.8
Strongly disagree	5	6	2.2	2.2	100.0
	•	3	1.1	MISSING	
TOTAL		274	100.0	100.0	100.0
VALID CASES	271	MISSING CASES 3			

Corresponding Report Table

Table 4. Response to Statement, "Apex Company is an asset to our community."

Response	No.	Pct.
Strongly agree	41	15
Agree	175	65
No opinion	34	13
Disagree	15	5
Strongly disagree	6	2
Total	271	100

© CENGAGE LEARNING 2013

a manufacturer of consumer products headquartered in Des Moines, Iowa, is considering building an addition to its factory there and wants to gauge local opinion before making a commitment.

On the printout, you'll see the following column headings:

- *Value Label:* Shows the five alternatives given on the questionnaire.
- *Value:* Shows the code used to identify each of these five alternatives.
- *Freq:* Shows the number of respondents who checked each alternative.
- *Pct:* Shows the percentage of each response, based on the total number of respondents (N = 274), including those who left this item blank.
- *Valid Pct:* Shows the percentage of each response, based on the total number of respondents who answered this particular question (N = 271).
- *Cum Pct:* Shows the cumulative percentage—that is, the sum of this response plus those above it (e.g., 79.7% of the respondents either agreed or strongly agreed with the statement).

The researcher must determine whether the "Pct" or "Valid Pct" column is more appropriate for the analysis. In most cases, choose "Valid Pct" column, which ignores any blank responses. These numbers were selected for the table at the bottom of Figure 13.

Your reader must be able to understand each table on its own, without having to read the surrounding text. Thus, at a minimum, each table should contain a table number, a descriptive but concise title, column headings, and body (the items under each column heading). If you need footnotes to explain individual items within the table, put them immediately below the body of the table, not at the bottom of the page. Similarly, if the table is based on secondary data, type a source note below the body, giving the appropriate citation. Common abbreviations and symbols are acceptable in tables.

Cross-Tabulation Analysis

Cross-tabulation analysis enables you to look at two or more groups of data simultaneously.

In some cases, the simple question-by-question tabulation illustrated in the table in Figure 13 would be enough for the reader's purpose. However, in most cases, such simple tabulations would not yield all of the useful information from the data. Most data can be further analyzed through **cross-tabulation**, a process by which two or more pieces of data are analyzed together.

The table in Figure 14 shows not only the total responses (both the number and the percentages) but also the percentage responses for the subgroups according to marital status, sex, and age. A quick "eyeballing" of the table shows that there do not seem to be any major differences in the perceptions of married versus single respondents. However, there does seem to be a fairly sizable difference between male and female respondents: males have a much more positive view of the company than do females.

Figure 14 Cross-Tabulation Analysis

Table 4. Response to Statement, "Apex Company is an asset to our community."										
	Total		Marital Status		Sex		Age			
	Total	Pct.	Married	Single	Male	Female	Under 21	21–35	36–50	Over 50
Strongly agree	41	15.1%	14.0%	17.6%	15.7%	10.4%	21.7%	8.4%	12.0%	28.4%
Agree	175	64.6%	67.5%	58.8%	67.6%	46.3%	47.8%	65.1%	69.1%	61.0%
No opinion	34	12.6%	11.2%	15.4%	11.4%	20.9%	17.5%	13.0%	14.3%	9.2%
Disagree	15	5.5%	5.1%	5.5%	4.0%	13.4%	13.0%	8.4%	4.0%	0.7%
Strongly disagree	6	2.2%	2.2%	2.7%	1.3%	9.0%	0.0%	5.1%	0.6%	0.7%
Total	271	100.0%	100.0%	100.0%	100.0%	100.0%	100.0%	100.0%	100.0%	100.0%

If the table in Figure 14 were one of only a few tables in your report, it would be just fine the way it's shown. However, suppose that the statement "Apex Company is an asset to our community" is one of a dozen attitude items, each of which requires a similar table. It is probably too much to expect the reader to study a dozen similar tables; in such a situation, you should consider simplifying the table.

Sometimes tabular data needs to be condensed for easier and faster comprehension.

You can use several approaches to simplify a table. You should recognize right from the start, however, that whenever you simplify a table (that is, whenever you merge rows or columns or simply delete data), your table loses some of its detail. The goal is to gain more in comprehensibility than you lose in specificity. Your knowledge of the readers and their needs will help you determine how much detail to present.

With that in mind, consider the simplified version of this table shown in Figure 15. The two positive responses ("strongly agree" and "agree") have been combined into one "agree" row, as have the two negative responses. Combining not only simplifies the table, but also prevents some possible interpretation problems.

Given the original table in Figure 14, for example, would you consider the following statement to be accurate?

Less than half of the females agree that Apex Company is an asset to their community.

Ethics in Communication

Technically, the statement is accurate, because the 46.3% who "agree" is *less* than half. However, the statement leaves an incorrect impression because more than half of the females (57%—those who "agree" *and* who "strongly agree") believe that Apex Company is an asset to their community. Presenting an incomplete picture could be considered unethical if used inappropriately. This conclusion is made clear in Figure 15.

Table 4. Response to Statement, "Apex Company is an asset to our community." (*N* = 271; all figures in percent)								
		Marital Status		Sex		Age		
	Total	Married	Single	Male	Female	Under 21	21–50	Over 50
Agree	80	82	77	83	57	69	77	90
No opinion	12	11	15	12	21	18	14	9
Disagree	8	7	8	5	22	13	9	1
Total	100	100	100	100	100	100	100	100

Figure 15
Simplified Table

© CENGAGE LEARNING 2013

Note also that the two center age groups ("21–35" and "36–50") have been combined into one age group ("21–50"). Because the company's products are geared mainly to this large age group, the company wanted to compare the responses of this important group with the responses of the less important younger and older groups.

Two other changes help simplify the table. First, only percentages are provided, which eliminates the need for the percentage sign after each number (readers can compute the raw numbers for themselves, because the sample size is shown in the table subtitle). Second, each percentage is rounded to its nearest whole—a practice recommended for most business reports when presenting percentages that total 100%.

More data is not always better than less data.

Follow these practices when rounding numbers:

- Any number with a decimal less than 0.50 gets rounded *down* to the next nearest whole number; any number with a decimal greater than 0.50 gets rounded *up*.

- To avoid bias, odd numbers with a decimal of exactly 0.50 get rounded *up*; even numbers with a decimal of exactly .50 get rounded *down*.

- If your table shows the total percentages and your rounding efforts result in totals that do not equal 100% (such as 99% or 101%), you have the option of either (1) showing the actual resulting totals or (2) readjusting one of the rounded numbers (the one that will cause the least distortion to the number) to "force" a 100% total.

Simplifying this table (reducing Figure 14 to Figure 15) has deleted two of the ten columns and two of the five rows—for a net decrease of 49% in the number of individual bits of data presented. When this reduction is multiplied by the number of similar tables in the report, the net effect is rather dramatic.

Arranging Data in Tables

As discussed earlier, the check-off alternatives in your questionnaire items should be arranged in some logical order, most often either numerical or alphabetical, to avoid possibly biasing the responses. Once you have the data in hand, however, it is often helpful to the reader if you rearrange the data from high to low.

In Figure 16, for example, the categories have been rearranged from their original *alphabetical* order in the questionnaire into *descending* order in the report table. Note also that the four smallest categories have been combined into a miscellaneous category, which always goes last, regardless of its size. Finally, note the position and format of the table footnote, which may be used to explain an entry in the table.

 Choose a logical order for your data, which may differ from your original questionnaire.

Figure 16 Arranging Data in Tables

From This Survey Response:

6. In which of the following categories of clerical workers do you expect to hire additional workers within the next three years? (Check all that apply.)

211	bookkeepers and accounting clerks
31	computer operators
30	data-entry clerks
24	file clerks
247	general office clerks
78	receptionists and information clerks
323	secretaries/administrative assistants
7	statistical clerks
107	typists and word processors

To This Report Table:

TABLE 2. COMPANIES PLANNING TO HIRE ADDITIONAL CLERICAL WORKERS, BY CATEGORY (*N* = 326)

Category	Pct.*
Secretaries/administrative assistants	99
General office clerks	76
Bookkeepers and accounting clerks	65
Typists and word processors	33
Receptionists and information clerks	24
Miscellaneous	28

*Answers total more than 100% because of multiple responses.

© CENGAGE LEARNING 2013

Preparing Charts

Well-designed charts and graphs (technically, *graphs* are shown on graph paper; however, the two terms are used interchangeably) can improve reader comprehension, emphasize certain data, create interest, and save time and space. Charts help readers understand main points from large amounts of statistical data.

Because of their visual impact, charts receive more emphasis than tables or narrative text. Use charts when the overall picture is more important than the individual numbers. Also, charts are ideal when using visual support for an oral presentation; tables with a lot of data are difficult to read when projected onto a screen.

However, avoid using too many charts. In a written report, because charts have strong visual appeal, the more charts you include, the less impact each chart will have. Also, tables may be a better choice for some data. Research indicates that managers have more confidence in their decisions based on data from tables alone as opposed to data from graphs alone, but managers have the most confidence when both formats are used.[15] In another study, respondents chose more accurate answers about data displayed in tables than data in charts.[16] Charts will highlight data and add visual appeal to your reports, but be sure to use them to complement your text.

Designing Simple, Clear Charts

When creating a chart for a report or to support an oral presentation, first determine the main point you wish to convey. For a persuasive report, use your audience analysis skills to decide what is most important to the audience, and then design a chart to emphasize this information.

 Keep charts simple to achieve immediate comprehension.

The chart in Figure 17 focuses on a narrow question—technology use among hotel managers.[17] The chart is easy to read and follow.

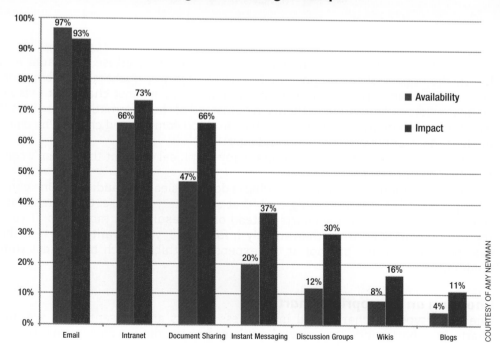

Availability and Impact of Technology Use Among Hotel Manager Sample

COURTESY OF AMY NEWMAN

Figure 17
Clear, Simple Chart from a Written Report

Figure 18 Chartjunk

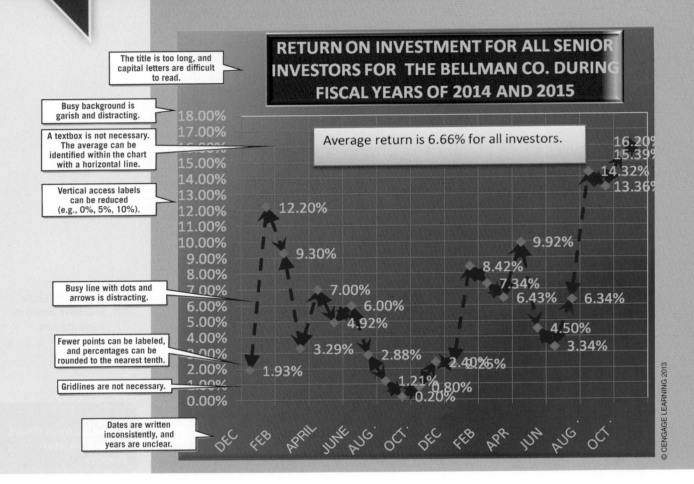

The title is too long, and capital letters are difficult to read.

Busy background is garish and distracting.

A textbox is not necessary. The average can be identified within the chart with a horizontal line.

Vertical access labels can be reduced (e.g., 0%, 5%, 10%).

Busy line with dots and arrows is distracting.

Fewer points can be labeled, and percentages can be rounded to the nearest tenth.

Gridlines are not necessary.

Dates are written inconsistently, and years are unclear.

RETURN ON INVESTMENT FOR ALL SENIOR INVESTORS FOR THE BELLMAN CO. DURING FISCAL YEARS OF 2014 AND 2015

Average return is 6.66% for all investors.

© CENGAGE LEARNING 2013

Cramming too much information into one chart will confuse the reader and lessen the impact of the graphic. In *The Visual Display of Quantitative Information*, Edward Tufte, an expert in information design, warns against **chartjunk**—visual elements that call attention to themselves instead of the information on a chart.[18] Avoid using too many, too large, too garish, and too complicated charts. The chart in Figure 18 is impossible to read—and ugly.

Charts should explain data. Eliminate any graphical element that doesn't contribute to your message.

An ethical manager ensures that charts don't mislead the audience. One common problem is presenting only data that supports your case. Of course, data selection is part of creating charts instead of full results in a table. And, if your report is persuasive rather than merely informative, you'll want to present the best possible picture—but not at the expense of ethics, which may affect your credibility.

Ethics in Communication

Choosing an Appropriate Chart Type

The main types of charts used in business reports and presentations are line charts, bar charts, and pie charts. All of these present data to show comparisons.

Data without context has little meaning. If you learned that a company reported a $307,000 profit in the fourth quarter, would you be impressed? It's a good sum of money, but what if this is $100,000 less than the previous three quarters? At a minimum, you would want to know how this figure compares to results from previous quarters—and possibly how this compares to competitors' profits.

Choose a chart type—or other graphic—to meet your communication objectives. A human resources manager may use different types of charts in a presentation to senior management (Figure 19).

Regardless of their type, label all your charts in a report as *figures,* and assign them consecutive numbers, separate from table numbers. Although tables are captioned at the top, charts may be captioned at the top or bottom. Charts preceded or followed by text or containing an explanatory paragraph are typically captioned at the bottom. As with tables, you may use commonly understood abbreviations.

Figure 19 Chart Types for Different Purposes

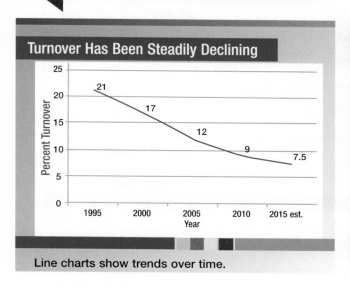

Line charts show trends over time.

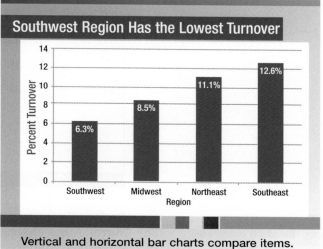

Vertical and horizontal bar charts compare items.

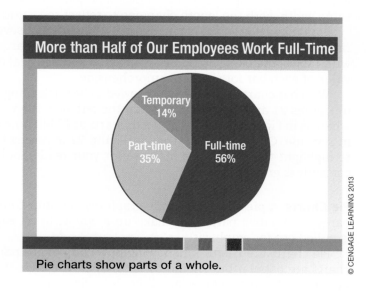

Pie charts show parts of a whole.

Use line charts to highlight trends.

Line Charts A **line chart** is a graph based on a grid of uniformly spaced horizontal and vertical lines. The vertical dimension represents values; the horizontal dimension represents time. Line charts show changes or trends in data over long periods of time, as illustrated in Figure 20.

Both axes should be marked off at equal intervals and clearly labeled. The vertical axis should begin with zero, even when all the amounts are quite large. In some situations, it may be desirable to show a break in the intervals. Fluctuations of the line over time indicate variations in the trend; the distance of the line from the horizontal axis indicates quantity.

**Figure 20
Line Chart**

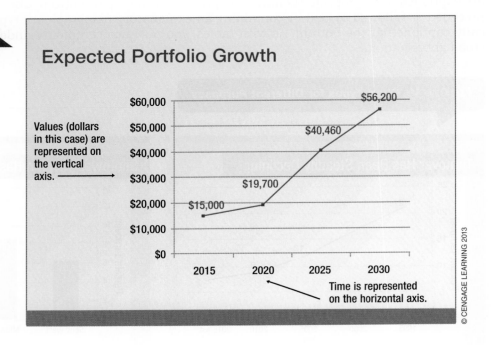

Bar charts compare the magnitude of items.

Bar Charts A **bar chart** is a graph with horizontal or vertical bars representing values. Bar charts are one of the most useful, simple, and popular graphic techniques. They are particularly appropriate for comparing the magnitude or size of items, either at a specified time or over a period of time. The bars should all be the same width, with the length changing to reflect the value of each item.

Bars may be grouped (as in Figure 17) to compare several variables over a period of time or may be stacked to show component parts of several variables. As with tables, the bars should be arranged in some logical order. Include the actual value of each bar for quicker comprehension.

Ethics in Communication

With bar charts, data is easily skewed to be misleading. Compare the bar charts in Figures 21 and 22. In Figure 21, on the left side, the vertical axis starts at zero, whereas in Figure 22, the vertical axis starts at $3 billion, exaggerating the increase in revenue. Of course, the arrow in Figure 22 is misleading too! It's a good idea to highlight the percentage increase for your reader, but the angle of the arrow certainly is greater than 4.5%.

Pie Charts A **pie chart** is a circle graph divided into component wedges. It compares the relative parts that make up a whole. In an **exploding pie**, one wedge is pulled out for emphasis.

As a rule, use between three and five components in a pie chart.

Pie charts are useful for showing how component parts add up to a total. Pie charts are popular but should be used when you have three to five or so component parts. More categories are difficult to distinguish.

Figures 21 and 22 The Effects of Vertical Axis Scales

Increase in Cash Balance in Q1 2013 (in $ billions)

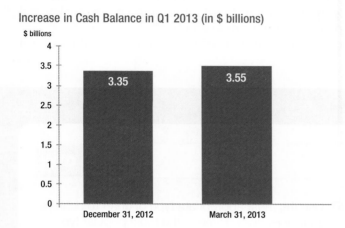

Increase in Cash Balance in Q1 2013 (in $ billions)

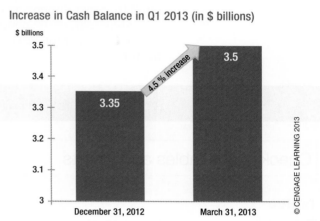

© CENGAGE LEARNING 2013

Begin "slicing" the pie at the 12 o'clock position and move clockwise in some logical order (often in order of descending size). The labels should be placed either inside each wedge or directly opposite the wedge but outside the pie. You may use a separate legend or key, but labels are easier to comprehend.

To distinguish each wedge, use shading, cross-hatched lines, different colors, or some other visual device (Figure 23).

Three-dimensional graphs contribute to chartjunk and are difficult to interpret. Because graphs are often used to display only two-dimensional data (horizontal and vertical), the third dimension (depth) has no significance. Similarly, three-dimensional pie charts, which are shown slanted away from the viewer

Figure 23 Pie Chart

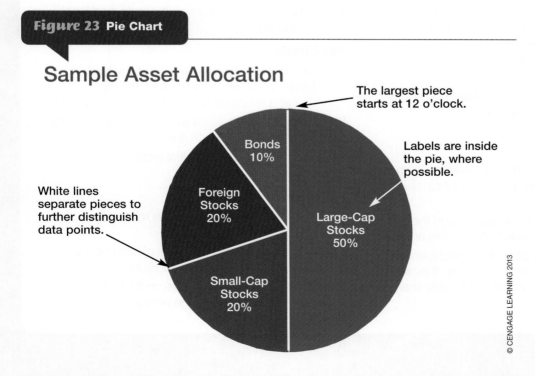

Sample Asset Allocation

© CENGAGE LEARNING 2013

rather than vertically, can be misleading because of perspective—the slices farthest away appear smaller than they actually are.

Such graphics gain attention and provide a general impression but do not convey the precise meanings needed in business communications. One experiment found that two-dimensional graphs communicated information more quickly and accurately than corresponding three-dimensional graphs.[19]

The Checklist for Tables and Charts summarizes the most important points on this topic.

Checklist for Tables and Charts   `GO`

Tables

☑ Use tables to present a large amount of numerical data in a small space and to permit easy comparisons of figures.

☑ Number tables consecutively and use concise but descriptive table titles and column headings.

☑ Ensure that the table is understandable by itself—without reference to the accompanying narrative.

☑ Arrange the rows of the table in some logical order (most often, in descending order).

☑ Combine smaller, less important categories into a miscellaneous category, and put it last.

☑ Use cross-tabulation analysis to compare different subgroups.

☑ Use only as much detail as necessary; for example, round figures off to the nearest whole to increase comprehension.

☑ Use easily understood abbreviations and symbols as needed.

☑ Ensure that the units (e.g., dollars, percentages, or tons) are identified clearly.

Charts

☑ Use charts only when they will help the reader interpret the data better—never just to make the report look better.

☑ Label all charts as *figures*, and assign them consecutive numbers (separate from table numbers).

☑ Keep charts simple. Strive for a single, immediate, correct interpretation, and keep the reader's attention on the *data* in the chart rather than on the chart itself.

☑ Use the most appropriate type of chart to achieve your objectives. Three of the most popular types of business charts are line, bar, and pie charts.

Line Charts

☑ Use line charts to show changes in data over a period of time and to emphasize the movement of the data—the trends.

☑ Use the vertical axis to represent amount and the horizontal axis to represent time.

☑ Mark off both axes at equal intervals and clearly label them.

☑ Begin the vertical axis at zero; if necessary, use slash marks (//) to show a break in the interval.

☑ If you plot more than one variable on a chart, clearly distinguish between the lines, and label each clearly.

Bar Charts

☑ Use bar charts to compare the magnitude or relative size of items (rather than the trend), either at a specified time or over a period of time.

☑ Make all bars the same width; vary the length to reflect the value of each item.

☑ Arrange the bars in a logical order and clearly label each.

Pie Charts

☑ Use pie charts to compare the relative parts that make up a whole.

☑ Begin slicing the pie at the 12 o'clock position, moving clockwise in a logical order.

☑ Label each wedge of the pie, indicate its value, and clearly differentiate the wedges.

INTERPRETING DATA

As the name visual *aids* implies, charts act as a *help*—not a substitute—for the narrative presentation and interpretation. When analyzing the data, first determine whether the data does, in fact, answer your question. You'll waste time preparing elaborate tables and other visual aids if your data is irrelevant, incomplete, or inaccurate. Use the process in Figure 24 to interpret your data.

LO5 Interpret data for the report reader.

Figure 24 Three Steps in Interpreting Data

Scenario: Imagine that you're trying to determine the exercise habits of college students. Perhaps you're considering opening a fitness center or offering individual yoga classes.

For this example, let's also assume that you gathered only three pieces of information: a paraphrase from a newspaper article, a chart you developed from a recent study published in a journal article, and primary data from a questionnaire you distributed on campus.

Step 1: Isolation

Look at each piece of data in isolation. If the newspaper article were the only piece of data you collected, what would that mean for your business idea? For example, if the article discussed students throughout the United States, what, if any, conclusions could you draw about your local campus? Follow the same process for the study and your questionnaire, examining each in isolation, without considering any other data.

Step 2: Context

Look at each piece of data in combination with the other bits. For example, the newspaper article may lead you to believe that few students exercise regularly, but 67% of students who responded to your questionnaire reported belonging to a gym. What could this combination of data mean (for example, perhaps students belong to a gym but rarely go)? If your data sources reinforce each other, you can use stronger, more conclusive language in your analysis. If not, you may want to use less certain language or perhaps not draw any conclusions at all.

Step 3: Synthesis

Synthesize all the information you've collected. When you consider all the facts and their relationships together, what do they mean for your business idea? Do you have enough data to conclude whether the business has a good chance of success? If so, you're ready to begin the detailed analysis and presentation that will help the reader—perhaps a business investor—understand your findings. If not, you must backtrack and start the research process again.

© CENGAGE LEARNING 2013

Don't just present tables and figures. Interpret important points for your reader.

Determine the meaning of each finding by itself, in conjunction with each other finding, and in conjunction with all other findings.

Making Sense of the Data

As a report writer, you cannot simply present the raw data without interpreting it. The data in your tables and charts helps to answer a question, and the report writer must make the connection between that data and the answer to the question. In the report narrative, you don't have to discuss *all* the data in the tables and charts; that would be boring and insulting to the reader's intelligence. But you must determine the important implications of your data, and then identify and discuss them for the reader.

What types of important points do you look for? Almost always, the most important finding is the overall response to a question (rather than the responses of the cross-tabulation subgroups). And almost always the category within the question that receives the largest response is the most important point. So discuss this question and this category first. Let's take another look at the Apex example (Figure 25).

Figure 25
Simplified Table

Table 4. Response to Statement, "Apex Company is an asset to our community."
(*N* = 271; all figures in percent)

	Total	Marital Status		Sex		Age		
		Married	Single	Male	Female	Under 21	21–50	Over 50
Agree	80	82	77	83	57	69	77	90
No opinion	12	11	15	12	21	18	14	9
Disagree	8	7	8	5	22	13	9	1
Total	100	100	100	100	100	100	100	100

© CENGAGE LEARNING 2013

At a minimum, discuss the overall response and any important cross-tab findings.

In Figure 25, the major finding is this: four-fifths of the respondents believe that Apex Company is an asset to their community. If you give the exact figure from the table (here, 80%), you can use less precise language in the narrative—"four-fifths" in this case, or in other cases "one in four," or "a slight majority." Doing so helps you avoid presenting facts and figures too quickly. Pace your analysis because the reader may struggle to understand data presented too quickly or too densely.

Once you've discussed the overall finding, discuss the cross-tabulation data as necessary. Look for any of these features:

- Trends
- Unexpected findings
- Data that reinforces or contradicts other data
- Extreme values
- Data that raises questions

If these features are important, discuss them. In our example, there were no major differences in the responses by marital status, so you would probably not need to discuss them. However, you would need to discuss the big difference in responses between males and females. If possible, present data or draw any valid conclusions regarding the *reasons* for these differences.

Finally, point out the trend that is evident with regard to age: the older the respondent, the more positive the response. If it's important enough, you might display this trend in a graph for more visual effect.

Sometimes you will want to include descriptive statistics (such as the mean, median, range, and standard deviation). At other times, your data will require inference (significance) testing to determine whether the differences found in your sample data are also likely to exist in the general population.

After all of your data collection and analysis, you'll likely know more about the topic than your reader does. Help the reader by pointing out the important implications, findings, and relationships of your data. With your guidance, the reader will draw the conclusions you have.

Considering the Ethical Dimension

Everyone involved in the reporting situation has a responsibility to act in an ethical manner.

In gathering, analyzing, and reporting data, everyone involved has both rights and obligations. The researcher has the right to expect that respondents will be truthful in their responses and has an obligation not to deceive respondents. The organization that is paying for the research has the right to expect that the researcher will provide valid and reliable information and has an obligation not to misuse that data. And consumers of information—readers of data analysis—have a right to expect an accurate portrayal of the research.

Unethical practices in managing data can have serious consequences. A pharmaceutical company that bribes drug trial participants to get positive results may bring an unsafe product to market. A credit card company that reveals only "teaser" interest payments—before rates increase—may force a family into bankruptcy. And a company that exaggerates financial results may damage its reputation and ultimately cause the stock to decline.

A study linking autism to a vaccine was published in a respected British medical journal in 1998. However, in early January 2011, the study was called "an elaborate fraud" based on misrepresentations and altered data. The researcher was stripped of his medical license, but not before rates for the vaccine, which prevents measles, mumps, and rubella, fell sharply, causing measles cases to increase dramatically in the following years.[20]

If you want your research to solve problems and help in decision making, everyone involved must use common sense, good judgment, and an ethical mindset to make the project successful.

The **3Ps** In Action

Displaying Nutritional Information

Purpose

Imagine that you work for Wally's, a fast-food restaurant chain, as the marketing manager for the salad menu. To increase sales, you would like to promote certain salad items as healthy choices. Although nutrition information is available on the website in a table, you would like to create one chart to show lower-calorie menu items more visually.

Process

1. **What is the purpose of your communication?**
   To show that Wally's has several healthy menu choices.

2. **Who is your audience?**
   Wally's current customers and people who may shy away from the restaurant, thinking that all menu items are high in fat and calories.

3. **Which data points will you include?**
   From the nutrition table for salads, I'll select the following items to highlight:

- On-the-Ranch Salad with Grilled Chicken, 320 calories
- On-the-Ranch Salad (without chicken), 140 calories
- BLT Salad with Grilled Chicken, 260 calories
- BLT Salad (without chicken), 140 calories
- Caesar Salad with Grilled Chicken, 220 calories
- Caesar Salad (without chicken), 90 calories
- Fruit & Nut Salad, 210 calories

Other salad items, for example, with fried chicken, are higher in calories, but I will not include those.

4. **In what order will you present the data?**
   I'll order the items from the least caloric to the most caloric.

5. **What chart type is most appropriate for your purpose?**
   I'll use a bar chart to compare items to each other and to a common take-out tuna fish sandwich (383 calories).[21]

Product

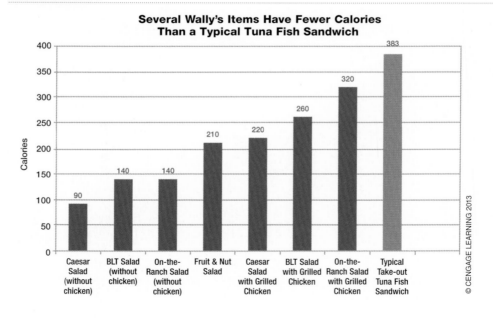

Several Wally's Items Have Fewer Calories Than a Typical Tuna Fish Sandwich

© CENGAGE LEARNING 2013

Developing a Questionnaire about Dessert Items

The 3Ps
In Practice

Purpose

The regional director of Wally's, a fast-food restaurant, has asked you, the manager of two stores, to survey customers for feedback about dessert items. The purpose of the survey is to determine how much customers enjoy current menu selections and what new items they would like to see on the menu. Develop a questionnaire that customers can complete during their visit to one of your stores.

Process

1. Brainstorm for 10 minutes. List every possible question you might ask the customers; don't worry at this point about the wording of the questions or their sequence.
2. Review your questions. Are all of them necessary to get information about dessert preferences?
3. Edit your questions to ensure that they are clear and unbiased.
4. Arrange the questions in some logical order.
5. Where possible, format each question with check-off responses, arranging the responses in some logical order.
6. Do any of the questions ask for sensitive information, or are any of them difficult to answer? If so, how will you handle these questions?
7. What information other than the questions themselves should you include on the questionnaire?

Product

Draft, revise, format, and proofread your questionnaire. Submit both your questionnaire and your answers to the process questions to your instructor.

Summary

L01   Find relevant sources for a report.

Search for data that will achieve your purpose, for example, to solve a problem or make a decision. By factoring the problem, you'll determine what primary and secondary data are needed to answer important questions. Where available, choose library databases over broad Internet searches to get the best sources.

L02   Evaluate the quality of data.

The quality of information on the Internet varies widely. When evaluating web resources, consider authority, accuracy and reliability, purpose/objectivity, coverage, and currency. When using research studies as secondary sources, first consider the purpose of the study, how the data was collected and analyzed, how consistent the data is with other studies, and how old the data is.

L03   Develop a questionnaire and cover letter.

Primary data is collected by various survey methods, mainly questionnaires, telephone inquiries, and interviews. Ensure that all survey questions are necessary, clearly worded, complete, and unbiased. Organize the questions and possible responses logically, provide clear directions, and choose an attractive format. The cover letter or email should be persuasive and explain why it is in the reader's interest to answer the survey.

L04   Construct tables and charts.

Data is converted into information by careful analysis and is interpreted in the report in narrative form and by visual aids. Each table you construct from the data should be interpretable by itself, without reference to the text. Often you will want to analyze two or more fields of data together in the same table to help identify relationships. Include only as much data in a table as is helpful, keeping the table as simple as possible.

Use well-designed line, bar, and pie charts to increase reader comprehension, emphasize certain data, create interest, and save time and space. Avoid using too many, too large, too garish, or too complicated charts.

L05   Interpret data for the report reader.

Do not analyze every figure from the table in your narrative. Instead, interpret the important points from the table, pointing out the major findings, trends, and contradictions. Avoid misrepresenting your information. A competent reporter of business information is an ethical reporter of business information.

Exercises

L01 Find relevant sources for a report.

1. Find relevant sources to support a business decision.

Choose one of the following small business situations:

- You own a clothing store and want to know whether to offer hats.
- You own an ice cream store and want to know whether to offer products other than ice cream (e.g., other desserts or soda).
- You own a jewelry store and want to know which precious gems are most popular (and what quantities you should order).
- You own a stationery store and want to know how to stock greeting cards—which are most popular?

- You own a sporting goods store and want to know the most popular bicycle brands by age group.

- You own a computer repair business and want to know what services customers will want.

  Or, of course, you can choose another situation that interests you.

  Conduct research and find a few articles to help you make your decision. Provide a list of the most relevant sources you found.

2. Compare search results on Google, Google Scholar, and a library database.

Enter a few key words into Google, Google Scholar, and a library database. You may use a scenario from Exercise 1 or choose a different situation. Try to get the most relevant, reliable results from each search by narrowing results a few times.

3. Find data to decide whether to open a store.

You have been asked to determine the feasibility of opening a frozen yogurt store in Greenville, North Carolina. Answer the following questions, using the latest figures available. Provide a citation for each source.

a. What were the number of stores and the total sales last year for TCBY, a frozen yogurt franchise?

b. What is the population of Greenville, North Carolina? What percentage of this population is between the ages of 18 and 24?

c. What is the per capita income of residents of Greenville?

d. What is the name and address of the president of TCBY?

e. What is the climate of Greenville, North Carolina?

f. How many students are enrolled at East Carolina University?

g. What is the market outlook for frozen yogurt stores nationwide?

h. What is the most current journal or newspaper article you can find on this topic?

4. Write a memo to improve accuracy in reporting.

Imagine that you're the chief editor for *The Baltimore Sun*. Use the Mike Wise situation discussed in this chapter to reinforce principles for evaluating information from the Internet (see Figures 5 and 6). Write a memo to all reporters. You might start by briefly summarizing the situation; then, use the questions presented in "Evaluating Web Resources" to write a few paragraphs as reminders for the reporters. Try to put the questions into your own words and make the principles relevant to experienced reporters.

LO2 Evaluate the quality of data.

5. Evaluate the quality of Internet resources.

Select two Internet resources and evaluate them based on the five criteria: authority, accuracy and reliability, purpose/objectivity, coverage, and currency. You might search for news about a company that interests you. Use the questions for "Evaluating Web Resources," and submit a brief summary of your analysis to your instructor.

6. Distinguish between high- and low-quality Internet sources.

Imagine that a person you admire is coming to speak on campus. You have been selected to introduce the speaker to your entire graduating class. Of course you want to ensure you have accurate information about this person. Search the Internet for information and identify at least five resources. Use the questions in "Evaluating Web

Resources" to determine the quality of the information. Write a brief summary of your analysis and submit it to your instructor.

7. Evaluate studies for a report.

Imagine that you're the corporate communications vice president for Harley-Davidson Motor Company. To promote motorcycle use in the United States, you're planning a communication campaign focused on safety. Your objective is to overcome the public's perception that motorcycles are dangerous.

You decide to include some scholarly research to support your point of view. But, of course, you want to present an ethical argument, so you'll evaluate each study carefully. Use the following questions from "Evaluating Research Studies" to ensure the studies meet your quality standards:

- What was the purpose of the study?
- How was the data collected?
- How was the data analyzed?
- How consistent is the data with that from other studies?
- How old is the data?

Write a few paragraphs that you plan to put on the Harley-Davidson website. Remember your objective: you want people to believe that motorcycles are safe (or, at least aren't as dangerous as people perceive them to be). Include references to the articles you decide to use so that your instructor can evaluate your choices.

L03 Develop a questionnaire and cover letter.

8. Create a questionnaire about a new restaurant.

As the marketing vice president of Piedmont Seafood Restaurants, you are considering opening a new restaurant in Ft. Collins, Colorado. You currently have 15 restaurants in surrounding states, and last year you opened a Piedmont in Denver. The Denver restaurant has been very successful, so you want to expand to other suitable areas.

To determine the suitability of a seafood restaurant in Ft. Collins, you are preparing a short questionnaire to be completed by people living in the Ft. Collins area. Your restaurant features a full seafood menu, with fresh seafood flown in daily. You are a full-service restaurant with a family-style atmosphere. Your prices range from $7.99 for a children's combo plate to $19.99 for your top-priced meal. The average price for a lunch or dinner would be $14.50.

Working with a partner, prepare a short questionnaire to be completed by the residents of Ft. Collins. You should have a title for your questionnaire and a brief introduction. Then ask six to ten appropriate questions that are clearly worded and unbiased. Put the questions in a logical sequence, and make sure the response options are mutually exclusive and exhaustive. Submit the questionnaire to your instructor for evaluation.

9. Write a cover letter for your questionnaire.

Prepare a cover letter to introduce the questionnaire prepared for Exercise 8. The letter should encourage readers to complete the questionnaire and return it quickly in the stamped, addressed envelope. It should also lay some groundwork for establishing potential customers if the restaurant becomes a reality. If the demand is sufficient, a Piedmont Seafood Restaurant could be opening in Ft. Collins soon.

10. Write a questionnaire about ice cream flavors.

You are planning to open an ice cream parlor. You want to have a wide variety of flavors for your patrons to select from, so you are going to ask potential customers to identify their favorite flavors of ice cream.

a. Write a question that presents an exhaustive list of ice cream flavors. You also want to know how much people are willing to pay for a single scoop of ice cream and a double scoop of ice cream.

b. Prepare questions that list the various price ranges people would be willing to pay for a single scoop of ice cream and a double scoop of ice cream. Make sure the questions are exhaustive and mutually exclusive.

c. Finally, you want to know what other ice cream novelty items your store should offer. Write a question that gathers this information.

   Make sure the options for each question are listed in an appropriate order.

11. Write a questionnaire about a new store.

Assume that you have been asked to write a report on the feasibility of opening a packaging and shipping store, such as a UPS Store, in your town. Because students at your school would be a major source of potential customers for your store, you decide to survey the students to gather relevant data. Working in a group of four or five, develop a two-page questionnaire and a cover letter that you could mail to a sample of these students.

   Ensure that the content and appearance of the questionnaire follow the guidelines given in this chapter. Pilot-test your questionnaire and cover letter on a small sample of students; then revise it as necessary and submit it to your instructor.

12. Convert your questionnaire to an online survey.

Go to a free online survey site (such as www.surveymonkey.com or www.zoomerang .com), and reformat the questionnaire you developed in Exercise 11 as an online survey. Your instructor may ask you to administer this questionnaire online by emailing it to a few students.

13. Create an online survey for your classmates.

Working in small groups, imagine that you're planning a start-up business targeted to students. First, decide on your business concept. This can be anything: a service (e.g., laundry or grocery shopping) or a product (e.g., custom T-shirts or imported hats).

   Next, write 8–12 questions to determine whether your idea will be popular. Remember to use the principles for writing effective questions described in this chapter.

   When you're satisfied that your questions meet the criteria for well-designed questionnaires, create a free online survey on a site such as www.surveymonkey.com or www.zoomerang.com. Distribute the survey to your classmates. (See the next exercise for a related activity.)

   Finally, with your group, analyze the responses and make a preliminary judgment about whether your business would be successful.

14. Evaluate your classmates' online surveys.

For Exercise 13, you worked in a group to create a survey for other students in your class. Pair up with another group to evaluate each other's questionnaire. As you're completing the other group's questionnaire, take notes to evaluate each question. In class, meet with your partner group and provide each other with feedback on your questionnaires. Which questions were most effective, and why? Which questions were least effective, and why?

L04   Construct tables and charts.

15. Analyze data and construct a table.

Next year, Broadway Productions will move its headquarters from Manhattan to Stamford, Connecticut, in the building where Tri-City Bank occupies the first floor. The bank hopes to secure many Broadway Productions employees as customers and has conducted a survey to determine their banking habits. The handwritten figures on the questionnaire in Figure 26 show the number of respondents who checked each alternative.

a. Is a table needed to present the information in Question 1?

b. Would any cross-tabulation analyses help readers understand the data in this questionnaire? Explain.

Figure 26
Survey Results

BROADWAY PRODUCTIONS QUESTIONNAIRE

1. Do you currently have an account at Tri-City Bank?
   _58_ yes
   _170_ no

2. At which of the following institutions do you currently have an account?
   (Please check all that apply.)
   _201_ commercial bank
   _52_ employee credit union
   _75_ savings and loan association
   _6_ other (please specify: _____)
   _18_ none

3. In terms of convenience, which one of the following bank locations do you consider most important in selecting your main bank?
   _70_ near home
   _102_ near office
   _12_ near shopping
   _31_ on way to and from work
   _13_ other (please specify: _____)

4. How important do you consider each of the following bank services?

	Very Important	Somewhat Important	Not Important
Bank credit card	88	132	8
Check guarantee card	74	32	122
Convenient ATM machines	143	56	29
Drive-in service	148	47	33
Free checking	219	9	0
Overdraft privileges	20	187	21
Personal banker	40	32	156
Telephone transfer	6	20	202
Trust department	13	45	170

5. If you have changed banks within the past three years, what was the major reason for the change?
   _33_ relocation of residence
   _4_ relocation of bank
   _18_ dissatisfaction with bank service
   _7_ other (please specify: _____)

   Thank you so much for your cooperation. Please return this questionnaire in the enclosed envelope to Customer Service Department, Tri-City Bank, P.O. Box 1086, Stamford, Ct 06902.

c. Construct a table that presents the important information from Question 4 of the questionnaire in a logical, helpful, and efficient manner. Give the table an appropriate title and arrange it in final report format.

16. Create a chart to compare data.

According to Mars, Inc., each bag of M&M's should contain the percentage of colors shown in Figure 27. Purchase five small bags of M&M's and separate the M&M's in each bag by color. Compare your percentage of occurrence of colors to that shown as the M&M standard. Create a chart showing the comparison.

Figure 27 **M&M Color Distribution**

What Colors Come in Your Bag?

30%   20%   20%   10%   10%   10%

"M&M's"® Milk Chocolate Candies Color Chart

Source: http://global.mms.com/us/about/products/milkchocolate.jsp

M&M'S AND M IN A CIRCLE ARE REGISTERED TRADEMARKS OF MARS, INCORPORATED AND ITS AFFILIATES. THESE TRADEMARKS ARE USED WITH PERMISSION. MARS, INCORPORATED IS NOT ASSOCIATED WITH CENGAGE LEARNING.

17. Evaluate charts in a business publication.

Find three or more charts in business articles from newspapers or magazines (e.g., *Business Week* or *Fortune*). Make a copy of each chart and the written information associated with it. Evaluate the charts based on the principles presented in this chapter. What are the strengths and weaknesses of each visual? What changes, if any, should be made to the charts to make them more understandable and helpful? Submit a copy of each article and your evaluation of the charts' effectiveness to your instructor.

18. Determine which type of visual is best.

For the following situations, select the most appropriate visual aid for presenting the data, and explain why it is the best option. Consider a line chart, bar chart, pie chart, table, or map.

a. To show the daily sales for your small computer business

b. To show the proportion of your budget spent on each of the four fixed costs for your company during the year

c. To show the results of six survey questions asking people's opinion regarding the economy

d. To show the comparisons of the first quarter's net sales for departments A, B, and C

e. To show the locations of your international offices

f. To show total sales by region and the percentage of increase or decrease from the previous year

g. To show the average annual rainfall in selected cities in the nation

19. Construct a chart from data presented in a table.

Imagine that you own an independent paint and home decorating store. To determine which product lines bring in the most revenue, you have created the following table.

Product	Revenue Contribution
Wallpaper	10%
Paint	49%
Tools and supplies	24%
Home accents	4%
Stain	13%

To communicate this information to store employees, create a chart from this data.

L05 Interpret data for the
report reader.

20. Interpret data.

Write a one- or two-sentence interpretation of the data for each of the five questions shown in Figure 26 (Exercise 15). Then, assume you need to present the important information from this questionnaire in one paragraph of no more than 50 or 60 words. Compose this summary paragraph.

21. Make sense of data.

As a marriage counselor, you have gathered the following statistics:

a. The average age at which women marry for the first time has increased by 1.5 years in the last decade.

b. The average age at which men marry for the first time has increased by 2.5 years in the last decade.

c. The number of people getting married for the first time has dropped by 13% in the last decade.

d. The number of divorces has increased by 22% in the last decade.

e. The average number of years couples remain married has decreased by 2.8 years in the last decade.

f. The number of people who were divorced more than once has increased 26% in the last decade.

g. The number of women between the ages of 20 and 50 entering the work force has increased by 12% in the last decade.

h. The number of men between the ages of 20 and 50 entering the work force has decreased by 8%.

i. The amount of debt for married couples has increased by more than 31% (an all-time high) during the last decade.

This is a lot of data, but what does it all mean? In groups of four or five people, discuss possible answers to the following questions. What trends can be identified in the data? What could the trends mean? How do the pieces of data relate to each other? Could one factor be causing another? If so, which ones? Before drawing any conclusions, what additional information would be helpful? What kind of visual aid would be best for showing these changes in the last decade?

22. Determine whether statements accurately represent data.

The following sentences interpret the table in Figure 25. Analyze each sentence to determine whether it represents the data in the table accurately.

a. Males and females alike believe Apex is an asset to the community.

b. More than one-fifth of the females (22%) did not respond.

c. Age and the generation gap bring about different beliefs.

d. Married males over age 50 had the most positive opinions.

e. Females disagree more than males, probably because most of the workers at Apex are male.

f. Female respondents tend to disagree with the statement.

g. Apex should be proud of the fact that four-fifths of the residents believe the company is an asset to the community.

h. Thirteen percent of the younger residents have doubts about whether Apex is an asset to the community.

i. More single than married residents didn't care or had no opinion about the topic.

j. Overall, the residents believe that 8% of the company is not an asset to the community.

23. Identify possible misrepresented statistics.

Politicians, businesspeople, and others love to quote statistics to support their viewpoints. Locate three news stories in which someone quotes statistics to support a particular case. Then find an unbiased source that either confirms or refutes those statistics. Write a memo to your instructor discussing your findings. Include a copy of both the original news articles and your supporting statistics.

PersuadeCafé

Let's revisit PersuadeCafé, the coffee and pastry company. Now that you have pitched an idea and received feedback, you'll want to research and develop the idea further.

On the PersuadeCafé intranet site, you'll find information and data that will be useful for you to support your proposal: the current menu, revenue trends, stock performance, the number of stores, customer and employee survey data, and other background information. Review everything available to you.

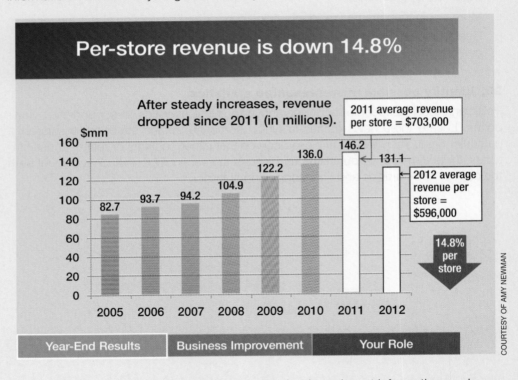

How will you make sense of the data, research other relevant information, and present findings in ways that support your idea?

Notes

1. "McDonald's, The Marketing Process," *The Times* 100, 2006, www .thetimes100.co.uk/downloads/ mcdonalds/mcdonalds_11_full.pdf, accessed September 2, 2010.

2. Jillian Madison, "McDonalds [sic] Menu Items from Around the World," Food Network Humor, July 9, 2009, http://foodnetworkhumor .com/2009/07/mcdonalds-menu- items-from-around-the-world-40- pics/, accessed August 31, 2010.

3. "McDonald's, The Marketing Process."

4. "McDonald's, The Marketing Process."

5. Adapted and used with permission from the author, Grace Lee.

6. A journal is a scholarly periodical published by a professional association or a university, and a *magazine* is a commercial periodical published by a for-profit organization. Although the distinction is sometimes useful in evaluating secondary sources, the two terms are used interchangeably in this chapter to refer to any periodical publication.

7. Andy Alexander, "Post Columnist Mike Wise Suspended for Fake Twitter Report," Omblog, *The Washington Post*, August 31, 2010, http://voices.washingtonpost .com/ombudsman- blog/2010/ 08/post_columnist_mike_wise_ suspe.html, accessed September 3, 2010.

8. Michael David Smith, "Washington Post's Mike Wise Fabricates Story to Prove Point," AOL News, August 30, 2010, http://www.aolnews .com/2010/ 08/30/washington-posts- mike-wise- fabricates-a-story-to- prove-a-point/, accessed July 8, 2011.

9. Geoffrey Nunberg, "Teaching Students to Swim in the Online Sea," *New York Times*, February 13, 2005, sec. 4, p. 4; and Judy Foreman, "A Wealth of E-Health: There's a Ton of Medical Data on the Internet, But How Much Is Reliable?" *Los Angeles* Times, November 29, 2004, p. F3.

10. Adapted from "Evaluating Web Resources," Nestlé Library, School of Hotel Administration, Cornell University, August 2010.

11. Charles Seife, *Proofiness: The Dark Arts of Mathematical Deception* (New York: NY, Viking Penguin, 2010).

12. Robert Rosenthal and Ralph L. Rosnow, *The Volunteer Subject* (New York: NY, John Wiley, 1975), pp. 195–196.

13. Stephani K.A. Robson and Sheryl E. Kimes, "Don't Sit So Close to Me: Restaurant Table Characteristics and Guest Satisfaction," *Cornell Hospitality Reports* 9, no. 2. (January 2009).

14. Used with permission.

15. "Financial Presentation Format and Managerial Decision Making: Tables Versus Graphs," *Management Communication Quarterly* 2 (November 1988): 194–216.

16. Matthias Schonlau and Ellen Peters, "Graph Comprehension," Working Paper, Rand Labor and Population, September 2008, www.rand.org/ pubs/working_papers/2008/RAND_ WR618.pdf, accessed September 6, 2010.

17. Judi Brownell and Amy Newman, "Hospitality Managers and Communication Technologies: Challenges and Solutions." *Cornell Hospitality Reports* 9, no. 18 (December 2009).

18. Edward Tufte, *The Visual Display of Quantitative Information* (Cheshire, CT: Graphics Press, 1983).

19. Theophilus B. A. Aldo, "The Effects of Dimensionality in Computer Graphics," *Journal of Business Communication* 31 (December 1994): 253–265.

20. "Retracted Autism Study an 'Elaborate Fraud,' British Journal Finds," CNN, January 5, 2011, http://cnn .com/2011/HEALTH/01/05/autism. vaccines/index.html, accessed January 30, 2011.

21. Calorie King, "Panera Bread's Sandwiches & Burgers: Cafe Sandwiches, Tuna Salad on Honey Wheat Bread," www.calorieking.com/foods/calories- in-sandwiches-burgers-cafe- sandwiches-tuna-salad-on-honey- wheat-bread-full_f-ZmlkPTY1MDUz .html, accessed December 22, 2010.

Chapter 10

Planning the Report (10) Selecting a Report Format (10) Organizing the Report (10) Outlining the Report (10) Drafting the Report (10) Drafting the Body (10) Introduction (10) Findings (10) Writing the Report (10) Summary, Conclusions, and Recommendations (10) Drafting Supplementary Sections (10) Title Page (10) Cover Letter, Memo, or Email (10) Executive Summary (10) Table of Contents (10) Appendix (10) References (10) Developing an Effective Writing Style (10) Documenting Your Sources (10) Footnotes and Endnotes (10) Author-Date Format (10) Refining Your Draft

LEARNING OBJECTIVES

After you have finished this chapter, you should be able to

L01 Determine an appropriate report format and organization.

L02 Draft the report body and supplementary pages.

L03 Use an effective writing style.

L04 Document sources accurately.

L05 Revise, format, and proofread the report.

"Consumers Union's staff of 652 is roughly divided into two camps: technicians who devise and perform tests and editors/writers who translate the findings into readable prose."

— THE WALL STREET JOURNAL[1]

Chapter Introduction: Information and Advocacy from Consumer Reports

Do you want to buy a new plasma TV or a car? Since 1936, Consumer Reports has provided expert, objective information about almost anything consumers buy.

Testing everything from paper towels to treadmills, the organization's National Research Center puts products through the ringer. How well do the car brakes work going from 60 mph to 0 on wet pavement? How intuitive are the iPhone buttons?

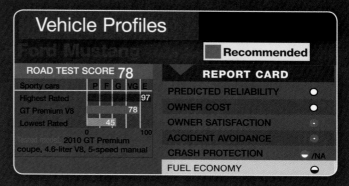

Consumer Reports' graphics make it easy for buyers to compare products.

After collecting the data, the organization translates its scientific research to easy-to-understand reports. Complex information becomes accessible to the public with Consumer Reports' simple explanations, "highs" and "lows" of each product, and at-a-glance graphic, such as the one shown here about the Ford Mustang. The standardized circle system makes it easy to compare products across a variety of criteria.

Consumer Reports helps people make smarter decisions with their money—and the company serves a role in consumer advocacy. The organization's research influences government recalls of defective products, such as glass bakeware that shattered and spinning candleholders that caught on fire. Fulfilling its mission of consumer protection, the organization also has influenced financial regulation overhaul and health care reform.[2]

Providing independent, well-researched opinions in an understandable way makes Consumer Reports a highly valued source for today's wary consumers.

PLANNING THE REPORT

Reports are a tough sell to today's business audience. Decision makers may prefer shorter documents and give little attention to the detail you labored over for your report. However, interpreting and presenting information is critical for major decisions, which may affect people's lives and cost millions—or billions—of dollars.

Recent reports about texting while driving have brought attention to the issue and may save lives. Reports by credible sources, such as the Pew Internet Research Center, tell us how many people text while driving: 34% of teens and 47% of adults who text.[3] Other reports tell us the impact of this behavior: 16,000 deaths were caused by texting while driving within a five-year period.[4] Armed with this data, researchers write reports that are translated for the public and—with any luck—make a difference in how we live. Writing a report is one of the most challenging and arguably the most important of the business communication tasks.

A billboard discourages texting while driving, a problem identified by credible data sources and reports.

When you write a report, you'll follow the same process we discussed for other types of business writing: planning, drafting, revising, and proofreading. Although you'll spend plenty of time planning the report (even before you collect data), presenting the results requires its own stage of planning. You need to decide what format to use, how to organize the content, and what headings to include.

LO1 Determine an appropriate report format and organization.

Communication Technologies

Reports may be primarily text or a mix of text and graphics.

Selecting a Report Format

When you picture a report, a primarily text-based document may come to mind. Reports written in programs such as Microsoft Word are still common, but more companies, particularly financial services and consulting firms, are using programs such as PowerPoint for reports that combine text and graphics. When printed, these reports are sometimes called **decks**. Also, reports may be strictly numerical, such as an expense report, which is created in a program such as Excel. In this chapter, we'll focus on text-based and more graphical reports.

Although both formats are fairly formal documents, significant differences exist. A text-based report (e.g., Figure 1),[5] is written in narrative (paragraph)

Figure 1
Cover and One Page of a Report with Primarily Text

McKinsey&Company

Education
Closing the talent gap: Attracting and retaining top-third graduates to careers in teaching

Header includes the report title, subtitle, and page number. These could appear in the footer at the bottom of the page instead.

Education
Closing the talent gap: Attracting and retaining top-third graduates to careers in teaching

9

Top performing nations recruit 100% of their new teachers from the top third. In the U.S., it's 23%—and 14% in high poverty schools.

Introduction: A moment of opportunity

American education policy is experiencing one of its most promising moments in memory, with national attention centered on whole system reform for arguably the first time. We are learning important lessons from hundreds of schools that achieve outstanding results with high-poverty students, the Race to the Top competition is beginning to spur innovation at system-wide scale, a broad state-based movement is underway to adopt common standards in core subjects, and new systems of data-driven performance management are being devised or introduced in many districts. Most important, the community of stakeholders who work to boost student achievement is focusing on effective teaching as a central strategy to improve education outcomes.

Research shows that of all the controllable factors influencing student achievement, the most important by far is the effectiveness of the classroom teacher. Stakeholders now recognize the importance of effective teachers—and of how far we are from a systemic approach to producing them. For example, few school systems evaluate teachers in ways that differentiate them and inform teaching practice with integrity and insight.[2] Many school districts and states, including Race to the Top competitors, are now working to measure, evaluate, reward, coach, and replicate effectiveness in teaching, and to build a cadre of school leaders who are capable of helping teachers to improve instructional practices. Although many school systems are just beginning the hard work of designing and implementing such human capital reforms, and many have yet to begin, the importance of effective teaching is now central to the U.S. reform debate.

This focus on teachers and teaching is broadly consistent with McKinsey & Company's work with school systems in over 50 countries, and in our global research on school system excellence. Leaders in the world's best-performing school systems believe that the "quality of an education system cannot exceed the quality of its teachers," and they have taken a strategic and systematic approach to attracting, developing, retaining, and training the most talented educators. Each top-performing country accomplishes this in its own way, but they all have the same aim: getting effective teachers in front of students of all socio-economic backgrounds, and retraining those teachers for a career in teaching.

While more Americans now recognize the importance of effective teaching, most of the U.S. initiatives to promote it seek to improve the effectiveness of teachers already in the classroom, not to upgrade the caliber of young people entering the profession. Top-performing nations such as Singapore, Finland, and South Korea have made a different choice, treating teaching as a highly selective profession. They recruit, develop, and retain what this report will call "top third+" students as one of their central education strategies, and they've achieved extraordinary results.

After recruiting from the top third, these countries rigorously screen students on other qualities they believe to be predictors of teaching success, including perseverance, ability to motivate others, passion for children, and organizational and communications skills. That's the "plus" in top-third+. These countries recognize that coming from the top third of

[2] Among many recent analyses of the U.S. teaching profession, perhaps the most influential has been *The Widget Effect*, by the New Teacher Project, which documents the stark inadequacy of teacher evaluations.

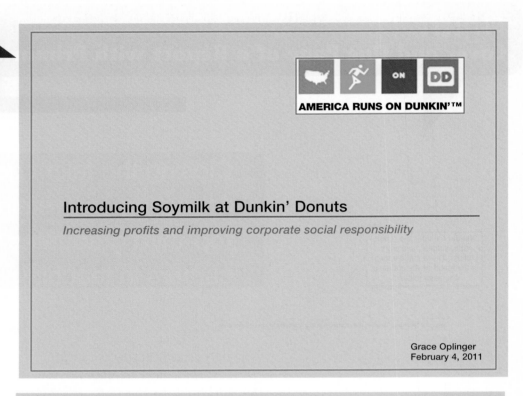

Figure 2
Title and One Slide from a Report Created in PowerPoint

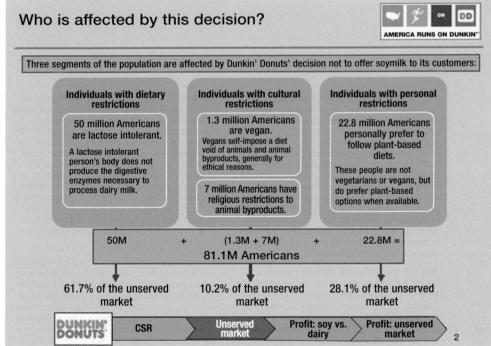

form, with headings and subheadings separating each section. In a PowerPoint report (e.g., Figure 2),[6] each slide, with a distinct title, becomes a separate page of the report, and very little, if any, paragraph text is used. Instead, text is written in bulleted form, often incorporated into graphical elements, such as tables or shapes.

The reports in Figures 1 and 2 have different purposes for different audiences. The McKinsey report (Figure 1) was publicized through newspaper articles to influence education policymakers. The Dunkin' Donuts report (Figure 2) was designed as a proposal to influence internal company decision makers.

The McKinsey example in Figure 1 is easy to read and easy to follow. Although primarily text, the report includes several graphics, which we'll see later in this chapter.

However, comparing Figures 1 and 2, you can see why PowerPoint reports are becoming more popular. In many ways, these reports are easier to create and easier to read. With more graphics and less dense text, the format has much more visual appeal and is far more skimmable than a paragraph-based report. But don't confuse these reports with PowerPoint slides that you would project on a screen or monitor during an oral presentation; the Dunkin' Donuts example is far too dense for such a presentation, which we'll discuss in the next chapter.

For less formal reports, such as a proposal to your manager, you may include the report within an email message or as an extension of a memo. As an example, let's revisit Grace Lee's idea of adding hot food items at Jason's Deli from Chapter 7. You may remember that Grace's manager rejected her idea in Chapter 8. But let's imagine that she had taken a different approach: rather than presenting her idea in a short email (as in Chapter 7), she writes a more formal proposal. In Figure 3, Grace expands on her idea by adding research and presents the proposal as a memo to the owner.[7] This example is more formal than her original email but less formal than a traditional text-based report or the PowerPoint format.

Which format you choose depends on audience needs, organizational norms, and type of content. For an audience accustomed to more traditional reports, a primarily text document may be best; however, for a more progressive audience who is pressed for time, the PowerPoint format may be a better choice. If your company typically produces text-based reports, then that format may be preferable. If you are illustrating your points with extensive charts and images, then the PowerPoint format probably is an easier medium to use.

Another example of a hybrid report page and more formatting guidelines are in the Reference Manual.

Less formal reports, such as internal proposals, may be written within an email or memo.

Sometimes this format is called a memo-report.

Organizing the Report

A songwriter doesn't necessarily start at the first bar and work toward the last. He or she may find a beautiful refrain and then fill in the rest later. For report writing, you may have collected data in some order, but that's not necessarily the best sequence in which to present the data to your audience.

The four most common ways to organize your findings are according to time, location, importance, and criteria. Of course, you may choose other patterns for organizing data; for example, you can move from the known to the unknown or from the simple to the complex. The purpose of the report, the type of content, and your knowledge of the audience will help you select the organizational framework that will be most useful.

Most reports are organized by time, location, importance, or criteria.

Time

Chronology, or time sequence, is appropriate for agendas, meeting minutes, schedules, and status reports. For informational reports—to simply inform rather than persuade your reader—discussing events in order is an efficient way to organize and is easy to follow. The following example uses time to show the history of Countrywide Financial.

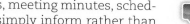
Organize your report by time only when it is important for the reader to know the sequence of events.

Countrywide Financial: A Case Study

- Founded by Loeb and Mozilo: 1969
- Enormous Returns to Investors: 1982–2003
- Aggressive Pursuit of Home Loans: 2000–2008
- Spectacular Demise: 2008–2009

Figure 3   Proposal in Memo Format

To: Jason Myers
From: Grace Y. Lee
Date: September 17, 2013
Subject: Proposal to Expand the Menu: Adding Hot Food Choices

> Includes a clear, specific recommendation in the subject line.

> Includes a brief introduction to gain attention; includes the recommendation early on.

Jason's Deli and Restaurant has done tremendously well as a salad bar and deli restaurant since its grand opening in 2005. However, guest count and revenue have been declining in the past year. To boost sales, I recommend that Jason's redesign the menu to include hot food choices. By doing so, Jason's can benefit in the following ways:

> Uses bullets to highlight main points: the benefits to the owner of adopting the proposal.

- Increase revenue and profit
- Distinguish the café from direct and indirect competitors
- Expand our consumer market

> Uses a brief transition sentence to motivate action.

I'm confident that you will recognize this potential business opportunity to improve our restaurant's financial situation.

> Organizes around the three main benefits.

Increase Revenue and Profit

> Uses a topic sentence as the main point of the first paragraph (direct and easy to skim); addresses costs —a potential obstacle— right up front.

You can increase Jason's revenue and profit by investing in a hot foods buffet. Before profiting from a hot foods buffet installment, you may wonder about the costs of investment. Although the average cost of buffet carts ranges from $5,400 to $8,800, the benefits of higher revenue and profits outweigh this cost.[1]

> Uses another good topic sentence (here and throughout); includes credible reference as evidence of key points.

We can expect Jason's to bring in higher revenue with a hot foods buffet. In fact, *Restaurant & Travel News* reports that hot food items, on average, weigh 20-30% more than cold food items. Additionally, consumers are more likely to load up on a variety of these heavier hot foods in their "pay-per-pound" containers as opposed to cold salad accompaniments.[2] For example, a container full of hot food selections may weigh 2 pounds whereas a container full of basic salad ingredients, deli meats, and cold pastas may weigh 1.6 pounds. At $6.49 per pound, the container of hot food will bring in an extra $2.60. Multiply those figures by the hundreds of pounds of food we sell in one day, and you can identify the benefits of hot foods generating more revenue.

> Could provide a larger figure here (perhaps for a week) to show the significance.

> Provides another clear, direct argument, but could estimate weekly, monthly, or annual increases

Further, hot food items have a lower food cost percentage, which ultimately contributes to increasing profits for Jason's. Accordingly, Hotel News Resource reports that batch cooking hot foods has as low as 15-20% food costs compared to the 25-30% food cost of fresh produce and deli meats.[3] Our average food cost is 28%, consistent with this research for fresh produce and deli. If we incorporate a hot foods buffet, we can expect our food costs to decrease dramatically. Because food cost and labor are our two primary expenses, lowering our food cost will in turn increase our total profits.

---

[1] "Kitchen & Bars for Outdoor Living," *Vermont Islands,* www.vermontislands.com, accessed April 21, 2011.
[2] "How Do Restaurant Buffets Make Money?" *Pricing for Profit,* www.pricingforprofit.com/pricing-strategy-blog/how-do-restaurant-buffets-make-money.htm, accessed September 17, 2009.
[3] Joe Dunbar, "Food & Beverage: Hot Food Cost Topic," Hotel News Resource, *Hotel Industry News,* www.hotelnewsresource.com/article36259.html, accessed September 18, 2009.

Figure 3 (Continued)

Organizes the section around a second benefit.

Uses direct organization for all paragraphs within each section.

Could strengthen evidence by indicating how many people participated in the survey.

Admits potential objections and addresses them well in this paragraph.

Distinguish Jason's from Competitors

In addition to increasing revenue and profit, a hot foods menu will distinguish Jason's from direct and indirect competitors in the town center. Only 3 of 12 vegetarian and deli restaurants surrounding Jason's have hot item selections. By being the only salad bar, vegetarian, and deli restaurant that offers an assortment of hot and cold foods, we can have the advantage of menu variety over our competitors.

For example, on Yelp.com, a user review website for restaurants, Jason's is classified as a salad bar, deli, and vegetarian joint—along with 27 other restaurants in the town center; however, adding a "traditional American" tag, after installing a hot foods menu, would separate Jason's from 21 of our competitors.[4]

Expand Our Consumer Market

In addition to distinguishing Jason's from local competitors, our hot food selections can expand our consumer market by appealing to more people. According to a consumer choice study by *Restaurants & Institutions* publications, menu variety is a highly influential factor in consumer dining decisions.[5] Holding all other factors constant, the larger and more diverse the salad bar or buffet, the more the restaurant appeals to the public. More specifically, *Hotels Magazine* suggests an increase in consumer demand for savory foods and hot comfort foods—a trend expected to continue for several years.[6]

On a more local scale, I conducted a small survey this summer of business people at City Center and discovered that most men preferred a hot lunch to a cold salad or sandwich; however, they were often too busy to bother dining at restaurants or ordering take-out. Rather, businessmen usually purchased lunch from quick-service or fast-casual restaurants. Therefore, if we offer restaurant-quality hot foods in a grab-and-go buffet, we could reach out to this untapped market.

On the other hand, women make up the majority of our calorie-conscious guests who may not be initially inclined to purchase hot foods (which are perceived to be high in calories and fat). Yet a study conducted at Columbia and Harvard University revealed that people tend to indulge the occasional urge for guilt-free eating. Women who strictly maintained a low-calorie, low-fat diet would build up "wistful feelings of missing out on life's pleasures."[7] As such, our hot foods buffet will be available to women who want to indulge their occasional urges for guilt-free meals.

In summary, a hot foods menu and buffet at Jason's will make more money, distinguish the café from local competitors, and expand market reach and appeal. With further research on costs and methods to implement this idea, I am certain the addition of hot food items will contribute to a successful, long-term change.

I look forward to hearing your reaction to this idea and to talking about next steps.

[4] "Jason's Deli," New York Restaurants, Dentists, Bars, Beauty Salons, Doctors, www.yelp.com/biz, accessed April 21, 2011.

[5] "Top of the Food Chains: Consumers' Choice in Chains 2009, Restaurants and Institutions," *Foodservice Industry News, Recipes, Research, Restaurants & Institutions.* www.rimag.com/article/CA6686573.html, accessed September 19, 2009.

[6] "Experts Offer Top Food Trends For Hotels and Restaurants," *HOTELS—The Magazine Of The Global Hotel Industry*, www.hotelsmag.com/article/ca6616400.html, accessed September 20, 2009.

[7] "Why It's Good to Indulge the Urge to Splurge," Times Online, Women | Fashion, Health, Beauty, Body & Soul, http://women.timesonline.co.uk/tol/life_and_style/women/fashion/article6091793.ece, accessed September 19, 2009.

Sequence is an easy way to organize topics but isn't appropriate in all situations. For example, just because you *record* data in sequence, it may not be the most efficient way to *present* that data to your readers. Assume, for example, that you are writing a progress report on a recruiting trip you made to four college campuses. The first passage, given in time sequence, is hard to follow and provides information about timing that isn't relevant to the reader.

NOT On Monday morning, I interviewed one candidate for the budget analyst position and two candidates for the junior accountant position. Then, in the afternoon, I interviewed two candidates for the asset manager position and another for the budget analyst position. Finally, on Tuesday, I interviewed another candidate for budget analyst and two for junior accountant.

BUT On Monday and Tuesday, I interviewed three candidates for the budget analyst position, four for the junior accountant position, and two for the asset manager position.

Location

Like the use of time sequence, the use of location as the basis for organizing a report is often appropriate for simple informational reports. Discussing topics according to their geographical or physical location (e.g., describing an office layout) may be the most efficient way to present the data.

The following example, Renovation Plans for the SAS Dallas Office, uses location to organize the topics; however, the writer probably is using a second variable—for example, time (when the projects will be started or completed) or importance (how much each project will cost). In most cases, you'll use more than one variable for organizing between and within sections.

> **Renovation Plans for the SAS Dallas Office**
> - Converting the Cafeteria to Office Space
> - Replacing the Roof
> - Redecorating the Executive Suite
> - Upgrading the Bathroom Facilities

Importance

For the busy reader, the most efficient organizational plan may be to have the most important topic discussed first, followed in order by topics of decreasing importance. The reader then gets the major idea up front and can skim the less important information as desired or needed. This organizational plan is routinely used by newspapers, where the most important points are discussed in the lead paragraph, and in proposals such as Grace Lee's about Jason's Deli.

The following example uses level of importance to organize information for a progress report about the SAS renovation.

> **Progress on SAS Renovation Project**
> - Renovation Is on Budget
> - Time Schedule Has Slipped One Month
> - Houston Office Was Added to Project

For some types of proposals, the opposite plan (a less direct structure) might be more effective. As we discussed earlier in the book, if you determine that your audience will be highly resistant to your idea, you may convince them in small steps, starting with the least objectionable point.

Criteria

For most analytical and recommendation reports, where the purpose is to analyze the data, draw conclusions, and recommend a solution, the most logical arrangement is by criteria. For these reports, you may develop a hypothesis and break down factors or causes of a problem. The following example, Selecting a Consultant for the Communication Audit, uses criteria against which the writer evaluates consultants.

The most logical organization for most analytical and recommendation reports is by criteria.

> ### Selecting a Consultant for the Communication Audit
> - Although the Most Expensive, McKinsey Offers the Most Depth
> - Deloitte Has Experience with the Northeast Region
> - Towers Watson Is the Least Expensive Option

By focusing attention on the criteria, you help lead the reader to the same conclusion you reached. This strategy is another good option if your reader might be resistant to your recommendations.

Select an organizational plan that helps the reader follow easily, understand the information, and accept the conclusions presented.

Presenting Conclusions and Recommendations

Once you've decided how to organize the findings of your study, you must decide where to present the conclusions and recommendations resulting from these findings. The differences among findings, conclusions, and recommendations are illustrated in Figure 4.

The conclusions and recommendations answer research questions raised in the introduction.

Most business reports for American audiences use the direct organization plan, with the conclusions and recommendations up front. This is the preferable structure for your manager, for audiences who will be receptive to your conclusions and recommendations, and for readers to have context before reading the details of your report. However, the indirect style may be appropriate in some situations. Consider the indirect style when your audience prefers the indirect style (e.g., some international audiences), when your audience may be resistant to your conclusions and recommendations, or when the topic is so complex that the reader needs detailed explanations to understand your conclusions.

Choose the direct plan (conclusions and recommendations first) for most business reports.

Of course, you can use a hybrid approach. For example, instead of putting all the conclusions and recommendations either first or last, you might split them up, discussing each in the appropriate subsection of your report. Or, even though you

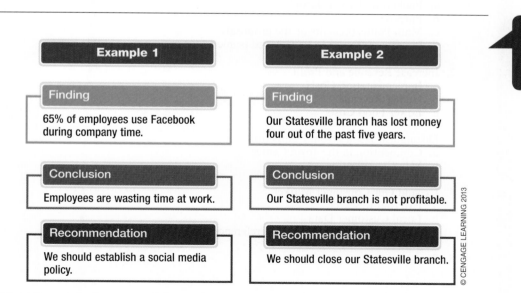

Figure 4
Examples of Findings, Conclusions, and Recommendations

Example 1	Example 2
Finding	**Finding**
65% of employees use Facebook during company time.	Our Statesville branch has lost money four out of the past five years.
Conclusion	**Conclusion**
Employees are wasting time at work.	Our Statesville branch is not profitable.
Recommendation	**Recommendation**
We should establish a social media policy.	We should close our Statesville branch.

© CENGAGE LEARNING 2013

write a report using an indirect plan, you may add an executive summary or cover letter or email to communicate the conclusions and recommendations to your audience before the report is read.

Outlining the Report

 The outline provides a concise visual picture of the structure of your report.

Although we introduced the concept of outlining in Chapter 4, the process is more complex for a longer, formal report. An outline is a useful step to help you plan which points are to be covered, in what order they will be covered, and how the topics relate to the rest of the report.

Consider your outline a working draft to be revised as you compose the report. The wording doesn't matter too much at this point; you just want to have the major and minor topics identified. You may use any combination of multilevel numbers, letters, or bullets for your outline. Figure 5 shows an outline of Grace Lee's proposal for Jason's Deli.

Use descriptive and parallel headings for unity and coherence.

Headings help orient your reader and give your report unity and coherence. As you refine your outline, you'll choose the actual wording for your headings and decide how many you'll need.

Talking and Generic Headings

Imagine reading proposals from four energy auditors about your company's property. Each wants to sell you energy-saving solutions, such as a new heating system

Figure 5   Proposal in Outline Format

Proposal to Expand the Menu: Adding Hot Food Choices

1. Introduction
   a. Background about Jason's
   b. Purpose
   c. Main Points (benefits of the proposal)
   d. Preview of Topics to Be Covered (same as the main points in this case)

2. Increase Revenue and Profit
   a. Implementation Costs
   b. Higher Revenue
   c. Lower Food Costs

3. Distinguish Jason's from Competitors
   a. Competition in the Town Center
   b. Yelp Classifications

4. Expand Our Consumer Market
   a. External Research
   b. Local Customer Data
   c. Possible Downside: Women's Preferences

5. Summary

or new windows. Sure, headings such as "Costs," "Advantages," and "Disadvantages," explain major sections of the reports, but they're hardly descriptive—and they do nothing to distinguish one report from the others.

The Dunkin' Donuts report uses **talking headings** to identify not only the topic of the section but also the major conclusion. Immediately following each slide title, which is in question form, the author tells the reader the answer. More commonly, talking headings appear as slide titles. Also used in newspapers and magazines, talking headings are especially useful for direct organization—the reader can simply skim the headings (or titles of each slide) to understand the major conclusions of the report. For PowerPoint reports, titles typically are written as full sentences, and they may span two lines.

Generic headings, on the other hand, identify only the topic of a section, without giving the conclusion. Reports written in an indirect pattern would use generic headings, similar to the headings used for Renovation Plans for the SAS Dallas Office:

- Converting the Cafeteria to Office Space
- Replacing the Roof
- Redecorating the Executive Suite
- Upgrading the Bathroom Facilities

Now compare the previous headings to those used for the progress report, which are talking headings:

- Renovation Is on Budget
- Time Schedule Has Slipped One Month
- Houston Office Was Added to the Project

Do you see the difference?

Parallelism

As illustrated above, you may phrase your headings in a variety of ways. Noun phrases are probably the most common form of heading, but you may also choose participial phrases, partial statements (which omit a verb), statements, or questions.

Whichever form of heading you select, be consistent within each level of heading. If the first major heading (a first-level heading) is a noun phrase, all first-level headings should be noun phrases. If the first major heading is a talking heading, the others should be too. As you move from level to level, you may switch to another form of heading if this works better, but all headings within the same level must be parallel.

Length and Number of Headings

For text-based reports, four to eight words is about the right length for most headings. Headings that are too long lose their effectiveness; the shorter the heading, the more emphasis it receives. Yet headings that are too short are ineffective because they do not convey enough meaning.

Similarly, choose an appropriate number of headings. For text-based reports, having too many headings weakens the unity of a report—they chop the report up too much, making it look more like an outline than a reasoned analysis. Having too few headings, however, overwhelms the reader with an entire page of solid text, without the chance to stop periodically and refocus on the topic.

 Use headings to break up a long report and refocus the reader's attention.

For a PowerPoint report, the pages should act as natural section divisions, with slide titles serving as headings. Too little content on one page will make the report look empty, whereas too much content will be confusing to your reader.

Balance

Maintain a sense of balance within and among sections. It would be unusual to give one section of a report five subsections and give the following section none.

Similarly, it would be unusual to have one section five pages long and another section only half a page long. Also, ensure that the most important ideas appear in the highest levels of headings. If you are discussing four criteria for a topic, for example, all four should be in the same level of heading—presumably in first-level headings.

When you divide a section into subsections, it must have at least two subsections. You cannot logically have just one second-level heading within a section because when you divide something, it divides into more than one part.

LO2 Draft the report body and supplementary pages.

DRAFTING THE REPORT

The final product—the written report—is the only evidence the reader has of your efforts.

You may have spent months—or years—collecting data, but your final report is the only way your audience knows how much time and effort you dedicated to the project. Even your skillful analysis of the data will be lost unless your written report explains the significance of your data and helps the reader reach a decision and solve a problem.

Everything you learned in Chapter 4 about the writing process applies directly to report writing—choosing a productive work environment; scheduling a reasonable block of time; letting ideas flow quickly during the drafting stage, without worrying about style, correctness, or format; and leaving time for revising. However, report writing requires several additional considerations as well.

Drafting the Body

The report body consists of the introduction; the findings; and the summary, conclusions, and recommendations. As stated earlier, the conclusions may go first (e.g., in an executive summary) or last in the report. Each part may be a separate chapter in long reports or a major section in shorter reports.

Introduction

The introduction sets the stage for understanding the findings that follow. The McKinsey report on teachers uses an introduction to provide background information about the topic, the purpose and need for the report, and a preview of topics covered.

The topics and amount of detail in an introduction vary according to the type and complexity of the report and the audience's needs. You might not cover related studies, but you might add a section about methodology (procedures to gather and analyze the data). PowerPoint reports omit the introduction entirely, merging this information into the executive summary or first page of the deck.

The introduction presents the information the reader needs to make sense of the findings.

Findings

Don't just present your findings; analyze and interpret them for the reader.

The findings are the major contribution of the report and make up the largest section. Discuss and interpret relevant primary and secondary data you gathered. Organize this section using one of the plans discussed earlier (e.g., by time, location, importance, or criteria). Using objective language, present the information clearly, concisely, and accurately.

Most reports will display numerical information in tables and figures (such as bar, line, or pie charts). The information in these displays should be self-explanatory; that is, readers should understand it without having to refer to the text.

However, all tables and figures should be mentioned and explained in the text so that the text, too, is self-explanatory. All references should be numbered (e.g., "as shown in Table 4"). Be careful with phrases such as "as shown below" because the table or figure might actually appear at the top of the following page.

Summarize important information from the display. Give enough interpretation to help the reader comprehend the table or figure, but don't repeat all the information it contains. Discuss data most relevant to your main points, pointing out important items, implications, trends, contradictions, unexpected findings, and similarities and differences.

The McKinsey report on teachers describes several graphics thoroughly. In one part of the report, shown in Figure 6, the authors explain a table of information—how policies to attract and retain teachers in other countries compare to those of the United States. The explanation continues on the next page of the report.

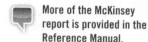 **More of the McKinsey report is provided in the Reference Manual.**

Figure 6 Description of a Table in the McKinsey Report

Applying lessons from global best-performing systems to the U.S.

Although Singapore, Finland, and South Korea follow their own unique strategies to recruit and retain top third+ students, they share some common practices that offer lessons for the U.S. (see exhibit 4).

Key finding: The world's best-performing systems recruit 100% of their teachers from the top tier of graduates and create a mutually reinforcing balance between high selectivity and attractive working conditions.

First, all of these top-performing countries make admissions to teacher training highly selective, accepting only a small fraction of applicants to teacher training colleges. The government monitors the demand for teachers and funds teacher education to match it, so that those admitted into training are assured jobs. They thus create a selectivity "gate" early in the pipeline of teachers' development, and then spend several years ensuring that university students whom they know will enter teaching are well prepared, with rigorous, extensive and practical training. Most American teachers, in contrast, enter the profession

Exhibit 4: International comparisons of policies aimed at attracting and retaining teachers.

✓ Significant priority in the country; best-in-class practices

Policies to attract/retain top teachers	Singapore	Finland	S. Korea	U.S.
❶ Selective admissions to teacher training	✓	✓	✓	Most programs not selective
❷ Government-paid teacher training	✓	✓		Students finance own education
❸ Government regulates supply of teachers to match demand	✓	✓	✓	Oversupply of teachers
❹ Professional working environment	✓	✓	✓	Variable working conditions
❺ Competitive compensation	✓		✓	Compensation not attractive to many students
❻ Cultural respect accorded to teaching	✓	✓	✓	Respect not comparable to other nations
❼ Teaching considered as a career	✓	✓	✓	Relative high attrition in early years
❽ Robust opportunities for career advancement	✓			Limited opportunities for advancement
❾ Performance pay for teachers	✓		✓	Limited performance pay

SOURCE: Interviews; McKinsey research

The table or figure should be placed immediately *below* the first paragraph that refers to the graphic. (Of course, if the display contains supplementary information, you may place it in an appendix rather than in the body of the report itself.) Avoid splitting a table or figure between two pages. If not enough space is available on the page for the display, continue with the narrative to the bottom of the page and then place the display at the very top of the following page.

Use emphasis, subordination, preview, summary, and transition to make the report read clearly and smoothly. Avoid presenting facts and figures so fast that the reader is overwhelmed with data. How much does the reader need to know? How much is too much? Be sure to make the transition from your own work on the project to what the reader needs to know.

Summary, Conclusions, and Recommendations

The length of your report summary depends on the length and complexity of the report. A one- or two-page report may need only a one-sentence or one-paragraph summary.

Longer or more complex reports, however, should include a more extensive summary. You may briefly review the issues and provide an overview of the major findings. For the McKinsey report, the last page suggests areas for further research and ends with a short conclusion to encourage action (Figure 7).

Repeating the main points or arguments immediately before presenting the conclusions and recommendations reinforces the reasonableness of those conclusions

Figure 7 Conclusion of the McKinsey Report

46

*A top third+ strategy for the teaching
profession should be part of the debate.*

Areas for further research

This work raises questions for further study:

Regional and local labor markets for top-third students. We focused on the nation as a whole, but teachers are hired primarily in local labor markets. Research might examine which elements of teaching's value proposition are most important in particular geographies. For example, the nation-wide average compensation we surveyed would almost certainly not be perfect fits for the biggest urban districts or for poorer rural areas, given disparities in the cost of living. States or districts pursuing a top-third strategy might find it useful to develop region specific "demand curves" for local talent.

Economy-wide salary structure. One strong hypothesis emerging from this research is that a higher income potential for top-third students in the U.S. has a large impact on the salaries needed to attract top third students to teaching. A more detailed comparison of U.S. and top-performing nation wage structures could shed light on this issue.

Retention scenarios. Some experts believe that it takes around two to three years for top talent to deliver in the classroom, and that compensation boosts once effectiveness is demonstrated are essential for retention. It would be worth examining options for raising and restructuring compensation between years two and three and, say, five to seven, to retain top students who become top classroom performers. Singapore's differential pay practices and retention bonuses might offer a model, in which a top third+ recruitment strategy and rigorous performance management reinforce one another.

Teacher effectiveness "plateaus." Top-performing nations don't appear to share the view of some U.S. researchers that a teacher's gains in effectiveness stop after three years. Because this judgment can affect many aspects of a national or regional human capital strategy, this question may merit further examination, perhaps in a collaborative effort with top-performing nations.

Conclusion

With more than half of America's teacher corps turning over in the next decade, the nation should be asking, "Who should teach?" Most world-class organizations have a talent strategy: concrete ideas about the human resources they need to succeed, and how to recruit and retain this talent. American education has long followed a more haphazard approach, with its teacher corps the byproduct of broad social and economic trends rather than any conscious design. Recruiting approaches that worked 30 or 40 years ago won't suffice today. Every country must find its own path and operate in a unique cultural setting. But the extraordinary success of the top-performing nations, who view their teachers as integral to their economic strategies, suggests that the composition of America's teacher corps deserves a national debate. Shifts in America's talent strategy for teaching would take years to fully implement, making it critical to start the conversation now. We hope this research can contribute to the discussion.

and recommendations. To avoid boring your reader (and sounding unimaginative), rephrase wording used earlier in the report.

If your report only analyzes the information presented and does not make recommendations, you might label the final section of the report "Summary" or "Summary and Conclusions." If your report includes both conclusions and recommendations, ensure that the conclusions stem directly from your findings and that the recommendations stem directly from the conclusions. Either way, end your report with a clear concluding statement. Don't leave your reader wondering if more pages will follow.

For direct-style reports, such as proposals, the summary repeats conclusions or recommendations presented in the executive summary. The Dunkin' Donuts PowerPoint report ends with a summary of the two main benefits of offering soy at all locations (Figure 8).

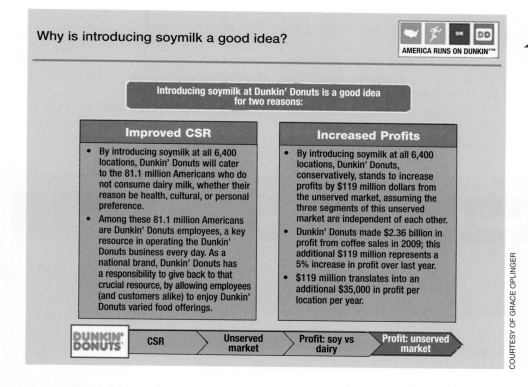

Figure 8
Summary Slide for the Dunkin' Donuts Report

COURTESY OF GRACE OPLINGER

Drafting Supplementary Sections

What additional components are included in reports? Depending on the length, formality, and complexity of the report, you may include additional sections to supplement the report body.

Title Page

Include a title page for text-based and PowerPoint reports, but not for reports that are typed within a memo or letter format (such as the Jason's Deli memo). The title page typically includes the title (and perhaps subtitle) of the report, the company name and logo, the writer's name (and perhaps the reader's name—as well as titles and departments), and the date the report was written. As the first impression of your report, the title page should look attractive and inviting to read, as are those in Figures 1 and 2. The McKinsey report includes additional pages with acknowledgements, the report date, and authors' names (shown in the Reference Manual).

Communication Technologies

Write the cover letter, memo, or email using the direct plan.

Cover Letter, Memo, or Email

Unless you're hand-delivering your report to the reader, you should include a cover note. Whether the report is formal or informal, use a conversational, personal style of writing for the cover note. Write a cover letter if you're sending a printed report to someone outside the company; a memo for a printed internal report; and, most commonly, an email (with the report attached) to someone outside or within the company.

Consider saving your report as a PDF file before attaching it to an email message. This way, your formatting will be preserved, and your report won't be changed without your permission.

In your email (or letter or memo), provide a summary of the report. State up front that the report is attached, and then briefly discuss background information, for example, that the report responds to a request. Perhaps give an overview of the conclusions and recommendations of the report (unless you want the reader to read the evidence supporting these conclusions and recommendations first). Briefly discuss any other information that will help the reader understand and make use of the report (e.g., "The report covers data through March; when we receive the data for April, we'll send you an update"). Include a goodwill ending, for example, "Thank you for the opportunity to present this proposal," or "If you would like to discuss the report in detail, I would be happy to schedule a meeting," or "Please let me know how I can help in the future."

A sample cover email for an internal report by a human resources manager is shown in Figure 9. The email uses the direct organizational plan, summarizing the main points of the report.

Figure 9   Cover Email for a Report

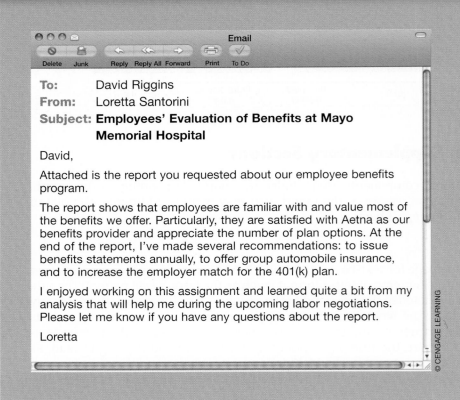

Executive Summary

An **executive summary**, also called an *abstract* or *synopsis*, is a condensed version of the body of the report (including introduction, findings, and any conclusions or recommendations). Although some readers may scan the entire report, most will read the executive summary carefully—and some will read *only* the executive summary. Some companies that do original research make an executive summary of a report publicly available, while charging a hefty fee (e.g., $2,500) for the detailed findings.

The executive summary may be read more carefully than the report itself.

Like the cover letter, memo, or email, the executive summary is an optional part of the report, most commonly used for long and direct-plan reports. Because the executive summary saves the reader time, this part should be short—no more than 10% of the entire report. Think of the executive summary as a standalone document: assume that the reader will not read the whole report, so include as much useful information as possible.

Use the same writing style for the summary as you used in the report. Figure 10 shows the executive summary for the Dunkin' Donuts report. For comparison, the four-page executive summary from the McKinsey report is in the Reference Manual at the end of the book. This may seem long but is just about the right length (10% of the 48-page report).

Executive Summary   AMERICA RUNS ON DUNKIN™

This report outlines why Dunkin' Donuts should earnestly consider introducing soymilk at its 6,400 locations. If Dunkin' Donuts decides to pursue this suggestion and offers soymilk in addition to dairy milk options, the company can benefit in two ways:

- Increased yearly profits
- Improved corporate social responsibility

Currently, Dunkin' Donuts remains one of the few major national coffee chains that does not offer soymilk. Two repercussions of this decision exist: it is neglecting a large portion of the population, and thus voluntarily impairing its corporate social responsibility; and it is foregoing potential coffee sales, and thus voluntarily sacrificing its own profit-generating potential.

By not offering soymilk, Dunkin' Donuts neglects three groups of people:

1. Individuals who have a dietary restriction that prevents them from consuming dairy milk
2. Individuals who have a cultural restriction that prevents them from consuming animal byproducts
3. Individuals who have a personal preference to follow a plant-based diet

If Dunkin' Donuts pursues this suggestion and decides to offer soymilk at its 6,400 locations, the company will conservatively see an increase in yearly profits of $119 million: an additional $35,000 per location and an increase in annual profits by 5%.

COURTESY OF GRACE OPLINGER

Figure 10
Executive Summary for the Dunkin' Donuts Report

Table of Contents

Long reports with many headings and subheadings usually benefit from a table of contents. Use the same wording in the table of contents that you use in the body of the report. Typically, only two or three levels of headings are included in the table of contents—even if more levels are used in the body of the report.

Page numbers in the table of contents identify where each section begins. You may find it useful to automate the pagination in a program such as Microsoft Word. This way, the page numbers in the table of contents automatically update as you edit the report.

Communication Technologies

Appendix

> An appendix might include supplementary reference material not important enough to go in the body of the report.

You may include supplementary information or documents in an appendix at the end of a report. For example, you might include a copy of the cover letter and questionnaire used to collect data or supplementary tables that might be helpful to the reader but that are not important enough to include in the body of the report. Label each appendix separately, by letter—for example, "Appendix A: Questionnaire" and "Appendix B: Cover Letter." In the body of the report, refer by letter to any items placed in an appendix.

References

The reference list contains all of your secondary sources cited in the report. The reference list for the Dunkin' Donuts report is shown in Figure 11. For a printed report, you may remove the hyperlinks to web addresses and keep the plain text.

A good indication of a report writer's scholarship is the accuracy of the reference list—in terms of both content and format—so proofread this part of your report carefully. The reference list is the very last section of the report.

**Figure 11
Reference Page for the Dunkin' Donuts Report**

References

AMERICA RUNS ON DUNKIN'™

Dunkin' Brands, "Corporate Social Responsibility," Dunkin' Donuts company website, www.dunkindonuts.com, accessed November 2010.

Imaner, "Vegan Statistics," Vegan Village, http://www.imaner.net/panel/statistics.htm, accessed November 2010.

Jeremy Foltz, "The Economics of the Soy Milk Market," Food Systems Research Group, University of Wisconsin, June 15, 2005, http://www.aae.wisc.edu/foltz/ls%20Soy%20Milk.pdf, accessed November 2010.

National Digestive Diseases Information Clearinghouse, "Lactose Intolerance," NDDIC website, http://digestive.niddk.nih.gov/ddiseases, accessed November 2010.

Stephen Rodrick, "Average Joe," NYMag, November 20, 2005, http://nymag.com/nymetro/news/bizfinance/biz, accessed November 2010.

VegAdvantage, "Facts," VegAdvantage website, http://www.vegadvantage.com/, accessed November 2010.

COURTESY OF GRACE OPLINGER

L03 Use an effective writing style.

DEVELOPING AN EFFECTIVE WRITING STYLE

An effective writing style will improve how well your report is received.

Tone

Regardless of the structure of your report, the writing style is typically more objective and less conversational than a letter or an email. Avoid colloquial expressions, attempts at humor, subjectivity, bias, and exaggeration.

NOT The company *hit the jackpot* with its new MRP program.

BUT The new MRP program saved the company $125,000 the first year.

NOT He *claimed* that half of his projects involved name-brand advertising.

BUT He stated that half of his projects involved name-brand advertising.

Pronouns

Formal language, which focuses on the information rather than on the writer, typically is used for reports. Where you can, use third-person pronouns and avoid using *I, we,* and *you.* However, if your perspective is emphasized or using *you* improves the readability of the report, you may use these pronouns as well.

First- and second-person pronouns can be used sparingly in most business reports.

You can avoid the awkward substitute "the writer" by revising the sentence. Most often, it is evident that the writer is the person doing the action communicated.

Informal	I recommend that the project be canceled.
Awkward	The writer recommends that the project be canceled.
Formal	The project should be canceled.

Using the passive voice is a common device for avoiding the use of *I* in formal reports, but doing so weakens the impact. Instead, revise some sentences to avoid overuse of the passive voice.

Informal	I interviewed Jan Smith.
Passive	Jan Smith was interviewed.
Formal	In a personal interview, Jan Smith stated . . .

You will probably also want to avoid using *he* as a generic pronoun when referring to an unidentified person. Chapter 2 discusses several ways to use gender-neutral language.

Verb Tense

Use the verb tense (past, present, or future) that is appropriate at the time the reader *reads* the report—not necessarily at the time that you *wrote* the report. Use past tense to describe procedures and to describe the findings of other studies already completed, but use present tense for conclusions from those studies.

 Verb tenses should reflect the reader's (not the writer's) time frame.

When possible, use the stronger present tense to present the data from your study. You can assume that your findings continue to be true—if your findings are no longer true, then you should probably not use them in the report.

NOT These findings *were based* on interviews with 62 football fans.

BUT These findings *are based* on interviews with 62 football fans.

NOT Three-fourths of the managers *believed* quality circles *were* effective at the plant.

BUT Three-fourths of the managers *believe* quality circles *are* effective at the plant.

Procedure	Nearly 500 people *responded* to this survey.
Finding	Only 11 percent of the managers *received* any specific training on the new procedure. *(The event happened in the past.)*
Conclusion	Most managers *do not receive* any specific training on the new procedures.

Emphasis and Subordination

Wouldn't it be nice if all of your data pointed to one conclusion? That rarely happens—and if it does, you might question the accuracy of your data. More likely, you'll have a mix of data and will have to evaluate the relative merits of each point for your reader. To help your reader understand how important you view each point, use the emphasis and subordination techniques learned in Chapter 5 when discussing your findings.

Consider an excerpt from a research report and how the authors show the relative importance of their findings (Figure 12).[8]

 Use emphasis and subordination ethically—not to pressure the reader.

Figure 12
How Authors Use Emphasis and Subordination

> **A sixth of cell phone owners have bumped into someone or something while using their handhelds.**
>
> **Of the 82% of American adults who own cell phones, fully 17% say they have bumped into another person or an object because they were distracted by talking or texting on their mobile phones. That amounts to 14% of all American adults who have been so engrossed in talking, texting, or otherwise using their cell phones that they bumped into something or someone.**

Devote an appropriate amount of space to a topic.
This section (with two more paragraphs) takes up only one-third of a page. Data about cell phone distractions while driving fill the remaining 3.5 pages of the findings section of the report.

Position your major ideas first for the direct plan.
This section appears last in the report, after the more dangerous cell phone behaviors.

Use language that directly tells what is more and less important.
Words such as "fully" express the authors' view of the data. Without this emphasis, the reader might interpret 17% to be a smaller number.

© CENGAGE LEARNING

Ethics in Communication

Use emphasis and subordination to let the reader know what you consider most and least important—but *not* to inappropriately sway the reader. If the data honestly leads to a strong, definite conclusion, then by all means make your conclusion strong and definite. But if the data permits only a tentative conclusion, then say so.

Also avoid overstating conclusions by using weak descriptions. Words such as *plethora, constantly,* and *countless* are inaccurate and could make your reader question your results—or worse, distrust you personally.

Coherence

One of the difficulties of writing any long document—especially when the document is drafted in sections and then put together—is making the finished product read smoothly and coherently, like a unified presentation rather than a cut-and-paste job. The problem is even greater for team-written reports, discussed in Chapter 2.

One way to achieve coherence in a report is to use previews, summaries, and transitions regularly. At the beginning of each major section, preview what is discussed in that section. At the conclusion of each major section, summarize what was presented and provide a smooth transition to the next topic. For long sections, the preview, summary, and transition might each be a separate paragraph; for short sections, a sentence might suffice.

Note how preview, summary, and transition are used in the following example of a report section opening and closing.

Use previews, summaries, and transitions to achieve coherence and unity.

Training System Users

The training program can be evaluated in two ways: the opinions of the users and the cost of training as a percentage of total system costs. . . . *(After this topic preview, several paragraphs follow that discuss the opinions of the users and the cost of the training program.)*

Even though a slight majority of users now feel competent in using the system, the training falls far short of the 20 percent of total system cost recommended by experts. This low level of training may have affected the precision of the data generated by the MRP system. *(The first sentence summarizes this section, and the second provides a transition to the next.)*

Don't depend on your heading structure for coherence. Your report should read smoothly and coherently without the headings. For variety and to reflect a sophisticated writing style, avoid repeating the exact words of the heading in the subsequent narrative, and avoid using the heading as part of the narrative.

NOT **The two departments should be merged.** The reason is that there is a duplication of services.

BUT **The two departments should be merged.** Merging the two departments would eliminate the duplication of services.

Always introduce a topic before dividing it into subtopics. You should never have one heading following another without some intervening text; these are called **stacked headings**. (The exception to this guideline is that the heading "Introduction" may be used immediately after the report title or subtitle.) Instead, use a **section overview** to preview for the reader how the topic will be divided before you actually make the division. For a direct-plan report, section overviews will also highlight main points to follow. Compare the stacked headings and section overview in Figure 13.

Stacked headings lack introductory text for a section.

Selecting a Consultant for the Communication Audit

Although the Most Expensive, McKinsey Offers the Most Depth
text text text text text text text text text text text text text text text text

Deloitte Has Experience with the Northeast Region
text text text text text text text text text text text text text text text text

Towers Watson Is the Least Expensive Option
text text text text text text text text text text text text text text text text

Figure 13
Avoiding Stacked Headings with a Section Overview

Section overviews highlight main points covered under subheadings.

Selecting a Consultant for the Communication Audit

McKinsey is the best choice for the communication audit. Competitors Deloitte and Towers Watson offer advantages, but McKinsey has the most depth in this area.

Although the Most Expensive, McKinsey Offers the Most Depth
text text text text text text text text text text text text text text text text

Deloitte Has Experience with the Northeast Region
text text text text text text text text text text text text text text text text

Towers Watson Is the Least Expensive Option
text text text text text text text text text text text text text text text text

© CENGAGE LEARNING

L04 Document sources
accurately.

DOCUMENTING YOUR SOURCES

When you write a report, you'll include information from other sources that must be documented.

Unless you identify a source, your audience will assume all ideas are your own. Documenting your sources will save you from embarrassment and potentially worse consequences: at school, you may be violating a code of academic integrity, and at work, you may lose credibility or—in some situations—your job.

Why We Document Sources

Ethics in Communication

A Harvard student's falsifications landed him with criminal charges including larceny for accepting $50,000 in financial aid and prizes. Adam Wheeler's "life of deception," reported by *The New York Times*, included rounding up his SAT scores by a few hundred points, faking letters of recommendation, and claiming that he wrote "numerous books."[9] This is an extreme case but offers a word of caution for smaller transgressions.

When writing for business audiences, we document sources for several reasons:

- To avoid accusations of plagiarism
- To give credit to the originator of information
- To demonstrate the validity of our work with credible sources
- To instruct readers where to find additional information

International Communication

Plagiarism is using another person's words or ideas without giving proper credit. Although each country has different laws regarding the use of others' written work, in the United States, copyright and other laws guide how we treat writers' words—as legal property. Using words without permission or acknowledgement is considered theft.

Documentation is identifying sources by giving credit to another person, either in the text or in the reference list, for using his or her words or ideas. For many business reports, secondary information may be the *only* data you use. This is entirely acceptable, but you must provide appropriate documentation whenever you quote, paraphrase, or summarize someone else's work.

What Has to Be Documented

All content from secondary sources (information or ideas that aren't your own) must be documented: articles, books, website content, blogs, quotations, graphics, interviews, and so on. However, you do not need to cite information considered common knowledge, for example, "Customer satisfaction is important in the retail industry" or information that is easily verifiable, for example, "Isadore Sharp is the founder of Four Seasons." If in doubt, it's always safer to provide a reference.

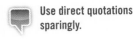

Use direct quotations sparingly.

Most of your references to secondary data should be in the form of paraphrases. A **paraphrase** is a summary or restatement of a passage in your own words. A **direct quotation**, on the other hand, contains the exact words of another. Use direct quotations (always enclosed in quotation marks) only for definitions or for text that is written in a unique way or is not easily paraphrased. The beginning of this section refers to Adam Wheeler's "life of deception," a quotation that is unique, precise, and not easily improved upon.

Paraphrasing involves more than just rearranging words or leaving out a word or two. Instead try to understand the writer's idea and then restate it in your own language. When you paraphrase, change the sentence structure, and do not use any three consecutive words from the original source, unless the words represent, for example, a company name that cannot be changed.

In February 2010, a *New York Times* reporter, Zachery Kouwe, was accused of plagiarizing *Wall Street Journal* reporter Amir Efrati's work.[10] In the following example, you can see that Kouwe's version of the story is too close to the original:

> Mr. Efrati wrote:
> The family members agreed not to transfer or sell property or assets valued at more than $1,000 or incur debts and obligations greater than $1,000 without approval of the trustee.

> Mr. Kouwe wrote:
> Under the agreement, the family members cannot transfer or sell property or assets valued at more than $1,000 or incur debts and obligations greater than $1,000 without approval of Mr. Picard.

This is just one of six examples of plagiarism *The Wall Street Journal* noted within one article.

Although all secondary sources must be documented, unpublished sources (e.g., not in a journal or on a website) do not need a formal citation. Instead, provide enough text to explain the source, as in these examples:

> According to the company's "Telephone Use Policy," last updated in March 2012, the company "has the right to monitor calls not made within normal business hours."

> The contractor's letter of May 23, 2013, stated, "We agree to modify Blueprint 3884 by widening the southeast entrance from 10 feet to 12 feet 6 inches for a total additional charge of $273.50."

Occasionally, enough information can be given in the narrative so that a formal citation is unnecessary even for published sources. This format is most appropriate when only one or two sources are used in a report.

> In the second edition of *Economic Facts and Fallacies*, Thomas Sowell discusses the discrepancy in pay between men and women.

After you cite a source once, you may mention it again on the same or even on the next page without another citation, as long as the reference is clear.

How to Document Sources

The three major forms for documenting the ideas, information, and quotations of other people in a report are footnotes, endnotes, and author-date references. The method you select depends on organizational norms, the formality of the report, the audience—and, for school reports, your instructor's guidelines.

Footnotes and Endnotes

Footnotes and endnotes are the business standard for documenting sources. For writers, footnotes and endnotes are easy to create in programs like Microsoft Word; for readers, footnotes are easy to view because they appear on the same page as the referenced text. Endnotes follow the same format as footnotes but simply shift the reference to the end of the paper. This is useful when you have so many footnotes on one page that your text is dwarfed by the citations. In this case, endnotes may be preferable for a better design and easier reading.

When you use footnotes, you do not need a separate bibliography or reference page. Although footnotes are ideal for text-based reports, they tend to clutter slide design in PowerPoint reports, so a separate reference page for graphical reports is preferable.

Communication Technologies

Footnotes appear as superscript text at the end of each sentence—or part of a sentence—that requires a citation. In the example in Figure 14, footnotes cite two different sources within one paragraph. If one source is used for an entire paragraph, you do not need to add a footnote after each sentence; instead, you may use only one footnote at the end of the paragraph. Notice that footnotes appear after all punctuation.

Figure 14
Two Footnotes within a Paragraph of the McKinsey Report

The U.S., by contrast, recruits most teachers from the bottom two-thirds of college classes, and, for many schools in poor neighborhoods, from the bottom third. Tellingly, relatively little research in the U.S. has addressed this issue, and the research that does exist is decidedly mixed in its conclusions. A growing body of research suggests that a teacher's cognitive ability, as measured by standardized test scores, grades, and college selectivity, correlates with improved student outcomes, particularly in mathematics. Paradoxically, other credible research finds such effects either statistically insignificant or small.[4] Moreover, recent research on the "value-added" impact of different teachers suggests that such variations are much larger than the effects of any single teacher attribute that can be observed before teachers are in the classroom, leading some to argue that recruiting or selecting great teachers is less important than observing them once in the classroom and either retaining or dismissing them according to their performance.[5]

Author-Date Format

For the author-date format, the writer inserts at an appropriate point in the text the last name of the author and the year of publication in parentheses, for example, (Yuan, 2013). Complete bibliographic information is then included in the References section at the end of the report. More typically used for APA and MLA formats, these in-text citations may interrupt the flow of a paragraph.

For footnotes, endnotes, and author-date formats, a variety of approaches may be used to describe the original source. See the Reference Manual for a simplified way to identify the author, title of the work, publication, date, and other information that tells your reader that your source is credible and retrievable. Regardless of the method, ensure that the citations are accurate, complete, and consistently formatted.

Ethics in Communication

Distortion by Omission

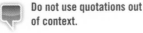
Do not use quotations out of context.

It would be unethical to leave an inaccurate impression, even when what you do report is true. Distortion by omission can occur when using quotations out of context, when omitting relevant background information, or when including only the most extreme or most interesting data. It would be inappropriate, for example, to include quotations from an employee's comments on a company gossip blog and imply that his or her views represent all or most employees.

Be especially careful to quote and paraphrase accurately from interview sources. Provide enough information to ensure that the passage reflects the interviewee's *intention*. Here are examples of possible distortions:

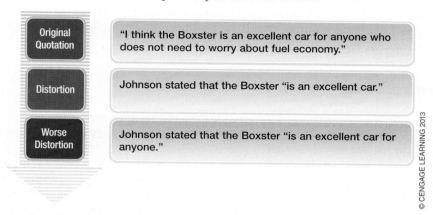

Original Quotation	"I think the Boxster is an excellent car for anyone who does not need to worry about fuel economy."
Distortion	Johnson stated that the Boxster "is an excellent car."
Worse Distortion	Johnson stated that the Boxster "is an excellent car for anyone."

© CENGAGE LEARNING 2013

L05 Revise, format, and proofread the report.

REFINING YOUR DRAFT

Once you have produced a first draft of your report, put it away for a few days. This will give you a fresh perspective and will help you find new ways of communicating your ideas.

Revising

As you revise your draft, don't try to correct all problems in one review. Instead, look at this process as having three steps, as discussed in Chapter 5—revising for content, style, and correctness (Figure 15).

 Revise for content, style, and correctness—three steps.

Figure 15
Steps for Revising

1. Revise for content.

- Have you included sufficient information to support each point?
- Have you excluded extraneous information (regardless of how interesting it might be or how hard you worked to gather the information)?
- Is all information accurate?
- Is the information presented in an efficient and logical sequence?

2. Revise for style.

- Are words clear, simple, and concise?
- Are you using a variety of sentence types?
- Do your paragraphs have unity and coherence, and are they of reasonable length?
- Have you maintained an overall tone of confidence, sincerity, and objectivity?
- Have you used appropriate emphasis and subordination?

3. Revise for correctness.

- Do you find any errors in grammar, spelling, punctuation, and word usage?
- Does a colleague catch any errors you may have overlooked?

© CENGAGE LEARNING 2013

Formatting

Use a consistent, logical format, keeping the needs of the reader in mind.

The physical format of your report, such as spacing and fonts, affects the readability of your final project. For example, regardless of the format used, make sure the reader can instantly tell which are major headings and which are minor headings. You can differentiate among headings by using different fonts, font sizes, enhancements (such as bold or italic), horizontal alignment, and color.

In the Reference Manual, you'll find additional examples and guidelines for formatting text-based and PowerPoint reports.

Proofreading

Do not risk destroying your credibility by failing to proofread carefully.

How would you react if you saw a typographical or data error in a report? Some managers and prospective clients may let this go, but others will judge the writer negatively.

After making all your revisions and formatting the pages, give each page one final proofreading. Check closely for errors and appearance. Do you have blank lines, extra page breaks, or inconsistent use of fonts and colors? Although not 100% helpful, run the spelling checker a final time after making all changes.

If you have a grammar software program, evaluate your writing electronically. Like the spell checker, the grammar checker is not 100% accurate, but it will check for passive voice, sentence length, misuse of words, unmatched punctuation (e.g., an opening parenthesis not followed by a closing parenthesis), and readability. Use every tool you have to ensure that your report reflects the highest standards of scholarship and diligence.

Let your pride of authorship show through in every facet of your report. Appearances and details count. Review your entire document to ensure that you can answer "yes" to every question contained in the Checklist for Reviewing Your Report Draft.

Checklist for Reviewing Your Report Draft

GO

Introduction

☑ Is the report title accurate, descriptive, and honest?

☑ Is the research problem or the purpose of the study stated clearly and accurately?

☑ Is the scope of the study identified?

☑ Are all technical terms, or any terms used in a special way, defined?

☑ Are the procedures discussed in sufficient detail?

☑ Are any questionable decisions justified?

Findings

☑ Is the data analyzed completely, accurately, and appropriately?

☑ Is the analysis free of bias and misrepresentation?

☑ Is the data *interpreted* (its importance and implications discussed) rather than just presented?

☑ Are all calculations correct?

☑ Is all relevant data included and all irrelevant data excluded?

☑ Are all sources properly documented and consistently formatted?

☑ Are visuals correct, needed, clear, appropriately sized and positioned, and correctly labeled?

Supplementary Pages

☑ Is the executive summary short, descriptive, and in proportion to the report itself?

☑ Is the table of contents accurate, with correct page numbers and wording that is identical to that used in the report headings?

☑ Is any appended material properly labeled and referred to in the body of the report?

Writing Style and Format

☑ Does the overall report take into account the needs and desires of the reader?

☑ Is the material appropriately organized?

☑ Are the headings descriptive, parallel, and appropriate in number?

☑ Are emphasis and subordination used effectively?

☑ Does each major section contain a preview, summary, and transition?

☑ Has proper verb tense been used throughout?

☑ Has an appropriate level of formality been used?

☑ Are all references to secondary sources properly documented?

☑ Is each needed report part included and in an appropriate format?

☑ Is the length of the report appropriate?

☑ Are the paragraphs of an appropriate length?

☑ Have the principles of document design been followed to enhance the report's effectiveness?

☑ Is the report free from spelling, grammar, and punctuation errors?

☑ Does the overall report provide a positive first impression?

Summary, Conclusions, and Recommendations

☑ Is the wording used in the summary consistent with that used earlier to present the data initially?

☑ Are the conclusions drawn supported by ample, credible evidence?

☑ Do the conclusions answer the questions or issues raised in the introduction?

☑ Are the recommendations reasonable in light of the conclusions?

☑ Does the report end with a sense of completion and convey an impression that the project is important?

The **3Ps**
In Action

Interpreting Data for Consumers

Purpose

Imagine that you work for a company that tests and rates consumer products. Using the information in the table, you are asked to write a paragraph about the best small and subcompact cars for fuel efficiency. This will be part of a larger report on vehicles and fuel economy.

BEST & WORST IN FUEL ECONOMY

BEST

Rank	Make & Model	Overall mpg	City mpg	Highway mpg
	SUBCOMPACT CARS Overall mpg = 30 or higher			
1	Smart ForTwo Passion	39	30	44
2	Toyota Yaris (sedan)	32	23	41
3	Toyota Yaris (hatchback)	30	22	38
4	Honda Fit (base)	30	21	39
	SMALL CARS Overall mpg = 28 or higher			
1	Honda Insight EX	38	29	45
2	Honda Civic Hybrid	37	26	47
3	Toyota Corolla LE	32	23	40
4	Honda Civic EX	28	18	43
5	Mazda3 i Touring (sedan)	28	18	40
6	Kia Forte EX	28	19	38

© CENGAGE LEARNING 2013

Process

1. **If you had space to make only one statement about this table, what would it be? This could be the first sentence of the paragraph.**
   Small and subcompact cars get 28 miles per gallon (mpg) or better overall; however, figures range from 47 mpg for highway driving to 18 mpg for city driving.

2. **What data will you highlight from the table?**
   I will discuss the differences within categories (both small and subcompact cars). Also, I'll highlight the dramatic differences between city and highway miles per gallon. For consumers who drive one more than the other, these differences may influence their buying decision.

3. **Assume that the next report section discusses sporty cars/roadsters. Write a summary/transition sentence at the end of the paragraph.**
   Although not as efficient as small and subcompact cars, sporty cars/roadsters offer good options for consumers looking to get more than 27 overall mpg.

Product

Small and subcompact cars get 28 miles per gallon (mpg) or better overall; however, figures range from 47 mpg for highway driving to 18 mpg for city driving. Within the small car category, the Honda Insight gets the highest mpg for city driving (29 mpg) and the second highest for highway driving (45 mpg). Of the subcompacts, Smart ForTwo Passion is the winner, with 30 mpg city and 44 mpg highway. For heavy highway drivers, the Honda Civic Hybrid—a small car that beats all subcompacts with 47 highway mpg—is worth a look. Heavy city drivers might avoid the Mazda3 i Touring and Honda Civic EX, which get only 18 city mpg, the lowest within the small and subcompact categories. Although not as efficient as small and subcompact cars, sporty cars/roadsters offer good options for consumers looking to get more than 27 overall mpg.

Writing an Executive Summary for a PowerPoint Report

The **3Ps**
In Practice

Purpose

Imagine that you work for a company that tests and rates consumer products, and you are asked to create a report using presentation slides (such as PowerPoint) about the best sporty cars/roadsters for fuel efficiency. Before writing the entire report, you decide to write a one-page executive summary for your manager's review.

	BEST		
Rank Make & Model	**Overall mpg**	**City mpg**	**Highway mpg**
SPORTY CARS/ROADSTERS Overall mpg = 27 or higher (tested with manual transmission)			
1 Mini Cooper (base)	33	24	41
2 Nissan Sentra SE-R Spec V	30	23	39
3 Mini Cooper S (hatchback)	30	22	38
4 Mini Cooper S (convertible)	30	22	37
5 Lotus Elise	29	24	33
6 Mazda MX-5 Miata Grand Touring	28	20	35
7 Kia Forte Koup SX	27	19	37
8 Volkswagen GTI	27	19	36
9 Honda Civic Si	27	19	35

© CENGAGE LEARNING 2013

Process

1. List several main points from the sporty cars/roadsters table that you will include in your executive summary.
2. How will you organize these points?
3. Write a talking heading for each of your main points.
4. What bulleted text will you include under each main point?

Product

Prepare your executive summary in presentation slide format for your instructor's review.

Summary

L01   Determine an appropriate report format and organization.

Reports may be formatted as primarily text documents or as a combination of text and graphics, as in a report created in PowerPoint or other presentation software. The most common ways to organize the findings of a report are by time, location, importance, and criteria. Conclusions should be presented at the beginning of the report unless the reader prefers the indirect plan, the reader will not be receptive toward the conclusions, or the topic is complex. Report headings should be composed carefully—in terms of their type, parallelism, length, and number.

L02   Draft the report body and supplementary pages.

The body of the report consists of the introduction; findings (the major part of the report); and, as needed, the summary, conclusions, and recommendations. Long, formal reports might also require such supplementary components as a title page, cover note, executive summary, table of contents, appendix, and reference list.

L03   Use an effective writing style.

Use an objective writing style, appropriate pronouns, and accurate verb tenses that reflect the reader's time frame (rather than yours, as the writer). Use emphasis and subordination techniques to help alert the reader to what you consider important; and use preview, summary, and transitional devices to help maintain coherence.

L04   Document sources accurately.

Use direct quotations sparingly; most references to secondary data should be paraphrases. Provide appropriate documentation whenever you quote, paraphrase, or summarize someone else's work by using footnotes, endnotes, or the author-date method of citation. Do not omit important, relevant information from the report.

L05   Revise, format, and proofread the report.

Delay revising the report until a few days after completing the first draft. Revise in three distinct steps: first for content, then for style, and finally for correctness. The report's format should enhance the report's appearance and readability and should be based on the organization's and reader's preferences. After all revisions and formatting have been completed, give each page one final proofreading.

Exercises

L01   Determine an appropriate report format and organization.

1. Determine which report format is best.

For each of the following scenarios, which report format would you choose and why? If you would use a primarily text-based report format, identify whether you would create a separate document (with a cover note) or include the report within the body of a letter, memo, or email. (Note: You will find more than one "correct" answer, but whichever you choose, be prepared to justify your response.)

Scenario	Report Format	
1. You work for a conservative university as the head of the residence halls for students. You write a report to the dean of students to provide unsolicited information about the number of false fire alarms in the 16 campus dorms. Your purpose is to request an upgraded fire alarm system for all dorms.	☐ Create a PowerPoint Report	☐ Create a Primarily Text-Based Report ☐ Create a separate document ☐ Include within a letter ☐ Include within a memo ☐ Include within an email
2. You work as a consultant, and you're trying to win new business from a prospective client, a software maker. You propose a training program to improve customer service skills for call center representatives. The estimated costs are $15,000.	☐ Create a PowerPoint Report	☐ Create a Primarily Text-Based Report ☐ Create a separate document ☐ Include within a letter ☐ Include within a memo ☐ Include within an email
3. You work for an independent clothing store and have been asked to compare the number of items made in China, South American countries, and the United States. The report will be sent to the store manager, who works on site, and the owner, who is located in another state.	☐ Create a PowerPoint Report	☐ Create a Primarily Text-Based Report ☐ Create a separate document ☐ Include within a letter ☐ Include within a memo ☐ Include within an email
4. You work for a regional bank and have been asked to research new ATMs. Your report will be sent to the chief technology officer and the head of the consumer banking division.	☐ Create a PowerPoint Report	☐ Create a Primarily Text-Based Report ☐ Create a separate document ☐ Include within a letter ☐ Include within a memo ☐ Include within an email

2. Explain the different report formats.

Imagine that a colleague asks for your help in deciding what format to use for a report for a prospective client. Write an email describing the differences between a primarily text-based report and a PowerPoint report. Without knowing more about the situation, you probably can't advise which is best, but be sure to include criteria for choosing the most appropriate format. In other words, what considerations should your colleague use when making the decision?

3. Convert an executive summary from a text-based report to a PowerPoint report.

Imagine that you wrote the introduction of the McKinsey report (see the Reference Manual for the full three-page introduction). When you showed your draft to your manager, he or she asked you to rewrite it for a PowerPoint report. Your manager believes that your client would prefer this format.

4. Create a report outline.

As a financial advisor, you provide expert advice for your clients. A new client has asked you to evaluate a potential investment opportunity: purchasing an existing used bookstore in Norfolk, VA. Before you begin your research, you write a very preliminary report outline, which will help you determine what data and other information you need to gather. Working in small groups, first brainstorm what information would be valuable in helping your client make the decision. Next, create an outline of major topics, with at least two minor topics under each.

5. Convert generic headings to talking headings.

From a preliminary outline for a report, you have the following major and minor generic headings. Convert these to talking headings that you'll include in your final report. You may add information to make each heading more descriptive. Either research each topic or, if your instructor allows, make up information just for the purpose of the exercise.

- Obesity in the United States
  - Adult Obesity
  - Childhood Obesity
- Contributors
  - Fast Food
  - School Lunches
  - Processed Food

L02   Draft the report body and supplementary pages.

6. Write an introduction for a report.

T&C, a consumer products company, has long been known for its product development prowess. You were recently hired by the company's public affairs department to manage the development of a new and unusual product: a book about the history of T&C's product development. The company plans to use this book for new employee training. You believe that making the book available to a wider audience would enhance T&C's reputation without giving away any of its secrets. You also know that you will need professional help to research the book—based on information in your archives and on interviews with current and former employees—and to write it.

Doing a bit of research, you learn that you can choose among four companies specializing in corporate histories: Winthrop Group in Cambridge, Massachusetts; History Associates in Rockville, Maryland; History Factory in Chantilly, Virginia; and Business History Group in Columbia, Maryland. Before your boss will approve this expensive project, you need to prepare a brief report showing the services offered by each company, some clients served by each, and your recommendations for which company seems the best fit given T&C's requirements.

How will you conduct more research? What do you need to know to make a recommendation? What is the purpose of your report? Describe your audience. What data will you include in the report? Using your knowledge of report writing, draft an introduction to this report.

7. Draft a report section.

You are the vice president of marketing for Excelsior, a mid-sized, U.S. consulting firm that specializes in strategic planning services. The CEO of your firm, Victor Trillingham, has asked you to prepare an extensive report on the feasibility of Excelsior's entering the international market.

One strategy you're considering is marketing to large multinational companies. As part of your research, you have data on the world's 25 largest public companies (see Figure 16).[11] You're interested in the non-U.S. firms in this group that have the largest sales.

Plan to create a text-based report. At this point, compose only the section that presents and discusses this data. Include a table of the largest, non-U.S. firms (in terms of sales). Discuss the data in terms of the largest companies, their countries of origin, and similar factors. Format the section in appropriate report format (beginning with page 5 of your report); provide an effective heading for this section, topic sentences, a summary, and a transition to the next section, which discusses the largest companies in terms of their major products and services.

Figure 16
Largest 25 Global Companies

Rank	Company	Country	Sales	Profits	Assets	Market Value
1	JPMorgan Chase	United States	$115.5 B	$17.4 B	$2,117.6 B	$182.2 B
2	HSBC Holdings	United Kingdom	$103.3 B	$13.3 B	$2,467.9 B	$186.5 B
3	General Electric	United States	$150.2 B	$11.6 B	$751.2 B	$216.2 B
4	ExxonMobil	United States	$341.6 B	$30.5 B	$302.5 B	$407.2 B
5	Royal Dutch Shell	Netherlands	$369.1 B	$20.1 B	$317.2 B	$212.9 B
6	PetroChina	China	$222.3 B	$21.2 B	$251.3 B	$320.8 B
7	ICBC	China	$69.2 B	$18.8 B	$1,723.5 B	$239.5 B
8	Berkshire Hathaway	United States	$136.2 B	$13 B	$372.2 B	$211 B
9	Petrobras-Petróleo Brasil	Brazil	$121.3 B	$21.2 B	$313.2 B	$238.8 B
10	Citigroup	United States	$111.5 B	$10.6 B	$1,913.9 B	$132.8 B
11	BNP Paribas	France	$130.4 B	$10.5 B	$2,680.7 B	$88 B
12	Wells Fargo	United States	$93.2 B	$12.4 B	$1,258.1 B	$170.6 B
13	Banco Santander	Spain	$109.7 B	$12.8 B	$1,570.6 B	$94.7 B
14	AT&T	United States	$124.3 B	$19.9 B	$268.5 B	$168.2 B
15	Gazprom	Russia	$98.7 B	$25.7 B	$275.9 B	$172.9 B
16	Chevron	United States	$189.6 B	$19 B	$184.8 B	$200.6 B
17	China Construction Bank	China	$58.2 B	$15.6 B	$1,408 B	$224.8 B
18	Wal-Mart Stores	United States	$421.8 B	$16.4 B	$180.7 B	$187.3 B
19	Total	France	$188.1 B	$14.2 B	$192.8 B	$138 B
20	Allianz	Germany	$142.9 B	$6.7 B	$838.4 B	$62.7 B
21	Bank of China	China	$49.4 B	$11.9 B	$1,277.8 B	$143 B
22	ConocoPhillips	United States	$175.8 B	$11.4 B	$156.3 B	$109.1 B
23	Sinopec-China Petroleum	China	$284.8 B	$10.9 B	$148.7 B	$107.7 B
24	Volkswagen Group	Germany	$168.3 B	$9.1 B	$267.5 B	$70.3 B
25	Agricultural Bank of China	China	$49.4 B	$9.5 B	$1,298.2 B	$134 B

8. Draft supplementary report sections.

Continuing in your role as vice president of marketing for Excelsior (from Exercise 7), add supplementary sections for your report to the CEO.

a. Assuming that the report will be submitted tomorrow, prepare a title page.

b. Using the data you analyzed in the previous exercise, draw conclusions and make recommendations. Then write a cover memo to accompany the report. Include brief statements of your conclusions and recommendations.

c. Decide whether you need an appendix; if so, note what it should contain.

9. Write an email report with new analysis.

Excelsior's CEO has read your report written in Exercise 8. He would like the data on the companies you identified as potential clients analyzed from a different perspective: he wants you to group the companies according to the countries in which they are based. Put the data into a table and, from your findings, draw conclusions about the geographic concentration of prospects. Write a brief report—within the body of an email—to the CEO; include your table and your conclusion.

10. Research secondary data and write a PowerPoint report.

Your client is a community foundation, which provides funding to small, local, not-for-profit organizations. With an endowment of $1 million, the foundation is looking for sound investments to grow the possible funds available to support the community. Choose any publicly traded company that interests you, and research whether this company would be a worthy investment for some of the foundation's endowment funds. Your purpose is to identify *whether* the company is a good choice—you do not need to give a positive recommendation.[12]

To formulate your argument, you might research some of the following about your company of choice:

* Background Information: What does your client need to know about the company?
* Mission and Vision: Does the company align with the foundation's mission?
* Stock Trend and Analysts' Recommendations: Is this a sound investment likely to give positive returns?
* Growth Trends: What do you know about the company's revenue and profits? What plans (e.g., for new products and new locations) might be relevant to the foundation?
* Management: Does the company have a strong, stable management team capable of running the company well in the future?
* Current News: What news items about the company might be relevant to the decision?

Prepare a PowerPoint report to the foundation's board of directors. Include a title page, executive summary, table of contents, several pages of findings, and a summary.

11. Write a short report within an email.

The Federal Trade Commission, a government agency that protects consumers, has hired you to summarize the issue of rising U.S. consumer debt. Your task is to write a short report within the body of an email that the agency will send to other government constituencies. The agency wants to highlight the importance of their work by showing the seriousness of the problem.

Working in groups of three or four, complete the following:

a. Independently research current data about consumer debt. Be sure to use credible sources, primarily government and academic research.

b. As a group, discuss your research and select the most relevant data for your purpose. In your short report, you won't be able to cover all data, so be selective and focus on three or four points.

c. Create an outline for your email report.

d. Draft the first paragraph, which will include the purpose and main points (your conclusions).

e. Draft the email and share your version with the rest of the class.

f. Vote on which group's email works best. What makes this email most effective?

12. Adjust the tone of a report section.

L03 Use an effective writing style.

You are a consultant working in the education division of a major firm. One of your group's clients is a federal government agency trying to increase how much time people spend reading. As part of the argument—and the final report—your client asks you how much time people spend on social networking sites, particularly Facebook.

You find this interesting story online. It's a good starting point, but to present this in a credible way for your client, you'll need to find updated data and, of course, present the data using a more objective tone. Write one or two paragraphs with the most recent data you can find.

Back in July, we reported that Facebook had become the Internet's ultimate time waster, with users spending an average of 4 hours, 39 minutes on it per month, more than any other site on the web.

Since then, however, that number has only gone up. According to numbers from Nielsen Online, users spent an average of 5 hours, 46 minutes on Facebook in the month of August. To put that in perspective, that's **triple the amount of time they spent on Google!**

In fact, the next closest site in Nielsen's top 10 is Yahoo, which, despite still having huge traffic in time consuming areas like news, sports, and financial data, could only get users to stick around for 3 hours and 14 minutes on average during the month. YouTube, surprisingly, only occupied 1 hour and 17 minutes of the average user's time.[13]

13. Explain the relative importance of data.

Imagine that you work as the facilities manager for the Dubai International Airport (DXB). You would like to generate support to expand the airport. As part of your evidence, you would like to use the data in Figure 17.[14]

Using techniques of emphasis and subordination, write one or two paragraphs to prove your point: DXB is a growing airport. You can make a strong argument about increasing traffic based on this data, but be careful about overstating the case and drawing conclusions that can't be substantiated by this data alone.

**Figure 17
World's Busiest
Airports**

Rank	City/Country/Code	Passengers	% CHG (From previous year)
1	ATLANTA GA, US (ATL)	89,331,622	1.5
2	BEIJING, CN (PEK)	73,891,801	13.0
3	CHICAGO IL, US (ORD)	66,665,390	3.3
4	LONDON, GB (LHR)	65,884,143	(0.2)
5	TOKYO, JP (HND)	64,069,098	3.4
6	LOS ANGELES CA, US (LAX)	58,915,100	4.2
7	PARIS, FR (CDG)	58,167,062	0.4
8	DALLAS/FORT WORTH TX, US (DFW)	56,905,066	1.6
9	FRANKFURT, DE (FRA)	53,009,221	4.1
10	DENVER CO, US (DEN)	52,211,242	4.1
11	HONG KONG, HK (HKG)	50,410,819	10.6
12	MADRID, ES (MAD)	49,786,202	2.8
13	DUBAI, AE (DXB)	47,180 628	15.4
14	NEW YORK NY, US (JFK)	46,495,876	1.4
15	AMSTERDAM, NL (AMS)	45,211,749	3.8
16	JAKARTA, ID (CGK)	43,981,022	18.4
17	BANGKOK, TH (BKK)	42,784,967	5.6
18	SINGAPORE, SG (SIN)	42,038,777	13.0
19	GUANGZHOU, CN (CAN)	40,975,253	10.6
20	SHANGHAI, CN (PVG)	40,582,356	27.2
21	HOUSTON TX, US (IAH)	40,475,058	1.2
22	LAS VEGAS NV, US (LAS)	39,397,359	(2.6)
23	SAN FRANCISCO CA, US (SFO)	39,254,634	5.1
24	PHOENIX AZ, US (PHX)	38,552,409	1.9
25	CHARLOTTE NC, US (CLT)	38,143,078	10.4
26	ROME, IT (FCO)	36,228,490	7.4
27	SYDNEY, AU (SYD)	35,992,164	7.6
28	MIAMI FL, US (MIA)	35,698,025	5.3
29	ORLANDO FL, US (MCO)	34,877,507	3.5
30	MUNICH, DE (MUC)	34,721,605	6.2

Total Passengers: arriving and departing passengers and direct transit passengers counted once.

Source: Airports Council International World, Montreal

14. Write a section overview.

Assume that you're writing a report with the following headings within one section. Write a brief section overview after the major heading to preview topics within the section and summarize the main points. Avoid using the same wording; instead, rephrase the sub-headings to form a meaningful section overview.

> **The Alliam Hotel can conserve water by making a few minor changes.**
> - Install Dual-Flush Toilets
> - Install Oxygen-Assisted Shower Heads
> - Capture Rainwater for Landscaping

15. Determine whether information has to be documented.

Imagine that you're writing a case study report about the bookseller Barnes and Noble. Which of the following information has to be documented in a report?

- Barnes and Noble's corporate headquarters is located at 122 Fifth Avenue, New York, NY.
- The company's online division uses the website www.bn.com.
- The company's online division generates 10% of the company's revenue.
- William Lynch is the CEO of Barnes and Noble.
- Barnes and Noble closed its Lincoln Center store in New York City.
- Most stores are between 10,000 and 60,000 square feet.

L04 Document sources accurately.

16. Paraphrase sources for a report.

Imagine that you're writing a report about pet overpopulation. You find these excerpts on the Humane Society website and want to incorporate the information into your report. Paraphrase the text into your own words.

- *Four million cats and dogs—about one every eight seconds—are put down in U.S. shelters each year. Often these animals are the offspring of cherished family pets. Spay/neuter is a proven way to reduce pet overpopulation.*
- *Between six and eight million dogs and cats enter U.S. shelters every year—far too many to all find homes.*[15]

17. Use footnotes to document sources.

Assume you are writing a report and have used the following secondary sources.

- An article written by Mary Morgan on pages 45–48 of the April 2, 2013, edition of *Business Week* entitled "How Big Profits Compare."
- A quotation by Taylor Scott in an article entitled "Holiday Profits—Boom or Bust" on page A2, column 1, of the April 17, 2013, edition of the *The Atlanta Herald.*
- Statistics from page 233 in a book entitled *Service over Profit: Who Wins?* written by Cameron Della Santi in 2013 and published by Harper Publishing in New York.
- A quote from an interview conducted on March 30, 2012, with T. Warren Towes, a professor of economics at the University of Wisconsin.

Using these sources and the guidelines in the Reference Manual, prepare footnotes for your report.

For Exercises 18–21, follow your instructor's directions in terms of report length, format, degree of formality, and supplements.

18. Use secondary sources to write a report about female leaders in business.

2020 Women on Boards is an organization dedicated to raising the percentage of women on corporate boards to at least 20% by the year 2020. As part of the organization's work, imagine that it wants to include case studies of female leaders and wants your help in writing these reports. The reports will be publicly accessible on its website.

Identify three women who are presidents or CEOs of companies listed on the New York Stock Exchange. Provide information on their backgrounds. Did they make it to the top by rising through the ranks, by starting the firm, by taking over from a family member, or by following some other path?

Analyze the effectiveness of these three individuals. How profitable are the firms they head in relation to others in the industry? Are their firms more or less profitable now than when they assumed the top job? Finally, try to uncover data regarding their management styles—how they see their role, how they relate to their employees, what problems they've experienced, and so on.

From your study of these three individuals, are there any valid conclusions you can draw? Write a report objectively presenting and analyzing the information you've gathered.

19. Use secondary sources to write a report about typing skills.

You are the director of training for an aerospace firm located in Seattle. Your manager, Charles R. Underwood, vice president of human resources, is concerned that so many of the firm's 2,000 employees use their computers for hours each day but still do not know how to touch-type. He believes the hunt-and-peck method is inefficient and increases the possibility of making errors when inputting data, thus lowering the data's reliability.

He has asked you to recommend a software program that teaches the user how to type. He is specifically interested in a program that is geared to adults, is educationally sound, and can be learned on an individual basis without an instructor present.

Identify and evaluate three to five keyboarding software programs that meet these criteria, and write a report recommending the best one to Underwood. Justify your choice.

20. Use primary and secondary sources to write a report about your future career.

Explore a career position that interests you. Determine the job outlook, present level of employment, salary trends, typical responsibilities, educational or experience requirements, and so on. If possible, interview someone holding this position to gain first-hand impressions. Then write up your findings in a report to your instructor. Include at least five secondary sources and at least three tables or graphs in your report.

21. Use primary sources to write a report about student housing.

Darlene Anderson, a real estate developer and president of Anderson and Associates, is exploring the feasibility of building a large student-apartment complex on a lot her firm owns two blocks from campus. Even though the city planning commission believes there is already enough student housing, Anderson thinks she can succeed if she addresses specific problems of present housing. She has asked you, her executive assistant, to survey students to determine their views on off-campus living.

Specifically, she wants you to develop a ranked listing of the most important attributes of student housing. How important to students are such criteria as price, location (access to campus, shopping, public transportation, and entertainment), space and layout, furnishings (furnished versus unfurnished), social activities, parking, pets policy, and so on?

In addition, the architect has drawn a plan that features the following options: private hotel-like rooms (sleeping and sitting area and private bath but no kitchen); private one-room efficiency apartments; one-bedroom, two-person apartments; and four-bedroom, four-person apartments. Which of these arrangements would students most likely rent, given their present economic situations? Would another alternative be more appealing to them?

Develop a questionnaire and administer it either in hard copy or online to a sample of students. Then analyze the data and write a report for Anderson.

22. Proofread part of a report.

Assume that the following passage is part of an informational report that you have prepared. Proofread it carefully for spelling errors, misused words, and grammar errors. Rewrite the passage showing the corrections you made.

> Our lawyers have reviewed the wording of the contacts you sent us. They're advise is to except provisions 1 thru 8 and 11 thorough 15. The remainder of the provisions (9 and 10) require farther negotiation.
>
> The number of people we want to include in these talks has not yet been determined. We do expect, however, to have fewer people involved now then in our proceeding meetings.
>
> Marcia Nash, our chief legal council, will be your principal contact during these negotiations. Please telephone her at 555-7376 to sit a mutually beneficial time for us too meet early next month. We are eager to settle this matter soon.

L05 Revise, format, and proofread the report.

Company Scenario

PersuadeCafé

PersuadeCafé

After all of your good research for PersuadeCafé's Business Improvement Program, you're ready to begin writing a report—a business improvement proposal.

At this point, you may want to refer back to Chapter 4, the Writing Process, to make sure you apply the planning principles discussed earlier. You will certainly want to consider your audience for the proposal, and you'll find Executive Profiles, with brief bios, on the PersuadeCafé intranet site. Before you start writing, make sure you're clear about your purpose and what you hope to achieve: you want your idea to be implemented!

Also, consider what format you'll use for the report. Will this be a text-based document or a PowerPoint report? Your instructor may ask for a particular format.

How will your executive summary reflect your main points? As you draft the report, make sure you have reinforced these main points so you produce a cohesive, convincing report.

Executive Profiles		
Jacqueline Marcus CEO and President	Christopher O'Connor VP, Business Development	Mark Parsons Chief Technology Officer

In 2002, Jackie Marcus joined PersuadeCafé as CEO and president. As the company's first external hire in this position, Jackie has taken a rather conservative approach to growing the company. Although she has been adamant about continuing the strategic plan of opening one store per month, she has not historically encouraged or rewarded innovation. However, now that PersuadeCafé is facing unprecedented financial challenges, Jackie recognizes that the company must change. She is more open to new ideas but only if they are well substantiated.

With an MBA from Stanford Business School, Jackie is known for her financial rigor and commitment to disciplined business processes. Jackie's previous work experience includes twelve years as COO of Peet's Coffee & Tea.

Notes

1. Gwendolyn Bounds, "Meet the Sticklers," Wall Street Journal Online, May 5, 2010, http://online.wsj .com/article/SB1000142405274870 3866704575224093017379202.html, accessed March 19, 2011.

2. Consumer Reports Website, www .consumerreports.org, accessed December 30, 2010.

3. Mary Madden and Lee Rainie, "Adults and Cell Phone Distractions," Pew Research Center, June 18, 2010, www.pewinternet.org/Reports/ 2010/Cell-Phone-Distractions/ Major-Findings/1-Texting-while- driving.aspx?view=all, accessed December 29, 2010.

4. Stephanie Hanes, "Texting Caused Total 'Distracted Driving' Deaths to Rise, Study Finds," CS Monitor, September 23, 2010, www.csmonitor .com/USA/Society/2010/0923/ Texting-caused-total-distracted- driving-deaths-to-rise-study-finds, accessed December 29, 2010.

5. Byron Auguste, Paul Kihn, and Matt Miller, "Closing the Talent Gap: Attracting and Retaining Top-Third Graduates to Careers in Teaching," McKinsey and Company, September 2010, www.mckinsey.com/clientser- vice/Social_Sector/our_practices/ Education/Knowledge_Highlights/~/ media/Reports/SSO/Closing_the_ talent_gap.ashx, accessed March 23, 2011.

6. Used with permission from the author, Grace Oplinger.

7. Used with permission from the author, Grace Lee.

8. Mary Madden and Lee Rainie, "Adults and Cell Phone Distractions," Pew Internet, June 18, 2010, www.pewinternet.org/Reports/2010/ Cell-Phone-Distractions.aspx, accessed December 29, 2010.

9. Jacques Steinberg and Katie Zezima, "Campuses Ensnared by 'Life of Deception,'" The New York Times, May 18, 2010, www.nytimes.com/2010/05/19/ education/19harvard.html, accessed December 31, 2010.

10. John Koblin, "Robert Thomson's Letter to Bill Keller About Zachery Kouwe's 'Apparent Plagiarism,'" The New York Observer Media Mob, February 15, 2010, www.observer .com/2010/media/robert-thomsons- letter-bill-keller-about-zachery- kouwes-apparent-plagiarism, accessed April 2010.

11. "The Forbes Global 2000," Forbes .com, April 23, 2011, www.forbes .com/2005/03/30/05f2000land.html, accessed June 20, 2011.

12. Adapted from an assignment by Prof. Daphne Jameson, Cornell University.

13. Adam Ostrow, "People Spend 3× More Time on Facebook than Google," Mashable, September 17, 2009, www.mashable.com/2009/ 09/17/facebook-google-time-spent/, accessed December 30, 2010.

14. Top 30 Airports, Airports Council International, 2010. Used with permission.

15. The Humane Society of the United States Website, "Pet Overpopula- tion," www.humanesociety.org/ issues/pet_overpopulation/, accessed December 30, 2010.

LEARNING OBJECTIVES

After you have finished this chapter, you should be able to

L01 Plan a presentation.

L02 Organize a presentation.

L03 Plan a team and online presentation.

L04 Develop effective visual support.

L05 Practice and deliver a presentation.

"A young man sitting next to us . . . has the word TED shaved into the side of his head. . . ."

— TED TALKS VIEWER[1]

Chapter Introduction: TED Talks

Imagine paying $6,000—by invitation only—to listen to four days of presentations. That's exactly what people do to hear some of the world's most inspiring and engaging speakers at the annual TED Conference.[2] The event celebrates "Ideas Worth Spreading" in the fields of technology, entertainment, and design.

The good news is that you can watch these presentations for free at the TED website (www.ted.com). Watch brain researcher Jill Bolte Taylor explain her "Stroke of Insight": how she experienced her own brain functions shutting down. "Dr. Jill" uses unusual visual support—a human brain with the spinal cord attached. Or you can listen to Jane McGonigal, the game designer, convince her audience that playing online games will help solve world problems like "hunger, poverty, climate change, global conflict, obesity." Or maybe you would enjoy hearing Thelma Golden, curator at the Studio Museum in Harlem, discuss "How Art Gives Shape to Cultural Change."[3]

Whatever topics interest you, you'll learn something by watching the TED videos, and you can incorporate these experts' delivery techniques into your own presentations.

Almost everyone in business is required to give a presentation occasionally.

THE ROLE OF BUSINESS PRESENTATIONS

You may have heard that one of Americans' top fears is public speaking—perhaps it's one of yours. But presentations are inescapable in business for training employees, winning new business, and getting support for an idea. Just about everyone in business will give at least one major presentation and many smaller ones each year to employees, clients, managers, and colleagues. Your presentation skills will also be useful for your personal life—for volunteer organizations and at community meetings.

Whether you're a CEO addressing thousands of shareholders or a first-line manager speaking with a small group of employees, the costs of ineffective presentations are immense. Weak presentations waste time and money and reflect poorly on the speaker. Investors lose confidence, training programs fail, sales are lost, and good ideas aren't implemented.

Making presentations involves good planning, logical organization, effective collaboration, proficient technology use, meaningful visual support, and strong delivery skills.

LO1   Plan a presentation.

PLANNING THE PRESENTATION

One sure way to fail at making presentations is to try to "wing it." Without proper planning, you may end up embarrassing yourself as did Stephen Duckett, former CEO of Alberta Health Services in Western Canada. Following criticism about hospital emergency room wait times, Duckett evaded speaking with reporters by repeatedly referring to a cookie he was eating. While the YouTube video was accumulating over 300,000 hits, Duckett was "released from his contractual obligations."[4]

To avoid reporters' serious questions about health care, a former company CEO continuously referred to the cookie he was eating.

© BIG ZEN DRAGON/SHUTTERSTOCK.COM

As we discussed for writing, planning a presentation involves determining the purpose of the presentation, analyzing the audience, and selecting a delivery method. These steps will help you decide what to include in your presentation, how to adjust the presentation to the audience, and how much time you'll devote to the project.

More formal presentations typically take more time to prepare. Complex topics or proposals with high stakes require more formal presentations—with extensive research, a carefully thought-out organizational plan, and well-planned visuals. Also, the larger the audience and the greater the audience's opposition to your ideas, the more formal the presentation should be. Finally, if you're speaking to an international audience, you will need to take their needs and expectations into consideration and will probably prepare a more formal presentation.

Purpose

Keeping your purpose in mind helps you decide what information to include and what to omit, in what order to present this information, and which points to emphasize and subordinate. Most business presentations have one of four purposes: to report, explain, persuade, or motivate. In the examples in Figure 1, you can see how a sales manager might use each.

 Most presentations are to report, explain, persuade, or motivate.

When the presentation is over, the sales manager determines whether the presentation was successful in fulfilling its purpose. Does the senior management team understand the sales report? Do the associates complete expense reports properly? Does the client change suppliers? Do associates work harder to win incentives? No matter how well or how poorly you spoke, and no matter how impressive or ineffective your visual support, the important question is whether you accomplished your purpose.

To Report

Updating the audience on a project or event

Example: At a senior management team meeting, the sales manager provides a monthly report of actual sales against targets.

To Explain

Detailing how to carry out a process or procedure

Example: The sales manager shows sales associates how to accurately complete expense reports.

To Persuade

Convincing the audience to purchase something or to accept an idea

Example: The sales manager encourages a new client to use the company's services.

To Motivate

Inspiring the audience to take some action

Example: At a monthly sales team meeting, the sales manager gets the associates excited about a new incentive plan.

Figure 1
Example of a Sales Manager Making Four Presentations with Different Purposes

© CENGAGE LEARNING 2013

Audience Analysis

Analyze the audience in terms of demographics, level of knowledge, and psychological needs.

In addition to identifying such demographic factors as the size, age, and organizational status of your audience, you will also have to determine their level of knowledge about your topic and their psychological needs (values, attitudes, and beliefs). These factors provide clues to everything from the overall content, tone, and types of examples you should use to the types of questions to expect, and even the way you should dress.

The principles you use to analyze your audience are the same as those discussed in the chapters on writing messages and reports. Consider the effect of your message on your audience and your credibility with them. The key is to put yourself in your audience's place so that you can anticipate their questions and reactions. The "you" attitude applies to oral as well as to written communication.

Large audiences require a more formal presentation.

The larger your audience, the more formal your presentation will be. When you speak to a large group, you should speak more loudly and more slowly and use more emphatic gestures and larger visuals. Usually, you should allow questions only at the end of your talk. If you're speaking to a small group, you can be more flexible about questions, and your tone and gestures will be more like those used in normal conversation. Also, when presenting to small groups, you have more options for visual support.

If your audience is unfamiliar with your topic, you should use clear, easy-to-understand language, with extensive visuals and many examples. If the audience is more knowledgeable, you can proceed at a faster pace. Suppose, however, that you have an audience composed of both novices and experts. One option, of course, would be to separate the two groups and to give two presentations—each geared to the level of that particular audience. This strategy—breaking up groups—requires more time and planning but usually is well worth the effort in order to achieve your purpose.

The best approach may be to tailor your presentation to the key decision maker in the group—often the highest-ranking person. Take time especially to understand this decision maker's needs, objectives, and interests as they relate to your objective.

Delivering a presentation to an international audience presents additional challenges. If your presentation is in English, and your audience speaks English as a second or third language, you will want to prepare and practice carefully, and follow this advice:

International Communication

- Use simple, clear language and a slower pace of delivery.
- Avoid acronyms, euphemisms, humor, and gestures that might not translate well.
- Check jargon with your host ahead of time to make sure the terms will be understood by the local audience, and define any questionable words.
- Enlist your host or an audience member who speaks English well to help translate rough parts for other listeners.
- Gauge the audience's response throughout so that you can make adjustments.
- Include several forms of visuals that the audience can follow during your presentation and take with them to read later.

The audience's psychological needs will also affect your presentation. If, for example, you think your listeners will be hostile—either to you personally or to your message—then you'll have to oversell yourself or your proposal. Instead of giving one or two examples, you'll need to give several. In addition to establishing your own credibility, you may need to quote other experts to bolster your case.

The same content presented to different audiences has to be tailored to each. If you were the sales manager, your monthly sales report to the senior management team would emphasize your strong sales results against targets. But you would probably reposition the monthly sales data as a motivational presentation to the sales associates. Sample agenda slides for these two presentations are shown in Figure 2; you can see how the audience and purpose of the presentation determine the content.

Figure 2
Agenda Slide Tailored to Different Audiences

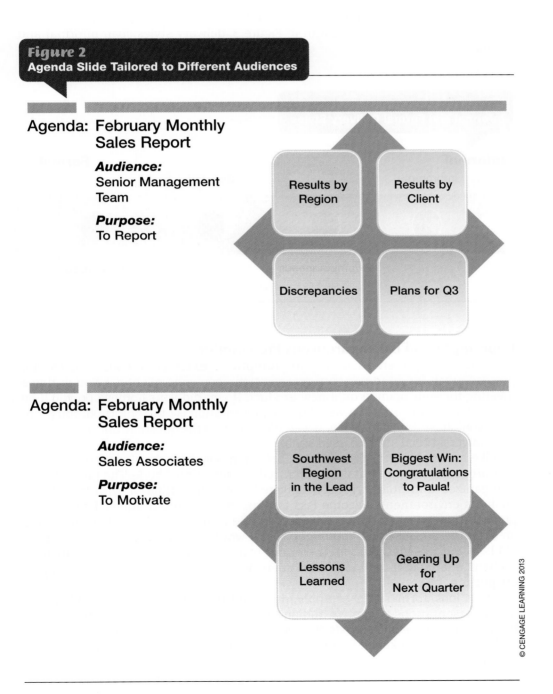

Try not to go into a presentation cold. Meeting with decision makers before your presentation can help predispose the audience in your favor, or at least tell you what resistance you might encounter. For example, if you know that a prospective client is unhappy with the service provided by the current vendor, you can spend more time talking about your company's high level of service.

Delivery Method

At some point during your planning, you'll decide how to deliver your presentation. Plotted along a continuum in Figure 3, delivery styles span informal and formal formats.

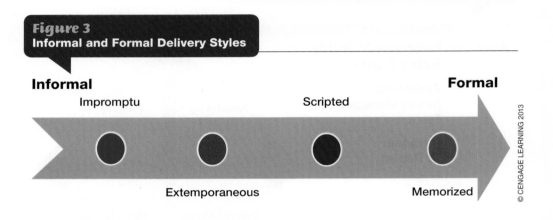

Figure 3
Informal and Formal Delivery Styles

Informal   Formal
Impromptu   Scripted

Extemporaneous   Memorized

© CENGAGE LEARNING 2013

Use an extemporaneous style—speaking from an outline—for most business presentations.

Impromptu and Extemporaneous Presentations

Most business presentations are **impromptu** or **extemporaneous**. You cannot prepare much for an impromptu presentation—someone might ask you during a meeting for your opinion on a new product. If you did your homework, you'll be able to answer the question well, but the presentation is quite informal. You probably won't have any visuals if you weren't expecting the question, and you'll speak in a conversational, unrehearsed style.

Like an impromptu presentation, an extemporaneous presentation requires an unrehearsed style—but is an enhanced conversational style. The presentation is organized and fluid, typically delivered from an outline or with visuals. As business environments become less formal, so have presentations. Even a sales presentation, which could be considered quite formal, should be delivered using an extemporaneous style. You might miss a word here and there or use a couple of fillers, but this method is far preferable to a stilted, formal style. Trying to build a client relationship or motivate a team with a memorized speech would be off-putting.

Steve Jobs, former CEO of Apple, mastered the extemporaneous style in his many presentations to captive audiences. One admirer even wrote a book about his style: *The Presentation Secrets of Steve Jobs: How to Be Insanely Great in Front of Any Audience*. Jobs had a knack for making complex technical information simple—and exciting.

Former Apple CEO Steve Jobs used an extemporaneous delivery style.

© AP IMAGES/PAUL SAKUMA

Preparation for extemporaneous presentations requires good notes, useful visuals, or both. With presentation software, such as PowerPoint, your slides can function as your outline. The most adept business presenters do not need additional notes, unless covering highly detailed or technical information.

If you do use notes, choose a structure and format that work for you. Consider writing only key phrases rather than complete sentences; you compose the exact wording as you speak. You also may include notes to yourself, such as when to pause, which phrases to emphasize, and when to change a slide.

Write your notes as a formal outline on full sheets of paper or as notes on index cards. If you use full pages, use larger type and avoid all capital letters, which are harder to read, and staples, which require you to flip pages and can be distracting. Either way, you can make your notes less obtrusive by placing them on a desk or by holding them low on your body with one hand while you gesture with the other.

Scripted and Memorized Presentations

In a few business situations, a **scripted** or **memorized** style may be appropriate. For a scripted presentation, the presenter reads directly from notes, as you see business leaders do at news conferences. For crisis situations, for example, this is a good approach to make sure you don't say anything on camera that you'll later regret. You also may read notes for ceremonial speeches, for example, at a retirement dinner. Finally, you may read notes for a small part of an extemporaneous presentation, for example, for highly technical information. But avoid reading for most business presentations, which diminishes eye contact, confidence, and connection with the audience.

Very few situations call for a memorized speech. Memorizing takes time, is risky, and like a scripted presentation, makes the speaker sound mechanical rather than like an accessible, authentic, adaptable business professional.

Whichever method you choose, the key to a successful delivery is practice, practice, practice. Less experienced presenters may write out the entire speech and then practice it until they can recite whole paragraphs or thoughts with ease. Experienced presenters may work from notes right from the start. Either way, each time the presenters do a run-through, they are using different words until they sound confident, fluid, and conversational, as if they barely rehearsed at all.

L02 Organize a presentation.

ORGANIZING THE PRESENTATION

For most presentations, the best way to begin is simply to brainstorm: write down every point you can think of that might be included in your presentation. Don't worry about the order or format—just get it all down.

Later, separate your notes into three categories: opening, body, and ending. As you begin to analyze and organize your material, you may find that you need additional information or research.

The Opening

Your opening should introduce the topic, identify the purpose, and preview the presentation.

The first 90 seconds of your presentation are crucial to capture the audience's attention. The audience will be observing and making judgments about your dress, posture, facial expressions, voice qualities, visuals, and of course, what you're saying. Begin immediately to build a relationship with your audience—not just for the duration of your presentation, but for the long term. Because the opening is so crucial to establish rapport, many professionals write out the entire opening and practice it until they are extremely familiar with it.

The kind of opening that will be effective depends on your topic, how well you know the audience, and how well they know you. If, for example, you're giving a weekly status report on a project, you can immediately announce your main points (e.g., that the project is on schedule and proceeding as planned) and go immediately to the body of your remarks. If, however, you're presenting a new proposal to senior managers, you'll first have to introduce the topic and provide background information.

Consider capturing attention with a creative opening. The examples in Figure 4 are for a presentation to union employees about absenteeism.

Effective openings include a quotation, question, hypothetical situation, story, startling fact, or visual.

Use your judgment with these catchy openings. You might make a strong first impression—or you might immediately lose the audience. Pay careful attention to the organizational culture and know your audience well before choosing one of these approaches.

Strong visuals in your presentation can serve as an alternative, engaging opening. When the Dunkin' Donuts report from Chapter 10 was used for an oral presentation instead of a written report, the presenter captured attention with a strong opening slide (Figure 5).[5] Shown after the title slide but before the agenda, this slide uses builds (or animations) to display an "X" over each container—a visual way to explain the lack of options for soymilk drinkers.

See the Reference Manual for the entire Dunkin' Donuts presentation.

Don't start your presentation with an apology or excuse (e.g., "I wish I had more time to prepare my remarks today" or "I'm not really much of a speaker"). The audience may agree with you! Also avoid apologizing for a cold or scratchy

Quote a well-known person.

"Comedian Woody Allen once said that 90% of the job is just showing up."

Ask a question.

"If we could cut our absenteeism by half during the next six months, how much do you think each of us would receive in our end-of-year bonus checks?"

Present a hypothetical situation.

"Imagine that as you were leaving home this morning to put in a full day at work, your son told you he was too tired to go to school because he had stayed up late last night watching the Super Bowl. What would be your reaction?"

Relate an appropriate anecdote, story, joke, or personal experience.

"My cousin recently left a job and was surprised that her old position wasn't filled. She asked a former coworker why this was, and he said, 'When you quit, you didn't leave a vacancy!' Perhaps the reason my cousin didn't leave a vacancy was that…"

Give a startling fact.

"A company our size loses an average of $9 million per year because of absenteeism."

Use a dramatic prop or visual.

(Showing an empty chair) "What do you think is the true cost of this chair to our company?"

© CENGAGE LEARNING 2013

Figure 4
Creative Openings for a Presentation to Union Employees about Absenteeism

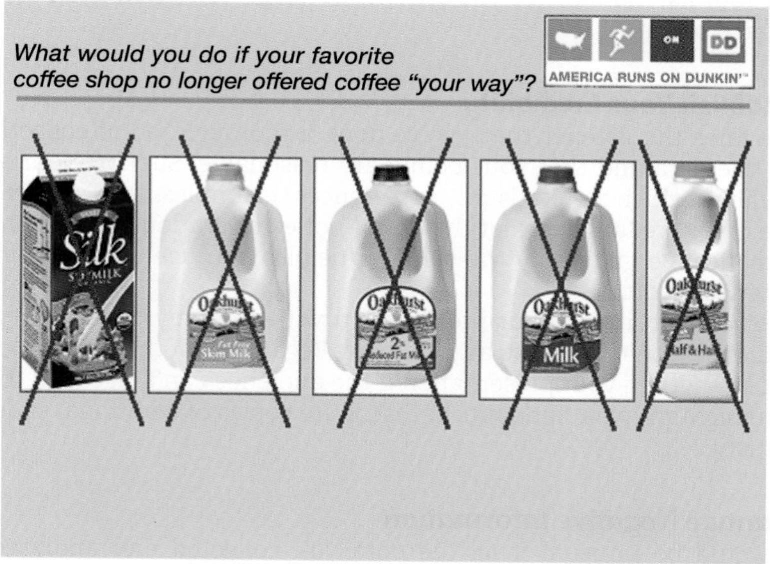

Figure 5
Engaging Opening Presentation Slide

COURTESY OF GRACE OPLINGER

voice unless it will be obvious to your audience. Why start off by telling your audience to question your credibility or delivery skills?

For most business presentations, let the audience know up front what you expect of them. Are you simply presenting information for them to absorb, or will the audience be expected to react in some way? Are you asking for their endorsement, their resources, their help, or what?

For direct-plan presentations, make sure your main point is right up front. If you want the audience to invest in your new ice cream shop, tell them early on what you want and what they can expect, for example, "I'm going to show you how a minimum investment of $50,000 will bring you returns of 10% to 15% beginning in year two."

Your opening should lead into the body of your presentation by previewing your content: "Today, I'll cover four main points. First, . . ." Typically, this will be your agenda for the presentation. Let the audience know the scope of your presentation. For example, if you're discussing the pros and cons of a plant closing from a financial perspective, tell the audience that your analysis does not consider implications for employees. You also might acknowledge up front that your topic may be controversial. Launching into a presentation about layoffs without some recognition that people's lives will be affected may be viewed as callous and can turn off your audience.

The Body

The body of your presentation conveys the real content. Here you'll develop the points you introduced in the opening, giving background information, specific evidence, examples, implications, consequences, and other information.

Organize the body logically, according to your topic and audience needs.

Choose a Logical Sequence
Just as you do when writing a letter, email, or report, choose an organizational plan that suits your purpose and your audience's needs. The most commonly used organizational plans are described in Figure 6.

Whatever organizational plan you choose, make sure that your audience knows at the outset where you're going and is able to follow you throughout the presentation. In a written document, signposts such as headings tell the reader how the parts fit together. In an oral presentation, frequent and clear transitions tell your listeners where you are within the presentation and how points connect to each other.

Establish Your Credibility
Convince the listener that you've done a thorough job of collecting and analyzing the data and that your points are reasonable. Support your arguments with credible evidence—statistics, experiences, examples, and support from experts. Use objective language; let the data—not exaggeration or emotion—persuade the audience. Be guided by the same principles you use when writing a persuasive letter or report.

Avoid saturating your presentation with so many facts and figures that your audience won't be able to absorb them. Regardless of their relevance, statistics will not strengthen your presentation if the audience can't digest all the data. Instead, you might prepare handouts or distribute copies of additional slides with detailed statistics.

Ethics in Communication

Manage Negative Information
It would be unusual if *all* the data you collected and analyzed support your proposal. (If that were the case, persuasion would not be needed.) What should

Figure 6
Typical Organizational Plans for Presentations

Criteria	Introduce each criterion in turn, and show how well each alternative meets that criterion (typically used for presenting proposals).
Direct Sequence	Give the major conclusions first, followed by the supporting details (typically used for presenting routine information).
Indirect Sequence	Present the reasons first, followed by the major conclusion (typically used for hostile or highly resistant audiences).
Chronology	Present the points in the order in which they occurred (typically used in status reports or when reporting on some event).
Cause/ Effect/ Solution	Present the sources and consequences of some problem, and then pose a solution (useful for problem solving).
Order of Importance	Arrange the points in order of importance, and then pose each point as a question and answer it (an effective way of helping the audience follow your arguments).
Elimination of Alternatives	List all alternatives, and then gradually eliminate each one until only one option remains—the one you're recommending (useful to guide decision making).

© CENGAGE LEARNING 2013

you do, then, about negative information, which, if presented, might weaken your argument? You cannot simply ignore negative information. To do so would surely open up a host of questions and subsequent doubts that would seriously undermine your position.

Steve Jobs couldn't ignore serious complaints about the iPhone. When people claimed that an earlier version dropped calls, he didn't shy away from the criticism. Instead, at a press conference, Jobs acknowledged that "phones aren't perfect." He then compared the iPhone to other smartphones, which he said also "lose signal strength if you hold it a certain way." Jobs cleverly used the negative feedback to show the iPhone's relative strength.[6]

When faced with negative information, think about your own analysis of the data. Despite criticism, you still believe in your idea. The best approach is to present all the important information—pro and con—and to show through your own analysis that your recommendations are still valid. Use the techniques you learned in Chapter 5 about emphasis and subordination to let your listeners know which points you consider major and which you consider minor.

 Do not ignore negative information.

Although you should discuss the important negative points, you may safely omit discussing minor ones. But be prepared to discuss all issues that the audience may raise during the question-and-answer session.

The Ending

Finish on a strong, upbeat note, leaving your audience with a clear and simple message.

The ending of your presentation is your last opportunity to achieve your objective. Don't waste it. A presentation without a strong ending is like a joke without a punch line. In closing his press conference about the iPhone, Steve Jobs drew attention away from the criticism and spoke about the customer: "We love our users. We really love them. And we try very hard to surprise and delight them. . . . We love our customers, and we're going to try to take care of every single one. . . ."[7]

Your closing should summarize the main points of your presentation, especially if it has been a long one. Let the audience know the significance of what you've said. Draw conclusions, make recommendations, or outline the next steps. Leave the audience with a clear and simple message.

To add punch to your ending, you may want to use one of the same techniques discussed for opening a presentation. You might tell a story or show a dramatic visual. However, resist the temptation to end with a quotation. Quotations are overused, and you want your listeners to remember *your* words—not someone else's.

After you've developed some experience in giving presentations, you'll be able to judge fairly accurately how long to spend on each point so that you can finish on time. Until then, practice your presentation with a stopwatch. If necessary, insert reminders at critical points in your notes, indicating where you should be at what point. Avoid having to drop important sections or rush through the conclusion of your presentation because you misjudged your timing.

Finish on a strong, upbeat note. Avoid fading out with a weak "That's about all I have to say" or "I see that our time is running out." Your audience may most remember your last words—choose them carefully and deliver them confidently.

Humor in Business Presentations

Use humor if it is appropriate and you are adept at telling funny stories.

Memory research indicates that when ideas are presented with humor, the audience can recall more details of the presentation and retain the information longer.[8] Humor also creates a connection between the speaker and the audience.

Most of us couldn't be stand-up comedians, even if we wanted to be. If you're not a good storyteller, practicing in front of an audience isn't the best choice. But if you believe that you can use humor effectively, doing so might add just the right touch to your presentation.

If you tell an amusing story, it must always be in good taste and appropriate to the situation. Unless you're writing for an episode of *South Park*, never tell an off-color or sexist joke; use offensive language; single out an ethnic, racial, or religious group; or imitate a foreign accent in telling a story. Also avoid humor if your presentation topic is serious or has negative consequences for the audience.

Ethics in Communication

Even comedians can go wrong in telling jokes. Sarah Silverman, known for her humor about taboo topics, was invited to a TED conference but failed miserably. Her jokes about wanting to adopt a "retarded" child with a terminal illness offended many in the audience, including Chris Anderson, the conference coordinator (Figure 7).[9]

Personalize an amusing story to make it relate more directly to your topic.

Personal, unexpected stories are often best for getting a good laugh. Self-deprecating humor shows that you're human and can laugh at yourself. But be careful not to damage your credibility. Joking about your lack of PowerPoint skills won't reflect

Figure 7
TED Conference Coordinator Tweets About Sarah Silverman

I know I shouldn't say this about one of my own speakers, but I thought Sarah Silverman was god-awful...

about 20 hours ago from web
Retweeted by 41 people

ʝ Reply ↩ Retweet

TEDchris
Chris Anderson

© TWITTER.COM

well on your presentation. Instead, surprise the audience by telling a story about yourself that becomes funny. Don't warn the audience that a joke is coming, which could disappoint them.

Relate your story to the next part of your presentation. If the audience laughs, this transition will be smooth. If the audience doesn't laugh—it happens—then just continue on with confidence.

Even if you're an expert joke teller, use humor sparingly. You want your audience to remember your ideas—not how funny you are.

PLANNING TEAM AND ONLINE PRESENTATIONS

L03 Plan a team and online presentation.

Most of your presentations probably will be solo performances in front of live audiences, but you may present as part of a team or via the Internet.

Team Presentations

Team presentations are common for communicating about complex projects. For example, presenting a large company's marketing strategy to management or updating the five-year plan may require the expertise and time of several people.

Team presentations, like team writing projects, require extensive planning, close coordination, and a measure of maturity and goodwill. Just as you would for team writing assignments, discussed in Chapter 2, delegate responsibilities according to each person's strengths. Not everyone has to have equal time in front of the audience, but it's odd to have one person speak for 20 minutes and another for only 3. Most important, your presentation should come across as coherent and well coordinated.

Achieving Coherence

Because people have different speaking styles, sounding like one cohesive unit is a challenge for team presentations. Group members should decide beforehand on the presentation tone, format, organization, and visuals. They should also agree on what to wear, how to handle questions, and how to transition from one speaker to another.

 Make your team presentation look as though it were prepared and given by a single person.

Use a presentation template to maintain one "look and feel" for all slides. Have one editor review all slides for consistency throughout the presentation.

Practicing the Team Presentation

A full-scale rehearsal with visuals—in the room where the presentation will be made—is crucial for team presentations. If possible, record the rehearsal on video so that you can review it later. Schedule your final practice session early enough that you will have time to make changes—and then run through the presentation once more, if possible.

Critiquing the performance of a colleague requires tact, empathy, and goodwill; and accepting such feedback requires grace and maturity. Revisit the guidelines for Commenting on Peer Writing in Chapter 2—similar techniques apply to oral presentations.

Coordinate introductions, transitions, and positioning. Will the first speaker introduce all team members at the beginning, or will speakers introduce themselves as they get up to speak? How will you transition to the next speaker and pass off the slide remote, if you're using one? Where will each of you stand? When others are speaking, consider sitting down rather than creating a police lineup in which presenters nervously look at their notes and mouth the words to their upcoming section.

This team is being photographed, but during a presentation, people who aren't presenting should sit down to avoid looking like a "police lineup."

© DATACRAFT CO LTD/PHOTOLIBRARY

Also plan how you'll handle questions. Will you take questions throughout the presentation or ask the audience to wait until the end? If a question comes up during the presentation that you know a team member will answer during a subsequent segment, avoid stealing the team member's thunder. Instead, respond, for example, with "Dylan will cover that point in a few minutes." If a question is asked of the group itself, the team leader should determine who will answer it. Refrain from adding to another member's response unless what you have to contribute is truly an important point not covered in the original answer.

Finally, consider yourself on stage during the entire team presentation—no matter who is presenting. If you're waiting for your turn, pay attention to the presenter (even though you may have heard the content a dozen times), and try to read the audience for nonverbal signs of confusion, boredom, or disagreement.

Communication Technologies

Online Presentations

Whether solo or with a team, you may deliver presentations over the Internet. Online presentations have many of the challenges of online meetings, discussed in Chapter 3, with a few more complications.

People may lose attention more quickly during a web presentation delivered to several locations. You might consider shorter presentations: perhaps two half-hour sessions rather than a one-hour session, or a half-hour with you as the presenter and then a half-hour for discussion in local offices.

Keep the audience engaged—even more so for an online presentation than an in-person presentation. Check in with the people at each location periodically if you don't hear from them, to make sure they are still interested and are following along.

As the presenter, you will be perceived as the person in control. Having good technology support—someone who knows the system well—is a bonus, but know the system yourself so you can confidently take control if problems occur.

Always have a backup plan for the worst-case scenario. If the video goes out, how can you continue your presentation? Send your slides in advance, arrange for a speakerphone, and have another system ready if yours fails.

DEVELOPING VISUAL SUPPORT FOR BUSINESS PRESENTATIONS

LO4 Develop effective visual support.

Most business presentations include some visual support. Visuals complement your message, increase comprehension, and make your presentation easier to follow—for you as well as your audience. When you are asked to give a presentation for a business audience, the default is to use PowerPoint or some other presentation software, projected onto a screen or large monitor.

But slides aren't right for every presentation. A demonstration of safety procedures to line workers should use the equipment as a model. A layoff announcement might include a handout with information employees can take home. And a motivational speech might use no visuals other than a dynamic, inspiring presenter.

When visuals are used, they must be done well, or they'll detract from your presentation. Presentation slides should be clear, easy to follow, attractive—and well integrated into the presentation. Handouts should provide the right amount of information at the right time.

Creating Presentation Slides

Although PowerPoint is the business standard, many tools are available for creating presentations. Some people prefer Apple's Keynote to PowerPoint. Google Docs is making some headway into the presentation market, with its easy-to-use and easy-to-share program. Or, as an alternative to linear slides, Prezi, a web-based program, uses one large canvas for transitioning and zooming in and out. In Prezi, you can incorporate a variety of text, images, videos—any object you would use in presentation slides. Here, we'll focus on PowerPoint, but most of the principles discussed in this section apply equally to other presentation tools.

Communication Technologies

Present Your Main Points Clearly

For direct-plan presentations—which most business presentations will be—you'll want your main points up front and reinforced throughout your slides.

Highlight your main points up front in a slide presentation.

Figure 8
Clear Main Points in a Slide Presentation

Your **title slide** should convey what your presentation is about and, if relevant, what result you expect from the presentation. Notice that the presentation is also customized to the audience by mentioning the investment group's name.

A **main point slide**, presented before the agenda slide, conveys the most important message to the audience—what they can expect from their investment. You don't always have to use a main point slide, but this extra step will make your communication objective clear. Showing a separate slide also ensures that you don't rush through your introduction but instead give your audience enough time to understand your key messages.

Next, your **agenda slide** describes main points. Rather than generic headings, such as Market, Products, Competition, and Financials, you can use talking headings, as we discussed in Chapter 10. Using talking headings for all of your slides will reinforce your main points throughout.

© CENGAGE LEARNING 2013

Let's use an example of an entrepreneurial venture: seeking investors for Ithaca's Ice Cream Shoppe. In Figure 8, a title slide, main point slide, and agenda slide present clear messages from the start.

Make Your Presentation Easy to Follow

Developing a well-organized presentation is only half the battle; now you have to reflect that clear organization through your visuals. Clear organization keeps your audience—and you as the presenter—focused.

In your slide presentation, you can include **divider slides** or a **slide tracker**. With divider slides, you repeat your agenda slide, highlighting each topic as you cover it. Divider slides are particularly useful for team presentations as you transition to new topics as well as different presenters.

An alternative to divider slides is a slide tracker to show where you are within the presentation. A slide tracker shows the major divisions of your presentation and is repeated on all slides after the agenda. With each section of the presentation highlighted as you get to it, a tracker is the audience's guide. Notice how "Profits and Costs"—the second section of the Dunkin' Donuts presentation—is highlighted in Figure 9. Although trackers typically appear at the bottom of a slide, they may appear at the top, as in Figure 10. The Facebook example was

Figures 9 and 10
Slide Trackers

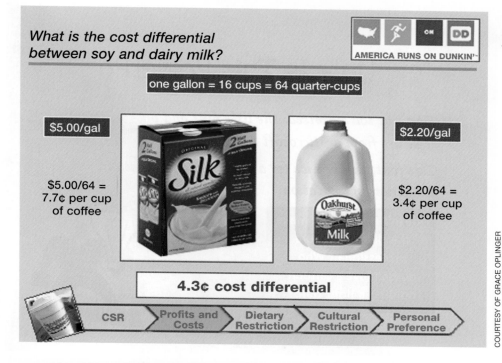

COURTESY OF GRACE OPLINGER

© KRASKA/SHUTTERSTOCK.COM; © TERRI MILLER/E-VISUAL COMMUNICATIONS, INC.

part of a presentation encouraging Starbucks to use Facebook as a communication tool for their employees. With the changing tabs at the top, the design fits the topic nicely.

Choose an Attractive, Appropriate Design

Design is never as important as content, but visual appeal can affect your credibility and, at times, the audience's understanding. The incredibly ugly slide in Figure 11 is difficult to read and not appropriate for a business presentation.

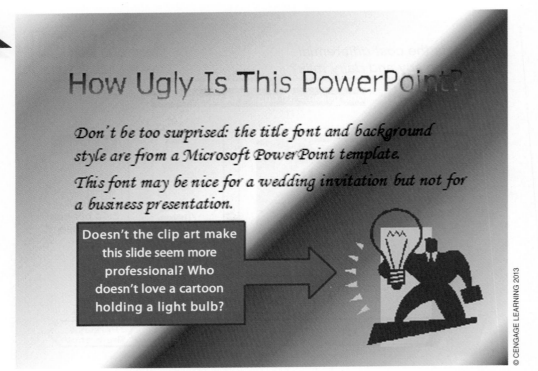

**Figure 11
Ugly Slide Example**

© CENGAGE LEARNING 2013

 Adjust slide design templates for a unique, custom look.

Compare the ugly slide to those in Figure 12. The Go Mein slides, for a new restaurant concept, use complementary colors, a cohesive design, simple photographs, and shapes as visual cues.[10]

Unless your company has a standard design that you must use, you can use one of the many templates available for presentation slides. A template is a good starting point for your slide design, but the few offered with a program such as PowerPoint get old fast. Adapt templates by, at a minimum, adjusting the colors, changing the fonts, and choosing a different background.

Figure 13 shows a customized design with a simple color palate. You may use more colors, but avoid too many that conflict with each other. You might also consider a color scheme that reflects your company's colors. Because 5% to 10% of the population is color blind, avoid using shades of red and green next to each other—they're too hard to distinguish.[11]

Simple backgrounds are best for slides. Choose a solid color, gradient, or very light image that travels the edges of the slide but doesn't interfere with text or other graphics. You may use either a dark background with light text or dark text on a light background.

If possible, look at your slides projected in the room where you'll deliver your presentation. All projectors show colors slightly differently, which could affect, for

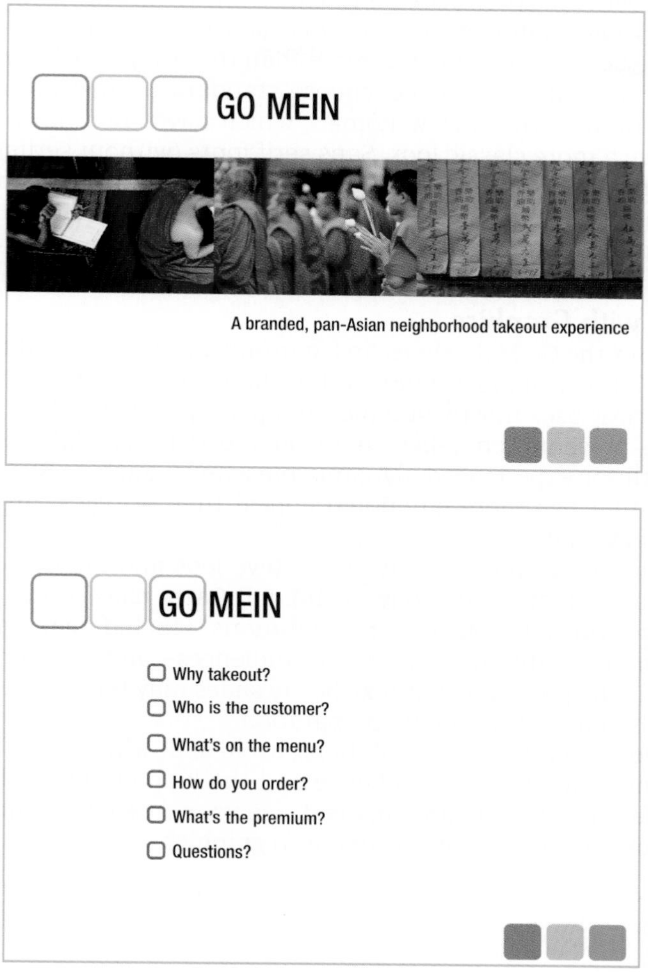

Figure 12
Original, Beautiful Slide Design

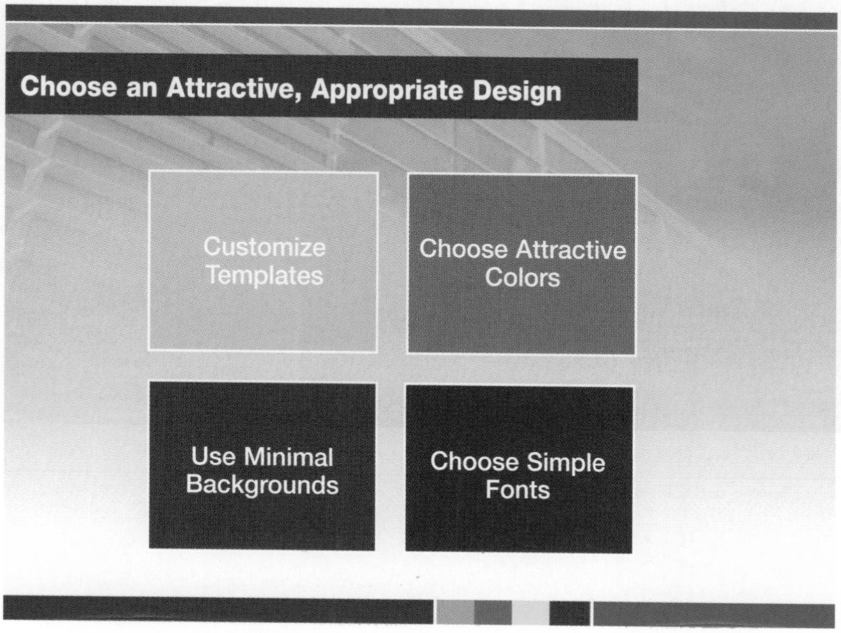

COURTESY OF MICHAEL POLLAK; © TIM HALL/AXIOM PHOTOGRAPHIC AGENCY/GETTY IMAGES; © PAUL EDMONDSON/ PHOTOGRAPHER'S CHOICE/GETTY IMAGES; © STEVEN L. RAYMER/NATIONAL GEOGRAPHIC/GETTY IMAGES

Figure 13
Custom Slide Design with a Simple Color Palette

© CENGAGE LEARNING 2013

example, your company's logo. Also, only with the appropriate room lighting can you determine whether your color contrast is sufficient.

Choose no more than two fonts for your slides. One font for a slide title and another for the body works well, but more than that may look busy. Unless you're presenting for a creative audience, choose standard business fonts. Serif fonts, such as Cambria and Times New Roman, which have small lines connecting to the letters, have a more classic look. Sans serif fonts (without serifs), such as Arial and Calibri, present a more modern look. Sometimes sans serif fonts are easier to read on a projected screen, so check the fonts when you do your presentation run-through in the room.

Replace Text with Graphics

The approach for the Go Mein slides (in Figure 12) differs from traditional business presentations but is gaining ground. Rather than showing lots of bulleted text on a slide, the creator uses mostly graphics and perhaps a few, select words. For this approach, the presentation relies more on the delivery skills of the speaker. This works well for experienced, dynamic presenters, such as Steve Jobs, and for presentations that use more emotional appeal than a logical argument, which may require heavy data.

Contrasting the presentation styles of Steve Jobs and Bill Gates, of Microsoft fame, we see a stark difference (Figure 14). Bill Gates uses content-heavy slides, which are more typical for business presentations.[12] Including more text on slides is useful for more traditional topics and audiences—and will serve as a better guide for you as the presenter. But text-heavy slides may tempt you to read off the slides rather than rely on your own preparation.

Even for more traditional presentations, avoid slide after slide of bulleted text. This is mind-numbing for your audience and the kind of approach that inspires jokes about "death by PowerPoint." Instead, use your creativity—and tools such as SmartArt in PowerPoint—to convert text into graphics.

> **Avoid too much bulleted text on slides.**

Figure 14
Comparing Use of Visuals

Figure 15
Graphics Show How Points Relate to Each Other

Higher
Staffing
Levels

Streamlined
Workflow

Better
Product
Design

Increased
Profits

© CENGAGE LEARNING 2013

Graphics make your slides more visually appealing and, more important, show your audience how concepts relate to each other, as in Figure 15. As a bulleted list, the text would miss the point: that these three improvements will lead to more profits.

Also consider using photos or other graphics to replace text. The Go Mein presentation makes good use of photos to illustrate points. But avoid irrelevant photos and goofy clip art, which detract from your main points. Unless you're presenting to elementary school students, stick with more professional images.

Equally mind-numbing as text-heavy slides are large tables of data projected for your audience. A table of dense numbers is fine for a printed report, but not for a slide. Columns and rows of numbers are hard to see and do nothing to help your audience make sense of the data. Instead, convert tables into charts, as we discussed in Chapter 9.

Finally, you can use graphics to highlight data, and add animations to help the audience follow along. Change colors and text enhancements, such as boldface, to draw attention to key points as you review a slide. And use animations to control when the audience sees certain text and graphics.

But keep animations simple and avoid overusing them. Nobody needs to see a line of text circle around the slide, accompanied by a Lady Gaga song, before it finally lands next to a bullet. Similarly, you don't need to control every word for your audience. Presenters who bring in one line of an agenda slide at a time are keeping their audience in suspense for no reason—and missing the chance for the audience to see the big picture of the presentation and read at their own pace.

In general, the more white space and simplicity, the better. Keep your slides clean so they are easy for your audience to grasp quickly.

Write Simply and Clearly

When you do use text, keep it simple and clear. Edit relentlessly to keep just the most important points. The example in Figure 16 shows how you can convert paragraph text to bulleted text.

 Simple, clear writing will make your slides easier to read.

Figure 16
Converting Paragraph Text to Bulleted Text

Three major initiatives will ensure that profits increase over the next 12 months. First, we must increase our staffing levels. We are currently operating at 100% capacity, yet we cannot keep up with demand, which has increased over 20% in the past six months alone. Second, we need to improve our workflow. We have people duplicating work in several departments, and this is leading not only to wasted time but also inconsistent output. Finally, we need better product design. Customer feedback tells us that our design should be simpler and easier to use. With a product return rate of 14%, we're losing our reputation for quality.

How to Increase Profits over the Next 12 Months

- Increase Staffing Levels
  - Operating currently at 100% capacity
  - Failing to keep up with increasing demand
- Streamline Workflow
  - Duplicating work in several departments
  - Causing wasted time and inconsistent output
- Improve Product Design
  - Ignoring customer feedback
  - Receiving 14% product returns
  - Losing reputation for quality

© CENGAGE LEARNING 2013

In the bulleted text in Figure 16, notice how parallel phrasing is used for each level of bullets, just as you would do for a written report. Use all of your proficient revising and editing skills to perfect the few words you include on your slides.

By further simplifying this text, you can create a graphic suitable for a presentation slide. In Figure 17, a graphic shows these three strategies for increasing profits as sequential steps—a different approach from that used in Figure 15. This slide loses the detail from the bulleted text but may work better for some situations. How much text you include on your slide depends on your audience and your delivery skills.

Using Presentation Slides

Use visuals to support your presentation—not to detract from you as the speaker.

Delivering your presentation with slides requires practice and a bit of choreography. When you present to an audience, your slides are just one visual—you are the main attraction. Use your visuals as support, with the main focus on you.

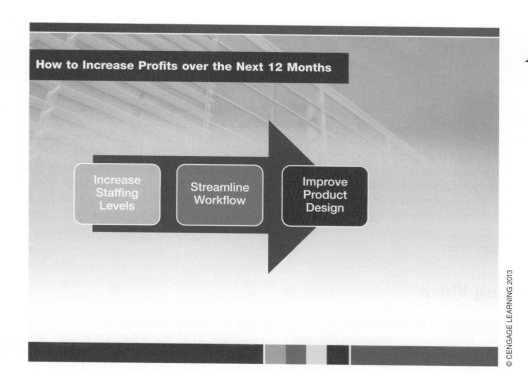

Figure 17
Converting Text to a Graphic

© CENGAGE LEARNING 2013

Depending on the room and screen or monitor, positioning yourself may be a challenge. Make sure the audience can see you and the slides easily, and always avoid walking in front of the slides and having your back to the audience. Try standing on the left side (from the audience's point of view) for English-speaking audiences, who read from left to right. With this setup, the audience looks toward the left to view you, glances slightly to the right to refer to the slides, and then moves back left to you again. Ideally, you'll find at least two places where you can stand so that you can move around during your presentation. To draw attention to slides occasionally, you can refer to the slide with your body, an arm gesture, or a laser pointer.

When using slides for your presentation, avoid standing or walking in front of the projection.

© ROBERT LLEWELLYN/PHOTOLIBRARY

Consider when you'll display your slides. You may want to have your title slide up when people enter the room, or you may want to connect with the audience and introduce your topic before showing your first slide. Also, you don't need your slides up during the entire presentation. When telling a story, discussing a controversial topic, or answering questions, consider blanking the slide temporarily to engage the audience so that you can walk in front of the screen projection. During a PowerPoint slideshow on a PC or a Mac, you can hit the Shift key + B to blank the slide, and then hit these keys again when you're ready to continue. Or you can use the remote for a projector to "blank" or "mute" the light for the same effect.

Use a remote to control your slides. A remote lets you walk around freely, so you're not tied to the computer. To advance slides, you don't need to point your remote to the screen or the projector—it's not a TV. Just continue with your natural hand and arm gestures, and push the button when you're ready to go to the next slide. Give yourself time to practice using the remote so you're smooth when the big day comes.

Communication Technologies

Video can engage the audience, illustrate a point, and make an emotional appeal.

Using Video

Including video in a presentation is a good way to engage the audience, illustrate a point, and make an emotional appeal. If you want in-store customer service associates to improve their sales skills, you could show a video of interactions with customers. If you want to convince an audience about the dangers of climate change, you might show a polar bear swimming through oceans of water looking for ice (as you may have seen in movies and commercials).

But don't use video just to break up your presentation. Your video should have a clear purpose—otherwise, it may detract from your presentation. Irrelevant or, worse, silly videos may make your audience question why your content isn't strong enough to stand alone. Use just enough to make your point, editing content to keep only the relevant points.

When you do use video, integrate it into the presentation. Tell your audience what to expect—why you're showing it, generally what it's about, and how long it will be. At the end, again explain the relevance, transitioning back to your main point.

Practice using the video smoothly and seamlessly. Embed videos into your presentation slides rather than switching or linking to YouTube. Embedded videos will look far more professional and will eliminate embarrassing downtime during your presentation.

Finally, practice using the video in your presentation room. A video that works on your home computer may not work on the room's computer. Also check the sound so you can set the volume level in advance, to make sure your audience won't miss the first few seconds of your video.

Creating and Using Handouts

Audience handouts supplement your presentation, provide space for note taking, and are a permanent record of your presentation.

Audience handouts—printed copies of slides, notes, tables, or illustrations—help the audience follow a presentation and provide a "takeaway."

Many presenters will distribute copies of the slides (the deck). The deck can include the projected slides or a report version of the slides that has more content. To save paper, you might print two or three slides to a page, leaving space for notes, as long as the slides are still legible. Before you print 100 copies, make sure the colors print well. Colors will look different printed and, if you're printing in black and white, some colors may be difficult to see.

Additional handouts to supplement the slides may be useful. You might include full tables of data, for example, that were not projected on the screen.

When is the best time to distribute your handout—before, during, or after your presentation? If the audience needs to understand complex information as context for your presentation, send handouts ahead of time. If you'll refer to material during your presentation, distribute handouts immediately before the presentation. This has an obvious disadvantage: the audience may refer to the notes rather than you during the presentation. Instead, you may choose to wait until the end of your presentation to distribute any handouts. This will keep the audience focused on you but may frustrate people who want to take notes throughout. Use your judgment and your knowledge of the audience to make the best decision and leave a positive impression.

 The content and purpose of your handout determine when it should be distributed.

PRACTICING AND DELIVERING THE PRESENTATION

L05 Practice and deliver a presentation.

Now that you have prepared your presentation, you should practice so that you can deliver it with confidence.

Practicing the Presentation

Choose simple language for oral presentations. Because the audience has only one chance to understand the information, use shorter sentences and simpler vocabulary for oral presentations than for written presentations. A long sentence that reads easily on paper may leave the speaker breathless when spoken. Instead, use a conversational style, including contractions, and avoid using words that you may have trouble pronouncing.

 Use appropriate language, voice qualities, gestures, and posture.

Practicing your presentation will build your confidence and help you engage your audience rather than put them to sleep.

© PETER HANSEN/SHUTTERSTOCK.COM

Record your rehearsal on video to help you review and modify your voice qualities, gestures, and content. Play back the video several times, paying attention to your voice qualities (especially speed and pitch), pauses, grouping of words and phrases, and pronunciation. The recording will help you judge and adjust these qualities.

For important presentations, plan on a minimum of three run-throughs. The first run-through should focus on continuity (does everything you say make sense when you say it aloud?) and approximate timing. If necessary, cut out a point so that you have time for a solid, well-rehearsed, and non-rushed summary and conclusion. Schedule your practice sessions far enough ahead of time to allow you to make changes. Your first run-through should probably be private, or perhaps with one close friend or colleague listening to give feedback. Then, when you're satisfied, you can include more people.

Become familiar enough with your message that a few notes or a graphic will keep you on track. Practice the most important parts (introduction, summary of key points, conclusion) the most number of times.

Speak in a conversational tone—but enhanced and slightly slower.

Practice using the extemporaneous delivery style: a conversational tone, but at a slightly slower rate than normally used in conversation. For interest and to fit the situation, vary both your volume and your rate of speaking, slowing down when presenting important or complex information and speeding up when summarizing. Use periodic pauses to emphasize important points. Use correct diction, avoid slurring or dropping off the endings of words, and practice pronouncing difficult names.

Use appropriate gestures in a way that feels natural.

Occasional hand and arm gestures are important for adding interest and emphasis, but only if they are appropriate and appear natural. If you never "talk with your hands" in normal conversation, it is unlikely you will do so naturally while presenting. Generally, one-handed gestures are more effective and less distracting than two-handed ones.

Use natural hand and arm gestures to add interest and emphasize points in your presentation.

© JON FEINGERSH PHOTOGRAPHY INC/BLEND IMAGES/PHOTOLIBRARY

Avoid annoying and distracting mannerisms and gestures, such as jingling coins or keys in your pocket; coughing or clearing your throat excessively; wildly waving or tightly clasping your hands; nervously swaying or pacing; playing with your hair or jewelry; or peppering your remarks with fillers, such as *um*, *uh*, *like*, or *you know*.

Practice smiling occasionally, standing tall and naturally, with your body balanced. Rest your hands by your side or in any natural, quiet position. Your voice and demeanor should reflect professionalism, enthusiasm, and self-confidence.

Delivering the Presentation

Dress comfortably—just slightly dressier than your audience.

Your clothing is a part of the message you communicate to your audience, so dress appropriately—in comfortable business attire. More conservative dress is always a better choice than flamboyant or revealing clothes. As the presenter, dress just slightly better than the audience, but don't go overboard. If the office is a casual setting, you don't have to wear a suit.

If you're speaking after a meal, eat lightly and avoid heavy sauces, desserts, and alcoholic beverages. As you're being introduced, take several deep breaths to clear your mind, walk confidently to the front of the room, take enough time to arrange yourself, look slowly around you, establish eye contact with several members of the audience, and then, in a loud, clear voice, begin your presentation.

You should know your presentation well enough that you can maintain eye contact easily with your audience, including people in all corners of the room. Lock in on one person and maintain eye contact for at least three seconds—or until you have completed a thought.

If you lose your place in your notes or script, relax and take as much time as you need to regroup. If your mind goes blank, try to keep talking—even if you repeat what you've just said. The audience will probably think you intentionally repeated the information for emphasis, and the extra time may jog your memory. If this doesn't work, simply skip ahead to another part of your presentation that you do remember; then come back later to the part you omitted.

Overcoming Speech Anxiety

According to author Mark Twain, "There are two types of speakers—those who are nervous and those who are liars." For some people, giving a presentation makes them feel faint or nauseated ("butterflies in the stomach"); makes their hands or legs shake and their palms sweat; gives them a rapid, loud heart beat; makes their face or neck look red and blotchy; or makes them speak too fast and in a high-pitched voice. If you have experienced these symptoms, you're not alone.

The Oscar-winning movie *The King's Speech* portrayed England's King George VI, who suffered with a stammer. The film raised awareness of how many people—even kings—suffer from speech anxiety and other hurdles to speaking in public.

In the movie *The King's Speech*, Geoffrey Rush coaches Colin Firth as King George VI, who had a severe stammer and terrible speech anxiety.

© WEINSTEIN COMPANY/COURTESY EVERETT COLLECTION

Fortunately, behavior-modification experts have found that of the full range of anxiety disorders, people can most predictably overcome their fear of public speaking.[13] The trick is to use this natural stress to your advantage.

Recognize that you have been asked to make a presentation because someone thinks you have something important to say. You should feel complimented. Unless you're an exceptionally good or exceptionally bad speaker, the audience will more likely remember *what* you say rather than how you say it. Most of us fall somewhere between these two extremes as presenters.

To avoid anxiety, practice, develop a positive attitude, and concentrate on friendly faces.

The best way to minimize any lingering anxiety is to over-prepare. The more familiar you are with the content of your speech and the more trial runs you've made, the better you'll be able to concentrate on your delivery once you're actually in front of the group. You may want to memorize the first several sentences of your presentation just so you can approach those critical first moments (when anxiety is highest) with more confidence.

Practice mental imagery. Several times before your big presentation, sit in a comfortable position, close your eyes, and visualize yourself giving your speech. Picture yourself speaking confidently, loudly, and clearly in an assured voice. If you can imagine yourself giving a successful speech, you will be able to do so.

Before your presentation, take a short walk to relax your body. While waiting for your presentation to begin, let your arms drop loosely by your sides and shake your wrists gently, all the while breathing deeply several times. As you begin to speak, look for friendly faces in the crowd, and concentrate on them initially.

Some nervousness is good. It gets the adrenaline flowing and gives your speech an edge. If you do find that you're exceedingly nervous as you begin your speech, don't say, "I'm so nervous, my hands are shaking." The audience probably didn't notice.

Answering Questions

One advantage of oral presentations over written reports is the opportunity to engage in two-way communication. The question-and-answer session is an important part of your presentation, so prepare to answer even the toughest of questions.

Decide whether you'll take questions throughout your presentation or only at the end. Holding questions until the end helps you avoid being interrupted and losing your train of thought, or possibly running out of time and not being able to complete your prepared content. Also, a question may be answered later in your presentation. However, for senior-level audiences, prospective clients, complex topics, and informal settings, you should take questions throughout your presentation. In these situations, you'll be able to adapt your presentation based on questions and can help audiences understand the content without getting too lost.

Plan your answers to possible questions ahead of time.

As you prepare your presentation, anticipate questions you might get from the audience. Make a list of them and think through possible answers. If your list of questions is very long, consider revising your presentation to incorporate some of the answers into your prepared presentation.

Always listen carefully to the question; repeat it, if necessary, for the benefit of the entire audience; and look at the entire audience as you answer—not just at the questioner. If necessary, make notes to refer to while answering. Treat each questioner with unfailing courtesy. If the question is antagonistic, be firm but fair and polite. If you don't know the answer to a question, say so and promise to have the answer within a specific period.

If no one asks a question, you either did a superb job of explaining your topic, or no one wants to be the first to ask a question. If you suspect the latter, to break the ice you might start the questions yourself by saying something like "One question I'm frequently asked is. . . ." Or you may ask someone ahead of time to ask the first question if no one else does.

When your presentation is over and you're back in your office, evaluate your performance. Use the Checklist for Oral Presentations to benefit from the experience. What seemed to work well and what not so well? Analyze each aspect of your presentation—from initial research through delivery. Regardless of how well the presentation went, work to improve your performance next time.

Checklist for Oral Presentations

GO

Planning the Presentation

☑ Determine whether an oral presentation will be more effective than a written report.

☑ Determine your purpose. What response do you want from your audience?

☑ Analyze your audience in terms of demographic factors, level of knowledge, and psychological needs.

☑ Select an appropriate delivery method.

Organizing the Presentation

☑ Brainstorm. Write down every point you think you might cover in the presentation.

☑ Separate your notes into the opening, body, and ending. Gather additional data if needed.

☑ Write an effective opening that introduces the topic, discusses the points you'll cover, and tells the audience what you hope will happen as a result of your presentation.

☑ In the body, develop the points fully, giving background data, evidence, and examples.

☑ Organize main points logically.

☑ To maintain credibility, discuss any major negative points and be prepared to discuss any minor ones.

☑ Pace the presentation of data to avoid presenting facts and figures too quickly.

☑ Finish on a strong, upbeat note by summarizing your main points, adding a personal appeal, drawing conclusions and making recommendations, discussing what needs to be done next, or using some other logical closing.

☑ Use humor only when appropriate and only if you are effective at telling amusing stories.

Planning Team and Online Presentations

☑ Spend adequate time preparing for a team presentation to ensure coherence. Coordinate introductions, transitions, positioning—and how you'll handle questions.

☑ When delivering a presentation online, consider shorter segments, plan ways to keep the audience engaged, and practice using the technology.

Developing Visual Support

☑ Create visuals to complement your presentation.

☑ Present main points clearly and reinforce them throughout your presentation with divider slides or a slide tracker.

☑ Customize a slide design template to create something original and relevant to your presentation. Choose simplicity over complexity.

☑ Where possible, replace text with graphics for easier reading and to show how your points relate to each other.

☑ Supplement your presentation with video and handouts, as appropriate for your audience and objectives.

Practicing and Delivering the Presentation

☑ Rehearse your presentation extensively, simulating the actual speaking conditions as much as possible and using your visual aids.

☑ Use simple language, short sentences, and an extemporaneous delivery style.

☑ Stand tall and naturally, and speak in a loud, clear, enthusiastic, and friendly voice. Vary the rate and volume of your voice.

☑ Use correct diction and appropriate gestures.

☑ Dress appropriately—in comfortable, business-like, conservative clothing.

☑ Maintain eye contact with the audience, including all corners of the room in your gaze.

☑ To avoid anxiety, practice extensively, develop a positive attitude, and concentrate on the friendly faces in the audience.

☑ Plan your answers to possible questions ahead of time. Listen to each question carefully, and address your answer to the entire audience.

The 3Ps In Action

Giving Feedback to a Speaker

Purpose

You are a colleague of Salman Khan, one of the expert speakers at the TED Conference introduced at the beginning of this chapter.[14] Imagine that you're watching Khan's presentation as a practice run-through, and plan to provide written feedback.

Process

1. **What is the purpose of Salman Khan's presentation?**
   To discuss how he uses video for education. The title is "Let's Use Video to Reinvent Education."

2. **Describe the audience.**
   The TED audience is a highly selective group who pays a considerable fee to attend the conference. The secondary audience is online viewers (over 100,000 on YouTube).

3. **What is the main point of the presentation?**
   By assigning video as homework, teachers can provide more one-on-one feedback in the classroom. Khan has used this successfully in math classes to customize learning for each student.

4. **How is the presentation best organized?**
   - Open with video examples to engage the audience and provide an example of Khan's work (YouTube videos about mathematics).
   - Give brief background information about his early YouTube videos:
     – Tell the story of his cousins' reaction to his videos.
     – Read comments from other viewers; highlight the experience of the child with autism.
     – Incorporate humor in this section.
   - Explain how he uses video in his classes.
   - Show examples of available data:
     – Show knowledge maps and explain how concepts build on each other for individual learners.
     – Show the dashboard of data from the Los Altos school and explain peer tutoring.
     – Show diagnostic data that teachers receive, and explain differentiated learning.
   - Explain how this process "humanizes the classroom" and changes the current paradigm of education.
   - Introduce the concept of a global classroom, with peers tutoring each other around the world.
   - Respond to questions from Bill Gates.

5. **What is the best delivery style for the presentation purpose and audience?**
   Extemporaneous. This should sound like a well-organized, well-rehearsed conversation. Visuals provide examples of videos and available data.

Product

Presentation Feedback

	Not at All	Somewhat	Yes	Definitely
1. The organization works well for the topic and is easy to follow. COMMENTS: *The organization is logical and easy to follow. For a short presentation, the transitions are smooth and subtle. For a longer presentation, Khan may use more explicit transitions.*	1	2	3	(4)
2. The content is clear and is well supported with details and examples. COMMENTS: *The content is relevant for the TED audience, and Khan provides excellent examples and feedback from people who have benefited from his videos. To strengthen the content, Khan could include more of the teacher's perspective—testimonials may give more credibility and another view to support his ideas.*	1	2	(3)	4
3. The delivery style is engaging and appropriate for the TED audience. COMMENTS: *Khan uses an engaging, conversational style, which works well for the TED audience. His pace and volume are appropriate, and he makes good use of movement and space. He appears calm and confident.*	1	2	3	(4)
4. Visual support is relevant and interesting. COMMENTS: *Starting with video examples is a great idea to engage the audience. The visuals that show the dashboard diagnostic data went a bit quickly. These could be simplified for the short time frame.*	1	2	(3)	4

Preparing for a TED Conference Presentation

Purpose

Imagine that you are one of the select few who are invited to speak at a TED Conference. Choose a topic you are passionate about—a hobby, a particular company, a movie, or something else that interests you. Prepare your presentation and deliver it in person or by video.

Process

1. What is the purpose of your presentation?
2. Describe your audience.
3. What level of knowledge is your audience likely to have about your topic?
4. How will you capture your audience's attention in the first minute of your presentation? Draft your opening section.
5. What points will you cover in the body of your presentation, and in what order?
6. Write a closing section that summarizes your points and reinforces the purpose of your presentation.
7. What delivery techniques will you use to make your presentation as dynamic as the TED presenters' speeches?
8. What visuals will you use? Try to avoid traditional presentation slides with heavy text in favor of a simpler, more graphical style.
9. If you were to give your presentation via the Internet to the class, how would you prepare?

Product

Using your knowledge of oral presentations, prepare an outline for this presentation, and submit it to your instructor for feedback. Then, prepare visuals and practice your presentation. When you're ready, deliver your presentation to the class. You might deliver part of your presentation in person in front of the class—and part via the Internet.

Summary

L01 **Plan a presentation.**

To plan a presentation, determine the purpose, analyze the audience, and plan the delivery method. Most business presentations are impromptu and extemporaneous rather than scripted or memorized.

L02 **Organize a presentation.**

Organizing the presentation requires developing an effective opening, developing each point logically in the middle, and closing on a strong, confident note. Use your opening remarks to capture the interest of your audience and build rapport. In the body, choose a logical sequence and deal effectively with any negative information. At the end, summarize your main points and outline the next steps. At any point in your presentation, you may use humor if it is appropriate to the situation.

L03 **Plan a team and online presentation.**

When making a team presentation, allow enough time to prepare, assign responsibilities, and rehearse sufficiently to ensure that the overall presentation has coherence and unity.

When giving an online presentation, keep the audience engaged, be proficient with the technology, and have a backup plan in case the technology fails.

L04 **Develop effective visual support.**

Visuals complement your presentation and help the audience understand your message. When creating presentation slides, present your main points clearly, make your presentation easy to follow, choose an attractive design, replace text with graphics and numbers with charts, and write simply and clearly. Practice using your visuals until you can deliver your presentation seamlessly.

Videos and handouts also can complement your presentation. Use these supplements to further enhance your oral delivery.

L05 **Practice and deliver a presentation.**

Practice your presentation as much as necessary. Use an extemporaneous delivery style—an enhanced conversational tone. Use appropriate hand and arm gestures, but avoid annoying and distracting mannerisms and gestures.

When delivering your presentation, dress appropriately, speak in a clear and confident manner, and maintain eye contact with the audience. If needed, follow the recommended techniques for dealing with speech anxiety. Plan answers to possible questions, and determine beforehand when you will take questions.

Exercises

1. Adapt a presentation for different audiences.

Imagine that you work for a university as the head of transportation. You want to encourage people to take the bus, rather than park on campus, because spots are limited. Prepare agenda slides for two different audiences: faculty and students.

Your presentation may include the challenges of parking on campus, the bus schedule, a cost comparison between driving and taking the bus, and any other information you believe may be relevant to persuade each of your audiences.

L01 Plan a presentation.

2. Prepare a presentation to a Brazilian audience.

The manager of a Brazilian bank has approached your school about the possibility of sending 30 of its managers to your institution to pursue a three-month intensive course in written and oral business communication. The purpose of the course is to make the Brazilian managers better able to interact with their American counterparts.

As the assistant provost at your institution, you have been asked to give a six- to eight-minute presentation to the four Brazilian executives who will decide whether to fund this program at your institution. The purpose of your presentation is to convince them to select your school.

Prepare a title and outline for your presentation.

3. Prepare a presentation to a South Korean audience.

Imagine that you invented a new product that you would like to sell to the South Korean market. The product can be anything consumers might find useful. The audience consists of wealthy individuals from South Korea.

Plan the presentation and determine the timing and method of delivery (the purpose and audience have already been determined). Prepare an outline and submit this to your instructor. In addition to the outline, write a cover memo explaining why you made certain decisions regarding cultural differences.

4. Identify methods of delivery.

For each of the following situations, which delivery method—impromptu, extemporaneous, scripted, or memorized—would be best?

Situation	Ideal Delivery Method
The HR director asks you to present to a group of new employees starting next month, to explain what your department does.	
The VP of your division walks over to your desk with two clients and asks you to describe a new product you're developing.	
You're extremely nervous about an upcoming presentation and are preparing your first two sentences.	
By conference call to 150 analysts across the country, you're explaining why third-quarter profits are down.	

5. Practice different delivery styles.

In small groups, practice each of the four delivery styles. First, each of you chooses a topic that interests you; this can be a hobby, volunteer work, or an aspect of business. Second, prepare to deliver two or three sentences of a presentation about the topic, using the three delivery styles for which you can prepare: extemporaneous, scripted, and memorized. Of course, you'll have to change what you say for each method.

Taking turns, have each person present the four styles using this approach:

1. Deliver your memorized speech.
2. Deliver your scripted presentation.
3. Deliver your extemporaneous presentation.
4. Wait until a team member asks you a related question, and then deliver your response using the impromptu style.

After your presentations, discuss what you learned. Which methods were easiest and most natural for you to deliver? Which were most difficult? How can you adjust to different styles, even though you may be more comfortable with one than the others?

6. Plan a presentation for graduate school.

You decided at the last minute to apply to graduate school to work toward a master's degree in public administration. Even though you have a 3.4 GPA (on a 4.0 scale), you were denied admission because you had not taken the GMAT, which is a prerequisite for admission.

You have, however, been given ten minutes to appear before the Graduate Council to try to convince them to grant you a temporary waiver of this requirement and permit you to enroll in graduate classes next term, during which time you will take the GMAT. The Graduate Council consists of the director of the public administration program and two senior faculty members.

a. What is the purpose of your presentation?
b. What do you know, or what can you surmise, about your audience that might help you prepare a more effective presentation?
c. What points will you include in your presentation?
d. What method of delivery should you use?

7. Prepare an outline for a report presentation.

Review an analytical or recommendation report you prepared in Chapter 10. Assume that you have been given 15 minutes to present the most important information from your written report to a committee of your managers who will not have an opportunity to read the report. What sequencing will you use for your presentation? Prepare an outline for your instructor's feedback.

L02 Organize a presentation.

8. Prepare presentation notes.

Prepare a three-minute oral presentation on a business topic of your choice. First, write out the complete presentation. Next, select several excerpts of the complete script to be used as notes for your presentation. Then, prepare an outline of notes for your presentation. Submit all three versions of the presentation to your instructor for evaluation.

9. Develop an opening for a presentation.

This chapter listed six types of effective openings for an oral presentation—quotation, question, hypothetical situation, story, startling fact, and visual aid. Select two of these methods, and develop effective openings for the same oral presentation. First, plan your presentation by describing your purpose; second, perform an audience analysis by identifying the demographics, the knowledge level, and the psychological needs of a potential audience; third, prepare two effective openings for your presentation, and explain why you selected these types.

10. Deliver a response to the interview question "Tell me about yourself."

First impressions happen particularly quickly during a job interview. Some recruiters will begin your interview with a general question: "Tell me about yourself." Sometimes called "elevator speeches," these presentations can be stressful and awkward if you're unprepared. But once you've developed and practiced a script, you can use parts of it in everyday situations, feeling more natural and confident each time.

Prepare a brief response (30–45 seconds) to the question, and deliver it to the rest of the class. To prepare your notes, you might include the following:

* Year and major or special interests in school
* Work or internship experience
* Skills and abilities
* Anything else you believe is relevant or significant about you (e.g., sports or other interests, hometown)
* What you're looking for (e.g., a summer job in a high-end restaurant)

Also consider these questions:

* What about you will be most relevant and interesting to this person?
* What do you think is this person's attitude toward you?
* What do you want him or her to remember most about you?

After your presentation, write a self-assessment memo that addresses the following questions:

* What did you do that you feel most proud of? What parts of your presentation were most powerful?
* What parts of the presentation do you feel least confident about?
* If you had the opportunity to prepare and deliver this message again, what would you do differently to improve your presentation?

LO3　Plan a team and online presentation.

11. Deliver a speech as part of a team panel.

Prepare a two-minute speech (using note cards) on the business topic of your choice. Then form into groups of six or seven to make up the head table. A few minutes before starting, randomly select roles to be played: host, head table guests (with professional titles), and a guest speaker. The rest of the class will serve as the audience.

The person selected to be the host should quickly obtain the professional titles and names of the people at the head table. Then the host should seat the members of the head table in their chairs. The host should then introduce the people at the head table—including the speaker. The speaker should then give his or her two-minute speech. After the speech is finished, the host should present the speaker with a token of appreciation.

Next, a member of the audience should be selected for an award, such as employee of the year, and the host should invite him or her to the podium to receive the award and to make a short impromptu acceptance speech.

Roles can be changed to allow others to be host, guest at the head table, speaker, or employee of the year. Have everyone submit his or her notes for the two-minute speech whether or not he or she actually spoke.

12. Divide speaking responsibilities for a team presentation.

In teams of three or four, plan how to divide parts of a presentation. Your topic is international copyright laws, and your audience consists of an international group of businesspeople who are concerned about using others' intellectual property. Follow these steps to plan your team presentation:

a. Brainstorm a list of topics for your presentation. Consider what would be valuable to your audience.

b. Create an outline of topics for your presentation. Plan on a logical sequence.

c. Identify how much time you would dedicate to each topic.

d. Select topics to cover in your presentation according to knowledge level and interests. Also select someone to open and close the presentation.

After you have finished your plan, discuss your team process. Is everyone happy with how responsibilities were shared and how the team worked together? Why or why not?

13. Prepare and deliver a team presentation.

Divide into teams of four or five students. Your instructor will assign you to either the pro or the con side of one of the following topics:

- Drug testing should be mandatory for all employees.
- All forms of smoking should be banned from all public spaces.
- Employers should provide flextime (flexible working hours) for all office employees.
- Employers should provide on-site child care facilities for the preschool children of their employees.
- Employees who work with the public should be required to wear a company uniform.

Assume that your employee group has been asked to present its views to a management committee that will make the final decision regarding your topic. The presentations will be given as follows:

a. Each side (beginning with the pro side) will have eight minutes to present its views.

b. Each side will then have three minutes to confer.

c. Each side (beginning with the con side) will deliver a two-minute rebuttal—to refute the arguments and answer the issues raised by the other side.

d. Each side (beginning with the pro side) will give a one-minute summary.

e. The management committee (the rest of the class) will then vote by secret ballot regarding which side (pro or con) presented its case more effectively.

Gather whatever data you think will be helpful to your case, organize it, divide up the speaking roles, and prepare speaker notes. (*Hint:* It might be helpful to gather information on both the pro and the con sides of the issue in preparation for the rebuttal session, which will be given impromptu.)

14. Prepare for an online presentation with remote offices.

Imagine that you work as the purchasing manager who is planning a presentation about a new process for ordering equipment costing over $100,000. Your audience will be the office managers in four locations: the United States (where you are based), Toronto, Geneva, and London. To save travel expenses, you decide to deliver the presentation online through Skype, Google Voice and Video Chat, or another web program.

List the steps you will take to prepare for the presentation. Include everything you would do, up to the point of starting the presentation.

15. Practice delivering and participating in an online presentation.

Working in groups of three or four, have one person deliver a short presentation over the web to the rest of the team. At least two of you (one will be the presenter) will have to sign up for a free account on Skype, Google Voice and Video Chat, or another web program.

Select a presenter, who will be in a separate room from the rest of the team. The presenter can choose any topic relevant to the rest of the team, and this can be an informal presentation.

During the presentation, the rest of the team takes notes on the following. After the presentation, the audience gives feedback to the presenter.

Presentation Feedback

	Not at All	Somewhat	Yes	Definitely
1. Engaged the audience throughout. COMMENTS:	1	2	3	4
2. Demonstrated proficiency with the technology. COMMENTS:	1	2	3	4
3. Used a backup plan effectively. COMMENTS:	1	2	3	4

16. Prepare for an online presentation to fail.

As you did for the previous exercise, plan for one person in another room to present to two or three team members over the web. But this time, imagine that the technology fails. When you begin the presentation, you can see each other, but the audience can't hear you. (Turns out, people on the receiving end had their speakers off—but you don't know that.)

Plan for this to happen, and arrange an alternative (e.g., a speakerphone or a cell phone that has a good speaker). Role-play this situation as realistically as possible. How will the presenter smoothly transition to the alternative?

After the presentation, discuss how well the speaker handled the situation. Discuss lessons you learned for the future.

LO4 Develop effective visual support.

17. Convert a report to slides for an oral presentation.

If you wrote a report using presentation software (discussed in Chapter 10), this is your chance to change it so that you can use it for an oral presentation. Convert heavy text to graphics, convert tables to charts, and edit text until it's concise and readable.

You may find the Dunkin' Donuts slides for an oral presentation (in the Reference Manual) helpful for a comparison.

18. Reduce text on a slide.

If a colleague showed you this slide, how would you help him or her change it? In pairs, work together to reduce the text on this slide to make it easier to read, more logically organized, and more graphical.

LEONARD'S ART GALLERY

- Leonard, the art gallery's chief curator, was born into the business.
- His father and uncle founded the gallery in 1961.
- He was in charge of selecting both art and artists for each gallery show.
- Gallery shows were held six times a year, once every two months.
- Summer and winter months were tough times to sell art.
- Art sold best at the gallery's annual spring opening.
- Leonard's last major sale covered the gallery's operating costs for the coming year.
- Leonard was named after his mother's favorite painter, Leonardo da Vinci.

© CENGAGE LEARNING 2013

19. Convert paragraph text to graphics.

Imagine that you want to present the ideas for using video in presentations from this chapter to a group of people. Convert the Using Video section of this chapter to one slide. Use only a few words, and arrange them in a graphical way.

20. Create a customized slide template.

You are the owner of a mid-sized insurance company. You have 25 agents who travel throughout the country, making presentations to small groups of people (10 to 20) regarding retirement programs.

You want to create a template that all agents can use for their presentations. Your agents have been making their own slides or using no visuals at all, but you want consistency across all regions.

Invent a company name and logo, and then create a template that all agents can use. Choose a design, colors, and a few standard graphics. Include five or six slides in your sample deck—title slide, agenda slide, two or three examples of graphical slides (for example, with SmartArt in PowerPoint), and a closing slide.

21. Evaluate visuals used for a presentation.

Attend a business meeting, a city council meeting, a student council meeting, a business conference, an executive lecture presentation, or some other event where oral presentations will be taking place.

Evaluate the visuals that were used in the presentation. What, if any, visuals were used? Did the presenter have handouts? When were the handouts distributed? How effective were the visuals? What changes could have improved the visuals? Write a one-page memo to your instructor, addressing these and other aspects of how the presentation was delivered.

22. Prepare visuals for a presentation about sales letters.

You are the trainer for a course on effective advertising techniques that is being offered to franchise owners of your Mexican fast-food chain. As part of the course, you are scheduled to present a 30-minute session on writing effective sales letters. You decide to use the sales letter section of Chapter 7 in this book as the basis for your presentation. Prepare four to six slides that you might use for your presentation to the 25 participants in the course. Submit a printed deck to your instructor.

23. Embed a video into a presentation.

If you don't have experience embedding a video into a presentation, research how to embed one into your favorite presentation program (PowerPoint, Keynote, Prezi, or another program). Search YouTube videos and other sources to find step-by-step instructions.

Select any YouTube video or other video that gives you embedding code. Practice inserting it into a new presentation.

For the class, demonstrate how you embedded the video.

24. Integrate a video into a presentation.

Create a presentation to convince your classmates to donate to or volunteer for your favorite not-for-profit organization. Create a title slide, main point slide, agenda slide, a few content slides, and a summary slide.

Find a short (2- to 3-minute) video to complement your message and provide emotional appeal. Embed the video into your presentation, and deliver the presentation, integrating the video seamlessly. For a smooth delivery, introduce your video, and then transition back to the rest of your presentation when the video ends.

25. Discuss whether to use a handout.

Revisit a presentation you delivered recently. In small groups, discuss whether you used a handout, and your rationale. If you had to deliver the presentation again today, would you distribute a handout? Explain your response to your teammates.

26. Create a handout.

Imagine that you're planning a presentation to a group of employees. You want to explain the new, online, time-off request system. Employees will use the system to request vacation time as well as personal days, such as for a doctor's appointment, that they have scheduled in advance. Employees can enter their requests between two weeks and one year before the scheduled time.

Create a handout that will supplement your presentation to employees. In addition to the information above, provide employees with a link to the system and instructions for accessing the system. You can invent these. If you're ambitious, you may create mock-ups of screenshots and include those as well.

27. Research speech anxiety.

Working in groups of three or four, develop at least three slides for a presentation on how to overcome speech anxiety. The presentation would be to ten people in a small boardroom. Use the Internet and other sources as well as information from this chapter for your slides. Remember to use an appropriate background color and to keep the special effects simple. Submit the slides to your instructor for evaluation.

L05   Practice and deliver a presentation.

28. Practice a presentation and track your progress.

Practice an upcoming presentation several times—at least once in the room where you will deliver it. Each time you practice, write notes about your observations and plans for improvements. You might use a simple format such as the following:

	Location	Timing	Major Strengths	Areas to Improve
Practice Round 1				
Practice Round 2				
Practice Round 3				
Practice Round 4				
Practice Round 5				

29. Anticipate and respond to questions about textbook content.

Prepare a three-minute presentation, using an outline, on any section of any chapter in this text. Before making the presentation, write a list of the questions you anticipate being asked and possible answers to those questions. Then, in groups of four or five, take turns delivering your presentation.

After each presentation, the audience should ask the presenter questions about his or her topic. Did the presenter anticipate the questions the group asked? If so, did he or she have effective answers? If not, how did he or she handle the questions that were asked?

Submit a memo to your instructor. The memo should include your outline, a list of the questions you anticipated, your answers to those questions, the actual questions asked (if different from the ones anticipated), and your answers to those questions. Also give your instructor a short post-presentation evaluation of what you did well and what changes you would make to improve your presentation.

30. Prepare a presentation and respond to questions from prospective employees.

Ken Shwartz wants you, the new director of human resources, to recruit more production workers for his hat embroidery company, Ahead Headgear. Based in New Bedford, Massachusetts, Ahead creates caps and visors for golf courses, resorts, and tournaments. Founder and CEO Shwartz has turned Ahead into one of the fastest growing small businesses in the United States.

In just a few years, the company has gone from a start-up operation to a firm that earns more than $18 million in annual sales. However, filling open production jobs can be a struggle. "We have a very high-tech company, but younger workers don't seem to want our production jobs," he tells you. "They equate us with the old, dirty sewing factories."

You decide to make a presentation about Ahead at the next Southern Massachusetts Job Fair, which typically attracts 1,000 high school graduates. You are allotted five minutes to speak to the audience and another five minutes for a question-and-answer period. What kinds of questions do you anticipate? List at least six questions you expect to be asked. Using the Internet or other sources, research Ahead Headgear to find the answers to these questions.

31. Provide feedback.

Using this presentation feedback form, evaluate your own and a peer's presentation. In your comments for each category, be sure to focus on both strengths and areas for development.

Presentation Feedback

	Not at All	Somewhat	Yes	Definitely
1. The organization works well for the topic and is easy to follow. COMMENTS:	1	2	3	4
2. The content is clear and is well supported with details and examples. COMMENTS:	1	2	3	4
3. The delivery style is engaging and appropriate for the audience. COMMENTS:	1	2	3	4
4. Visual support is relevant and interesting. COMMENTS:	1	2	3	4

PersuadeCafé

After all of your hard work proposing an idea for PersuadeCafé, researching the situation, and producing a report, imagine that you're lucky enough to present your recommendation to the executive management team.

Develop your slides to focus on your main points and reinforce your oral delivery. How will you use text and graphics to support your business improvement idea?

As you design your slides, you might consider PersuadeCafé's graphical style. You can see this from the intranet site, menu, and Jackie Marcus's slides. You don't have to use her slides as a template, but for consistency, your visuals should have the look and feel of the company.

Notes

1. Joseph Huff-Hannon, Salon.com, "Inside TED," February 18, 2010, www.salon.com/life/feature/2010/02/18/ted_conference, accessed June 28, 2010.

2. Joseph Huff-Hannon.

3. TED Website, www.ted.com, accessed June 28, 2010.

4. Frank Landry, "Cookie-Eating Health Boss Loses Job," *Toronto Sun*, November 24, 2010, www.torontosun.com, accessed January 1, 2010.

5. Used with permission from Grace Oplinger.

6. "iPhone 4 Press Conference VIDEO: Watch Steve Jobs Announce iPhone 4 Free Case Offer," Huffington Post, July 16, 2010, www.huffingtonpost.com/2010/07/16/iphone-4-press-conference_n_649827.html, accessed March 15, 2011.

7. Steve Jobs, "Apple Events, July 16 Press Conference," http://events.apple.com.edgesuite.net/100716iab73asc/event/index.html, accessed March 15, 2011.

8. Kerry L. Johnson, "You Were Saying," *Managers*, February 1989, 19.

9. Jack McKenna, "The TED v. Sarah Silverman Fight Turns Really Retarded," TechCrunch, February 15, 2010, www.techcrunch.com, accessed January 2, 2011.

10. Used with permission from Michael Pollak.

11. Lynn Russell and Mary Munter, *Guide to Presentations*, 3rd ed., (Upper Saddle River, NJ: Pearson, 2011), 86.

12. Garr Reynolds, "Gates, Jobs, & the Zen Aesthetic," Presentation Zen Blog, November 5, 2005, http://presentationzen.blogs.com, accessed January 4, 2011.

13. Jolie Solomon, "Executives Who Dread Public Speaking Learn to Keep Their Cool in the Spotlight," *The Wall Street Journal*, May 4, 1990, B1.

14. Salman Kahn, "Let's Use Video to Reinvent Education," TED Blog, March 9, 2011, http://blog.ted.com/2011/03/09/lets-use-video-to-reinvent-education-salman-khan-on-ted-com/, accessed July 11, 2011.

Chapter 12

LEARNING OBJECTIVES

After you have finished this chapter, you should be able to

LO1 Write and format a résumé.

LO2 Write a cover letter or inquiry email.

LO3 Present yourself well during an employment interview.

LO4 Follow up throughout the selection process.

LO5 Practice business etiquette in the workplace.

"The hiring process at Google has a lot of mystique behind it, but actually it's pretty simple."

— GOOGLE RECRUITING VIDEO[1]

Chapter Introduction: Getting Hired at Google

I f you're like a lot of students, Google seems like a great place to work—and it is, according to *Fortune Magazine* and undergraduate students' rankings.[2,3] Google offers challenging work, a globally diverse work-

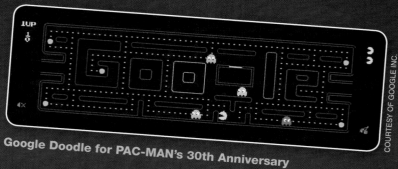

Google Doodle for PAC-MAN's 30th Anniversary

COURTESY OF GOOGLE INC.

force, and plenty of perks. According to Eric Schmidt, CEO, Google, "The goal is to strip away everything that gets in our employees' way. We provide a standard package of fringe benefits, but on top of that are first-class dining facilities, gyms, laundry rooms, massage rooms, haircuts, carwashes, dry cleaning, commuting buses—just about anything a hardworking employee might want."[4]

Google can afford to be selective in hiring future "Googlers." The company has received over 1 million applications in a year and has hired as few as 5,000.[5] According to people close to the company, you can make yourself more attractive by writing an interesting, in-depth cover letter and by having Googlers recommend you.[6]

Starting with a phone interview and often ending with at least four in-person, on-site interviews, the hiring process can be arduous for prospective employees. Google involves a committee of people to ensure the best possible hiring decision. Although this is an extensive process, the company typically communicates decisions within two weeks—worth the wait if you want to work for one of the most sought-after companies in the world.[7]

PUTTING YOUR BEST SELF FORWARD

Applying for a job puts all of your communication skills to the test. This is your chance to impress an employer and land your dream job. Because companies receive many résumés for each open position, how you represent yourself during the employment process will determine whether you are the selected candidate.

Typically, a company will follow a selection process such as that shown in Figure 1. Of course, this process varies by company and position, but these are the usual steps from when a company identifies a hiring need to when a new employee starts the job. Throughout this process, you are putting your best self forward and—if the process goes well—continuously communicating with your future employer.

Communication skills play an important role in the selection process.

PREPARING YOUR RÉSUMÉ

L01 Write and format a résumé.

Your **résumé** summarizes your history and qualifications for a job. The best résumé is tailored to show how your education and work experience have prepared you for a specific job.

The purpose of the résumé is to get you an interview, and the purpose of the interview is to get you a job. You will not likely be hired based on the résumé alone, but your résumé and cover letter will set you apart from potentially thousands of job applicants, as we saw in the Google example.

The purpose of a résumé is to get you a job interview—not to get you a job.

Over 2,500 recruiters in the United States and Canada were asked for their résumé "pet peeves." Their top ten are listed in Figure 2 and offer good advice for preparing your résumé.[8]

In addition to these missteps, one of the worst mistakes you can make on your résumé is lying about your experience or academic background. Lying is common but has severe consequences. Forty-nine percent of managers reported catching lies on résumés, and 57% of those immediately dismissed the candidate.[9]

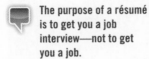
Ethics in Communication

CareerBuilder.com asked hiring managers "to share the most memorable or outrageous lies they came across on résumés." Figure 3 shows what they reported.[10]

Résumé Length

How long should your résumé be? One consideration is how much time employers spend reviewing a résumé: about 60 seconds.[11] This probably seems absurd, considering how much time and energy you'll devote to perfecting your résumé over the years, but this is enough time for an experienced recruiter to quickly decide whether you meet the minimum qualifications for the job.

Most recruiters prefer a one-page résumé for entry-level positions.

Most recruiters prefer one-page résumés from students and new graduates. However, two-page résumés are becoming more acceptable now.[12] If you have been working for a few years and are applying for a higher-level position, then you can continue your résumé onto a second page.

Figure 1
Typical Selection Process

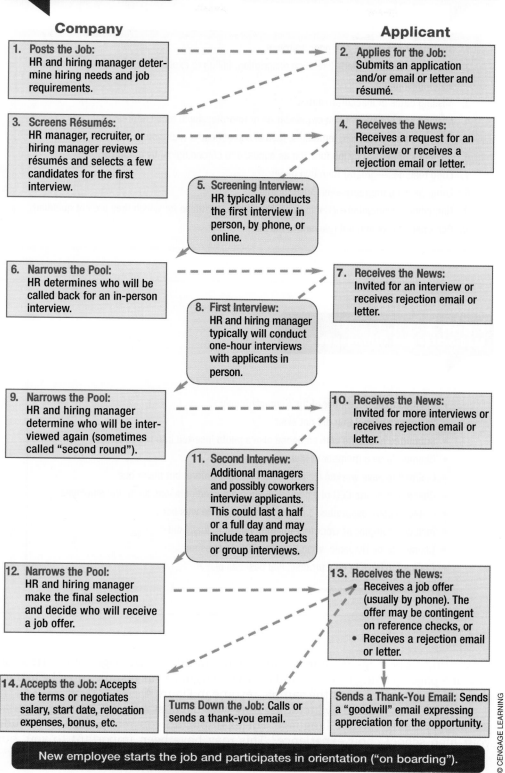

Company

1. **Posts the Job:**
HR and hiring manager determine hiring needs and job requirements.

2. **Applies for the Job:**
Submits an application and/or email or letter and résumé.

3. **Screens Résumés:**
HR manager, recruiter, or hiring manager reviews résumés and selects a few candidates for the first interview.

4. **Receives the News:**
Receives a request for an interview or receives a rejection email or letter.

5. **Screening Interview:**
HR typically conducts the first interview in person, by phone, or online.

6. **Narrows the Pool:**
HR determines who will be called back for an in-person interview.

7. **Receives the News:**
Invited for an interview or receives rejection email or letter.

8. **First Interview:**
HR and hiring manager typically will conduct one-hour interviews with applicants in person.

9. **Narrows the Pool:**
HR and hiring manager determine who will be interviewed again (sometimes called "second round").

10. **Receives the News:**
Invited for more interviews or receives rejection email or letter.

11. **Second Interview:**
Additional managers and possibly coworkers interview applicants. This could last a half or a full day and may include team projects or group interviews.

12. **Narrows the Pool:**
HR and hiring manager make the final selection and decide who will receive a job offer.

13. **Receives the News:**
• Receives a job offer (usually by phone). The offer may be contingent on reference checks, or
• Receives a rejection email or letter.

14. **Accepts the Job:** Accepts the terms or negotiates salary, start date, relocation expenses, bonus, etc.

Turns Down the Job: Calls or sends a thank-you email.

Sends a Thank-You Email: Sends a "goodwill" email expressing appreciation for the opportunity.

Applicant

© CENGAGE LEARNING

New employee starts the job and participates in orientation ("on boarding").

Figure 2
Recruiters' Top Ten Résumé Pet Peeves

1. Spelling errors, typos, and poor grammar
2. Too duty oriented—reads like a job description, failing to explain the job seeker's relevant accomplishments
3. Missing dates or inaccurate dates
4. Missing contact information or inaccurate or unprofessional email addresses
5. Poor formatting—boxes, templates, tables, use of header and footers, etc.
6. Résumés organized by job function as opposed to chronological by employer
7. Long résumés—greater than two pages
8. Long, dense paragraphs—no bullet points
9. Unqualified candidates—candidates who apply to positions for which they are not qualified
10. Personal information not relevant to the job

© CENGAGE LEARNING

Figure 3
Memorable and Outrageous Lies

- Claimed to be a member of the Kennedy family
- Invented a school that did not exist
- Submitted a résumé with someone else's photo inserted into the document
- Claimed to be a member of Mensa
- Claimed to have worked for the hiring manager before, but never had
- Claimed to be the CEO of a company when the candidate was an hourly employee
- Listed military experience dating back to before he was born
- Included samples of work that the interviewer actually did
- Claimed to be Hispanic when he was 100% Caucasian
- Claimed to have been a professional baseball player

© CENGAGE LEARNING

Writing a one-page résumé doesn't mean cramming two pages of information into one page by using tiny text and narrow margins. Your résumé must be attractive and easy to read, as is the sample résumé in Figure 4.

Shorten your résumé by including only what is most relevant to the particular job and by using concise language. For example, do you really need to include your high school choir experience? This may have been important to you, but

Figure 4 Sample Résumé 1 (Chronological)

Uses a simple, creative design; includes clear contact information and a professional email address.

Starts with educational background, most relevant for a graduating student.

Highlights experience to differentiate his candidacy.

Uses bold type to emphasize job title, which is more important than the names of this applicant's employers.

Chooses present tense verbs to describe current responsibilities.

Chooses past tense verbs to describe previous experience.

Includes relevant skills and hobbies (optional).

Marcus C. Benini
1445 College Avenue
Palos Hills, IL 60465
708.555.4539
mbenini@555.com

Education
Moraine Valley Community College, Palos Hills, IL
- Associate in Science Degree (A.S.), 3.8 G.P.A., Expected Graduation 2012
- Dean's List All Semesters
- Coursework: International Business, Fundamentals of Accounting, Business Mathematics, Financial Accounting, Computer Applications in Accounting

The American International University in Rome
Study Abroad, High School Program, Summer 2010
- Lived with a host family for three weeks
- Studied Italian and Introduction to Business Management

Employment
Moraine Valley Community College
Teaching Assistant, Computer Applications in Accounting, (2011-present)
- Assist professor with grading 150 papers each semester
- Hold daily office hours for students
- Provide tutoring on challenging course material

Lakewatch Apartments
Property Accountant (2009-2012)
- Processed all accounts payable including taxes, mortgages, and monthly bills
- Maintained cash receipt journals for various properties
- Processed and deposited rental income
- Maintained general ledger and reconciled all bank statements
- Produced special reports for the partners and investors

Other
- Notary Public, State of Illinois
- Proficient in Peachtree and Microsoft Word, Excel, and Outlook
- Proficient Italian
- Hobbies include guitar, tennis, model airplanes

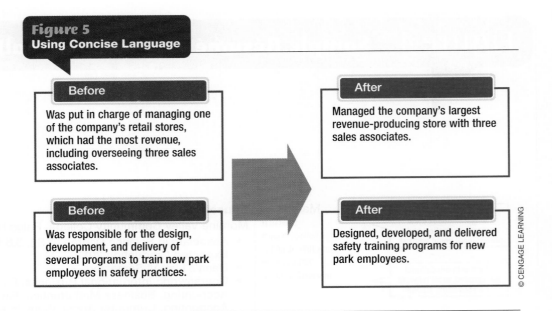

Figure 5
Using Concise Language

Before	After
Was put in charge of managing one of the company's retail stores, which had the most revenue, including overseeing three sales associates.	Managed the company's largest revenue-producing store with three sales associates.
Was responsible for the design, development, and delivery of several programs to train new park employees in safety practices.	Designed, developed, and delivered safety training programs for new park employees.

© CENGAGE LEARNING

perhaps you have more relevant, more recent experience. The before and after examples in Figure 5 show how to describe your experience concisely. In both of these examples, revising the text using principles from Chapter 5 saves valuable résumé space.

On the other hand, don't make your résumé *too* short. A résumé that doesn't fill a page highlights your lack of experience. If you haven't worked many jobs, include more detail for the experience you do have, list your coursework, and write more about your extracurricular activities. You also may use a slightly larger font, more spacing, and more design features (within reason).

Résumé Format

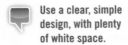

Use a clear, simple design, with plenty of white space.

Although the content of your résumé is obviously more important than the format, a recruiter will get a strong first impression from your design. The format should make your résumé easy for the recruiter to scan and quickly determine whether your background meets the job qualifications. Include lots of white space, easy-to-read fonts, and tasteful design features (for example, columns or horizontal lines). To highlight important content, use font enhancements (bold or italics), bullets, and varied spacing.

You can start with a résumé template in Microsoft Word or another program, but customize the template for your own style. Some of these formats are not appropriate for business positions. The example in Figure 6 is too graphical to be considered a professional résumé.

When you go to a career fair or an interview, bring copies of your résumé. Print it onto white or off-white, 8½ × 11-inch, 20-pound, résumé paper using a high-quality laser printer. For traditional companies, skip the fancy stationery and bright colors. Unless you're applying for a creative position (such as an advertising job), err on the side of conservatism.

Make sure that your résumé is 100% error free.

Finally, your résumé and cover letter must be 100% free from error—in content, spelling, grammar, and format. Ninety-nine percent accuracy is simply not good enough when seeking a job. One survey of large-company executives

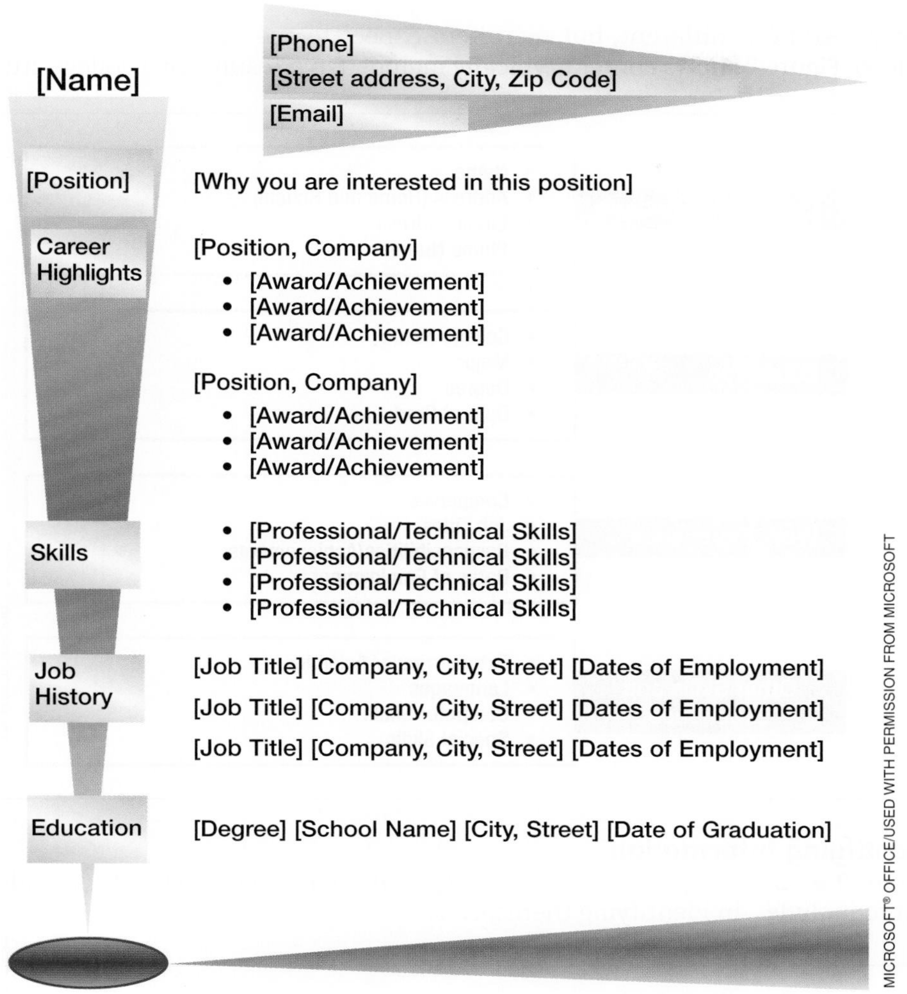

Figure 6
Inappropriate Résumé Template

[Name]

[Phone]
[Street address, City, Zip Code]
[Email]

[Position]   [Why you are interested in this position]

Career Highlights
[Position, Company]
- [Award/Achievement]
- [Award/Achievement]
- [Award/Achievement]

[Position, Company]
- [Award/Achievement]
- [Award/Achievement]
- [Award/Achievement]

Skills
- [Professional/Technical Skills]
- [Professional/Technical Skills]
- [Professional/Technical Skills]
- [Professional/Technical Skills]

Job History
[Job Title] [Company, City, Street] [Dates of Employment]

[Job Title] [Company, City, Street] [Dates of Employment]

[Job Title] [Company, City, Street] [Dates of Employment]

Education
[Degree] [School Name] [City, Street] [Date of Graduation]

MICROSOFT® OFFICE/USED WITH PERMISSION FROM MICROSOFT

showed that one or two typos are enough for 76% of executives to decide not to interview an applicant. Figure 7 shows a few outrageous errors on real résumés.[13]

Proofread carefully. Show right from the start that you're the type of person who takes pride in your work.

Figure 7
Real Errors on Résumés

Hope to hear from you, shorty.

Have a keen eye for derail

Dear Sir or Madman

I'm attacking my résumé for you to review.

I am a rabid typist.

My work ethics are impeachable.

Nervous of steel

Following is a grief overview of my skills.

GPA: 34.0

Graphic designer seeking no-profit career

Include the information employers want; exclude the information they do not want.

Résumé Content

Every résumé is different, but recruiters expect to see some standard parts included. Figure 8 shows content typically included in a résumé of a college student.

Figure 8
Typical Résumé Content

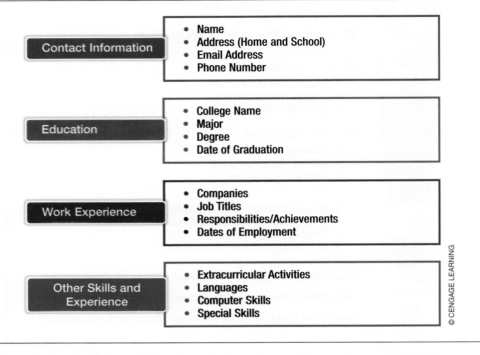

Contact Information	• Name • Address (Home and School) • Email Address • Phone Number
Education	• College Name • Major • Degree • Date of Graduation
Work Experience	• Companies • Job Titles • Responsibilities/Achievements • Dates of Employment
Other Skills and Experience	• Extracurricular Activities • Languages • Computer Skills • Special Skills

© CENGAGE LEARNING

Identifying Information

Figure 9 addresses questions students typically have about what to include—or not to include—in identifying themselves.

Figure 9
Q&A About Identifying Information

Should I include my family's address?	This is optional. If you live on a college campus away from home, companies probably won't send letters to your family's house, but you may include their address if, for example, you're in the process of moving, or your campus mail is unreliable.
Should I include background information about myself, such as my age and ethnicity?	For U.S. résumés, do not include a photograph or any such personal information (e.g., age, ethnicity, religion, sex, marital status, whether you have children). Because it's illegal to hire or not hire someone on the basis of these characteristics, you should not include them.
Can I include my nickname instead of my given name? How about my middle name?	Include your given name so that employers can easily check references. You may also include a nickname if it's significantly different from your given name, for example, "Matsuko (Mike) Takahashi." Include your middle name or middle initial if you use it when signing your name.

© CENGAGE LEARNING

Job Objective

Job objectives on résumés seem to be falling out of favor.[14] Some recruiters believe an objective is obvious—you want the job for which you're applying. Also, you can explain your career objective in your cover letter. Depending on the industry, you might omit an objective, and instead, start with your educational background after your identifying information.

However, you could use an objective to clarify your career goals if, for example, your experience doesn't match the job for which you're applying. Or, instead of an objective, some career professionals suggest a summary of qualifications (shown in Sample Résumé 2 in Figure 11), which identifies your key skills and experience. This is more typical for applicants who have more significant full-time work experience.

If you do include an objective, write one that is clear and specific—but not so specific that you exclude yourself from positions that may interest you.

NOT
- A position that offers an opportunity for growth.
- A challenging position in a progressive organization.
- A responsible position that lets me use my education and experience and that provides opportunities for increased responsibilities.

BUT
- A paid, one-semester internship in marketing or advertising in the Atlanta area.
- A sales position in a medium-sized manufacturing firm.
- An opportunity to apply my accounting education and Spanish-language skills outside the United States.
- A public relations position requiring well-developed communication, administrative, and computer skills.

Education

Figure 10 addresses typical questions from students about the education section of a résumé.

Work Experience

The work experience section of your résumé shows how your previous jobs have prepared you for a future job. Most résumés, for example, Sample Résumé 1, use the chronological format to list work history, starting with the most recent position. In a recent study, HR and other company representatives were asked, "What style of résumé does your company prefer?" An overwhelming 92% responded that they prefer a chronological résumé.[15] By far, this is the most common type of résumé—particularly for college students.

 Employers prefer the chronological résumé style.

In some situations, a functional résumé—organized around skills or job functions—is a better choice. Functional résumés are most appropriate when you're changing industries, moving into an entirely different line of work, or re-entering the workforce after a long period of unemployment. In these situations, functional résumés emphasize your skills rather than your employment history and let you show how these skills have broad applicability to other jobs.

Figure 10 Q&A About Education

Which should come first—my education or experience?	Unless you have extensive work experience, your education is probably your strongest job qualification and therefore comes first on the résumé. After your first full-time job, you might start with your experience and move the education section to the bottom of your résumé.
What if I didn't graduate yet?	You may include language such as "Expected date of graduation." (See Sample Résumé 1 for an example.)
Should I include my grade-point average?	Include your grade-point average if it will set you apart from the competition (generally, at least a 3.3 or 3.5 on a 4.0 scale). If you made the dean's list, write which semesters you achieved this distinction.
Should I include the name of my high school and grade-point average or rank?	After freshman year in college, you can probably omit your high school information unless it might attract attention from a recruiter (e.g., if you attended a highly selective or unique school or if you were valedictorian). By your junior or senior year, you may find that you have more worthy information (work and leadership experience) to fill your one-page résumé.
Should I include a list of classes?	Include classes when you need to fill space or when the classes will distinguish you in some way. Listing core classes that every student takes may not be a differentiator when recruiters are flipping through résumés from students at the same school.

© CENGAGE LEARNING

Sample Résumé 2 (Figure 11) is an example of a functional résumé.[16] For Dina Fowler, a functional résumé is a good choice because she has changed careers—and now wants to make another switch (from a nonprofit organization to a for-profit company). With a chronological format, Dina's résumé would highlight her previous jobs, which do not match her current job objective. Instead, Dina needs to emphasize the *skills* that qualify her for a future position.

Choose the functional format sparingly. Remember that one of the top pet peeves of U.S. and Canadian employers is "résumés organized by job function as opposed to chronological by employer." Functional formats cause recruiters to have to fill-in-the-blanks of your work experience. It's a clever disguise for an imperfect history but makes the screening process more difficult for recruiters.

The purpose of describing your work history is to show prospective employers what you've learned that will benefit his or her organization. From your research about the job you're seeking, highlight your skills and experience that will transfer to the new position. For example, if a position description emphasizes teamwork, be sure to describe examples of your work with others.

 Regardless of which type of organizational pattern you use, provide complete information about your work history.

NOT ▶ Updated the employee directory.

BUT ▶ Worked with liaisons in all departments to update the employee directory.

 Show how your work experience qualifies you for the type of job for which you are applying.

Complete sentences are not necessary. Instead, start your descriptions with action verbs, using present tense for current responsibilities and past tense for

Figure 11 Sample Résumé 2 (Functional)

States her desire to move back to the private sector. Should explain in her cover letter, too.

Provides an overview of her skills.

Organizes around major skill areas relevant to the position she seeks.

Weaves in examples from her experience, where relevant.

Dina Fowler   dinafowler555@gmail.com
612 Madeline Road, Apt. 3B, Newark, NJ 07102   **(973) 555-9648**

POSITION OBJECTIVE

A fundraising or community outreach position for a progressive company

QUALIFICATIONS SUMMARY

Highly organized senior manager with professional experience in the corporate, nonprofit, and government sectors. Proven ability to successfully manage projects and develop diversified fundraising strategies. Exceptional presentation skills; adept at communicating at all organizational levels and with community partners.

SELECTED ACCOMPLISHMENTS

Nonprofit Leadership and Fundraising

- Provided leadership, management, and vision for Bailey Community Center; coordinated fundraising drives, program development, volunteer services, and daily operations; worked with community coalitions and served as the primary spokesperson.

- Created and implemented comprehensive fundraising plan to diversify revenue sources, evaluate results, and engage board members in soliciting donations.

- Instituted new major donor solicitations and direct-mail fundraising campaigns resulting in 20% increase in annual fundraising revenues.

- Researched and secured new foundation and government grants through meticulous proposal writing. Managed and improved profit margin of large-scale fundraising events.

- Implemented structured volunteer services including recruitment, communications, and appreciation events for almost 100 regular volunteers at Bailey.

Project Management

- Administered all aspects of scholarship program for low-income students attending college. Managed collaboration between Newark County and private scholarship foundation, applicant recruitment, selection process, and annual press event.

- Organized and expanded annual conference on issues concerning homelessness; increased attendance 25% to almost 450 participants over three years; managed logistics and tasks for volunteer committee.

Figure 11   (Continued)

Dina Fowler   **page 2**

- Recommended and advocated for public policy changes. Tracked developments in policy on the local, state, and national levels to advise executive director on appropriate positions.

- Coordinated coalition of over 50 nonprofit and advocacy agencies to work for passage of community housing legislation.

- Worked on corporate-wide, human resources computer system conversion for Black & Decker. Analyzed and redesigned all business processes for most effective use of new technology and alignment with corporate standards.

Training and Education

- Created and managed new computer training department for 2,800 employees at the University of Maryland; responsible for computer and furniture procurement, internal marketing, scheduling, enrollment, training delivery, and management reporting.

- Designed and delivered hands-on computer training in PeopleSoft HRMS; and Microsoft Word, Excel, PowerPoint, and Access.

- Developed, marketed, and presented training programs on hunger and homelessness issues for hundreds of people in law enforcement, social service agencies, schools, corporations, and religious organizations.

WORK HISTORY

2010 – present	Assistant Executive Director, Newark Coalition for the Hungry and Homeless, Newark, NJ
2007 – 2010	Executive Director, Bailey Community Services Center, Newark, NJ
2003 – 2007	Computer Instructor, University of Maryland, College Park, MD
2000 – 2003	Programmer/Analyst, Black & Decker Corporation, Baltimore, MD

EDUCATION AND SKILLS

Rutgers University, Rutgers Business School, B.S. in Management, 2002

Intermediate Spanish

Annotations:

Provides a summary of her history toward the end of the résumé.

Should explain in her cover letter why she moved from an "executive director" to "assistant" (e.g., because it's a much larger corporation). Otherwise, this could be a red flag.

Should explain in her cover letter that she attended school part-time to complete her degree.

© CENGAGE LEARNING

previous job responsibilities or accomplishments. Use concrete words such as the following to explain your work experience:

accomplished	constructed	increased	produced
achieved	coordinated	instituted	purchased
administered	created	interviewed	recommended
analyzed	delegated	introduced	renovated
applied	designed	investigated	reported
approved	determined	led	researched
arranged	developed	maintained	revised
authorized	diagnosed	managed	screened
budgeted	directed	modified	secured
built	edited	negotiated	simplified
changed	established	operated	sold
communicated	evaluated	organized	supervised
completed	generated	oversaw	trained
conceived	guided	planned	transformed
concluded	hired	prepared	updated
conducted	implemented	presented	wrote

Use concrete, achievement-oriented words to describe your experience.

Avoid weak verbs such as *attempted, hoped,* and *tried.* When possible, list specific accomplishments, giving numbers or dollar amounts. Highlight accomplishments that have direct relevance to the desired job.

Stress specific accomplishments directly related to the desired job.

> **NOT** ▶ I was responsible for a large sales territory.

> **BUT** ▶ Managed a six-county sales territory; increased sales 13% during first full year.

> **NOT** ▶ I worked as a clerk in the cashier's office.

> **BUT** ▶ Balanced the cash register every day; was the only part-time employee entrusted to make nightly cash deposits.

> **NOT** ▶ Worked as a bouncer at a local bar.

> **BUT** ▶ Maintained order at Nick's Side-Door Saloon; resolved several disputes without police intervention.

> **NOT** ▶ Sold tickets for Art Reach.

> **BUT** ▶ Sold more than $1,000 worth of tickets to annual benefit dance; introduced "Each One, Reach One" membership drive that increased membership every year during my three-year term as membership chair.

In the experience section, you may include unpaid internships and volunteer work. Employers will not likely care whether you were paid for jobs listed under "Experience"—they are just interested in the skills you developed. Include relevant volunteer work that may have helped you develop skills in managing time, working with groups, handling money, organizing tasks, and managing people. However, employers may consider it a stretch to include volunteer work under "Work Experience." Instead, consider adding a section called "Other Relevant Experience" or broadening the "Work Experience" title to "Relevant Experience."

Include relevant unpaid positions.

If you started your own business, include it in the work experience section. Emphasize your entrepreneurial skills, but be careful about overstating your experience (for example, referring to yourself as "CEO, President, and COO"). Here's one description of a start-up business.

Cathy Lin Bracelets, New York, NY
Founder and Owner

- Managed business to produce over $15,000 annual revenue last fiscal year
- Designed and sold custom bracelets for over 250 customers since inception
- Marketed through flyers and word-of-mouth
- Maintained all records in Microsoft Excel
- Managed large inventory of handmade beads

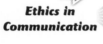

Ethics in Communication

Your résumé represents you in the best possible light. Of course you'll highlight your strengths and minimize your weaknesses. However, be careful about taking credit for accomplishments that weren't yours (or yours alone) and about exaggerating responsibilities. A simple telephone call can verify any statement on your résumé. During an interview, the employer will push for details about your past responsibilities. It will be obvious if you didn't do what you claim on your résumé. This may be embarrassing for you—and for your school.

Other Relevant Information

Figure 12 addresses questions students typically have about other information to include on a résumé.

Figure 12
Q&A About Other Relevant Information

What should I call the last section on my résumé where I have additional skills?	Here are a few options: "Leadership and Other Experience," "Other Relevant Experience," "Extracurricular Activities," or "Other Skills and Qualifications." Choose a heading that summarizes your additional qualifications for the job.
What type of information should I include?	Include anything relevant to the job or interesting to an employer: professional, athletic, or social clubs and organizations; volunteer experience; language skills; honors and awards; and computer skills, particularly programs important for an industry. If you held a leadership position in a club or organization, include the title and perhaps some of your responsibilities.
Should I include high school information here? I was on the varsity football team for three years (or I was the president of the chess club for two years).	After your college freshman year, you may want to omit all high school information. Unless the activity is very relevant to the job (e.g., you started a culinary club, and you're applying for a job as a prep chef), you will probably have more recent and relevant information from college to emphasize.
How do I represent my language skills?	Consider these categories to describe your language skills: basic, conversational, intermediate, proficient, fluent. If you're unsure, ask your language instructor for an assessment. Also, imagine yourself in front of an interviewer who is fluent in this language. How would you do?
Where do I include my study abroad experience?	You may include your study abroad experience in the last section or within the education section at the beginning of your résumé. Consider including the university name, location, dates, and possibly your coursework.
Should I include names of references or "References on Request" on my résumé?	You should omit both. Including information about references on your résumé is considered a waste of valuable résumé space.[17] Just prepare a list of people who can vouch for you so you're ready when an employer asks.

Applications for international jobs often require a **CV**, or **curriculum vitae**, a longer version of a résumé. Although personal information, such as height, weight, marital status, and children, is more common on CVs than on résumés, this information is not required and is best omitted.

Keywords

Keywords on your résumé may make the difference between getting an interview and landing in the reject pile. If you post your résumé on a site such as Monster .com, employers may use keywords to search for qualified candidates. Also, most large companies—and some small—have an **applicant tracking system**, which will search your résumé for keywords. Only 3% of companies surveyed recently prefer scannable résumés (a text-only format),[18] but if this format is requested, you'll certainly want to use good keywords that will be automatically selected by a database. Here are a few tips when considering keywords for your résumé:

Choose nouns for describing your work experience.

- Think of nouns instead of verbs (users rarely search for verbs). Browse other online résumés, job postings, and industry publications to find industry-specific terms.

- Put keywords in proper context, weaving them throughout your résumé. This is a more sophisticated approach than listing them in a block at the beginning of the résumé.

- Use a variety of words to describe your skills, and don't overuse important words. In most searches, each word counts once, no matter how many times it is used.

As a starting point, look at a few job postings. From a job posting, you can determine which words may be most important to employers (see highlighted words in Figure 13). Then, you can incorporate these words into bulleted descriptions

---

Figure 13
Key Words in an Ad

Human Resources Recruiter

Core Job Responsibilities:
- Write job descriptions and identify job requirements
- Screen résumés
- Conduct screening interviews in person and online
- Conduct in-person behavioral interviews
- Organize candidates' interview schedules with managers
- Make selection decisions working with managers
- Manage high school and college intern programs
- Work with an assistant for administrative support

Qualifications and Skills:
- Bachelor's degree required
- Strong interpersonal skills
- Ability to work with all levels of management
- Proficient use of Microsoft Office software
- Strong writing and editing skills
- Experience working with a recruitment management system a plus
- Meticulous organization and follow-up skills
- Professional in Human Resources (PHR) certification preferred

KEYWORDS: job descriptions, selection decisions
- Worked with managers to write job descriptions and make final selection decisions.

KEYWORDS: résumés, intern
- Screened résumés of interns and full-time applicants to determine qualifications.

KEYWORDS: interviews, online, intern
- Conducted interviews in person, by phone, and online for full-time and intern hires.

KEYWORDS: Microsoft Office, recruitment management system
- Used Microsoft Office products (Word, Excel, and PowerPoint) and Earrow Recruitment Management System (RMS).

KEYWORDS: bachelor's degree, PHR
- Earned a bachelor's degree from the University of North Carolina, 2012, and earned a PHR (Professional in Human Resources) certification in 2013.

KEYWORDS: interpersonal, writing, organization
- Impeccable organizational skills, strong business writing skills, and excellent interpersonal communication skills.

on a résumé (Figure 14). Weaving these keywords into your cover letter also may increase your chances of being selected and will ensure a cohesive approach to your application.

Because your résumé is about you, it is perhaps the most personal business document you'll ever write. Use everything you know about effective communication to tell your story in the best way possible.

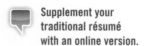

Communication Technologies

Résumés on the Web

Although you may submit your résumé through your school's career management system, through a company website, or as an attachment to an email, you may create an online résumé and supplemental materials as well.

Online Résumé and Portfolio

Supplement your traditional résumé with an online version.

Online résumés that link to supplemental materials are becoming more popular. In an email, you can link to an online résumé, which you can store on sites such as Monster, Résumé Bucket, or Google Docs. Sample Résumé 3 (Figure 15) is a creative version designed and stored at VisualCV (www.visualcv.com).[19] With links and examples of your work, you'll tell a prospective employer more extensive information about you.

Figure 15 Sample Résumé 3 (Online)

View My VisualCV Online: http://www.visualcv.com/adambarrera

Adam Barrera

Automotive Analyst – Social Media

Houston, United States
Detroit, United States (July 2010)
Last Updated: 30 April 2010

m: +1.713.443.0708

adam-vcv@highmileage.org

Breaking News and Video Reviews

ExpoTV	AutoTrader.com	YouTube	Speed:Sport:Life

Honest video critique and analysis of new vehicles targeted toward tech-savvy car shoppers.	Concise short-form coverage of SEMA, Seattle, and Los Angeles auto shows.	Owner community-focused niche coverage aimed at engaging passionate enthusiasts.	Time-critical industry news, accurately relayed through rich media.

Welcome

I'm Adam, a proud recent graduate of the Jack Valenti School of Communication at the University of Houston. During my years spent delivering auto industry analysis and commentary, I've most enjoyed connecting impassioned car enthusiasts with the brands they love.

I've helped GM connect with fans via live video during the Camaro launch, webcast and live-Tweeted a cross-country drive in the Ford Fiesta, and even microblogged my experience drifting a pre-production Mustang in Japan. My #firstshots campaign aims to bring -- and succeeds in bringing -- the first live photos of vehicles revealed at auto shows. At the New York International Auto Show, RebelIndustries noticed my unprompted interaction with Mazda fans and subsequently invited me to run Mazda's Twitter feed for the brief hours before my outbound flight.

Reaching car buyers via newsprint, digital ink, and broadcast television has always been a rush, but I recognize that I'm most exhilarated -- and effective -- when acting as a brand ambassador. I'm moving to Detroit to pursue a full-time career in automotive public relations. If you can help me achieve that dream, get in touch using the methods above. Let's save car culture!

Honors and Accolades

1st Place - Excellence in Video
Awarded by Texas Auto Writers Association, 14 November 2008
Independent judges bestowed top honors upon my coverage of the New York International Auto Show.

Editor's Pick
Awarded by ExpoTV on 12 November 2007 and 7 May 2008
"An excellent and comprehensive review of this compact car, inside and out."

Live Updates, 24/7!

twitter

Experience today's freshest metal firsthand through a constantly updated, mostly unedited, and inherently honest video microblog. Counter-commentary is always welcome. Visit highmileage on Twitter!

I'm great at using social media to report breaking automotive news 1ST! A live list of my exclusives: highmileage1ST

Automotive Videojournalism

2010 Mazda 3 x 2010 Kia Forte Review

You Tube

Self-filmed, scripted, edited and captioned comparison of these fun-focused compact sedans.

2009 Dodge Journey Review

You Tube

Self-filmed, scripted, edited, and produced critique of this versatile people-mover.

2008 Texas Auto Writers Association Excellence in Video Winner: 2008 New York International Auto Show – Dream Cars

You Tube

This video won first place in the 2008 TAWA Excellence in Video competition. Check out my coverage of the '08 NYIAS on

Figure 15 (*Continued*)

View My VisualCV Online: http://www.visualcv.com/adambarrera

These reviews were prominently featured as a "showcase review" on ExpoTV's homepage.

2006 Solo II Season Champion – C Street Prepared
Awarded by <u>South Texas Border Region Sports Car Club of America</u>. January 2007

Autowriters.com Spotlight
Profiled in <u>Autowriters.com</u> newsletter, July 2006
This industry publication asked to print a <u>biography detailing my burgeoning career</u>.

Interactive Work History

ExpoTV

Circulation: 30 Million Nationwide – New York City, United States   2006 – 2009

Automotive Category Leader

– <u>Critiqued new vehicles</u> while leveraging the powerful medium of video to ensure fairness and accuracy.
– Engaged userbase by moderating <u>category questions</u>, maintaining an <u>automotive blog</u>, and providing video <u>production guides</u>.
– <u>Covered NY Int'l. Auto Show</u> in 2007 and 2008 by researching vehicles, focusing content, and anchoring show. <u>Distributed to 30 million</u> digital-cable homes throughout VOD.

University of Houston Daily Cougar

Circulation: 40,000 – Houston, United States   2005 – 2006

Staff Reporter – Health, Engineering, Consumer

• Uncovered -- <u>and ended</u> -- unfair foodservice pricing.
• Highlighted student <u>Society of Automotive Engineers' accomplishments</u>.
• Sought out <u>unique health stories</u> and <u>placed them into student-relevant context</u>.
• Covered Houston Auto Show from <u>2005</u>–<u>2008</u>.

Interactive Education History

University of Houston – Jack Valenti
School of Communication

Houston, United States   Aug 2003 – May 2008

B.A. – Linguistics; B.A. – Print Journalism

Curriculum emphasized <u>journalism ethics</u>, <u>automotive cultural studies</u>, <u>emerging language trends.</u>

Skills Honed in the Field

• Strong relationships with colleagues, production personnel, and most auto manufacturers' PR teams. References available.
• Proficient in, and comfortable with, the video production process. Shooting, editing, scripting, and production using the Adobe suite and PC tools.
• Optimistic disposition. Unique awareness of manufacturers' obligations and buyers' expectations.
• Eager to adopt emerging media platforms to reach as many audiences as possible.

Selected Print Articles

<u>Behind Domed Doors: At GM, R&D means "Research and Design"</u>. Speedsportlife.com, 13 August 2009. Teaser coverage intended to augment social media coverage of this event.

<u>2009 Pikes Peak International Hill Climb: Before the Hillside Shifts.</u> Speedsportlife.com, 29 July 2009. Event coverage enriched with historical context and cultural commentary.

ExpoTV's Digital Cable On-Demand channel!

Car Temperature PSA

Self-produced PSA. NEVER leave a child alone in a hot car!

Automotive Photojournalism

Modern Nissan Design Details

You Tube

Zama, Japan

Ford Escape Hybrid

Published in Auto Finance News, Pikes Peak, United States

Mazda RX-7

Houston, United States

Video Résumé

In addition to an online résumé, you might consider producing a video résumé (Figure 16). Video résumés are a good way to show more of your personality, particularly for jobs that require strong people skills. You could try your hand at producing your own video and uploading it to YouTube, or you might choose a more sophisticated approach through a dedicated video résumé website.

> Video résumés are becoming more popular.

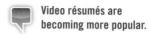
Figure 16
Video Résumé on YouTube

COURTESY OF DAVID PEDERSEN

WRITING COVER LETTERS AND INQUIRY EMAILS

> LO2 Write a cover letter or inquiry email.

When you send your résumé to a potential employer, you will typically include a cover letter. This may be sent as an email with the résumé attached, which is the most preferable way for employers to receive your résumé.[20] Or you may be asked by on-campus recruiters to submit a cover letter with your résumé so they can see a writing sample and how you present yourself. Also, to expand your job search, you will likely contact people who don't have advertised jobs. We'll look at formal cover letters and these inquiry emails next.

Cover Letters

> Use the cover letter (often your first contact with an employer) to tailor your qualifications to one specific job.

A **cover letter** tells a prospective employer that you are interested in and qualified for a position within the organization. An effective cover letter will achieve the following:

- Express your interest in the company and the position
- Highlight how your background specifically matches job qualifications
- Reveal some of your personality
- Demonstrate your business writing skills
- Provide the employer with logistical information: how you can be reached and when you're available to work

Your cover letter is a sales letter—you're selling your qualifications to the prospective employer. This is your chance to differentiate yourself and pique the employer's interest in you as a candidate. Ideally, a recruiter reads your cover letter and thinks, "I'd like to meet this person." You want to sound confident and professional, without being too boastful or presumptuous.

Typically, cover letters for entry-level jobs are one page long, as in the Sample Cover Letter (Figure 17). This should be enough space to achieve your goals.

Figure 17   Sample Cover Letter

140 West Hill Avenue
Fullerton, CA 92832

Uses traditional formatting for a letter.

October 17, 2013

Brenda Diaz
Young & Rubicam
285 Madison Avenue
New York, NY 10017

Dear Ms. Diaz:

Begins with a catchy way to express interest.

For two years, I've been hoping Young & Rubicam would visit the Fullerton campus, so I was excited to see the summer position posting for Public Relations Assistant. As a junior concentrating in PR, I have read several case studies about Y&R, and I would like to see your work firsthand. From my coursework and PR experience, I'm confident that I have the strong written and oral communication skills you require for the position.

Summarizes his background and why he is writing.

Includes topic sentence for recruiters who skim.

In addition to excelling in my PR-focused courses, I have been selected as a teaching assistant for two classes: Public Relations Writing and Writing for Mass Media. In Public Relations Writing, we wrote social media press releases, which challenged us to present companies in a positive light and capture media attention. In Writing for Mass Media, we worked with a real client—a local not-for-profit organization—to help it get publicity for a capital campaign. In both classes, I developed my writing skills and learned the importance of clear, concise communication.

Describes how his education may be relevant to the position.

Emphasizes skills that are required for the position.

As a teaching assistant, I review students' draft assignments and give them feedback to improve their writing. Working as a TA has developed my oral communication skills. I now feel confident in giving students positive feedback while encouraging them to improve.

Describes relevant work experience and what he learned.

Last summer, I worked with a small communications strategy firm in New York City. At Hiltzik Strategies, I worked closely with the owner to develop communication plans for high-profile clients such as Alec Baldwin. During the summer, the company dealt with a crisis situation, and I learned a great deal about how to respond quickly to avoid negative publicity.

Explains his particular interest in Y&R.

This summer I'd like to experience working with a larger company, and Y&R would be ideal. I'm sure I can contribute my written and oral communication skills—and my enthusiasm and strong work ethic—to have a successful experience with the company.

Closes with logistical information and his plan to follow up.

My résumé describes more of my work experience and leadership activities on campus. I am available to work anytime between May 15 and August 15. I will call you next week to follow up, or you may reach me at 213-555-6720 or at ps555@fullerton.edu. Thank you, and I look forward to speaking soon.

Sincerely,

Peter Steinberg

© CENGAGE LEARNING

Although it's often still referred to as a "letter," a cover letter may be sent as an email message. Forty-one percent of employers prefer receiving a résumé by email.[21] In this case, it's best to attach your résumé as a PDF file so that your formatting will be retained. You also should shorten your traditional cover letter and place the body text (without the letter formatting) within the email, rather than attaching it as a file. This avoids the receiver having to open two attachments. Compare the Sample Cover Letter (Figure 17) with the Sample Email (Figure 18) to see the difference.

Communication Technologies

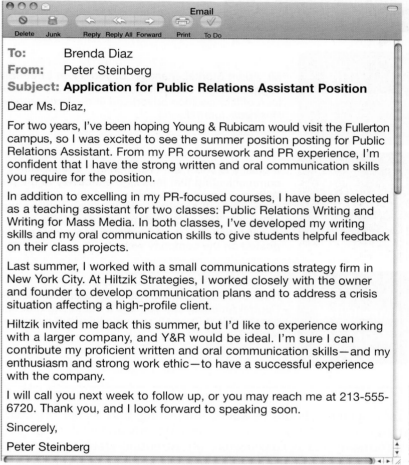

Figure 18
Sample Email

To: Brenda Diaz
From: Peter Steinberg
Subject: **Application for Public Relations Assistant Position**

Dear Ms. Diaz,

For two years, I've been hoping Young & Rubicam would visit the Fullerton campus, so I was excited to see the summer position posting for Public Relations Assistant. From my PR coursework and PR experience, I'm confident that I have the strong written and oral communication skills you require for the position.

In addition to excelling in my PR-focused courses, I have been selected as a teaching assistant for two classes: Public Relations Writing and Writing for Mass Media. In both classes, I've developed my writing skills and my oral communication skills to give students helpful feedback on their class projects.

Last summer, I worked with a small communications strategy firm in New York City. At Hiltzik Strategies, I worked closely with the owner and founder to develop communication plans and to address a crisis situation affecting a high-profile client.

Hiltzik invited me back this summer, but I'd like to experience working with a larger company, and Y&R would be ideal. I'm sure I can contribute my proficient written and oral communication skills—and my enthusiasm and strong work ethic—to have a successful experience with the company.

I will call you next week to follow up, or you may reach me at 213-555-6720. Thank you, and I look forward to speaking soon.

Sincerely,

Peter Steinberg

© CENGAGE LEARNING

Address and Salutation

Your letter should be addressed to an individual rather than to an organization or department. Ideally, your letter should be addressed to the person who will interview you and who will likely be your manager if you get the job. Make sure you have the right name—and the correct spelling—and position title. In your salutation, use a courtesy title (such as *Mr.* or *Ms.*) along with the person's last name. If you're unsure of the person's gender, spell out the full name: "Dear Chris Warren." If you don't have someone's name, use a generic title: "Dear Human Resources Manager" or "Dear Hiring Manager."

Opening

The opening paragraph of a **solicited cover letter** is fairly straightforward. Because the organization has advertised the position, it wants to receive quality applications, so use a direct organization: state (or imply) the reason for your letter, identify the position for which you're applying, and indicate how you learned about the opening.

 Use the direct organizational plan for writing a solicited cover letter.

Tailor your opening to the job and to the specific organization. For conservative companies (e.g., financial services), use a restrained opening. For more creative work (e.g., sales, advertising, and public relations), you might start out on a more imaginative note. Finally, for **unsolicited cover letters**, which you initiate rather than responding to a job posting, you must first get the reader's attention. Try talking about the company—a recent project or a new product launch—and then show how you can contribute to the corporate effort (Figure 19).

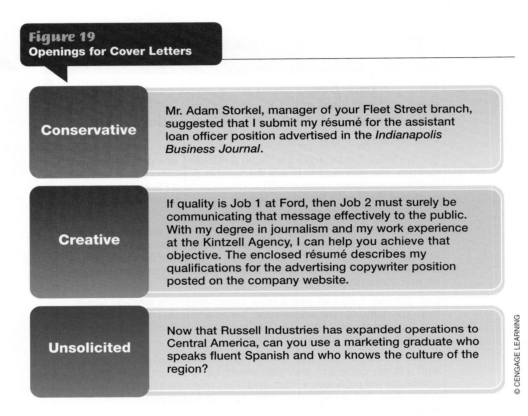

Figure 19
Openings for Cover Letters

Conservative — Mr. Adam Storkel, manager of your Fleet Street branch, suggested that I submit my résumé for the assistant loan officer position advertised in the *Indianapolis Business Journal*.

Creative — If quality is Job 1 at Ford, then Job 2 must surely be communicating that message effectively to the public. With my degree in journalism and my work experience at the Kintzell Agency, I can help you achieve that objective. The enclosed résumé describes my qualifications for the advertising copywriter position posted on the company website.

Unsolicited — Now that Russell Industries has expanded operations to Central America, can you use a marketing graduate who speaks fluent Spanish and who knows the culture of the region?

© CENGAGE LEARNING

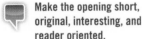 Make the opening short, original, interesting, and reader oriented.

Your opening should be short, interesting, and reader oriented. Avoid tired openings such as "Please consider this letter my application for. . . ." Maintain an air of formality and avoid being too cute. Attention-grabbing gimmicks send a non-verbal message to the reader that the applicant may be trying to deflect attention from a weak résumé.

Body

 Don't repeat all the information from the résumé.

In a paragraph or two, highlight your strongest qualifications and show how they can benefit the employer. Show—don't tell; provide specific, credible evidence to support your statements, using different wording from that used in the résumé. Give an example to make the bullets on your résumé come alive and help the recruiter visualize your experience.

> **NOT** As stated on my résumé, I sometimes went on sales calls.

> **BUT** Once, I went on a sales call with the president of Scholastic, Inc.'s Education division, and we closed a $150,000 deal—the largest for the Ugo software product. From observing the sales manager, I learned. . . .

Your letter also should reflect modest confidence rather than a hard-sell approach. Avoid starting too many sentences with *I*.

NOT I am an effective supervisor.

BUT Supervising a staff of five bank tellers taught me. . . .

NOT I am an accurate person.

BUT In my two years of experience as a student research assistant, none of the spreadsheets I maintained ever came back with corrections.

NOT I took a class in business communication.

BUT The communication strategies I learned in my business communication class will help me resolve customer issues as a customer service representative at Allegheny Industries.

Refer the reader to the enclosed résumé. Subordinate the reference to the résumé and emphasize instead what the résumé contains.

NOT I am enclosing a copy of my résumé for your review.

BUT As detailed in the enclosed résumé, my extensive work experience in records management has prepared me to help you "take charge of this paperwork jungle," as mentioned in your classified ad.

Closing

Close your letter by asking for a personal interview. Indicate flexibility regarding scheduling and location. Provide your phone number and email address, either in the last paragraph or immediately below your name and address in the closing lines.

Politely ask for an interview.

> After you have reviewed my qualifications, I would appreciate your letting me know when we can meet to discuss my employment with Connecticut Power and Light. I will be in the Hartford area from December 16 through January 4 and could come to your office at any time that is convenient for you.

Or you might try a more proactive approach. Because companies receive so many résumés, one way to distinguish yourself is to follow up with a phone call.

> I will call your office next week to see whether we can arrange a meeting to discuss my qualifications for the financial analyst position.

Use a standard closing, such as "Sincerely." For letters you send through the mail, leave enough space to sign the letter, and then type your name. For a version you send by email, just skip a line, and type your name below "Sincerely."

Inquiry Emails

When you don't know of a specific position available but want to express interest in a company, you can send an email—sometimes called a **networking email** or request for an informational interview. This is a good way to find job openings that may not be advertised or simply to learn more about a company and professionals in your area of interest. You might find an appropriate contact through one of the following:

Write networking emails to expand your job search.

- Your school's alumni database
- Friends and family
- The company's website
- Articles about the company

**Figure 20
Sample Inquiry
Email**

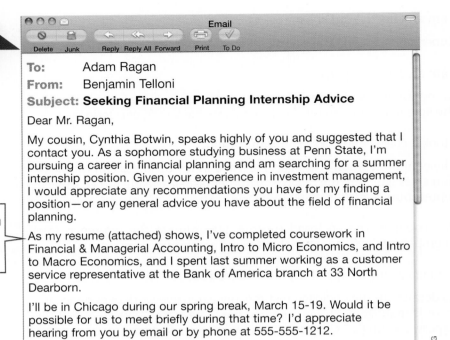

To: Adam Ragan
From: Benjamin Telloni
Subject: Seeking Financial Planning Internship Advice

Dear Mr. Ragan,

My cousin, Cynthia Botwin, speaks highly of you and suggested that I contact you. As a sophomore studying business at Penn State, I'm pursuing a career in financial planning and am searching for a summer internship position. Given your experience in investment management, I would appreciate any recommendations you have for my finding a position—or any general advice you have about the field of financial planning.

As my resume (attached) shows, I've completed coursework in Financial & Managerial Accounting, Intro to Micro Economics, and Intro to Macro Economics, and I spent last summer working as a customer service representative at the Bank of America branch at 33 North Dearborn.

I'll be in Chicago during our spring break, March 15-19. Would it be possible for us to meet briefly during that time? I'd appreciate hearing from you by email or by phone at 555-555-1212.

Thank you for your consideration.

Regards,

Benjamin Telloni

> In an email, spell resume without the accents to avoid problems with character recognition. It's acceptable to use this spelling in your cover letters too.

© CENGAGE LEARNING

Typically, an inquiry email is shorter than a cover letter (Figure 20).

You may not hear back from everyone who receives your inquiry email, but it's worth a shot. Making these connections is a good way to practice your networking skills.

The Checklist for Writing Cover Letters summarizes guidelines presented in this section.

Checklist for Writing Cover Letters   GO

☑ Use your cover letter to show how the qualifications listed in your résumé have prepared you for the specific job for which you're applying.

☑ If possible, address your letter to the individual in the organization who will interview you.

☑ When applying for an advertised opening, begin by stating (or implying) the reason for the letter, identify the position for which you're applying, and tell how you learned about the opening.

☑ When writing an unsolicited cover letter, gain the reader's attention by showing that you are familiar with the company and can make a unique contribution to the business.

☑ In one or two paragraphs, highlight your strongest qualifications and relate them directly to the needs of the specific position. Refer the reader to the enclosed résumé.

☑ Treat your letter as a persuasive sales letter: provide specific evidence, stress reader benefits, avoid exaggeration, and show confidence in the quality of your product.

☑ Close by tactfully asking for an interview.

☑ Maintain an air of formality throughout the letter.

☑ Make sure the finished document presents a professional, attractive, and conservative appearance and that it is 100% error free.

PREPARING FOR A JOB INTERVIEW

Almost all employers require at least one employment interview before extending a job offer, even for summer internships. Employers use interviews to verify information on the résumé, learn more about your experience, and get to know you personally. Your skills and experience are important, but many companies today are also looking for an **organizational fit**—someone who will work well within the organizational culture.[22] Be yourself—and be likable. If you have the right experience but present yourself as too arrogant or too timid, you may lose the chance.

Of course, the interview is a good opportunity for you too. You're evaluating the organization as much as the interviewer is evaluating you. Is this the right fit for *you*? You'll learn about the company from the questions the interviewer asks, how he or she reacts to you and your responses, and how he or she answers your questions.

Researching the Organization

You wouldn't walk into a potential customer's office without knowing about the company. The same is true for your interview. Learn everything you possibly can about the organization. Research the specific organization in depth, using the research techniques you developed from Chapter 9. Learn about the company's products and services, history, financial health, corporate structure, locations, and recent news.

You might find interesting information about the company through social media. Look at career websites, such as Glassdoor and Vault, where employees post comments. Many of these are petty and griping, but repeated comments may tell you about the inner workings of the company. Also explore analysts' ratings and customers' reviews and comments.

Think about the context of the company's competitors and the industry. By relating what you've learned about the company into the broader perspective of the industry, you can discuss issues affecting the company more intelligently. No one is impressed by the interviewee who, out of the blue, spouts, "I see your stock went up $5 last week." However, in response to the interviewer's comment about the company's recent announcement of a new product line, it would be appropriate to say, "I saw that the stock spiked last week." If you raise former employees' snarky comments, the interviewer may feel defensive. But if an interviewer from Time Warner Cable admits to a lot of change recently, you can simply say, "Yes, I saw some employee comments online about layoffs. I saw that Verizon also had layoffs this year." Bring up information that flows naturally into the conversation. If you don't get a chance to talk about what you learned, at least you'll know a lot about the company, which will help you make an informed decision about whether to accept a job.

Practicing Interview Questions

Recruiters and hiring managers use different techniques to interview candidates. In addition to standard interviews, many companies use behavioral interviews, case-based interviews, and unfortunately, stress interviews.

LO3 Present yourself well during an employment interview.

 Learn as much as you can about the organization—your possible future employer.

Avoid "showing off" your knowledge of the organization.

Standard Interviews

Practice your response to typical interview questions.

Some interviews are fairly straightforward. The interviewer may review your résumé with you, asking questions about your experience (e.g., "What did you like about working for Walgreens?"). With standard and all interview questions, the employer is interested not only in the content of your responses but also in *how* you react to the questions themselves and *how* you communicate your thoughts and ideas.

Before your interview, practice answering each of the questions in Figure 21. You may want to set up a video camera so you can watch yourself and assess how you look and sound.

**Figure 21
Standard Interview
Questions**

- Tell me about yourself.
- Tell me something about yourself that I won't find on your résumé.
- What are you most proud of?
- Why did you leave your job at _____?
- Why would you like to work for our organization?
- Why should we hire you?
- What are your long-range career objectives?
- What type of work do you enjoy doing most? Least?
- What accomplishment has given you the greatest satisfaction?
- What would you like to change in your past?
- What courses did you like best and least in college?
- Specifically, how does your education or experience relate to this job?

Behavioral Interviews

Respond to behavioral interview questions by giving a "STAR."

Behavioral (or structured) interviews are based on the theory that past behavior predicts future performance. More than 80% of companies use this reliable technique.[23] Behavioral interview questions are highly specific questions related to **competencies** (knowledge, skills, or abilities) identified for a job. When interviewers ask these questions, they are looking for a specific example that demonstrates your ability to fulfill key job requirements. The best response follows a "STAR" format:

- **S**ituation or **T**ask: What brief context is important for the interviewer to understand?
- **A**ction: How did you handle the situation? What did you do?
- **R**esult: How did the situation turn out? How can you prove that your action was appropriate in the situation?

You'll find more sample interview questions at www.cengagebrain.com.

Two typical job competencies, behavioral interview questions, and sample responses are shown in Figure 22.

You can prepare for a behavioral interview by doing the following:

- Determine possible competencies for the job: look at the job description, which may list requirements.
- Plan between 10 and 15 examples: think about your work and school experience. What specific examples could you provide that might fit behavioral interview questions?
- Practice in front of a video camera: rehearse your examples and see how you come across.

Competency Area: Initiative

Sample Behavioral Interview Question:
"Tell me about a time when you saw a problem and took initiative to solve it."

Sample Response:
"[**Situation**] Sure, when I was working for Tasty Treats Bakery last summer, we had a lot of very busy times when 15 to 20 customers were waiting. It was chaotic in the store because we didn't have enough space for a line, and people argued about who was first. [**Action**] I suggested to the owner that we implement a 'Take-a-Number' system so customers could be served in order of when they arrive. She was concerned about the cost and how it would work, so I researched three systems and explained the process in more detail. [**Result**] By the end of the summer, she had called two of the manufacturers in for quotes. When I visited the bakery over winter break, I saw she had installed a system! I felt very proud that I could contribute to the business in this way."

Notes:
With some variations, this situation could apply to different behavioral interview questions. For example, if you were asked for a time when you persuaded someone to make a change, you could focus more on the steps you took to convince the owner. Or if you were asked for an example of a problem you solved, you could focus more on the result for the owner, for example, that the business was running more smoothly and fewer customers left without ordering.

Competency Area: Teamwork

Sample Behavioral Interview Question:
"Tell me about a time you worked as part of a team that didn't function too well. What did you do about it?" (Note that behavioral questions may ask for negative examples. In these situations, you should be honest and focus on how you learned from the experience.)

Sample Response:
"[**Situation**] For my marketing class in school, I worked with three other students to create a marketing plan. We started off well by assigning responsibilities and deadlines, but one student didn't submit her work on time. This was a problem for all of us because she was supposed to do the initial research, and this held up the rest of our work. [**Action**] I jumped in and did her work because I was worried about the project and wanted to move it along. [**Result**] We finished the marketing plan on time and got a 'B+,' but looking back, I'm not sure this was the best solution—everyone should participate equally, and this student got the same grade as the rest of us but didn't pull her weight. We didn't think this was fair."

Notes:
At this point during the interview, you may present another example to demonstrate what you learned from the experience and how you improved your teamwork skills. You may ask the interviewer for permission to give another example, and then describe the situation:

"[**Situation**] I had a similar situation for a finance project just last semester, but this time I did two things differently. [**Action**] First, I set up a wiki for the team so we could track everyone's progress throughout the project. This made accountability easier because when someone didn't complete a part of the assignment, it was public, and this put more pressure on each team member. Second, when one person didn't do his part on time, instead of jumping in, I took the initiative to talk to the student to see what was going on. He was having trouble finding data we needed, so I helped him but didn't complete the work for him. [**Result**] He was a couple of days late, but I'm glad he contributed his assigned part to the project. The team received an 'A,' and I think it's partly because everyone contributed fairly equally."

Figure 22
Sample Behavioral Interview Questions and Responses

Prepare for case interviews by following expert advice.

Case Interviews

Some companies—particularly management consulting firms—use case interviews that present you with a problem to be solved. These companies are testing your analytical skills, creativity, problem-solving skills, ability to think on your feet, logic and reasoning, quantitative skills, and of course, your communication skills. For these types of interviews, your approach to solving the problem may be as important as the solution you offer.

Case questions may be quite complex and are typically between 20 and 40 minutes.[24] Questions may be short, such as a question asked during one interview at Google, "How many pieces of luggage go through JFK on an average day?" or long, such as "One of our clients, a retailer in the jewelry and luxury watch market, has experienced declining profits in the past 12 months. How would you go about assessing this problem?"

It's best to prepare for this type of interview. McKinsey & Company, the management consulting firm, offers practice cases online and tips and common mistakes for case interviews (Figure 23).[25]

Figure 23 Acing a Case Interview

The Case Interview (from McKinsey & Company)

Tips	Common Mistakes
• Listen to the problem. • Begin by setting a structure. • Stay organized. • Communicate your train of thought clearly. • Step back periodically. • Ask for additional information when you need it. • Watch for cues from the interviewer. • Be comfortable with numbers. • Don't fixate on "cracking the case." • Use business judgment and common sense. • Relax and enjoy the process.	• Misunderstanding the question or answering the wrong question. • Proceeding in a haphazard fashion. • Asking a barrage of questions. • Force-fitting familiar business frameworks to every case question. • Failing to synthesize a point of view. • Not asking for help.

Stress Interviews

Some companies simulate a stressful environment to see how well you work under pressure. In these situations, your interviewer may ask you pointed or inappropriate questions, interrupt you, or be sarcastic and just generally rude.

Try to maintain your composure if this happens. Keep telling yourself that you're qualified for the job and can handle the interview. You're under no obligation to answer inappropriate questions, and you have every right to defend your performance and experience. If an interviewer rolls his eyes and says, "You really don't have the background to work here," be clear and confident: "Yes, I do. I have strong analytical skills from my experience at. . . ."

Of course, you may decide that a company that chooses to use stress interviews isn't the place for you. If you are offered the job, you have no obligation to take it.

Managing a Video or Phone Interview

Video interviews are becoming more common because the technology has improved and companies want to reduce travel expenses.

Communication Technologies

© CARLOSSELLER/SHUTTERSTOCK.COM

Video interviews are becoming increasingly popular.[26] Zappos, the online shoe company, for example, has used video interviews to save about $1,000 on travel expenses per job candidate.[27,28]

With a webcam, you can connect with a recruiter just as you would in person, and you should prepare for the interview the same way. In addition, practice with a friend or family member to get comfortable with the technology and to ensure that you look and sound professional. Dress as you would for an in-person interview, and make sure you're in a quiet, neat area without distractions or interruptions, such as someone knocking on your door.

Instead of a video interview, companies may request a phone interview, particularly for initial screening. Typically, these interviews are shorter than in-person interviews and may include general or, sometimes, behavioral questions. Avoid distractions and background noise just as you would for a video interview. But the real challenge may be not having nonverbal cues from your interviewer, such as nodding and smiling—or trying to jump in. You might keep your answers shorter to allow the interviewer to interrupt; otherwise, you could be way off track and not know it.

 Prepare for a video or phone interview with a friend.

Preparing Your Own Questions

During the interview, many of your questions about the organization or the job will probably be answered. However, some of the best interviews are more like conversations—you may ask questions throughout.

During one 45-minute interview at Google, the candidate was asked questions for only 15 minutes. For the remaining 30 minutes, the interviewer expected him to lead with questions. As this candidate said, "It was important that I had many questions prepared that were relevant to my position and Google on a macro and micro level."[29] Good thing he did his homework.

Prepare several questions about the company and the job.

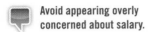

Figure 24
Possible Questions to Ask During an Interview

- How would you describe a typical day on the job?
- What opportunities exist for ongoing training and development?
- What are your expectations of new employees?
- How would my performance in this position be measured?
- What makes someone successful in this position?
- What are the organization's plans for the future?
- What do you see as the biggest opportunities and challenges for this division/company?
- To whom would I report? Would anyone report to me?
- What are the advancement opportunities for this position?

Avoid appearing overly concerned about salary.

Asking questions such as those in Figure 24 shows the recruiter that you're engaged in the interview and interested in the job and company. But avoid asking about salary, vacation time, and benefits during the initial interview. You'll have plenty of time for these questions later, after you have convinced the organization to offer you the job. You also may be able to find salary ranges on your own: ask your college career office staff, and check sites such as www.salary.com for approximations.

Finally, know when the interview is over. If the recruiter seems to be wrapping up, you may have to end your questions.

Dressing for Success

Making a good first impression during the interview is critical. In one study, executives said they form a positive or negative impression of a candidate within the first ten minutes of a job interview.[30]

Business attire usually means a suit—a suit and tie for men and either a pant suit or skirt suit for women.

© ISTOCKPHOTO.COM/LISE GAGNE

To make a good first impression, pay careful attention to your dress, grooming, and posture. You want the interviewer to remember what you had to say and not what you wore. Although different positions, companies, industries, and parts of the country and world have different norms, in general, choose well-tailored, clean, conservative clothing for the interview.

 Choose a well-tailored, clean, conservative outfit for the interview.

For most business interviews, men should dress in a black, blue, or gray suit and a white or pale blue shirt with a subtle tie, dark socks, and black shoes. Women should dress in a black, blue, or gray tailored suit with a light-colored blouse and medium heels.

Business casual attire varies widely by organization. Err on the side of more conservative dress for job interviews, as shown here (except for the guy in jeans—a formal jacket doesn't necessarily make jeans acceptable).

© ISTOCKPHOTO.COM/CHRIS SCHMIDT

When recruiters ask you to wear "business casual," you can skip the jacket and tie. A tailored shirt or conservative sweater with a skirt or dress pants will probably work well.

Avoid excessive or distracting jewelry, heavy perfumes or cologne, and elaborate hairstyles. Impeccable grooming is a must: wash and iron your clothes, shine your shoes, brush your hair, and make sure your breath is fresh.

For business positions, most interviewers want to see that you can conform to organizational norms. You'll convey this with conservative clothes.

CONDUCTING YOURSELF DURING THE INTERVIEW

Observe the organizational environment very carefully and treat everyone you meet, including the receptionist and the interviewer's assistant, with scrupulous courtesy. Be natural but professional. When shown into the interview room, greet the interviewer by name, with a firm handshake, direct eye contact, and a smile.

At the beginning of an interview, address the interviewer as "Mr." or "Ms.," switching to a first name if the interviewer gives you permission ("Call me Terry"). If you're not asked to be seated immediately, wait until the interviewer is seated and then take your seat. Lean forward a bit in your seat, and maintain comfortable eye contact with the interviewer. Avoid taking notes, except perhaps for a specific name, date, or telephone number.

Assume a confident, courteous, and conservative attitude during the interview.

Once the interview starts, do your best to relax, while maintaining a professional image. One overly anxious applicant scattered a recruiter's jar of paper clips all over his office. He was embarrassed, and he didn't get the job. With enough practice—during mock interviews on campus or with a friend—you should be well prepared for even the toughest questions. Listen carefully to each question rather than focusing on what you'll say next. Imagine that you're talking with a trusted friend of the family.

Act appropriately for a job interview. Don't go in with the attitude that "You're lucky to have me here." The interviewer might not agree. Follow the interviewer's lead, letting him or her determine which questions to ask, when to move to a new area of discussion, and when to end the interview. But you needn't fawn or grovel either. You're *applying*—not begging—for a job. If the match works, both you and the employer will benefit.

Answer each question honestly. Keep your mind on the desired job and how you can show that you're qualified. Don't try to oversell yourself, or you may end up in a job for which you're unprepared. However, if the interviewer doesn't address one of your skills, try to work it into the discussion. At the end of an interview, many recruiters will ask you, "Is there anything else we didn't cover that you'd like to tell me?" That's your chance to talk about the business fraternity you joined or the speaker series you started.

If asked about your salary expectations, try to avoid giving a number. Instead, say that you would expect to be paid in line with other employees at your level of expertise and experience. If pressed, however, be prepared to reveal your salary expectations, preferably using a broad range.

When discussing salary, talk in terms of what you think the position and responsibilities are worth rather than what you think *you* are worth. If salary is not discussed, be patient. Few people have ever been offered a job without first being told what they would be paid.

You might participate in a group interview, with several people asking you questions. If possible, find out about this practice ahead of time so that you can prepare yourself mentally. Address your responses to everyone, not just to the person who asked the question or to the most senior person present.

As shown in the typical selection process in Figure 1, it's also likely that you'll be interviewed more than once—with either multiple interviews the same day or, if you survive the initial interview, a "second [or third] round" of more intense, longer interviews. When you apply for a full-time job, most companies that interview on campus will invite you to the corporate office or local property for more interviews. Multiple interviewers will talk to each other about you, so be sure to give consistent responses.

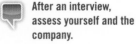

After an interview, assess yourself and the company.

Immediately after the interview, conduct an assessment of your performance and the company so you can improve for future interviews and make a decision about the company (Figure 25). Asking such questions—about yourself and the company—puts you back in control and helps you continuously develop your interview skills.

Assess Yourself	Assess the Company
How was your appearance and attire? Did you dress appropriately for the interview and company? How would you dress differently in the future?	How do you feel about the company? Is this a place you could see yourself working?
What qualifications are most important in this job? How can you change your cover letter, résumé, or responses to address these more directly?	How was your relationship with the interviewer and people on the team? Did you connect with them?
Which questions did you answer best? How can you present these descriptions or examples in future interviews?	What are the job responsibilities? Could you see yourself doing this job for the next two to three years?
Which questions did you have trouble answering? How can you address these differently?	How does this company compare to others you're considering? What are the advantages and disadvantages?
What questions did the recruiter ask about your résumé? What should you clarify or delete as a result?	Do you think you'll get a job offer? What would you do?

Figure 25
Questions to Ask Yourself After an Interview

FOLLOWING UP THROUGHOUT THE PROCESS

L04 Follow up throughout the selection process.

Communication throughout the selection process can be challenging. You're dealing with busy HR people and companies who—let's face it—don't always do the best job of keeping you informed. Even Google, which prides itself on timely communication, assured some candidates they would hear back within two weeks, but it was "about a month" in at least one situation.[31]

Without being overly aggressive, you can take some initiative throughout the selection process. As you saw in the Sample Cover Letter, calling a week or so after you send a résumé is perfectly appropriate and may differentiate you from other applicants. You might leave a voice mail such as the following:

> "Hello, Ms. Catona. This is Catherine Lin. I recently sent a résumé for the Finance Management Trainee position, and I'm excited about the opportunity to work for Bank on Me. I'd like to talk about my qualifications, particularly my relevant experience at Ernst & Young, and possibly set up an interview. You can reach me at 555-555-1212. Thank you, and I look forward to hearing from you."

You may not hear back from Ms. Catona, but she will likely remember your name as she reads through the stack of résumés—and perhaps she'll give yours a second look.

During the process of setting up interviews, be sure to express your appreciation and enthusiasm for the job, and try to be as flexible as possible.

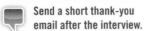
Send a short thank-you email after the interview.

After each interview, send a thank-you email by the next day. Decisions may be made quickly, so you want the chance to influence them. In one study, 15% of hiring managers said they wouldn't hire an applicant who didn't send a thank-you note; 32% said they would still consider the applicant but would think less of him or her.[32] In another study, 88% of executives said a thank-you note influences their decision, but only half of candidates send them.[33] Clearly, sending a note is an easy way for you to differentiate yourself.

Send a customized thank-you email that expresses genuine appreciation for the interview, reiterates your interest in the job, and reinforces your qualifications. If the interview coordinator doesn't give you email addresses for your interviewers, ask for a business card at the end of each interview. A sample email is shown in Figure 26.

Sending a printed letter as well is a nice touch but should not substitute for an email, which will arrive much more quickly. You also may send a handwritten note in special circumstances, for example, when you make a personal connection with the interviewer.

Figure 26   Sample Thank-You Email

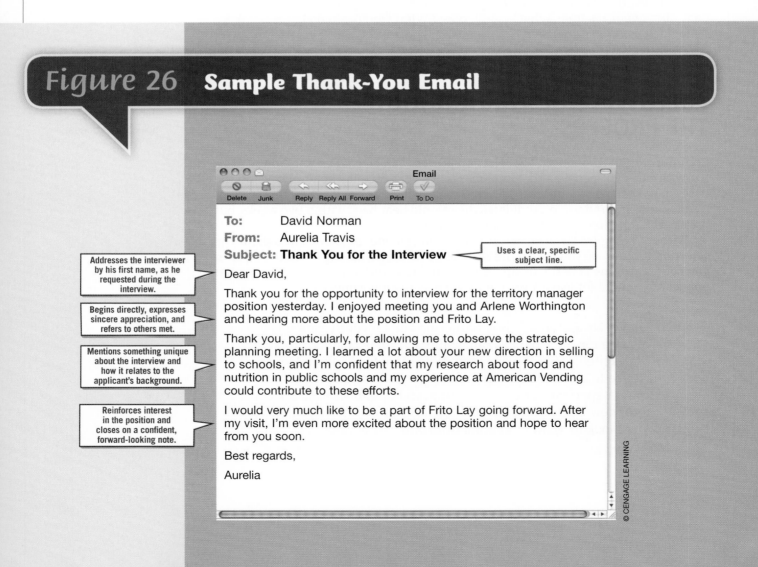

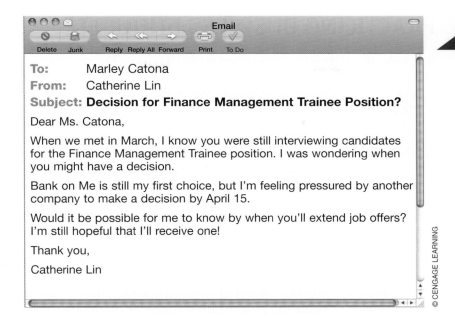

© CENGAGE LEARNING

Figure 27
Follow-Up Email

If you don't hear back from the interviewer by the deadline he or she gave you for making a decision, call or send an email for an update. If no decision has been made, your inquiry will keep your name and your interest in the interviewer's mind. If someone else has been selected, you need to know so that you can continue your job search. You might send an email such as the example in Figure 27, which is polite, yet pushes for a decision.

The Checklist for Job Interviews summarizes key points from this section.

Checklist for Job Interviews   GO

Preparing for a Job Interview

☑ Before going on a job interview, learn everything you can about the organization.

☑ Practice answering common interview questions, and prepare questions of your own to ask.

☑ Select appropriate clothing to wear.

☑ Control your nervousness by being well prepared and on time.

Conducting Yourself During the Interview

☑ Throughout the interview, be aware of the nonverbal signals you are communicating through your body language.

☑ Answer each question completely and accurately, always trying to relate your qualifications to what the company needs.

☑ Assess your performance, your résumé, and your cover letter, and make improvements for the next interview.

Following up Throughout the Process

☑ Call to follow up on a submitted résumé.

☑ Send a thank-you email after each interview.

☑ Call or email to politely ask for a decision if you don't hear back after an interview.

LO5   Practice business etiquette in the workplace.

PRACTICING BUSINESS ETIQUETTE

Business etiquette refers to appropriate behavior in a business setting. By following good etiquette, we present a professional image and interact properly with others at work. As a business professional, you want to represent yourself as a serious employee who can be trusted—and promoted.

 Learn what is considered appropriate behavior in your organization.

Each organization has its own rules about what is considered appropriate in terms of dress, interactions with senior-level managers, punctuality, and other subtle forms of communication in the workplace. In addition, every country and every culture has its own rules, and these may vary even within an organization. What's considered acceptable in the IT department (e.g., casual dress and abbreviations in instant messages), may be perceived negatively in the sales department. Generally, these rules are not written down but are learned informally or through observation. Executives typically set the bar for business etiquette, so following their lead will help you determine appropriate behavior.

Business etiquette differs from social etiquette. Flirting, drinking too much, and telling questionable jokes may be acceptable at a party with your friends, but not at a business function. When in doubt, use a high standard of acceptability—err on the side of being too proper rather than risk offending someone or embarrassing yourself.

Meeting and Greeting

When you meet people for the first time, take the initiative to introduce yourself. If someone is hosting you, then he or she should make the introduction—as you should for others—but if you're new to a job, at a conference, meeting with a new client, or attending a training program, introduce yourself to people around you. This initiative shows confidence and simply will help you meet more people at your company or in your industry.

When introducing others, the basic rule is to present the lower-ranking person to the higher-ranking person, regardless of age or gender: "[CEO], this is my new assistant." The format for an introduction might be like this: "Helen, I'd like you to meet Carl Byrum. Carl just began working here as a junior account manager. Carl, this is Helen Smith, our CEO." Or in a social situation, you might just say, "Rosa, this is Gene Stauffer. Gene, Rosa Bennett." The appropriate response to an introduction is "Hello, Gene," "I'm glad to meet you, Gene," or, more formally, "It's a pleasure to meet you, Gene." Typically, in the United States, the two people will then shake hands.

 Use a person's name in the conversation to help remember it.

To help remember someone's name, repeat it when you shake hands. If you cannot remember someone's name, when the person approaches you, simply extend your hand and say your name. The other person will typically respond by shaking your hand and also giving his or her name. In the potentially awkward situation when you introduce two people but remember only one person's name, simply say, "Have you met Carly from Accounting?"

Whenever you see someone who may not remember you, you can help avoid embarrassment by introducing yourself and helping jog the person's memory: "Hello, Mr. Wise, I'm Eileen Wagoner. We met at the Grahams' party last month."

 Exchange business cards at the end of a business encounter.

Today, most American businesspeople have business cards, although the protocol for exchanging them isn't as strict here as it is in some other countries. In business settings, present your card at the end of the encounter to communicate your interest in continuing the relationship. Never present your card during a meal (wait until it is over), and never offer your card at any time during a social function.

Dining

Whether in the employee cafeteria or at a fine restaurant, these guidelines will help you enjoy your business meal.

Before the Meal

- If you host a meal, choose a restaurant appropriate for the person and within your company's policy, to be sure you'll get reimbursed. Also ask your guest whether he or she has dietary restrictions that may affect your choice.
- Be sure to make reservations. You don't want to be embarrassed by showing up at a restaurant that cannot accommodate you and your guests.
- If a maitre d' (headwaiter) seats you and your guest, your guest should precede you to the table. If you're seating yourselves, take the lead in locating an appropriate table. Give your guest the preferred seat, facing the window with an attractive view or facing the dining room if you're seated next to the wall.
- If you're the host, to signal the waiter that you're ready to order, close your menu and lay it on the table. The host's order is generally taken last.
- Go light on the liquor. You may order wine for the table if others would like to indulge, but keep your own drinking to a minimum.
- When the food arrives, guests should not begin eating until the host begins. Never begin eating until everyone has been served. If yours is the only dish not yet served because of a delay, it's polite to invite others to begin rather than wait. They may or may not do so.

During the Meal

- A business meal is about the conversation—not the food. Stay engaged in the conversation throughout the meal.
- Your mother was right: never talk with your mouth full. Take small bites so you can participate in the conversation.
- Take your host's lead for topics. Sometimes, business meals are more social, and discussing too much business is considered inappropriate.

At a formal place setting, the glass on the right side and the bread plate on the left side are yours.

- Your glass is at your right; your bread plate is on the left. When using silver-ware, start from the outside in (the smaller fork is for your salad). When passing food or condiments, pass to the right, offering items to someone else before you serve yourself. If you *must* use salt (only after tasting the food), ask someone to please pass it to you, rather than reach across the table. And when asked to pass the salt or pepper, pass both together.

- To get the server's attention, say "Excuse me" when he or she is nearby, or catch the server's eye and quietly signal for him or her to come to the table, or ask a nearby server to ask yours to come to your table.

- Don't put your elbows on the table while eating, although you may do so between courses.

- If you leave the table during the meal, leave your napkin on your chair. At the end of the meal, place the napkin, unfolded, on the table.

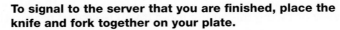

To signal to the server that you are finished, place the knife and fork together on your plate.

© PAVEL IGNATOV/SHUTTERSTOCK.COM

- Place the knife across the top edge of the plate, with the cutting edge toward you when it is not being used; don't keep silverware leveraged on the table and plate like oars. To signal to the server that you have finished, place your knife and fork together on the plate.

After the Meal

- For business meals, it's typically inappropriate to take leftovers home. If the server asks, politely decline.

- The person who extended the invitation is expected to pay the bill. When the server comes with the check, indicate that you will accept it. If it's placed on the table, just pick it up. If it's unclear who will pay, you should always offer. If your host declines your offer, say a polite, "Thank you."

- If someone else paid, be sure to say "Thank you" before you get up from the table.

- Tip between 15% and 20% of the bill before tax. If you can't calculate this in your head, bring a tip card with you or subtly check your smartphone. If you checked coats, leave $1 per coat, and if you used valet parking, tip the attendant $2.

- If you were the guest, send a thank-you note immediately after the meal. Be sure to write more than a token note, mentioning something special about the décor, food, service, and company.

Giving Gifts

Giving gifts to suppliers, customers, or workers is typical at many firms, especially in December during the holiday period. Although gifts are often appreciated, check your company's policy. Many companies restrict both giving and receiving gifts to avoid improprieties.

 Avoid giving gifts that are extravagant or personal or that might be perceived as a bribe.

Most people would consider a gift appropriate if it meets the four criteria in Figure 28.

A manager is more likely to give his or her employee a gift than the other way around. More likely, coworkers will contribute to a gift for the boss on special occasions.

Figure 28
Criteria for an Appropriate Business Gift

 It is an impersonal gift. Gifts that can be used in the office or in connection with work are nearly always appropriate. For example, a notepad is appropriate; lingerie is not!

 It is for past favors. Gifts should be used to thank someone for past favors, business, or performance—*not* to create obligations for the future. Giving a fruit basket to a prospective customer who has never ordered from you before might be interpreted as a bribe.

 It is given to everyone in similar circumstances. Singling out one person for a gift and ignoring others in similar positions could be embarrassing or cause bad feelings.

 It is not extravagant. A very expensive gift might make the recipient uneasy, create a sense of obligation, and call into question your motives for giving. Inviting a customer and his family on a cruise is not appropriate and is likely against both companies' policies.

© CENGAGE LEARNING

 Take responsibility to manage information about you on the Internet.

Managing Your Online Reputation

Your professional image also will be judged by your **online reputation**—how you are represented on the Internet. It's your responsibility to make sure that the web tells your story well.

Starting with the recruiting process, companies search for information about you online. In a recent study, a whopping 79% of HR representatives/recruiters answered "All the time" or "Most of the time" in response to the question, "Do you review online reputational information about candidates when evaluating them for a potential job/college admission?"[34] We can expect these numbers to increase as more information is available online.

You can protect yourself by managing your online reputation as follows:

- Google yourself to see what others see.
- Manage your privacy settings on Facebook and other social networking sites.
- Avoid posting questionable content about yourself.
- Post positive content (an online résumé, a blog) that shows your strengths.

Once you're hired, you'll still want to be careful about what you post online. As discussed in Chapter 1, avoid writing anything that might be perceived as offensive or critical of your employer, coworkers, or customers. For example, a restaurant server got fired after complaining on her Facebook page about receiving a $5 tip.[35] And in Chapter 1, you read about the Best Buy employee who got suspended for posting videos. Companies have been criticized and, in some cases, sued for their reaction to online posts, but why spoil your professional image and put your job in jeopardy?

Working in an Office

Be respectful of others' space.

How you behave around the office will determine how people feel about you as a coworker and as a business professional. Although you want to be friendly—and be yourself—you also want to be perceived as someone who is respectful of others.

Tight quarters—and some strange personalities—cause people to annoy their coworkers in the movie _Office Space_.

© 20TH CENTURY FOX FILM CORP. ALL RIGHTS RESERVED./COURTESY EVERETT COLLECTION.

Office space is a precious commodity today, and people value their own work area, which, for millions of people, is a cubicle. Because cubicles offer little privacy, courtesy is especially important. Follow these guidelines:

- Always knock or ask permission before entering someone's cubicle, and never wander into someone's unoccupied cubicle without permission.
- Never shout a comment to someone in the next cubicle. If it's inconvenient to walk over, email, send an IM, or call instead.

- Do not leave valuables in your cubicle unattended.
- Avoid talking on the phone or to visitors too loudly, and avoid strong perfumes or colognes.
- Finally, honor the occupant's privacy by not staring at his or her computer screen or listening to private conversations.

Always be aware of how others behave in the workplace. Whether you're waiting for an elevator or to get a second cup of coffee, pay attention to social cues. How much small talk do people engage in? What are their conversations about? What's common practice when people come into work and when they leave for the day? The best way to fit in socially is to observe others and, as long as the behavior is professional and acceptable to you personally, adapt to the environment.

By practicing effective business communication and respecting others at work, you'll be a successful business professional—and may be next in line for that big promotion.

Sending a Thank-You Note

Purpose

Imagine that you just interviewed for your dream job—designing graphics for your favorite company's website. The interview went well, and you want to send an inspired thank-you note to seal the deal.

Process

1. In what format will you send the thank-you note?

Email—this is how all of my communication with the company has taken place so far, and I want the hiring manager to receive it quickly.

2. Write an opening paragraph for your email to capture attention and convey the purpose up front.

Thank you for such an interesting and educational interview today. I didn't know that your chief graphic designer started as a college intern! This job would be the perfect place for me to start my own career—and I believe I would be a great fit for the company.

3. How will you reinforce your relevant skills and other qualifications for the job?

I'm glad you liked the logos I developed in the past. Having worked with nine diverse companies to design unique logos, I look forward to applying my creativity to develop new graphics.

4. How will you reinforce your education as a differentiator from other applicants?

As an advertising design major, I would bring a solid foundation in visual communication and design theory. My business coursework in marketing, finance, and communication supplement my design skills, making me a well-rounded candidate for the job.

5. Write the closing sentence.

Again, thank you for the opportunity to meet with you about the job. I'm excited about the chance to be a part of such a dynamic team and look forward to hearing from you soon.

Product

To: Karen Withers

From: Sanjay Maan

Subject: Thank You for the Interview

Dear Karen,

Thank you for such an interesting and educational interview today. I didn't know that your chief graphic designer started as a college intern! This job would be the perfect place for me to start my own career—and I believe I would be a great fit for the company.

I'm glad you liked the logos I developed in the past. Having worked with nine diverse companies to design unique logos, I look forward to applying my creativity to develop new graphics.

As an advertising design major, I would bring a solid foundation in visual communication and design theory. My business coursework in marketing, finance, and communication supplement my design skills, making me a well-rounded candidate for the job.

Again, thank you for the opportunity to meet with you about the job. I'm excited about the chance to be a part of such a dynamic team and look forward to hearing from you soon.

Best regards,

Sanjay

The
3Ps
In Practice

Writing a Résumé

Purpose

Assume that you are beginning your last semester of college before graduating. Using information about your education, work experience, and so on, prepare a résumé in an effective format.

Process

1. How will you word your name at the top of your résumé—for example, with or without any initials?

2. What is the title of your degree? The name of your college? The location of the college? Your major and minor? Your expected date of graduation (month and year)?

3. What is your grade-point average overall and in your major? Is either one high enough to be considered a selling point?

4. Have you received any academic honors, such as scholarships or being named to the dean's list? If so, list them.

5. Did you take any elective courses that are relevant to the job and that might differentiate you from other applicants? If so, list them.

6. List in reverse chronological order (most recent job first) the following information for each job you've held during college: company name, job title, location (city and state), and dates of employment. Describe your specific responsibilities in each position. Use short phrases, beginning each responsibility with an action verb, and showing, where possible, specific evidence of the results you achieved.

7. What additional information might you include, such as special skills, extracurricular activities, volunteer work, languages spoken, and so on?

Product

Using the information listed, draft, revise, format, and then proofread your résumé. Submit your résumé and your responses to the process questions to your instructor.

Summary

L01 Write and format a résumé.

The purpose of your résumé is to get you a job interview. Strive for a one-page document with a simple, readable format. Include your name, address, phone number, email address, information about your education and work experience, and special skills. Include other information only if it will help distinguish you favorably from the other applicants. Prefer the chronological organization for your work experience, and stress the skills and experiences that can be transferred to the job you want.

Consider creating an online or video version of your résumé to supplement your employment materials.

L02 Write a cover letter or inquiry email.

Compose a cover letter that discusses how your education and work experience qualify you specifically for the job. If possible, address your letter to the person who will interview you for the job. Because most employers prefer résumés by email, you may write your cover note within the body of an email message.

Adjust your letter or email opening to the situation and type of job. Then highlight your strongest qualifications, relating them to the needs of the position for which you're applying. Close by politely asking for an interview.

L03 Present yourself well during an employment interview.

If your cover letter is successful, you will be invited for an interview. For a successful interview, prepare by researching the company, and practice answering and asking questions. Prepare for all types of interviews: standard, behavioral, case, and stress. For behavioral interviews, which are most common, practice giving specific examples from your experience in this format: situation/task, action, and result.

L04 Follow up throughout the selection process.

After the interview is over, evaluate your performance so you can do better the next time. Also evaluate your résumé and cover letter and revise them if necessary. Take the time to write a personalized thank-you note, and consider following up if you do not hear from the employer within the timeframe promised.

L05 Practice business etiquette in the workplace.

Business etiquette is a guide to help people behave appropriately in business situations. To be effective in business, learn how to make introductions, conduct business lunches, give suitable gifts, and maintain good working relationships around the office. Check your online reputation to avoid embarrassment and to make sure you are well represented wherever an employer may look.

Exercises

1. Improve your résumé.

Exchange résumés with a partner. Using the principles in this chapter, analyze your partner's résumé. Imagine that you're a human resources manager who reviews hundreds

L01 Write and format a résumé.

of résumés every day. Use this checklist to provide feedback to your partner and suggest improvements:

Résumé Feedback

Criteria	Comments
• Formatting is attractive and easy to read.	
• Identifying information is clear.	
• Education section is accurate and emphasizes key points.	
• Work experience section is well organized.	
• Work experience section includes companies, job titles, and dates.	
• Bulleted job responsibilities start with action verbs and are phrased clearly.	
• Job responsibility descriptions highlight accomplishments.	
• Other activities are relevant and clearly explained.	
• Résumé is 100% accurate.	

2. Customize your résumé for a job.

One way to land a job is to apply for opportunities posted through your school's career center. But you can supplement your search by reaching out to other companies that interest you. Using your school's career center, the Internet, and library research tools, brainstorm a list of companies where you would like to work. On Hoovers (www.hoovers .com), for example, you can search for companies by industry or location. After you identify companies that interest you, take a look at their career websites. What positions are available? How do they describe the organizational culture?

If a company and position seem like a fit for you, then prepare a customized résumé. You might change, for example, which past jobs you include on your résumé, how you describe your responsibilities, and which extracurricular activities or skills you include. Imagine yourself receiving the résumé. Does it seem like a fit for the organization and culture?

3. Create an online résumé.

Transform your résumé to an online version. Upload files, for example, relevant reports and presentations you have completed. Include links to companies and organizations with which you have been affiliated. And link to any relevant online content, for example, a video you have created or a blog you maintain. Include anything that would represent you well and provide a potential employer with more information about you and your experience.

4. Customize a cover letter.

After you identify a company and position that interests you and for which you're qualified, write a customized cover letter. How will you express interest in this specific company? Which experiences will you highlight?

L02 Write a cover letter or inquiry email.

5. Change your cover letter to an email message.

Change a cover letter you wrote previously (or the one you wrote for Exercise 4) to a version you'll send as an email. What changes will you make in the salutation and formatting? How can you reduce the length? How will you change the tone to make it more appropriate for an email message?

6. Rewrite a networking email.

Imagine that your friend, Ron, asks you to review a draft networking email before he sends it. His goal is to get a summer internship in the marketing department of the company. What advice would you give to your friend? If you were Ron, how would you revise the email?

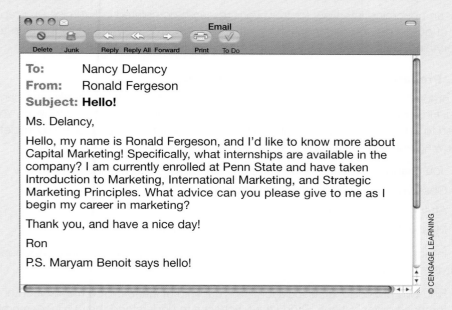

To: Nancy Delancy
From: Ronald Fergeson
Subject: **Hello!**

Ms. Delancy,

Hello, my name is Ronald Fergeson, and I'd like to know more about Capital Marketing! Specifically, what internships are available in the company? I am currently enrolled at Penn State and have taken Introduction to Marketing, International Marketing, and Strategic Marketing Principles. What advice can you please give to me as I begin my career in marketing?

Thank you, and have a nice day!

Ron

P.S. Maryam Benoit says hello!

© CENGAGE LEARNING

7. Expand your network.

To expand your job search, you might reach out to people you know. If you haven't already, sign up for a free account on LinkedIn, the professional social networking site. Create your profile and invite people you know and trust to join your network.

Search for groups on LinkedIn that reflect your career interests. Join two or three, and observe the discussion for one week. Then, begin participating in the discussion. See how you can add value and learn more about your field.

8. Write networking emails.

Find a few executives with whom you would like to network. For this exercise, you can decide—based on your own career goals—what you would like to get out of the experience: a visit to the company's headquarters, a chance to meet with an executive to see what it's like to work for your dream company, more information about a field that interests you, or a summer internship. Just be realistic and avoid placing too much burden on someone you don't know.

To find people to contact, you might search your college's alumni database, ask friends or family for recommendations, look at companies' websites, or search online for people's names and titles. The more people you include, the more likely you will get responses.

Prepare a draft generic email. Then, tailor the email to each executive on your list. Think about ways to connect with each person to encourage a positive response.

L03 Present yourself well during an employment interview.

9. Research a potential employer.

Assume that your favorite company has invited you to interview. To prepare for the interview, research the company by reviewing its website, reading news stories, and exploring websites such as Hoovers, Vault, and Glassdoor. Concentrate on information most likely to help you during the interview.

Now assume that another student, who is also interested in the company, asks you what you have learned. You're such a nice person that you're willing to tell him or her everything! Write an email to this student summarizing your research.

10. Prepare a list of questions for a potential employer.

For an upcoming interview (or from your research completed in Exercise 9), prepare a list of questions you might ask during the interview. You may not have the time to ask everything, but prepare a long list, just in case.

11. Prepare a career preparation portfolio.

To prepare for your job search, conduct research and meet with people who can help you. First, target specific people within companies where you might like to work. You will need to send a few networking emails to ask for assistance. Your goal is to complete the following activities within one or more companies:

- Job shadow someone in the company who holds a job that interests you.
- Observe a meeting or formal presentation.
- Attend a training program.
- Meet with people in your field (informational interviews).

In addition, to understand your field of interest, pursue professional development activities, such as the following:

- Find two professional associations for your field of interest. You may search online for these organizations. Study their websites to understand the purpose, membership, and mission of each organization.
- Attend a local meeting of one of the professional organizations that interests you.
- Find two professional journals within your field of interest, and study one article from each.
- Search for news stories or credible blogs about your field. Study what these sources say about important trends or developments within your field.

Prepare a portfolio of your work, and submit it to your instructor. You might be instructed to include the following:

- A cover memo summarizing what you learned from these activities
- Observations from your job shadowing experience
- Copies of handouts or presentation decks you received during meetings or training programs
- Notes from your informational interviews
- Observations about professional associations in your field

- Notes from the professional association meeting you attended
- Summaries of journal articles you read
- An analysis of trends and developments that might affect your career choice in the future

Organize your portfolio in a way that makes sense to you—not necessarily in the order presented here. Include a table of contents for your materials and a title page.

12. Practice a behavioral interview.

To prepare for this exercise, identify between 10 and 15 examples of stories from your experience, as described in this chapter. Then, in class, work in groups of three to practice answering a behavioral interview question. Take turns, with one of you asking the question, another responding, and the third person observing and taking notes, using the checklist below to evaluate the candidate's response:

Content & Organization	❑ **Did you get a complete story (STAR)?**
	❑ **Did it demonstrate the competency you were looking for?**
	❑ **Was it well organized?**
	❑ **Did you get the right amount of detail (enough, not too much)?**
	❑ **COMMENTS:**
Delivery	❑ **Easy to understand**
	❑ **Good eye contact**
	❑ **Appropriate pace**
	❑ **Good volume**
	❑ **Effective hand gestures**
	❑ **Few fillers (*uh, um*)**
	❑ **Appropriate pauses**
	❑ **COMMENTS:**

Here are a few behavioral interview questions you may ask your partner:

- Tell me about a time when you worked well as part of a team. What was your role, and what was the result of the team's work?
- Please tell me about a situation when you had a difficult problem to solve. What did you do, and how did it turn out?
- Please give me an example of a positive interaction you had with a customer. What was the situation, what did you do, and how did it turn out?
- What do you consider your greatest strength in communicating with others? Can you give me an example of when you used this skill or technique, and tell me how it worked out?
- Tell me about a time when you took a leadership role. What was the situation, what did you do, and what was the result?
- Please give me an example of a difficult decision you made recently. How did you go about making the decision, and what was the result?

13. Practice dressing up for an interview.

With your classmates, agree on a date when everyone will come to class dressed for a job interview. If you're shy, you can meet in small groups to give each other feedback. If you're bold, have a fashion show. One person at a time can walk in front of the class for feedback. Be kind, of course! Give each other tips on professional attire and grooming.

14. Leave a voice mail message.

Imagine that you are following up on a cover letter you sent. Use the guidelines in this chapter to leave a short, professional voice mail message on your instructor's office phone that shows your initiative and enthusiasm for the job.

15. Write a thank-you email.

Imagine that you had a great interview for your ideal job. Write a thank-you email to your interviewer to reinforce your interest in the position and your qualifications. Send the email to your instructor for feedback.

16. Follow up after an interview.

Have you had an interview in the past, and the interviewer never got back to you? Or have you sent a résumé and not received a response? Think about one of these situations, and write an email to follow up. Exchange drafts with a partner to make sure your request is clear and your tone is appropriate.

17. Discuss options for gifts.

Working in small groups, discuss your experience with giving gifts at work. Have you ever given or received a gift in a workplace? Who were the people involved, and what were the gifts? Discuss whether you believe, in retrospect, that these gifts were appropriate.

18. Practice introducing people at work.

Assume the role of Pat Gibson, Catering Director for Writeaway Hotels. You're expecting Carly Singleton, an event manager and important potential client from Atlanta, for a business meeting at 10 a.m. Carly will be accompanied by Eunji Shun, who reports to her. You've met both of them once before. Working with other students who will play these roles, make the following introductions:

a. Carly Singleton and Ian Mendoza (Pat's manager)

b. Carly Singleton and Margaret Bryant (Ian's assistant)

c. Eunji Shun and Ian Mendoza (Pat's manager)

d. Eunji Shun and Jay Chan (summer intern)

19. Practice eating a business meal.

Imagine that you're taking two or three clients out for lunch. With your classmates, arrange a meeting time at a local restaurant or a dining hall on campus. Assign roles: one of you will be the host, and the others will play various levels within the client organization—director, assistant director, and manager.

If you go to a dining hall, imagine that you have to explain to your guests what is available and the process for getting food and returning trays and silverware. Invite your guests to go ahead of you and direct them where to sit, being sensitive to their preferences.

If you go to a restaurant, follow guidelines from this chapter for ordering food. Perhaps the host can pay (but then get reimbursed by the guests).

Company Scenario

Bank on Me

Bank on Me, a financial services company, is hiring for its Finance Management Training Program. In this company scenario, you'll see employment communication from the other side of the table—the employer's perspective—and will learn to do the following:

- Evaluate employment communication against given job requirements.
- Practice interviewing skills as a company recruiter or as a job applicant.
- Participate in a decision-making meeting.
- Communicate positive and negative hiring decisions.

This is a good opportunity for you to apply what you learn to your own communication during a hiring process. At www.cengagebrain.com, you'll find these materials:

- Job description for finance management trainee
- Résumés and cover letters for five candidates
- Three voice mail messages (two from candidates who said they would call and one from a candidate's mother!)
- Interviewer's Guide
- Hiring Decision Matrix (shown below)

**Bank on Me
Hiring Decision Matrix**

Instructions: Please rate each candidate's qualifications against the criteria defined in the "Finance Management Trainee" job description. For each criterion, click on "Choose an item" to select a rating from the drop-down list. Write a few comments to explain and support your rating (the box will expand).

	Finance Coursework	Finance Experience	Leadership Experience	Degree and GPA	Communication Skills	Attention to Detail (assessed from the cover letter and résumé)	Proficiency in Excel	Spanish Language	Candidate Ranking (1 = highest, 5 = lowest)
Marcus Benini	Choose an item. Comments:	Choose an item. Comments:	Choose an item. Comments:	Choose an item. Comments:	Choose an item. Comments:	Choose an item. Comments:	Choose an item. Comments:	Choose an item. Comments:	Choose an item.
Laurie Carpenter	Choose an item. Comments:	Choose an item. Comments:	Choose an item. Comments:	Choose an item. Comments:	Choose an item. Comments:	Choose an item. Comments:	Choose an item. Comments:	Choose an item. Comments:	Choose an item.
Catherine Lin	Choose an item. Comments:	Choose an item. Comments:	Choose an item. Comments:	Choose an item. Comments:	Choose an item. Comments:	Choose an item. Comments:	Choose an item. Comments:	Choose an item. Comments:	Choose an item.
Landon Lowry	Choose an item. Comments:	Choose an item. Comments:	Choose an item. Comments:	Choose an item. Comments:	Choose an item. Comments:	Choose an item. Comments:	Choose an item. Comments:	Choose an item. Comments:	Choose an item.
Ana Santos	Choose an item. Comments:	Choose an item. Comments:	Choose an item. Comments:	Choose an item. Comments:	Choose an item. Comments:	Choose an item. Comments:	Choose an item. Comments:	Choose an item. Comments:	Choose an item.

Your instructor may assign these activities for you to engage in this scenario:

- Analyze the employment information from the five candidates and complete the hiring matrix.
- Interview one of the candidates (or play the role of a candidate being interviewed).
- Make a hiring decision as part of a team of interviewers.
- Communicate a positive or negative hiring decision with a phone call, email, or both.

Notes

1. Google Recruiting Video, www .google.com/jobs/joininggoogle/ hiringprocess/, accessed June 9, 2010.
2. "100 Best Companies to Work For," *Fortune*, February 8, 2010, http:// money.cnn.com/magazines/ fortune/bestcompanies/2010/, accessed June 9, 2010.
3. "The World's Top 50 Most Attractive Employers," Universum, www .universumglobal.com, accessed June 9, 2010.
4. Google Benefits, Google Website, www.google.com, accessed June 9, 2010.
5. "What Works," CNN in the Money, January 28, 2007, http://edition.cnn .com, accessed June 9, 2010.
6. Email interview with Google applicant, June 13, 2010.
7. Google Hiring Process, www.google .com, accessed June 15, 2010.
8. "Recruiter 'Pet Peeve' Survey," Resume Doctor, www.resumedoctor .com, accessed August 27, 2010.
9. "Nearly Half of Employers Have Caught a Lie on a Resume, CareerBuilder Survey Shows," Career Builder, July 30, 2008, www.careerbuilder.com, accessed July 10, 2010.
10. CareerBuilder.com.
11. Jason Ferrara, "Are Employers Looking at Your Résumé?" Career Builder, March 27, 2009, www .careerbuilder.com, accessed August 26, 2010.
12. "Resumes Inching Up," Accountemps, News Release, http:// accountemps.com, accessed August 26, 2010.

13. "Have a Keen Eye for Derail," Accountemps, News Release, http:// accountemps.com, accessed August 26, 2010.
14. Barbara Safani, "Your Resume Is Ready for the Attic," The Ladders, June 7, 2010, www.theladders.com, accessed June 16, 2010.
15. Nancy M. Schullery, Linda Ickes, and Stephen E. Schullery, "Employer Preferences for Résumés and Cover Letters," *Business Communication Quarterly*, vol. 72, no. 2 (June 2009), 163–176.
16. Adapted and used with permission from the author.
17. Tania Khadder, "Five Signs Your Resume Is Passé," www.monster .com, accessed June 10, 2010.
18. Schullery et al.
19. Adam Barrera, Visual CV, www .visualcv.com/adambarrera, accessed December 20, 2010.
20. Schullery et al.
21. Schullery et al.
22. "Targeted Selection: Meeting Today's Selection Challenges," Development Dimensions International, White Paper, www.ddiworld.com, accessed August 26, 2010.
23. "Survey Signals Sharp Rise in Behavioral Interviewing," Novations, January 18, 2008, www.novations .com, accessed June 15, 2010.
24. "What is a Case Interview?" Ace the Case, www.acethecase.com, accessed June 11, 2010.
25. "Techniques and Tricks," McKinsey & Company, www.mckinsey.com, accessed June 11, 2010.
26. Andrew R. McIlvaine, "Lights, Camera . . . Interview," Human

Resource Executive Online, September 16, 2009, www.hreonline .com, accessed June 11, 2010.
27. Courtney Friel, "Job Hunt: Interviewing on the Web," Fox News, December 22, 2009, http://liveshots .blogs.foxnews.com, accessed June 11, 2010.
28. Ric Romero, "Webcam Job Interviews Growing in Popularity," KABC-TV Los Angeles, CA, March 15, 2010, http://abclocal .go.com, accessed June 11, 2010.
29. Email interview with Google applicant, June 13, 2010.
30. "Survey: Employers Form Opinions of Interviewees Within 10 Minutes," Business & Legal Resources, April 12, 2007, http://hr.blr.com, accessed August 26, 2010.
31. Email interview.
32. Rosemary Haefner, "No Thank You Could Mean No Job," CareerBuilder .com, September 29, 2009, www .careerbuilder.com, accessed August 26, 2010.
33. "Thanks, But No Thanks," Accountemps, August 9, 2007, www .accountemps.com, accessed August 26, 2010.
34. "Data Privacy Day: Perceptions Study," Cross-Tab Marketing Services, January 2010, www .microsoft.com/privacy/dpd/ research.aspx, accessed September 9, 2010.
35. "Waitress Fired for Gripe About Tip on Facebook," Associated Press, May 17, 2010, www.msnbc.msn. com/id/37192342/, accessed September 9, 2010.

Reference Manual

A   Language Arts Basics

LAB 1: PARTS OF SPEECH

We use words, of course, to communicate. Of the hundreds of thousands of words in an unabridged dictionary, each can be classified as one of just eight parts of speech: noun, pronoun, verb, adjective, adverb, preposition, conjunction, or interjection. These eight parts of speech are illustrated in the sentence below:

Interjection Pronoun Adverb Verb Preposition Adjective Noun Conjunction Noun

Oh, I eagerly waited for new computers and printers.

Many words can act as different parts of speech, depending on how they are used in a sentence. (A *sentence* is a group of words that contains a subject and predicate and that expresses a complete thought.)

Consider, for example, the different parts of speech played by the word *following*:

We agree to do the *following*. *(noun)*

I was only *following* orders. *(verb)*

We met the *following* day. *(adjective)*

Following his remarks, he sat down. *(preposition)*

All words do not serve more than one function, but many do. Following is a brief introduction to the eight parts of speech.

1.1 Nouns   A *noun* is a word that names something—for example, a person, place, thing, or idea:

Person:	employee, Mr. Watkins
Place:	office, Chicago
Thing:	animal, computer
Idea:	concentration, impatience, week, typing

The words in italics in the following sentences are all nouns.

Olaf promoted his *idea* to the *vice president* on *Wednesday.*

Problem solving is just one of the *skills* you'll need as an *intern.*

How much does one *quart* of *water* weigh on our bathroom *scales?*

The animal *doctor* treated my *animal* well in *Houston.*

If you were asked to give an example of a noun, you would probably think of a *concrete noun*—that is, a *physical* object that you can see, hear, feel, taste, or smell.

An *abstract noun,* on the other hand, names a quality or concept and not something physical.

Concrete Noun	Abstract Noun
book	success
stapler	patience
computer	skills
dictionary	loyalty

A *common noun,* as its name suggests, is the name of a *general* person, place, thing, or idea. If you want to give the name of a *specific* person, place, thing, or idea, you would use a *proper noun.* Proper nouns are always capitalized.

Common Noun	Proper Noun
man	Rodolfo Escobar
city	Los Angeles
car	Corvette
religion	Judaism

A *singular noun* names one person, place, thing, or idea. A *plural noun* names more than one.

Singular Noun	Plural Noun
Smith	Smiths
watch	watches
computer	computers
victory	victories

1.2 Pronouns   A *pronoun* is a word used in place of a noun. Consider the following sentence:

Anna went to *Anna's* kitchen and made *Anna's* favorite dessert because *Anna* was going to a party with *Anna's* friends.

The noun *Anna* is used five times in this awkward sentence. A smoother, less monotonous version of the sentence substitutes pronouns for all but the first *Anna:*

Anna went to *her* kitchen and made *her* favorite dessert because *she* was going to a party with *her* friends.

The words in italics in the following sentences are pronouns. The nouns to which they refer are underlined:

<u>Angélica</u> thought *she* might get the promotion.

None of the <u>speakers</u> were interesting.

<u>Juan</u> forgot to bring *his* slides.

1.3 Verbs   A *verb* is a word (or group of words) that expresses either action or a state of being. The first kind of verb is called an *action verb*; the second kind is known as a *linking verb.* Without a verb, you have no sentence because the verb makes a statement about the subject.

Most verbs express action of some sort—either physical or mental—as indicated by the words in italics in the following sentences:

Iram *planted* his garden while Lian *pulled* weeds.

I *solved* my problems as I *baked* bread.

Jeremy *decided* he should *call* a meeting.

A small (but important) group of verbs do not express action. Instead, they simply link the subject with words that describe it. The most common linking verbs are forms of the verb *to be*, such as *is, am, are, was, were,* and *will.* Other forms of linking verbs involve the senses, such as *feels, looks, smells, sounds,* and *tastes.* The following words in italics are verbs (note that verbs can comprise one or more words):

Rosemary *was* angry because Ivanov *looked* impatient.

If Franz *is having* a party, I *should have been* invited.

Jason *had* already *seen* the report.

1.4 Adjectives   You can make sentences consisting of only nouns or pronouns and verbs (such as "Dogs bark."), but most of the time you'll need to add other parts of speech to make the meaning of the sentence clearer or more complete. An *adjective* is a word that modifies a noun or pronoun. Adjectives answer questions about the nouns or pronouns they describe, such as *how many?, what kind?,* and *which one?* (*Articles* are a special group of adjectives that include the words *a, an,* and *the.*)

As shown by the words in italics in the following sentences, adjectives may come before or after the nouns or pronouns they modify:

Seventeen applicants took the *typing* test.

The interview was *short,* but *comprehensive.*

She took the *last* plane and landed at a *small Mexican* airport.

1.5 Adverbs   An *adverb* is a word that modifies a verb (usually), an adjective, or another adverb. Adverbs often answer the questions *when?, where?, how?,* or *to what extent?* The words in italics in the following sentences are adverbs:

Please perform the procedure *now. (When?)*

Put the papers *here. (Where?)*

Alice performed *brilliantly. (How?)*

I am *almost* finished. *(To what extent?)*

The *exceedingly* expensive car was *very carefully* protected.

In the last sentence, the adverb *exceedingly* modifies the adjective *expensive* (how expensive?) and the adverb *very* modifies the adverb *carefully* (how carefully?).

Many (but by no means all) adverbs end in –ly, such as *loudly, quickly, really,* and *carefully.* However, not all words that end in –ly are adverbs; for example, *friendly, stately,* and *ugly* are all adjectives.

1.6 Prepositions   A *preposition* is a word (such as *to, for, from, of,* and *with*) that shows the relationship between a noun or pronoun and some other word in the sentence. The noun or pronoun following the preposition is called the *object* of the preposition, and the entire group of words is called a *prepositional phrase*. In the following sentences, the preposition is shown in italics; the entire prepositional phrase is underlined:

> The ceremony occurred *on* the covered bridge.

> The ceremony occurred *under* the covered bridge.

> Lucia talked *with* Mr. Hines.

> Lucia talked *about* Mr. Hines.

1.7 Conjunctions A *conjunction* is a word (such as *and, or,* or *but*) that joins words or groups of words. For example, in the sentence "Ari and Alice are brokers," the conjunction *and* connects the two nouns *Ari* and *Alice*. In the following sentences, the conjunction is shown in italics; the words it joins are underlined:

> Francesca *or* Teresa will attend the conference. *(joins two nouns)*

> Chang spoke quietly *and* deliberately. *(joins two adverbs)*

> Harriet tripped *but* caught her balance. *(joins two verbs)*

1.8 Interjections An *interjection* is a word that expresses strong emotions. Interjections are used more often in oral communication than in written communication. If an interjection stands alone, it is followed by an exclamation point. If it is a part of the sentence, it is followed by a comma. You should not be surprised to learn that some words can serve as interjections in some sentences and as other parts of speech in other sentences. In the following sentences, the interjection is shown in italics:

> *Good!* I'm glad to learn that the new employee does good work.

> *Oh!* I didn't mean to startle you.

> *My,* I wouldn't do that.

> *Gosh,* that was an exhausting exercise. *Whew!*

Application

Note: For all LAB application exercises, first photocopy the exercise and then complete the exercise on the photocopied pages.

Directions Label each part of speech in Sentences 1–8 with the abbreviation shown below.

adjective	*adj.*
adverb	*adv.*
conjunction	*conj.*
interjection	*interj.*
noun	*n.*
preposition	*prep.*
pronoun	*pron.*
verb	*v.*

1. Oh, don't tell me I missed my flight.

2. My, your new chair is comfortable.

3. When I received your package, I was relieved. Whew!

4. Gosh! I could not believe the depth of the raging water in the river.

5. When the quail and her chicks came into the yard, the hen carefully

   checked the area for predators.

6. Alas! By the time he received her report, the decision had been made.

7. I was disappointed we missed your input to the decision-making process,

   but I hope you can meet the deadline next time.

8. Valerie Renoir, the major conference speaker, was delayed at O'Hare and

   did not arrive at the hall until 2 p.m.

LAB 2: PUNCTUATION—COMMAS

Punctuation serves as a roadmap to help guide the reader through the twists and turns of your message—pointing out what is important (italics or underscores), subordinate (commas), copied from another source (quotation marks), explained further (colon), considered as a unit (hyphens), and so on. Sometimes correct punctuation is absolutely essential for comprehension. Consider, for example, the different meanings of the following sentences, depending on the punctuation:

What's the latest, Dope?
What's the latest dope?

The social secretary called the guests names as they arrived.
The social secretary called the guests' names as they arrived.

Our new model comes in red, green and brown, and white.
Our new model comes in red, green, and brown and white.

The play ended, happily.
The play ended happily.

A clever dog knows it's master.
A clever dog knows its master.

We must still play Michigan, which tied Ohio State, and Minnesota.
We must still play Michigan, which tied Ohio State and Minnesota.

"Medics Help Dog Bite Victim"
"Medics Help Dog-Bite Victim"

The comma rules presented in LAB 2 and the other punctuation rules presented in LAB 3 do not cover every possible situation; comprehensive style manuals, for example, routinely present more than 100 rules just for using the comma rather than just the 11 rules presented here. These rules cover the most frequent uses of punctuation in business writing. Learn them—because you will be using them frequently.

Commas are used to connect ideas and to set off elements within a sentence. When typing, leave one space after a comma. Many writers use commas inappropriately. No matter how long the sentence, make sure you have a legitimate reason before inserting a comma.

COMMAS USED *BETWEEN* EXPRESSIONS

Three types of expressions (an expression is words or groups of words) typically require commas between them: independent clauses, adjacent adjectives, and items in a series.

2.1 Independent Clauses   Use a comma between two independent clauses joined   *, ind*
by a coordinate conjunction (unless both clauses are short and closely related).

> Mr. Karas discussed last month's performance, and Ms. Daniels presented the sales projections.

> The meeting was running late, but Mr. Chande was in no hurry to adjourn.

> *But:* The firm hadn't paid and John was angry.

The major coordinate conjunctions are *and, but, or,* and *nor.* An independent clause is a subject-predicate combination that can stand alone as a complete sentence.

Do not confuse two independent clauses joined by a coordinate conjunction and a comma with a compound predicate, whose verbs are not separated by a comma. *Hint:* Cover up the conjunction with your pencil. If what's on both sides of your pencil could stand alone as complete sentences, a comma is needed.

> **No comma:**   Mrs. Ames had read the report_but had not discussed it with her colleagues. *("Had not discussed it with her colleagues" is not an independent clause; it lacks a subject.)*

> **Comma**:   Mrs. Blanco had read the report, but she had not discussed it with her colleagues.

2.2 Adjacent Adjectives   Use a comma between two adjacent adjectives that   *, adj*
modify the same noun.

> He was an aggressive, unpleasant manager.

> *But:* He was an aggressive_and unpleasant manager. *(The two adjectives are not adjacent; they are separated by the conjunction "and.")*

Do not use a comma if the first adjective modifies the combined idea of the second adjective plus the noun. *Hint:* Mentally insert the word "and" between the two consecutive adjectives. If it does not make sense, do not use a comma.

> Please order a new bulletin board for the executive_conference room.

Do not use a comma between the last adjective and the noun.

> Wednesday was a long, hot, humid_day.

, ser   **2.3 Items in a Series**   Use a comma between each item in a series of three or more. Do not use a comma after the last item in the series.

> The committee may meet on Wednesday, Thursday, or Friday_of next week.
>
> Carl wrote the questionnaire, Anna distributed the forms, and Jacinto tabulated the results_for our survey on employee satisfaction.

> Some style manuals indicate that the last comma before the conjunction is optional. However, to avoid ambiguity in business writing, you should insert this comma.
>
> *Not:* We were served salads, macaroni and cheese and crackers.
>
> *But:* We were served salads, macaroni and cheese, and crackers.
>
> *Or:* We were served salads, macaroni, and cheese and crackers.

COMMAS USED *AFTER* EXPRESSIONS

Two types of expressions typically require commas after them: introductory expressions and complimentary closings in letters.

, intro   **2.4 Introductory Expressions**   Use a comma after an introductory expression. An *introductory expression* is a word, phrase, or clause that comes before the subject and verb of the independent clause. When the same expression occurs at the end of the sentence, no comma is used.

> No, the status report is not ready. *(introductory word)*
>
> Of course, you are not required to sign the petition. *(introductory phrase)*
>
> When the status report is ready, I will call you. *(introductory clause)*
>
> *But:* I will call you when the status report is ready.

> Do not use a comma between the subject and verb—no matter how long or complex the subject is.
>
> To finish that boring and time-consuming task in time for the monthly sales meeting_was a major challenge.
>
> The effort to bring all of our products into compliance with ISO standards and to be eligible for sales in Common Market countries_required a full year of detailed planning.

, clos   **2.5 Complimentary Closing**   Use a comma after the complimentary closing of a business letter formatted in the standard punctuation style.

> Sincerely,   Cordially yours,
>
> Yours truly,   With warm regards,

> With standard punctuation, a colon follows the salutation (such as "Dear Ms. Jones:") and a comma follows the complimentary closing. With open punctuation, no punctuation follows either the salutation or complimentary closing.

COMMAS USED *BEFORE* AND *AFTER* EXPRESSIONS

Numerous types of expressions typically require commas before *and* after them. Of course, if the expression comes at the beginning of a sentence, use a comma only after the expression; if it comes at the end of a sentence, use a comma only before it.

2.6 Nonrestrictive Expressions   Use commas before and after a nonrestrictive expression. A *restrictive expression* is one that limits (restricts) the meaning of the noun or pronoun that it follows and is, therefore, essential to complete the basic meaning of the sentence. A *nonrestrictive expression,* on the other hand, may be omitted without changing the basic meaning of the sentence.

, nonr

Restrictive:	Anyone *with some experience* should apply for the position. ("With some experience" restricts which "anyone" should apply.)
Nonrestrictive:	Anne Suárez, *a clerk with extensive experience*, should apply for the position. (Because Anne Suárez can be only one person, the phrase "a clerk with extensive experience" does not serve to further restrict the noun and is, therefore, not essential to the meaning of the sentence.)
Restrictive:	Only the papers *left on the conference table* are missing. (identifies which papers are missing)
Nonrestrictive:	Lever Brothers, *one of our best customers*, is expanding in Europe. ("One of our best customers" could be omitted without changing the basic meaning of the sentence.)
Restrictive:	The manager *using a great deal of tact* was Ellis.
Nonrestrictive:	Ellis, *using a great deal of tact*, disagreed with her.

An *appositive* is a noun or noun phrase that identifies another noun or pronoun that comes immediately before it. If the appositive is nonrestrictive, insert commas before and after the appositive.

Restrictive:	The word *plagiarism* strikes fear into the heart of many. ("Plagiarism" is an appositive that identifies which word.)
Nonrestrictive:	Mr. Bayrami, *president of the corporation*, is planning to resign. ("President of the corporation" is an appositive that provides additional, but nonessential, information about Mr. Bayrami.)

2.7 Interrupting Expressions   Use commas before and after an interrupting expression. An *interrupting expression* breaks the normal flow of a sentence. Common examples are *in addition, as a result, therefore, in summary, on the other hand, however, unfortunately,* and *as a matter of fact*—when these expressions come in the middle of the sentence.

, inter

You may, of course, cancel your subscription at any time.

One suggestion, for example, was to undertake a leveraged buyout.

I believe it was John, not Nicolette, who raised the question.

It is still not too late to make the change, is it?

Aida's present salary, you must admit, is not in line with those of other network managers.

But: You must admit_Aida's present salary is not in line with those of other network managers.

If the expression does not interrupt the normal flow of the sentence, do not use a comma.

There is no doubt that you are qualified for the position.

But: There is, no doubt, a good explanation for his actions.

, date

2.8 Dates

Use commas before and after the year when it follows the month and day. Do not use a comma after a partial date or when the date is formatted in day-month-year order. If the name of the day precedes the date, also use a comma *after* the name of the day.

> The note is due on May 31, 2007, at 5 p.m.
>
> *But:* The note is due on May 31 at 5 p.m.
>
> *But:* The note is due in May 2007.
>
> *But:* The note is due on 31 May 2007 at 5 p.m.
>
> Let's plan to meet on Wednesday, December 15, 2007, for our year-end review.

, place

2.9 Places

Use commas before and after a state or country that follows a city and between elements of an address in narrative writing.

> The sales conference will be held in Phoenix, Arizona, in May.
>
> Our business agent is located in Brussels, Belgium, in the P.O.M. Building.
>
> You may contact her at 500 Beaufort Drive, LaCrosse, VA 23950. *(Note that there is no comma between the state abbreviation and the ZIP code.)*

, dir ad

2.10 Direct Address

Use commas before and after a name used in direct address. A name is used in *direct address* when the writer speaks directly to (that is, directly addresses) another person.

> Thank you, Ms. Zhao, for bringing the matter to our attention.
>
> Ladies and gentlemen, we appreciate your attending our session today.

, quote

2.11 Direct Quotation

Use commas before and after a direct quotation in a sentence.

> The president said, "You have nothing to fear," and then changed the subject.
>
> "I assure you," the human resources director said, "that no positions will be terminated."

If the quotation is a question, use a question mark instead of a comma.

> "How many have applied?" she asked.

Application

Directions Insert any needed commas in the following sentences. Above each comma, indicate the reason for the comma. If the sentence needs no commas, leave it blank.

Example: As a matter of fact, *(intro)* you may tell her yourself.

1. A comma comes between two adjacent adjectives that modify the same noun but do not use a comma if the first adjective modifies the combined idea of the second adjective and the noun.

2. Stephen generated questions and I supplied responses.

3. At the request of your accountant we are summarizing all charitable deductions in a new format.

4. By asking the right questions we gained all the pertinent information we needed.

5. Everyone please use the door in the rear of the hall.

6. His bid for the congressional seat was successful this time.

7. I disagree with Gabriela but do feel some change in policy is needed.

8. I feel as a matter of fact that the proposed legislation will fall short of the required votes.

9. Ethan will prepare the presentation graphics and let you know when they are ready.

10. Determining purpose analyzing the audience and making content and organization decisions are critical planning steps.

11. It is appropriate I believe to make a preliminary announcement about the new position.

12. A goodwill message is prompt direct sincere specific and brief.

13. Look this decision affects me as much as it does you.

14. The teacher using one of her favorite techniques prompted the student into action.

15. Subordinate bad news by using the direct plan by avoiding negative terms and by presenting the news after the reasons are given.

16. My favorite destination is Atlanta Georgia.

17. The team presented a well-planned logical scenario to explain the company's status.

18. Evan plans to conclude his investigation and explain the results by Friday but would not promise a written report until Tuesday.

19. We appreciate your business.

Sincerely

Medea Haddad

20. Those instructors who were from southern schools were anxious to see the results of the study completed in Birmingham.

21. A group of teachers from Michigan attended the conference this year.

22. Our next training session will be located in Madison Wisconsin sometime in the spring.

23. The next meeting of our professional organization will be held in the winter not in the spring.

24. The brochure states "Satisfaction is guaranteed or your money will be freely refunded."

25. The department meeting you will note will be held every other Monday.

26. This assignment is due on April 20 which is one week before the end of the semester.

27. I need the cabinets installed by the week before my family arrives.

28. To qualify for promotion will require recommendations and long hours of preparation.

29. To qualify for promotion you will need recommendations from previous managers.

30. To earn an award for outstanding sales is an achievable goal for Mary.

31. To earn an award for outstanding sales Mary must set intermittent goals that are attainable.

32. Dave was promoted in his job by working hard.

33. Shayna's sister was born on June 6 1957, in Munster Indiana.

34. Ted could paint the house himself or he could hire a professional to do the job.

35. I am telling you Esther that your report has been misplaced.

LAB 3: PUNCTUATION—OTHER MARKS

HYPHENS

Hyphens are used to form some compound adjectives, to link some prefixes to root words (such as *quasi-public*), and to divide words at the ends of lines. When typing, do not leave a space before or after a regular hyphen. Likewise, do not use a hyphen with a space before and after to substitute for a dash. Make a dash by typing two hyphens with no space before, between, or after. Most word processing programs automatically reformat two hyphens into a printed dash.

3.1 Compound Adjective   Hyphenate a compound adjective that comes *before* a noun (unless the adjective is a proper noun or unless the first word is an adverb ending in *-ly*).

— adj

> We hired a first-class management team.
>
> *But:* Our new management team is first_class.
>
> The long-term outlook for our investments is excellent.
>
> *But:* We intend to hold our investments for the long_term.
>
> *But:* The General_Motors warranty received high ratings.
>
> *But:* Huang presented a poorly_conceived proposal.

Note: Don't confuse compound adjectives (which are generally temporary combinations) with compound nouns (which are generally well-established concepts). Compound nouns (such as *Social Security, life insurance, word processing,* and *high school*) are not hyphenated when used as adjectives that come before a noun; thus, use *income_tax form, real_estate agent, public_relations firm,* and *data_processing center.*

3.2 Numbers   Hyphenate fractions and compound numbers 21 through 99 when they are spelled out.

— num

> Nearly three-fourths of our new applicants were unqualified.
>
> Seventy-two orders were processed incorrectly last week.

SEMICOLONS

Semicolons are used to show where elements in a sentence are separated. The separation is stronger than a comma but not as strong as a period. When typing, leave one space after a semicolon and begin the following word with a lowercase letter.

3.3 Independent Clauses with Commas   If a misreading might otherwise occur, use a semicolon (instead of a comma) to separate independent clauses that contain internal commas. Make sure that the semicolon is inserted *between* the independent clauses—not *within* one of the clauses.

; comma

> *Confusing:* I ordered juice, toast, and bacon, and eggs, toast, and sausage were sent instead.
>
> *Clear:* I ordered juice, toast, and bacon; and eggs, toast, and sausage were sent instead.
>
> *But:* Although high-quality paper was used, the photocopy machine still jammed, and neither of us knew how to repair it. *(no misreading likely to occur)*

3.4 Independent Clauses Without a Conjunction   Use a semicolon between independent clauses that are not connected by a coordinate conjunction (such as *and, but, or,* or *nor*). You have already learned to use a comma before coordinate conjunctions when they connect independent clauses. This rule applies to independent clauses *not* connected by a conjunction.

; no conj

> The president was eager to proceed with the plans; the board still had some reservations.

But: The president was eager to proceed with the plans, but the board still had some reservations. *(Use a comma instead of a semicolon if the clauses are joined by a coordinate conjunction.)*

Bannon Corporation exceeded its sales goal this quarter; furthermore, it rang up its highest net profit ever.

But: Bannon Corporation exceeded its sales goal this quarter, and, furthermore, it rang up its highest net profit ever. *(Use a comma instead of a semicolon if the clauses are joined by a coordinate conjunction.)*

; ser   **3.5 Series with Internal Commas**   Use a semicolon after each item in a series if any of the items already contain a comma. Normally, we separate items in a series with commas. However, if any of those items already contain a comma, we need a stronger mark (semicolon) between the items.

The human resources department will be interviewing in Dallas, Texas; Stillwater, Oklahoma; and Little Rock, Arkansas, for the new position.

Among the guests were Henry Halston, our attorney; Phaedra Hart-Wilder; and Isabella Grimes, our new controller.

COLONS

A colon is used after an independent clause that introduces explanatory material and after the salutation of a business letter that uses the standard punctuation style. When typing, leave one space after a colon; do not begin the following word with a capital letter unless it begins a quoted sentence.

: exp   **3.6 Explanatory Material**   Use a colon to introduce explanatory material that is preceded by an independent clause.

His directions were as follows: turn right and proceed to the third house on the left.

I now have openings on the following dates: January 18, 19, and 20.

Just remember this: you may need a reference from her in the future.

The fall trade show offers the following advantages: inexpensive show space, abundant traffic, and free press publicity.

Expressions commonly used to introduce explanatory material are *the following, as follows, this,* and *these.* Make sure the clause preceding the explanatory material can stand alone as a complete sentence. Do not place a colon after a verb or a preposition that introduces a list.

NOT ▶ My responsibilities were: opening the mail, sorting it, and delivering it to each department.

BUT ▶ My responsibilities were opening the mail, sorting it, and delivering it to each department.

: salut   **3.7 Salutations**   Use a colon after the salutation of a business letter that uses the standard punctuation style.

Dear Ms. Havelchek: Dear Human Resources Manager: Dear Rubén:

Never use a comma after the salutation in a business letter. (A comma is appropriate only in a personal letter.) With standard punctuation, a colon follows the salutation and a comma follows the complimentary closing. With *open* punctuation, no punctuation follows the salutation or complimentary closing.

APOSTROPHES

Apostrophes are used to show that letters have been omitted (as in contractions) and to show possession. When typing, do not space before or after an apostrophe (unless a space after is needed before another word).

Remember this helpful hint: whenever a noun ending in s is followed by another noun, the first noun is probably a possessive, requiring an apostrophe. However, if the first noun *describes* rather than establishes ownership, no apostrophe is used.

Bernie's department *(shows ownership; therefore, an apostrophe)*

the sales department *(describes; therefore, no apostrophe)*

3.8 Singular Nouns   To form the possessive of a singular noun, add an apostrophe plus s.   *'sing*

my accountant's fee	a child's toy
the company's stock	Eva's choice
Alzheimer's disease	Mr. and Mrs. Yuan's home
a year's time	the boss's contract
Ms. Morris's office	Liz's promotion
Gil Hodges's record	Carl Bissett Jr.'s birthday

3.9 Plural Nouns Ending in S   To form the possessive of a plural noun that ends in s (that is, most plural nouns), add an apostrophe only.   *'plur + s*

our accountants' fees	both companies' stock
the Dyes' home	two years' time

3.10 Plural Nouns Not Ending in S   To form the possessive of a plural noun that does not end in s, add an apostrophe plus s (just as you would for singular nouns).   *'plur − s*

the children's hour	the men's room
the alumni's contribution	

Hint: To avoid confusion in forming the possessive of plural nouns, first form the plural; then apply the appropriate rule.

Singular	Plural	Plural Possessive
employee	employees	employees' bonuses
hero	heroes	heroes' welcome
Mr. and Mrs. Lake	the Lakes	the Lakes' home
woman	women	women's clothing

3.11 Pronouns   To form the possessive of an indefinite pronoun, add an apostrophe plus s. Do not use an apostrophe to form the possessive of personal pronouns.   *'pro*

It is *someone's* responsibility.

But: The responsibility is *theirs*.

I will review *everybody's* figures.

But: The bank will review *its* figures.

Note: Examples of indefinite possessive pronouns are *anybody's, everyone's, no one's, nobody's, one's,* and *somebody's*. Examples of personal possessive pronouns are *hers*, *his*, *its*, *ours*, *theirs*, and *yours*. Do not confuse the possessive pronouns *its*, *theirs*, and *whose* with the contractions *it's*, *there's*, and *who's*.

> *It's* time to put litter in *its* place.
>
> *There's* no reason to take *theirs*.
>
> *Who's* determining *whose* jobs will be eliminated?

'ger **3.12 Gerunds**   Use the possessive form for a noun or pronoun that comes before a gerund. (A gerund is the *–ing* form of a verb used as a noun.)

> Garth questioned *Karen's* leaving so soon.
>
> *Stockholders'* raising so many questions delayed the adjournment.
>
> Mr. Matsumoto knew Karl and objected to *his* going to the meeting.

PERIODS

Periods are used at the ends of declarative sentences and polite requests and in abbreviations. When typing, leave one space after a period (or any other punctuation mark).

.req **3.13 Polite Requests**   Use a period after a polite request. Consider a statement a polite request if you expect the reader to respond by *acting* rather than by giving a yes-or-no answer.

> Would you please sign the form on page 2.
>
> May I please have the report by Friday.
>
> But: Would you be willing to take on this assignment? *(This sentence is a real question, requiring a question mark. You expect the reader to respond by saying "yes" or "no.")*

QUOTATION MARKS

Quotation marks are used around direct quotations, titles of some publications and conferences, and special terms. Type the closing quotation mark after a period or comma but before a colon or semicolon. Type the closing quotation mark after a question mark or exclamation point if the quoted material itself is a question or an exclamation; otherwise, type it before the question mark or exclamation. Capitalize the first word of a quotation that begins a sentence.

"quote **3.14 Direct Quotation**   Use quotation marks around a direct quotation—that is, around the exact words of a person.

> "When we return on Thursday," Luis said, "we need to meet with you."
>
> But: Luis said that when we return on Thursday, we need to meet with you. *(no quotation marks needed in an indirect quotation)*
>
> Did Helen say, "He will represent us"?
>
> Helen asked, "Will he represent us?"

3.15 Term   Use quotation marks around a term to clarify its meaning or to show that it is being used in a special way.

"*term*

> Net income after taxes is known as "the bottom line"; that's what's important around here.

> The job title changed from "chairman" to "chief executive officer."

> The president misused the word "effect" in last night's press conference.

3.16 Title   Use quotation marks around the title of a newspaper or magazine article, chapter in a book, report, conference, and similar items.

"*title*

> Read the article entitled "Wall Street Recovery."

> Chapter 4, "Market Segmentation," of *Industrial Marketing* is of special interest.

> The theme of this year's sales conference is "Quality Sells."

> The report "Common Carriers" shows the extent of the transportation problems.

> *Note:* The titles of *complete* published works are shown in italics (see below). The titles of *parts* of published works and most other titles are enclosed in quotation marks.

ITALICS (OR UNDERLINING)

Before the advent of word processing software, underlining was used to emphasize words or indicate certain titles. Today, the use of italics is preferred for these functions.

3.17 Titles   Italicize the title of a book, magazine, newspaper, and other *complete* published works.

<u>*Title*</u>

> Liang's newest book, *All That Glitters,* was reviewed in the *New York Times* and in the *Los Angeles Times.*

> The cover story in last week's *Time* magazine was "Is the Economic Expansion Over?"

ELLIPSES

An ellipsis is an omission. Three periods, with one space before and after each, are used to show that something has been left out of a quotation. Four periods (the sentence period plus the three ellipsis periods) indicate the omission of the last part of a quoted sentence, the first part of the next sentence, or a whole sentence or paragraph. Here is an example of a quotation from Bank of America CEO Brian Moynihan:[1]

Complete Quotation:

Our quarterly results show that we are making progress on our strategy to align around our three core customer groups—consumers, businesses, and institutional investors—and create the financial institution that customers tell us they want, built on a broad relationship of clarity, transparency, and helping them manage through challenging times. We improved our capital foundation

---

[1]Dawn Kawamoto, "Bank of America Earnings Beat Wall Street Estimates," Daily Finance, July 16, 2010, http://www.dailyfinance.com/2010/07/16/bank-of-america-earnings-beats-wall-street-estimates/, accessed July 26, 2011.

through retained earnings, and credit quality improved even faster than expected. We have the most complete financial franchise in the world, and we are focused on executing our strategy and delivering outstanding long-term value to our customers and shareholders.

Shortened Quotation:

Our quarterly results show that we are making progress on our strategy to align around our three core customer groups . . . and create the financial institution that customers tell us they want, built on a broad relationship of clarity, transparency, and helping them manage through challenging times. . . . We have the most complete financial franchise in the world, and we are focused on executing our strategy and delivering outstanding long-term value to our customers and shareholders.

Note: The typing sequence for the first ellipsis is *space period space period space period space*. The sequence for the second ellipsis is *period space period space period space period space*.

3.18 Omission   Use ellipsis periods to indicate that one or more words have been omitted from quoted material.

According to *Business Week,* "A continuing protest could shut down . . . Pemex, which brought in 34% of Mexico's dollar income last year."

Application

Directions Insert any needed punctuation (including commas) in the following sentences. Underline any expression that should be italicized. Above each mark of punctuation, indicate the reason for the punctuation. If the sentence needs no punctuation, leave it blank.

Example: We received our money's worth.

1. Bernice tried to use the new software but she had trouble with the computer.

2. Juanita Johnsons raising the expectations for promotion was hotly debated.

3. The short term goal of the department was improvement in software utilization.

4. It was a poorly designed office.

5. Approximately one half of the orders came from Spokane Washington.

6. Bertram preferred soda hamburgers and fries but iced tea, hot dogs and onion rings were served instead.

7. The classes started on time the school was entirely on schedule.

8. Did you met Sally Henley our manager Paul Krause and Ana Chávez our attorney?

9. Remember this the best recommendation is a job well done.

10. Dear Mr. Weatherby

11. Did you get the total from the sales department?

12. Jason s boss will distribute the new guidelines for his department.

13. Within two years time the neighborhood will double in size.

14. Locking the door to the department was someones responsibility.

15. Fabiáns guiding the discussion was a departure from the regular procedure.

16. Would you please sort these responses for me

17. The teacher said The samples you submitted were excellent.

18. Would you believe he misspelled the word their in his report?

19. The article entitled Technology for Fitness should be required reading.

20. Time magazine features a person of the year each December.

21. I want her to know she is a highly respected employee.

22. The meeting s date was rescheduled.

23. If the tickets sell we will tell Mrs. Zimfer she will take it from there.

24. The hotels guests thought the conference rooms temperatures were too cold.

25. They were watching the demonstration nevertheless they didn't understand
     the last section.

26. Can we keep this off the record?

27. You will receive the materials tomorrow but stop by today to see Alberto
     our corporate trainer for a quick preview.

28. I can do this for you either on December 5 2005 or January 13 2006.

29. This is a once in a lifetime opportunity for our employees families.

30. Mr. Henry will see you after the meeting Mr. Perez will not be available.

LAB 4: GRAMMAR

Suppose the vice president of your organization asked you, a systems analyst, to try to locate a troublesome problem in a computer spreadsheet. After some sharp detective work, you finally resolved the problem and wrote a memo to the vice president saying, "John and myself discovered that one of the formulas were incorrect, so I asked he to revise it."

Instantly, you've turned what should have been a "good-news" opportunity for you into, at best, a "mixed-news" situation. The vice president will be pleased that you've uncovered the bug in the program but will probably focus entirely too much attention on your poor grammar skills.

Grammar refers to the rules for combining words into sentences. The most frequent grammar problems faced by business writers are discussed below. Learn these common rules well so that your use of grammar will not present a communication barrier in the message you're trying to convey.

COMPLETE SENTENCES

4.1 Fragment   Avoid sentence fragments.

> **NOT** ▶ He had always wanted to be a marketing representative. Because he liked to interact with people.

> **BUT** ▶ He had always wanted to be a marketing representative because he liked to interact with people.

Note: A fragment is a part of a sentence that is incorrectly punctuated as a complete sentence. Each sentence must contain a complete thought.

4.2 Run-on Sentences   Avoid run-on sentences.

> **NOT** ▶ Fidélia Padilla is a hard worker she even frequently works through lunch.

> **NOT** ▶ Fidélia Padilla is a hard worker, she even frequently works through lunch.

> **BUT** ▶ Fidélia Padilla is a hard worker; she even frequently works through lunch.

> **BUT** ▶ Fidélia Padilla is a hard worker. She even frequently works through lunch.

Note: A run-on sentence is two independent clauses run together without any punctuation between them or with only a comma between them (the latter error is called a *comma splice*).

MODIFIERS (ADJECTIVES AND ADVERBS)

An adjective modifies a noun or pronoun; an adverb modifies a verb, an adjective, or another adverb.

4.3 Modifiers   Use a comparative adjective or adverb (*-er, more,* or *less*) to refer to two persons, places, or things and a superlative adjective or adverb (*-est, most,* or *least*) to refer to more than two.

The Datascan is the fast**er** of the two machines.

The XR-75 is the slow**est** of all the machines.

Rose Marie is the **less** qualified of the two applicants.

Rose Marie is the **least** qualified of the three applicants.

Note: Do not use double comparisons, such as "more faster."

AGREEMENT (SUBJECT/VERB/PRONOUN)

Agreement refers to correspondence in number between related subjects, verbs, and pronouns. All must be singular if they refer to one, plural if they refer to more than one.

4.4 Agreement   Use a singular verb or pronoun with a singular subject and a plural verb or pronoun with a plural subject.

> The four **workers have** copies of **their** assignments.

> Roger's **wife was** quite late for **her** appointment.

> **Mr. Kucera and Ms. Downs plan** to forgo **their** bonuses.

> Included in this envelope **are a contract and an affidavit.**

Note: This is the general rule; variations are discussed below. In the first sentence, the plural subject (*workers*) requires a plural verb (*have*) and a plural pronoun (*their*). In the second sentence, the singular subject (*wife*) requires a singular verb (*was*) and a singular pronoun (*her*). In the third sentence, the plural subject (*Mr. Kucera and Ms. Downs*) requires a plural verb (*plan*) and a plural pronoun (*their*). In the last sentence, the subject is *a contract and an affidavit—not envelope.*

4.5 Company Names   Treat company names as singular.

> **NOT** ▶ Bickley and Bates **has** paid for **its** last order. **They** are ready to reorder.

> **BUT** ▶ Bickley and Bates **has** paid for **its** last order. **It** is now ready to reorder.

4.6 Expletives   In sentences that begin with an expletive, the true subject follows the verb. Use *is* or *are*, as appropriate.

> There **is** no **reason** for his behavior.

> There **are** many **reasons** for his behavior.

Note: An expletive is an expression such as *there is, there are, here is,* and *here are* that comes at the beginning of a clause or sentence. Because the topic of a sentence that begins with an expletive is not immediately apparent, such sentences should be used sparingly in business writing.

4.7 Intervening Words   Disregard any words that come between the subject and verb when establishing agreement. See, however, Rule 4.8 regarding special treatment of certain pronouns.

> Only **one** of the mechanics **guarantees his** work. (not *their work*)

> The **appearance** of the workers, not their competence, **was** being questioned.

> The **administrative assistant,** as well as the clerks, **was** late filing **her** form. (not *their forms*)

Note: First determine the subject; then make the verb agree. Other intervening words that do not affect the number of the verb are *together with, rather than, accompanied by, in addition to,* and *except.*

4.8 Pronouns   Some pronouns (*anybody, each, either, everybody, everyone, much, neither, no one, nobody,* and *one*) are always singular. Other pronouns (*all, any, more, most, none,* and *some*) may be singular or plural, depending on the noun to which they refer.

Each of the laborers **has** a different view of **his or her** job.

Neither of the models **is** doing **her** job well.

Everybody is required to take **his or her** turn at the booth. (not *their turn*)

All the **pie has** been eaten.   **None** of the **work is** finished.

All the **cookies have** been eaten.   **None** of the **workers are** finished.

4.9 *Subject Nearer to Verb*   If two subjects are joined by correlative conjunctions (*or, either/or, nor, neither/nor,* or *not only/but also*), the verb and any pronoun should agree with the subject that is nearer to the verb.

Either Pablo or **Harold is** at **his** desk.

Neither the receptionist nor the **operators were** able to finish **their** tasks.

Not only the actress but also the **dancer has** to practice **her** routine.

The tellers or the **clerks have** to balance **their** cash drawers before leaving.

Note: The first noun in this type of construction may be disregarded when determining whether the verb should be singular or plural. Pay special attention to using the correct pronoun; do not use the plural pronoun *their* unless the subject and verb are plural. Note that subjects joined by *and* or *both/and* are always plural: *Both* **the actress and the dancer have** to practice **their** routines.

4.10 *Subjunctive Mood*   Verbs in the subjunctive mood require the plural form, even when the subject is singular.

I wish the situation **were** reversed.

If I **were** you, I would not mention the matter.

Note: Verbs in the subjunctive mood refer to conditions that are impossible or improbable.

CASE

Case refers to the form of a pronoun and indicates its use in a sentence. There are three cases: nominative, objective, and possessive. (Possessive-case pronouns are covered under "Apostrophes" in the section on punctuation in LAB 3.) Reflexive pronouns, which end in *-self* or *-selves*, refer to nouns or other pronouns.

4.11 *Nominative Case*   Use nominative pronouns (*I, he, she, we, they, who, whoever*) as subjects of a sentence or clause and with the verb *to be.*

The customer representative and **he** are furnishing the figures. (**he** *is furnishing*)

Mrs. Quigley asked if Oscar and **I** were ready to begin. (**I** *was ready to begin*)

We old-timers can provide some background. (**we** *can provide*)

It was **she** who agreed to the proposal. (**she** *agreed*)

Who is chairing the meeting? (**he** *is chairing*)

Mr. Lentzner wanted to know **who** was responsible. (**she** *was responsible*)

Guadalupe is the type of person **who** can be depended upon. (**she** *can be depended upon*)

Note: If you have trouble determining which pronoun to use, ignore the plural subject or substitute another pronoun. See the reworded clauses in parentheses.

4.12 Objective Case   Use objective pronouns (*me, him, her, us, them, whom, whomever*) as objects in a sentence, clause, or phrase.

> Thomas sent a fax to Mr. Baird and **me.** (*sent a fax to* **me**)

> This policy applies to Eric and **her.** (*applies to* **her**)

> Habib asked **us** old-timers to provide some background. (*Habib asked* **us** *to provide*)

> The work was assigned to **her** and **me.** (*the work was assigned to* **me**)

> To **whom** shall we mail the specifications? (*mail them to* **him**)

> Guadalupe is the type of person **whom** we can depend upon. (*we can depend upon* **her**)

Note: For *who/whom* constructions, if *he* or *she* can be substituted, *who* is the correct choice; if *him* or *her* can be substituted, *whom* is the correct choice. Remember: *who-he, whom-him.* The difference is apparent in the final examples shown here and under "Nominative Case," Rule 4.11: **who** *can be depended upon* versus **whom** *we can depend upon.*

4.13 Reflexive Pronouns   Use reflexive pronouns (*myself, yourself, himself, herself, itself, ourselves, yourselves,* or *themselves*) to refer to or emphasize a noun or pronoun *that has already been named.* Do not use reflexive pronouns to *substitute for* nominative or objective pronouns.

> I **myself** have some doubts about the proposal.

> You should see the exhibit **yourself.**

> **NOT** Virginia and **myself** will take care of the details.

> **BUT** Virginia and **I** will take care of the details.

> **NOT** Maya Louise administered the test to Thomas and **myself.**

> **BUT** Maya Louise administered the test to Thomas and **me.**

Application

Directions Select the correct words or words in parentheses.

1. (Who/Whom) is your favorite new chef? Laura Buraston, who along with Frederico Fox, (are/is) a new chef in Tucson. Some of my friends (has/have) eaten at their restaurants. Laura, they say, is the (better/best) of the two.

2. Merchant Associates is presenting (its/it's/their/there) seminar in Kansas City. The associates will work with seven or eight participants in developing (their/there) portfolios. Not only Dr. Merchant but also his associates (is/are) willing to mentor faculty members. Dr. Merchant asked all participants to acknowledge the invitation with written responses to (he/him).

3. If I (was/were) you, I would be (more/most) helpful with organizing the conference. You can work directly with Sandra and (me/myself). After all, Sandra knows that it was (I/me) (who/whom) made key contacts. This opportunity is open to the type of person (who/whom) we can depend on.

4. The report on sales volume (is/are) finally on my desk. (Us/We) managers may be somewhat apprehensive about these reports, but sales results tend to predict (who/whom) can be depended upon.

5. Not only the lawyer but also the manager (was/were) able to attend the conference on ethics. Everybody in the firm (is/are) trying to participate as a way to improve (their/his or her) performance. Each of the employees (is/are) eager to attend the next session.

6. There (was/were) several students in the class (who/whom) challenged whether each of the assignments (was/were) comparable in complexity. The professor asked (us/we) group leaders to evaluate the students' concerns.

7. Neither the professors nor the dean (was/were) able to meet Dr. Phyllis Hart, the conference speaker, at the airport. In fact, neither of the professors (was/were) able to pick her up at the hotel either. However, Dean Dye, as well as two other professors, (is/are) escorting her to the banquet.

8. Martin's and Ricardo's groups are the (more quicker/most quicker/quicker/quickest) in the class. Ricardo's group is the (more slow/most slow/slower/slowest) of these two groups. In any case, all of the jobs (has/have) been submitted for both groups.

9. (Who/Whom) will you ask to participate in the evaluation process? If I (was/were) you, I'd consider Hillary. While Jane is the (more/most) competent software expert we have available, Hillary is the type of team player (who/whom) can provide the leadership we need.

10. I wish it (was/were) possible for Machiko and (I/me/myself) to see both Marty and Alex in (his/their) last performance this season. Machiko and (I/me/myself) have always had a gathering in our home after they finished. Watching their reactions to the reviewers' comments as they were given (is/are) exciting, but as we are leaving too, it remains to be seen (who/whom) will assume that function next year.

Directions Revise the following paragraph to eliminate any fragments and run-on sentences.

FunTimes by Travel Log is a prepaid vacation program designed with families in mind. Club owners have permanent usage rights in a continually growing system of outstanding resorts. Unlike the traditional time-share plans. Members may select any of the club resorts as a destination with optional access to other resorts through exchange programs, the owners may select additional vacation sites, both in the United States and internationally. The membership fee entitles an owner to a fixed number of points each year, up to three years' worth can be accumulated so a selected vacation can be upgraded or lengthened. Future points can be "borrowed" for use on a current vacation. Reservations may be made up to 13 months in advance these features make this plan an economical and flexible way to create family vacation memories.

LAB 5: MECHANICS

Writing mechanics refer to those elements in communication that are evident only in written form: abbreviations, capitalization, number expression, spelling, and word division. (Punctuation, also a form of writing mechanics, was covered in LABs 2 and 3.) While creating a first draft, you need not be too concerned about the mechanics of your writing. However, you should be especially alert during the editing and proofreading stages to follow these common rules.

ABBREVIATIONS

Use abbreviations according to organizational norms for business writing. Be sure that your audience will understand your abbreviation, or follow the rule "When in doubt, write it out." When typing, do not space within abbreviations except to separate each initial of a person's name. Leave one space after an abbreviation unless another mark of punctuation follows immediately.

5.1 Not Abbreviated   In narrative writing, do not abbreviate common nouns (such as *acct., assoc., bldg., co., dept., misc.,* and *pkg.*) or the names of cities, states (except in addresses), months, and days of the week.

5.2 With Periods   Use periods to indicate many abbreviations.

No.	8:00 a.m.	4 ft.
Dr. M. L. Peterson	P.O. Box 45	e.g.

5.3 Without Periods   Write some abbreviations in all capitals, with no periods—including all two-letter state abbreviations used in addresses with ZIP codes.

CPA	IRS	CT
TWA	MBA	OK

Note: Use two-letter state abbreviations in bibliographic citations.

CAPITALIZATION

The function of capitalization is to emphasize words or to show their importance. For example, the first word of a sentence is capitalized to emphasize that a new sentence has begun.

5.4 Compass Point   Capitalize a compass point that designates a definite region or that is part of an official name. (Do not capitalize compass points used as directions.)

Margot lives in the **S**outh.

Our display window faces **w**est.

Is **E**ast Orange in **W**est Virginia?

5.5 Letter Part   Capitalize the first word and any proper nouns in the salutation and complimentary closing of a business letter.

Dear **M**r. **F**edorov:	**S**incerely **y**ours,
Dear **M**r. and **M**rs. **A**mes:	**Y**ours **t**ruly,

5.6 Noun Plus Number   Capitalize a noun followed by a number or letter (except for page and size numbers).

Table 3	**p**age 79
Flight 1062	**s**ize 8D

5.7 Position Title   Capitalize an official position title that comes before a personal name, unless the personal name is an appositive set off by commas. Do not capitalize a position title used alone.

Vice **P**resident Alfredo Tenegco	Shirley Wilhite, **d**ean,
our **p**resident, Joanne Rathburn,	The **c**hief **e**xecutive **o**fficer retired.

5.8 Proper Noun   Capitalize proper nouns and adjectives derived from proper nouns. Do not capitalize articles, conjunctions, and prepositions typically of four or fewer letters (for example, *a, an, the, and, of,* and *from*). The names of the seasons and the names of generic school courses are not proper nouns and are not capitalized.

Xerox copier	**A**mherst **C**ollege (*but:* the **c**ollege)
New **Y**ork **C**ity (*but:* the **c**ity)	the **M**exican border
the **F**ourth of **J**uly	**F**riday, **M**arch 3,
Chrysler **B**uilding	**B**ank of **A**merica
First-**C**lass **S**torage **C**ompany	**M**argaret **A**dams-**W**hite
business **c**ommunication	the **w**inter holidays

5.9 Quotation   Capitalize the first word of a quoted sentence. (Do not capitalize the first word of an indirect quotation.)

According to Hall, "**T**he goal of quality control is specified uniform quality."

Hall thinks we should work toward "**s**pecified uniform quality."

Hall said that **u**niform quality is the goal.

5.10 Title   In a published title, capitalize the first and last words, the first word after a colon or dash, and all other words except articles, conjunctions, and prepositions of four or fewer letters.

"**A W**ord to the **W**ise"

Pricing **S***trategies:* **T***he* **L***ink with* **R***eality*

NUMBERS

Authorities do not agree on a single style for expressing numbers—whether to spell out a number in words or to write it in figures. The following guidelines apply to typical business writing. (The alternative is to use a *formal* style, in which all numbers that can be expressed in one or two words are spelled out.) When typing numbers in figures, separate thousands, millions, and billions with commas; and leave a space between a whole-number figure and its fraction unless the fraction is a character on the keyboard or is created automatically by your word processing software.

5.11 General   Spell out numbers for zero through ten and use figures for 11 and higher.

the first three pages	ten complaints
18 photocopies	5,376 stockholders

Note: Follow this rule only when none of the following special rules apply.

5.12 Figures   Use figures for

- dates. (Use the endings *-st, -d, -rd,* or *-th* only when the day precedes the month.)
- all numbers if two or more *related* numbers both above and below ten are used in the same sentence.
- measurements—such as time, money, distance, weight, and percentage. Be consistent in using either the word *percent* or the symbol %.
- mixed numbers.

May 9 (or the 9th of May)	10 miles
4 men and 18 women	*But:* The **18** women had **four** cars.
$6	5 p.m. (or 5 o'clock)
5 percent (or 5%)	6½
	But: 6 3/18

5.13 Words   Spell out

- a number used as the first word of a sentence.
- the smaller number when two numbers come together.
- fractions.
- the words *million* and *billion* in even numbers.

Thirty-two people attended.	nearly two-thirds of them
three 41-cent stamps	150 two-page brochures
37 million	$4.8 billion

Note: When fractions and the numbers 21 through 99 are spelled out, they should be hyphenated.

SPELLING

Correct spelling is essential to effective communication. A misspelled word can distract the reader, cause misunderstanding, and send a negative message about the writer's competence. Because of the many variations in the spelling of English words, no spelling guidelines are foolproof; there are exceptions to every spelling rule. The five rules that follow, however, may be safely applied in most business writing situations. Learning them will save you the time of looking up many words in a dictionary.

5.14 Doubling a Final Consonant   If the last syllable of a root word is stressed, double the final consonant when adding a suffix.

Last Syllable Stressed		Last Syllable Not Stressed	
prefer	prefe**rr**ing	happen	happe**n**ing
control	contro**ll**ing	total	totaling
occur	occu**rr**ence	differ	differed

5.15 One-Syllable Words   If a one-syllable word ends in a consonant preceded by a single vowel, double the final consonant before a suffix starting with a vowel.

Suffix Starting with Vowel		Suffix Starting with Consonant	
ship	shi**pp**er	ship	ship**m**ent
drop	dro**pp**ed	glad	gla**d**ness
bag	ba**gg**age	bad	ba**d**ly

5.16 Final E   If a final *e* is preceded by a consonant, drop the *e* before a suffix starting with a vowel.

Suffix Starting with Vowel		Suffix Starting with Consonant	
come	co**m**ing	hope	hop**e**ful
use	us**a**ble	manage	manag**e**ment
sincere	since**r**ity	sincere	sincer**e**ly

Note: Words ending in *ce* or *ge* usually retain the *e* before a suffix starting with a vowel: *notic**e**able, advantag**e**ous.*

5.17 Final Y   If a final *y* is preceded by a consonant, change *y* to *i* before any suffix except one starting with i.

Most Suffixes		Suffix Starting with i	
company	compan**i**es	try	tr**y**ing
ordinary	ordinar**i**ly	forty	fort**y**ish
hurry	hurr**i**ed		

5.18 *EI and* IE *Words*   Remember the rhyme:

Use i before *e*	bel**ie**ve	y**ie**ld
Except after *c*	rec**ei**ve	dec**ei**t
Or when sounded like *a*	fr**ei**ght	th**ei**r
As in *neighbor* and *weigh.*		

WORD AND PARAGRAPH DIVISION

When possible, avoid dividing words at the end of a line, because word divisions tend to slow down or even confuse a reader (for example, *rear- range* for *rearrange* or *read- just* for *readjust*). However, when necessary to avoid grossly uneven right margins, use the following rules. Most word processing software programs have a hyphenation feature that automatically divides words to make a more even right margin; you can change these word divisions manually if necessary. When you are typing, do not space before a hyphen.

5.19 Compound Word   Divide a compound word either after the hyphen or where the two words join to make a solid compound.

    self- service   free- way   battle- field

5.20 Division Point   Leave at least two letters on the upper line and carry at least three letters to the next line.

    ex- treme   typ- ing

5.21 Not Divided   Do not divide a one-syllable word, contraction, or abbreviation.

straight   shouldn't

UNESCO   approx.

5.22 Syllables   Divide words only between syllables.

re-sources   knowl- edge

Note: When in doubt about where a syllable ends, consult a dictionary.

5.23 Web Addresses   Avoid breaking a URL (web address) or email address to a second line. If you must, break it before a period. Never add a hyphen, which the reader may misunderstand to be part of the address.

5.24 Paragraphs   If it is necessary to divide a paragraph between two pages, leave at least two lines of the paragraph at the bottom of the first page and carry forward at least two lines to the top of the next page. Do not divide a three-line paragraph.

Application

Directions   Rewrite the following paragraphs so that all words and numbers are expressed correctly. Do not change the wording in any sentences.

1. 100 of our elementary students will receive passes to Holly's Heartland Amusement Park today. Mrs. freda t. albertson, principal, indicated students from every grade were randomly selected to receive the free passes. The students represent about a 1/5 of the school's population.

2. As of Sept. 1st, nearly ¾ of our parents have attended at least one learning style orientation seminar. The School Psychologist, John Sibilsky, summarized the response of the participants and reported a favorable evaluation by ninety-six parents.

3. The Athletes for Freedom participants sponsored 12 2-hour presentations in a 3-week period. The last stop was east St. Louis, before the long ride home.

4. As reported on Page 2 of today's newspaper, the price of a barrel of oil has continued to climb. According to president Victoria payton, the price is 1 ½ times higher than last year.

5. This month's issue of Time magazine reports an interview with justin lake who said, "Service to our country is measured by many things, but a gift of time is one of the more significant." Our employees gave a total of two-hundred-ninety-five hours.

Directions   Correct the one misspelling in each line.

1. preferring	controlling	occurence
2. shipper	droped	baggage
3. totalling	badly	shipment
4. differred	happening	gladness
5. sincerity	sincerly	noticeable
6. trying	fortyish	ordinarly
7. deceit	yeild	believe
8. advantagous	hopeful	companies

9.	changeable	boundary	arguement
10.	catagory	apparent	criticize
11.	recommend	accomodate	weird
12.	plausable	indispensable	allotted
13.	camouflage	innocence	seperately
14.	nickle	miniature	embarrassing
15.	liaison	exhilarated	inadvertant

Directions Write the following words, inserting a hyphen or blank space at the first correct division point. If a word cannot be divided, write it without a hyphen.

Examples: mis-spelled
        thought

1.	freeway	chairperson	lien
2.	express	exploitation	right
3.	MADD	soared	solitary
4.	wouldn't	mayor-elect	reliance
5.	agree	recourse	Ohio
6.	www.homemadesimple.com		
7.	Saddlebrooke_tripticket@yahoo.com		

LAB 6: WORD USAGE

The following words and phrases are often used incorrectly in everyday speech and in business writing. Learn to use them correctly to help achieve your communication goals.

In some cases in the following list, one word is often confused with another similar word; in other cases, the structure of our language requires that certain words be used only in certain ways. Because of space, only brief and incomplete definitions are given here. Consult a dictionary for more complete or additional meanings.

6.1 Accept/Except *Accept* means "to agree to"; *except* means "with the exclusion of."

I will **accept** all the recommendations **except** the last one.

6.2 Advice/Advise *Advice* is a noun meaning "counsel"; *advise* is a verb meaning "to recommend."

If I ask for her **advice,** she may **advise** me to quit.

6.3 Affect/Effect *Affect* is most often used as a verb meaning "to influence" or "to change"; *effect* is most often used as a noun meaning "result" or "impression."

The legislation may **affect** sales but should have no **effect** on gross margin.

6.4 All Right/Alright Use *all right*. (*Alright* is considered substandard.)

The arrangement is **all right** (not *alright*) with me.

6.5 A Lot/Alot   Use *a lot*. (*Alot* is considered substandard.)

We used **a lot** (not *alot*) of overtime on the project.

6.6 Among/Between   Use *among* when referring to three or more; use *between* when referring to two.

Among the three candidates was one manager who divided his time **between** London and New York.

6.7 Amount/Number   Use *amount* to refer to money or to things that cannot be counted; use *number* to refer to things that can be counted.

The **amount** of consumer interest was measured by the **number** of coupons returned.

6.8 Anxious/Eager   Use *anxious* only if great concern or worry is involved.

Andrés was **eager** to get the new car although he was **anxious** about making such high payments.

6.9 Any One/Anyone   Spell as two words when followed by *of*; spell as one word when the accent is on *any*.

Anyone is allowed to attend **any one** of the sessions.

Between   See *Among/Between*.

6.10 Can/May   *Can* indicates ability; *may* indicates permission.

I **can** finish the project on time if I **may** hire an additional secretary.

6.11 Cite/Sight/Site   *Cite* means "to quote" or "to mention"; *sight* is either a verb meaning "to look at" or a noun meaning "something seen"; *site* is most often a noun meaning "location."

The **sight** of the high-rise building on the **site** of the old battlefield reminded Monica to **cite** several other examples to the commission members.

6.12 Complement/Compliment   *Complement* means "to complete" or "something that completes"; *compliment* means "to praise" or "words of praise."

I must **compliment** you on the new model, which will **complement** our line.

6.13 Could of/Could've   Use *could've* (or *could have*). (*Could of* is incorrect.)

We **could've** (not *could of*) prevented that loss had we been more alert.

6.14 Different from/Different than   Use *different from*. (*Different than* is considered substandard.)

Your computer is **different from** (not *different than*) mine.

6.15 Each Other/One Another   Use *each other* when referring to two; use *one another* when referring to three or more.

The two workers helped **each other,** but their three visitors would not even look at **one another.**

Eager   See *Anxious/Eager*.

Effect   See *Affect/Effect*.

6.16 *e.g./i.e.* The abbreviation *e.g.* means "for example"; *i.e.* means "that is." Use *i.e.* to introduce a restatement or explanation of a preceding expression. Both abbreviations, like the expressions for which they stand, are followed by commas. (Many writers prefer the full English terms to the abbreviations because they are clearer.)

The proposal has merit; **e.g.,** it is economical, forward-looking, and timely.

Or: The proposal has merit; for example, it is economical, forward-looking, and timely.

Unfortunately, it is also a hot potato; **i.e.,** it will generate unfavorable publicity.

Or: Unfortunately, it is also a hot potato; that is, it will generate unfavorable publicity.

6.17 *Eminent/Imminent* *Eminent* means "well-known"; *imminent* means "about to happen."

The arrival of the **eminent** scientist from Russia is **imminent.**

6.18 *Enthused/Enthusiastic* Use *enthusiastic.* (*Enthused* is considered substandard.)

I have become quite **enthusiastic** (not *enthused*) about the possibilities.

Except   See *Accept/Except.*

6.19 *Farther/Further* *Farther* refers to distance; *further* refers to extent or degree.

We drove 10 miles **farther** while we discussed the matter **further.**

6.20 *Fewer/Less* Use *fewer* to refer to things that can be counted; use *less* to refer to money or to things that cannot be counted.

Alvin worked **fewer** hours at the exhibit and therefore generated **less** interest.

Further   See *Farther/Further.*

6.21 *Good/Well* *Good* is an adjective; *well* is an adverb or (with reference to health) an adjective.

Joe does a **good** job and performs **well** on tests, even when he does not feel **well.**

i.e.   See *e.g./i.e.*

Imminent   See *Eminent/Imminent.*

6.22 *Imply/Infer* *Imply* means "to hint" or "to suggest"; *infer* means "to draw a conclusion." Speakers and writers *imply*; readers and listeners *infer.*

The president **implied** that changes will be forthcoming; I **inferred** from his tone of voice that these changes will not be pleasant.

6.23 *Irregardless/Regardless* Use *regardless.* (*Irregardless* is considered substandard.)

He wants to proceed, **regardless** (not *irregardless*) of the costs.

6.24 *Its/It's* *Its* is a possessive pronoun; *it's* is a contraction for "it is."

It's time to let the department increase **its** budget.

6.25 Lay/Lie   Lay (principal forms: *lay, laid, laid, laying*) means "to put" and requires an object to complete its meaning; *lie* (principal forms: *lie, lay, lain, lying*) means "to rest."

Please **lay** the supplies on the shelf.   I **lie** on the couch after lunch each day.

I **laid** the folders in the drawer.   The report **lay** on his desk yesterday.

She had **laid** the notes on her desk.   The job has **lain** untouched for a week.

Less   See *Fewer/Less.*

Lie   See *Lay/Lie.*

6.26 Loose/Lose   *Loose* means "not fastened"; *lose* means "to be unable to find."

Do not **lose** the **loose** change in your pocket.

May   See *Can/May.*

Number   See *Amount/Number.*

One Another   See *Each Other/One Another.*

6.27 Passed/Past   *Passed* is a verb (the past tense or past participle of *pass*, meaning "to move on or by"); *past* is an adjective, adverb, or preposition meaning "earlier."

The committee **passed** the no-confidence motion at a **past** meeting.

6.28 Percent/Percentage   With figures, use *percent*; without figures, use *percentage.*

We took a commission of 6 **percent** (or 6%), which was a lower **percentage** than last year.

6.29 Personal/Personnel   *Personal* means "private" or "belonging to one individual"; *personnel* means "employees."

I used my **personal** time to draft a memo to all **personnel.**

6.30 Principal/Principle   *Principal* means "primary" (adjective) or "sum of money" (noun); *principle* means "rule" or "law."

The guiding **principle** is fair play, and the **principal** means of achieving it is a code of ethics.

6.31 Real/Really   *Real* is an adjective; *really* is an adverb. Do not use *real* to modify another adjective.

She was **really** (not *real*) proud that her necklace contained **real** pearls.

6.32 Reason Is Because/Reason Is That   Use *reason is that.* (*Reason is because* is considered substandard.)

The **reason** for such low attendance **is that** (not is *because*) the weather was stormy.

Regardless   See *Irregardless/Regardless.*

6.33 Same   Do not use *same* to refer to a previously mentioned item. Use *it* or some other wording instead.

We have received your order and will ship **it** (not *same*) in three days.

6.34 Set/Sit   *Set* (principal forms: *set, set, set, setting*) means "to place"; *sit* (principal forms: *sit, sat, sat, sitting*) means "to be seated."

Please **set** your papers on the table.	Please **sit** in the chair.
She **set** the computer on the desk.	She **sat** in the first-class section.
I have **set** the computer there before.	I had not **sat** there before.

6.35 Should of/Should've   Use *should've* (or *should have*). (*Should of* is incorrect.)

We **should've** (not *should of*) been more careful.

Sight   See *Cite/Sight/Site.*

Sit   See *Set/Sit.*

Site   See *Cite/Sight/Site.*

6.36 Stationary/Stationery   *Stationary* means "remaining in one place"; *stationery* is writing paper.

I used my personal **stationery** to write a letter about the **stationary** bike.

6.37 Sure/Surely   *Sure* is an adjective; *surely* is an adverb. Do not use *sure* to modify another adjective.

I'm **surely** (not *sure*) glad that she is running and feel **sure** that she will be nominated.

6.38 Sure and/Sure to   Use *sure to.* (*Sure and* is considered substandard.)

Be **sure to** (not *sure and*) attend the meeting.

6.39 Their/There/They're   *Their* means "belonging to them"; *there* means "in that place"; and *they're* is a contraction for "they are."

They're too busy with **their** reports to be **there** for the hearing.

6.40 Theirs/There's   *Theirs* is a possessive pronoun; *there's* is a contraction for "there is."

We finished our meal, but **there's** no time for them to finish **theirs.**

They're   See *Their/There/They're.*

6.41 Try and/Try to   Use *try to.* (*Try and* is considered substandard.)

Please **try to** (not *try and*) attend the meeting.

Well   See *Good/Well.*

6.42 Whose/Who's   *Whose* is a possessive pronoun; *who's* is a contraction for "who is."

Who's going to let us know **whose** turn it is to make coffee?

6.43 Your/You're   *Your* means "belonging to you"; *you're* is a contraction for "you are."

You're going to present **your** report first.

Application

Directions Select the correct words in parentheses.

1. I will (accept/except) your (advice/advise), but the (affect/effect) of doing so may bring (alot/a lot) of change.

2. The seminar was (all right/alright), but (among/between) Ludwig and me, most participants were (anxious/eager) to complete the training.

3. The (amount/number) of political activity generated (fewer/less) interest than anticipated.

4. (Any one/Anyone) of the students (may/can) apply that (principal/principle) if (theirs/there's) time.

5. The first (sight/cite/site) for the new office (could of/could've) (complimented/complemented) the surrounding community, mainly because it is (different from/different than) the typical building.

6. The program will succeed; (e.g./i.e.), it is positive, forward-looking, and cost effective.

7. The group members supported (each other/one another) and were (enthused/enthusiastic) about their presentation.

8. The CEO (implied/inferred) that arrangements with an (eminent/imminent) scientist have been finalized, and (irregardless/regardless) of the number who are invited, we will be included.

9. How much (farther/further) can we pursue this if (its/it's) not (passed/past) on through regular channels?

10. Please (lay/lie) your (loose/lose) change on the dresser, and I'll be (real/really) pleased.

11. You (should of/should've) taken advantage of the opportunity to refinance your home under the lower (percent/percentage) rates.

12. The new investment program is open to all (personal/personnel) and will (sure/surely) build security for (their/there) future.

13. The reason for the increase in deli foods in grocery stores is (that/because) more people are buying food prepared outside the home.

14. I use my personal (stationery/stationary), and please (try to/try and) use yours.

15. Tell Henri to be (sure and/sure to) lock up before he leaves and (sit/set) the late afternoon mail on my desk.

16. We have the document and will forward (it/same) to the actuary so that (you're/your) department is included in the transaction.

17. (Who's/Whose) turn is it to clean the refrigerator because it (sure/surely) needs it?

18. I'll follow the guidelines you (advise/advice), (except/accept) the one involving the (eminent/imminent) staff change in sales.

19. There was wide disparity (between/among) the five candidates, but they supported (each other/one another).

20. Dr. Zhoa was excited about the new job but (eager/anxious) about the research required.

21. Be sure the (cites/sights/sites) are interesting because we want to do a (good/well) job.

22. What did you (imply/infer) from her (compliment/complement)?

23. The (principle/principal) reason for (their/there/they're) success is the lawyer, (whose/who's) a specialist in international law.

24. A (stationery/stationary) pump for the well was (complemented/complimented) by a mobile emergency back up.

25. They wanted us to work (less/fewer) hours so the (number/amount) of savings could be increased.

B Formatting Business Documents

FORMATTING LETTERS AND MEMOS

The most common features of business letters and memos are discussed in the following sections and illustrated in Figure 1.

Letter and Punctuation Styles

The *block style* is the simplest letter style to type because all lines begin at the left margin. In the *modified block style,* the date and closing lines begin at the center point. Offsetting these parts from the left margin enables the reader to locate them quickly.

The *standard punctuation style*—the most common format—uses a colon after the salutation and a comma after the complimentary closing. The *open punctuation style,* on the other hand, uses no punctuation after these two lines.

Stationery and Margins

Most letters and memos are printed on standard-sized stationery, 8½ × 11 inches. The first page is printed on letterhead stationery, which shows the company logo at the top and the company address either at the top or at the bottom. Subsequent pages are printed on good-quality plain paper.

Side, top, and bottom margins should be 1 to 1¼ inches (the typical default in programs such as Microsoft Word). Vertically center one-page letters and memos. Set a tab at the center point if you're formatting a modified block style letter.

Required Letter Parts

The required letter parts are as follows:

Date Line Type the current month (spelled out), day, and year on the first line. Begin either at the center point for modified block style or at the left margin for the block style.

Inside Address The inside address gives the name and location of the person to whom you're writing. Include a personal title (e.g., *Mr., Mrs., Miss,* or *Ms.*). If you use the addressee's job title, type it either on the same line as the name (separated from the name by a comma) or on the following line by itself. In the address, use the two-letter U.S. Postal Service abbreviation, typed in all capitals with no period, and leave one space between the state and the ZIP code. Type the inside address at the left margin; skip between one and four lines below the date, depending on

Figure 1 Written Message Formats

Block style letter

food bank of the Southern Tier

May 18, 2011

Ms. Amy Newman
Cornell University
331 Statler Hall
Ithaca, NY 14853

Dear Ms. Newman:

Please accept my deepest gratitude for your generous in-kind gift of food. Your gift will help feed our Southern Tier neighbors in need. The Food Bank's network of hunger-relief agencies is currently serving more households than in previous years. Within the last year, existing clients needed assistance more frequently than before, and our network experienced an increase in first-time users, many of them employed but unable to make ends meet, as well as seniors who struggle to live on fixed incomes.

Without people like you, we would not be able to keep up with the increasing demand for emergency food assistance. I am very thankful that we have such wonderful, caring donors who want to alleviate the stress that some families face.

Thank you for your generosity and support for the Food Bank's hunger-relief efforts.

Sincerely,

Natasha R. Thompson
President & CEO

NRT/lce

Modified block style letter

food bank of the Southern Tier

May 18, 2011

Ms. Amy Newman
Cornell University
331 Statler Hall
Ithaca, NY 14853

Dear Ms. Newman:

Please accept my deepest gratitude for your generous in-kind gift of food. Your gift will help feed our Southern Tier neighbors in need. The Food Bank's network of hunger-relief agencies is currently serving more households than in previous years. Within the last year, existing clients needed assistance more frequently than before, and our network experienced an increase in first-time users, many of them employed but unable to make ends meet, as well as seniors who struggle to live on fixed incomes.

Without people like you, we would not be able to keep up with the increasing demand for emergency food assistance. I am very thankful that we have such wonderful, caring donors who want to alleviate the stress that some families face.

Thank you for your generosity and support for the Food Bank's hunger-relief efforts.

Sincerely,

Natasha R. Thompson
President & CEO

NRT/lce

Interoffice memo (page 1)

Calaway Movers

To: All Calaway Staff
From: Bill Calaway, CEO
Subject: Reorganizing Our Sales Teams
Date: September 9, 2013

As we discussed on the web conference last week, we are reorganizing the corporate office to focus more closely on customer needs. Instead of sales functions serving regional customers, we will organize around types of customers: consumer, small business, and corporate. This will allow Calaway to tailor our products and services to specific customer groups and leverage services within customer segments. The former regional model worked well for a long time, but we have outgrown this structure and must adapt, particularly to our growing base of corporate clients, who demand more customized services from Calaway.

Our goal is to make this transition as smooth as possible. Over the next 90 days, we will implement the transition plan:

- **Transfer sales representatives to new divisions (by October 15)**

  Each sales representative will be moved from our current regional teams to a new team: consumer, small business, or corporate. Managers will work closely with representatives to determine strengths, experiences, and preferences.

- **Identify account type (by October 31)**

  All sales representatives will categorize current accounts for the new divisions: consumer, small business, and corporate.

- **Transition accounts to new teams (by November 30)**

  Where accounts are changing sales representatives, we will follow this process:

  ○ For small business accounts, the former and new sales representative will send an email to the account contact, followed by a phone call and visit (if possible) by the new sales representative.

  ○ For corporate accounts, the former sales representative will send an email and schedule a conference call or visit by the account contact and new sales representative.

Seamless communication with our clients during this transition is essential. Each segment is working on email templates to ensure that our communication is clear and consistent across all divisions.

Interoffice memo (page 2)

Sales Reorganization   Page 2   September 9, 2013

I am pleased to announce the following leaders in the newly formed sales organization:

- **Melissa Chowdhury, Vice President, Sales**

  Formerly the vice president of the Northeast region, Melissa will oversee all sales functions. Melissa will report directly to me, and the following sales directors will report to Melissa.

- **Bruce Gorman, Director, Consumer Accounts**

  Bruce will move from the Midwest region to oversee the new Consumer Accounts division.

- **Ryan Korman, Director, Small Business Accounts**

  Ryan will move from the Southern region to oversee the Small Business Accounts division.

- **Manny Fernandez, Director, Corporate Accounts**

  Formerly director, customer service, Manny will oversee the Corporate Accounts division.

Please join me in congratulating these folks in their new roles.

I am very excited about the future of Calaway. With our new organizational structure, we will continue to grow—and move people safely to new homes and offices across the country. I look forward to taking this journey with all of you.

the size of the letter. For international letters, type the name of the country in all-capital letters on the last line by itself.

Salutation   Use the same name in both the inside address and the salutation. If the letter is addressed to a job position rather than to a person, use a generic greeting, such as "Dear Human Resources Manager." If you typically address the reader in person by first name, use the first name in the salutation (for example, "Dear Cara:"); otherwise, use a personal title and the surname only (for example, "Dear Ms. Currigan:"). Leave one blank line before and after the salutation.

Body   Single-space the lines of each paragraph and leave one blank line between paragraphs.

Page 2 Heading   Insert the page number in the header or footer, centered or on the right side. Omit the page number on page 1. You should carry forward to a second page at least two lines of the body of the message.

Complimentary Closing   Begin the complimentary closing at the same margin point as the date line. Capitalize the first word only, and leave one blank line before and approximately three blank lines after, to allow room for your signature before your full typed name.

Signature   Sign your name legibly in blue or black ink.

Writer's Identification   The writer's identification (name or job title or both) begins approximately on the fourth line immediately below the complimentary closing. Do not use a personal title. The job title may go either on the same line as the typed name, separated from the name by a comma, or on the following line by itself.

Reference Initials   When used, reference initials (the initials of the typist) are typed at the left margin in lowercase letters without periods, with one blank line before. Do not include reference initials if you type your own letter.

Envelopes   Business envelopes have a printed return address. You may type your name above this address, if you wish. Use plain envelopes for personal business letters; you should type the return address (your home address) at the upper left corner, or use an address label. On large (No. 10) envelopes, begin typing the mailing address 2 inches from the top edge and 4 inches from the left edge. On small (No. 6¾) envelopes, begin typing the mailing address 2 inches from the top edge and 2½ inches from the left edge. Fold 8½ × 11 letters in thirds and small notepaper in half to fit the envelope.

Optional Letter Parts

Optional letter parts are as follows:

Subject Line   You may include a subject line in letters (identified by the words *Subject* or *Re* followed by a colon) to identify the topic of the letter. Type it below the salutation, with one blank line before and one after.

Numbered or Bulleted Lists in the Body   You may include a numbered list (if the sequence of the items is important) or a bulleted list (when the sequence is not important). Single-space each item, and double-space or use 6-point spacing between items. Leave one blank line before and after the list.

Enclosure Notation   You may use an enclosure notation if items are included in the envelope and are not obvious. Type "Enclosure" (or "Attachment" if the items are physically attached) on the line immediately below the reference initials, and as an option, add the description of what is enclosed.

Delivery Notation   You may type a delivery notation (e.g., *By Certified Mail, By Fax, By Federal Express*) a single space below the enclosure notation.

Copy Notation   If someone other than the addressee is to receive a copy of the letter, type a copy notation ("c:") immediately below the enclosure notation or reference initials, whichever comes last. Then follow the copy notation with the names of the people who will receive copies.

Postscript   If you add a postscript to a letter, type it as the last item, preceded by one blank line. The heading "P.S." is optional. Postscripts are used most often in sales letters.

Memo Header Format

Internal memos may be printed, attached to email messages, or uploaded onto company intranet sites. Double-space the memo header and include the following:

To: Type the first and last name of the receiver or a group name, for example, "All Employees." You may include a job title after a receiver's name and a comma, for example, "Jason Matthews, CFO."

From: Type your first and last name. If you wrote a title after the receiver's name, include yours here. For printed memos, you may sign your initials after your name if this is standard in your organization.

Date: Type the full date: Month, day, year

Subject: Include a descriptive subject line as you would for an email message.

FORMATTING PRIMARILY TEXT REPORTS

If the reader or organization has a preferred format style, use it. Otherwise, follow these generally accepted guidelines for formatting text-based business reports. Additional pages (1–12 of the 48 pages) from the McKinsey report discussed in Chapter 10 are shown in Figure 2.

Figure 2 Pages 1–12 from the McKinsey Report

McKinsey&Company

Education

Closing the talent gap: Attracting and retaining top-third graduates to careers in teaching

An international and market research-based perspective

Acknowledgements

A number of the world's top-performing school systems have made great teaching their 'north star.' They have strategic and systematic approaches to attract, develop, retain, and ensure the efficacy of the most talented educators, and they make it a priority to attract and retain top graduates to a career in teaching. The aim of this paper is to describe how these high-performing school systems have accomplished this, and to share the results of original market research on what it would take to attract and retain top students to teaching in the United States.

The authors wish to acknowledge the following experts for their counsel: Cindy Brown, Alice Cain, Michael Casserly, Linda Darling-Hammond, Segun Eubanks, Michael Fullan, Drew Gitomer, Dan Goldhaber, Robert Gordon, Kati Haycock, Rick Hess, Eric Hanushek, Kevin Huffman, Peter Kannam, Dan Katzir, Ee-gyeong Kim, Joel Klein, Wendy Kopp, Matt Kramer, Jari Lavonen, Arthur Levine, Sing Kong Lee, Yi Qi, Andrew Rotherham, Pasi Sahlberg, Andreas Schleicher, Jon Schnur, Kate Walsh, Ellen Winn, Ludger Woessmann, Josh Wyner, and Lu Cheng Yang.

The authors also wish to deeply thank our colleagues Michelle Rosenthal, Tamara Charm, Chris Crittenden and Jennifer Smith for their significant contributions to this report. The following colleagues also provided valuable input and leadership: Michael Barber, Kartik Jayaram, Lenny Mendonca, Andy Moffit, Mona Mourshed, and Fenton Whelan.

The preparation of this report was co-funded by McKinsey and Proof Points, a non-profit organization designed to support state-level education reform. This work is part of the fulfillment of McKinsey's social sector mission to help leaders and leading institutions to understand and address important and complex societal challenges. As with all McKinsey research, results and conclusions are based on the unique outlook and experience base that McKinsey experts bring to bear.

Closing the talent gap: Attracting and retaining top-third graduates to careers in teaching

An international and market research-based perspective

September 2010

Byron Auguste
Paul Kihn
Matt Miller

Figure 2 (Continued)

The U.S. could dramatically increase the portion of top third new hires in high needs districts.

Executive Summary

When McKinsey & Company analyzed "How the World's Best School Systems Stay on Top" (2007), we found a few common themes. Perhaps the most important was that "the quality of an education system cannot exceed the quality of its teachers." This simple statement conveys a profound truth—and masks considerable complexity. Research has shown that of all the controllable factors in an education system, the most important by far is the effectiveness of the classroom teacher. The world's best-performing school systems make great teaching their "north star." They have strategic and systematic approaches to attract, develop, retain, and ensure the efficacy of the most talented educators—and they make sure great teachers serve students of all socio-economic backgrounds.

The U.S. does not take a strategic or systematic approach to nurturing teaching talent. Buffeted by a chaotic mix of labor market trends, university economics, and local school district and budget dynamics, we have failed to attract, develop, reward or retain outstanding professional teaching talent on a consistent basis.

Fortunately, improving "teacher effectiveness" to lift student achievement has become a major reform theme in American education. Many school districts and states, including some "Race to the Top" competitors and other education stakeholders like local teacher unions and charter management organizations, are finding new ways to measure, evaluate, reward, coach, and replicate effectiveness in teaching. Yet most such efforts focus either on improving the effectiveness of teachers who are already in the classroom—that is, people who have chosen teaching given the current nature of the profession—or on retaining the best performers and dismissing the least effective. Little attention has been paid to altering the value proposition of

teaching to draw young people with strong academic backgrounds to the career.

McKinsey's work with school systems in more than 50 countries suggests this is an important gap in the U.S. debate, because the world's top performing school systems—Singapore, Finland and South Korea—make a different choice. They recruit, develop and retain what this report will call "top third+" students as one of their central education strategies, and they've achieved extraordinary results. These systems recruit 100% of their teacher corps from the top third of the academic cohort, and then screen for other important qualities as well. In the U.S., by contrast, 23% of new teachers come from the top third, and just 14% in high poverty schools, which find it especially difficult to attract and retain talented teachers. It is a remarkably large difference in approach, and in results.

Paradoxically, U.S. research on whether teachers' academic backgrounds significantly predict classroom effectiveness is very mixed, and it suggests that merely sprinkling teachers with top-third academic credentials into our existing system will not by itself produce dramatic gains in student achievement. No single reform can serve as a "silver bullet." Nonetheless, the extraordinary success of top-performing systems suggests a "top third+" strategy deserves serious examination as part of a comprehensive human capital strategy for the U.S. education system. Moreover, given that roughly half of the teacher corps will be eligible for retirement in the next decade, the question "who should teach?" in the U.S. seems especially timely. The research presented here suggests the need to pursue "bold, persistent experimentation" (in Franklin D. Roosevelt's famous words) to attract and retain top graduates to the teaching profession, so the U.S. can learn whether more teachers with such backgrounds, working in the right school system context, can help

Figure 2 (Continued)

6

lift student achievement to the levels top-performing nations now enjoy.

This report asks what lessons we might learn from nations that succeed in delivering world-class educational outcomes with top talent in teaching—Singapore, Finland, and South Korea—and what an American version of such a strategy might entail. We conducted market research among teachers and "top-third" college students to understand what it would take to attract and retain such talent, how to do so cost-effectively, and what complementary system changes would maximize the efficacy of such a strategy. Finally, we offer ideas on how to start down a path to achieve this aspiration.

Singapore, Finland and South Korea do many things differently than does the U.S. to recruit and retain top-third+ students. These nations make admissions to rigorous teacher training programs highly selective; some also pay for these programs' tuition and fees, and give students a salary or a living stipend while they train. In addition, government closely monitors the demand for teachers and regulates supply to match it, so that teachers who complete this selective training are guaranteed jobs in the profession. They offer competitive compensation, so that the financial rewards from teaching suffice to attract and retain top third students given the dynamics of these nations' labor markets. They offer opportunities for advancement and growth in a professional working environment, and bestow enormous social prestige on the profession. Officials in Singapore, Finland and South Korea view the caliber of young person they draw to teaching as a critical national priority.

McKinsey's market research with 900 top-third college students and 525 current teachers with similar backgrounds shows that it would take major new efforts for the U.S. to attract and retain more top third+ talent to teaching. Most students see teaching

as unattractive in terms of the quality of the people in the field, professional growth and compensation. Among the 91 percent of top-third college students who say they are not planning to go into teaching, the most important job attributes include prestige and peer group appeal, but compensation is the biggest gap between teaching and their chosen professions. Our research suggests that improving compensation and other features of teaching careers could dramatically increase the portion of top-third new hires in high-needs schools and school districts, and retain these teachers in much greater numbers with complementary changes, such as better school leaders and working conditions.

We have explored cost-effective ways to pursue such a strategy, although they are not necessarily inexpensive. We examined reform scenarios informed by our market research on how many more top-third students would choose to teach if certain aspects of the profession changed, and if such efforts were targeted in various ways, along with some indicative cost scenarios for a large urban district (of 50,000-150,000 students) and an "average" state (representing 1/50th of the U.S. student population). *Please note that these scenarios do not represent recommendations, but are meant to show a range of options for recruiting and retaining top-third students that could inform discussion.*

In one scenario, for example, the U.S. could more than double the portion of top-third+ new hires in high-needs schools, from 14% today to 34%, without raising teacher salaries. In this scenario, teachers would not pay for their initial training; high-needs schools would have effective principals and offer ongoing training comparable to the best professional institutions; districts would improve shabby and sometimes unsafe working conditions; the highest-performing teachers would receive

Figure 2 (Continued)

Education
Closing the talent gap: Attracting and retaining top-third graduates to careers in teaching   7

> *If teachers drawn from the top third at much greater scale could help close the achievement gap, the economic and social returns could be enormous.*

performance bonuses of 20%; and the district or state would benefit from a marketing campaign promoting teaching as a profession. The cost of this scenario for an illustrative large district with half of its schools serving high poverty students might be roughly $10-30 million per year at current student-teacher ratios; for an "average" state, the cost would be $66 million (half of one percent of current K-12 spending). If the same scenario was applied to "turnaround" schools—the lowest-performing one in 20 schools targeted by the Obama Administration—which serve roughly 5% of students, a similar result would follow at a cost of $1-3 million per year in the district, or $20 million for the state (or two-tenths of one percent of current K-12 spending).

Given the real and perceived gaps between teachers' compensation and that of other careers open to top students, drawing the majority of new teachers from among top-third+ students likely would require substantial increases in compensation. For example, our market research suggests that raising the share of top-third+ new hires in high-needs schools from 14% to 68% would mean paying new teachers around $65,000 with a maximum career compensation of $150,000 per year. At current student-teacher ratios, and applied to all current teachers as well, this would cost roughly $100-290 million for the large urban district and $630 million for the average state. It would be considerably less expensive to focus such an effort on "turnaround" schools.

The predictions emerging from our market research are inexact, to be sure. But if our estimates are close to correct, a top-talent strategy would involve substantial costs, and would therefore likely require the country to reexamine many elements of its human capital system, including student-teacher ratios, the basis and structure of teacher compensation over time, and per-pupil school-funding formulas

and levels. The cost of top-third initiatives could be reduced significantly, however, by accepting higher student/teacher ratios, raising the salaries of only those teachers deemed effective by comprehensive evaluations, transitioning existing teachers to this pay structure on an "opt-in" basis, or by finding ways to reallocate less effective K-12 spending. Further research might reveal less expensive ways to use prestige and peer groups to attract top talent to high-needs schools for a career, as Teach for America has done for shorter stints, or whether well-defined paths for advancement within the profession could have an analogous impact on retention.

Beyond cost-effectiveness is the question of how the system must change to produce more truly effective teachers—or how to put the "+" in a "top-third+" strategy. The three countries we examine use a rigorous selection process and teacher training more akin to medical school and residency than to a typical American school of education. A U.S. version of a top-talent strategy might aim to transform schools of education directly, give districts the power to demand better-equipped educators, or rely more heavily on identifying effective and ineffective teachers early in their careers. Singapore's integration of a top-third approach with rigorous performance management systems, moreover, shows these can be mutually reinforcing strategies: a nation need not choose between drawing high-caliber talent to the profession and assuring that this talent delivers results in the classroom. For an American "top-third+" strategy to be effective, it would need to address not only the attraction and retention of top-third graduates to teaching, but also the many levers that support the efficacy of teachers once they are in the classroom.

Our research makes a compelling case for exploring top third+ strategies with pilots in high-needs districts or in a state, perhaps via a new "Race to the Top Third"

Figure 2 (Continued)

8

grant competition, or through collaborations among
school systems, philanthropic institutions, and other
education stakeholders. Given the complexity of
the issues, and the regional and national dimensions
of the talent pool, the research also suggests there
would be benefits to creating a National Teaching
Talent Plan. A commission assigned to this task
might propose next steps and timelines for phasing
in changes in how we recruit, prepare, retain, and
reward teachers, informed by global best practice.

Progress will require research, experimentation
and learning, but the economic and social returns
from getting it right could be enormous. McKinsey
research last year found that the achievement gap
between the U.S. and top performing nations—a
burden borne most directly by low-income and
minority students—imposes the economic equivalent
of a "permanent national recession" on the United
States.[1] In our education system research and work
in more than 50 countries, we have never seen an
education system achieve or sustain world-class
status without top talent in its teaching profession.
If the U.S. is to close its achievement gap with the
world's best education systems—and ease its own
socio-economic disparities—a top-third+ strategy for
the teaching profession must be part of the debate.

[1]   "The Economic Impact of the Achievement Gap in America's Schools" McKinsey and Company (2009).

Figure 2 (Continued)

Education
Closing the talent gap: Attracting and retaining top-third graduates to careers in teaching

9

*Top performing nations recruit
100% of their new teachers from
the top third. In the U.S., it's 23%—
and 14% in high poverty schools.*

Introduction: A moment of opportunity

American education policy is experiencing one of its most promising moments in memory, with national attention centered on whole system reform for arguably the first time. We are learning important lessons from hundreds of schools that achieve outstanding results with high-poverty students, the Race to the Top competition is beginning to spur innovation at system-wide scale, a broad state-based movement is underway to adopt common standards in core subjects, and new systems of data-driven performance management are being devised or introduced in many districts. Most important, the community of stakeholders who work to boost student achievement is focusing on effective teaching as a central strategy to improve educational outcomes.

Research shows that of all the controllable factors influencing student achievement, the most important by far is the effectiveness of the classroom teacher. Stakeholders now recognize the importance of effective teachers—and of how far we are from a systemic approach to producing them. For example, few school systems evaluate teachers in ways that differentiate them and inform teaching practice with integrity and insight.[2] Many school districts and states, including Race to the Top competitors, are now working to measure, evaluate, reward, coach, and replicate effectiveness in teaching, and to build a cadre of school leaders who are capable of helping teachers to improve instructional practices. Although many school systems are just beginning the hard work of designing and implementing such human capital reforms, and many have yet to begin, the importance of effective teaching is now central to the U.S. reform debate.

This focus on teachers and teaching is broadly consistent with McKinsey & Company's work with school systems in over 50 countries, and in our global research on school system excellence. Leaders in the world's best-performing school systems believe that the "quality of an education system cannot exceed the quality of its teachers," and they have taken a strategic and systematic approach to attracting, developing, retaining, and training the most talented educators. Each top-performing country accomplishes this in its own way, but they all have the same aim: getting effective teachers in front of students of all socio-economic backgrounds, and retaining those teachers for a career in teaching.

While more Americans now recognize the importance of effective teaching, most of the U.S. initiatives to promote it seek to improve the effectiveness of teachers already in the classroom, not to upgrade the caliber of young people entering the profession. Top-performing nations such as Singapore, Finland and South Korea have made a different choice, treating teaching as a highly selective profession. They recruit, develop and retain what this report will call "top third+" students as one of their central education strategies, and they've achieved extraordinary results.

After recruiting from the top third, these countries rigorously screen students on other qualities they believe to be predictors of teaching success, including perseverance, ability to motivate others, passion for children, and organizational and communications skills. That's the "plus" in top-third+. These countries recognize that coming from the top third of graduates

---

2   Among many recent analyses of the US teaching profession, perhaps the most influential has been *The Widget Effect*, by The New Teacher Project, which documents the stark inadequacy of teacher evaluations.

Figure 2 (Continued)

10

"Recruiting top students into teaching should be a national objective"

- Joel Klein, chancellor of schools, New York City.

does not automatically translate into classroom effectiveness, and they invest systematically in developing the skills of those they select to teach. At the same time, however, they view high academic achievement as a critical threshold criteria in deciding who will be allowed entry to the profession.[3]

The U.S., by contrast, recruits most teachers from the bottom two-thirds of college classes, and, for many schools in poor neighborhoods, from the bottom third. Tellingly, relatively little research in the U.S. has addressed this issue, and the research that does exist is decidedly mixed in its conclusions. A growing body of research suggests that a teacher's cognitive ability, as measured by standardized test scores, grades and college selectivity, correlates with improved student outcomes, particularly in mathematics. Paradoxically, other credible research finds such effects either statistically insignificant or small.[4] Moreover, recent research on the "value-added" impact of different teachers suggests that such variations are much larger than the effects of any single teacher attribute that can be observed before teachers are in the classroom, leading some to argue that recruiting or selecting great teachers is less important than observing them once in the classroom and either retaining or dismissing them according to their performance.[5]

Research on Teach For America, which recruits top college graduates and screens them for other "plus" factors, suggests that its teachers are more effective on average than other teachers of

similar experience levels, with the largest impact on achievement in mathematics.[6] As with many other issues in the data-poor U.S. education system, the research is inconclusive, but it does suggest that an increase in "top third+" teaching talent would need to be combined with other system reforms to raise student achievement.

The debate will continue, but it is worth noting that officials in top-performing countries have little doubt that recruiting teachers from the top third+ is critical to their success. They tend to point to superior results rather than research, along with a commonsense notion that effective teaching requires a mastery of subject matter, psychology, and how to tailor pedagogical styles for different students, all of which they consider higher-order skills associated with academic success.

Based on this international evidence, along with the absence of a compelling research consensus in the U.S., we believe that bold system-level experimentation, coupled with rigorous evaluation, would be required to determine the potential for the integration of a "top third+" talent strategy in the panoply of reforms now being undertaken in the U.S. Individual school districts, charter management organizations, and state education systems—collaborating with universities and other teacher training institutions, teacher unions, social entrepreneurs, education philanthropists, and the U.S. Department of Education—could devise and implement strategies to ensure that effective teachers

---

3   We recognize that "top third" students can be defined in a number of ways. For the purposes of clarity for our market research, top third is defined in this report by a combination of SAT, ACT, and GPA scores.

4   For a summary of this research literature visit sso.mckinsey.com.

5   For an example of this value-added research, see Gordon, Kane, and Staiger (2006). "Identifying Effective Teachers Using Performance on the Job." Brookings Institute.

6   See, for example, Zeyu Xu, Jane Hannaway, Colin Taylor (2008). "Making a Difference? The Effect of Teach for America on Student Performance in High School." Urban Institute Working Paper.

Figure 2 (Continued)

are the consistent norm for students of all socio-economic backgrounds in their systems. In tandem, research on the results of these initiatives should inform strategies nationwide.

Several developments make an inquiry into the composition of America's teacher corps timely. More than half of today's teachers—roughly 1.8 million of 3.3 million—will be eligible to retire within the next decade, providing a rare window of opportunity to shape the next generation of teachers.[7] High-poverty schools have perennially struggled to attract great teachers, particularly in the so-called "STEM" subjects of science, technology, engineering and math. Employers are increasingly demanding that students be equipped with the higher-order skills and critical thinking for the 21st-century workplace. Meanwhile, an achievement gap persists between American students and those in top-performing nations. McKinsey research last year found that this gap—a burden borne most directly by low-income and minority students—imposes the economic equivalent of a "permanent national recession" on the United States.[8]

These opportunities and challenges suggest the moment is ripe to think more closely about the composition of the teacher corps. "Recruiting top students into teaching should be a national objective," says Joel Klein, chancellor of schools in New York City. "If your human capital isn't at the top, that makes all the other hills harder to climb."

After briefly reviewing the current situation in the U.S., this report offers case studies of top-performing nations—Singapore, Finland and South Korea—to understand how they recruit and retain top-third+ students. Next, we review the findings of new market research conducted by McKinsey with top-third college students and current teachers in the U.S. This research shows what it would take to attract and retain such students as teachers, and illustrates options for policymakers who seek to adopt top third+ strategies at the school district, state or national level. The report concludes by discussing some implications of these findings for education stakeholders, and by suggesting a program of bold experimentation and further research at multiple levels of the American education system.[9]

7   Richard M. Ingersoll, Ph.D., University of Pennsylvania, original analysis for NCTAF of Schools and Staffing Survey.

8   "The Economic Impact of the Achievement Gap in America's Schools" McKinsey and Company (2009).

9   A companion document containing McKinsey's more detailed findings and analyses is available at sso.mckinsey.com.

Figure 2 (Continued)

12

The U.S. situation:
A profession buffeted by change

The U.S. attracts most of its teachers from the bottom two-thirds of college classes, with nearly half coming from the bottom third, especially for schools in poor neighborhoods. Department of Education data shows that only 23% of new teachers overall—and about 14% of those in high-poverty schools—come from the top third of graduates.[10] This reality, so different from what we find in the world's highest-performing school systems, is not the result of a conscious strategic choice. On the contrary, it is the by-product of the labor market trends of the past 40 years, the economics and culture of higher education and school districts, and budget dynamics.

Experienced observers in the U.S. say this is a dramatic change from the situation up through the 1960s and mid 1970s, when the academic quality of the teacher corps was effectively "subsidized" by discrimination, because women and minorities didn't have as many opportunities outside the classroom. In addition, the difference in starting salaries between teaching and other professions wasn't as large. In 1970 in New York City, for example, a starting lawyer going into a prestigious firm and a starting teacher going into public education had a differential in their entry salary of about $2,000. Today, including salary and bonus, that starting lawyer makes $160,000, while starting teachers in New York make roughly $45,000.

The late Sandra Feldman, president of the American Federation of Teachers from 1997 to 2004, and herself a product of this earlier era, was open about the problem in an interview in 2003. "You have in the schools right now, among the teachers who are

going to be retiring, *very* smart people," she said. "We're not getting in now the same kinds of people. It's disastrous. We've been saying for years now that we're attracting from the bottom third."

As these observations suggest, U.S. teacher recruitment has been buffeted in recent decades by a kind of "double whammy." Broader career opportunities have opened up for women and minorities, so that people who in previous eras became teachers now become doctors, lawyers, engineers, scientists and businesspeople. It's striking to consider that in the 1970s, more than half of college-educated working women were teachers, compared with around 15% today. At the same time, just as these labor market changes have forced teaching to compete with a wide array of lucrative professions, average teacher salaries have fallen significantly as a percentage of GDP per capita over the past 30 years,[11] reducing the relative rewards of teaching (see exhibit 1). Today starting teacher salaries average $39,000 nationally, and rise to an overall average of $54,000, with an average maximum salary of $67,000. This does not compare favorably to other professional options for top college graduates, particularly in major metropolitan areas (see exhibit 2 for an international comparison).

The American teaching profession also suffers from a lack of prestige. The Department of Education reports that about 80% of teachers enter the profession through traditional certification paths in schools and departments of education. While some of the nation's over 1,450 schools, colleges and departments of

10   Derived from the US Department of Education, NCES, 2001 Baccalaureate and Beyond Longitudinal Survey.

11   This measure amounts to an index that allows easy comparability across professions as well as countries, as discussed later in the report.

Margins

For traditional text reports in programs such as Microsoft Word, use a 2-inch top margin for the first page of each special part (for example, the table of contents, the executive summary, the first page of the body of the report, and the first page of the reference list). Leave a 1-inch top margin for all other pages and at least a 1-inch bottom margin on all pages. Use 1- to 1¼-inch side margins on all pages. The McKinsey report uses larger top margins to allow for callout text.

Spacing and Fonts

Business reports are typically typed single-spaced. Although you may indent at the beginning of paragraphs, this is not necessary. Instead, all paragraphs may be left justified with one line space between paragraphs as in the McKinsey report example.

Use a standard business font such as Times New Roman 12, Arial 10, or Calibri 11.

Report Headings

The number of levels of headings used will vary from report to report. Reports written within a memo or letter may have only first-level subheadings, with no part titles or other headings. Long reports may have as many as four levels of headings. With different fonts, colors, or enhancements (e.g., bold or italic), make sure that the reader can easily tell which are major headings and which are subordinate headings.

Headers, Footers, and Page Numbers

Business reports typically have the report title (and perhaps the subtitle) and page number in either the header or footer of body pages. Some reports may include the date, the name of the writer or organization, or a copyright notice. Whether these appear in the header or footer depends on organizational standards and the writer's preference.

The title page of a report is counted as page 1, but no page number is shown. Subsequent preliminary pages may take lowercase Roman numerals; for example, the executive summary might be page ii, and the table of contents might be page iii. Or, Arabic numbers may begin on the first page of the report body. The McKinsey report does not follow either convention; rather, Arabic numerals appear following the report cover.

FORMATTING REPORTS IN PRESENTATION SOFTWARE

Your organization may have a standard template for reports created in presentation software such as PowerPoint. Because these reports are more graphical, formatting standards tend to be more flexible. General guidelines for formatting these reports are shown in Figure 3.

Figure 3 Guidelines for Formatting a PowerPoint Report

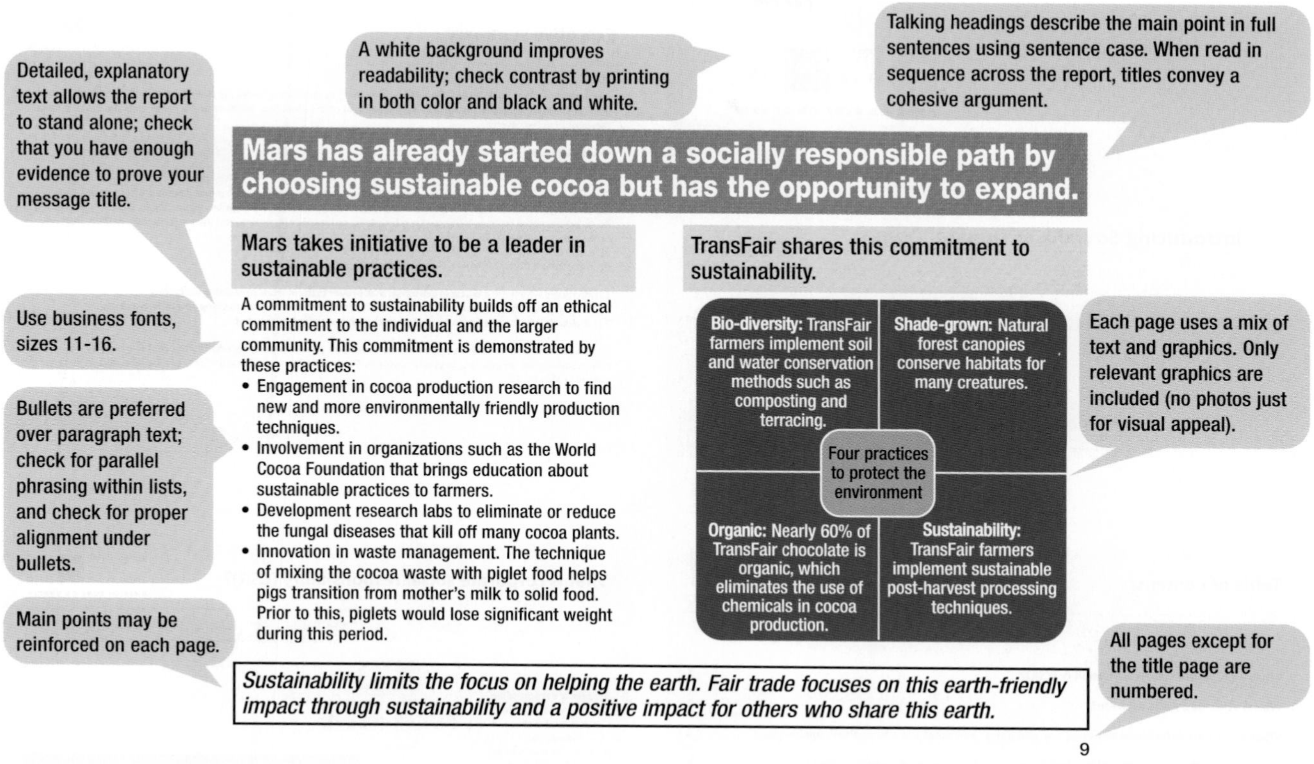

Detailed, explanatory text allows the report to stand alone; check that you have enough evidence to prove your message title.

A white background improves readability; check contrast by printing in both color and black and white.

Talking headings describe the main point in full sentences using sentence case. When read in sequence across the report, titles convey a cohesive argument.

Mars has already started down a socially responsible path by choosing sustainable cocoa but has the opportunity to expand.

Mars takes initiative to be a leader in sustainable practices.

A commitment to sustainability builds off an ethical commitment to the individual and the larger community. This commitment is demonstrated by these practices:
- Engagement in cocoa production research to find new and more environmentally friendly production techniques.
- Involvement in organizations such as the World Cocoa Foundation that brings education about sustainable practices to farmers.
- Development research labs to eliminate or reduce the fungal diseases that kill off many cocoa plants.
- Innovation in waste management. The technique of mixing the cocoa waste with piglet food helps pigs transition from mother's milk to solid food. Prior to this, piglets would lose significant weight during this period.

TransFair shares this commitment to sustainability.

Bio-diversity: TransFair farmers implement soil and water conservation methods such as composting and terracing.

Shade-grown: Natural forest canopies conserve habitats for many creatures.

Four practices to protect the environment

Organic: Nearly 60% of TransFair chocolate is organic, which eliminates the use of chemicals in cocoa production.

Sustainability: TransFair farmers implement sustainable post-harvest processing techniques.

Use business fonts, sizes 11-16.

Bullets are preferred over paragraph text; check for parallel phrasing within lists, and check for proper alignment under bullets.

Main points may be reinforced on each page.

Each page uses a mix of text and graphics. Only relevant graphics are included (no photos just for visual appeal).

All pages except for the title page are numbered.

Sustainability limits the focus on helping the earth. Fair trade focuses on this earth-friendly impact through sustainability and a positive impact for others who share this earth.

9

Reports created in presentation software are intended as stand-alone documents without a presenter to explain the detail. Therefore, compared to slides used to complement an oral presentation, a report will be far denser with text and graphics and may use standard business font sizes. For comparison, the full Dunkin' Donuts report (Figure 4) and oral presentation slides (Figure 5) are shown. Both were created in PowerPoint, but the content and formatting are quite different.

DOCUMENTING SOURCES

As discussed in Chapter 10, most business documents cite sources within the text using footnotes or endnotes. To appropriately describe a source, use the guidelines in Figure 6, which are consistent with those recommended by Harvard Business School; these are an updated version of guidelines recommended by *The Chicago Manual of Style*. If your source material (for example, a blog post) isn't included in this chart, use a format that mirrors these, or you can find additional guidelines in the *Harvard Business School Citation Guide* (www.library.hbs.edu/guides/citationguide.pdf).

Figure 4 Dunkin' Donuts Report

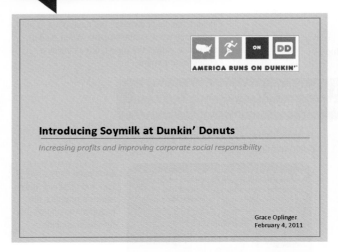

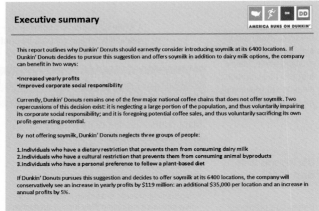

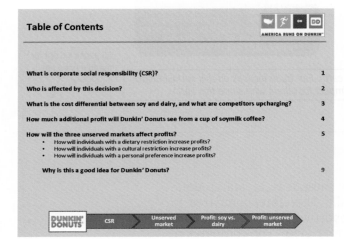

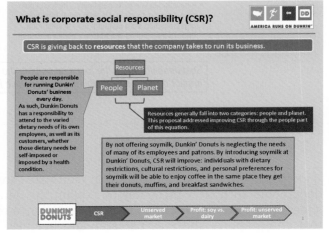

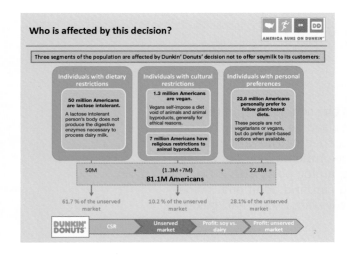

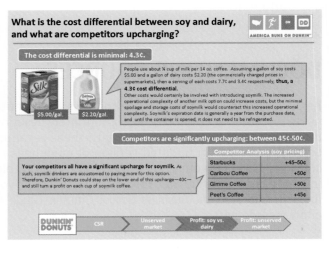

Figure 4 (Continued)

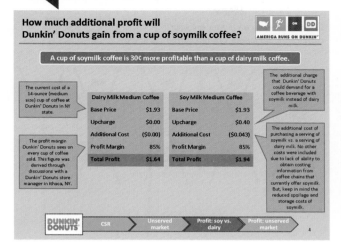

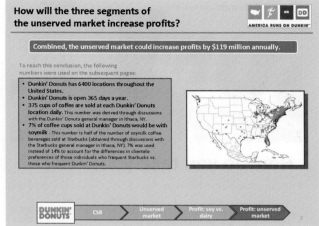

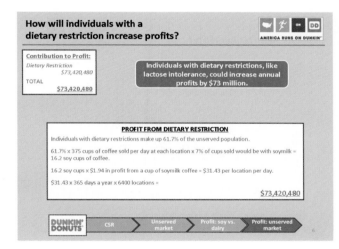

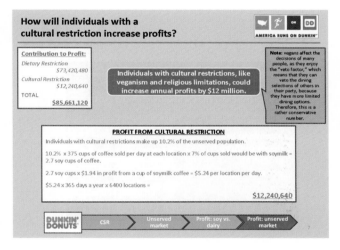

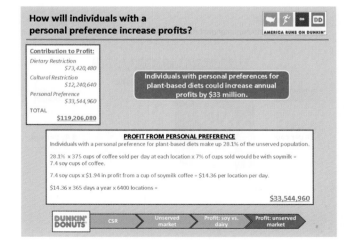

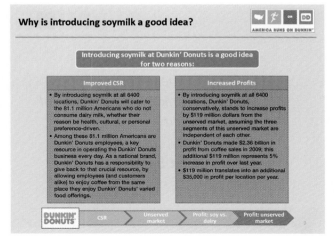

Figure 5 Dunkin' Donuts Slides for a Presentation

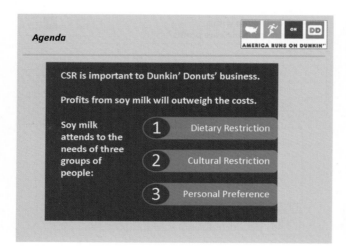

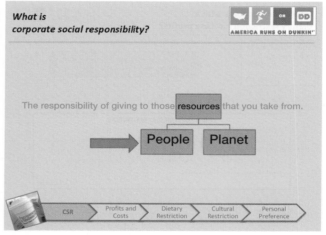

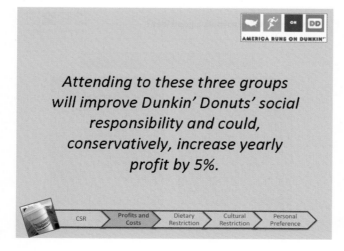

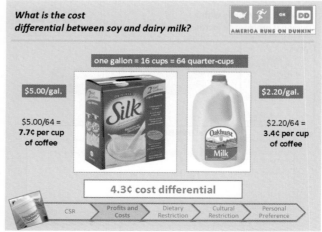

Figure 5 (Continued)

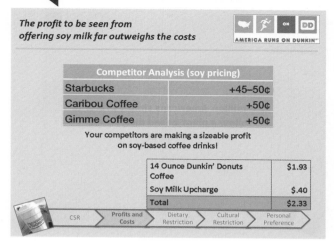

The profit to be seen from offering soy milk far outweighs the costs

AMERICA RUNS ON DUNKIN'

Competitor Analysis (soy pricing)	
Starbucks	+45–50¢
Caribou Coffee	+50¢
Gimme Coffee	+50¢

Your competitors are making a sizeable profit on soy-based coffee drinks!

14 Ounce Dunkin' Donuts Coffee	$1.93
Soy Milk Upcharge	$.40
Total	$2.33

CSR | Profits and Costs | Dietary Restriction | Cultural Restriction | Personal Preference

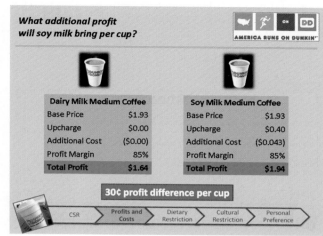

What additional profit will soy milk bring per cup?

AMERICA RUNS ON DUNKIN'

Dairy Milk Medium Coffee	
Base Price	$1.93
Upcharge	$0.00
Additional Cost	($0.00)
Profit Margin	85%
Total Profit	$1.64

Soy Milk Medium Coffee	
Base Price	$1.93
Upcharge	$0.40
Additional Cost	($0.043)
Profit Margin	85%
Total Profit	$1.94

30¢ profit difference per cup

CSR | Profits and Costs | Dietary Restriction | Cultural Restriction | Personal Preference

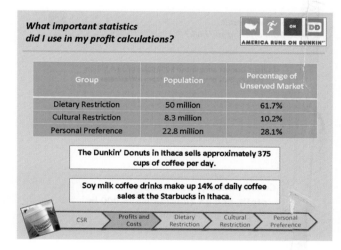

What important statistics did I use in my profit calculations?

AMERICA RUNS ON DUNKIN'

Group	Population	Percentage of Unserved Market
Dietary Restriction	50 million	61.7%
Cultural Restriction	8.3 million	10.2%
Personal Preference	22.8 million	28.1%

The Dunkin' Donuts in Ithaca sells approximately 375 cups of coffee per day.

Soy milk coffee drinks make up 14% of daily coffee sales at the Starbucks in Ithaca.

CSR | Profits and Costs | Dietary Restriction | Cultural Restriction | Personal Preference

Contribution to Profit:
TOTAL $

AMERICA RUNS ON DUNKIN'

50 million Americans are lactose intolerant.

CSR | Profits and Costs | Dietary Restriction | Cultural Restriction | Personal Preference

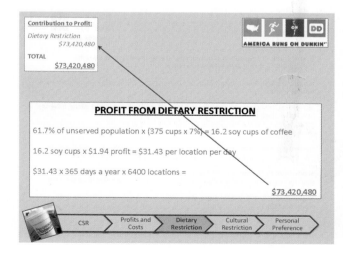

Contribution to Profit:
Dietary Restriction
    $73,420,480
TOTAL
    $73,420,480

AMERICA RUNS ON DUNKIN'

PROFIT FROM DIETARY RESTRICTION

61.7% of unserved population x (375 cups x 7%) = 16.2 soy cups of coffee

16.2 soy cups x $1.94 profit = $31.43 per location per day

$31.43 x 365 days a year x 6400 locations =

$73,420,480

CSR | Profits and Costs | Dietary Restriction | Cultural Restriction | Personal Preference

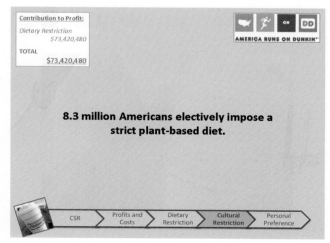

Contribution to Profit:
Dietary Restriction
    $73,420,480
TOTAL
    $73,420,480

AMERICA RUNS ON DUNKIN'

8.3 million Americans electively impose a strict plant-based diet.

CSR | Profits and Costs | Dietary Restriction | Cultural Restriction | Personal Preference

Figure 5 (Continued)

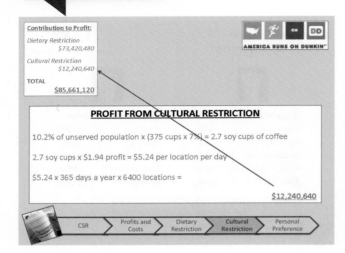

Contribution to Profit:

Dietary Restriction
      $73,420,480

Cultural Restriction
      $12,240,640

TOTAL
      $85,661,120

AMERICA RUNS ON DUNKIN'

PROFIT FROM CULTURAL RESTRICTION

10.2% of unserved population x (375 cups x 7%) = 2.7 soy cups of coffee

2.7 soy cups x $1.94 profit = $5.24 per location per day

$5.24 x 365 days a year x 6400 locations =

                                        $12,240,640

CSR > Profits and Costs > Dietary Restriction > Cultural Restriction > Personal Preference

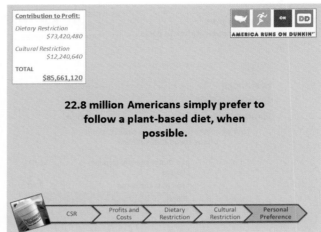

Contribution to Profit:

Dietary Restriction
      $73,420,480

Cultural Restriction
      $12,240,640

TOTAL
      $85,661,120

AMERICA RUNS ON DUNKIN'

22.8 million Americans simply prefer to follow a plant-based diet, when possible.

CSR > Profits and Costs > Dietary Restriction > Cultural Restriction > Personal Preference

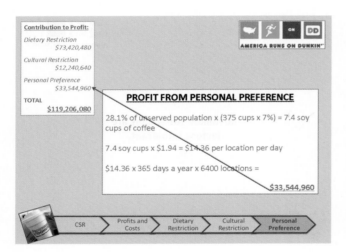

Contribution to Profit:

Dietary Restriction
      $73,420,480

Cultural Restriction
      $12,240,640

Personal Preference
      $33,544,960

TOTAL
      $119,206,080

AMERICA RUNS ON DUNKIN'

PROFIT FROM PERSONAL PREFERENCE

28.1% of unserved population x (375 cups x 7%) = 7.4 soy cups of coffee

7.4 soy cups x $1.94 = $14.36 per location per day

$14.36 x 365 days a year x 6400 locations =

                                        $33,544,960

CSR > Profits and Costs > Dietary Restriction > Cultural Restriction > Personal Preference

By how much will profit increase from offering soy milk?

AMERICA RUNS ON DUNKIN'

Dunkin' Donuts announced 2009 sales of $4.4 billion dollars, 63% of which came from coffee sales.

63% x $4.4 billion x 85% profit margin = $2.36 billion dollars.

$119,206,080 from the introduction of soy-based milk products.

Conservatively, a 5% increase in yearly profit, and an additional $35,000 in profit per location each year.

AMERICA RUNS ON DUNKIN'

References

AMERICA RUNS ON DUNKIN'

Dunkin' Brands, "Corporate Social Responsibility," Dunkin' Donuts company website, www.dunkindonuts.com, accessed November 2010.

Imaner, "Vegan Statistics," Vegan Village, http://www.imaner.net/panel/statistics.htm, accessed November 2010.

Jeremy Foltz, "The Economics of the Soy Milk Market," Food Systems Research Group, University of Wisconsin, June 15, 2005, http://74.125.155.132/scholar?q=cache:Q01P3AFdOUEJ:scholar.google.com/+prefer+soy+over+dairy+milk&hl=en&as_sdt=20000000000, accessed November 2010.

National Digestive Diseases Information Clearinghouse, "Lactose Intolerance," NDDIC website, http://digestive.niddk.nih.gov/ddiseases/pubs/lactoseintolerance/, accessed November 2010.

Stephen Rodrick, "Average Joe," NYMag, November 20, 2005, http://nymag.com/nymetro/news/bizfinance/biz/features/15139/, accessed November 2010.

VegAdvantage, "Facts," VegAdvantage website, http://www.vegadvantage.com/, accessed November 2010.

Type of Reference Material	How to Format the Footnote	Notes/Alternatives
Article from a periodical	Bruce J. McNeil, "The Life and Times of Split-Dollar Life Insurance," *Journal of Deferred Compensation*, Vol. 16, No. 3 (2011), pp. 16–73.	Although some traditional citation formats suggest including the database you used to find articles (for example, Factiva or ProQuest), this is not necessary for footnoting in business writing.
Article from a newspaper accessed online	Jane L. Levere, "In-Flight Food Tries to Be Tasty," *The New York Times*, April 12, 2010, www.nytimes.com, accessed April 24, 2010.	If you retrieved this article from the print newspaper, you would include the section and page number instead of the website and accessed date. If the article doesn't identify an author, you would simply start with the title.
Article from a website	Juliana Shallcross, "Hotel Indigo San Diego Gets iPad Happy," *HotelChatter*, April 12, 2010, www.hotelchatter.com, accessed April 24, 2010.	To keep footnotes short and save space, you may shorten most URLs to include only the main site reference, as long as the reader can find the original source easily.
Content from a website	Marriott International, Inc., "Who We Support," Marriott company website, www.marriott.com, accessed April 28, 2013.	Providing the date accessed is particularly important for content that exists only online because pages may be moved or removed. You also may include the day of the month if the site contents change frequently.
Notes from a class discussion	Robert J. Kwortnik, "Services as Experiences," HADM 2430 class discussion, September 10, 2012, Cornell University, School of Hotel Administration, Ithaca, NY.	To cite PPT slides or handouts, simply replace "class discussion" with the name of the source material.
Personal conversations or interviews	Abigail Mauer, conversation with author, Hoboken, NJ, July 29, 2013.	Another variation may be, "Abigail Mauer, phone interview by author, July 29, 2013."
Book	Timothy R. Hinkin, *Cases in Hospitality Management: A Critical Incident Approach*, 2nd Edition (New York: Wiley, 2005), p. 72.	For books and articles with more than three authors, include only the first author's name, followed by "et al.," to mean "and others."

Figure 6 Footnote Formatting

C Common Types of Reports

Management needs comprehensive, up-to-date, accurate, and understandable information to achieve the organization's goals. Much of this information is communicated in the form of reports. The most common types of business reports are periodic reports, proposals, policies and procedures, and situational reports. Each of these types is discussed and illustrated in the following sections.

PERIODIC REPORTS

Three common types of periodic reports are routine management reports, compliance reports, and progress reports.

Routine Management Reports

Every organization requires its own set of recurring reports to provide the knowledge base from which decisions are made and problems are solved. Some of these routine management reports are statistical, consisting sometimes of just spreadsheets; other management reports are primarily narrative. Examples of routine management reports are quarterly earnings, annual headcount, and monthly revenue.

Compliance Reports

Many state and federal government agencies require companies doing business with them to file reports showing that they are complying with regulations in such areas as affirmative action, contacts with foreign firms, labor relations, occupational safety, financial dealings, and environmental concerns. Completing these compliance reports is often mostly a matter of gathering the needed data and reporting the information honestly and completely. Typically, very little analysis of the data is required.

Progress Reports

Interim progress reports are often used to communicate the status of long-term projects. They are submitted periodically to management for internal projects, to the customer for external projects, and to the investor for an accounting of venture capital expenditures. Typically, these reports (1) tell what has been accomplished since the last progress report, (2) document how well the project is adhering to the schedule and budget, (3) describe any problems encountered and how they were solved, and (4) outline future plans. Often these reports will be produced using project management software and will include at-a-glance charts.

PROPOSALS

A proposal is a written report with the purpose of persuading the reader to accept a suggested plan of action. Two types of business proposals are project proposals and, less common, research proposals.

Project Proposals

A manager may write a project proposal, for example, to persuade a potential customer to purchase goods or services from the writer's company, to persuade the federal government to locate a new research facility in the headquarters city of the writer's company, or to persuade a foundation to fund a project to be undertaken by the writer's company. Any of these proposals may be solicited or unsolicited.

Government agencies and many large companies routinely solicit proposals from potential suppliers. For example, the government might publish an RFP (request for proposal) stating its intention to purchase 5,000 microcomputers, giving detailed specifications regarding the features it needs on these computers, and inviting prospective suppliers to bid on the project. Similarly, the computer manufacturer that submits the successful bid might itself publish an RFP to invite parts manufacturers to bid on supplying some component the manufacturer needs for these computers.

Unlike solicited proposals, unsolicited proposals typically require more background information and more persuasion. Because the reader may not be familiar with the project, the writer must present more evidence to convince the reader of the merits of the proposal.

When writing a proposal, keep in mind that the proposal may become legally binding. In spelling out exactly what the writer's organization will provide, when, under what circumstances, and at what price, the proposal report writer creates the *offer* part of a contract that, if accepted, becomes binding on the organization.

As discussed in Chapter 10, proposals vary in length, organization, complexity, and format. Most, however, include the following sections:

1. *Background:* Introduce the problem you're addressing and discuss why it merits the reader's consideration. Provide enough background information to show that a problem exists and that you have a viable solution.

2. *Objectives:* Provide specific information about what the outcomes of the project will be. Be detailed and honest in discussing what the reader will get in return for a commitment of resources.

3. *Procedures:* Discuss in detail exactly how you will achieve these objectives. Include a step-by-step discussion of what will be done, when, and exactly how much each component or phase will cost. (Alternatively, you may include costs in an appendix.)

4. *Qualifications:* Show how you, your organization, and any others who would be involved in conducting this project are qualified to do so. If appropriate, include testimonials or other external evidence to support your claims.

5. *Request for approval:* Directly ask for approval of your proposal. Depending on the reader's needs, this request could come either at the beginning or at the end of the proposal.

6. *Supporting data:* Include as an appendix to your proposal any relevant but supplementary information that might bolster your arguments.

Research Proposals

Because research is a cost to the organization in terms of labor time and expenses, senior management may want to know what they will gain in return for expending these resources. Thus, a research proposal is a structured presentation of what you plan to do in research, why you plan to conduct the research, and how you plan to accomplish it

Figure 7
Sample Research
Proposal

STAFF EMPLOYEES' EVALUATION OF THE BENEFITS
PROGRAM AT MAYO MEMORIAL HOSPITAL

A Research Proposal by Lyn Santos
January 23, 2013

Employee benefits are a rapidly growing and an increasingly important form of employee compensation for both profit and nonprofit organizations. According to a recent U.S. Chamber of Commerce survey, benefits now constitute 37% of all payroll costs, costing an average of $10,857 a year for each full-time employee.[1] As has been noted by one management consultant, "The success of employee benefits programs depends directly on whether employees need and understand the value of the benefits provided."[2] Thus, an organization's employee benefits program must be monitored and evaluated if it is to remain an effective recruitment and retention tool.

Mayo Memorial employs 2,500 staff personnel who have not received a cost-of-living increase in two years. Thus, staff salaries may not have kept pace with industry, and the hospital's benefits program may become more important in attracting and retaining good workers. In addition, the contracts of three staff unions expire next year, and the benefits program is typically a major area of bargaining.

PROBLEM

To help ensure that the benefits program is operating as effectively as possible, the following problem will be addressed in this study: What are the opinions of staff employees at Mayo Memorial Hospital regarding their employee benefits? To answer this question, the following subproblems will be addressed:

1. How knowledgeable are the employees about the benefits program?
2. What are the employees' opinions of the benefits presently available to them?
3. What benefits would the employees like to have added to the program?

---

[1] Enar Ignatio, "Can Flexible Benefits Promote Your Company?" *Personnel Quarterly*, Vol. 20, September 2006, p. 812.
[2] Ransom Adams and Seymour Stevens, *Personnel Administration*, All-State, Cambridge, MA, 2002, p. 483.

Although research proposal formats vary depending on your purpose and audience, Figure 7 shows an example of a simple research proposal. It includes the following sections:

1. *Heading:* Provide a neutral, descriptive title for your project, being careful not to promise more than you can deliver. Include as a subtitle "A Research Proposal," your name, and the submission date.

2. *Introduction:* Establish a definite need for your study. Include here the background information about the problem, explaining enough to establish a situation and to orient the reader. For credibility, include any information from published sources that helps to establish a need for your project.

Figure 7
(Continued)

2

SCOPE

Although staff employees at all state-supported hospitals receive the same benefits, no attempt will be made to generalize the findings beyond Mayo Memorial. In addition, this study will attempt to determine employee preferences only. The question of whether these preferences are economically feasible is not within the scope of this study.

PROCEDURES

A random sample of 200 staff employees at Mayo Memorial Hospital will be surveyed to answer the three subproblems. In addition, personal interviews will be held with a compensation specialist at Mayo and with the chair of the Staff Personnel Committee. Secondary data will be used to (a) provide background information for developing the questionnaire items and the interview questions, (b) provide a basis for comparing the Mayo benefit program with that of other organizations, and (c) provide a basis for comparing the employees' opinions of the Mayo benefit program with employee opinions of programs at other organizations.

CONCLUSION

The information will be analyzed, and appropriate tables and charts will be developed. Conclusions will be drawn and recommendations made as appropriate to explain the staff employees' opinions about the benefit program at Mayo Memorial Hospital.

3. *Problem:* On the basis of what you said in the previous section, a problem needs answering. Introduce the problem statement and then, using neutral language, state in question form the specific problem to be investigated (avoid yes-or-no questions because your problem is probably more complex than that). Then introduce the subproblems, again in the form of questions, and list them in logical order. Taken together, the answers to your subproblems must provide a complete and accurate answer to your problem statement.

4. *Scope:* The scope of the problem describes the boundaries you have established for your research problem. The scope (also called "delimitations") indicates those parts of the topic that normally might be considered a part

of such a study but that you do not wish to include in your study. Your report title and problem statement must reflect any major delimitations imposed on your study. If you are using any terms in your study that may be subject to different interpretations or that may be unfamiliar to the reader, define them here.

5. *Procedures:* Explain how you will conduct your investigation. Describe your sources of data and methods of collection. Regardless of how you organize this section, plan your procedures carefully and present them in such a way that the reader has confidence that they will enable you to provide an accurate and complete answer to your problem statement.

6. *Conclusion:* Don't leave the reader hanging by ending your report abruptly. Include an appropriate ending paragraph that provides a sense of closure for your research proposal.

7. *Footnotes:* Include the published sources referred to in your proposal.

POLICIES AND PROCEDURES

Policies are broad operating guidelines that govern the general direction and activities of an organization; procedures are the recommended methods or sequential steps to follow when performing a specific activity. An organization's attitude toward promoting from within a company would constitute a policy, and the steps to be taken to apply for a promotion would constitute a procedure. Policy statements are typically written by top management, while procedures may be written by the managers and supervisors who are involved in the day-to-day operation of the organization.

Policy

Begin a policy statement by setting the stage; that is, justify the need for a policy. Your justification should be general enough that the policy covers a broad range of situations but not so general that it has no real "teeth." Ensure that the reader knows exactly who is covered by the policy, what is required, and any other needed information. Finally, show how the reader, the organization, or *someone* benefits from this policy. You will find sample policies online or through professional associations. These are good starting points, but always have legal counsel review a policy before publishing it to employees or clients.

Procedure

Write procedures in a businesslike but not formal manner, using the active voice. Imagine that you are explaining the procedure orally to someone. Go step by step through the process, explaining, when necessary, what should *not* be done as well as what should be done. Try to put yourself in the role of the reader. How much background information is needed; how much jargon can safely be used; what reading level is appropriate? Anticipate questions and problems. Use pictures and diagrams as appropriate.

Don't assume that the reader knows anything about the process, but likewise don't assume that the reader is completely ignorant. Because it would be impossible to answer every conceivable question, concentrate on the high-risk components—those tasks that are difficult to perform or that have serious safety or financial implications if performed incorrectly.

Minimize the amount of conceptual information included, concentrating instead on the practical information. (Remember that a person can learn to drive a car safely without needing to learn how the engine propels the car forward.) Usually, numbered steps are appropriate, but use a narrative approach if it seems more effective.

After you have written a draft, have several employees who are typical of those who will use the document read and comment on it. If the document is a policy, ask them questions to see if they really understand the policy. If it is a procedure, have them follow the steps to see if they work. Revise as necessary.

An example of a procedure is given in Figure 8. Could you follow this procedure and get the desired results?

Figure 8 Sample Procedure

PROCEDURE FOR HIRING A TEMPORARY EMPLOYEE

Employee	Action
Requester	1. Requests a temporary employee with specialized skills by filling out Form 722, "Request for a Temporary Employee." 2. Secures manager's approval. 3. Sends four copies of Form 722 to labor analyst in Human Resources.
Labor Analyst	4. Checks overtime figures of regular employees in the department. 5. If satisfied that the specific people are necessary, checks budget. 6. If funds are available, approves Form 722, sends three copies to buyer of special services in Human Resources, and files the fourth copy.
Buyer of Special Services	7. Notifies outside temporary help contractor by phone and follows up the same day with a confirming letter or email. 8. Negotiates a mutually agreeable effective date. 9. Contacts Human Resources by phone, telling it of the number of people and the effective dates.
Human Resources	10. Notifies Security, Badges, and Gate Guards. 11. Returns one copy of Form 722 to the requester. 12. Provides a temporary ID.
Temporary Help Contractor	13. Furnishes assigned employee or employees with information on the job description, the effective date, and the individual to whom to report.
Temporary Employee	14. Reports to receptionist one half-hour early on the effective date.

SITUATIONAL REPORTS

In any organization, unique problems and opportunities appear that require one-time only reports. Many of these situations call for information to be gathered and analyzed and for recommendations to be made. These so-called *situational reports* are perhaps the most challenging for the report writer. Because they involve a unique event, the writer has no previous reports to use as a guide; he or she must decide what types of information and how much information are needed and how best to organize and present the findings. A sample situational report is shown in Figure 9.

**Figure 9
Sample Situational
Report**

A COMPARISON OF THE PHYSICAL FITNESS LEVELS OF MOUNT PLEASANT ACADEMY STUDENTS WITH NATIONAL NORMS

Danielle K. Kizer

Recent studies reveal a nation of physically unfit children. One research study revealed that one-third of the youth were not physically active enough for aerobic benefit.[1] As past fitness studies have shown schoolchildren to be unfit, the purpose of this study was to determine how Mount Pleasant Academy students (encompassing grades three through six) compared to national norms in physical fitness.

To make this comparison, all 146 MPA students (75 boys and 71 girls) were administered the American Alliance for Health, Physical Education, Recreation, and Dance *Health-Related Physical Fitness Test*. This test consisted of four subtests, each of which was treated as a subproblem of this study.

DISTANCE-RUN TEST

The cardiorespiratory maximum functional capacity and endurance of the students were measured by the Distance-Run Test. Students were instructed to run one mile in the fastest possible time. Walking was permitted, but the objective was to cover the distance in the shortest possible time.

The boys' scores tended to exceed the girls' scores, indicating better fitness for the boys. The weakest age group was the 11-year-old students; all of the students in this age group scored in the lower two quartiles. Seventy percent of the boys and 87 percent of the girls scored at or below the 50th percentile. Overall, the scores displayed by MPA students were below average.

SKINFOLD FAT TEST

The second test administered was the Skinfold Fat Test. This test measured the level of fat in a student's body. Two skinfold fat sites (triceps and subscapular) were used because they are easily measured and are highly correlated with total body fat.

The majority of the students scored below the 50th percentile for healthfulness. In fact, three-fourths of the students evidenced higher-than-average levels of body fat. The leanest group of students comprised the 11-year-old boys and girls. As a whole, boys had higher levels of body fat than girls.

MODIFIED SIT-UP TEST

The Modified Sit-Up Test, the third test used in this study, evaluated a student's abdominal muscular strength and endurance. Students completed their sit-ups lying on their backs with knees flexed, feet on the floor, and heels 12 to 18 inches above the buttocks.

Figure 9
(Continued)

2

The 8- and 9-year-old students scored the highest—specifically, the 8-year-old boys and the 9-year-old girls. Half of the students scored at or below the 50th percentile. The students appeared most physically fit when this test was used, but half of the class still scored at or below national averages.

SIT-AND-REACH TEST

The final test, the Sit-and-Reach Test, was used to measure flexibility of the lower back and posterior thighs. The students sat with knees fully extended and reached directly forward, palms down, as far as they could along the measuring scale.

The girls' scores on this test were higher than the boys' scores. The younger age groups also showed greater levels of flexibility than the other students. Eighty percent of the 8-year-old girls and 86 percent of the 9-year-old girls scored in the top two quartiles. Overall, 68 percent of the girls scored above the 50th percentile compared to 27 percent of the boys. Mount Pleasant Academy students' Sit-and-Reach Test scores for the girls were above average, but the boys' scores were markedly low.

SUMMARY, CONCLUSIONS, AND RECOMMENDATIONS

As shown in Table 1, the students at MPA scored below the 50th percentile on the Distance-Run and the Skinfold Fat Test. Stronger scores were shown on the Modified Sit-Up Test, but half of the class scored below average. The boys' Sit-and-Reach Test scores were below average, but 68 percent of the girls scored above the 50th percentile.

TABLE 1. PERCENTAGE OF MPA STUDENTS SCORING BELOW THE NATIONAL AVERAGE

Test	Total (N = 146)	Boys (N = 75)	Girls (N = 71)
Distance-Run	78	70	87
Skinfold Fat	66	68	64
Modified Sit-Up	51	54	45
Sit-and-Reach	53	73	32
Mean	62	66	57

On the whole, the physical-fitness level of the students at Mount Pleasant Academy is below the average set by the American Alliance for Health, Physical Education, Recreation, and Dance.

Students who scored below average on any test should be encouraged to strive for higher performance—through counseling, individualized exercise routines, and all school activities. Improvements in physical fitness should become a priority to help reduce the risk of injury or disease and to improve overall health and physical fitness.

[1] Clarence Hershberger, "An Unhealthy State of Affairs," *Physical Education*, September 2005, pp. 19–37.

D   Glossary

A

Abstract word A word that identifies an idea or feeling instead of a concrete object. (1)

Active voice The sentence form in which the subject performs the action expressed by the verb. (5)

Agenda A list of topics to be covered at a meeting, often including the name of the person responsible for covering each topic and the timing for each topic. (3)

Agenda slide A slide that presents the topics or main points of a presentation. (11)

Aggregator A program that collects online information from multiple sources and distributes it through one site. (6)

Applicant tracking system A system that companies use to track job applicants and résumés. (12)

Audience The receiver of a message. (1)

B

Bar chart A graph with horizontal or vertical bars representing values. (9)

Behavioral interviews Interviews based on the theory that past behavior predicts future performance (also called *structured interviews*). (12)

Benefits Advantages a potential customer receives from a product or service. (7)

Brainstorming Jotting down ideas, facts, and anything else—without evaluating the output—that might be helpful in constructing a message. (4)

Buffer A neutral and supportive opening statement designed to lessen the impact of negative news. (8)

Business etiquette A guide to appropriate behavior in a business setting. (12)

Business report An organized presentation of information used to make decisions and solve problems. (9)

C

Cascading communication When information starts at the top of the organization and flows down to each level in sequence. (1)

Central selling theme The major reader benefit that is introduced early and emphasized throughout a sales letter. (7)

Chartjunk Visual elements that call attention to themselves instead of information on a chart. (9)

Cliché An expression that has become monotonous through overuse. (5)

Coercion Using force or intimidation to get someone to comply. (4)

Coherence When each sentence of a paragraph links smoothly to the sentences before and after it. (5)

Communication The process of sending and receiving messages. (1)

Competencies The knowledge, skills, and abilities identified for a specific job. (12)

Complex sentence A sentence that has one independent clause and at least one dependent clause. (5)

Compound sentence A sentence that has two or more independent clauses. (5)

Concrete word A word that identifies something the senses can perceive. (1)

Conference call A meeting held using a speakerphone for people in two or more locations (also called a *teleconference*). (3)

Conflict Disagreements or arguments that may occur within a team. (2)

Conformity Agreement to ideas, rules, or principles. (2)

Connotation The subjective or emotional feeling associated with a word. (1)

Consensus Reaching a decision that best reflects the thinking of all team members. (2)

Consumer-generated media (CGM) Any media (e.g., video, images, blogs) about a company posted by consumers for public viewing (also called *user-generated content*). (1)

Corporate social responsibility (CSR) A form of self-regulation whereby a company considers the public's interest (people, planet, as well as profit) in their business practices. (1)

Cover letter Communication that tells a prospective employer that an applicant is interested in and qualified for a position within the organization. (12)

Cross-cultural communication Communication between cultures—when a message is created by someone from one culture to be understood by someone from another culture (also called *intercultural communication*). (2)

Cross-tabulation A process by which two or more items of data are analyzed together. (9)

Culture The customary traits, attitudes, and behaviors of a group of people. (2)

Curriculum vitae (CV) A longer version of a résumé that is more typical for international (and academic) jobs. (12)

D

Dangling expression Any part of a sentence that does not logically connect to the rest of the sentence. (5)

Deck A printed report or slides created in PowerPoint, Keynote, or other presentation tools. (10)

Denotation The literal, dictionary meaning of a word. (1)

Derived benefits Similar to benefits—how marketers refer to benefits customers receive from a product or service. (7)

Destination The point when control passes from the sender to the receiver. (1)

Direct organizational plan A plan in which the major purpose of the message is communicated first, followed by any needed explanation and details. (6)

Direct quotation The exact words of another person. (10)

Divider slide A slide repeated throughout a presentation, highlighting each topic as it is covered. (11)

Documentation Identifying sources (to give credit) to another's words or ideas. (10)

Downward communication The flow of information from managers to their employees. (1)

Drafting Composing a preliminary version of a message. (4)

E

Editing The stage of revision that ensures that writing conforms to standard English. (4)

Empathy The ability to project oneself into another person's position and to understand that person's situation and feelings. (5)

Ethics A system of moral principles that go beyond legal rules to tell us how to act. (1)

Ethnocentrism The belief that one's own cultural group is superior. (2)

Ethos A persuasive appeal based on credibility. (7)

Euphemism An expression used in place of words that may be offensive or inappropriate. (1)

Executive summary A condensed version of the report body (also called an *abstract* or *synopsis*). (10)

Expletive An expression such as *there is* or *it has been* that begins a clause and for which the pronoun has no antecedent. (5)

Exploding pie chart A pie chart with one wedge pulled out for emphasis. (9)

Extemporaneous presentation A presentation delivered using an unrehearsed, enhanced, conversational style. (11)

Extranet A private computer network for a select group of people outside of the company (e.g., for customers or franchisees). (1)

F

Factoring Breaking a problem down to determine what data needs to be collected. (9)

Feature An aspect of how a product or service works. (7)

Filter Perception based on one's knowledge, experience, and viewpoints. (1)

Formal communication network The transmission of information through downward, upward, and lateral paths within an organization. (1)

G

Generic heading A report heading that identifies only the topic of a section without giving the conclusion. (10)

Geolocation Identifying where objects are physically located. (1)

Goodwill message A message that is sent out of a sense of kindness. (6)

Google Alert An email update provided by Google when online content matches the user's predefined search terms. (6)

Grapevine The flow of information through nonofficial channels within the organization (also called the *informal communication network*). (1)

Groupthink A hindrance to team performance that happens when individuals think too similarly. (2)

H

Horizontal communication The flow of information among peers within an organization (also called *lateral communication*). (1)

I

Impromptu presentation A presentation delivered without preparation. (11)

Inclusion Creating an environment where all people are valued and can contribute to their fullest potential. (2)

Indirect organizational plan A plan in which the reasons or rationale are presented first, followed by the major idea. (6)

Individual ethics Ethics defined by a person, which are based on family values, heritage, personal experience, and other factors. (1)

Informal communication network The flow of information through nonofficial channels within the organization (also called the *grapevine*). (1)

Information Meaningful facts, statistics, and conclusions. (9)

Intercultural communication Communication between cultures—when a message is created by someone from one culture to be understood by someone from another culture (also called *cross-cultural communication*). (2)

Internal paraphrase Summarizing a speaker's comments to oneself. (3)

Intranet A private computer network within a company or organization for employee access. (1)

J

Jargon Technical terminology used within specialized groups. (1)

L

Lateral communication The flow of information among peers within an organization (also called *horizontal communication*). (1)

Letter A written message mailed to someone outside (or external to) an organization. (4)

Line chart A graph based on a grid, with the vertical axis representing values and the horizontal axis representing time. (9)

Logos A persuasive appeal based on logic. (7)

M

Main point slide An optional slide in a presentation shown before an agenda slide to convey the most important message to the audience. (11)

Main points The major conclusions of a message. (4)

Mashups Web applications or pages that combine content from different sources. (1)

Mechanics Elements in communication that show up only in writing (e.g., spelling, punctuation, abbreviations, capitalization, number expression, and word division). (5)

Medium How a message is transmitted—for example, an email or phone call. (1)

Memo A written message sent to someone within (or internal to) an organization. (4)

Memorized presentation A presentation delivered from memory. (11)

Message The information (either verbal or nonverbal) that is communicated. (1)

Microblogs A type of blog used for short messages with timely information. (1)

Mind mapping Generating ideas for a message by connecting them in a graphical way. (4)

Minutes An official record of a meeting that summarizes what was discussed, what decisions were made, and what actions participants will take. (3)

Multicommunicating Overlapping conversations using various forms of communication. (1)

Multiculturalism A philosophy of appreciating diversity among people, typically beyond differences in countries of origin. (2)

Multimedia The integration of several forms of media (e.g., text, video, and graphics). (1)

N

Networking email An email sent to a person at a company or in a field of interest for the purpose of obtaining career information or job leads. (12)

Noise Environmental or competing elements that distract one's attention during communication. (1)

O

Online meeting A meeting held using a web-based service, such as WebEx. (3)

Online reputation How a company or an individual is represented on the Internet. (12)

Organization The sequence in which topics are presented in a message. (4)

Organizational fit A match between a prospective employee and a particular organizational culture. (12)

P

Parallelism Using similar grammatical structure to express similar ideas. (5)

Paraphrase A summary or restatement of a passage in one's own words. (10)

Passive voice The sentence form in which the subject receives the action expressed by the verb. (5)

Pathos A persuasive appeal based on emotion. (7)

Persuasion Using communication to change another person's beliefs, feelings, or behaviors. (4)

Pie chart A circle graph divided into component wedges. (9)

Plagiarism Using another person's words or ideas without giving proper credit. (10)

Platitude A trite, obvious statement. (5)

Podcast Portable audio or video content for individuals to download and listen to at their computer or on a mobile device. (1)

Preview An overview of what the audience can expect in a message. (4)

Primary audience The most important receiver of a message (e.g., the decision maker). (4)

Primary data Data collected by the researcher to solve a specific problem. (9)

Professional ethics Ethics defined by an organization. (1)

Purpose The reason for which a message is created. (4)

Q

Questionnaire A written instrument containing questions to obtain information from recipients. (9)

R

Receiver benefits The advantages a reader would derive from granting the writer's request or from accepting the writer's decision. (5)

Redundancy The unnecessary repetition of an idea that has already been expressed or intimated. (5)

Résumé A representation of an applicant's education, work history, and other qualifications. (12)

Revising Modifying the content and style of a draft to increase its effectiveness. (4)

Rhetorical question A question asked to get the reader thinking about the topic; a literal answer is not expected. (7)

S

Scripted presentation A presentation delivered by reading from notes. (11)

Secondary audience Receivers of a message who are not the *primary audience* but who will also read and be affected by a message. (4)

Secondary data Data (published or unpublished) collected by someone else for another purpose. (9)

Section overview Text that previews for the reader how a section will be divided and—for direct-plan reports—what main points will follow. (10)

Service recovery Responding to a service failure in a way that turns an upset customer into a satisfied customer. (7)

Simple sentence A sentence that has one independent clause. (5)

Situational ethics Ethics that are based on particular circumstances. (1)

Situational report A report that is produced only once to address unique problems and opportunities. (9)

Slang An expression, often short-lived, that is identified with a specific group of people. (1)

Slide tracker An image on the slide that repeats on every slide after the agenda to show the major divisions of a presentation, highlighting each topic as it is presented. (11)

Social ethics Ethics defined by society. (1)

Social loafing The psychological term for avoiding individual responsibility in a group setting. (2)

Social media A blending of technology and social interaction. (1)

Social networking sites Websites where communities of people who share common interests or activities can form relationships (a subset of *social media*). (1)

Solicited cover letter A cover letter that responds to a position advertised by a company. (12)

Solicited sales letter A company's reply to a request for product or service information from a potential customer. (7)

Stacked headings Two consecutive headings without intervening text. (10)

Stimulus An event that creates a need to communicate. (1)

Style How an idea is expressed (rather than the substance of the idea). (5)

Survey A data-collection method that gathers information through questionnaires, telephone inquiries, or interviews. (9)

Synchronous Simultaneous or at the same time (antonym: asynchronous). (1)

T

Table An orderly arrangement of data into columns and rows. (9)

Talking heading A report heading that identifies the major conclusion of a section. (10)

Team A group of individuals who depend on one another to accomplish a common objective. (2)

Teleconference A meeting held using a speakerphone for people in two or more locations (also called a *conference call*). (3)

Title slide The first slide of a presentation, which usually includes the title, date, name of presenter, company, and audience. (11)

Tone How the writer's attitude toward the reader and the subject of the message is reflected. (5)

Topic sentence The main idea of a paragraph, usually introduced at the beginning of a passage. (5)

U

Unity When all parts of a paragraph work together to develop a single idea consistently and logically. (5)

Unsolicited cover letter A cover letter that is initiated by an individual searching for a job. (12)

Unsolicited sales letter A way to promote a company's products or services to potential customers who have not expressed any interest. (7)

Upward communication The flow of information from lower-level employees to upper-level employees or managers. (1)

User-generated content (UGC) Any media (e.g., video, images, blogs) about a company posted by consumers for public viewing (also called *consumer-generated media*). (1)

V

Videoconference A video-based meeting using videophones, smartphones, desktop programs, or dedicated services such as telepresence suites. (3)

Visual aids Tables, charts, photographs, or other graphic materials. (9)

Vlog A video form of a blog. (1)

VoIP Voice over Internet Protocol—a technology for making phone calls over the Internet. (3)

W

Web 2.0 Web applications that facilitate online interaction. (1)

Wiki A website where anyone with access can edit content directly. (1)

Writer's block The inability to focus one's attention on the writing process and to draft a message. (4)

Y

"You" attitude Emphasizing what the reader wants to know and how the reader will be affected by the message. (5)

Index

Page references followed by f indicate figure

D

Dangling expression, 145, 532
Data, 286
  analyzing, 293f, 299
  arranging in tables, 302, 302f
  collection of, 293–294
  currency of, 293f
  displaying, 298–308
  ethical dimension and, 311
  identifying types of, 288–289
  interpreting, 309–322, 309f
  making sense of, 309–310, 310f
  primary, 289
  questionnaires and, 293–298
  research study and, 293f
  secondary, 288
Databases, 289
Date line, letters and, 503
Dates, commas and, 476
Davis, Gary 141
Decisions, 38, 255–257, 267, 286
Decks, PowerPoint 326, 532
Delimitations. *see* Scope
Delivery method, presentations and,
    372–374, 372f, 392, 395
Delivery notation, as a letter part, 506
Delivery skills, 77
Deloitte Film Festival, 17
Denotation, 10, 532
Derived benefits, 224, 532
Design
  presentations and, 384–386, 385f
  of résumé, 418
Destination, 6f, 7, 532
Dewey, Wright and Howe, 68
Different from/Different than, 497
Dining, and business etiquette, 449–451
Direct address, commas and, 476
Direct approach, 113, 115f, 190f
Direct organizational plan, 182, 216f, 532
  business reports and, 333
  indirect plans *vs.*, 253
  main points in presentations,
    381–382, 382f
  persuasive messages and,
    214–215, 220
  to present an idea, 215f
  presentations, 376
  presenting bad news immediately,
    251–254, 251f, 252f
  reports and, 339, 341
  section overviews, 345, 345f
  talking headings and, 335
  for writing solicited cover letter, 433
  Yahoo's memo using, 268f
Direct quotation, 346, 476, 482, 533
Direct sequence, presentations and, 377f
Disney, 37, 39f
Disrespectful comments, addressing, 59
Distractions, 12, 13, 77, 116f
Diversity, 4f, 37, 46, 51–58
Diversity Resource Groups, 37
Divider slides, 383, 533
Division point, spelling and, 494
Documentation, 346–349, 533
Doodle program, 89f
Doubling a final consonant,
    spelling and, 493
Dove Evolution viral video, 73
Downward communication, 7–9, 8f, 533
Drafting, 533
  the appendix, 342
  the body of the report, 336–339
  checklist for, 125
  cover letter and memo, 340
  email, 117, 340

executive summary, 341
references, 342
the report findings, 336
the report introduction, 336
supplementary sections, 339–342
table of content, 341
title page, 339
writing process and, 106, 106f,
    114–123, 115f
Dress, 392, 441, 442–443
Drucker, Peter, 72
Duckett, Stephen, 368
Dunkin' Donuts, 518–519f
  executive summary for, 341f
  reference page for, 342f
  slides for a presentation, 520–522f
  slide trackers in, 383f
  summary slide for, 339f
  title and slide from, 328f, 329, 335

E

Each Other/One Another, 497
eBay, 70, 71
Eckert, Bob, 209
Editing, 124, 533
Education, on résumé, 421, 422f
Efrati, Amir, 347
e.g/i.e, 498
EI and IE words, spelling and, 494
Ekman, Paul, 72
Electrolux vacuum cleaners
    advertisement, 11
Electronic communication. *see*
    Email; Instant messaging (IM);
    Text messaging
Elimination of alternatives, as
    organizational plan, 377f
Ellipses, 483–485
Email, 7, 18f, 58
  about security breach, 252f
  communicating bad news via, 250–251
  communicating via, 14–15, 58
  as competing noise, 13
  cover letter and, 340, 340f
  cover letter as, 433
  employees participating in
    Wikis and, 44
  follow-up, 447f
  as formal communication network, 9
  Goldman's, 20
  guidelines for drafting, 117
  ineffective request, 185
  inquiry, 435–436, 436f
  Intel bad news in, 267
  for a meeting, 88f
  networking, 435
  poorly and well-written, 119f
  questionnaires and writing,
    297–298, 298f
  revised request, 186f
  revising, 167
  sample of, 433f
  sample thank-you, 446f
  writing, 117–119
  Yahoo! layoff, 268f
Eminent/Imminent, 498
Emotional appeal, persuasion and, 212
Emotionalism, avoiding, 218
Emotional messages, 18f
Emotions, 5, 12, 13, 74, 77, 212
Empathy, 163, 533
Emphasis, data and, 343–344, 344f
Emphasis technique, 160–161
Employees, 4f, 8f
  communicating with, 108
  companies decisions and, 267

diversity among, 51
engaging online with, 81
Starbucks CEO bad news
    email to, 267
tailoring persuasive message to, 211
use of instant messaging, 15
written and oral communication of, 4
Enclosure notation, as a letter part, 506
Enclosures, referring to, 226–227
Ending, 340, 378
Endnotes, 347–348, 517
End of message (EOM), email messages
    and, 117
Enthused/Enthusiastic, 498
Envelopes, as a letter part, 505
Environment, 38, 116f. *see also* Business
    environment; Working environment
Environmental noise, 13
Errors, 124, 419f
Ethical behavior, 22
Ethical decision making, framework for,
    23–24, 23f
Ethical language, 225
Ethical persuasion, 110, 213–214, 213f
Ethics, 533
  communication and, 21–24, 75, 190,
    213, 311 *see also Topics of Interests codes
    marked throughout the chapter*
  organizations and, 4f
  team members and, 41–42
Ethisphere Institute, 22
Ethnicity, communication and, 53–54
Ethnocentrism, 46, 533
Ethos, 211, 212, 533
Euphemisms, 11–12, 12f, 533
Europe, communication in, 58f, 85f
European Americans, 53
Evidence, 108, 217f, 225
Excuse, opening for presentation
    and, 374
Executive summary, 341, 508–511f, 533
Experience section, in résumé, 425
Expert opinion, 217f
Explanation, presentations and, 369f
Explanatory materials, colons and, 480
Expletives, 150, 487, 533
Explicit communication, 47
Exploding pie charts, 306, 533
Expressions
  dangling, avoiding, 145
  inappropriate use of, 11–12
  redundancy and wordy, avoiding, 147
  reports and, 342
  transitional, 156
Extemporaneous presentation, 372–373,
    372f, 392, 533
External stimulus, 5
Extranet, 15, 533
Eye contact, 72, 78, 373

F

Facebook, 15, 16f, 18, 80, 121–123
Facebook Connect, 80
Face-to-face communication, 14, 15,
    18, 18f, 58
Face-to-face meetings
  best and worst of, 86f, 89f
  communicating bad news and, 250
  preference of, 84–85
  telephone *vs.*, 82
Facial expressions, 7, 72
Factoring, 286, 533
Facts, 255f, 375f, 376
Family values, 22
Farther/Further, 498
Favors, 218, 261, 261f